6. Can a local account be used in a trust relationship? Explain.

7. In a complete trust domain model that uses 4 different domains, what is the total number of trust relationships required to use a complete trust domain model?

Exam Questions

The following questions are similar to those you will face on the Microsoft exam. Answers to these questions can be found in section Answers and Explanations, later in the chapter. At the end of each of those answers, you will be informed of where (that is, in what section of the chapter) to find more information..

1. ABC Corporation has locations in Toronto, New York, and San Francisco. It wants to install Windows NT Server 4 to encompass all its locations in a single WAN environment. The head office is located in New York. What is the best domain model for ABC's directory services implementation?

   A. Single-domain model

   B. Single-master domain model

   C. Multiple-master domain model

   D. Complete-trust domain model

2. JPS Printing has a single location with 1,000 users spread across the LAN. It has special printers and applications installed on the servers in its environment. It needs to be able to centrally manage the user accounts and the resources. Which domain model would best fit its needs?

A. Single-domain model

B. Single-master domain model

C. Multiple-master domain model

D. Complete-trust domain model

5. What must be created to allow a user account from one domain to access resources in a different domain?

A. Complete Trust Domain Model

B. One Way Trust Relationship

C. Two Way Trust Relationship

D. Master-Domain Model

Answers to Review Questions

1. Single domain, master domain, multiple-master domain, complete-trust domain. See section, Windows NT Server 4 Domain Models, in this chapter for more information. (This question deals with objective Planning 1.)

2. One user, one account, centralized administration, universal resource access, synchronization. See section, Windows NT Server 4 Directory Services, in this chapter for more information. (This question deals with objective Planning 1.)

6. Local accounts cannot be given permissions across trusts. See section, Accounts in Trust Relationships, in this chapter for more information. (This question deals with Planning 1.)

Answers to Review Questions: For each of the Review and Exam questions, you will find thorough explanations located at the end of the chapter.

Exam Questions: These questions reflect the kinds of multiple-choice questions that appear on the Microsoft exams. Use them to become familiar with the exam-question format and to help you determine what you know and what you need to review or study more.

Suggested Readings and Resources

The following are some recommended readings on the subject of installing and configuring NT Workstation:

1. Microsoft Official Curriculum course 770: *Installing and Configuring Microsoft Windows NT Workstation 4.0*

   • Module 1: Overview of Windows NT Workstation 4.0

   • Module 2: Installing Windows NT Workstation 4.0

2. Microsoft Official Curriculum course 922: *Supporting Microsoft Windows NT 4.0 Core Technologies*

   • Module 2: Installing Windows NT

   • Module 3: Configuring the Windows NT Environment

3. *Microsoft Windows NT Workstation Resource Kit Version 4.0* (Microsoft Press)

   • Chapter 2: Customizing Setup

   • Chapter 4: Planning for a Mixed Environment

4. Microsoft TechNet CD-ROM

   • *MS Windows NT Workstation Technical Notes*

     • MS Windows NT Workstation Deployment Guide – Automating Windows NT Setup

     • An Unattended Windows NT Workstation Deployment

5. Web Sites

   • www.microsoft.com/train_cert

Suggested Readings and Resources: The very last element in each chapter is a list of additional resources you can use if you wish to go above and beyond certification-level material or if you need to spend more time on a particular subject that you are having trouble understanding.

Use of the Microsoft Approved Study Guide Logo on this product signifies that it has been independently reviewed and approved in complying with the following standards:

- ◆ Acceptable coverage of all content related to Microsoft exam number 70-100, entitled Analyzing Requirements and Defining Solution Architectures.
- ◆ Sufficient performance-based exercises that relate closely to all required content.
- ◆ Technically accurate content, based on sampling of text.

MCSD

Solution
Architectures

Randy Cornish
Derek Ferguson
Denny Dayton
Eeraj J. Qaisar

New
Riders

MCSD Training Guide: Solution Architectures

International Standard Book Number: 0-7357-0026-5

Library of Congress Catalog Card Number: 99-63015

Printed in the United States of America

03 02 01 00   7 6 5 4 3 2

Interpretation of the printing code: The rightmost double-digit number is the year of the book's printing; the rightmost single-digit number is the number of the book's printing. For example, the printing code 99-1 shows that the first printing of the book occurred in 1999.

Trademarks

Warning and Disclaimer

PUBLISHER
David Dwyer

EXECUTIVE EDITOR
Mary Foote

ACQUISITIONS EDITOR
Amy Michaels

DEVELOPMENT EDITOR
Chris Zahn

MANAGING EDITOR
Sarah Kearns

PROJECT EDITOR
Jennifer Chisholm

COPY EDITOR
Barbara Hacha

INDEXER
Kevin Fulcher

TECHNICAL EDITORS
Randy Cornish
Mike Draganza
Corby Jordan
Eeraj J. Qaisar

SOFTWARE DEVELOPMENT SPECIALIST
Craig Atkins

COMPOSITORS
Ron Wise
Wil Cruz

Contents at a Glance

Table of Contents

8 Developing the Conceptual Design for a Solution   331

PART II: Defining Solutions

Study and Exam Prep Tips   633

PART IV: Appendixes

About the Authors

Randy Cornish is an experienced Visual Basic developer and architect with more than 22 years in the computer industry (including more than 13 years with Digital Equipment). As an independent consultant, he has worked with many companies in the Chicagoland area over the past 10 years, with a focus on Microsoft technologies. In addition to coding and architecting COM solutions, Randy has done classroom teaching, training material development, and managing high performance teams. Randy is an MCP in Visual Basic, Access, and Windows. His hobbies are reading, volleyball, bowling, and telling his daughter, "No, you can't have a dog." Dog-lovers can send complaints to: RLCornish@cs.com.

Derek Ferguson is Software Project Manager for InterAccess, Chicago's largest and oldest Internet Service Provider (ISP). He is a Microsoft Certified Solutions Developer (MCSD) as well as a Certified Lotus Notes Principal Programmer (CLPP) and currently is working on Sun Certified Java Developer (SCJD) status.

Derek received his B.S. in Computer Science from DePaul University and has written professionally on a wide variety of technical subjects, ranging from Microsoft Access 2000 to Java database connectivity.

You may visit his page on the World Wide Web at www.EvilOscar.com, or contact him via E-mail at dferguson@interaccess.com.

Denny Dayton is a MCSD and an MCT, and works as a solution developer and trainer with Rainier Technology, focusing on *n*-tier inter- and intra-net applications built using COM. Denny has been working with this technology, in its many incarnations, for four years.

Eeraj J. Qaisar has a degree in Chemical Engineering from AMU-Aligarh (India). He is also a MCSD with product specialization in VB5.0 and SQL Server 6.5. He currently works for MediaServ.com—a Microsoft Certified Solutions Partner as a solutions consultant. He can be reached at eeraj@hotmail.com.

ABOUT THE TECHNICAL EDITORS

Mike Draganza is a Microsoft Certified Solution Developer. He lives in Costa Mesa (Orange County), CA with his wife, Robin, and two kids, Natalie, 10, and Lauren, 8. When he is not programming or reading about programming, he enjoys tennis and golf. He currently works as a contract programmer for Boeing. His programming experience runs the gamut of Windows technologies: COM and ATL, ActiveX, MFC and Win32.

Corby Jordan has been in the technology industry for 7 years, working with such companies as Intel, Autodesk, and Boeing. As an MCT, he has trained hundreds of professionals seeking to become MCSE's and MCSD's. He is currently working as the IT Lead Project Manager at IRSC, with a focus on developing multi-tier applications. He lives in southern California with his wife, Michele, and his three kids, Caitlin, Sophia, and Symeon.

Dedications

Randy Cornish:

To my parents, Sandy and John, who instilled in me a love for reading and writing. It is a gift I appreciate every day of my life.

Derek Ferguson:

To my wife, Erin, who is everything that is good, noble, and true in this world. And to my cat, Oscar…who—I'm pretty certain—is the Devil incarnate. :-)

Denny Dayton:

To Nikki, who agreed not to throw the laptop into the ocean.

Acknowledgments

Randy Cornish:

I would like to thank the following people for making my contribution to this book possible.

I'd like to thank Nancy Maragioglio for bringing me into the New Riders family. I'd like to thank Amy Michaels and Mary Foote for giving me the chance to contribute to this book. I would like to give a special thanks to Chris Zahn for his almost daily guidance, his open-mindedness, and his ability to pull us all through a very challenging book.

I'd like to thank my teammates for the last two years: Patrick, Sundar, Curt, Cindy, Jay, Kenny, Paul, Alex, Srinivas and Linda. It has been a pleasure and a privilege to work with each and every one of them. The intermingling of ideas and approaches made me a better architect. We pushed each other to new heights because nobody wanted to let down the team.

Most importantly, I'd like to thank my wife and my daughter, Crystal and Mandy. They had to put up with a less pleasant version of my former self who spent more time in front of a laptop than is natural. "I love you and I'm back."

Derek Ferguson:

I'd like to thank Hoyt Hudson, CTO of InterAccess, for giving me a chance when I was just a kid out of college. Also at InterAccess, I'd like to thank my next-door neighbor, Ken Savich, for enduring the Who's Tommy many, many times over the last couple months.

Thanks also to Ari Kaplan for all his help during the (now semi-legendary) Infranet conversion. There is much in this book that was learned "the hard way" on that project.

In the publishing world—which I've found (like college) often only bears an accidental resemblance to the "real world"—I cannot thank my agent, Chris VanBuren, enough. Also, many, many, many thanks to Amy Michaels and Chris Zahn at Macmillan for inspiring me with their boundless positivism (where do you get it from?!).

Finally, I'd like to thank Marillion for being the greatest Progressive Rock band ever.

Denny Dayton:

I'd like to take the opportunity to thank a few people. First of all, I'd like to thank my parents, who managed to have faith as I wandered through a college career, and also Dennis, Calvin, Richard, and the rest of the developers at Rainier for building an environment where it is okay to ask "Is this really the way we should do this?" Finally, of course, thanks to my wife, Nikki, who I married during the course of writing this book, and who put up with my bringing my laptop on our honeymoon in Hawaii.

Eeraj J. Qaisar:

I would like to thank my friend Abhijit Mandrekar for his help in technical review. FatMan (dad), mom, and Rahul—thanks for your support and help!

Tell Us What You Think!

As the reader of this book, you are our most important critic and commentator. We value your opinion and want to know what we're doing right, what we could do better, what areas you'd like to see us publish in, and any other words of wisdom you're willing to pass our way.

As the Executive Editor for the Certification team at New Riders Publishing, I welcome your comments. You can fax, email, or write me directly to let me know what you did or didn't like about this book—as well as what we can do to make our books stronger.

Please note that I cannot help you with technical problems related to the topic of this book, and that due to the high volume of mail I receive, I might not be able to reply to every message.

When you write, please be sure to include this book's title and authors, as well as your name and phone or fax number. I will carefully review your comments and share them with the authors and editors who worked on the book.

Fax: 317-581-4663

Email: `certification@mcp.com`

Mail: Mary Foote
         Executive Editor
         Certification
         New Riders Publishing
         201 West 103rd Street
         Indianapolis, IN 46290 USA

How to Use This Book

New Riders Publishing has made an effort in the second editions of its Training Guide series to make the information as accessible as possible for the purposes of learning the certification material. Here, you have an opportunity to view the many instructional features that have been incorporated into the books to achieve that goal.

CHAPTER OPENER

Each chapter begins with a set of features designed to allow you to maximize study time for that material.

List of Objectives: Each chapter begins with a list of the objectives, as stated by Microsoft.

Objective Explanations: Immediately following each objective is an explanation of it, providing context that defines it more meaningfully in relation to the exam. Because Microsoft can sometimes be vague in its objectives list, the objective explanations are designed to clarify any vagueness by relying on the author's test-taking experience.

OBJECTIVES

Microsoft provides the following objectives for "Connectivity":

Add and configure the network components of Windows NT Workstation.

▶ This objective is necessary because someone certified in the use of Windows NT Workstation technology must understand how it fits into a networked environment and how to configure the components that enable it to do so.

Use various methods to access network resources.

▶ This objective is necessary because someone certified in the use of Windows NT Workstation technology must understand how resources available on a network can be accessed from NT Workstation.

Implement Windows NT Workstation as a client in a NetWare environment.

▶ This objective is necessary because someone certified in the use of Windows NT Workstation technology must understand how NT Workstation can be used as a client in a NetWare environment and how to configure the services and protocols that make this possible.

Use various configurations to install Windows NT Workstation as a TCP/IP client.

▶ This objective is necessary because someone certified in the use of Windows NT Workstation technology must understand how TCP/IP is important in a network environment and how Workstation can be configured to use it.

CHAPTER 4

Connectivity

OUTLINE

Chapter Outline: Learning always gets a boost when you can see both the forest and the trees. To give you a visual image of how the topics in a chapter fit together, you will find an outline at the beginning of each chapter. You will also be able to use this for easy reference when looking for a particular topic.

STUDY STRATEGIES

▶ Disk configurations are a part of both the planning and the configuration of NT Server computers. To study for Planning Objective 1, you will need to look at both the following section and the material in Chapter 2, "Installation Part 1." As with many concepts, you should have a good handle on the terminology and know the best applications for different disk configurations. For the objectives of the NT Server exam, you will need to know only general disk configuration concepts—at a high level, not the nitty gritty. Make sure you memorize the concepts relating to partitioning and know the difference between the system and the boot partitions in an NT system (and the fact that the definitions of these are counter-intuitive). You should know that NT supports both FAT and NTFS partitions, as well as some of the advantages and disadvantages of each. You will also need to know about the fault-tolerance methods available in NT—stripe sets with parity and disk mirroring—including their definitions, hardware requirements, and advantages and disadvantages.

Of course, nothing substitutes for working with the concepts explained in this objective. If possible, get an NT system with some free disk space and play around with the Disk Administrator just to see how partitions are created and what they look like.

You might also want to look at some of the supplementary readings and scan TechNet for white papers on disk configuration.

▶ The best way to study for Planning Objective 2 is to read, memorize, and understand the use of each protocol. You should know what the protocols are, what they are used for, and what systems they are compatible with.

As with disk configuration, installing protocols on your NT Server is something that you plan for, not something you do just because it feels good to you at the time. Although it is much easier to add or remove a protocol than it is to reconfigure your hard drives, choosing a protocol is still an essential part of the planning process because specific protocols, like spoken languages, are designed to be used in certain circumstances. There is no point in learning to speak Mandarin Chinese if you are never around anyone who can understand you. Similarly, the NWLink protocol is used to interact with NetWare systems; therefore, if you do not have Novell servers on your network, you might want to rethink your plan to install it on your servers. We will discuss the uses of the major protocols in Chapter 7, "Connectivity." However, it is important that you have a good understanding of their uses here in the planning stage.

Study Strategies: Each topic presents its own learning challenge. To support you through this, New Riders has included strategies on how to best approach studying in order to retain the material in the chapter, particularly as it is addressed on the exam.

INSTRUCTIONAL FEATURES WITHIN THE CHAPTER

These books include a large amount of different kinds of information. The many different elements are designed to help you identify information by its purpose and importance to the exam and also to provide you with varied ways to learn the material. You will be able to determine how much attention to devote to certain elements, depending on your goals. By becoming familiar with the different presentations of information, you will know what information will be important to you as a test-taker and which information will be important to you as a practitioner.

EXAM TIP

Only One NTVDM Supports Multiple 16-bit Applications Expect at least one question about running Win16 applications in separate memory spaces. The key concept is that you can load multiple Win16 applications into the same memory space only if it is the initial Win16 NTVDM. It is not possible, for example, to run Word for Windows 6.0 and Excel for Windows 5.0 in one shared memory space and also run PowerPoint 4.0 and Access 2.0 in another shared memory space.

Exam Tip: Exam Tips appear in the margins to provide specific exam-related advice. Such tips may address what material is covered (or not covered) on the exam, how it is covered, mnemonic devices, or particular quirks of that exam.

Note: Notes appear in the margins and contain various kinds of useful information, such as tips on the technology or administrative practices, historical background on terms and technologies, or side commentaries on industry issues.

8   Chapter 1   PLANNING

INTRODUCTION

Microsoft grew up around the personal computer industry and established itself as the preeminent maker of software products for personal computers. Microsoft has a vast portfolio of software products, but it is best known for its operating systems.

Microsoft's current operating system products, listed here, are undoubtedly well-known to anyone studying for the MCSE exams:

◆ Windows 95

◆ Windows NT Workstation

◆ Windows NT Server

NOTE

Strange But True Although it sounds backward, it is true: Windows NT boots from the system partition and then loads the system from the boot partition.

Some older operating system products—namely MS-DOS, Windows 3.1, and Windows for Workgroups—are still important to the operability of Windows NT Server, so don't be surprised if you hear them mentioned from time to time in this book.

Windows NT is the most powerful, the most secure, and perhaps the most elegant operating system Microsoft has yet produced. It languished for a while after it first appeared (in part because no one was sure why they needed it or what to do with it), but Microsoft has persisted with improving interoperability and performance. With the release of Windows NT 4 which offers a new Windows 95-like user interface, Windows NT has assumed a prominent place in today's world of network-based computing.

WINDOWS NT SERVER AMONG MICROSOFT OPERATING SYSTEMS

▶ As we already mentioned, Microsoft has three operating system products now competing in the marketplace: Windows 95, Windows NT Workstation, and Windows NT Server. Each of these operating systems has its advantages and disadvantages.

WARNING

Don't Overextend Your Partitions and Wraps It is not necessary to create an extended partition on a disk; primary partitions might be all that you need. However, if you do create one, remember that you can never have more than one extended partition on a physical disk.

Looking at the presentation of the desktop, the three look very much alike—so much so that you might have to click the Start button and read the banner on the left side of the menu to determine which operating system you are looking at. Each offers the familiar Windows 95 user interface featuring the Start button, the Recycling

Objective Coverage Text: In the text before an exam objective is specifically addressed, you will notice the objective is listed to help call your attention to that particular material.

Warning: When using sophisticated information technology, there is always potential for mistakes or even catastrophes that may occur through improper application of the technology. Warnings appear in the margins to alert you to such potential problems.

STEP BY STEP

5.1 Configuring an Extension to Trigger an Application to Always Run in a Separate Memory Space

1. Start the Windows NT Explorer.

2. From the View menu, choose Options.

3. Click the File Types tab.

4. In the Registered File Types list box, select the desired file type.

5. Click the Edit button to display the Edit File Type dialog box. Then select Open from the Actions list and click the Edit button below it.

6. In the Editing Action for Type dialog box, adjust the application name by typing **cmd.exe /c start /separate** in front of the existing contents of the field (see Figure 5.15).

FIGURE 5.15
Configuring a shortcut to run a Win16 application in a separate memory space.

Figure: To improve readability, the figures have been placed carefully so they do not interrupt the main flow of text.

---

14   Chapter 1   PLANNING

You must use NTFS if you want to preserve existing permissions when you migrate files and directories from a NetWare server to a Windows NT Server system.

Windows 95 is Microsoft's everyday workhorse operating system. It provides a 32-bit platform and is designed to operate with a variety of peripherals. See Table 1.1 for the minimum hardware requirements for the installation and operation of Windows 95. Also, if you want to allow Macintosh computers to access files on the partition through Windows NT's Services for Macintosh, you must format the partition for NTFS.

MAKING REGISTRY CHANGES

To make Registry changes, run the REGEDT32.EXE program. The Registry in Windows NT is a complex database of configuration settings for your computer. If you want to configure the Workstation service, open the HKEY_LOCAL_MACHINE hive, as shown in Figure 3.22.

The exact location for configuring your Workstation service is

    HKEY_LOCAL_MACHINE\System\CurrentControlSet\Services\
    LanmanWorkstation\Parameters

To find additional information regarding this Registry item and others, refer to the Windows NT Server resource kit.

This summary table offers an overview of the differences between the FAT and NTFS file systems.

In-Depth Sidebar: These more extensive discussions cover material that perhaps is not directly relevant to the exam, but is useful as reference material or in everyday practice. In-Depths may also provide useful background or contextual information necessary for understanding the larger topic under consideration.

CASE STUDIES

Case studies are the central element in the Solution Architectures exam. You are presented with case studies throughout this book so you can gain the experience that you will need to pass the 70-100 exam. Each case study presents an information technology situation that requires you to recognize the important facts that are relevant for answering the types of questions presented on the exam. See Appendix E, "Quick Tips for Analyzing an Exam Case Study," for more explanation of case studies.

CASE STUDY: NEW RIDER IMPORTERS

BACKGROUND

New Rider Importers is a multinational firm specializing in the acquisition and retail sale of consumer goods from all over the Earth. Over the last 20 years, it has grown from a single storefront in Chicago to more than 1,000 retail outlets in more than 60 countries! The coming of the "global economy" is having a profound impact on the business of New Rider Importers—good and bad.

PROBLEM STATEMENT

As it has become easier for people to travel around the world, it has become much harder for New Rider Importers to locate items that would otherwise be unavailable to its customers.

CFO

"There's no two ways about it. Sales are down—way down! The stuff that we have in our stores simply isn't getting there fast enough to be 'fashionable!' I'm projecting that if we don't increase our revenues within the next few months, we are going to have to start seriously looking at cutting out some of our stores!"

Checkout Assistant

"I'm tired of always telling people that we don't have the stuff they want. It's been six months now since we had Mexican jumping beans in our toy section. If the past is any indication, we will probably get them in another three months—long after the jumping bean craze is over!"

Purchasing Agent

"I keep hearing these complaints about the stores not having whatever is fashionable in their areas at the moment, but what do they expect us to do? With stores spread out all over the world, we have to cater to more different tastes than you would ever dream possible. And, even if I knew that everyone in New York was suddenly interested in Japanese plum candy, for example, how could I possibly know that our stores there are fresh out of it? Chances are that I'm 4,000 miles away at the time, trying to work out a deal for whatever the 'big thing' was six months ago."

CURRENT SYSTEM

The system currently used by New Rider Importers has evolved from a number of smaller pieces that have been written in an ad hoc fashion over time.

Customer

The process begins when a customer visits a New Rider Importers store. Eventually, the customer finds a product that he or she would like to purchase. The customer brings this to the front counter. At this point, the checkout assistant processes the sale and the customer is ready to go.

Purchasing Agent

Purchasing agents travel the globe looking for items that they think might be salable in countries where New Rider Importers has stores. When goods are found and a deal is made, it is entered into the laptop systems that the

---

CHAPTER SUMMARY

KEY TERMS

Before you take the exam, make sure you are comfortable with the definitions and concepts for each of the following key terms:

• FAT

• NTFS

• workgroup

• domain

This chapter discussed the main planning topics you will encounter on the Windows NT Server exam. Distilled down, these topics revolve around two main goals: understanding the planning of disk configuration and understanding the planning of network protocols.

◆ Windows NT Server supports an unlimited number of inbound sessions; Windows NT Workstation supports no more than 10 active sessions at the same time.

◆ Windows NT Server accommodates an unlimited number of remote access connections (although Microsoft only supports up to 256); Windows NT Workstation supports only a single remote access connection.

Key Terms: A list of key terms appears at the end of each chapter. These are terms that you should be sure you know and are comfortable defining and understanding when you go to take the exam.

Chapter Summary: Before the Apply Your Learning section, you will find a Chapter Summary that wraps up the chapter and reviews what you have learned.

EXTENSIVE REVIEW AND SELF-TEST OPTIONS

At the end of each chapter, along with some summary elements, you will find a section called "Apply Your Knowledge" that gives you several different methods with which to test your understanding of the material and review what you have learned.

Chapter 1 PLANNING   23

APPLY YOUR KNOWLEDGE

This section allows you to assess how well you understood the material in the chapter. Review and Exam questions test your knowledge of the tasks and concepts specified in the objectives. The Exercises provide you with opportunities to engage in the sorts of tasks that comprise the skill sets the objectives reflect.

Exercises

1.1 Synchronizing the Domain Controller

The following steps show you how to manually synchronize a backup domain controller within your domain. (This objective deals with Objective Planning 1.)

Estimated Time: Less than 10 minutes.

1. Click Start, Programs, Administrative Tools, and select the Server Manager icon.

2. Highlight the BDC (Backup Domain Controller) in your computer list.

3. Select the Computer menu, then select Synchronize with Primary Domain Controller.

12.2 Establishing a Trust Relationship between Domains

The following steps show you how to establish a trust relationship between multiple domains. To complete this exercise, you must have two Windows NT Server computers, each installed in their own domain. (This objective deals with objective Planning 1.)

Estimated Time: 10 minutes

1. From the trusted domain select Start, Programs, Administrative Tools, and click User Manager for Domains. The User Manager.

FIGURE 1.2
The login process on a local machine.

2. Select the Policies menu and click Trust Relationships. The Trust Relationships dialog box appears.

4. When the trusting domain information has been entered, click OK and close the Trust Relationships dialog box.

Review Questions

1. List the four domain models that can be used for directory services in Windows NT Server 4.

2. List the goals of a directory services architecture.

3. What is the maximum size of the SAM database in Windows NT Server 4.0?

4. What are the two different types of domains in a trust relationship?

5. In a trust relationship which domain would contain the user accounts?

Exercises: These activities provide an opportunity for you to master specific hands-on tasks. Our goal is to increase your proficiency with the product or technology. You must be able to conduct these tasks in order to pass the exam.

Review Questions: These open-ended, short-answer questions allow you to quickly assess your comprehension of what you just read in the chapter. Instead of asking you to choose from a list of options, these questions require you to state the correct answers in your own words. Although you will not experience these kinds of questions on the exam, they will indeed test your level of comprehension of key concepts.

6. Can a local account be used in a trust relationship? Explain.

7. In a complete trust domain model that uses 4 different domains, what is the total number of trust relationships required to use a complete trust domain model?

Exam Questions

The following questions are similar to those you will face on the Microsoft exam. Answers to these questions can be found in section Answers and Explanations, later in the chapter. At the end of each of those answers, you will be informed of where (that is, in what section of the chapter) to find more information..

1. ABC Corporation has locations in Toronto, New York, and San Francisco. It wants to install Windows NT Server 4 to encompass all its locations in a single WAN environment. The head office is located in New York. What is the best domain model for ABCís directory services implementation?

   A. Single-domain model

   B. Single-master domain model

   C. Multiple-master domain model

   D. Complete-trust domain model

2. JPS Printing has a single location with 1,000 users spread across the LAN. It has special printers and applications installed on the servers in its environment. It needs to be able to centrally manage the user accounts and the resources. Which domain model would best fit its needs?

A. Single-domain model

B. Single-master domain model

C. Multiple-master domain model

D. Complete-trust domain model

5. What must be created to allow a user account from one domain to access resources in a different domain?

A. Complete Trust Domain Model

B. One Way Trust Relationship

C. Two Way Trust Relationship

D. Master-Domain Model

Answers to Review Questions

1. Single domain, master domain, mulriple-master domain, complete-trust domain. See section, Windows NT Server 4 Domain Models, in this chapter for more information. (This question deals with objective Planning 1.)

2. One user, one account, centralized administration, universal resource access, synchronization. See section, Windows NT Server 4 Directory Services, in this chapter for more information. (This question deals with objective Planning 1.)

6. Local accounts cannot be given permissions across trusts. See section, Accounts in Trust Relationships, in this chapter for more information. (This question deals with Planning 1.)

Exam Questions: These questions reflect the kinds of multiple-choice questions that appear on the Microsoft exams. Use them to become familiar with the exam question formats and to help you determine what you know and what you need to review or study more.

Answers and Explanations: For each of the Review and Exam questions, you will find thorough explanations located at the end of the section.

Suggested Readings and Resources

The following are some recommended readings on the subject of installing and configuring NT Workstation:

1. Microsoft Official Curriculum course 770: *Installing and Configuring Microsoft Windows NT Workstation 4.0*

   • Module 1: Overview of Windows NT Workstation 4.0

   • Module 2: Installing Windows NT Workstation 4.0

2. Microsoft Official Curriculum course 922: *Supporting Microsoft Windows NT 4.0 Core Technologies*

   • Module 2: Installing Windows NT

   • Module 3: Configuring the Windows NT Environment

3. *Microsoft Windows NT Workstation Resource Kit Version 4.0* (Microsoft Press)

   • Chapter 2: Customizing Setup

   • Chapter 4: Planning for a Mixed Environment

4. Microsoft TechNet CD-ROM

   • *MS Windows NT Workstation Technical Notes*

      • MS Windows NT Workstation Deployment Guide – Automating Windows NT Setup

      • An Unattended Windows NT Workstation Deployment

5. Web Sites

   • www.microsoft.com/train_cert

   • www.prometric.com/testingcandidates/ assessment/chosetest.html (take online

Suggested Readings and Resources: The very last element in every chapter is a list of additional resources you can use if you want to go above and beyond certification-level material or if you need to spend more time on a particular subject that you are having trouble understanding.

Introduction

MCSD Training Guide: Solution Architectures is designed for developers whose goal is certification as a Microsoft Certified Solutions Developer (MCSD). It covers the Analyzing Requirements and Defining Solution Architectures exam (#70-100). This exam measures your ability to analyze business requirements in various scenarios and then define technical solution architectures that will optimize business results by using Microsoft development tools.

This book is your one-stop shop. Everything you need to know to pass the exam is in here, and Microsoft has approved it as study material. You do not have to take a class in addition to buying this book to pass the exam. However, depending on your personal study habits or learning style, you may benefit from buying this book *and* taking a class.

Be aware that Microsoft advises that exam takers have a minimum of two years experience in the following areas:

- ◆ Analyzing customer needs and creating requirements specifications documents for client/server solutions in multiple business domains

- ◆ Process modeling, data modeling, component design, and user interface design

- ◆ Designing, developing, and implementing a client/server solution

- ◆ Knowledge of the functionality of both Microsoft Office and Microsoft Back Office Applications

- ◆ Integration of new systems and applications into legacy environments

- ◆ Developing Microsoft Windows and Web applications

Although oriented toward the exam, this book also teaches the basics of client/server development.

HOW THIS BOOK HELPS YOU

This book takes you on a self-guided tour of all the areas covered by the Solutions Architectures exam and teaches you the specific skills you'll need in order to achieve your MCSD certification. You'll also find helpful hints, tips, real-world examples, and exercises, as well as references to additional study materials. Specifically, this book is set up to help you in the following ways:

- ◆ **Organization.** The book is organized by individual exam objectives. Every objective you need to know for the Solution Architectures exam is covered in this book. We have attempted to present the objectives in an order that is as close as possible to that listed by Microsoft. However, we have not hesitated to reorganize them where needed to make the material as easy as possible for you to learn. We have also attempted to make the information accessible in the following ways:

  - The full list of exam topics and objectives is included in this introduction.

  - Each chapter begins with a list of the objectives to be covered.

  - Each chapter also begins with an outline that provides you with an overview of the material and the page numbers where particular topics can be found.

- The objectives are repeated where the material most directly relevant to it is covered (unless the whole chapter addresses a single objective).

- Information on where the objectives are covered is also conveniently condensed on the tear card at the front of this book.

◆ **Instructional Features**. This book has been designed to provide you with multiple ways to learn and reinforce the exam material. Following are some of the helpful methods:

- *Case Studies*. Given the case study basis of the exam, we designed this *Training Guide* around them. Case studies appear in each chapter and also serve as the basis for exam questions.

- *Objective Explanations*. As mentioned previously, each chapter begins with a list of the objectives covered in the chapter. In addition, immediately following each objective is an explanation of that objective in a context that defines it more meaningfully.

- *Study Strategies*. The beginning of the chapter also includes strategies for how to approach studying and retaining the material in the chapter, particularly as it is addressed on the exam.

- *Exam Tips*. Exam tips appear in the margin to provide specific exam-related advice. Such tips may address what material is covered (or not covered) on the exam, how it is covered, mnemonic devices, or particular quirks of that exam.

- *Review Breaks and Summaries*. Crucial information is summarized at various points in the book in lists or tables. Each chapter ends with a summary as well.

- *Key Terms*. A list of key terms appears at the end of each chapter.

- *Notes*. These appear in the margin and contain various kinds of useful information such as tips on technology or administrative practices, historical background on terms and technologies, or side commentary on industry issues.

- *Warnings*. When you use sophisticated information technology, there is always the potential for mistakes or even catastrophes to occur because of improper application of the technology. Warnings appear in the margin to alert you to such potential problems.

- *In-depths*. These more extensive discussions cover material that may not be directly relevant to the exam but that is useful as reference material or in everyday practice. In-depths may also provide useful background or contextual information necessary for understanding the larger topic under consideration.

- *Exercises*. Found at the end of the chapters in the "Apply Your Knowledge" section, exercises are performance-based opportunities for you to learn and assess your knowledge.

◆ **Extensive practice test options.** The book provides numerous opportunities for you to assess your knowledge and practice for the exam. The practice options include the following:

- *Review Questions*. These open-ended questions appear in the "Apply Your Knowledge" section at the end of each chapter. They allow you to quickly assess your comprehension of what you just read in the chapter. Answers to the questions are provided later in the section.

- *Exam Questions.* These questions also appear in the "Apply Your Knowledge" section. They cover a case study. Use them to practice for the exam and to help you determine what you know and what you need to review or study further. Answers and explanations for them are provided.

- *Practice Exam.* A practice exam is included in the "Final Review" section. The "Final Review" section and the Practice Exam are discussed next.

- *ExamGear.* The special Training Guide version of the ExamGear software included on the CD-ROM provides further practice questions.

> **NOTE**
> **Details on ExamGear, Training Guide Edition** For a description of the New Riders ExamGear test simulation software, see Appendix D, "Using the ExamGear, Training Guide Edition Software."

◆ **Final Review.** This part of the book provides you with three valuable tools for preparing for the exam.

- *Fast Facts.* This condensed version of the information contained in the book will prove extremely useful for last-minute review.

- *Study and Exam Prep Tips.* Read this section early on to help you develop study strategies. It also provides you with valuable exam-day tips and information on new exam/question formats such as adaptive tests and simulation-based questions.

- *Practice Exam.* A practice test is included. Questions are written in styles similar to those used on the actual exam. Use it to assess your readiness for the real thing.

The book includes several other features like a section titled "Suggested Readings and Resources " at the end of each chapter that directs you toward further information that could aid you in your exam preparation or your actual work. There are valuable appendices as well, including a glossary (Appendix A), an overview of the Microsoft certification program (Appendix B), and a description of what is on the CD-ROM (Appendix C).

The Microsoft Solution Architectures exam is structured around case studies and is really more of a reading comprehension exam than any other Microsoft exam you may have taken. For this reason, we've included Appendix E, "Quick Tips for Analyzing an Exam Case Study," which provides you with an overview of the approach you should take to reading and understanding the case studies on the exam. These and all the other book features mentioned previously supply you with thorough exam preparation.

For more information about the exam or the certification process, contact Microsoft:

Microsoft Education: 800-636-7544

Internet:
ftp://ftp.microsoft.com/Services/MSEdCert

World Wide Web:
http://www.microsoft.com/train_cert

CompuServe Forum: GO MSEDCERT

WHAT THE ANALYZING REQUIREMENTS AND DEFINING SOLUTION ARCHITECTURES EXAM (#70-100) COVERS

The Analyzing Requirements and Defining Solution Architectures exam (#70-100) covers six main topics. These include analyzing business requirements, defining the technical architecture for a solution, developing the conceptual and logical design for an application, developing data models, designing a user interface and user services, and deriving the physical design. Each of these main topic areas is covered in one or more chapters.

Six themes recur throughout this book and the Microsoft exam. These are referred to as the "PASS ME" themes:

◆ Performance

◆ Availability

◆ Security

◆ Scalability

◆ Maintainability

◆ Extensibility

In Chapter 3, "PASS ME Analysis," you learn how the analysis phase of your project should take into account requirements for each of these six areas. In Chapter 7, "Testing the Technical Architecture," you learn how to test the design of your technical architecture using them as well. Chapter 8, "Developing the Conceptual Design for a Solution," uses PASS ME to develop a complete conceptual design for a new solution. And finally, in Chapter 13, "PASS ME and the Physical Design," you explore the impact that various physical design decisions may have on the capability of your solutions to satisfy user requirements reflecting each of the "PASS ME" aspects.

The exam objectives are listed by topic area in the following sections.

Analyzing Business Requirements

Analyze the scope of a project. Considerations include:

◆ Existing applications

◆ Anticipated changes in environment

◆ Expected lifetime of solution

◆ Time, cost, budget, and benefit trade-offs

Analyze the extent of a business requirement.

◆ Establish business requirements.

◆ Establish the type of problem, such as a messaging problem or communication problem.

◆ Establish and define customer quality requirements.

◆ Minimize Total Cost of Ownership (TCO).

◆ Increase Return on Investment (ROI) of solution.

◆ Analyze current platform and infrastructure.

◆ Incorporate planned platform and infrastructure into solution.

◆ Analyze impact of technology migration.

◆ Plan physical requirements, such as infrastructure.

◆ Establish application environment, such as hardware platform, support, and operating system.

◆ Identify organizational constraints, such as financial situation, company politics, technical acceptance level, and training needs.

◆ Establish schedule for implementation of solution.

◆ Identify audience.

Analyze security requirements.

◆ Identify roles of administrator, groups, guests, and clients.

◆ Identify impact on existing environment.

◆ Establish fault tolerance.

◆ Plan for maintainability.

◆ Plan distribution of security database.

◆ Establish security context.

◆ Plan for auditing.

◆ Identify level of security needed.

◆ Analyze existing mechanisms for security policies.

Analyze performance requirements. Considerations include:

◆ Transactions per time slice

◆ Bandwidth

◆ Capacity

◆ Interoperability with existing standards

◆ Peak versus average requirements

◆ Response-time expectations

◆ Existing response-time characteristics

◆ Barriers to performance

Analyze maintainability requirements. Considerations include:

◆ Breadth of application distribution

◆ Method of distribution

◆ Maintenance expectations

◆ Location and knowledge level of maintenance staff

◆ Impact of third-party maintenance agreements

Analyze extensibility requirements. Solution must be able to handle the growth of functionality.

Analyze availability requirements. Considerations include:

◆ Hours of operation

◆ Level of availability

◆ Geographic scope

◆ Impact of downtime

Analyze human factors requirements. Considerations include:

◆ Target users

◆ Localization

◆ Accessibility

◆ Roaming users

◆ Help

◆ Training requirements

◆ Physical environment constraints

◆ Special needs

Analyze the requirements for integrating a solution with existing applications. Considerations include:

◆ Legacy applications

◆ Format and location of existing data

◆ Connectivity to existing applications

◆ Data conversion

◆ Data enhancement requirements

Analyze existing methodologies and limitations of a business. Considerations include:

- Legal issues
- Current business practices
- Organization structure
- Process engineering
- Budget
- Implementation and training methodologies
- Quality control requirements
- Customer's needs

Analyze scalability requirements. Considerations include:

- Growth of audience
- Growth of organization
- Growth of data
- Cycle of use

Defining the Technical Architecture for a Solution

Given a business scenario, identify which solution type is appropriate. Solution types are single-tier, two-tier, and *n*-tier.

Identify which technologies are appropriate for implementation of a given business solution. Considerations include:

- Technology standards such as EDI, Internet, OSI, COMTI, and POSIX
- Proprietary technologies
- Technology environment of the company, both current and planned

- Selection of development tools
- Type of solution, such as enterprise, distributed, centralized, and collaborative

Choose a data storage architecture. Considerations include:

- Volume
- Number of transactions per time increment
- Number of connections or sessions
- Scope of business requirements
- Extensibility requirements
- Reporting requirements
- Number of users
- Type of database

Test the feasibility of a proposed technical architecture.

- Demonstrate that business requirements are met.
- Demonstrate that case scenarios are met.
- Demonstrate that existing technology constraints are met.
- Assess impact of shortfalls in meeting requirements.
- Develop appropriate deployment strategy.

Developing the Conceptual and Logical Design for an Application

Construct a conceptual design that is based on a variety of scenarios and that includes context, workflow process, task sequence, and physical environment models. Types of applications include:

- SDI, MDI, console, and dialog desktop applications
- Two-tier, client/server, and Web applications
- *n*-tier applications
- Collaborative applications

Given a conceptual design, apply the principles of modular design to derive the components and services of the logical design.

Incorporate business rules into object design.

Assess the potential impact of the logical design on performance, maintainability, extensibility, scalability, availability, and security.

Developing Data Models

Group data into entities by applying normalization rules.

Specify the relationships between entities.

Choose the foreign key that will enforce a relationship between entities and will ensure referential integrity.

Identify the business rules that relate to data integrity.

Incorporate business rules and constraints into the data model.

Identify appropriate levels of denormalization.

Develop a database that uses general database development standards and guidelines.

Designing a User Interface and User Services

Given a solution, identify the navigation for the user interface.

Identify input validation procedures that should be integrated into the user interface.

Evaluate methods of providing online user assistance, such as status bars, ToolTips, and Help files.

Construct a prototype user interface that is based on business requirements, user interface guidelines, and the organization's standards.

- Establish appropriate and consistent use of menu-based controls.
- Establish appropriate shortcut keys (accelerated keys).

Establish appropriate type of output.

Deriving the Physical Design

Assess the potential impact of the physical design on performance, maintainability, extensibility, scalability, availability, and security.

Evaluate whether access to a database should be encapsulated in an object.

Design the properties, methods, and events of components.

HARDWARE AND SOFTWARE YOU'LL NEED

Although neither this book nor the exam specifically requires that you use any particular technology, one of the tools that Microsoft mentions as relevant to the exam is Microsoft Visual Studio. In order to run Visual Studio, your computer should meet the following criteria:

- On the Microsoft Hardware Compatibility List
- Pentium 90MHz (or better) processor

◆ 600MB (or larger) hard disk

◆ VGA (or Super VGA) video adapter and monitor

◆ Mouse or equivalent pointing device

◆ CD-ROM drive

◆ Network Interface Card (NIC) or modem connection to Internet

◆ Presence on an existing network, or use of a two-port (or more) miniport hub to create a test network

◆ Internet access with Internet Explorer 4 (Service Pack 1) or later

◆ 24MB of RAM (32MB recommended)

◆ Windows NT Option Pack recommended

◆ Microsoft SQL Server 6.5 (or better) optional

◆ Microsoft SNA Server optional

It is easier to obtain access to the necessary computer hardware and software in a corporate business environment. It can be difficult, however, to allocate enough time within the busy workday to complete a self-study program. Most of your study time will occur after normal working hours, away from the everyday interruptions and pressures of your regular job.

ADVICE ON TAKING THE EXAM

More extensive tips are found in the Final Review section titled "Study and Exam Prep Tips," but keep this advice in mind as you study:

◆ **Read all the material.** Microsoft has been known to include material not expressly specified in the objectives. This book has included additional information not reflected in the objectives in an effort to give you the best possible preparation for the examination— and for the real-world experiences to come.

◆ **Complete the exercises in each chapter.** They will help you gain experience using the specified methodology or approach. All Microsoft exams are task- and experienced-based and require you to have experience actually performing the tasks upon which you will be tested.

◆ **Use the questions to assess your knowledge.** Don't just read the chapter content; use the questions to find out what you know and what you don't. You also need the experience of analyzing case studies. If you are struggling at all, study some more, review, and then assess your knowledge again.

◆ **Review the exam objectives.** Develop your own questions and examples for each topic listed. If you can develop and answer several questions for each topic, you should not find it difficult to pass the exam.

Exam-Taking Advice Although this book is designed to prepare you to take and pass the Solution Architectures certification exam, there are no guarantees. Read this book, work through the questions and exercises, and when you feel confident, take the Practice Exam and additional exams using the ExamGear, Training Guide Edition test simulator. This should tell you whether you are ready for the real thing.

When taking the actual certification exam, make sure you answer all the questions before your time limit expires. Do not spend too much time on any one question. If you are unsure, answer it as best as you can; then mark it for review so you can go back to it when you have finished the rest of the questions.

Remember, the primary object is not to pass the exam—it is to understand the material. If you understand the material, passing the exam should be simple. Knowledge is a pyramid: To build upward, you need a solid foundation. This book and the Microsoft Certified Professional programs are designed to ensure that you have that solid foundation.

Good luck!

NEW RIDERS PUBLISHING

The staff of New Riders Publishing is committed to bringing you the very best in computer reference material. Each New Riders book is the result of months of work by authors and staff who research and refine the information contained within its covers.

As part of this commitment to you, the NRP reader, New Riders invites your input. Please let us know if you enjoy this book, if you have trouble with the information or examples presented, or if you have a suggestion for the next edition.

Please note, however, that New Riders staff cannot serve as a technical resource during your preparation for the Microsoft certification exams or for questions about software- or hardware-related problems. Please refer instead to the documentation that accompanies the Microsoft products or to the application's Help systems.

If you have a question or comment about any New Riders book, there are several ways to contact New Riders Publishing. We will respond to as many readers as we can. Your name, address, or phone number will never become part of a mailing list or be used for any purpose other than to help us continue to bring you the best books possible. You can write to us at the following address:

New Riders Publishing
Attn: Mary Foote
Executive Editor
201 W. 103rd Street
Indianapolis, IN 46290

If you prefer, you can fax New Riders Publishing at 317-581-4663.

You also can send email to New Riders at the following Internet address:

certification@mcp.com

Thank you for selecting *MCSD Training Guide: Solution Architectures*!

ANALYZING REQUIREMENTS

This chapter addresses the following exam objective listed by Microsoft as part of the Analyzing Business Requirements section of the exam:

Analyze the scope of a project. Considerations include the following:

- **Existing applications**

- **Anticipated changes in environment**

- **Expected lifetime of solution**

- **Time, cost, budget, and benefit trade-offs**

► This objective encourages you to think about the size of your project. You need to consider how much effort you and your team are likely to expend developing a given solution. This is largely determined by the systems the organization has in place and the level of business resources made available to you. You might consider whether the project is small, medium, or large, knowing that a small, simple system would require a different degree of effort than a larger, more complicated one.

► You also should try to determine in advance how significant the impact of a solution is likely to be on a given customer. Keep foremost in your mind the future plans of the customer's organization as you are determining this impact.

► As you make your project analysis, you may find that the nature of your customer's existing applications have something of a "wildcard" effect. If the applications are well-designed and properly implemented, your job may be easier than you anticipate. If not, the effort required to build your solution could be what you expected or greatly increased.

CHAPTER 1

Analyzing Project Scope

▶ Similarly, anticipated changes in your customer organization's environment can either increase or reduce the scope of your project. Newer hardware and operating systems can improve performance or cause insurmountable incompatibilities with existing code. Organizational restructuring can improve the flow of communication and decision-making within your customer's organization or confuse your working environment to the point of gridlock.

▶ It is also important for this objective that you understand the effects of a solution's expected life-time on your project's scope. In general, solutions with shorter expected life spans need to be delivered quicker—even at the expense of additional "bells and whistles." Longer-term solutions have more time to prove their worth, can take a little longer to finish, and should probably include a few more features.

▶ Finally, this objective requires an understanding of the subtle relationships between the resources of time, cost, budget, and benefits. Because the meaning of "cost" versus "budget" may not be immediately clear, we have chosen to distinguish these in our text by referring to them as "labor" and "money." This chapter shows you how to estimate the impact on one or more resources when another resource is increased or decreased.

▶ Remember that one benefit of going into an organization that has little or no computer technology in place is the absence of existing technology that may be difficult to work with. The downside to this, unfortunately, is the absence of potentially useful technology, which means you may need to build everything yourself.

▶ Be able to distinguish between the two types of organizations that have information systems already in place. In some cases, this technology is useful and an asset in the construction of your solution. In others, it is obsolete or poorly built and a hindrance to your efforts.

▶ Understand how anticipated changes in your solution's environment, expectations for its life span, and the resource trade-offs required for its development all play a part in determining the form that your solution must eventually take.

INTRODUCTION

This chapter introduces you to the study of business problem definition. Here you will find everything you need to tackle the subject matter on the exam, except for the recurring "PASS ME" themes, which are discussed at length in the next chapter.

This chapter focuses on determining the scope of a project. You may wonder how you can figure out how much work is involved in building a solution before you have even determined the nature of the problem. The answer lies in the fact that on the exam, as in this book, questions of "scope" generally refer to those factors influencing your project that are extrinsic to the problem itself.

Microsoft is one of the most successful corporations in history. It seems logical, then, to consider how Microsoft is able to consistently produce solutions that are both high in quality and low in price. The answer lies largely in the company's approach to business problem definition and analysis.

This logic may confuse you at first. After all, Microsoft's success has been built mainly on the production of pre-packaged software for mass-market consumption. What does this have to do with building custom solutions for individual business customers?

The answer is quite a lot. By the end of this chapter, you will see more clearly these "universal truths" of business problem definition. Along the way, you will discover many places where some "truths" seem more important than others on the Microsoft exam.

CASE STUDY: THE OSCARNET

BACKGROUND

The OscarNet is a Seattle-based Internet Service Provider (ISP), claiming about 25,000 customers in and around the Seattle metropolitan area. The majority of the company's revenues come from the sale of dialup accounts that allow customers to access the Internet via the OscarNet's network.

PROBLEM STATEMENT

Although the OscarNet's approach to selling dialup accounts has served it well in the past, the time has come to update the company's signup processes.

VP of Sales
"I can't even begin to tell you how many sales we've lost because people don't want to wait to get our software in the mail. When people decide that they want Internet access, they want it yesterday. And then, even once they've gotten our software and signed up with it, the system makes them wait until 5:00 P.M. to start using it!"

Inside Sales Representatives
"It's not really such a bad old system, but I do have my suspicions about its accuracy. I know for a fact that I sold 15 business monthly dialup accounts last month, and I only got commissions on 12 of them! I hate to complain, but that is real money out of my pocket, you know?"

Billing Clerk
"I guess the system works out pretty well for us, except for when we do our monthly consistency checks. It seems that a lot of accounts get created on our system that never get billed. The training I got when I started here said that this would happen if we didn't put all of our applications into the system correctly. But I've forgotten a lot of the correct procedures since then and all the people who knew the procedures are gone."

CURRENT SYSTEM

The system the OscarNet uses to create new dialup accounts was created when the company was in its infancy. Some of the automated bits have been patched to use newer technology since that time. Many pieces still require considerable human intervention and activity.

Customer
The process of signing up for a dialup account with the OscarNet usually begins with a telephone conversation between the potential customer and an Internal Sales Representative. The salesperson takes the relevant information and arranges to mail the customer the company's special signup software.

When the software arrives a few days later, the customer is able to use it to call the OscarNet's special signup server. The signup server uses a PPP networking connection to support customer signup via a web browser. After the customer enters the relevant information for a second time, the system responds that the new account will be active at 5:00 P.M.

CASE STUDY: THE OSCARNET

Receptionist

The receptionist at the OscarNet is responsible for creating the dialup accounts on the company's network. Throughout the day, the receptionist checks the information coming through the signup server for accuracy. At the end of the day, all the valid requests are put into the account-creation application and become available for customer use. If the receptionist is out sick or unavailable for any reason, requests are processed the following day. This happens only three or four times a year but never fails to generate customer complaints.

Billing Clerk

The billing clerks are responsible for entering into the billing system the accounts created on the OscarNet's network. Throughout the day, sales representatives from Internal Sales provide the billing clerks with paper applications taken from customers over the phone. The clerks then manually enter the information into the billing system.

At the end of the day, the billing system generates labels that allow the billing clerks to ship the software to the customers so they can use their accounts.

Dialup Sales Manager

The current account-creation process often results in discrepancies between existing accounts and those actually getting billed. Resolving these discrepancies is one of the jobs of the Dialup Sales Manager. The manager also is responsible for paying sales commissions at the end of every month on the basis of reports generated by the billing system.

ENVIRONMENT

The environment under which the OscarNet's current system operates is a curious mixture of old and new technologies.

VP of Sales

"I know that whatever computer they're using to answer the signup software calls is really old. Our billing system has a really nice, big computer, though. And, of course, all of our sales staff have adequate desktop machines."

Programmer

"When someone dials in to the signup server, we've got a bunch of Active Server Pages that take their information and dump it into Access databases. The receptionist copies it out of there and pastes it (via Telnet) into a PERL application that we have running on our UNIX servers. This may seem a bit primitive, but we've found that it is the most fool-proof way to have non-technical individuals perform file transfers."

Development Manager

"We're running our billing system on a 4-processor Alpha computer with 256MB of memory running NT 4. The signup server, on the other hand, is an old 486 with just 16MB, also running NT 4. It's got four modems for taking calls, and it communicates with callers using our own proprietary networking protocol. Hopefully, we'll be swapping that out for a Pentium with plenty of memory soon.

continues

CASE STUDY: THE OSCARNET

continued

We've got about 50 desktops running Windows 98 here with CPUs that vary from 100 to 200 MHz, but we've standardized their memory at least—they all have exactly 32MB."

ENVISIONED SYSTEM

Everyone at the OscarNet has ideas about what should be included in any new system for creating new dialup accounts.

VP of Sales

"I think it goes almost without saying that all dialup accounts should get created as soon as they are ordered. That way, we wouldn't even have to send out software."

Programmer

"Whatever we do is going to require a more reliable database for storing our dialup account information. Whenever we have tried to do account creation during business hours, the whole thing has wound up crashing. I guess the load on it at that time has just been too much for it to handle.

The new billing system we're buying in a few months should change everything. At the very least, it will interface better with other applications."

Dialup Sales Manager

"Most importantly, we absolutely must write versions of our signup software for the other Windows OS. However much it costs—we've got plenty left in the budget for whatever you can come up with.

So far, we only have it available for Windows 95, so what about all the NT users? Whenever I talk to these customers, this is one of the first things that they ask about. If we could just have something for them, I'd consider myself satisfied."

SECURITY

Being in the Internet business, there's no shortage of security experts at the OscarNet. Most of their experience has been directed at protecting themselves from the outside world, however, rather than internal security.

VP of Sales

VPs at the OscarNet generally are allowed full access to information pertaining to the people and tasks under their direct supervision. The VP of Sales is particularly concerned that only her Dialup Manager will be able to view commissions information for the sales staff as a whole. Of course, individual sales representatives should always be able to view their own information.

Billing Clerk

Only billing clerks are allowed to "comp" accounts, and they need the approval of the Dialup Manager to issue any kind of credit or refund.

CASE STUDY: THE OSCARNET

Inside Sales Representative

The inside sales representatives must be kept from altering each other's applications. Otherwise, it is just possible that one of them will try to put their name on someone else's application in order to get the commission payments. Sensitive information such as customer credit card numbers and passwords should, ideally, disappear from the applications after an appropriate amount of time.

PERFORMANCE

The process of account creation is the primary focus of all attempts to improve performance at the OscarNet. Forcing customers to wait until 5:00 P.M. to use their accounts on a business day is bad business practice. Making them wait until the following Monday for accounts requested after 5:00 P.M. on Friday is completely unacceptable.

VP of Sales

"Now that the initial rush to get on the Internet is over, I think we can pretty safely assume our days of exponential growth are over. On the other hand, we do have this DSL rollout up our sleeve that could bring in a lot of new small business and consumer business. So, I guess the new system should be able to handle a lot—even though it probably won't have to."

Programmer

"The billing clerks tend to use the system all day, every day—except for weekends, of course. So, since we have three of them, our billing system must continue to support at least three simultaneous users. The signup server, somehow or another, needs to expand upward to supporting at least 10 callers at a time."

Receptionist

"Whatever you do, I have to get out of here by 5:30 P.M. every day. You know the OscarNet's position on overtime pay!"

Development Manager

"Our dialup database is going to make improving account creation performance very difficult, at best. And the signup server only supports four modems. I bet a project to fix all of our problems would have to contain 100 tasks, at least!"

MAINTAINABILITY

A new system is useful only as long as it continues to function properly. Maintainability is the measure of how easy it will be to keep it functioning effectively.

continues

CASE STUDY: THE OSCARNET

continued

VP of Sales

"Well, for the time being at least, our entire operation is confined to the 2nd and 3rd floors of this one building. But, ideally, we'd like to bring our business partners in on as much of our signup technology as possible—eventually. I'm not sure how we can make sure that all of them always have the latest and greatest versions of our stuff, though."

Development Manager

"I guess keeping this whole thing running is going to fall to my staff. The five of us have a pretty good handle on PERL, Visual Basic, Active Server Pages, and HTML. I did a lot of C in college, but C++ is Greek to all of us!

Both of my staff members that usually work with the database and billing system are going off on a couple weeks of vacation tomorrow! Thankfully, we have full support contracts for both systems."

AVAILABILITY

At OscarNet, the user most concerned with system availability is the receptionist.

Receptionist

"I need some way to keep track of all the accounts that are being signed up for during business hours. Then, I need to be able to create all of them and get out of here as quickly as possible."

ANALYZING THE SCOPE OF A PROJECT

Analyze the scope of a project.

With this objective, you are concerned mainly with looking at the people, places, and things surrounding your problem area. You may find many opportunities to be seized as well as obstacles to be circumvented.

At this point, the most important thing is for you to understand how the various factors may affect your project. You do not yet need to be able to explain *exactly* how to capitalize on or survive them.

Which Applications Does the Organization Have?

The applications an organization has should have a profound impact on the kind of solutions you develop for them. If they have few or no applications, you find yourself starting with a clean slate. If they have a great deal already built, you may have a good or bad situation on your hands.

Starting from Scratch

A solution developer may feel a certain sense of despair on encountering a customer who has few (if any) applications already in place. Computer people often want to look at a system already in place, figure out what's wrong with it, and give it a good patch. When there isn't much to look at, people may ask, "Where do we even *begin?*"

Starting from scratch means that you need to work harder. Instead of looking for programs and machines that handle different tasks, you most likely need to interview users and trace paper paths.

The positive side to starting from scratch is that you have less technology with which to ensure compatibility. Software standards vary widely, and if the solution designers for the existing technology made bad choices, it could be blamed on you.

Think of the situation as the difference between writing a poem all by yourself and having to collaborate with someone else: You may have twice as much to write, but at least you never have to worry about your partner forcing you to rhyme something with "orange!"

Another benefit to starting from scratch is that people who have nothing tend to appreciate anything they get. If you go into an organization where people have been doing everything with fountain pens, imagine how thankful they will be when you give them erasable ballpoint pens! The same holds true with computer technology, an idea which is called *perceived Return-on-Investment* (ROI).

The final benefit of building a solution from scratch is that you have much more control. Any major design decisions that must be made are in your hands on a start-from-scratch project. That way you have the opportunity to get everything right from the start.

So, to summarize, when starting from scratch, you have

- More to build.

- Fewer interoperation problems.

- Greater perceived ROI.

- More research and analysis time.

- Opportunity to make all design decisions from the start.

Improving on a Good Situation

If the organization has an automated system in place, or if significant pieces of a manual system involve some automation, you may find your task easier or harder. First, consider the situation in which the existing automation is of some benefit to your efforts.

The first benefit of a situation in which automation already exists is the reduction of the amount you need to build. Even if you think it would take you too long to understand the existing system, think twice before starting from scratch.

To paraphrase Sun Tzu, "A single line of someone else's code is worth 1,000 of your own." Remember that using existing code saves you not only the writing time it takes, but also the analysis and planning it requires.

Of course, this benefit assumes that you know the systems you've inherited actually perform as expected. If you think you will need to spend considerable time testing to ensure proper system behavior, you might not think the existing systems are such an asset. In fact, if your testing produces too many specific errors, you might consider building something from scratch instead.

Just about the only drawback to walking into a project where most of the code has already been written for you is that the perceived ROI of your efforts is likely to be considerably lower. Figure 1.1 illustrates the lack of appreciation you may encounter in such situations. They were happy enough before that they don't really notice any improvement.

In a situation in which you have a *beneficial* set of previous applications, you have

◆ Least to build.

◆ Easier interoperation.

◆ Lower perceived ROI.

◆ Simplified analysis and design.

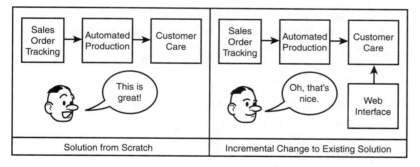

FIGURE 1.1
Lower perceived ROI in "already good" situations.

Coping with a Bad Situation

The final possibility is that the existing applications turn out to be more trouble than they are worth. This situation, for obvious reasons, is called *difficult*.

The situation might be difficult because the source code for the existing applications is no longer available or is so poorly documented that it is impossible to understand. The code also might be written in an obscure and/or obsolete computer language that no one on the project knows.

Although you still have less code to write than you would if you were starting from scratch, your team may want to consider rewriting existing code. You must take into account how deeply entwined the problem code is in the existing application environment. If the dependencies are few and well understood, it may be worth replacing the problem code. If you are not certain that the piece of the system in question is reasonably isolated, you must exercise extreme caution before making any alterations.

All of this is bound to make integration with your new solution more difficult. If the existing applications are using proprietary database-access standards, for example, you may have to write translation code. If the user interfaces for existing tools follow a peculiar standard (for example, having a Document menu at the far-right of the top menu bar rather than a File menu at the far-left), you need to decide whether to change your tools to match theirs, tolerate mismatching interfaces, or rewrite their tools.

The final big problem in inheriting an existing solution is that you probably need to make changes "on the fly." This means that the existing code is usually in use, which makes it much harder to alter without disturbing the important work of your organization.

What this all boils down to is a significantly lower *real* ROI for your project. The people involved in developing the solution must put in more time and effort, which costs more money. Even after the new solution is in place, the system may not work nearly as well as expected. Little bits of the old system that you thought were fully understood may operate differently than you expected, and problems may arise.

Here are the hallmarks of *difficult* existing applications:

◆ Less you *have* to build; possibly more you *should* build.

◆ More difficult interoperation.

◆ Lower real ROI.

◆ Changes must be made while the current system is still in use.

Which Situation Applies to OscarNet?

To determine which of the three situations best fits a specific case, you should first consider the presence of existing applications. In this case, you can see easily that there are at least some tools already in place—so you definitely won't be starting from scratch on this project.

This leaves two options, so you must now ask yourself whether the pieces already in place seem to help or hinder your efforts to build a better solution. The programmer's comments from the Envisioned System section, earlier in this chapter, seem most enlightening here: "Whatever we do is going to require a more reliable database for storing our dialup account information."

"The new billing system we're buying in a few months…will interface better with other applications."

Considering only these two remarks, you can see that any attempt to build a solution for the OscarNet will encounter a *difficult* set of existing applications.

What Changes Are They Planning?

After you have analyzed the existing applications of your chosen organization, consider how that organization is already planning to change. The changes referred to in this section are those that the organization was planning to make even without your solution. Failure to consider these can result in the production of a solution for a problem and a situation that no longer exists by the time the solution is delivered.

Getting Different Hardware

There are many different kinds of computer hardware: Central Processing Units (CPUs) that provide the "brain-power," memory for temporary storage, and disk space for storing permanent kinds of information. The organization you work with may be considering increasing or decreasing any of these three things. You must know for the exam what effects, if any, these plans may have on the scope of your project.

The organization may be planning a CPU change in particular or a change in processing power in general. Typically, this change involves buying new, faster computers and relegating the older ones to lighter, less important tasks. The change may, in more technically adept organizations, mean upgrading only the processing chips within the existing computers.

In general, more computer storage is better than less, reading and writing is better than only reading, and the faster the computer can do both of those things, the better! Backward compatibility with older media can reduce the scope of your project by easing the migration of data from the old system to the new. Finally, a technology that has multi-vendor standardization is much more likely to become dominant than one that is splintered because the pool of available resources (such as drivers, support, etc.) is that much larger.

The final way in which an organization can plan to change is by adding accessories to their information technology. This may mean changing the number of printers, scanners, OCR machines, voice-pattern security systems, and so on. You should consider which, if any, functions these accessories may provide that you could use in developing a solution. Keep in mind, however, that not everything a company adds is relevant to the task at hand, and you should resist the if-they-have-it,-we-have-to-use-it attitude.

Getting Different Operating Systems

Not all operating systems have the same features and capabilities, so you need to consider planned changes in this area very carefully.

There is a better-than-even chance that code written for one operating system will not run on another. The one notable exception to this may be Java, a language specifically designed to support operation on multiple platforms without modification or recompilation.

NOTE

DirectX Generating graphics is one of the most notoriously hardware-intensive tasks around. For this reason, software involved in these kinds of operations often directly access the video hardware inside computers. Windows usually tries to prevent this kind of activity, but provides DirectX for those applications where such access is required.

In general, code written for non-Microsoft operating systems will not operate correctly in a Windows environment without significant alteration.

Figure 1.2 shows that *most* of the applications written for a given Microsoft operating system will continue to operate without modification for one or two subsequent versions of the OS. The great barriers within the Microsoft family of operating systems come between the 16-bit (DOS and Windows 3.1) platforms and the 32-bit (95/98 and NT). Assume that 32-bit applications will not run on 16-bit platforms.

You also will find that many DOS applications need to read and write directly to and from system memory. Windows 95/98 tolerates this behavior, but Windows NT considers it a violation of "encapsulation." For this reason, it is not uncommon to find DOS applications that will not run on Windows NT.

A positive side to the acquisition of new operating systems may somewhat offset the incompatibility problems. The following additional features and services provided by new platforms may prove useful in the creation of your solution:

◆ A better user interface

◆ More efficient use of hardware

◆ Superior Internet integration

◆ Support for a wider range of hardware

Ideally, a new operating system supports a wider range of hardware, while making even better use of what it already has. Unfortunately, you may find that the new operating system, for whatever reason, places even greater demands upon your hardware than the previous one. You should, therefore, carefully consider the hardware requirements of any new operating system hand-in-hand with the other planned changes in your hardware. Later in this chapter, you learn how operating system and hardware changes affect the scope of your project.

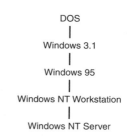

FIGURE 1.2
Microsoft Windows ladder of compatibility.

NOTE · **Encapsulation**   This is a principle of object-oriented programming that asserts that a properly designed object should not expose internal implementation to its consumers. Instead, only the necessary methods/properties of an object should be available to a consumer (through an interface), and the implementation is kept private.

Changing Organizational Structure

The last changes you should anticipate are organizational ones. These are changes to the structure and/or size of the company for which you are developing a solution. Organizational changes are often the hardest ones to see coming, and yet they can exert a profound influence on the scope of your project.

Probably the most dreaded organizational change is downsizing. In this situation, a company reduces the number of positions in an attempt to decrease expenses and save money.

Downsizing can increase the scope of your project. If the main players in your proposed solution are removed, you need to do a quick redesign. You can help minimize the potential damage of such an action by keeping the job positions and skills required for your solution as general as possible when downsizing is a significant possibility. Even the sponsor of your project could change jobs through downsizing, promotion, or a move to another company.

Downsizing can affect the scope of your project also by forcing you to spend additional time ensuring that your solution is easy to learn and use. If downsizing is a possibility, you may need to train a wider, less-skilled selection of employees to use your solution than you originally planned.

The ease-of-use concerns stem from the possibility that some of the people using your solution may be left doing the work of three former employees when all is said and done.

Downsizing can adversely affect the scope of your project by

- ◆ Creating additional problems.
- ◆ Removing essential players in your solution.
- ◆ Requiring that your solution be easy to learn and use.

The opposite of corporate downsizing is, of course, upsizing. This, too, can require that you expand the scope of your proposed solution. If you know in advance that a company will have twice its current level of business, or twice the number of people, by the time your solution is in place, you must consider the scalability of your technology. You learn more about analyzing scalability requirements in the next chapter.

Anticipating a Changing OscarNet

In order to prepare an effective solution, you need to look for three key changes: hardware, operating systems, and organizational changes. Is there any place in the case study where hardware changes specifically are mentioned?

When asked about the OscarNet's environment, the Development Manager said, "Hopefully, we'll be swapping [the signup server] out for a Pentium with plenty of memory soon." This means that right off the bat, you can expect at least one instance of increased processing power and another of increased storage.

When asked about performance, the same manager said, "The signup server only supports four modems." Whether plans already have been made is not clear, but it seems quite likely that additional modems are in the OscarNet's future. This would be an area to follow up on in interviews with the Development Manager.

You can see that OscarNet intends to increase their project scope on all three hardware points. But what about operating systems? In the entire case study, there is not a single mention of any unhappiness with their current operating systems. You can deduce, however, that they are looking to expand to other platforms because the following question was asked:

"What about all the NT users?"

The good news here is that the one or two development machines needed to produce software for external consumption should have little or no effect on the platforms used within the organization. So, in this case, you can view the availability of a few "alien" machines as irrelevant at worst.

Finally, have you been given any indication as to the future shrinkage or growth of the OscarNet's employment? Check out the VP of Sales' comments on Performance. First, the VP says that the Internet boom is over, so there won't be any growth worth worrying about. But then you hear about a new "miracle technology" that might cause a *huge* upswing in sales. The section closes by explaining that this is probably just a pipe dream.

As a general rule of thumb, a company seriously considering downsizing will be fairly confident that there is a need to cut costs. A company that wants to upsize will be just as sure that their fortunes are on the rise. In this case, the VP of Sales obviously is not confident of anything.

In situations like this one, the need for scalability never can be completely discounted. As the solution is designed, appropriate care must be taken to ensure that additional users and processes do not cause system failures.

The most immediate impact of this requirement is an increase in project scope. You examine additional ramifications of this requirement in the section on scalability in Chapter 2.

How Long Will They Need Your Solution?

Not every solution you build is intended to remain in operation until the organization closes its doors. Many fast-growing businesses have long-term strategies that specifically provide for the continual re-evaluation and replacement of their technology. You may find pros and cons to both extremes of life-span expectations.

Short-Term Solutions

In some cases, you develop a solution that all parties agree is a short-term answer. The positive side to this is that your maintenance and support burden is lighter than it would be with a long-term solution. The negative aspect is that demonstrating the value of your solution is a harder task.

Your support burden is lighter with a short-term solution because it won't be in use long enough for much to go wrong with it. The people who were there as it was being developed are likely to be around for the entire time it is in use. This means the system was probably designed and built to match the desires and abilities of the people using it.

Having the same people around is helpful also in that familiar users have a better understanding of the problem and the way in which your system solves it. For example, imagine a Check Verification system that makes sure personal checks written to a grocery store are written against sufficient funds. The people who were there before the system was in place will, no doubt, remember the endless stream of bounced checks that more than justifies the additional 30 second wait at the counter for your system to say either "Yes" or "No." Continuity of knowledge from the inception of the project through to its deployment is a large benefit.

A short-term solution is less likely to encounter significant changes in business processes. The longer that your target organization conducts its business in the same way as when you were developing your solution, the longer it will be before you get requests for modifications and extensions. This is a good thing.

In summary, short-term solutions help limit the scope of your project in the following ways:

◆ Shorter time for things to break

◆ More user "buy-in" to project success

◆ Better user understanding of the solution

◆ Fewer business changes for the system to cope with

Of course, short-term solutions also have negatives. The most notable of these is that the amount of time in which your solution must earn a Return on Investment (ROI) is shorter. This means that you must work harder to decrease your system's Total Cost of Ownership (TCO) while simultaneously increasing its value to the organization.

You learn much more about strategies for reducing TCO later in this chapter. For now, know that short-term solutions probably provide the best opportunities in business for the use of technologies that are "bleeding-edge" rather than leading edge. By "bleeding-edge," we are referring to any technology that is too young to have properly worked out the majority of its bugs. The so-called "dot-zero" versions of most software (1.0, 2.0, etc.) fall into this category. You should only consider this if there is a specific technology that holds promise for addressing a specific issue associated with your solution.

For example, in a situation where the same software must be used on many different platforms, you might consider using Visual J++. If your staff is less than expert in this language and its associated technology, you may find that it makes a better short-term solution than a long-term one. Why is this?

If you are certain that your short-term solution will not be used for continuing service, you won't have the same support obligations you would have in a long-term solution. Additionally, you won't have to live with mistakes as long. At the same time, you have reduced a very real cost using a new technology and extended the technical abilities of your staff. What a deal!

Figure 1.3 illustrates the dangers of continuing to use a solution built with experimental technologies. The iceberg represents a solution's life span, starting at the peak and ending with its short-term retirement at the waterline. The points on the iceberg's surface that are labeled with dates represent times the solution might fail because of design errors. Managers may be tempted to continue using the solution past its useful lifetime only if they fail to realize that the first two failures are merely the "tip of the iceberg."

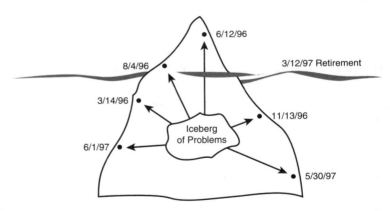

FIGURE 1.3
The danger of continuing to use prototypes.

NOTE

The App that Wouldn't Die The history of computer systems design is littered with temporary solutions that have gone on to become permanent solutions. Consider the Y2K bug: no one ever dreamt that the systems containing the problematic code would still be in use 30 years after they were developed. The moral to the story is that if you cut corners in the short term, you may be giving yourself enough rope to hang yourself with later if the solution fails to go out of service. Always remember, "code today like you will be dead tomorrow."

Long-Term Solutions

Building solutions intended for long-term use introduce an entirely new set of factors into determining project scope. On one hand, whatever solution you develop needs ample time to prove its worth. On the other hand, the maintenance obligation on a system that remains in service for a very long time can become a near-crippling burden if sufficient care is not exercised during the initial design stages.

The idea of a long-term solution having more time to demonstrate its value is, of course, wrapped up within the whole conception of Return on Investment. As you can see in Tables 1.1 and 1.2, equally capable solutions can end up with very different total ROIs when they are used for different lengths of time.

TABLE 1.1

CONTRASTING POTENTIAL ROIs FOR SHORT- AND LONG-TERM SOLUTIONS OF VARYING RATES OF RETURN

Rate of Return	Length of Use	Total ROI
$100/month	12 years	$144,000
$8.33/month	12 years	$1200
$1200/month	12 years	$2,073,600

TABLE 1.2

CONTRASTING POTENTIAL ROIs FOR SHORT- AND LONG-TERM SOLUTIONS OF VARYING LENGTH OF USE

Rate of Return	Length of Use	Total ROI
$100/month	12 months	$1200
$100/month	12 years	$144,000

In longer life-span solutions, business processes gradually change, leaving parts of your system obsolete or in need of maintenance. For example, consider the earlier Check Approval system, which is now experiencing the introduction of debit cards. To the extent that people stop writing personal checks, the entire value of retaining your system is continually called into question.

A worse problem is that, over time, people originally there for the development of the solution tend to leave. The people who replace them often do not understand your system nearly as well as the people who helped you build it, which means you get more questions and calls for support. Another problem can arise when the new people decide they don't like the system because they weren't involved in its creation and are constantly pushing for modifications.

The OscarNet

So what kind of life span are your employers at the OscarNet expecting from your solution? Take a moment to review the case study and see whether anyone gives a direct statement on the subject.

Companies rarely think of any solution as being designed for less than the span of eternity, so as you might expect, there is no direct statement about the life span of the solution in the case study. One clue can give you an idea about your solution's longevity, however:

"The new billing system we're buying in a few months should change everything," said the programmer while contemplating his envisioned system. Anything that truly stands a chance to "change everything" in a few months should be considered a strong indication that the solution will be retired soon and should therefore be considered short-term.

For this reason, the OscarNet's developers should avoid hard-coding too many things that depend upon the current billing system's interfaces. If this can be avoided, the amount of code from this system that can be reused in building whatever long-term solution follows is greatly increased.

Which Resources Will You Have to Trade?

Most business situations seem to have limited resources available for completing a seemingly unlimited number of tasks. The four resources you need to know for the exam are as follows:

◆ Time

◆ Labor

◆ Money

◆ Benefits

Figuring out in advance which trade-offs among resources might be required is one of the most important tasks in analyzing the scope of a project.

Time

The amount of time between the present and the time when your solution must be in place is referred to (rather obviously) as *time*. You can, therefore, gain more of this resource by pushing back the due date for your project. Similarly, you lose time whenever anything pulls your solution's "go live" date forward—such as an unexpected, urgent business need for it. You also can lose time when other projects push back the date you are able to begin work on the project.

Dependencies can affect the time you have available. If your solution requires the rollout of new hardware and the hardware install is delayed, the delay could affect your ability to meet your date.

Once you know the total number of hours required to complete your project, trading time for labor is a matter of answering the following question:

"How many hours per day do we need to work, in order to maintain our schedule?"

Too many projects start out with standard 40-hour weeks and end in a flurry of action-packed all-nighters. Needless to say, this is not the ideal way to work. The rule of thumb for software project management has always been, "Work to create an accurate estimate and then add at least a 20 percent 'contingency' adjustment." An accurate estimate should include (but not be limited to) design and development time, training time, administration time, overhead time (meetings often consume much more time than was forcasted), testing and Q&A time, deployment time, and, if appropriate, post-deployment support.

As Figure 1.4 shows, you can use this information to derive the appropriate hours per day required by dividing your total require-ment by the number of business days between now and when your solution must be finished. If you have more than one person working on the project in Figure 1.4, you should divide the answer appropriately.

As a rule, never plan overtime into your initial schedule. Scheduling your overtime takes away your ability to use it to make up for sched-ule slippage later in your plan.

Trading money for time is a matter of answering the question:

"How much money do we need to spend in order to maintain our schedule?"

You can buy yourself more time on a project in a number of ways. The most obvious way is by being willing to foot the bill for what-ever overtime or bonuses are required in order to get your people to put in additional hours. Another way is to purchase labor-saving tools, such as code generation software, data-flow modeling systems, etc.

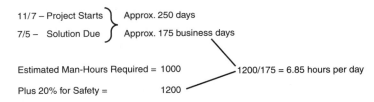

FIGURE 1.4
Effects of time on project scheduling.

The final trade-off that can be made with time is that of benefits. Benefits can be divided into two areas: scope and quality. You can determine the trade-off by asking two main questions. The first is *"How many new features does our schedule allow for?"*

Every feature that you add to the solution requires additional time. At some point, you must draw the line and say, "If we try to do any more in this phase of the project, we're going to miss our deadline." You then can decide (along with your client) to push the deadline back or drop some of the planned functionality.

The second question you can ask to weigh time and benefits is *"What level of quality can we assure within schedule?"*

In an ideal world, all solutions would be developed to a level of 100-percent perfection 100 percent of the time. Unfortunately, in the real world this is rarely possible. Before work begins, the organization building the solution and the solution provider must come to an understanding about the kind of quality required in order for the solution to be effective. The next chapter provides more information about this topic. Possible trade-offs against the resource of time include the following:

◆ Labor = hours per day & work days per week

◆ Money = overtime and bonuses & time-saving tools

◆ Benefits = number of features & degree of quality

Labor

Labor refers to anything companies call "Human Resources," considering not only the number of people available to work on a given project, but how good they are at their jobs. Labor also encompasses the degree of effort individuals are willing to exert in order to reach a solution, which has a great influence on the time investment.

Money interacts with time in decisions you make about how much to spend on incentives and time-saving tools, and time interacts with labor in the number and quality of people hired to work on a project. Putting twice the number of people on a job won't get it done in half the time, but adding people to a project often can hasten the results. The best people in any given field do not come cheap, however, and attempting to save money by hiring less competent individuals is one of the classic causes for project failure.

You also can trade money for labor by purchasing pre-packaged source code, data, or objects. Whenever you find yourself building something you suspect many people need, take the time to search for an existing, commercial product that fits your needs. Buying something is almost always cheaper than building it, which makes this one of the best ways to trade resources and reduce your project scope.

In addition to money, labor also can be traded against the benefits of any new system you might build. One consideration is the number of people you should bring in to produce whatever level of functionality you want from your planned solution. Another possibility is that you will hire too many (or the wrong) people and they will begin confusing each other by stepping on toes and egos.

Possible trade-offs against the resource of labor include the following:

◆ How many people can we afford to put on the project?

◆ What quality of people can we afford for the project?

◆ How much pre-built functionality can be bought rather than built?

◆ How many people does the project demand?

Money

The final resource you need to understand is money. You already have seen how money can interact with time and labor to produce significant effects on the scope of your project. The final aspect of money you should be familiar with is its direct relationship to the benefits resource.

The money you spend on a project comes in two forms: up-front and ongoing. The total of the costs is referred to as the *Total Cost of Ownership*. The benefits you derive from creating a solution and keeping it operational, minus the Total Cost of Ownership, is called your *Return on Investment*. You learn more about ROI later in this chapter, but you need to remember the following:

Benefits −TCO = ROI

Table 1.3 illustrates the many ways in which time, labor, money, and benefits can be traded against each other. The table presents a total of 6 possible combinations you need to remember for the exam.

TABLE 1.3

RESOURCE TRADE-OFF CONSIDERATIONS AND IMPLICATIONS

	Time	*Labor*	*Money*	*Benefits*
Time		Hours per day & Days per week	Incentives & Time-saving tools	Number of features & Quality of work
Labor	Hours per day & Days per week	—	Number and quality of people & Pre-built functionality	Number of people needed vs. Level of confusion
Money	Incentives & Time-saving tools	Number and quality of people & Pre-built functionality	—	Benefits – TCO = ROI
Benefits	Number of features & Quality of work	Number of people needed vs. Level of confusion	Benefits – TCO = ROI	—

Trading Resources at the OscarNet

To determine the proper balance of resources in a given situation, first try to determine which are plentiful (if any) and which are in short supply. Because problems usually are easier to find than reasons for optimism, start there! Do you see any reason to worry about sufficient time, labor, money, or benefits at the OscarNet?

Because you already determined that you are being asked to develop a short-term solution, you can say with great confidence that time is already in short supply. When the new billing system is purchased in a few months, the clients will no longer need the solution you are planning to build for them today!

With this information and the earlier discussion about the effect of short-term solutions on ROI, you can understand why this time pressure can make creating a visibly worthwhile solution difficult. Compounding matters, the amount of labor available for the completion of this task is not going to be all that it could be. Check out the Development Manager's comments in the Maintainability section:

"The five of us..."

This part of the statement tells you that five information systems people are usually available.

"Both of my staff that usually work with the database and billing system are going off on a couple weeks of vacation tomorrow!"

Five people minus two leaves three people available to work with you on this project. After you estimate the number of hours your project should require, divide the number by the number of people available to figure out how many hours per week each person would be responsible for contributing.

Is there any good news at the OscarNet? Fortunately, the organization has been saving up for a rainy day just like this one. If you can believe the Dialup Sales Manager's response to the question about the envisioned system, "...[they've] got plenty left in the budget for whatever you can come up with."

Analyzing the Scope of the OscarNet's Project

Now that you have learned about all the considerations for analyzing the scope of a project, a brief synthesis of the facts is appropriate. This synthesis provides you with an approach to the OscarNet's project that will continue throughout the following chapter.

A number of factors are working to increase the scope of the OscarNet's project. Most notable of these is the fact that your data is "bottled up" in obscure and poorly performing existing systems. Also, additional platforms are going to be introduced into the organization, which will require the existing IS staff to develop some additional skills.

You need to think of the solution you create as short-term, given the drastic changes planned in the corporate IS infrastructure. What the OscarNet may be thinking about the potential short-term use is not clear, however; they may be looking for something that can be used both before and after the changes are made. The impending change has created a shortage of time for the creation of this solution. This, combined with a pre-existing shortage of labor, completes the set of factors that may frustrate your attempts to build an effective solution at the OscarNet.

The list of things working in the OscarNet's favor is, unfortunately, somewhat shorter. First is the prospect of additional, superior hardware being brought into the organization. Also, a temporary abundance of cash is available for the completion of this project. Apparently these funds were put away for a "rainy day"... and it's raining!

Your wisest course of action for the OscarNet is to set up a heavy incentive program for early and on-time completion. Also, you should buy the appropriate time-saving tools. Finally, you may want to consider hiring some additional consultants to assist with the project, finances permitting.

CHAPTER SUMMARY

In this chapter, you learned to analyze the scope of a project. In the next chapter, you begin the task of analyzing the extent of business requirements. Chapter 2 also introduces you to the recurring PASS ME themes of the Microsoft exam.

As you learned in this chapter, analyzing the scope of a project requires that you look at the existing applications to understand their impact on the amount you must build, the level of integration, and the return on your investment. You also saw how anticipated changes in hardware, operating systems, and the target organization can affect the scope of your project. You learned how shorter and longer solution life spans require different approaches to cost, quality, and technology choice. And, finally, you explored the complex interactions that can occur when you must trade off the resources of time, labor, money, and benefits to get the best possible fit for your solution.

KEY TERMS

- Business requirement
- Scope

APPLY YOUR KNOWLEDGE

Exercises

1.1   Analyzing Project Scope

Exercise 1.1 helps familiarize you with the considerations involved in analyzing project scope.

Estimated Time: 10 minutes.

1. The leftmost column of Table 1.4 contains a list of situations you might encounter while designing a solution.

2. For each item on this list, place a check mark in the column labeled Scope Reducing if you believe that this is something that would be likely to reduce the scope of your project.

3. If you believe an item would be more likely to increase the scope of your project, place a check mark in the column labeled Scope Increasing.

4. When you are finished, you should have a total of six check marks in the Scope Reducing column and six under Scope Increasing.

TABLE 1.4

EXERCISE 1.1 WORKSPACE

Situation	*Scope Reducing*	*Scope Increasing*
The new solution needs many new features.		
The organization for which the solution is being built has no computer technology.		
The solution being built needs to remain in service for a very long time.		
All computers currently running Windows 98 will be upgraded to Windows 2000.		
The hardware currently in place will not be changed for many years.		
The systems currently in place are poorly documented and malfunction often.		
There is the distinct possibility of a corporate merger occurring soon.		
The systems currently in place at the organization are well-documented and always function properly.		
The solution being built will be needed only for a short time.		

APPLY YOUR KNOWLEDGE

Situation	Scope Reducing	Scope Increasing
The solution being built has a very flexible deadline for delivery.		
The staff involved in producing the new solution is willing to work long hours if needed.		
The organization has cut in half the budget for producing the new solution.		

The solution to the exercise is presented in Table 1.5.

TABLE 1.5

EXERCISE 1.1 SOLUTION

Situation	Scope Reducing	Scope Increasing
The new solution needs many new features.		X
The organization for which the solution is being built has no computer technology.	X	
The solution being built needs to remain in service for a very long time.		X
All computers currently running Windows 98 will be upgraded to Windows 2000.		X
The hardware currently in place will not be changed for many years.	X	
The systems currently in place are poorly documented and malfunction often.		X
There is the distinct possibility of a corporate merger occurring soon.		X
The systems currently in place at the organization are well-documented and always function properly.	X	
The solution being built will be needed only for a short time.	X	
The solution being built has a very flexible deadline for delivery.	X	
The staff involved in producing the new solution is willing to work long hours if needed.	X	
The organization has cut in half the budget for producing the new solution.		X

APPLY YOUR KNOWLEDGE

Review Questions

1. Suppose that the OscarNet didn't own a single piece of computer hardware or software. Which existing application situation would they then be in?

2. What would be the effect on your project's scope if the OscarNet planned to buy a new computer that was twice as powerful as the current one, but running an OS that was only half as efficient in its use of hardware? Assume that the new OS is completely compatible with all existing applications.

3. What would be the impact on your solution's ROI if the OscarNet decided not to buy a new billing system in a few months?

4. You are trying to determine how many "neat things" you can do in your new system without having to work past your deadline. What two resources are you trading off?

5. Suppose that everyone at OscarNet suddenly began calling in sick during your project. Which resource would be most in jeopardy?

6. Which resource would most likely be increased if the OscarNet made an Initial Public Offering (IPO) during the development of your solution?

7. What kind of change could potentially result from an Initial Public Offering (IPO) during the development of your solution?

8. You are evaluating the system that one of OscarNet's competitors uses for Internet signups. The system is both well documented and reliable. What is this competitor's existing application situation?

Exam Questions

1. How would you describe OscarNet's existing application situation if you were unable to find any documentation to assist you in evaluating it?

   A. Starting from scratch

   B. Improving on a good situation

   C. Coping with a bad situation

   D. Minor technology exists

2. Which of the following are aspects of short-term solutions that reduce project scope?

   A. More user buy-in

   B. More time to earn ROI

   C. Fewer business changes

   D. Less time to earn ROI

3. Which factor determining the scope of OscarNet's project would change if the new billing system were cancelled?

   A. Existing applications

   B. Planned organizational changes

   C. Length of service required for your solution

   D. Resource availability

4. Choose the valid resources and rank them in order from most to least available:

   People

   Time

   Labor

   Goodwill

   Money

   Customer Satisfaction

APPLY YOUR KNOWLEDGE

5. In the following table, draw lines between the different existing application situations and their effects on project scope.

QUESTION 5 WORKSPACE

Most difficult interoperation	No existing applications
Most to build	
Lowest perceived ROI	
Lowest real ROI	
Best opportunity to make all design decisions	Good existing applications
Least to build	
Greatest perceived ROI	
Least chance to make design decisions	
Simplest analysis and design	Bad existing applications

6. The need to upgrade from a 32-bit platform to a 64-bit one would entail which of the following kinds of changes?

    A. Hardware change

    B. OS change

    C. Organizational change

    D. System analysis

7. Imagine that while you are building their new signup system, OscarNet completely replaces their janitorial staff. What kind of change would this constitute?

    A. Hardware change

    B. OS change

    C. Organizational change

    D. System analysis

8. Which kind of solution is the best for experimenting with new technologies?

    A. Short-term

    B. Long-term

    C. One requiring many new features

    D. One requiring few new features

Answers to Review Questions

1. This situation is referred to as the "From Scratch" environment. Working in this environment may mean that you must build more yourself, but at least you won't have to work around existing technologies you don't like. See "What Applications Do They Already Have?"

2. The effect would be negligible. The inefficiency of the new OS would completely counteract the improvement in the computer's performance. See "What Changes Are They Planning?"

3. If the OscarNet weren't buying a new billing system in a few months, your system could become a long-term solution. This would give it more time to prove its worth and increase its potential ROI. See "How Long Will They Need Your Solution?"

4. Time versus benefits. In this case, time is represented by the need to make the deadline. Benefits are the "neat things" that you would like to add. See "Which Resources Will You Have to Trade?"

APPLY YOUR KNOWLEDGE

5. By calling in sick, OscarNet's employees are reducing the supply of labor available for completing the signup project. See "Which Resources Will You Have to Trade?"

6. Initial Public Offerings (IPOs) are stock sales that are intended to bring more money into an organization. In this case, then, the resource of money would stand to be increased by an IPO. See "Which Resources Will You Have to Trade?"

7. Although Initial Public Offerings (IPOs) are intended primarily to raise funds within a company, they also can have the effect of changing their organizational structures. One reason for this is the wide difference between the way public companies are required to do business and the way privately held corporations act. See "Which Resources Will You Have to Trade?"

8. OscarNet's competitor is fortunate enough to have a good existing application situation. Documentation and proper functioning are two of the most valuable aspects of any automated system. See "What Applications Do They Already Have?"

Answers to Exam Questions

1. **B.** The use of any computer technology at all at OscarNet makes A an impossible answer. Insofar as no actual problems have been reported with the technology currently in use, there is no reason to think that the current situation is a bad one. "Minor technology exists" is not even an existing application environment option from the text. See "What Applications Do They Already Have?"

2. **C, D.** The owner and drivers have considered the possibility of new laptops, but nothing final has been decided. See "What Changes Are They Planning?"

3. **B.** There is nothing to indicate that the solution will be short-term, as would be the case if a new system were already slated to come into play later. Instead, the owner actually states at one point that the new solution must "last us for a very long time." See "How Long Will They Need Your Solution?"

4. Most to least = Money, Time, Labor

   You know that money is readily available because the Dialup Sales Manager states that "we've got plenty left in the budget for whatever you can come up with." See "Which Resources Will You Have to Trade?"

5. No existing applications = Most to build, Greatest perceived ROI, Best opportunity to make all design decisions.

   Good existing applications = Lowest perceived ROI, Least to build, Simplest analysis and design.

   Bad existing applications = Most difficult inter-operation, Lowest real ROI, Least chance to make design decisions.

   See "What Applications Do They Already Have?"

6. **A, B.** 32-bit vs. 64-bit is primarily a hardware difference. Without an operating system capable of supporting it, however, a large bus size will go largely unused. You have no relationship between a change of this sort and changes to the organization itself. System analysis was not discussed in this chapter. See "What Changes Are They Planning?"

APPLY YOUR KNOWLEDGE

7. **D.** Organizational changes refer more to the creation, redefinition, and elimination of job positions than to changes in the specific personnel filling them. If OscarNet had decided to no longer retain janitors, this might have constituted an organizational change (though probably still not a relevant one). Hardware and OS changes are both technology, not business-based. System analysis was not discussed in this chapter. See "What Changes Are They Planning?"

8. **A.** The consequences of mistakes made while you are building a short-term solution are not nearly as dire as those that occur when you are building a long-term solution. You must live with bad decisions much longer as part of a long-term solution. The number of features required is completely irrelevant. See "What Changes Are They Planning?"

Suggested Readings and Resources

1. Davis, William. *Business Systems Analysis and Design.* Wadsworth, 1994.

   • Chapter 1: Information Systems Analysis

2. *Visual Studio Developing for the Enterprise,* Visual Basic 6, Enterprise Edition, Microsoft, 1998.

   • Chapter 1: What Is an Enterprise Application?

This chapter addresses the following exam objective listed by Microsoft as part of the Analyzing Business Requirements section of the exam:

Analyze the extent of a business requirement. The objective involves the following activities:

- **Establish business requirements**

- **Establish the type of problem; for example, messaging problems or communication problems**

- **Establish and define customer quality requirements**

- **Minimize Total Cost of Ownership (TCO)**

- **Increase the Return on Investment (ROI) of the solution**

- **Analyze the current platform and infrastructure**

- **Incorporate into the solution the planned platform and infrastructure**

- **Analyze the impact of technology migration**

- **Plan the physical requirements, such as the infrastructure**

- **Establish the application environment, including the hardware platform, support, and operating system**

- **Identify any organizational constraints, such as the financial situation, company politics, technical acceptance level, and training needs**

- **Establish the schedule for the implementation of solution**

- **Identify the audience**

CHAPTER 2

Analyzing the Extent of Business Requirements

▶ This objective is the lengthiest on the exam, but fortunately it can be boiled down to just a few fundamental concepts. By the end of this chapter, you should be able to describe, in varying degrees of detail, the business problem that is being solved.

You also should be able to identify all the business factors that are likely to exert an influence over the development of any solution, including whether management will even approve funding for the project.

▶ Be able to describe business problems in very general terms by using categorization. Asking the customer simple questions such as "Who does what?" and "Where, when, and how often is it done?" help you get a general description of the problem.

▶ Know the different kinds of costs that come from building and maintaining custom solutions. Learn ways to reduce them and look for other, more general methodologies for increasing ROI.

▶ Make sure that you can adequately analyze a given application environment, make your solution adaptable to changes in that environment, and explain the wider implications such changes might have.

▶ Understand the factors influencing your solution's physical requirements.

▶ Be able to identify the various audiences and organizational constraints and to express how they would most likely influence the development of your solution.

▶ Know the benefits and problems associated with scheduling faster and slower implementations of solutions.

INTRODUCTION

In this chapter, you turn your attention to analyzing the extent of business requirements. You learn how to describe problems in varying degrees of detail and to analyze the effects of various external factors on solution development. Finally, you get a peek at exam objectives on reducing solution costs while increasing Return on Investment (ROI).

This chapter continues the analysis of the OscarNet's case study from Chapter 1. You may want to review that chapter if you need additional case details.

ANALYZING THE EXTENT OF BUSINESS REQUIREMENTS

Analyze the extent of a business requirement.

With this objective, you begin defining the exact nature of the business problem. You develop a general, high-level description of the problem's type and a specific understanding of some of the problem's particulars. The rest of the problem is fully analyzed in the following chapter.

Establishing the Business Requirements

Business requirements enable you to define precisely the problem for which an organization wants a solution. They loosely correspond to the "who, what, when, where, why, and how" that journalists use to describe the facts of a news story.

As you collect the business requirement facts, you should document everything carefully and get sign-off whenever possible. Sign-off on any given design decision represents a semi-binding degree of official approval. This allows you to avoid much of the finger pointing that can occur later if things start to go wrong. Any changes requested to a design after sign-off should be carefully documented and subjected to another round of management sign-offs.

One of the most important documents you may produce while establishing business requirements is a *use case document*. A use case document presents a series of scenarios in which your new system might be used to solve various business problems. A typical use case for a record store inventory system, for example, could describe a situation in which a customer needs a refund. In addition to clearly stipulating the conditions under which such a situation might arise (for example, an overcharge or damaged merchandise), the use case should completely describe how your system will behave.

Exactly What Is the Problem?

Using the journalistic model noted earlier, stating the problem is equivalent to determining the "what" of a news story. You can best think of this as having two parts: The first part tells the way things are, and the second part tells the way things should be. These parts are often referred to in development methodologies as *as is* and *to be*. The difference between the two, then, is the proposed scope of the project, which is called the *transition plan*. Figure 2.1 illustrates this point with the case of an employee who insists on disturbing his cubicle-mate with loud music.

In the first frame of this illustration, music is drifting over the wall of a cubicle. This is a problem only because the person in the second cubicle does not want to hear it. In the middle frame, you see the way this should ideally work: The person in the other cube should be wearing headphones. By carefully examining the differences between these two situations, you can reduce the problem to its most basic description: The ill-mannered cubicle-mate is using speakers.

| The Way It Is... | The Way It Should Be... | The Problem... |

FIGURE 2.1
Problem = Ideal—Reality.

For example, if you were trying to explain a problem associated with running a small, regional airline, you might begin with, "Passengers stand in a long line to have their bags checked, walk a mile to the gate, and are then randomly seated by unfriendly staff." Then you would mention how you would like things to work; for example "Passengers should arrive at the terminal from which they are departing, give their bags to our friendly staff, and be seated according to their reservations."

The difference between the above two statements gives you the best statement of the problem possible:

"Passengers are arriving at the wrong location. They should be giving their bags to the airline staff rather than special receivers. Our airline staff needs to be friendlier. And, they need to seat according to reservation rather than whim."

Which Parts of the Business Are Involved?

Businesses consist of many occupations, normally organized into departments, divisions, and other hierarchical constructs. This discussion generalizes the parts of a business into four general areas: Production, Sales, Accounting, and Management.

Production represents the people who actually "create salable output" at an organization. In a car-making company, such as Ford or Chrysler, Production would mean the actual assembly lines. The people who design the items being produced and the systems that assist in their production also fall into this category. However, production can also be intangible. Many companies today are in the business of creating information or providing a service.

Sales, as you might expect, sells the things made by Production.

Accounting refers to the people in a company who are charged with recording the financial details of what everyone else in the organization is doing. This means keeping track of exactly how much Production is producing and how much Sales is selling. As with Production, people who build systems that assist in Accounting generally are also included in this category.

Finally, Management is chartered with motivating and guiding the workforce, using information to make the company more competitive and achieving financial performance to satisfy stockholder and owner objectives.

The parts of a business are as follows:

▶ Production—makes goods and/or provide services.

▶ Sales—sells whatever Production produces.

▶ Accounting—tracks financials of Production and Sales.

▶ Management—creates corporate strategies to make the business strong and profitable.

Determining which parts of a business are involved in a problem is simply a matter of looking at your description of the problem and "checking-off" areas of the company as you see them mentioned. In the airline example, the only parts that seem to be involved are Production: airport-designing staff, baggage-receiving staff, and airline staff.

In Which Situations Does the Problem Arise?

Having answered the "what" in the journalistic reference, you can now move on to the "when." Exactly when does the problem arise? You can best describe this by determining the frequency with which a problem occurs, the people involved, and the systems involved.

The frequency with which a problem occurs is one measure of the severity of the problem. If someone tells you that the computer locks-up occasionally, you are far more likely to view this as a serious problem if it happens every few minutes than if it happens once or twice a month.

In the airline example, it seems a safe bet that passengers always arrive at the baggage-check and, therefore, always have to wait in a long line and walk a long distance to the gate. Whether the airline staff is rude and inclined to seat passengers in a random manner is not clear from the information given and would, therefore, have to be deduced by careful observation.

Observations of this sort can be conducted via direct interview, in which you would simply ask the airline staff, "Is rude treatment of passengers something that you do on a daily basis, or something you save for special occasions?" Of course, there would be little or no reason for us to expect the airline staff to incriminate themselves by answering these kinds of questions honestly!

For this reason, among others, it is important that you interview as wide a cross-section of your target audiences as possible. The end-users who have to work with your solution should, of course, be interviewed. Also, you need to speak to the people responsible for supervising work that will be done with your solution.

A more accurate way of gathering this information is by looking at paper trails relating to the behavior being observed. In this case, you would go to the Complaints department and ask to look at their records. Finally, you can get the data through direct experience, which would require that you and/or others working on your project actually go through the system in which the problems have been reported. In this example, this might mean actually subjecting yourself to a certain number of flights!

The second aspect of describing the situations in which a problem arises is determining the people involved. This loosely corresponds to answering the journalistic question of "Who?." Because you have already named the parts of the business that are involved, this should be straightforward. You can begin by naming the general positions; in the example, this would be the airport-designers, the baggage-receivers, and the airline staff.

After you have named the general positions involved, you should try to determine whether specific individuals are responsible for some or all of these problems. You might discover, for example, that Larry Lester designed all the airports where passengers have to walk three miles from baggage-check to gate.

The final aspect you need to consider, as you sleuth out the situation, is the system involved. Start by naming all the hardware in use, and then find out which software is running on the equipment when the problem occurs.

In the airport example, a remote possibility is that something in the airport architect's computer setup requires such a sadistic approach to terminal layout. You would also investigate the hardware and software that produces seating reservations to ensure that there isn't some good reason why the airplane staff is unable to seat people as indicated. Perhaps federal safety laws are not being taken into account as reservations are assigned.

The aspects of a problematic situation include the following:

R E V I E W B R E A K

▶ Frequency—one measure of problem severity.

▶ People—general positions and specific individuals.

▶ Systems—hardware and software.

In What Locations Does the Problem Appear?

If there is anything unusual about the locations in which a solution must be deployed, you need to note this as well. Things you should consider include (but are not limited to) the number of locations involved and language issues.

The number of locations involved determines the degree of network connectivity you must obtain and implement in order for a solution to function properly. For example, a solution intended for use by an organization that operates in a single location—a carpet store, for instance—may not require any connections beyond its own location. On the other hand, a solution that must provide a common set of data to an organization disbursed across the planet—such as a major airline— requires some kind of network among all locations and data stores.

The most obvious example of a language issue occurs when software must be developed for foreign countries. People working in a language not their own may make mistakes, which means you need to devise some means for getting your solution's output appropriately translated for them.

Establishing the OscarNet's Business Requirements

Deriving a complete statement of the problem from a case study usually is not difficult on the Microsoft exam. You simply need to take the information given to you and rearrange it in a logical fashion. Here is one take on the OscarNet's situation. See whether you concur (you will have additional opportunities to do this in the Exercises and on the CD):

"The OscarNet's current system requires customers to call, wait for special software to arrive, and then wait until 5:00 P.M. on the day they sign up before they are able to use their accounts. Meanwhile, not all customers are getting billed properly and not all salespeople are getting paid the right commissions.

Ideally, customers should be able to sign up without calling or waiting for special software to arrive in the mail, and they should be able to use their new accounts immediately. This system should, somehow, be automated to a degree that makes it virtually impossible for customers not to get billed or salespeople not to get their commissions."

As you recall, the second part of establishing the business requirements for the case study requires that you identify the parts of the business that are involved. The creation of dialup accounts is a Production task, taking the inbound customer telephone calls is a Sales task, and billing people is an Accounting task. It looks, so far, as though Management is the only part of the company that is "off the hook" as far as this problem goes. Because dialup accounts are being constantly ordered and incorrectly fulfilled and billed, you can see that the frequency of these problems is constant—a most severe circumstance! The positions involved are the internal sales representative, billing clerk, and receptionist.

The last bit of information you receive about the problem describes the specifics of the company's hardware and software:

"Active Server Pages... take [customer] information and dump it into Access databases. The receptionist... pastes it (via Telnet) into a PERL application that we have running on our UNIX servers."

"We're running our billing system on a four-processor Alpha computer with 256MB of memory. The sign-up server ...is an old 486 with just 16MB. It's got four modems...and [uses] our own proprietary networking protocol.

We've got...50 desktops...with CPUs...from 100-200 MHz...they all have exactly 32MB."

Finally, you can see a little good news for the OscarNet in the geographic area where its problems arise. The *lingua franca* of Seattle is English, so language should not be much of an influence on their business requirements.

Establishing the Type of Problem

Once you understand the specific problems your target organization needs to resolve, you should classify them into more general types or categories. For this purpose, you will divide all problems into one of four categories: communications, calculation, automation, and storage and retrieval. The following sections describe each of these problem types for you in terms of inputs, processes, and output.

Communications Problems

A communications problem is any problem that revolves around the transfer of data between a certain number of points. The locations in question can be as close as different applications running on the same computer or they can be as far apart as ATM machines on opposite sides of the globe.

The transportation process can be as simple as handing a memo to a messenger on a bicycle or it can be as advanced as a satellite system relaying bits and bytes through the upper atmosphere.

Calculation Problems

A calculation problem is any problem in which the central requirement is that something be figured out. In this situation, data is inputted into the system and then subjected to a series of formulas and rules. Finally, information is produced as output.

Data in this sense means facts and figures that require further interpretation and manipulation in order to have value to the business. For example, it is a wonderful thing to know the total dollar values of your last 1,000,000 sales. However, if you were simply to send all of these values to management the next time that they ask, "How have our sales been doing?" you probably will not be satisfying their expectations!

Automation Problems

An automation problem occurs whenever the system focus is on getting a recurring task or process done quickly and correctly. The system must coordinate people, materials, and information in the creation of finished products.

The processes in an automation problem are often referred to as *workflows.* A workflow describes what is given to a specified person or process, what they are to do with it, and to whom or what they are then to give their output. For example, on an auto assembly line, a typical workflow might be the following:

1. The assembler receives a steering wheel and dashboard.

2. The assembler attaches the steering wheel to the dashboard.

3. The assembler gives the finished driver-side assembly to the Painter.

Figure 2.2 shows how this might look in the form of a flowchart, showing the process of creating driver-side assemblies. The final workflow in an automation problem's series of processes produces the output for the entire system. This may be given directly to the customer or sent to the Sales department for subsequent delivery to the customer.

Storage and Retrieval Problems

Storage and retrieval problems occur in an organization whenever data needs to be saved past the point in time when it is generated and later recalled for processing into information. This kind of problem is similar to a communications problem in that its output is ultimately the same as its input.

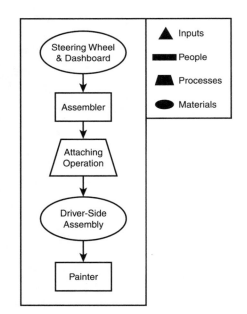

FIGURE 2.2
The workflow in flowchart form.

Table 2.1 gives you an overview of all problem types as they stand in relation to their inputs, processes, and outputs.

TABLE 2.1

COMPARISON OF PROBLEM TYPES

Problem	*Inputs*	*Processes*	*Outputs*
Communications	Data	Transportation	Data
Calculation	Data	Formulas and Rules	Information
Automation	People, Materials, and Information	Workflows	Products
Storage and Retrieval	Data	Storage and Retrieval	Data

Establishing the OscarNet's Type of Problem

Applying this kind of categorization to the case study requires re-reading your own statement of the problem. You should contrast every point in your description of the existing system to your description of that same point in the ideal situation. By determining the inputs, processes, and outputs of these points, you will be able to categorize your problem(s) appropriately.

You can analyze the OscarNet's problems as outlined in Table 2.2.

TABLE 2.2

ESTABLISHING THE OSCARNET'S PROBLEM TYPES

Problem	*Inputs*	*Processes*	*Outputs*	*Type*
Customers must call salespeople to sign up.	Customer's name, address, phone, etc. *(Data)*	Writing it down on paper applications *(Transfer)*	Customer's name, address, phone, etc. *(Data)*	Communications

continues

TABLE 2.2	*continued*			

ESTABLISHING THE OSCARNET'S PROBLEM TYPES

Problem	*Inputs*	*Processes*	*Outputs*	*Type*
Customers must wait until 5 P.M. to sign up.	Usernames, passwords, and the receptionist *(Information and People)*	Account creation *(Workflows)*	New dialup accounts *(Products)*	Automation
Customers are not always getting billed.	Billing information, salespeople, and billing clerks *(Information and People)*	Entering information into the billing system *(Workflows)*	Billing system entries *(Products)*	Automation
Salespeople are not always getting commissions.	Billing information, salespeople, and billing clerks *(Information and People)*	Entering information into the billing system *(Workflows)*	Billing system entries *(Products)*	Automation

Two interesting things should be noted here. First, two of the stated problems (customers not getting billed and salespeople not getting their commissions) really are different manifestations of the same problem. (You will see later in this chapter that, for purposes of ROI calculation, you still may want to think of these as separate issues.)

The other point is that only two types of problems are occurring at the OscarNet. Your solution, stated in the simplest form possible, needs only to provide better communications with which to sign-up new customers and a better automation mechanism for getting the accounts created and billed. Piece of cake!

The case study presents additional opportunities for improving the OscarNet's information systems. You might find it useful to see how many you can identify and list (including duplicates). Then try restating them in the proper technical terms.

Establishing and Defining Customer Quality Requirements

Different customers have different requirements for the quality of work you do for them. This isn't to say that you should ever knowingly put a solution into production that doesn't do what your customer needs done. You should be aware that organizations differ in the way they like to measure, document, and test software projects.

How Do They Want to Measure Your Progress?

The quality of your final product may be judged four different ways:

◆ Bugs per lines of code

◆ Error counts by severity

◆ Aesthetic appeal

◆ Integrity of the user interface

At this point, you are concerned primarily with analysis, so the exact means by which these goals are satisfied is not of direct importance. You should establish at this point, however, the exact criteria by which various system behaviors will be classified as "bugs," as opposed to "requests for enhancements." This is just one example of the importance of getting sign-offs on design decisions, as mentioned earlier in this chapter.

Judging the aesthetic appeal and integrity of your user interface also is an area for some concern during your initial analysis. You should carefully investigate the existence of any UI guidelines at your organization well before any screens are designed. Detailed guidelines may increase the difficulty of your project, on one hand, by requiring you to present information in ways that are less natural and intuitive to you and your people.

On the other hand, UI guidelines can simplify many design tasks by making many of the big decisions for you. For example, if existing UI guidelines require that all text be presented in black foreground over a white background, this is one less decision that you need to make.

How Do They Want to Document Your Efforts?

Just as organizations differ in the methods they use to measure software project progress, they also differ in the ways they document those projects. Unlike the earlier example, however, there are no real right or wrong ways to go about doing this. In general, the more documentation the better, and you can take any number of different approaches.

You may want to create software manuals to be used alone or used with other internal documentation. This kind of external technical documentation offers you more flexibility in what you can say (very few programming languages support graphics as internal documentation, for example) at the cost of having your explanations stored completely separately from their subject matter.

The other half of your documentation should focus on the process used to create your solution. Organizations vary widely in how much of this documentation they require and in which form it should take. Being familiar with a few of the most common forms should suffice for the exam. The three most common documentation requirements your target organization might have are the following:

◆ Design documents

◆ Review sessions and code walk-throughs

◆ Source control

A design document generally lists the features requested in a solution, followed by the exact steps needed to create them. In review sessions with their peers, developers conduct "walk-through" explanations of their code. With source control, developers can be required to "check-out" pieces of code from a central repository before working with it and "release" it when they are finished.

How Do They Want to Test Your Solution?

You should be familiar with two principal kinds of testing for the exam. The first is called *integration testing,* and the technical staff who are charged with creating the solution usually conduct the testing. The second is called *acceptance testing* and must, by definition, be performed by the people who will actually use the built solution.

In the strictest sense, integration testing is intended to ensure that all pieces of a solution will work correctly when put together. In a more general sense, it is usually intended to answer the larger question, "Have we really built what we planned to build?" To answer this question, the system must be proven to perform, without significant bugs or malfunctions, the tasks for which it was designed.

Acceptance testing must answer the question, "Did our solution provider's plans really take into account what we need?" If the answer to either of these questions is "No," disaster can occur. For this reason, you should conduct both kinds of testing on an on-going basis rather than waiting until everything has been built and it is too late to change anything easily.

The OscarNet's Quality Requirements

Case studies are unlikely to say exactly what kind of quality requirements are expected by a given organization. This means that you have to try to deduce what you can from little hints found here and there in the text. Can you find anything in the text that would indicate to you how the OscarNet likes to measure the progress of its software projects? (*Hint*: The development manager is most likely to be the person in charge of this.)

The quote "...a project to fix all of our problems would have to contain 100 tasks..." is what the development manager says in the section on Performance. You can deduce from this that the OscarNet is a task-counting organization, which bodes well for the approach to the solution you are about to build with the company.

What can you find out about end-user training at the OscarNet? (*Hint*: Remember that the two end-users in this case are the billing clerk and the internal sales representative.)

"...training I got when I started..."

"...[I] don't have any way of refreshing my memory."

Based on the billing clerk's comments on the existing system, you can deduce that the OscarNet prefers training to online help and manuals. If the OscarNet had manuals, the billing clerks could brush up on their understandings of the system.

NOTE

Unit Testing and Quality Assurance
In some organizations, two additional layers of testing may be added: unit testing and quality assurance. Unit testing precedes all other forms of testing and is intended to ensure that the individual components or pieces of a solution function as expected. For example, you would unit test an object intended to simulate bank accounts in isolation from all other components in a banking system.

You can conduct quality assurance testing before or with acceptance testing. The focus here is to ensure that the completed solution meets or exceeds organizational standards on a technical basis. The PASS ME themes of performance, availability, security, scalability, maintainability, and extensibility usually are measured very carefully during this phase. You might think of quality assurance as answering the question, "Does our solution meet the quality requirements that have been established?"

Minimizing Total Cost of Ownership (TCO)

As you learned in the section on making resource trade-offs, the total of up-front costs and ongoing costs is referred to as the *Total Cost of Ownership*. The next section explains how you can reduce these costs.

Reducing Up-Front Costs

Up-front costs are the obvious expenses that must be paid in order to create a solution. The key to reducing these expenses is to change as little as possible as slowly as possible. You can do this best by using for your project as much of the existing systems and staff as possible. You also can choose to push back the rollout date for your new system(s).

Working with existing systems saves you up-front expense because you have to develop less of a new system using your own resources. You can save money by designing your system to operate on existing hardware and operating systems. You can save money, labor, and time by designing your system to incorporate existing software.

The information technologies staff that already is a part of the organization for which you are developing a solution can reduce your up-front costs in a number of ways. First, any work they do is work you will not have to do yourself. Second, because they are familiar with the organization and its problems, they can invariably spot bad ideas quickly and help you develop realistic alternatives.

Reducing Maintenance Costs

Maintenance or ongoing costs represent the unexpected expenses involved in keeping a system operational over time. The primary cause of these expenses is system downtime and unavailability. The human intervention and administration needed to keep the system operational is also costly. The most pervasive costs, however, are those associated with trying to extend a system to do things that it should have been able to do right from the start.

The obvious way to reduce down-time costs is to manufacture your system to a high level of quality and reliability. This may involve something of a trade-off as the resources saved from possible future problems are gradually offset by some very real up-front expenses. Try to remain calm and focus on how nice things *will* be after the system is done—whenever that may be.

You can reduce the need for administration of your solution by planning from the beginning to automate many of the processes involved in the system. Similarly, you can reduce the costs associated with adding new features to your solution by planning for extensibility. You learn more about this in the next chapter because extensibility is one of the recurring PASS ME themes that you see throughout this book and the Microsoft exam.

REVIEW BREAK

Figure 2.3 shows the level of expense that generally can be expected to accompany a solution at varying stages in its lifespan.

The peak at the beginning of the diagram represents the cost of development and testing associated with the initial rollout of a system. This is followed by a short, steep period of decline as the initial problems that weren't caught by developer testing are found by end-users and resolved. The remainder of the graph shows the long, slow decline in cost that represents the subsequent "ironing out" of little bugs as the solution's life progresses. Notice that even though the graph slopes downward, the duration of the maintenance period over an extended time demonstrates that the majority of total costs are incurred *after* the solution is released.

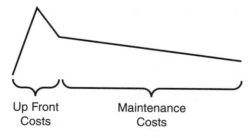

FIGURE 2.3
Ownership costs over time.

Reducing the OscarNet's TCO

The OscarNet seems less concerned about reducing the cost associated with a new system than with making absolutely certain that the current problems are given a definitive, once-and-for-all solution. Still, the information in the case study suggests at least a couple of techniques that can be employed to decrease the OscarNet's TCO.

One challenge you face in building this solution for the OscarNet is that the solution is meant to be short-term, as you previously learned. This means that you won't be able to invest the additional time you would need to ensure high levels of reliability.

Increasing the ROI of a Solution

The opposite side of the TCO coin is ROI, or Return on Investment. You learned in the section on making resource trade-offs that this is what remains after the Total Cost of Ownership for a system is subtracted from all the value the system produces during its life span.

You always can do a few general things to increase a solution's ROI. First, you can add more features. The greater the number of problems your solution solves, the more valuable it will be to the organization. Next, you can create high-quality documentation for your solution. This allows the organization to get higher usage levels and more value out of your solution. Finally, of course, you can increase the ROI of your solution by ensuring that there are as few errors in your code as possible.

You can take two main approaches to increasing the ROI of a solution you are developing. The first is to work strictly against issues arising out of the current problem. The second is to create your system in a way that leverages the reusability of components for future solutions.

Increasing ROI Against the Current Problem

In most organizations, the return on resources invested in the current system is most noticeable if you can get the same result from the same system that you are building. For this reason, we will cover this topic first. One approach to doing this is to solve all the easiest problems first. Another way would be to solve all the costliest problems first.

Solving the easiest problems first enables you to solve the greatest number of problems with the fewest resources. On the other hand, if you solve the most expensive problems first, you may get an even better ROI.

One example to illustrate both approaches is the way in which a space agency might allocate its research and development budget. Putting an emphasis on preventing flight disasters constitutes a case of solving the costliest problems first. Considering the billions of dollars required for a typical satellite and launch vehicle, this approach could easily pay for itself with a single averted disaster. On the other hand, a job like this easily could consume sufficient resources to stop work on other projects. (Recall NASA's launch hiatus in the aftermath of the Challenger tragedy.)

In contrast to this, the space agency might choose to use the Easiest Problems First approach by doing an "old-fashioned" (and familiar) single-use rocket launch rather than one involving the space shuttle. The benefit to this approach is that the actual number of problems that can be addressed is greater because each problem will consume fewer resources. NASA cannot do as much with single-launch craft as it can with the space shuttle, but it can launch the single-launch crafts (at a profit) many, many times more often.

Table 2.3 illustrates a situation in which one solution provider has chosen to use the Easiest Problems First approach and the other has decided to deal with the Costliest Problems First. When both solution providers are given only 200 hours in which to work, they wind up saving the organization equal amounts of money: $25,000 per year. The only difference between the two scenarios is that the second approach solves only one problem ($25k), whereas the first approach solves two ($10k + $15k = $25k).

NOTE

The 80/20 Rule Most management sciences have some variation on the Law of Diminishing Returns—in Software Engineering, this is known as the 80/20 rule. The 80/20 rule says that there is a point in every project where the benefits that might be gained in a solution by continuing to solve problems and add features is not worth the cost required. Hypothetically, this point occurs around the point at which 80 percent of all possible work has been completed and 20 percent remains. Given a choice between solving 80 percent of a customer's problems for $100,000 or 100 percent of the problems for $1,000,000, most customers will not hesitate to favor the cheaper solution!

TABLE 2.3

**SOLVING THE EASIEST PROBLEMS FIRST VS. THE
COSTLIEST PROBLEMS**

Hours Required to Fix	*Cost to Business (in $1,000 per Year)*	*Easiest Problems First*	*Costliest Problems First*
100	10	SOLVED	—
200	25	—	SOLVED
200	18	—	—
100	15	SOLVED	—
400	32	—	—

Increasing ROI Through Reusability of Components

You can also increase ROI by leveraging the reusability of components you create. The first step in working this way is to identify the pieces of code you will be building that are likely candidates for reuse. A good example of this would be a routine for generating an account number your billing system will accept. You should write this code only once, no matter how many times and places you may be using it.

Figure 2.4 shows a situation in which just four small components are being combined in varying ways to produce three full-featured applications. This kind of reuse is a key goal in all the most successful development shops. You may find places in the current system to reuse your code, which is an additional benefit.

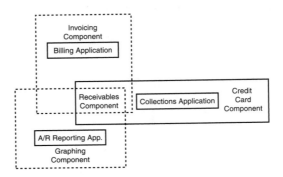

FIGURE 2.4
The value of component reuse.

In order to leverage your code against other problems, you first need to settle on a binary standard for your components. The two leading binary standards are ActiveX/COM from Microsoft and CORBA. Using a binary standard allows you to combine pieces written in different programming languages and distribute your pieces on different machines on your network.

You learn more about the specifics of building distributed applications in Chapters 9 through 13. For now, simply understand that it will allow the code you build as part of this project to be reused by many other projects written in different languages and running on different machines.

Increasing the ROI of the OscarNet's Solution

To determine the best way to increase the return on the OscarNet's investment in your new solution, you must estimate the cost of each of the four problems. At this stage, it is better not to combine the four problems into three by removing the duplicate because every department most likely has a different stake in the problems' solutions. Only by adding the different values the solution offers each department can you arrive at an accurate final estimate of ROI.

You estimate the number of hours required to solve each problem, apply both the EPF and CPF methods, and compare the results. You can try this procedure in the Exercises at the end of this chapter.

Analyzing the Current Application Environment

Earlier in the book, you learned how to incorporate planned changes to an application's environment into your estimated project scope. The application environment already in place must be analyzed just as thoroughly. You must understand fully all the hardware, operating systems, and internal support systems presently available for your solution's use.

Analyzing the Hardware

Hardware provides the "horsepower" behind the software. You need to make sure that the processor speeds of the computers your solution uses are up to the task. Too little CPU power can cause even the best applications to run unbearably slowly.

Storage space is another prime concern when you are evaluating hardware. You should ensure that the computers you are incorporating into your solution have sufficient memory and disk space. If they are short on memory, they will be accessing the disk that much more often. So, in this case, disk space becomes even more important.

The speed of your data-link is the final thing you should verify as sufficient for your needs. If you have written the rare modern application that exists in a vacuum without need of network resources, this probably will be less of a concern for you. For the rest of us, the faster the connection, the better!

Analyzing the Operating Systems

The way in which you evaluate the efficiency of an operating system's resource usage is similar to the way you analyzed project scope. Your analysis should touch specifically on the operating system's use of both the processor and physical storage.

As you know, an operating system's ease-of-use can have a significant effect on the frequency of support calls. One factor that enhances ease-of-use is having a GUI (graphical user interface). Other "good signs" include the following:

◆ Returning full-text errors rather than cryptic error numbers that must be looked up in printed manuals

◆ Being highly resistant to crashing

◆ Being widely used

◆ Offering permissions-based security

◆ Running each process in its own, isolated process-space

◆ Multitasking in a pre-emptive, rather than co-operative fashion

Windows NT is widely regarded as superior to Windows 98 in all of these points, with the possible exception of the full-text errors. Windows 98, however, offers plug and play hardware support and a wide variety of other conveniences aimed at the consumer market.

The final set of criteria you should apply in analyzing the operating systems' impact on the current application environment is the ease with which code can be written for them. First, you should consider the sheer number of tools available for programming for a given operating system (such as Visual Basic for Windows, Code-Warrior for Macintosh, and the gcc compiler for UNIX).

Secondly, consider the amount of information about the OS that is publicly available. The amount of available information relates directly to the wide use of the operating system. The more people using an OS, the more information resources are likely to exist for it.

Third, you need to look at the low-level services provided to applications running on a particular operating system. One example of an OS service is the text-boxes and buttons on a graphical user interface. If programmers had to build these entirely from scratch every time they used them, not many graphical applications would exist. Fortunately, modern operating systems provide pre-made "widgets" that make creating such objects as simple as making standard API (application programming interface) calls.

Analyzing the Internal Support Systems

After you build your solution, you need to keep it operational as long as the organization desires. The responsibility for this falls largely on the shoulders of so-called "internal support" at the organization. You should begin your analysis of this group's contribution to an existing application environment by determining the number of support personnel an organization has, how much they are likely to be needed, and how good they seem to be at their craft.

For the problems that the organization's people cannot solve themselves, find out what kinds of support agreements they have with their technology vendors. If they have no coverage, or less than you think adequate, you should look into the possibility of purchasing more.

Analyzing the OscarNet's Application Environment

The following list recaps what you already know about the OscarNet's existing hardware and operating systems:

◆ UNIX network servers provide dialup connectivity

◆ 4-processor, 256MB Alpha server for billing (NT)

◆ x486, 16MB with four modems for sign-up server (NT)

◆ 50 100-200MHz desktops, 32MB RAM (Windows 98)

Recall that the OscarNet already is planning to change certain aspects of this environment. Depending upon when you decide to implement your solution, your own applications may have to live in either or both environments. The next section explores how to cope with this challenge.

Incorporating the Planned Application Environment

When you are designing a solution, you must know whether the hardware, operating systems, or internal support systems of your target organization will soon be changing. If so, one of three scenarios is possible.

In the first scenario, your solution will no longer be needed after the changes, in which case you can design entirely for the existing application environment. The second case is that your solution will not be needed until after the changes have taken place, in which case you should design completely for the planned application environment. The third and final situation is that your solution will be needed in both environments, in which case you must plan for compatibility very carefully indeed!

Working with the Planned Hardware

When thinking about how you will incorporate planned hardware into your solution, you should try to arrange things so that your most complicated business logic runs on the computers with the most powerful CPUs. This means distributing your business objects on these computers in a distributed model. In a more traditional client/server model, this means putting the servers on these machines.

The same principles apply to where you choose to store your data. Machines with the most disk space are the most obvious choice. You should remember, however, that a machine with poor connectivity (accessible only via a 28.8k modem, for example) might not be the best place to store anything, given the difficulty of later reading from and writing to it.

Working with the Planned Operating Systems

In the previous section, you learned what constitutes strengths and weaknesses in operating systems. When you are planning to incorporate planned operating systems into your solution, you can use a few rules of thumb to help you.

All else being equal, you should put the more user-friendly operating systems on client computers because those systems will have the most direct human use. For your server computers, you should choose operating systems based of the performance boosts they offer.

Working with the Planned Support Systems

The company for which you are developing your solution may also have plans for altering their support systems. It will be your job, as a designer, to figure out how these changes can best be incorporated into your solution.

Your solution may require that more people be brought permanently on staff in order to support it. On the other hand, if your solution is particularly self-administering, some people who are now obliged to spend most of their time doing "help-desk" may find themselves free to pursue more rewarding tasks.

You learned in the last section that there are different kinds of external support that a company can use: extended contract or per-incident. This is your opportunity to assess the likelihood that your organization will need support for any of the third-party technologies that form a part of your solution. If the likelihood is particularly high, you may want to recommend a support contract.

The OscarNet's Planned Application Environment

In the case study, you are told nothing about the hardware on the UNIX server, so disregard it for the moment. The Alpha machine is obviously a "monster machine," so you will want to put any heavy processing required by your solution on it. The sign-up server is teetering on the verge of total obsolescence and is a prime candidate for complete retirement. The desktops seem to have adequate, if not amazing, processing power (by the standards of 1999).

Windows NT provides a wide range of features, but supporting these features consumes memory and processing cycles. On the Alpha server this is fine, but it seems a very bad choice for the sign-up server. Because the software already on that machine demands Windows (Active Server Pages), Windows 98 running Personal Web Server would be a good choice.

Analyzing the Impact of a Technology Migration

The path from one system to another is rarely completely free of bumps. Half the battle in overcoming these obstacles lies in being able to see them from a distance. For this reason, you should spend some time before any design decisions have been set in stone, to try to determine in advance what problems are likely to arise as you attempt to move from one technology to another.

Analyzing Training Needs

Most likely, you will find three distinct groups within your target organization that are in need of training after the migration has taken place. The first of these groups is the technical staff, the second is management, and the third is the end-user population. Many of the training requirements for these groups are the same, but there are sufficient differences to warrant a brief word of explanation.

The technical staff at your target organization will be concerned mainly with what they need to know in order to keep the system running after you have left. In cases where the new system is being built in cooperation with this staff, they are liable to need some additional training about any technologies you decide to use with which they are unfamiliar.

Of the remaining two groups, management's prime concern will be learning the high-level tasks that they need to know in order to extract the appropriate information from your system. Similarly, the end-users of your system will just want to focus on whatever low-level tasks they are required to perform in the completion of their daily work. Figure 2.5 shows the overall relationships between these very different kinds of users and the kinds of training that they will require.

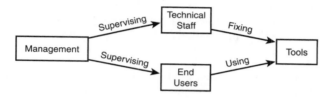

FIGURE 2.5
Training people according to their job tasks.

Determining What Additional Solutions May be Required

Once your solution is in place, other problems that were previously rare or nonexistent may become intolerable. Similar to training requirements, learning to anticipate these situations is the best means for eventually coping with them.

The most common problems that start wreaking havoc soon after a new solution has been put into place are usually the ones that have always been there. The slowness of fast-food service, for example, might go largely unnoticed for as long as an inefficient drive-through system is slowing down orders. Once the drive-through is repaired, however, customers are much more likely to notice the true source of their 15-minute wait for food.

The other kind of problem is the kind that is directly caused by your new solution. To continue with the fast-food example, this could occur when, after you have replaced the previous, tiny drive-through speaker with a 1000-watt Public Address system, customers start complaining of a persistent ringing in their ears after going through your drive-through. In this case, you have just exchanged one problem for another. In computer technology terms, this is like exchanging a slow, reliable technology (like dialing-up the Internet with a modem) for a faster, less reliable one (such as satellite-dish access).

Migrating the OscarNet's Technology

To figure out which kind of training will be needed after a technology migration, begin by asking exactly what everyone at that organization does. The technical staff at the OscarNet will be keeping your solution operational and might even help you build it, so at the very least they will need to get a good technical overview of the entire system. Management, meanwhile, will want to know how to continue tracking billing discrepancies and commissions. And, the billing clerks and internal sales representatives will need to know how to enter billing information and fill-out sales applications, respectively.

The additional solutions that might be required at the OscarNet are less obvious from the information given. Just for purposes of further explanation, an existing problem in this case might be something like customers noticing more busy signals because they are able to access their accounts quicker. A problem caused by your solution might be increased corporate expenses as sales commissions are no longer understated by lost information. And finally, the best example of a future problem with a future cause in this case might well prove to be the infamous Y2K bug causing widespread disasters and panic on January 1, 2000.

Planning Physical Requirements

The physical requirements for a solution include both traditional kinds of computer hardware: processing and storage. It is important to remember, however, that in the Internet age, connectivity is every bit as important as either of those physical requirements. Planning for these considerations at this early stage may seem impossible, but there are a few basic principles you can apply as your project progresses to help you think in the right terms.

How Much Processing Power?

You can consider a couple of things in determining how much processing power your solution is likely to require. The first of these is the nature of your logic, which is best estimated at this stage by considering the nature of your problem. You recall the four primary types of problem areas:

◆ Communications

◆ Calculation

◆ Automation

◆ Storage and Retrieval

Of the four, Calculation requires the most processing power. Automation may also require significant processing, depending on the exact nature of the procedures being automated.

Other things that eat up considerable CPU cycles are fancy graphical displays of information. This occurs exclusively in Calculation and Automation problems. This type of problem is also, almost by definition, generally a client-side or user-interface tier issue (depending upon which architecture you choose).

How Much Storage?

The amount of storage you will need for your solution is directly proportional to the amount of data your system will be managing. You should also take into account the number of users that will be accessing your system simultaneously because every user that connects to your data creates some degree of "overhead" on the computer hosting the data.

When the sheer amount of data is your prime concern, buy more disk space. When speed of access is everything, consider more RAM.

What Kind of Connectivity?

No connectivity is best in many cases. If your applications require no outside information apart from what can be typed into them (such as a checkbook balancing application), why subject yourself to the security risks associated with putting the system into a networked environment? On the other hand, what if you are trying to solve a Communications problem in which some form of connectivity is essential?

> **WARNING**
>
> **Calculation versus Storage and Retrieval**   If you find yourself needing a lot of processing power as you begin building what you think is a storage and retrieval problem, please reconsider your classification. Intense processing is a key indicator that data is being churned into information at some point, and this is beyond the scope of a storage and retrieval problem.

Building your own network is one way to approach the problem. If all the computers you want to connect are in a single office or building, a LAN (Local Area Network) is probably your best and cheapest choice. Most operating systems feature built-in support for at least some LAN protocols, and add-on software is readily available for the few that don't come equipped with those features.

If some of the computers you want to connect to are in separate buildings, however—or perhaps even in different cities, states, or provinces—you must consider getting a WAN (Wide Area Network). WANs use strong transmission media (microwaves, lasers, and so on) to connect multiple networks at great distances. The software for managing these is not as widely available and the development costs are great.

The perfect alternative in this situation is to use the Internet as a relatively free backbone for your organization's data transfers. For just a little more money, you can build a VPN (Virtual Private Network) that will encrypt your data for safe transmission across the Internet. Figure 2.6 depicts all three kinds of networks and the ways in which they might relate to each other.

Planning the OscarNet's Physical Requirements

Let's deal with the easiest part first. Because the OscarNet is, according to the case study, "...confined to the 2nd and 3rd floors of...one building," (to quote the VP of Sales), a LAN is the most natural choice for providing your solution with connectivity. In fact, you can deduce from the fact that they already have some kind of client-server billing system in place that they already have the connectivity they want.

As you may recall, Table 2.2 showed that two types of problems must be solved at the OscarNet: one Communications issue, and two Automation issues (one of which is listed again in a different permutation, making the total appear to be four). Neither of these is associated with particularly strong data requirements (like Storage and Retrieval) or processing (like Calculation). So, you can rightly adopt more of a "wait and see" attitude toward the physical requirements of a project such as this.

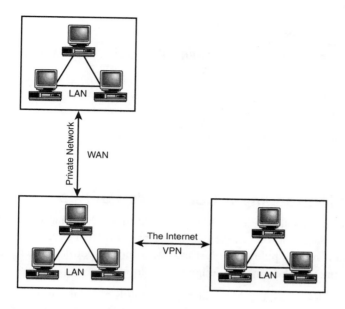

FIGURE 2.6
LANs, WANs, and VPNs.

Identifying Organizational Constraints

Organizational constraints are the little quirks about a company that make working there more difficult than it really needs to be. You look at several of these constraints in this section.

Assessing the Customer's Financial Situation

Many good reasons exist for you to be concerned with your customer's financial situation before you begin building a solution. On the exam, however, the questions are more likely to focus on the different approaches to building solutions you should take in different kinds of financial situations.

As Table 2.4 shows, a company can do harm to itself both by spending too little and too much. Similarly, a company also can heal itself by spending more or less. You should always try to build a solution that moves a sick organization in a healthier direction.

TABLE 2.4		
SIGNIFICANCE OF DIFFERENT FINANCIAL SITUATIONS		
Customer's Spending	*Healthy*	*Sick*
Conservative	Thrift and Efficiency	"Spiral of Death"
Liberal	Positioning for Expansion	Wasteful

Understanding a Company's Politics

Most technical people would sooner lock themselves in a room with a computer and the company vending machine than have to deal with company politics. Unfortunately, corporate politics does have an effect on the way you design your solutions.

The rules are simple. You will find two kinds of organizational decision-making flows: One is dynamic and the other is static. A company with dynamic decision-making flows is either changing itself constantly to adapt to changing market requirements or running around in a state of utter chaos and pandemonium. A company with static decision-making flows is either enjoying the benefits of consistency and reliability or quietly stagnating. Figure 2.7 compares the organizational charts of two different companies to show the difference between these two flows.

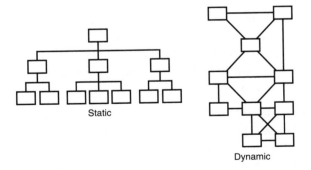

FIGURE 2.7
Static vs. dynamic decision-making flows.

The diagram on the left has a traditional, static decision-making flow that proceeds in a hierarchical fashion from top to bottom. The one on the right is a more dynamic affair, with people more free to network in the accomplishment of their work than might otherwise be possible. In a company with dynamic decision-making flows, your solutions must be able to change if and when the target organization requires. At the other extreme, you must be very careful that any changes in a company's decision-making brought about by your solution are ones the company can ultimately accept. When modifying your applications in ways that significantly alter data availability and/or decision-making capabilities, make sure to document all change requests and get the proper approvals.

Determining the Customer's Technical Acceptance Level

A customer's technical acceptance level is a measure of how comfortable that organization is acquiring and using new information systems. Some customers are almost too eager to try new things. Other customers would rather keep the systems they started with until the day they go out of business. Rarely will you find the "happy medium"—a customer willing to try new things, but only when business needs dictate.

The problem with organizations that are too eager to use leading-edge technologies is that they often go for "bleeding-edge" technologies; that is, technologies that have yet to have all the bugs worked out. These organizations also tend to choose fashionable tools over ones that stand the best chance of working. As you design your solution, resist the urge to satisfy company requests when it isn't in the organization's best interests.

Technologically resistant customers, on the other hand, tend to have two main reasons for disliking system-improvement. The first reason is a fear of breaking things that are currently working acceptably, if not perfectly. The second reason is reluctance to expose employees to newer technologies for fear that they will use the experience to go off and get better jobs.

Identifying Training Needs

The fear of employee-loss through better training is just one of the concerns that you need to address as you make your instructional plans. Other concerns you are likely to encounter are time and cost.

Proper training takes time and money. The fear that employees trained in the hottest new technologies are more likely to leave for better jobs has some validity. This additional cost should be factored into the maintenance portion of your solution's TCO.

When discussing this with your target organization's management, make the point that there is really nothing stopping highly motivated employees from pursuing training on their own. At least, if the company offers the training, there may be some gratitude on the part of those who receive the training. In fact, lack of training on new technologies can be one of the factors motivating employees to leave companies. The opportunity for "staying current," on the other hand, can motivate them to stay.

Identifying the OscarNet's Organizational Constraints

In the Case Study, nothing indicates the organization being in financial trouble. On the contrary, recall that in the section on the Envisioned System, the Dialup Sales Manager states "...[we've] got plenty left in the budget for whatever you can come up with."

The decision-making flows at the OscarNet are never specifically mentioned, but the two end-users do seem to have a lot of flexibility in the way they do their work. How else could so many applications be getting lost between Sales and Billing? A company as young as they are probably is also a good bet for a more dynamic decisional system.

Because of the OscarNet's position on money, you can be reasonably sure that training will not be a problem. Time, on the other hand, is of the essence because you are creating a short-term solution.

Establishing a Schedule for Solution Implementation

When you are building solutions, the conventional wisdom is that sooner is always better. Like most conventional wisdom, this is not always the case. Although completing a project slowly has definite drawbacks, there are also some advantages. Likewise, although you will find many advantages to getting a project done quickly, so too are there some definite drawbacks.

Doing It Faster

Perhaps the most obvious reason to get your solution in place as quickly as possible is that your target organization can start enjoying its benefits that much sooner. In the earlier section on ROI, you saw how the length of time a given solution was in service could drastically affect its return on investment.

If the problems your new system is intended to solve are severe, you may need to work as fast as you can. On the other hand, if the problems to be solved are trivial, you might consider that taking your time is much more likely to produce correct results down the road.

> **NOTE**
>
> **Parkinson's Law** It would probably be good for you to remember Parkinson's Law while contemplating any kind of work schedule. In short, this law states that any amount of work that needs to be done will expand to fill all time available for doing it! For this reason, it is sometimes a good idea to schedule deadlines a little ahead of when you actually need to meet them.

Doing It Slower

You have a couple of reasons to take things a little slower (if not easier) when building a solution. Both of these reasons have to do with making sure that your solution provides the highest levels of service and reliability when it does, finally, go into production.

Doing a conversion more slowly allows more time to adequately test your solution. As you saw in the previous section on customer quality requirements, two primary kinds of testing are used: integration and acceptance. In the case of a slower rollout, integration testing should be conducted on an on-going basis with a short period of intensified testing at the end. Acceptance testing, as always, should remain the responsibility of the customer.

If you have a slower rollout, you will not only have the benefit of more time for testing, but you should also be able to train more fully the people who will be using and maintaining the solution.

NOTE **Iterative Development**   Some solutions are creating using an iterative approach, in which a solution that meets at least some of the customer's requirements is shipped as soon as possible. This solution is then modified over time in response to customer requests for improvements. Slowly but surely, this tool grows to encompass all or most of the originally desired functionality. In this "slower" approach to solution creation, you are able to start giving your customer some of the benefits of your solution almost immediately. The downside is that you must live with any limitations resulting from your initial shortcuts until you have a chance to make changes in subsequent solution revisions.

Of course, there is some danger to a slower rollout. In addition to Parkinson's Law, you have to recognize and deal with the concept of "technology churning," which happens when cutting edge technology advances beyond your project while it is still in progress. For example, suppose that you began building a solution with cgi-scripts when that was the newest and best technology available. By the time you were done with the project, Active Server Pages had come on the scene and rendered your solution obsolete.

Scheduling the OscarNet's Solution Implementation

Given the short-term nature of the solution you are being asked to provide for the OscarNet, the only possible schedule that you can choose is "as soon as possible."

Identifying Your Audience

The last aspect of analyzing business requirements you need to know in this chapter involves identifying the audience for your project. Audiences consist of all the people who rely on your solution in order to complete their work. Some of these people are end-users, others are management, and still others are technical personnel.

End Users

End users are the people who put data into the system and get information out of it. The Accounting, Production, and Sales parts of a business are comprised mostly of end users.

Management

You deal with two main kinds of management in any organization: senior and project. Senior management is in charge of making strategic decisions about the proper allocation of corporate resources. Project management executes the strategies developed by senior management and takes status reports on progress toward various goals and milestones.

Senior managers are an audience for your solution because they require information from your systems in order to make their strategic decisions. Often you will find it difficult to get these people to participate fully in the design of your solutions because they tend to be very busy. You may have to try to deduce the kinds of information they need, based upon what you know about the existing systems and the people who are available to them.

Project managers, on the other hand, have more of a vested interest in the success of your systems. Any failure to find solutions for the problems that prevent them from achieving senior management's strategies invariably reflect poorly on them. For this reason, you should always include project managers in your list of solution audiences and try to get as much information from them about your tasks as possible.

Technical Staff

The technical staff members at the organization are the third group you should consider when determining the audience for your solution. The three kinds of technical staff you deal with are programmers, internal support, and administrators.

Programmers need the deepest understanding of your solution because they will be the ones left behind to make minor modifications and extensions to your systems after you have left.

Internal support will be in charge of answering most of the questions that end-users have about how to use your new systems. Typically, they provide the "buffer layer" that protects programmers from continual distraction by simple questions.

The people in charge of performing routine tasks required to keep your system operational (such as cleaning-up disk space, editing user accounts, and keeping the network running) are called *administrators*. Administrators do not have to work with your system when it is not working correctly, so these individuals need to know only what should be required under normal, operational circumstances.

Identifying Your Audience at the OscarNet

The positions mentioned in the case study break down along the lines represented in Table 2.5.

<table>
<tr><td colspan="3">TABLE 2.5</td></tr>
</table>

AUDIENCES AT THE OSCARNET

Position in Case Study	Part of Corporation	Audience Type
VP of Sales	Management	Management
Inside Sales Representative	Sales	End-User
Billing Clerk	Accounting	End-User
Receptionist	Production	End-User
Dialup Sales Manager	Sales	Management (Project)
Programmer	Production	Technical Staff
Development Manager	Management	Technical Staff

Notice that the VP of Sales is included in Management rather than Sales. This is an arguable decision and should be made largely on the basis of whether the position is ever directly involved in the sale of goods to customers. The Dialup Sales Manager is included in Sales rather than Management (under Part of Corporation) strictly on the basis of the fact that he said, "...Whenever I talk to these customers..." in the section on the Envisioned System.

Finally, Table 2.5 lists programmers as a part of Production because they invariably create (intangible) things. When development managers directly participate in code creation, they can be listed as part of Production as well.

CHAPTER SUMMARY

Analyzing the extent of a business requirement requires the consideration of many factors. First, you must formulate an exact description of the problem, answering the journalistic "who, what, when, where, why, and how" questions. Next, you should try to fit the problems into more general categories: Communications, Calculation, Automation, and Storage and Retrieval.

Having determined the nature of the problem, you then need to look at the various factors that affect the solutions you create. These

CHAPTER SUMMARY

factors include customer quality requirements for progress measurement, documentation, and testing. They also included ways to minimize TCO by cutting back on up-front and maintenance costs. This, in turn, affects ROI versus the current problem as well as others (through reusability of components).

Analyzing the current application environment at an organization requires looking at hardware, operating systems, and support availability. Incorporating all this into a solution requires a proper distribution of code, connectivity, and the various operating systems used as well as a keen understanding of options for external, as well as internal, support.

Because it is impossible to go from one set of systems to another without encountering some problems, this chapter included forewarnings about the unique needs for training and additional solutions you may encounter.

Planning physical requirements is a matter of taking processing power, connectivity, and storage into account. All these should be distributed according to the needs of your solution and the limitations imposed by your organization. Determining exactly what those constraints are requires assessing your target organization's financial situation, politics, technical acceptance level, and training needs.

In some case, after you have considered all of the factors, you will decide that a quick conversion is the best path to follow. At other times, you will opt for a slower course of action. This chapter explained that you should make this decision by carefully weighing the potential benefits of the new system against any possible loss of opportunities for training and testing.

Finally, no solution can adequately be planned without an intimate knowledge of the audience for that solution. You should take into account the needs of end-users, management, and technical staff when designing any solution.

KEY TERMS

- 80/20 rule
- Acceptance testing
- Costliest Problems First (CPF)
- Design document
- Downsizing / upsizing
- Easiest Problems First (EPF)
- Integration testing
- Iterative development
- Multi-threading
- Organizational constraint
- Quality Assurance
- Return on Investment (ROI)
- Review meeting
- Source control
- Technical acceptance level
- Total Cost of Ownership (TCO)
- Unit testing

APPLY YOUR KNOWLEDGE

Exercises

1.1   EPF vs. CPF

In Exercise 1.1, you get the chance to analyze a problem yourself, using both Easiest Problems First and Costliest Problems First approaches. By the end of the exercise, you should have a much better idea of how to increase your solution's ROI against the current problem.

Estimated Time: 10 minutes.

1. Study the "Hours Required to Fix" and "Cost to Business" columns in Table 2.6.

2. Imagine that you have only 1,000 hours before your solution must be delivered.

3. Going in order of fewest to most hours required to fix, put the word *SOLVED* in as many boxes in the EPF column as you can. When you can't fill in any more boxes without going over 1000 hours total, stop.

4. Going in order from highest cost to least, put the word SOLVED in as many boxes in the CPF column as you can. When you can't fill in any more boxes without going over 1000 hours total, stop.

5. Add the numbers in the Cost to Business column for every row where you put SOLVED in the EPF column. Now do the same for the CPF column.

6. When you compare the two totals, you should find that solving the Easiest Problems First is a better approach in this case.

TABLE 2.6

SOLVING THE EASIEST PROBLEMS FIRST VERSUS THE COSTLIEST PROBLEMS

Hours Required to Fix	Cost to Business (In $1,000 per Year)	Easiest Problems First (EPF)	Costliest Problems First (CPF)
300	15		
800	22		
200	28		
1200	3		
5500	7		
500	17		

See the solution in Table 2.7.

APPLY YOUR KNOWLEDGE

TABLE 2.7

SOLVING THE EASIEST PROBLEMS FIRST VERSUS THE COSTLIEST PROBLEMS

Hours Required to Fix	Cost to Business (In $1,000 per Year)	Easiest Problems First (EPF)	Costliest Problems First (CPF)
300	15	SOLVED	—
800	22	—	SOLVED
200	28	SOLVED	SOLVED
1200	3	—	—
5500	7	—	—
500	17	SOLVED	—

Review Questions

The following review questions conclude your examination of the OscarNet's case study. To refresh your memory regarding the details of this scenario, please refer to Chapter 1.

1. If you found out that significant bugs existed in the OscarNet's sign-up software, which part of the business would you hold accountable?

2. Suppose that the OscarNet needs a way to keep track of all the calls received by Sales during the course of the day. What kind of problem is this?

3. The OscarNet wants weekly reports about how many watts of electricity have been consumed by computers being used to create your solution. Is this a good way to measure your progress? Why or why not?

4. What kind of cost would you be reducing for the OscarNet if you agreed to build their initial solution for free?

5. Components designed to interface with the OscarNet's future billing system are already available. How can these be used to increase the ROI of your solution?

6. Someone at the OscarNet just suggested putting Linux on the salespeople's desktops. Can you think of a reason why this would be a bad idea?

7. Imagine that everyone currently in Internal Support at the OscarNet will be retiring in a few days. How would this affect your plans for incorporating the planned application environment?

8. Soon after you roll out your new solution, the President of the OscarNet begins complaining that he isn't getting enough sleep. Eventually you discover that his loss of sleep is due to the fact that your solution has earned him so much money that he has been able to buy every video game on the market and is playing them all night every night. What type of problem is this?

APPLY YOUR KNOWLEDGE

9. Suppose that two employees at the OscarNet currently are communicating across the office using two cans and a piece of string. If you plan to replace this with a new computer-messaging system, what kind of physical infrastructure needs should you evaluate?

10. How would you analyze the OscarNet's organizational constraints if everyone there needed to type every business action they took and have their bosses sign the documents in triplicate?

11. If someone told you that the OscarNet's new billing system had been delayed for several years, what would be some reasons for pushing back the rollout of your solution?

12. The programmers and Development Manager at the OscarNet have gotten angry and decided not to work on or use your new solution. What audience have you just lost?

Exam Questions

1. A document that describes a number of situations along with the desired behavior for your system in each one is known as what?

   A. Parkinson's Law

   B. Technology churning

   C. Use case document

   D. Sign-off document

2. Classify the following facts according to the aspect of business requirements they would impact. (Choose two facts per requirement.)

REQUIREMENTS AND CASE STUDY FACTS

Requirements	*Facts*
Parts of business involved	The sign-up server is running NT.
	Billing clerks mail out software.
Problematic situations	Salespeople are not getting their commissions.
	OscarNet is in Seattle.
	DSL may bring a lot more revenue.
Problematic locations	Billing system needs to handle at least three simultaneous users.
	Money has been put away for a sign-up server reworking.
Performance requirements	OscarNet's customers are all in Seattle.
	Billing clerks can COMP accounts.
Hardware and operating systems	Account creation application is written in PERL.
	Receptionist needs to leave by 5:30 P.M.
Internal support	Salespeople make sales over the phone.
	Customers are never getting billed.

APPLY YOUR KNOWLEDGE

Requirements	*Facts*
Customer's financial situation	The CPU on the sign-up server is an Alpha.
	The VP of Sales should be able to see commissions reports.
Security requirements	People at OscarNet are generally fairly computer literate.

3. Consider the flow of sign-up software from the CD burning personnel to the billing clerks responsible for mailing it out. Altering this system would be what kind of problem?

   A. Communications

   B. Calculation

   C. Automation

   D. Storage and Retrieval

4. Which of the actions listed below could be effective in reducing your solution's maintenance costs? (Choose two)

   A. Getting your solution built faster

   B. Ensuring that your system is thoroughly tested

   C. Adding automated diagnostic procedures

   D. Reducing your applications' disk usage

5. What is it called when technology progresses at such a fast pace that a project is rendered partially obsolete before it is even finished?

   A. Parkinson's Law

   B. Technology churning

   C. Use case document

   D. Sign-off document

6. The VP of Sales at OscarNet will probably require training after any technology migration your solution may require is implemented. What do you think the nature of this training might be?

   A. How to keep your systems running

   B. How to pull reports out of your solution

   C. How to extend your solution's functionality

   D. How your system assists in wine production

7. What is the name of the principle that claims "a task will expand to consume all time available for its completion"?

   A. Parkinson's Law

   B. Technology churning

   C. Use case document

   D. Sign-off document

8. If you were told that the new billing system at OscarNet is going to be operational one month sooner than you had previously thought, how would you be most likely to schedule rollout of your new solution?

   A. Faster, because it is a short-term solution and will have more time to cause problems

   B. Slower, because it is a short-term solution and will have less time to prove its value

APPLY YOUR KNOWLEDGE

   C. Faster, because it is a long-term solution and gimmicks are most important

   D. Slower, because it is a long-term solution and quality is most important

Answers to Review Questions

1. Production. This is the part of the company that is in charge of producing items for sale and internal use. Development, which is probably the department in question, is also usually considered a part of Production. See "Which Parts of the Business Are Involved?"

2. Storage and Retrieval. It would become a Calculation problem if the need ever arose to present the calls received in a graph or other useful types of information. See "Establishing the Type of Problem."

3. No, this is the worst way. Counting watts of electricity is measuring a resource consumed in the completion of your task. A better way would be to measure the by-products. The best way is to monitor the achievement of milestones. See "How Do They Want to Measure Your Progress?"

4. Up-front costs. See "Minimizing Total Cost of Ownership (TCO)."

5. You can increase the ROI of this solution by decreasing the TCO of other solutions (by providing pre-built functionality that reduces the up-front costs associated with building the other solutions). See "Increasing ROI Through Reusability of Components."

6. Linux is not very user-friendly. Unlike Windows and MacOS, the GUI in UNIX environments is not the default mode of operation. See "Analyzing the Operating Systems."

7. You need to figure out an alternate means for supporting your solution. You might recommend that your customer purchase support agreements for all the vendors that have technology included in your systems. Or, you might decide to make some kind of support directly available from your own organization's resources. See "Analyzing the Planned Support Systems."

8. This is a case of your solution creating additional problems. In this case, the benefit produced by your solution (more money) has aggravated a lack of discipline on the part of one of the target organization's employees (the President). See "Determining What Additional Solutions May be Required."

9. You should evaluate the physical requirement for connectivity. This means you need to consider whether a LAN, WAN, or Internet-link is needed. See "What Kind of Connectivity?"

10. This would be an example of very static decision-making flows. See "Understanding a Company's Politics."

11. Better training. More features. Improved testing. All of these could be made possible by the increased time resources available when you push back your deadline. See "Doing It Slower."

12. The technical staff. See "Identifying Your Audience."

Answers to Exam Questions

1. **C.** This is called a Use case document. Parkinson's Law is a scheduling concept. Sign-offs are important parts of your requirements documentation. See "Establishing the Business Requirements."

2. Parts of business involved:

   Billing clerks mail out software.

   Salespeople make sales over the phone.

   Problematic situations:

   Salespeople are not getting their commissions.

   Customers are not getting billed.

   Problematic locations:

   OscarNet is in Seattle.

   OscarNet's customers are all in Seattle.

   Performance requirements:

   Receptionist needs to leave by 5:30 P.M.

   Billing system needs to handle at least three simultaneous users.

   Hardware and operating systems:

   The sign-up server is running NT.

   The CPU on the sign-up server is an Alpha.

   Account creation application is written in PERL.

   Internal support:

   People at OscarNet generally are fairly computer literate.

   Customer's financial situation:

   Money has been put away for a sign-up server reworking.

   DSL may bring a lot more revenue.

   Security requirements:

   The VP of Sales should be able to see commissions reports.

   Billing clerks can COMP accounts.

3. **C.** Because the problem involves the movement of real, physical materials between participants, it must be considered an Automation problem. In order for it to be a Communications problem, data would have to be the only thing getting moved. The other two answers, although referring to valid problem types, are not correct. See "Establishing the Type of Problem."

4. **B, C.** Getting your solution built faster would introduce a greater chance of bugs, and this would make maintenance even worse. Reducing your applications' disk usage is completely irrelevant. On the other hand, ensuring that your system is thoroughly tested would reduce the chance of bugs. Adding automated diagnostics would help in the event that things break in spite of the precautions taken. See "Reducing Maintenance Costs."

5. **B.** Technology churning. Use case documents and sign-offs are two kinds of requirements documents. Parkinson's Law is a key principle in project scheduling. For more information, see "Doing It Slower."

APPLY YOUR KNOWLEDGE

6. **B.** Pulling useful information out of your solution is one of the things in which Management will be interested. This is to assist them in the making of strategic decisions. Keeping your system running and extending its functionality would be the domain of the organization's technical staff (if they had any). Using your system to assist in Internet connectivity would be of interest to end users. See "Analyzing Training Needs."

7. **A.** Parkinson's Law. Use case documents and sign-offs are important requirements documents. Technology churning is another concept that should influence the scheduling of your projects. For more information, see "Doing It Faster."

8. **D.** When developing a long-term solution, achieving quality is the most important thing. Between the two alternatives of a faster or slower rollout, the only one of these that makes sense is a slower approach. Moving faster increases the likelihood of introducing serious bugs and errors into your code. In a long-term solution, shortfalls in the quality of your code produce maintenance burdens that are much worse than those in short-term solutions. See "Establishing a Schedule for Solution Implementation."

Suggested Readings and Resources

1. Brooks, Frederick. *The Mythical Man-Month.* New York: Addison Wesley, 1975.

   - Chapter 2: The Mythical Man-Month

   - Chapter 3: The Surgical Team

   - Chapter 15: The Other Face

2. HCL Consulting Web site [http://www.microsoft.com/vbasic/prodinfo/ca sestudies/hclconsulting/default.htm]

3. Sodhi, Jag. *Software Requirements Analysis and Specifications.* New York: McGraw Hill, 1992.

   - Chapter 3: Importance of Requirements

   - Chapter 4: Requirements Paradigms

     - Sign-off—a semi-binding statement of official approval. Almost always in writing.

   - Use case document—a document describing a number of situations and the desired behavior for a solution built to operate under those circumstances.

   - Technology churning—the tendency of technological process to render lengthy projects obsolete even before they are completed.

4. McCarthy, Jim. *Dynamics of Software Development.* Redmond, WA: Microsoft Press, 1995.

5. McConnell, Steve. *Rapid Development.* Redmond, WA: Microsoft Press, 1996.

6. McConnell, Steve. *Software Project Survival Guide.* Redmond, WA: Microsoft Press, 1998

The exam objectives to be covered in this chapter are from the Analyzing Business Requirements area of the exam. They include the following:

Analyze performance requirements. Considerations include

- **Transactions per time slice**

- **Bandwidth**

- **Capacity**

- **Interoperability with existing standards**

- **Peak versus average requirements**

- **Response-time expectations**

- **Existing response-time characteristics**

- **Barriers to performance**

▶ This objective focuses on the many expectations that your customers (internal and external) may have about performance.

Analyze availability requirements. Considerations include

- **Hours of operation**

- **Level of availability**

- **Geographic scope**

- **Impact of downtime**

▶ Availability refers to the full spectrum of circumstances under which people are able to make use of your solution. Successful solution analysis requires a deep understanding of the circumstances under which your target organization would like your solution to be available. It also requires that you know what "bad things" can potentially happen if your system isn't available when it should be.

CHAPTER 3

"PASS ME" Analysis

Analyze security requirements.

- **Identify the roles of administrator, groups, guests, and clients.**
- **Identify the impact on the existing environment.**
- **Establish fault tolerance.**
- **Plan for maintainability.**
- **Plan the distribution of security database.**
- **Establish the security context.**
- **Plan for auditing.**
- **Identify the level of security needed.**
- **Analyze existing mechanisms for security policies.**

▶ The other points refer to specific approaches to security and their likely outcomes—both expected and unexpected.

Analyze scalability requirements. Considerations include the following:

- **Growth of audience**
- **Growth of organization**
- **Growth of data**
- **Cycle of use**

▶ Systems are generally described as processes, which produce output from input. The solutions that you develop must take into account changes in the amount of input over time. The degree to which this is needed is called scalability.

Analyze maintainability requirements. Considerations include

- **Breadth of application distribution**
- **Method of distribution**
- **Maintenance expectations**
- **Location and knowledge level of maintenance staff**
- **Impact of third-party maintenance agreements**

▶ Applications vary widely in the degree to which they require maintainability. To satisfy this objective, you must understand the many factors that can influence maintainability requirements.

Analyze extensibility requirements. The solution must be able to handle the growth of functionality.

▶ Every solution you build will probably need to have its functionality modified in some way during its useful life. All your customers will probably have slightly different requirements for how they would like to go about making such changes in the future. This objective will help you understand these requirements.

- ▶ Know the differences between real, perceived, and expected response-time characteristics.

- ▶ Be able to express performance requirements in terms of peak versus average requirements. Also be able to articulate the ways in which transaction intensity and frequency interact to determine a system's overall capacity.

- ▶ Understand the importance of interoperability with existing standards.

- ▶ Be able to recognize required hours of operation—whether they are limited, flexible, or continual.

- ▶ Make sure that you can adequately analyze the geographic scope of a proposed solution. This includes understanding the associated costs, the technical implications, and any cultural issues.

- ▶ Understand the different levels of downtime impact that different solutions entail.

- ▶ Remember the roles and responsibilities of all security audiences: administrators, groups, guests, and clients.

- ▶ Understand how the likelihood of a security breach and the potential impact of such an event combine to influence the level of security needed for a solution.

- ▶ Be able to determine the best way to distribute a security database. You should take into account who will have access during the process, as well as the nature of the process itself.

- ▶ Remember that security database backups and auditing are the two best ways to establish fault-tolerant security.

- ▶ Make sure that you understand the training and remote-access issues involved in the maintenance of security.

- ▶ Understand that increasing security in an organization will invariably increase the time required for the completion of tasks. You should also be able to articulate exactly why this is the case.

- ▶ Know the ways in which organizational growth can require your solution to scale. Also know the three main points in the cycle of use.

- ▶ Be able to state the pros and cons of trying to maintain a solution that is distributed in a single location. Be able to do the same for a solution in multiple locations.

- ▶ Understand the options available to you for distributing changes to your solution.

- ▶ Know the importance of reaching a clear understanding very early in your project regarding your customer's maintenance requirements and what part you will play in them.

- ▶ Be able to classify a maintenance staff's situation based upon their location and knowledge levels.

- ▶ Remember how modifications made to your solution can impact maintenance obligations. This includes your customer's warranty as well as your responsibilities for technical support.

- ▶ Make sure you remember the three primary methods for providing extensibility within your solution: source code, APIs, and components.

INTRODUCTION

In this chapter, we discuss the PASS ME themes found on the Microsoft exam. This acronym refers to the following system attributes:

- Performance
- Availability
- Security
- Scalability
- Maintainability
- Extensibility

In this chapter, we are still primarily concerned with defining business problems. In this context, we will use PASS ME to measure the degree to which these things should be provided for by any solution that you develop for the business problem at hand. It is not yet important that you fully understand *how* to achieve the required functionality in your finished system. Although each of the PASS ME concepts is discussed in detail in this chapter, it will help you to understand them better if we begin with some basic definitions.

Performance is a gauge of how much work your system can accomplish in a given amount of time. We look at various ways to measure this.

Availability determines when and how people can use your system to perform the work. The hours of operation, level of use, and geographic scope of your solution are all factors influencing its availability. We also look at features typical of solutions in which the consequences of downtime are minimal, moderate, and mission-critical.

Security is best described as the art of preventing people from doing anything that they aren't supposed to do. Sometimes these attempts are the result of innocent mistakes. At other times, they are willful attempts to access and/or destroy restricted bits of your system. Good security usually prevents this from succeeding, notes any such attempts, and tries not to get in the way of legitimate system use any more than is absolutely necessary.

Scalability is the degree to which any system you build can continue to function efficiently as its input levels rise and fall. For example, a checkbook-balancing program is said to be very scalable when it works as well with a business account, which processes millions of transactions a month, as it does with a personal account, which processes only a few transactions per month. In this chapter, we show you the many areas of growth that can require scalability. We also introduce you to the Cycle of Use, which enables you to determine the prospects for future increases and decreases in the use of your solution.

Maintaining a solution after it is in place at the target organization can often be more work than building it in the first place! The breadth of your application's distribution and the quality of the technical staff at your target organization are the two biggest determinants of how easy or difficult your task will be. The most important thing at the stage of defining business problems, however, is to arrive at a clear understanding of the customer's expectations in this regard.

Extensibility is a measure of how easy it is to add to the functionality of your solution after it is in place. This is different from maintainability, which merely aims to keep the same level of functionality available over time.

It is important to note that throughout this chapter, "customer" is a term that applies equally to internal (as well as external) clients. Few, if any, principles are applied to analysis by independent contractors that would not prove equally useful to internal developers.

CASE STUDY: NEW RIDER IMPORTERS

BACKGROUND

New Rider Importers is a multinational firm specializing in the acquisition and retail sale of consumer goods from all over the Earth. Over the last 20 years, it has grown from a single storefront in Chicago to more than 1,000 retail outlets in more than 60 countries! The coming of the "global economy" is having a profound impact on the business of New Rider Importers—good and bad.

PROBLEM STATEMENT

As it has become easier for people to travel around the world, it has become much harder for New Rider Importers to locate items that would otherwise be unavailable to its customers.

CFO

"There's no two ways about it. Sales are down—way down! The stuff that we have in our stores simply isn't getting there fast enough to be 'fashionable!' I'm projecting that if we don't increase our revenues within the next few months, we are going to have to start seriously looking at cutting out some of our stores!"

Checkout Assistant

"I'm tired of always telling people that we don't have the stuff they want. It's been six months now since we had Mexican jumping beans in our toy section. If the past is any indication, we will probably get them in another three months—long after the jumping bean craze is over!"

Purchasing Agent

"I keep hearing these complaints about the stores not having whatever is fashionable in their areas at the moment, but what do they expect us to do? With stores spread out all over the world, we have to cater to more different tastes than you would ever dream possible. And, even if I knew that everyone in New York was suddenly interested in Japanese plum candy, for example, how could I possibly know that our stores there are fresh out of it? Chances are that I'm 4,000 miles away at the time, trying to work out a deal for whatever the 'big thing' was six months ago."

CURRENT SYSTEM

The system currently used by New Rider Importers has evolved from a number of smaller pieces that have been written in an ad hoc fashion over time.

Customer

The process begins when a customer visits a New Rider Importers store. Eventually, the customer finds a product that he or she would like to purchase. The customer brings this to the front counter. At this point, the checkout assistant processes the sale and the customer is ready to go.

Purchasing Agent

Purchasing agents travel the globe looking for items that they think might be salable in countries where New Rider Importers has stores. When goods are found and a deal is made, it is entered into the laptop systems that the

CASE STUDY: NEW RIDER IMPORTERS

purchasing agents carry with them. When the agents return to their home offices, their laptop systems are then connected to the central computer for updates.

Checkout Assistant

The checkout assistants are usually able to answer pricing questions from their terminals. When it comes to locating merchandise within the store, however, the assistants must leave their checkoutregisters and look around the stores for the items. At the end of the day, the checkout assistants perform an "end-of-day" routine on their registers and go home.

Branch Manager

The managers of New Rider Importers's branches are responsible for reviewing their stores' sales figures directly at their home offices via the central computer.

ENVIRONMENT

New Rider Importers recently invested millions of dollars to upgrade all its computer equipment.

CFO

"I think FastBooks Pro is probably the best accounting software that I've ever used. I use a different version of it at home for managing my own finances, so it is great to have something here at work that is so similar.

One of the things I like best about it is the way that it automatically connects to the Internet and downloads information about all our accounts every time I start it.

Anyhow, to make most of my calculations, I find myself exporting a lot of information from FastBooks to put into Excel. The accounting system we had before FastBooks did all that kind of stuff, too. But it was so difficult to use that I am more than willing to accept this newer setup."

CIO

"We were able to get laptops for all our purchasing agents with this last upgrade—unfortunately, no modems. Fortunately, we already had one modem in each of our stores for their nightly updates with our central computer.

The computers that they use for cash registers all tend to be Pentium IIs, which is probably overkill, but we won't be upgrading again for a long time. On the other hand, the computers that we have in our home offices are all P120s. Maybe we'll have the money to upgrade those next time around.

The central computer is an IBM mainframe running MVS. I think that there must be something wrong with the way that we have it configured, though, because I have seem them running much faster at other organizations."

Software Engineer

"The software we built for our purchasing agents is all done in Visual Basic. That's nice from the standpoint that we can read the code pretty easily, but it is difficult to get updates and modifications out to them. Especially when they are constantly traveling all over the world!

continues

continued

The checkout assistants are using some kind of off-the-shelf software using CICS, though. That's easy enough to distribute changes to, because it is all connected to the central computer. But, it is a really old technology, and the only way to make changes to the software is through an application programmer's interface.

Another great point in its favor is that it hardly ever goes down. That's important to us because, being an international organization, we have people working in all time zones."

ENVISIONED SYSTEM

The need for a change at New Rider Importers is felt from the highest levels of management all the way down to the people working in the stores.

Branch Manager

"There has to be an easier way for me to keep track of what items we're running out of. Back in the days when we each only managed a handful of stores, it was more realistic for me to sort through all these reports. Now that we're managing double that number, it is just about impossible to catch all the stock shortages that are costing us sales."

CFO

"If there weren't so many stores for me to keep track of, it would be a lot easier to see trends and patterns. With all the different locations involved now, though, everything just seems like a bunch of numbers on paper. I've considered

bringing all our accounts into FastBooks. I'm concerned, however, that as the number of accounts grows, starting up the software will take forever as it downloads information about each one!"

Software Engineer

"The interface for that cash register software we use is really difficult to teach newly hired programmers. In fact, it isn't exactly easy even for those of us who've been here for a while. If we could figure out some way to do all the same things from Visual Basic without having to jump through hoops all the time, it would be great.

What I have in mind is a situation where pieces of VB code encapsulate access to the information currently stored on the IBM mainframe. The code would have to be accessed by computers all over the world and yet be centrally located to allow for easy maintenance."

SECURITY

Everyone at New Rider Importers is eager to avoid repeating a recent security incident involving the loss of an entire day's sales transactions!

Data Processing Manager

"Ultimately, I am responsible for all the security here at New Rider Importers. We found out during the last break-in just how expensive inadequate protection of our data could be. Whoever would have guessed that our sales staff would all pick such easily guessed passwords?

CASE STUDY: NEW RIDER IMPORTERS

I make a copy of our SAM database every weekend and keep it in the safe in my office. But, I haven't been able to review the logs for violations (or attempted violations) for the last month or so.

I once lost the password to my account, and it took my people six months to figure out how to get me back into the system. Fortunately for us, my Administrator's password had been hardcoded in several places, so we were able to find it right in the COBOL!"

Checkout Assistant

"I have to type a password into the system before I log in each morning. After that, I don't tend to think much about security—at least not computer security. My biggest concern is making sure that customers don't carry products out of the store without paying for them. People trying to rob the cash register when I'm not looking is another big concern of mine."

Purchasing Agent

"Security isn't something I ever even think about. I guess I'm personally concerned about someone trying to steal my laptop, but there wouldn't be much they could do with it if they did. They'd have to take it to my home office and connect to the main computer from there to do anything harmful!"

PERFORMANCE

Performance may seem at first like a single issue, but it can mean many things to different people.

Checkout Assistant

"I hate it when I enter a customer's purchase into the computer, and then I have to wait forever to get back a response. It happens with credit card purchases and checks, mostly. But, I've seen it act real slow with cash sometimes, too. If it ever shuts down completely, we're going to be in really big trouble!

I guess I would say I usually have to wait for about 45 seconds to get a response. That might not seem like very long, but when you have an anxious customer standing at the counter, it can seem like an eternity!"

CFO

"The stuff I use seems to do really well sometimes and is just awful at other times—particularly around tax season. When my assistant is running her tax reports, I've seen some of my daily work take twice as long to finish. For whatever reason, I can't seem to run more than three reports at a time, either."

Purchasing Agent

"I used to work for another import company, and its software ran much faster. For example, when we made a credit card purchase and entered it into our computers at my old company, we would get an approval code or a decline within just a few seconds. I would think that this stuff should run just as fast. I mean, how different can it be?"

continues

CASE STUDY: NEW RIDER IMPORTERS

continued

Software Engineer

"I've tracked the performance of all our systems pretty carefully for the last year or so and have noted some interesting phenomena. Although our CFO is usually able to run his reports at about 100 database calls per second, it falls to about half that around tax time.

At our stores, everything seems to run smoothly until more than three checkout assistants try to ring up customers at the same time. At that point, one of them is invariably made to wait while one of the others gets processed first. Unfortunately, this is all running on that package that we bought rather than on something we built ourselves. So, I have no idea why this is happening."

MAINTAINABILITY

It is important to understand right from the start of a project who will be responsible for maintaining what.

CFO

"All the stuff that I work with is right here in this building. I would like a system where if anything breaks, we can just call the people up who built it and have them send some people out here. Then, if there is anything new that should be added to any of our systems, they can just bring the disks with them."

CIO

"We have an awful lot of stores to worry about. It is completely impractical for me to try to send software upgrades to all of them via the post office.

Probably, we'll have to arrange to get everyone on a WAN and distribute changes that way. This might be expensive, so my data processing manager should be the only person who can authorize sending out changes this way."

AVAILABILITY

New Rider Importers has varying requirements for system availability.

Purchasing Agent

"I try to work during daylight hours and sleep at night, regardless of how jet-lagged I might be. So, I guess you won't ever have to worry about me needing my laptop at 2:00 a.m., no matter where I am.

My Global Positioning System, on the other hand, is of vital importance to me at all times. The last thing I want to do is accidentally drive off a mountain at night because my GPS is dead!"

ANALYZING PERFORMANCE REQUIREMENTS

Analyze performance requirements.

Some of the solutions that you build will need to offer outstanding performance. Others will be more lenient in their requirements.

In the introduction to this chapter, we defined performance as a measure of how much work your solution could do given a certain amount of time. For this reason, the concept of performance is very closely tied to that of efficiency.

Response-Time Characteristics

The central manifestation of performance, as far as most of your users are concerned, is a matter of response times. This refers to the length of time between a user making a request from a system and the user receiving a response from it. The amount of time it takes between asking your system, "How many taxis are in New York?" and receiving the answer, "Four thousand," is an example of response time.

You need to understand three kinds of response times for the Microsoft exam:

◆ Real response-times

◆ Perceived response-times

◆ Expected response-times

Real Response-Time

Real response-times measure how long it takes for your solution to actually do the work that it is being asked to do. We say that they are measured from the time that a request is made until the end of the response.

For example, if you asked your system to give a 10% raise to every taxi driver in New York, the real response-time would be reached only after your solution had actually given a raise to the very last taxi driver. This would, most likely, take the form of waiting for a lengthy database "update" query to finish.

NOTE

PASS ME Themes Remember that scalability is the second S in PASS ME. This chapter covers these themes in order, and we are currently discussing P—performance.

This is the most important kind of response time affecting the scalability of your solution. You learn more about what this means later in this chapter.

Perceived Response-Time

In contrast to real response-times, perceived response-time measures how long the users of your system *think* that it takes your solution to respond to their requests. In other words, we measure this from the time at which a user makes a request of your system until your solution produces some kind of response on the user interface.

To continue our previous example, we would be measuring perceived response-time if we waited only for the "OK!" message box to pop up on your system after the user asked for the 10% raise to be enacted. Now, if you could design your system in such a way that it responded "OK" before the entire update query finished, you could gain some improvement in perceived response-time.

Additional benefits are derived if the user could go on to work on something else at this point. Perhaps taxi driver records could be reviewed for traffic violations while the initial 10% raise request is still being processed on the server. This would allow more work to be accomplished.

Expected Response-Time

The final kind of response time is the expected response-time. This usually arises as the result of users having some experience with systems designed to solve similar problems. It usually takes the form of constant comparisons being made between the two, either for better or for worse.

If the person doing the taxi-driver raises in our example had given out similar raises the previous year, they would probably have an expected response-time. Notice that this would be true even if they were using the same system this year as last.

Sometimes, expected response-times can also be based on claims made by software vendors about underlying technology. If you had just spent millions of dollars for a database that claims to be able to return millions of rows per second, your expectation would certainly be set at that level.

To summarize, basically three comparisons can be made in expected response-times:

◆ Other systems

◆ Previous uses of the same system

◆ Published technical specifications

Response Times at New Rider Importers

In the case study section on performance, the software engineer gives us the best example of real response-time estimates. Her statement includes a measure of the number of database calls per second. She also tells us how many checkout assistants can use the system simultaneously before a bog-down occurs.

The CFO and the checkout assistant also have comments in the performance section, but both are examples of perceived response-times. Neither of these people dug into the technical details of the system enough to know what is actually happening "under the hood." We must assume, therefore, that their comments are based solely on what they have observed working through the user interfaces on their applications.

The CFO and the purchasing agent both lay out expected response-times. In the case of the CFO, the comparison is made between different uses of the same system: at tax-time and during the rest of the year. The purchasing agent compares the current system to one that he used at a previous job.

Measuring Performance

To accurately compare system performance instances, as in the case of expected response-times, a common method for measuring performance must first be agreed on. The following are two issues that seem common to all performance-measurement methodologies:

◆ Peak versus average requirements

◆ Capacity

Peak versus Average Requirements

A system's requirements for performance are likely to vary over time. The variation may take the form of a cycle that is daily, weekly, monthly, and so on, or it may be a gradual increase from the point of "rollout" until the system is no longer actively used by the organization.

Peaks represent the absolute hardest that your solution will ever have to work to meet your target organization's requirements. At a bank, this might be equivalent to the long lines at the drive-through window every night at 5 p.m. as people stop on their way home from work. In a larger perspective, it might represent the rush on the third day of every month when social security checks are issued.

Average requirements, on the other hand, represent the more normal periods of usage. You can determine the average by calculating a point somewhere in the middle between the extremely busy "peak" periods and the times when there is almost no usage at all.

All these measurements require some basic unit. Probably the most common unit for measuring performance is the number of transactions per time slice. In other words, you might determine that your peak requirement during rush hours at a bank consists of 300 checks per hour and four deposits per minute. Transactions may also represent numbers of simultaneous users, so you could set a peak performance requirement, for example, of 12 simultaneous teller stations in operation on the third day of every month.

Capacity

An issue closely related to peak performance is that of system capacity. Whereas peak performance requirements measure the most work that your system should be able to do, capacity measures the most that it actually can do. The three things determining capacity are transaction intensity, transaction frequency, and peak longevity.

It is important to realize that not all the transactions processed by your solution represent equal strains on your system's resources. It is possible, for example, that making a deposit to a customer's account in our bank example would require only two database accesses, whereas cashing a check might require five. This difference in resource consumption is called transaction intensity.

Transaction frequency, on the other hand, is a measure of how often a certain transaction must be handled by your system. If you find that your tellers are cashing 100 checks per night and making only 50 deposits, you would say that check cashing has a transaction frequency double that of deposit making.

Measuring Performance at New Rider Importers

Two of the commentators on performance at New Rider Importers made observations regarding average requirements, and the other two were looking at peaks. Can you tell which ones were which?

The checkout assistant and the purchasing agent were dealing with average requirements. The keyword in the case of the checkout assistant is "usually." She said, "I usually have to wait for about 45 seconds to get a response." This gives us no indication of the exact circumstances where things might work faster or slower, so we have to assume that this is an average.

The purchasing agent is talking about the system he previously used, and he says that it took a certain amount of time to produce the right responses. He doesn't say anything about it ever taking different amounts of time, however, so we will call this the average.

The CFO and the software engineer both looked at a peak requirement, however. In this case, the peak is determined by the onset of tax season. The CFO just has the general sense that things slow down on the system around this time. The software engineer gives the precise figure that "performance falls to about half what it usually is."

Interoperability with Existing Standards

The aspect of performance requirements most commonly forgotten is that of a new solution to subscribe to with the use of existing standards. These standards might be industry-wide, such as the ANSI standard for the C programming language, or they might be standards that exist only within your target organization, such as a requirement for the way that code should be commented and formatted.

Existing Standards at New Rider Importers

Several standard technologies are mentioned in our case study. We know that the CFO is using FastBooks and Excel; therefore, whatever data format is used by those applications should be thoroughly researched and used as much as possible by any new solution.

We know that Visual Basic was used for the purchasing agents' applications. Traditionally, three varieties of this language have been available in any released version: Standard (or Learning), Professional, and Enterprise. In addition, some significant differences exist between versions of Visual Basic before and after release 4. These variations may become an issue, or at least a decision point.

On the other hand, only one standard exists for MVS/CICS, which is maintained by IBM. To the extent that your solution will be able to accomplish its mission and maintain backward compatibility with this technology, you will be that much further toward the goal of meeting this final performance requirement.

Analyzing Availability Requirements

Analyze availability requirements.

The second part of our PASS ME analysis, the A, stands for availability. We previously defined availability as that aspect of your system that determines when and how people can use your system to perform work. In this section, we show how availability is really the sum of the following constituent requirements and factors:

◆ Hours of operation

◆ Level of availability

◆ Geographic scope

◆ Impact of downtime

Hours of Operation

In terms of the hours during which a solution is required to be available, only two kinds of requirements exist. The first case is that of 100% uptime requirements. Some examples of these kinds of systems are as follows:

◆ A cell-phone switching system

◆ An in-hospital paging system

◆ A military warning system

In contrast to this are the systems that simply do not require 100% uptime. Some of these are the following:

◆ NASDAQ computers (7 a.m. to 5 p.m.)

◆ An insurance-claims entry system (9 a.m. to 5 p.m.)

◆ A decision-support system (business hours)

Hours of Operation at New Rider Importers

The only person in our case study to speak specifically to the issue of availability is the purchasing agent. The information he gives us appears, at first, to make determining his needs very simple. He tells us that he always works during daylight hours, so we never need to worry about him using his laptop at 2 a.m. This indicates a system in which availability is not required to be 100%.

Level of Availability

It is rare for a system to be so simple in design that the entire thing can always be described as either "available" or "unavailable." Instead, a broad spectrum of availability usually exists between these two extremes, in which different portions of a system exist at different points in time. The points in this spectrum can be thought of as levels of availability and can have requirements that are both consistent and variable.

> **NOTE**
>
> **Time Zones and Availability**
> Consider for a moment the nature of the purchasing agents' jobs. We know that they travel around the world on a regular basis. We also know that different countries exist in different time zones. Finally, we know that the purchasing agents always work during daylight hours in whichever countries they happen to find themselves.
>
> If the purchasing agents had modems with which to connect to our central computers, the central computers have to be available 100% of the time!

Consistency

A consistently low requirement for availability typically indicates a system that is never going to get much use. Tax calculation software (which almost no one uses from May to January) or a fire alarm system in a large building are good examples of this kind of system. An information kiosk in the middle of Death Valley is also a good example of this kind of system.

A consistently high requirement for availability typically indicates a system that is always going to be in use. The rudder-control element of an airplane's navigational software is a good example. Certainly, instances may occur when it isn't important in what direction an airplane is heading, but few passengers would care to find out what these instances are.

Variable

Many systems will exist at different points on the "spectrum of availability" at different points in time. These systems are said to have variable availability requirements and must deal with special issues of threshold tolerance and efficient resource allocation.

To continue our airplane example, the perfect example of a variable availability requirement is the airplane's emergency landing systems. You wouldn't want these to be at all available 99.9% of the time, assuming that they do things (such as releasing oxygen masks, dumping fuel, and so on) that under normal flying conditions would be quite a bad idea. On the other hand, when you are in an emergency situation, you would certainly want them to be 100% available for as long as you needed them.

The length of time that you can continue using such a system after it has "come alive" is called threshold tolerance. A system that is used only in .01% of circumstances is unlikely to have the same performance endurance as one that is in use the rest of the time. When such a system stops working—that is, when the masks run out of oxygen in the preceding example, we say that the system has exceeded its threshold tolerance.

For this reason, it is particularly important that a solution with a variable availability requirement be able to consume resources with great efficiency. You can think of this in terms of the many power-saving features built into most laptops. Battery power is a system that you will use only some of the time, after all.

Level of Availability at New Rider Importers

Given the daily nature of the purchasing agents' work, it is probably safer to assume a consistently high availability requirement than a consistently low one.

Geographic Scope

The geographic scope of the solution that you are designing can affect its availability in many ways. Some of these are obvious; others can be extremely subtle.

Local Area

A solution that exists within a single office, an office building, or even a few close buildings is typically considered to be "local area." A local area solution can typically be connected using any of the regular LAN (local area network) topologies.

The main advantage to a local area system is the low cost associated with maintaining and upgrading it. These two advantages combine to greatly improve availability in such solutions by reducing the likelihood of breakage (through lack of maintenance) or obsolescence (through lack of upgrades).

Wide Area

Wide area systems refer to any solutions that are distributed on a scale greater than local area but something short of global. If you prefer, however, you may consider global solutions to be a special case of wide area systems.

The network mediums that are generally available for building such environments include microwaves and satellites. Technology such as this does not come cheaply.

Wide area solutions typically cost significantly more to maintain and upgrade. Therefore, a wide area system is much more likely to become unavailable because of breakage or obsolescence.

The Internet is rapidly replacing proprietary backbones in many major organizations. In these cases, corporate sites connect to the Internet using ISDN or DSL and transmit information to each other using VPN technology to ensure security.

Global

Probably the most challenging geographic scope for a system is also the one that provides the greatest opportunities for improvements in availability. This is the globally scoped solution. In this kind of system, some or all of the solution is actively used simultaneously in many parts of the world.

It is important to realize that connectivity infrastructures vary widely around the world and can profoundly impact the availability of your system. The two aspects of connectivity that should be taken into account by your design are quality of connectivity and cost.

The quality of network connectivity between different points on the Earth is not at all uniform. Many countries are still in their formative stages as far as information technology is concerned. Outages in these places are far more likely than in some Western nations. Make sure you take this possibility into account before deploying network-dependent applications to these countries.

The price that you have to pay to maintain network connections on a global scale can vary widely. The great opportunity is that you might be able to use the Internet as your backbone and thus spend little or nothing for your communications. If you are concerned about privacy and the possibility of information tampering, you can spend a little more and get a Virtual Private Network (VPN) that can encrypt and decrypt your transmissions for their journey across the Internet.

Geographic Scope of New Rider Importers

You won't get a question this easy on the Microsoft exam, even in your dreams! It should go without saying that New Rider Importers operates on a global scale, which means that in developing a solution for them, you will have to contend with infrastructure issues.

A good exercise in this is a consideration of whether modems are a good idea for the purchasing agents' laptops. For modems to be of use, the purchasing agents have to be in countries with reliable phone service. Calling directly to the home office entails a (potentially massive) long-distance fee. The other possibility, then, is to look for Internet Service Providers with dial-up locations in foreign countries.

In the next section of our PASS ME themes, we examine whether this is an acceptable solution from a security perspective.

Impact of Downtime

When downtime occurs for a system, it can have many possible results. Sometimes the impact is minimal; at other times it is disastrous. Usually, it falls somewhere between.

Minimal Impact

The impact of a downtime incident is said to be minimal when the effects on the business running the system are negligible. This is typically the case when whatever business was being attended to can be redone at a later point in time. To return to our banking example, this might be a case in which a customer can still be given a receipt for a deposit without the teller immediately putting the deposit into the computer.

The great opportunity afforded to you by minimal availability requirements is that you can reduce the degree of support that you make available to the target organization. This occurs because the constant availability of the solution is evidently not as important. One example is a library check-in computer—no money is lost if the system is not available; the lack of availability creates only an inconvenience. A decision support system for noncritical subjects (corporate picnic scheduling, perhaps) is another example of a situation requiring minimal availability.

Moderate Impact

A somewhat more serious level of significance occurs when downtime is known to have a moderate impact on business operations. Under these circumstances, business lost as a result of system downtime cannot usually be redone later. Only a less-than-essential nature for the business in question prevents this from being a "mission-critical" situation, which you learn about next.

In this banking scenario, the automatic teller machine in the drive-through is broken for a few hours. The customers who visit the bank during this time will not be able to get money without standing in line for a teller. This causes a distinct loss of customer satisfaction. However, this isn't going to cause a run on the bank, so it isn't mission-critical.

You should write code somewhat more carefully in this kind of setting. You can also keep your support obligations reduced, but you still have to provide some means of eventually rectifying the problem.

Mission-Critical Impact

The final level of impact for solution downtime is mission-critical. Like the preceding moderate case, this occurs when business missed cannot be redone at a later point in time. Unlike the moderate case, however, this is business that can have a show-stopping effect on the organization as a whole.

If the software used by the tellers in our banking example were to suddenly start producing inaccurate results, this could easily be mission-critical downtime, particularly if the numbers being produced were believable enough to continue being used. Customers walking away with thousands of dollars in inappropriate withdrawals would be enough to bring even the strongest of financial institutions to its knees.

In cases such as this, it is a good idea to write your code in such a way that a simple, independent "kernel" is in charge of everything and can itself almost never be broken. This should allow you to put your entire solution into some kind of "emergency mode" where at least the mission-critical transactions can still be processed. Finally, in this scenario you have no choice but to provide some path to 24-hour support for your target organization.

Some other examples of mission-critical impact situations are the following:

◆ Bank-to-bank electronic funds transfers

◆ Production-line automation systems

◆ Patient monitoring systems

At this point, it is helpful to see a side-by-side comparison of the three levels of downtime impact (see Table 3.1).

TABLE 3.1
IMPACT OF DOWNTIME ON SOLUTION AVAILABILITY

Impact Level	Effect on Business	Quality Standards	Support
Minimal	Can be delayed or missed without substantial business impact	Little or no redundancy, minimal testing, bugs/lines of code ratio not crucial	Limited or none
Moderate	Some unrecoverable loss to business in $ or intangibles	Redundancy, stronger or more intense testing cycles, bugs/lines of code monitored more closely	Support required, often with pagers or same-day support access
Mission critical-	Impact can cost significant $ or even put company at risk or loss of life	Full redundant systems, strong QA or mandated "certification," bug/lines of code measured closely (for example, NASA)	24-hour availability

Downtime at New Rider Importers

The most obvious place to look in the case study for this kind of information is in the "Availability" section. The only person commenting here is the purchasing agent, and he says "…if I can't get in during the day though, I can always enter my purchases later." This indicates that at least for his part of the system, the impact of downtime is minimal. This is because the nature of his business is repeatable.

However, if you examine the checkout assistant's comments on system performance, you get a different picture. She says, "If the system ever shuts down completely, we're going to be in really big trouble." In this case, we can probably deduce that "really big trouble" means not being able to conduct business. Customers would not be able to be checked out; therefore, no sales and no income for the store. In her case, the solution must be considered mission-critical.

ANALYZING SECURITY REQUIREMENTS

Analyze security requirements.

We previously defined security as preventing people from being able to do things with your solution that they shouldn't be allowed to do. In this section, the first S in PASS ME, you learn exactly how to go about determining what kinds of security your system will need to implement.

Establishing a Security Context

Establishing a security context refers to examining the environment in which security must be established and maintained. This requires that you begin by identifying the security roles at your target organization. Then you must analyze the existing mechanisms for instituting the proper security policies.

Identifying Audience Roles

Four audience roles should be considered in establishing a security context for your solution:

◆ Administrators

◆ Groups

◆ Guests

◆ Clients

Administrators are, perhaps, the most "powerful" of all the security audience members. They are the only people who are empowered to change security policies, permissions, and accounts.

Clients are internal users and applications that use your solution. They have their permissions and privileges set for them by the administrators at your target organization.

Guests also use your solution, but they are typically external to the organization for which your solution was developed. For example, it is not uncommon on a Windows NT server to create a guest account representing the privileges that should be granted to users accessing Web pages served from that machine.

Finally, groups are logical groupings of all the above. You could create a group called Programmers, for example, and put all the users into it that you would like to be able to make code modifications to your solution. The advantage to groups is that you can set permissions and privileges one time and have it apply to all members of your group.

Analyzing Existing Mechanisms for Security Policies

After you have identified the security audience roles at your target organization, you need to analyze their existing mechanisms for security policies. These typically include the following:

◆ Passwords

◆ Permissions

◆ Physical restrictions

The function of passwords is obvious. Permissions determine what users are and are not allowed to do with your solution. Permissions can be set at the individual client or guest level, or they can be set for an entire group.

Physical restrictions are mechanisms within the actual physical environment of your target organization that assist or inhibit the implementation of security. Some examples of physical security include

◆ An office firewall that blocks access to certain Web sites or newsgroups.

◆ An ATM machine that refuses to allow a withdrawal without having your ATM card inserted.

◆ A computer without a modem or a network card, thereby disallowing any kind of remote access.

Security Contexts at New Rider Importers

The data processing manager is the Administrator in the case study because he is "…responsible for all the security…at New Rider Importers."

Everyone else in the case study is a client because they all use the systems that are currently in place. The only exceptions to this are the customers themselves. The case study does not indicate that customers ever have any direct interaction with New Rider Importers's automated systems. But, if they did (through a Web site, for example) they would be considered guests.

The checkout assistant's comments in the "Security" section indicate that she, at least, has to use a password to access the system. Unfortunately, we can also see a physical problem with security in her job. Often, she must leave her register to assist customers in locating merchandise. This leaves her terminal unlocked and available for someone else in the store to violate the system's security using her account.

Identifying the Level of Security Needed

The nature of some systems requires the greatest degree of security possible. Others are more appropriately guarded with the least degree of effort possible. In this section, you learn how to identify the level of security needed by any solution that you are required to design and/or implement.

Risk Level

The first question you should ask yourself when trying to determine the appropriate level of security for a solution is "How likely is it that anyone will actually try violating my security?" In trying to answer this question, there are a few things you should consider.

If the machines hosting your solution have little or no network connectivity, your solution is much less likely to be attacked. Remember
that a computer that isn't connected to a modem or other network
connection can't be connected to by another computer, regardless
of what Hollywood depicts. On the other hand, as you add these
connections to computers that are important to your solution, your
chances of a security breach increase dramatically.

Physical access is the other way in which your security may be violated. A computer locked in a closet with a 10-foot-thick concrete
door is much less likely to have an attempt made against it directly
from its console.

The number of accounts and their required privileges is the final
great determiner of the likelihood of a security breach. The fewer
accounts that the administrator creates with access to the machines
implementing your solution, the safer your setup. Similarly, the less
these accounts are privileged to do on those machines, the better.

Estimating the Stakes

In addition to determining the likelihood of an attempt being made
to break your security, you should try to estimate the damage that
could be done by a successful break-in. A direct relationship should
exist between the level of disaster that a successful break-in would
represent and the effort that you expend in preventing it.

One kind of disaster to consider is the effect on your business of
having your information known. If you are a publicly traded company, could the promising results of your latest research make you
the potential target of a hostile takeover if your larger competitors
found out? Or could someone within your own organization use
similar information to conduct insider trading?

The other kind of disaster is the effect on your business if your
information were to be destroyed. Losing historical data can be bad
for purposes of forecasting and targeted marketing. The intentional
destruction of more current information and software could impact
profits or even put the company out of business.

Security Needed at New Rider Importers

To determine the security needed at New Rider Importers, we must begin by analyzing the risk levels that they face. We know that the checkout assistant's terminals are physically vulnerable and have some degree of connectivity to the central computer. The purchasing agents' laptops are perhaps even more vulnerable—but lack any such connectivity.

The stakes involved in the event of a successful break-in can be deduced by the data processing manager's comments regarding the previous break-in. He said, "We found out during the last break-in just how expensive poorly protecting our data could be." In fact, the case study tells us that the last break-in cost the company an entire day's worth of sales! This would indicate that a fairly substantial degree of security is needed.

Planning Distribution of Security Databases

A security database is where your solution stores the passwords and permissions for its audience members. For your solution's security to be effective, therefore, you must plan for some way to distribute your security database to all locations where your system will be used. This means first determining who should be allowed access to this information. Only then can you settle upon a specific means for transporting this information.

Who Has Access?

Determining who will have access to your security database includes machines as well as people. You should select the following:

- ▶ A home storage site
- ▶ Transporters
- ▶ Target sites

The home storage site is the machine where your security database is primarily stored. Transporters are the processes, people, and machines that are empowered to move the security database from its home storage site to the places where it will actually be read and used by your solution. The target sites represent the locations in which your security database will be read by your solution to determine what its clients should and should not be allowed to do.

How Is It Moved?

You can move your solution's security database in two ways. The first is manually. The other way is via automatic processes.

Manual transfers of your security database require finding a larger number of people within your target organization that can be personally entrusted with this data. Automated transfers take people out of the equation. In this case, a process is scheduled to run at specific times that copies the security database from its home storage site to the target sites.

Distributing the Security Database at New Rider Importers

The purchasing agents in the case study are not equipped with the hardware necessary for connecting remotely to your central computer. They don't have modems. Therefore, any automated process working with them will have to wait until they return to their home offices and update their security databases as they dump their purchase records.

The checkout assistants are in stores that share a single modem. The case study indicates that this is typically used only once at the end of each day. In this case, this would be the perfect opportunity for an automated system.

Everyone else in the case study works in a home office, so they have the option of either an automated or a manual process. Because there are many home offices and only one administrator (the CIO), the most likely setup would be an automated process to distribute the security database from the CIO's home office to all the other ones. From that point, specific people within each home office could be charged with the task of manually transferring the security database to each target site machine within the office.

Establishing Fault Tolerance

Things go wrong, even in systems that have been designed with reliability constantly in mind. The best solutions take steps to ensure that, even in event of disastrous failure, security is maintained.

The two most important steps that you can take to ensure that your system's security will be fault tolerant are

◆ Backing up your security database.

◆ Auditing your system's security logs.

Security Database Backups

Backing up your data is always a good idea. When it comes to your system's security database, it is a must. Because your security database contains the passwords and privileges for every account with access to your solution, losing it would be disastrous. Every account would have to be recreated, reassigned to the correct groups, and given the appropriate permissions all over again.

The more external to the functioning of your system you can make your backup procedures, the better. The best backups are performed by systems that function independently of your own. Perhaps this means a tape system running on a different computer, automatically programmed to begin every day at 3 a.m. and to make a copy of everything on your company's network.

One level beyond this is to arrange for separate storage of the backups as soon after they are made as possible. In this case, the computer in the previous example might not even belong to your organization, much less be located on the same premises. Instead, you could buy a professional backup service from a company specializing in such things.

Planning for Auditing

Auditing means reviewing whatever security logs are kept by your system for indications that security attempts have been attempted. Usually, you can tell by looking at logs whether the attempts failed or succeeded.

In the case of successful security breaches, finding them quickly is almost always the most important factor in reducing the damage. Passwords can be changed to prevent further break-ins. Permissions can be changed to make accessing sensitive information more difficult. The more frequently your administrator audits, the greater chance you stand of surviving even the most hostile of invasions.

Fault Tolerance at New Rider Importers

The data processing manager at New Rider Importers is "it" as far as security administration goes. From the case study, we can tell that he is currently responsible both for making all the backups of the security database and for doing all the auditing.

Planning for Maintainability

The best plans for securing your system are meaningless if they are impossible to maintain. You should create a plan for every solution you build that outlines a simple, yet effective, scheme for maintaining security. This plan should include a careful consideration of the pros and cons of granting remote access to the users (and maintainers) of your solution. You should also make an in-depth study of the kinds of training that will need to be provided to create a security-oriented corporate culture within your target organization.

Remote-Access Privileges

It is best to consider the possibility of leaving remote-access unusable most of the time, until it is needed. This might be accomplished as simply as turning off a modem, or it might be as complicated as changing the passwords on the remote-access account. Whatever you decide, it is a good idea to come to an understanding as soon as possible regarding what everyone's responsibilities and obligations in maintaining the security of your solution will be.

Training

The training you provide as part of your solution's rollout also greatly determines the maintainability of its security. The users of your system must understand how to choose good passwords. The administrators must understand how to choose permissions properly. And everyone at the organization must understand the importance of taking the appropriate physical precautions to prevent misuse of your solution.

Maintaining Security at New Rider Importers

Currently, only a single source of remote access exists at New Rider Importers—the single modem at each store. If this situation were to change in the future—if the purchasing agents were to get modems for their laptops, for example—security requirements would require reevaluation.

The most obvious training opportunity would be with the checkout assistants, helping them to find ways to protect their cash registers when they must assist customers. Perhaps they could lock the keyboards in their cash drawers. Perhaps the solution you build will allow them to temporarily "freeze" their displays so that only reentering their passwords will get them back in.

Identifying Impacts on an Existing Environment

Chances are, whatever security measures you take as part of deploying a new solution won't be the same as the ones already in use at your target organization. This requires some degree of flexibility on your part. It also requires some degree of adjustment on the part of your target organization.

In this section, we look at one of the biggest adjustments that your organization is likely to have to deal with—increased task-time requirements. Closely related to this is the potentially increased difficulty of using your solution. Finally, we examine a few of the many benefits to be gained by bringing a heightened level of security into an organization.

Increased Task-Time Requirements

Increasing the level of security currently in place at an organization will invariably increase the amount of time that it takes people using the newly secured systems to complete their work. The following are three things that typically consume the most additional time in such situations:

◆ Physical security

◆ Passwords

◆ Administration

Physical security can consume additional time by delaying access to the needed parts of your solution. For example, consider the introduction of a rule at a bank stating that tellers are no longer allowed to keep more than $2000 in cash in their "boxes" at a time. Any excess must be immediately brought to a supervisor and deposited into the branch's safe for additional protection.

Now, suppose you are a customer who comes into the bank every Friday and withdraws $3000 in cash for your weekend's leisure. I know that this is a difficult thing for most of us to imagine, but it's fun, isn't it? Anyhow, suppose for the sake of argument that it usually takes you one minute to get in and out of the bank. On the first Friday that you visit after the new rules go into effect, you will probably have to spend somewhat longer—say two minutes.

The teller in question will not have the cash on hand as he probably did in the past. Instead, he will have to go through some new security procedure to get your cash out of the branch's safe. This will, undoubtedly, take longer than just grabbing it out of his box for you.

Passwords are another cause of delays when implementing new security measures. To continue the preceding example, this would be equivalent to a new rule that required the entry of a password every single time that a teller cashed a check. Generally (assuming that the password is memorized), the delays associated with this kind of system behavior are not quite as significant as with physical restrictions.

NOTE **Resetting System Security** For a refresher on issues surrounding system security resets, refer to the previous section, "Remote-Access Privileges."

Finally, consider the time required to get an administrator's assistance when all else fails. This might mean that our hypothetical teller gets his supervisor in the odd instance that he forgets his password. Or, in an even worse scenario, it might mean that the supervisor calls *you* to reset the security on your solution's Administrator account.

Increased Difficulty

In addition to the time that your new security measures will consume, you should also expect an increase in the difficulty of using your solution. One aspect of this difficulty could lie in getting through whatever physical restrictions you decide to put in place. A moat filled with crocodiles surrounding your laptop would, for example, constitute a deterrent to potential thieves—not just for the time it would take them to swim across. They would also be somewhat concerned at the possibility of being eaten, or at the very least, severely nibbled on.

Similarly, the tellers who have to enter the branch's vault to make large withdrawals will not be concerned solely with the additional minutes that this might take. They will probably not enjoy taking the chance of accidentally setting off the bank's alarm system.

Passwords will also frustrate your users. At best, they constitute one more thing that they must remember to effectively perform their jobs. Often, even when they remember them, they will find that they have mistyped them; then they have to go back and try again. When they forget them, they will probably feel humbled and belittled by the experience of having to consult someone else to regain access to their own systems.

The most pervasive way in which additional security complicates matters, however, is the dreaded "permissions issues." This occurs when things refuse to work properly in a highly secured operating system, such as UNIX or NT, not because the code is wrong or the software improperly configured, but because the permissions on some file *somewhere* are set incorrectly. Many late nights have been spent by many system administrators hunting through thousands of files by hand to find the single weak link in the chain that is causing a system to not work properly.

Impacting the Environment at New Rider Importers

The best way that security can be increased here is by adding password protection to the register's software so that unauthorized personnel can't use it while the checkout assistant is away. This adds both time and difficulty to that job, but it may well prevent a very costly security breech.

ANALYZING SCALABILITY REQUIREMENTS

Analyze scalability requirements.

We now come to the final S in our PASS ME theme—scalability. Scalability is the degree to which any system you build can continue to function efficiently as its input levels rise and fall. You will encounter some requirement for this in virtually every system you build, because most organizations do not plan to remain at their present sizes indefinitely. The vast majority of companies have plans for continued growth, and the few that don't will most likely already be shrinking.

Growth

As an organization grows, the principal challenge to the scalability of your solution will be the presence of more of everything, including the following:

◆ Problems

◆ Users

◆ Data

Organizational Growth

That more problems will occur as an organization grows seems to go almost without saying. Geographic growth alone (meaning opening stores in additional states and/or countries) introduces strange new legal requirements that must be attended to. The challenges associated with organizing a larger organization also figure prominently into these additional problems.

Your solution will also have more users as your target organization grows. This is true, in the most basic sense, simply because more people will want to use your system. If every person using your system makes 50 database queries a day, adding more employees means adding that much more load to your database.

In a slightly larger sense, this is true because the people using your system will also demand more functionality from it. By this, we mean solutions to the new problems just cited.

Finally, the managers of your target organization, when faced with the continued growth of their company, will want to have more and more capability to track the usage of your system. Their hope here would be to gain insights into the best way that their organization can continue functioning.

The growth of a business can also require more scalability on the part of your system through increased data requirements. The most obvious of these requirements is the capability to handle more rows of data—more sales history items, for example.

Another kind of increased data requirement is more tables, with a corresponding increase in the complexity of joins required to get "the whole picture." You'll learn much more about database design later in this book. For now, suffice it to say that this would be the difference between a single table named "Sales" and multiple tables named "Northern Sales," "Southern Sales," "Eastern Sales," and "Western Sales." To get all your sales for a certain period, you would have to concatenate the results of at least four separate queries.

Growth at New Rider Importers

Several hints in the case study indicate that New Rider Importers has experienced organizational growth. As one example, in the "Envisioned System" section, the branch manager comments, "…we're managing double that number of stores." This means double the number of users and database queries, as we saw earlier.

We can also tell from the case study that additional problems exist. The main problem seems to center around the purchasing agents' inability to keep up with what the stores in the home locations are running out of, which indicates a need for additional functionality. All this is typical of scalability requirements.

The Cycle of Use

Solutions typically progress through a life cycle that brings them from youth to maturity to "retirement age." Given a specific stage in the cycle, you should also be able to list the features typical of that stage.

The New, Underused Stage

When a solution is first "rolled out" for general use, it is typically regarded with a mild degree of fear, uncertainty, and doubt (FUD). You will typically encounter the lowest levels of system usage at this point, except in the case where the new solution is intended as the sole replacement for a highly used, existing system. In these cases, the initial underused stage is completely skipped and the mature phase begins immediately.

Assuming that this is not the case, however, you will have your greatest opportunity for making revisions to your solution shortly after the initial rollout. However well you have tested your system beforehand, nothing quite compares to the test of actually having your solution out in the field and getting used by people in real-world situations.

The Mature, Highly Used Stage

If your system is intended to solve a problem that has never before been tackled by your target organization, it will reach this stage only after a certain level of initial distrust has abated. In general, the worse the users' experience during the "new" phase, the longer it will take to get to this phase. This is true even if all problems are resolved very early on in the process.

On the other hand, if your system is intended as the sole replacement for a highly used, existing system, you will begin this stage immediately upon rollout.

In this stage, which will probably constitute the vast majority of your solution's life span, you have the fewest opportunities to make changes to your system because the system will be used to a degree that makes downtime very difficult. The only changes that will be possible may very well be those that can be accomplished without disruptions in service. For more information on this, see the "Extensibility" section later in this chapter.

The strains on your system will probably reach their zenith during this stage; it is this stage that constitutes the truest measure of your solution's scalability. After this, "it's all downhill."

The Old, Disused Stage

As your system ages, it will gradually become less in line with the needs of your target organization. People will gradually shift to using other systems to complete the parts of their work that are no longer covered by your solution.

When your solution reaches this stage, most of your requirements for scalability should have passed.

New Rider Importers's Cycle of Use

At what point in the cycle of use is New Rider Importers's existing system? You might be inclined at first to say old and disused, because the organization is obviously looking to get rid of it. But this would not be accurate because nothing in the case study suggests that people have begun to shift to anything else. For all its problems, it appears that everyone at New Rider Importers is still using the current system.

We must, therefore, be looking at a situation in which a new system is intended to be the sole replacement for an existing, highly used system. This means that our new solution will skip the first stage of the cycle of use completely and come in right at a point of maturity.

ANALYZING MAINTAINABILITY REQUIREMENTS

Analyze maintainability requirements.

Your target organization will continue to change and evolve the entire time that it is using your solution. Your solution's capability to be changed in order to continue serving your target organization's needs is measured as its maintainability. You should be concerned about four main things when analyzing system maintainability requirements:

- ◆ Breadth of application distribution
- ◆ Method of distribution
- ◆ Maintenance expectations
- ◆ Location and knowledge level of maintenance staff

Breadth of Application Distribution

The breadth of your applications' distribution is closely related to the considerations on geographic scope that you learned earlier in this chapter. For our purposes here, however, we divide the possible distributions into fewer cases. The first case is that of the single-location distribution. The other, in contrast, is that of multiple locations.

Applications in a Single Location

A number of benefits accrue to the maintainability of your solution if it need be distributed no further than a single location. You may be able to have a maintenance staff actually on premises and ready to respond at only a moment's notice to any problems that arise. Furthermore, the difficulties that this staff will need to overcome to gain access to your solution will be much lighter than if they were in some remote locale. The opportunities are much greater for direct physical contact between the people doing the maintenance work and your solution.

Applications in Multiple Locations

On the other hand, if your solution must be distributed over multiple locations, you will have to be somewhat more clever to make sure that maintainability requirements are designed in. You might consider the need for your target organization to outsource the ongoing maintenance for your solution. For example, it might prove cheaper to use a consulting firm in Tasmania to mend a solution in Tasmania than to bring in experts from some other part of the world.

As with our earlier discussion on global issues in accessibility, a number of special concerns for maintainability occur when operating on a planet-wide basis. As before, you should appreciate the potential barriers presented by language right from the start. In this case, however, the primary barrier is likely to be in trying to provide technical support to people who don't speak the same language. In this same vein, it is also important to realize that agreeing to provide 9-to-5 support on a global basis can have many possible interpretations, given the wide range of time zones!

New Rider Importers's Breadth of Application Distribution

New Rider Importers has purchasing agents and stores operating in numerous countries around the world. For this reason, we cannot possibly think that they face anything less than a global situation when considering the maintenance of their automated solutions.

Method of Distribution

Many ways are possible to distribute whatever modifications to your systems are needed to keep them properly maintained. They must all address the same couple of basic concerns, however. The first of these concerns is whether a distribution will be done manually or through some automated means. The other concern is the nature of the media that will be used to propagate these changes.

How Is It Done?

Manual transmission of changes would be the most labor-intensive way of keeping your solution maintained. On the other hand, many people feel that the less automation is involved in a system, the less potential exists for things to go wrong. Whether this is the case is largely a matter of personal perspective.

Automated transmission of changes to your system will require substantially less human effort. However, there is a subtle issue with any system intended to automate distribution of your system maintenance. As your target organization changes, your distribution itself may become yet another system requiring maintenance work.

What Media Is Used

Two primary kinds of media can be used in distributing maintenance changes to your systems. The first and, perhaps, most common is removable storage. The other, somewhat newer media is network storage.

Removable storage is any kind of storage that can be written onto, disconnected from the source computer, reconnected to the target computer, and then read from. By this definition, even a fixed device such as a hard disk could be termed removable storage. For the

Microsoft exam, however, removable storage should refer only to the following items:

◆ Floppy disks

◆ CDs

◆ Removable hard disks (Zip, Iomega, and so on)

◆ DVDs

◆ Tape backups

The use of removable storage as a medium all but requires a manual process for distribution of your maintenance changes. It is certainly possible to automate the writing and reading of information to and from a removable media's surface. The actual transport of that media between computers, however, almost certainly requires some human intervention.

Eliminating the human element becomes entirely possible, though not necessary, when you choose a network as the media for your maintenance. A network connecting the computer that has the changes to the computer that needs them can make your updates go much faster and more smoothly. In this case, an automated process could potentially write modifications directly to the storage space on the target computer.

One of the best tools available for automating this kind of process is Microsoft's Systems Management Server (SMS). Requirements during your analysis phase that may signal a need for SMS include

◆ Large numbers of computers requiring maintenance upgrades.

◆ Multiple pieces of software required per upgrade.

◆ Fairly simple, repetitive tasks involved in upgrades.

◆ Reliable network connectivity.

◆ Limited human technical resources.

◆ Homogeneous, Microsoft-based computing environment.

Another alternative is to have a "third computer" on the network to which both the source and target computer have access. In this case, a person or automated process could write changes to the intermediate computer. Another person or automated process at the target

NOTE

Visual Studio 6 Distributions The use of removable storage media is directly supported by Visual Studio 6 in the form of Floppy/CD Setup files distribution. Automated distribution is covered by the remaining two options: Network Setup files and Internet Distributions. The first of these is intended primarily for use with shared drives behind a firewall on a private network utilizing a network protocol such as NetBEUI or IPX. Internet Distributions, on the other hand, automates the creation of .cab archives for use on publicly accessible Web servers.

computer would then know to look at the shared location on occasion to see what, if any, new code is available. It would then be the responsibility of this person or process at the target computer to make sure that the new changes are put into place properly.

New Rider Importers's Method of Distribution

The method of distribution used by New Rider Importers appears to be a manual one. We can't be sure what layers of automation might lay beneath the surface, but everything that we can read in the case study indicates that a large degree of human activity is required for changes to be propagated throughout the system.

We know, for example, that the purchasing agents must connect their laptops to the central computer when they return to their home offices. This is done so that a two-way update can take place. Without this bit of human effort, the software on the purchasing agents' laptops would remain fixed in its original form—without maintenance upgrades.

The checkout assistants seem to have it somewhat easier. According to the software engineer, their stuff is "…easy enough to distribute changes to, since it is all connected to the central computer." Still, CICS updates are done manually, so we must call this a manual system.

In both cases, some kind of network connectivity is used. Removable storage is not involved in any maintenance work at New Rider Importers.

Maintenance Expectations

It is best to determine as early in the design process as possible exactly what everyone expects in terms of maintenance obligations and responsibilities. The issue of customer expectations will probably work a little differently, depending on whether you are developing an internal solution or operating as a consultant.

Internal Situations

In general, internal customers will have almost unlimited expectations about your responsibilities for maintenance. The rule of thumb is: "You built it, you keep it running."

Cost-center analysis is now common in many organizations and should always be considered when analyzing maintenance requirements. In this kind of situation, the dollar cost associated with ongoing maintenance is tracked on a department-by-department or a branch-by-branch level. These numbers are then run against the profits generated by these organizational units to determine net profitability or liability.

In cases where cost-center analysis is in place, it is wise to determine at the requirements stage exactly whose budget maintenance tasks will come out of. If the department or branch requesting your solution will have to pay for its maintenance, easy maintenance may be a more important requirement to them!

Consulting Situations

The first thing that you should determine with your customer is which one of you will ultimately be responsible for propagating maintenance changes. As we saw in the previous section, there are many ways to go about doing this. If the method of choice is manual to any degree, a considerable amount of extra work will be required to accomplish a successful distribution.

One compromise agreement is where you agree to distribute maintenance changes to a single computer at the target organization. After this, it is strictly that organization's responsibility to get your changes in place on whatever other systems they may be running.

Expecting Maintenance at New Rider Importers

The CFO of New Rider Importers has made his wishes on maintenance very clear in the case study. He wants "...a system where if anything breaks, ...the people up who built it...send some people out here." So this is clearly more on the "yours" side of the yours/mine responsibility breakdown. His remarks seem to imply that you are building this application from the perspective of a consulting situation.

> **NOTE**
>
> **Error Logs** One thing that an organization may expect from both internal and external developers is that careful logs be kept of all errors reported. Under internal circumstances, this can be used as an additional part of cost-center analysis. It may serve a similar purpose for external developers, helping an organization to determine whether they have truly "gotten their money's worth."

Location and Knowledge Level of Maintenance Staff

The location and knowledge level of your maintenance staff will be one of the hardest maintainability requirements for you to judge objectively. Certainly, it is fairly easy to say "the customer is there and we are here." But to actually try measuring the knowledge level of your staff or that of your target organization can prove to be an enormous and risky undertaking.

One reason for this is the lack of agreed-upon standards within the computer science field. Obviously, if you are interested in Microsoft certification, you must yourself be aware of the difficulty in "proving yourself" in today's market. Certification represents the market's first steps toward rectifying this situation.

Another reason for concern is the seemingly constant turnover of IS personnel. No sooner will you have made an assessment of your staff's strengths and weaknesses than someone will have left or joined, thus throwing off your entire estimate.

For these reasons, among others, we have decided to refer to all three maintenance staff situations using positive terms: good, better, and best. The factors cited previously mean that you should temper all of the following with the proverbial grain of salt, and common sense, as always, should be allowed to override any written rule.

Good

Two factors contribute to a minimal level of acceptability for a given maintenance staff or an individual. The first of these is a minimal capability to get in touch with them. Perhaps this means that you are given only an email address or, only slightly better, a nondirect telephone number.

The second thing that justifies a minimum rating is a lack of knowledge on the part of the proposed maintainer(s). An example of maintainers at this level would be individuals who have worked with some IT technologies before, but not any of the ones involved in your solution. Maybe they have had experience supporting applications written using Microsoft Access, but never with SQL Server. You could be sure that they would understand the concept of databases, but they would probably not be able to easily stop and restart your server.

This level of maintenance staff should be accepted only for a solution with very low availability requirements. For a fuller description of what this means, you can refer to the previous section, "Availability."

Better

The next step up the ladder in terms of maintenance staff quality is a staff that actually has some kind of remote access to the solution in question. Their knowledge, however, may extend only to the basic technologies that were used in its initial construction.

For example, a team of C++ programmers and Oracle DBAs could be given a modem link to a solution built with Visual C++ and Oracle. With regard to availability, you can use this level of maintenance staff with systems that are somewhat more essential—but not mission-critical.

Best

For mission-critical applications, only the absolute best level of maintenance staff will meet your customer's requirements. This means arranging for the presence of an onsite maintenance crew. If you are building your solution in a consulting situation, your analysis should include an additional requirement: focusing on knowledge transfer and technology mentoring with existing IS personnel during solution development.

In addition, the staff of this crew should have an in-depth knowledge of the specific solution on which they will be operating.

At this point, it is probably be helpful to see a side-by-side comparison of the three levels of maintenance staff quality (see Table 3.2).

REVIEW BREAK

TABLE 3.2

VARYING QUALITIES OF MAINTENANCE STAFFS

Quality Level	Minimum Location Required	Minimum Knowledge Level Required	Minimum Contact Level Required	Maximum Appropriate Availability Requirement
Good	Anywhere	General computers	Phone/email	Minimal
Better	Anywhere	General solution technologies	Remote access privileges	Moderate
Best	Onsite	Solution	Direct	Mission-Critical

The Maintenance Staff at New Rider Importers

You should have come away from this section with a certain appreciation for the subtle relationship between maintenance staff requirements and availability requirements. The most natural place to begin determining what kind of maintenance staff is required by New Rider Importers, then, is to review what we said about its availability requirements.

The kind of availability that is of particular concern where maintenance staffs are involved is downtime. On this issue, we previously decided that New Rider Importers was divided into two halves. The purchasing agents have very low availability requirements and high downtime tolerances. The checkout assistants, on the other hand, have very high availability requirements and low downtime tolerances.

This means that the purchasing agents should be able to function with an email address and/or telephone number that they can contact when they are experiencing problems. This works out rather well because they will be spending most of their time in the field, anyway.

The checkout assistants require onsite support for any problems that occur during their use of the system. This is a little tricky because their system has two ends: the cash registers at the stores and the central computers at the home offices. Probably the best solution in this case is to train someone at each store in the most basic of system-restoration procedures because an outage at that end will affect, at most, a single store. At the home-office end, a fully trained maintenance staff fluent in the specifics of your solution should be on hand. An outage at this end could potentially bring down several stores at a time.

ANALYZING EXTENSIBILITY REQUIREMENTS

Analyze extensibility requirements. Solution must be able to handle the growth of functionality.

Like maintenance work, extending your solution involves writing additional code and rewriting some existing code. The major difference between the two lies in the purpose for which the new code is being created. If the purpose is to make sure that the system can keep the level of functionality with which it started, it is called maintenance. If, on the other hand, new functionality is being sought, it falls into the realm of extensibility.

You must know three important things about Extensibility (the final letter, E, in our PASS ME theme) to pass the Microsoft exam. These are as follows:

◆ The impact on maintenance obligations

◆ Methodologies

◆ Operational implications

Analyzing the Impact on Maintenance Obligations

In the previous section, "Maintainability," we looked at how to determine customer/solution-provider expectations right from the beginning. Attempts to extend the functionality of your solution after it is in place can have profound effects on the expectations that we set. As discussed earlier, requirements will probably vary slightly depending on whether you are building your solution as internal developers or as consultants.

Internal Situations

Signoffs obtained during the requirements analysis phase of your solution play a great part in determining future extensions. Theoretically, all requests for system extensions would have to agree with previous design signoffs.

For example, consider a banking system where a requirement to forbid negative deposits has been clearly documented and signed-off by senior management. If a later request were to come in to allow exactly this kind of activity, then our signoff should allow us to clearly categorize this as a Request for Extension (RFE) rather than as a common maintenance request.

Whereas external consultants could use this to require additional funds or to justify a lower prioritizing of the project, this is unlikely to occur in the case of internal developers. The most that is likely to happen is that, in a cost-center analysis report, these funds will be budgeted slightly differently than if they were being used in the eradication of "bugs."

Consulting Situations

The most important impact that extensibility will have on your customer's maintenance obligations is that they should be required to tell you what parts of your solution they have changed since you last worked with it. This is so that any differences in system behavior can be fully understood. Otherwise, a lengthy period of "code exploring" might be needed in order to refamiliarize your people with the solution before they can begin work.

Imagine a situation, for example, in which a bank's own developers have attempted to implement address verification on credit card advances. When your staff completed their part of the solution, no such functionality was present. Now, if something breaks and your staff has to return to work on the system, it would be nice for them to know about the address verification. Otherwise, the rejection of test data with bogus address information would appear quite mysterious!

If your solution is "warranteed" in any way, an even more important requirement for your customer is that they not attempt to extend the parts of your system that you place "off-limits" to them. You can think of these as the internal pieces that, like opening a television or other appliance, will "void their warranty" if they tinker with them. Situations such as this most often arise when "free, unlimited technical support" is included in the cost of a solution's license.

One such example is a system that stores all its data in a widely known and easily accessible database, such as SQL Server. If your solution has consistency requirements above and beyond those that are made obvious by the database schema, it makes sense to tell your customer not to edit the data in your system directly through the database (such as via ODBC). These kinds of requirements should be spelled out for your customers clearly, repeatedly, and in writing!

Maintenance Obligations at New Rider Importers

Because New Rider Importers has a CIO and at least one software engineer, we can deduce that it has at least some degree of in-house IS capability. For this reason, you will have to follow both of our admonitions and stress to them in the strongest possible terms what portions of your solution they are not to modify. And, for your part, you should endeavor to keep New Rider Importers's IS staff as informed as possible about the nature of your own modifications.

Extension Methodologies

You can choose to make your solution extensible in several ways. The most common methodologies include the following:

- ◆ Source code
- ◆ APIs
- ◆ Components

Source Code

Providing your target organizations with some or all of the source code for your solution is perhaps the most obvious way of making your system extensible. It is the most powerful and flexible way, but it is also the most dangerous!

Proper extensibility via source code requires extensive knowledge on the part of those charged with making the extensions. It requires, at the very least, a familiarity with whatever language(s) your solution is written in. Beyond that, it requires a certain level of solution-specific knowledge to understand enough of how your system works to be able to change it.

This all translates into a potentially higher training requirement for the solution provider. For more information on training, see Chapter 2, "Analyzing the Extent of Business Requirements." Additional documentation (primarily of the internal, commenting variety) should also be considered a strong requirement.

APIs

APIs (Application Programming Interface) are one level of abstraction further up the ladder from source code. By providing a set of APIs for your solution, you will allow your target organization's IS staff to call much of its functionality without the use of your source code.

The way this is typically done is by exposing (also known as "export-ing") functions originally built for internal use by your solution. For example, the banking application to which we keep returning might export a function called `addInterest`. This function would take an account number as input and run a process on the account to which it referred that added the interest to it for that month.

The advantage to this system is that it doesn't require your target organization to use your source code. In addition to the legal advantages in this, there is the decreased knowledge requirement for your target organization's maintenance staff. They don't even need to know the language(s) that your applications were written in!

Unfortunately, the absence of source code for your system will most likely require that much more external documentation. Giving your exposed functions intuitive names (like the function used in the pre-ceding example) will go a long way toward making your APIs easier to use. But even with these measures, the parameters taken by your functions will be difficult to understand without some degree of external documentation.

The other disadvantage to APIs is their distinct bias toward C language use. Although largely historical, technical reasons also exist as to why most exposed functions are most easily called from C. In target organizations where C is not the language of choice, however, APIs may not be the best choice for extensibility.

Components

Component technologies, such as COM, render the question of languages entirely mute. By implementing a binary standard, they allow pieces of your solution written in different languages to operate together perfectly.

In addition to the benefit of language independence, distributed technologies (such as DCOM) allow your solution's "pieces" to be location independent as well. This means that one piece running on one machine can call functions in another piece running on another machine anywhere else on the network!

In the case of COM and DCOM (the two Microsoft technologies that you are most likely to encounter on the exam), two other benefits should be mentioned. COM components allow the functionality of a system to be extended while that system is still in operation. Also, adding functions to COM components is guaranteed not to break applications expecting the old components.

Extending Your Solution at New Rider Importers

Nowhere in the case study does anyone mention an aptitude for the C programming language. Instead, we learn in the software engineer's comments that most of the purchasing agents' applications were written in Visual Basic. Visual Basic is an application with deeply built-in support for COM—so it would have to be a stronger contender for extending the solution's functionality.

This could also potentially provide the answer to a request from the case study. The software engineer, in the section "Envisioned System," says that she would like some way to access the cash register's functionality from Visual Basic. Building a few components that "wrapped" the needed functionality might be just the thing.

CHAPTER SUMMARY

We chose to organize the parts of Analyzing Business Requirements that were covered in this chapter according to the acronym PASS ME: Performance, Availability, Security, Scalability, Maintainability, and Extensibility. These themes recur throughout the Microsoft exam and will be seen many more times throughout this book.

Performance is a measurement of how much work your solution can do given a specified amount of resources. One of its main manifestations is in three varieties of response time, each of which differ from the other in terms of importance and how they are measured.

Measurement of performance is generally handled in terms of peak versus average requirements and capacity.

Availability determines when and where your solution is capable of doing the work described in the previous paragraph. In terms of "when," some organizations will require your solution to be available constantly; others either will not care or will specifically require it to be unavailable at certain times. Even within these categories, the specific level of availability required for your system may be consistently low, consistently high, or variable. The impact of downtime will also vary considerably.

The "where" of availability refers to the geographic scope of your solution. If it is a local-area solution, you will have to deal with various LAN topologies. If it is wide-area, but less than global, you will need a WAN. Global solutions also require WANs, but various issues of language, culture, and infrastructure may prove even more important.

Security requires that your solution be able to prevent people and process from doing things with it that you don't want them to be able to do. The first step in ensuring that this is the case, then, is to identify the people involved in the use of your system: administrators, groups, guests, and clients. Only then should you proceed to an assessment of exactly how much security your solution will need, based upon the likelihood of a break-in attempt and the magnitude of disaster that would occur in the case of a successful break-in.

After you have determined these things about your security requirements, you can begin planning an implementation with a plan for distributing your solution's security database. Your plan should

CHAPTER SUMMARY

include a provision for sufficient training to make sure that problems don't arise. It should also provide for backups and auditing to deal with the instances in which things still go wrong.

As your organization grows, your solution will require more and more of the scalability that you will, hopefully, have designed into it. It is important that you understand from the very beginning of your project exactly what potential for additional users, data, and problems may exist in your target organization. You also need to know at what point in the cycle of use your solution will be rolling out.

Maintainability is the measure of how easy or difficult it is to keep your solution in a usable state. This will be easiest in situations where the solution is in a single location with maintenance staff onsite at all times. In contrast, the most difficult solutions to maintain are the ones that are spread out over large geographical spaces within only distant contact of maintenance staff.

Extensibility is often confused with maintainability because both can require code modifications. In the case of extensions to your solution, however, the purpose is different from that of maintenance because the goal will be to add new features rather than to preserve ones that already exist. It is important to come to an understanding with your target organization as soon as possible regarding how you will divide the work on these extensions with them.

Several methods are available for providing levels of extensibility in your solutions. You could elect to give your customers some of your source code, but this is as dangerous to your company on a business level as it is to your solution on a technical level. Alternatively, you could provide a set of APIs for your system, but these can require much additional documentation and knowledge of the C programming language.

Components using COM are the solution most likely to be favored on the Microsoft exam. In the real world, they can provide language independence, location independence, and versioning support.

KEY TERMS

- Administrators/groups/guests/clients
- API
- Auditing
- Capacity
- Cycle of use
- Index
- LAN/WAN/VPN
- Mission-critical
- "PASS ME"
- Peak longevity
- Peak versus average requirements
- Real, perceived, and expected response times
- Threshold tolerance
- Transaction frequency
- Transaction intensity

APPLY YOUR KNOWLEDGE

Exercises

3.1 Analyzing Performance Requirements

In Exercise 3.1, we walk you through a careful comparison of some key performance characteristics. By the end of the exercise, you should have a very clear understanding of the differences between the three kinds of response times: peaks, averages, and capacities.

Estimated Time: 5 minutes.

1. Study Figure 3.1. This graph represents a median sampling of statistics for six users' system usage over an extended time.

2. Each mark in the figure starts at the point of the user's request and finishes at the point of a system response. Taken as a whole, each mark is reflecting real response-times.

3. Locate the transaction that had the longest real response-time.

   You should pick the transaction in the lower-right corner.

4. The empty boxes at the start of each transaction measure from the point of user request to UI response. This is the perceived response-time of the system.

5. Based on each user's first transaction, would the expected response-times generally be satisfied or disappointed? In most cases, you can tell that users would be disappointed—because the marks get longer as you move further to the right.

6. Count the total number of marks in the figure. Divide this number by 100 (the number of seconds indicated on the horizontal access) to get the average performance in transactions per time slice.

7. Find the point of the graph with the most simultaneous users.

   You should count 5. This represents the peak requirement for this kind of performance.

8. See whether you can locate the greatest point of transaction frequency on the graph.

   It occurs when User #2 generates three transactions within approximately 30 seconds.

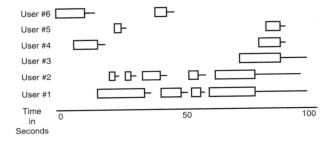

FIGURE 3.1
Graph for Exercise 3.1.

3.2 Taking Availability Requirements into Account

Exercise 3.2 is intended to let you practice developing schedules for system maintenance on a global basis. You should take away from this exercise an intuitive understanding of the difficulties inherent in performing global maintenance without disrupting important operations.

Estimated Time: 15 minutes.

1. You have to perform maintenance upgrades on six of the seven locations listed in Table 3.3. Chicago is your own office, so you may ignore it for the time being.

2. Begin by determining each city's time(s) of solution usage in terms of your own time zone.

APPLY YOUR KNOWLEDGE

3. Based on your calculations from the preceding step, determine the time(s) when each city is *not* going to be using your solution. Put this in the Adjusted Availability column of Table 3.4.

4. Organize the cities into three general groups ordered according to their downtime impact level. Put this in the Downtime Impact Rank column in Table 3.4.

5. Within each group, rank your cities from least to most time available for performing the needed upgrades. Put this in the Availability Subrank column of Table 3.4.

6. Assume that your staff can work on only one location at a time and that each city has been estimated to require two hours of maintenance work.

7. Multiply the preceding estimate by a factor of two to allow for unexpected difficulties. You now have 24 hours of maintenance to perform in exactly 24 hours.

8. Begin distributing your 24 hours of maintenance by giving four hours to the city with the most severe downtime impact level and the least time available for upgrade. Put this block in the Assigned Maintenance Window column of Table 3.4.

9. Proceed in giving out different four-hour blocks of time. You should progress gradually backward through your previous ordering until you are able to give the final four hours to the city with the least severe downtime impact level and the most time available for upgrade.

TABLE 3.3

GLOBAL BUSINESS SITES

City	Time Difference (in Hours)	Local Times When Solution Is Used	Downtime Impact Level
Moscow	Nine hours ahead	7:00 a.m.–7:00 p.m.	Moderate
Hawaii	Four hours behind	9:00 a.m.–5:00 p.m.	Moderate
London	Six hours ahead	9:00 a.m.–5:00 p.m.	Moderate
Los Angeles	Two hours behind	10:00 a.m.–4:00 p.m.	Minimal
Chicago	None	8:00 a.m.–6:00 p.m.	Minimal
Berlin	Seven hours ahead	7:00 a.m.–11:30 a.m. and 1:00 p.m.–5:00 p.m.	Mission-critical

APPLY YOUR KNOWLEDGE

TABLE 3.4

EXERCISE 3.2 WORKSPACE

City	*Adjusted Availability*	*Downtime Impact Rank*	*Availability Subrank*	*Assigned Maintenance Windows*
EXAMPLE #1	*2:00 a.m.–10:00 a.m.*	*1 (Mission-critical)*	*1.2*	*4:00 a.m.–8:00 a.m.*
EXAMPLE #2	*12:00 p.m.–8:00 p.m.*	*3 (Minimal)*	*3.1*	*3:00 p.m.–7:00 p.m.*
Moscow				
Hawaii				
London				
Los Angeles				
Chicago				
Berlin				

EXERCISE 3.2 ANSWER

City	*Adjusted Availability*	*Downtime Impact Rank*	*Availability Subrank*	*Assigned Maintenance Windows*
Moscow	10 a.m.–10 p.m.	2	2.2	3 p.m.–7 p.m.
Hawaii	9 p.m.–1 p.m.	2	2.1	12 a.m.–4 a.m.
London	11 a.m.–3 a.m.	2	2.1	8 p.m.–12 a.m.
Los Angeles	6 p.m.–12 p.m.	1	1.1	8 a.m.–12 p.m.
Chicago	6 p.m.–8 a.m.	1	1.2	4 a.m.–8 a.m.
Berlin	4:30 a.m.–6 a.m. and 10 a.m.–12 a.m.	3	3.1	10 a.m.–2 p.m.

APPLY YOUR KNOWLEDGE

3.3 Analyzing Security Role Requirements

Exercise 3.3 is intended to let you practice categorizing various positions according to security role.

Estimated Time: 5 minutes.

1. Review the left column in Table 3.5. Each entry in the list represents one of the security roles discussed in this chapter.

2. Review the right column in Table 3.5. Each entry in the list represents a characteristic of one or more of the roles listed on the left.

3. Draw a line between each role on the left and the related characteristic(s) on the right.

TABLE 3.5

TABLE FOR EXERCISE 3.3

Administrator	Can change accounts
	Can change permissions
Group	Always internal
	Collection for practicality's sake
Guest	Individual user
	Can change policies
Client	Always external

You should have matched up the roles and characteristics as follows:

Administrator = Can change accounts, can change permissions, always internal, can change policies.

Group = Collection for practicality's sake.

Guest = Always external, individual user.

Client = Always internal, individual user.

3.4 Recognizing Scalability Requirements in the Cycle of Use

In Exercise 3.4, you learn to organize the series of events that occur throughout a typical solution's cycle of use.

Estimated Time: 5 minutes.

1. Review the following list. Some of these represent steps in the cycle of use of a typical automated solution.

2. Pick the steps that you believe represent genuine cycle of use steps and make a list only of them.

3. Order these steps to progress from those that should happen first to those that should happen last.

   - Usage levels fall.
   - Schema are designed.
   - Opportunities for revision peak.
   - System strain peaks.
   - F.U.D.
   - Usage levels rise.
   - Logic is modularized.
   - Requirements are analyzed.
   - Users are interviewed.
   - Distrust subsides.
   - Needs change.
   - Opportunities for revision diminish.

APPLY YOUR KNOWLEDGE

Your solution should look like the following:

1. F.U.D.

2. Opportunities for revision peak.

3. Usage levels rise.

4. Distrust subsides.

5. Opportunities for revision diminish.

6. System strain peaks.

7. Needs change.

8. Usage levels fall.

3.5   Satisfying Maintainability Requirements in Multiple Locations

In Exercise 3.5, you choose appropriate maintenance distribution techniques and assign appropriate levels of staff to multiple locations.

Estimated Time: 5 minutes.

1. Figure 3.2 represents the layout of a small organization's branches and information technology resources. The large circle in Figure 3.2 that contains most of the other objects in the diagram represents the extent of one small company's only LAN.

2. Each box in Figure 3.2 represents one solution that has been deployed at the company. One of these is of minimal importance, one is of moderate importance, and the final one is of mission-critical importance.

3. Attached to each box is a label indicating whether that solution should receive maintenance updates via a Manual or an Automated approach.

4. The three smaller circles in Figure 3.2 each represent a group of technicians. One of these is Good, another is Better, and the final one is the Best.

5. Each of the arrows in Figure 3.2 indicates a different way in which the technicians (circles) can provide support for their associated solutions (squares). The three possibilities are direct contact, remote access, and telephone support.

6. These arrows also serve to indicate which of Visual Studio 6's distribution methods would be most appropriate for packaging maintenance software. The options are CD/Floppy, Network Setup files, and Internet distribution.

7. Using one of each kind of solution and technician, fill in every square and circle, respectively. Using one of each kind of support and distribution, label each arrow.

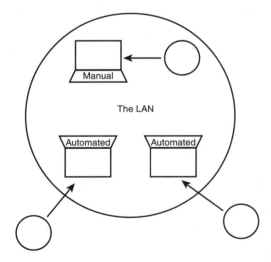

FIGURE 3.2
One company's information resources and locations.

APPLY YOUR KNOWLEDGE

Figure 3.3 illustrates the solution to the exercise.

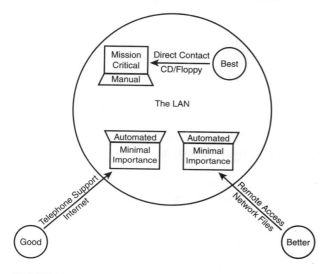

FIGURE 3.3
Solution to Exercise 3.5.

3.6 Analyzing Extensibility Methodology Requirements

Exercise 3.6 is intended to help you understand the various pros and cons associated with each method of extending your solutions.

Estimated Time: 5 minutes.

1. Review the left column in the following table. Each entry in the list represents one of the extension methodologies discussed in this chapter.

2. Review the right column in the following table. Each entry in the list represents a characteristic of one or more of the extension methodologies listed on the left.

3. Draw a line between each methodology on the left and the related characteristic(s) on the right, as shown in Table 3.6.

TABLE 3.6

METHODOLOGIES AND CHARACTERISTICS

Source code	Language independent
	Plagiarism danger
API	Uses exported functions
	C language-centric
Components	Versioning support
	Most flexible

Your solution should look like the following:

Source code = Plagiarism danger, most flexible.

API = Uses exported functions, C language-centric.

Components = Language independent, versioning support.

Review Questions

1. The checkout assistants at New Rider Importers are noticing slower and slower turnarounds on their requests to your system. What kinds of response times are being dealt with in these observations?

2. If your system is giving people slower responses during evening "rush hours," what kind of performance are you measuring?

3. Suppose the purchasing agents decide that they will now conduct all their business via the telephone from a single location. How would this affect the extent of your systems' availability requirements?

APPLY YOUR KNOWLEDGE

4. Imagine that a monsoon has made it impossible for many of New Rider Importers's purchasing agents to get in touch with their home offices. Of what global availability issue is this an example?

5. Someone has suggested that in the event of system outages, checkout assistants should be empowered to hand write receipts for customers and finish entering their transactions into the computer at a later point in time. How could this potentially affect the impact of downtime at New Rider Importers?

6. How would forbidding all uses of modems at New Rider Importers decrease the extent of your solution's security requirements?

7. What audience role would be doubled up if the CIO hired an assistant who had all the same privileges and permissions as the CIO?

8. Suppose that surveys of customer satisfaction show a dramatic improvement shortly after the removal of locks on the checkout assistants' cash drawers. What would be the most likely explanation for this phenomenon?

9. If all employees at New Rider Importers had stopped using the existing automated systems to perform their jobs, what stage of the cycle of life would it be in?

10. You tell New Rider Importers that you will require that they leave a modem set up to answer and connect to an account on their systems even after you have rolled-out their new solution. What is the likely reason for your request?

11. What can you do if New Rider Importers modifies all the parts of your solution that you specifically told them not to?

12. New Rider Importers want the greatest degree of control over the inner workings of your solution. They are not concerned about having to shut it down temporarily so that their changes can take effect. What methodology would you use to provide your solution with the required degree of extensibility?

Exam Questions

1. If the purchasing agent had never worked for another company before but still felt that system performance should be better, what kind of response times would he be talking about?

   A. Real

   B. Perceived

   C. Expected

   D. Derived

2. Which of the following maintenance methods are *not* involved in the CFO's use of FastBooks? (Choose two.)

   A. Manual processing

   B. Automatic processing

   C. Removable storage

   D. Network

3. Which of the following requirements would be most reduced by an assurance that the number of customers will *not* be increasing in the future?

   A. Extensibility

   B. Scalability

   C. Security

   D. Availability

APPLY YOUR KNOWLEDGE

4. What could have been done to prevent New Rider's sales staff from choosing easily crackable passwords?

    A. Technology partnerships

    B. Freezing workstations after five minutes of inactivity

    C. Limiting availability

    D. Improving training

5. The maximum number of reports that the CFO can run simultaneously may gauge what aspect of performance?

    A. Transaction frequency

    B. Maximization

    C. Capacity

    D. None of the above

6. How would you best describe the potential impact of downtime for the purchasing agent's GPS?

    A. Mission-critical

    B. Moderate

    C. Minimal

    D. All of the above

7. Select the minimal level of knowledge that would be acceptable in forming a maintenance staff for the purchasing agent's GPS.

    A. None

    B. General computers

    C. General technologies used in solution

    D. Solution specific

8. If the central computer at New Rider Importers used C rather than COBOL, which extension methodology would be much more likely?

    A. Source code

    B. API

    C. Components

    D. None of the above

9. The way that code is currently indented at New Rider Importers is an example of what kind of requirements?

    A. Geographic requirements

    B. Growth requirements

    C. Maintainability requirements

    D. Interoperability requirements

10. A typhoon knocking out all communications with New Rider's purchasing agents would be an example of which of the following?

    A. Audience growth's impact on maintainability

    B. Geographic scope's impact on maintainability

    C. Audience growth's impact on availability

    D. Geographic scope's impact on availability

11. If purchasing agents suddenly start selling less after stronger security measures are added to their laptops, how would you explain it?

    A. Security's cycle of use

    B. Security's impact on existing environments

    C. Security's breadth of application distribution

    D. Security's impact on maintenance obligations

APPLY YOUR KNOWLEDGE

12. Which concept in requirements analysis would predict that a solution's usage will rise, peak, and fall off during its lifetime?

    A. The cycle of use

    B. The chain of life

    C. Growth requirements

    D. Maintainability requirements

13. What great benefit would you anticipate if all New Rider's information technologies could be housed in a single location?

    A. Fewer opportunities for direct physical contact

    B. Fewer opportunities for performance evaluation

    C. Greater opportunities for direct physical contact

    D. Greater opportunities for performance evaluation

14. The company that originally wrote New Rider Importers telephone switch software is refusing to continue providing free technical support for it. They claim that it has been substantially rewritten in violation of the existing support contract. Of what is this an example?

    A. Availability requirements' impact on maintenance obligations

    B. Extensibility requirements' impact on maintenance obligations

    C. Maintenance obligations' impact on availability requirements

    D. Maintenance obligations' impact on extensibility requirements

Answers to Review Questions

1. Perceived response-times and expected response-times are the two kinds in question. Real response-times cannot be determined by end users because they require an intimate knowledge of the technologies being used "under the hood." Expected response-times are involved here insofar as expectations for present performance have been derived from past experience using the same system. See "Response-Time Characteristics."

2. Measuring performance at these times would mean looking at "peak" requirements. This stands in contrast to the average requirements that would be in effect during the slower, more common times. See "Measuring Performance."

3. If the purchasing agents all conducted business from a single location, you could redefine their availability requirements as being limited. The reason for this is that they will no longer be in the wide variety of time zones that had previously required 24-hour access to your systems. See "Level of Availability."

4. This is an issue of global differences in infrastructure. In some countries, severe weather will prove a considerable challenge in the establishment of reliable communications. See "Geographic Scope."

5. This suggestion would allow the checkout assistants to redo their work later, thus lessening the impact of downtime. This is a feature consistent with systems where the impact of downtime is minimal. See "Impact of Downtime."

6. The level of required security would be reduced. The reason for this is that the number of connections supported to the secured data would be

APPLY YOUR KNOWLEDGE

reduced, which represents a significant decrease in the likelihood of a security breach being attempted. See "Identifying the Level of Security Needed."

7. Administrator. This is the role that we decided, earlier in this chapter, was represented by the data processing manager. See "Establishing a Security Context."

8. The most likely cause is the quickening of customer service represented by removing a physical security measure. Physical security can require additional time for the completion of tasks because authorized personnel must deal with it before they can conduct business. See "Identifying Impacts on an Existing Environment."

9. A system meeting this description is said to be in the "old, disused" stage. Typically, this occurs when the cost of maintaining and extending a system has risen beyond the benefits to be gained. See "The Cycle of Use."

10. This probably means that you want to retain remote-access privileges so that you can participate in the maintenance of your solution. See "Maintenance Expectations."

11. You may be able to refuse to continue supporting your solution. This is why it is important to make specific legal arrangements for this contingency well in advance of your solution's final delivery. See "Analyzing the Impact on Maintenance Obligations."

12. Under these circumstances, giving New Rider Importers some portion of the source code for your solution may well be the best way to provide extensibility. Source code will definitely give

them the greatest control over your application's inner workings. See "Extension Methodologies."

Answers to Exam Questions

1. **C.** The purchasing agent would still be talking in terms of expected response-times because he would still have an expectation—regardless of whether it has a basis in past experience! It could not be a case of real response-times because no specific measurements are given. A case could be made for perceived response-times, but it is not the best choice because no user-interface observations are included. "Derived" is not even a valid kind of response-time. See "Response-Time Characteristics."

2. **A, C.** The CFO says that everything comes to him automatically off the Internet. The Internet is, indeed, a network. This leaves only removable storage and manual processes. See "Method of Distribution."

3. **B.** In this case, scalability would be the requirement most reduced by an assurance that the number of customers would not be increasing. This is true because additional customers would generate more input for the system (in the form of sales), which would require scalability. See "Growth."

4. **D.** Better training would have taught New Rider's staff the value of choosing difficult-to-guess passwords. It would also have covered the things that generally constitute easy-to-guess passwords. The other options may have contributed somewhat to overall security but would not have specifically assisted password selection in any way. See "Planning for Maintainability."

APPLY YOUR KNOWLEDGE

5. **C.** The CFO's reports are testing the capacity of the New Rider Importers system. This is because he is talking about the maximum number of reports that the system can generate simultaneously. Transaction frequency is a measure of how often transactions are presented to a solution. Maximization is a nonsense term in this context. See "Measuring Performance."

6. **A.** The impact of downtime in any situation where a life is at stake (from "driving off a mountain") must be estimated to be mission-critical. Moderate and minimal impacts would suggest less significance and are, therefore, incorrect. See "Impact of Downtime."

7. **D.** Any maintenance staff dealing with a mission-critical situation such as a GPS system for someone in dangerous terrain (such as the purchasing agent) must have a great deal of solution-specific knowledge. The other two options represent less-specific knowledge levels that are unacceptable. See "Location and Knowledge of Maintenance Staff."

8. **B.** A C-centric approach is typical of an Application Programmer's Interface (API). Source code would allow for modification of the solution itself. Component interfaces feature methods and properties, not functions. See "Extension Methodologies."

9. **D.** This would be an interoperability requirement. The reason for this is that any new code that is added to the information systems should try to match the existing coding style as much as possible. Geographic requirements and maintainability requirements also exist, but they are not related to this concept. Growth is a phenomenon that creates requirements for your solutions, but is now a requirement in itself. See "Interoperability with Existing Standards."

10. **D.** Typhoons are a fact of life in some geographic regions and completely absent from many others. The inability to access your solution would be an availability issue. See "Geographic Scope."

11. **B.** The people who use automated solutions on a daily basis tend to develop very specific approaches to their operation. Changing something as simple as security procedures can have profound effects on the ability of users to continue doing their jobs effectively. See "Impact on Existing Environments."

12. **A.** The cycle of use predicts that all solutions go through three distinct phases. The first is a new, underused phase. The second is a well-known, highly used stage. Finally, most solutions fall into a state where they no longer meet business requirements and are not often used. See "Cycle of Use."

13. **C.** If all New Rider's information technologies were housed in a single location, the opportunities for direct physical contact between maintenance personnel and people experiencing problems would be greater. This would, presumably, allow for quicker resolution of important issues. See "Location and Knowledge of Maintenance Staff."

14. **B.** This would be an example of attempts to extend a solution resulting in a "voided warranty" situation. In general, maintenance obligations are affected by requirements, not the other way around. See "Impact on Maintenance Obligations."

APPLY YOUR KNOWLEDGE

Suggested Readings and Resources

1. Brooks, Frederick. *The Mythical Man-Month.* Addison Wesley, 1975.

   - Chapter 11: Plan to Throw One Away

   - Chapter 16: No Silver Bullet

2. Pipkin, Donald. *Halting the Hacker.* Hewlett Packard Professional Books, 1997.

   - Chapter 8: Keeping the Hacker Contained

3. Pukite, Paul and Jan. *Modeling for Reliability Analysis.* Institute of Electrical Engineers, 1998.

   - Chapter 2: System Requirements and Design

   - Chapter 11: Maintainability Modeling

   - Chapter 12: Availability Modeling

This chapter addresses the following exam objective:

**Analyze human factors requirements.
Considerations include**

- **Target users**

- **Localization**

- **Accessibility**

- **Roaming users**

- **Help**

- **Training requirements**

- **Physical environment constraints**

- **Special needs**

▶ This objective is designed to remind you of a basic fact that is too often overlooked in software design. A solution almost never exists for its own sake. Typically, your software is being requested by a human being or a group of human beings (perhaps even several groups) who have a specific problem they need solved.

▶ The message is simple. If you do not consider these people, their problems, and their goals, a solution—no matter how beautifully conceived and designed—is likely to fail. So, as a designer, being aware of the unique characteristics of the users, understanding the business problem thoroughly, and meeting their needs (as opposed to the developer's needs) is critical.

CHAPTER 4

Human-Computer Interface Analysis

OUTLINE

▶ Be able to identify who the target user base is for your solution. Remember, if it does not solve the problems from the user's point of view, it solves nothing.

▶ Be able to identify your need for disconnected or roaming users in the application. Do they simply need to connect to the system from different machines in the offices, or do they need to be able to dial in from remote locations, working on the go?

▶ Be able to identify effective approaches for satisfying special needs of the target user group.

▶ Be able to decide what the appropriate level of training is for a target user group, based on their previous experience with systems.

▶ Know the various ways that users can be provided with help for the application.

▶ Understand the effects of localization, both from a development perspective and a target user perspective.

▶ Be able to effectively analyze a given physical environment, discovering how this will limit or enhance user-system interactions.

INTRODUCTION

This chapter introduces you to the process of defining the most important interface in any piece of software—the human-computer interface. First, the chapter focuses on the identification of the target user group and its requirements. In almost every case, the problem that software is asked to solve has originated with people in the business. Therefore, the needs of these people are crucial in deciding how to begin solving it. Different types of users will no doubt have very different needs for their system interface.

Second, we focus on issues of software localization. In essence, this is the process of making software that is equally friendly to users in different countries and different languages.

Third, we take a look at that portion of the human-computer interface that may be most important—and that seems, at times, most difficult to do well—the system help. As you will see, the exam presents us with many options for providing the user with assistance.

Finally, although it is fine to discuss the perfect means of providing these options to users, we also need to take a moment to reflect on how the physical environment in which the software will be deployed might affect, positively or negatively, our planned interface. As you will see, sometimes (in fact, most times) the best-laid plans go awry.

Every year, Microsoft spends millions of dollars researching what it calls the "most important interface in the computer industry." It isn't the latest and greatest Microsoft product rolling out of the pipe. Instead, it is the interface that exists between a user and the software he or she attempts to use. The central tenet of this emphasis is the assumption that a good solution gets a chance only if it is paired with a good interface between the user (human) and the system (the computer). Without that, no matter how good the design, no opportunity to display it will occur.

In Microsoft's opinion, it boils down to this: software design yields the interface, and this is where the proverbial rubber meets the road, where the end users are actually trying to use the system. If it is easy to use, intuitive, and helps them to accomplish their objectives, users are likely to forgive (or more accurately, never even discover) technical flaws in the application's design. In the opposite case, however, no amount of marketing and promotion of a design will save an application that users find confusing, unhelpful, or inflexible.

CASE STUDY: VITAMOBILE

BACKGROUND

VitaMobile is a Seattle-based vitamin supplement dealer. Normally, it provides more than $2,000,000 worth of these supplements to various consumers and wholesalers throughout the United States each year. Until now, all deals with consumers have been by mail, and all wholesalers have purchased from a small set of salespeople who travel to their clients to take orders and promote products. The majority of the company's revenue has been from wholesale, but it is planning to make an aggressive move in the consumer space, creating an Internet presence to allow online ordering of products.

PROBLEM STATEMENT

VitaMobile has had a successful wholesale division for several years, but the lack of direct contact with consumers has left that aspect of its business difficult to manage. The wholesale division, which formerly kept track of everything on paper, is feeling pressure to modernize to keep up with the demand and to decrease overhead.

VP of Sales

"It seems like fewer and fewer people are using commercial outlets for their purchases. They'd rather deal directly with manufacturers and cut out the middleman. This would be great for us, and it would let us cut prices to them while still increasing our profits. But we don't know who to market to; we've never had much luck with direct sales."

Sales Representatives

"The more I am working with these chains of health-food stores, the more I find them wanting to just do a quick once-over on last month's order and reorder the same thing. This ought to make my job a lot easier, but really it isn't. I have to go through all my invoices that get sent to me by the main office, find theirs, and then read through each item because they are all returned with codes instead of product names."

Billing Clerk

"The system doesn't seem to have anything wrong with it, exactly. However, when we get calls from customers, we have a lot of trouble with some of their requests because we can't figure out how to pull it up by their P.O. numbers. I know they tell us we can do it, but it doesn't seem to work, and no one ever showed us how. I'd look it up, but there are 10 three-ring binders in the back, gathering dust, that make up the 'help' system."

CURRENT SYSTEM

The current system at VitaMobile is centralized around the main office. Remote salespeople fax in orders that are input into the system. It was originally designed when more than 90 percent of the company's business was in the Seattle area.

The system itself is, from a technical standpoint, a mainframe system. The system runs under CICS and has a target of 20 connected IBM 3270 (or emulating) terminals. This program was actually purchased from another company before VitaMobile even began operating. It is at least 15 years old.

continues

CASE STUDY: VITAMOBILE

continued

Customer

The process is different depending on whether you are a wholesaler or a consumer.

As a consumer, you consult a print ad or receive order numbers by word-of-mouth; you send in a request order form to the company, along with a check or money order, for the amount of product you've ordered, plus shipping and handling. If the amount is incorrect or the product numbers are not valid, the order is returned to the sender, with an explanation that the order could not be processed.

Sales Representative

As a wholesaler, the order process begins with a visit from a member of the VitaMobile sales staff. This person discusses your needs with you and then takes out a form and fills in each item you would like to order. That evening, when the day is complete, this form gets faxed to the main office of VitaMobile. Assuming again that all is in order, the order is processed. If not, the sales rep is notified the next morning, and the customer is notified the next day.

Data Entry Clerk

The data entry clerk is responsible for two things. One is checking the mail for orders from consumers. If orders are present, the clerk is to verify and enter them into the terminal-based system. If not, he or she is to place the whole order into an "invalid order" bin to be processed and returned to the sender.

The data entry clerk is also responsible, at 4:00 p.m. Pacific Time, for checking the fax machine for incoming daily orders from the wholesale salespeople. The clerk takes the order and verifies that all products are valid. If not, it is set aside to be faxed back to the sales representative. If the orders are valid, the data is inputted as previously described.

Billing Clerk

Billing clerks process the payments made by both consumers and wholesalers. They also receive phone calls from wholesalers to discuss invoices when they are billed. They keep paper records of which invoices belong to which customer purchase order number because they aren't sure how to make the system look up a client's P.O. number.

VP of Sales

Because all the sales staff in the field are salaried, the VP of sales is responsible for monitoring the output of the sales staff and managing final disputes on billing or invoices. The VP is also responsible for generating new business for the sales staff and letting them know about the new leads.

ENVISIONED SYSTEM

If they are going to be building a new system for managing their orders, the VitaMobile staff has a lot of different ideas about how the new system needs to be structured.

CASE STUDY: VITAMOBILE

VP of Sales

"We need to be able to take in orders from consumers more easily. We also need to speed up the processing of orders from both the consumers and our wholesale customers."

Programmer

"The new system is going to need a better-designed database so that we can have different people accessing the same data. Also, if we really want to enable end-user commerce, we're going to have to put the catalog online as well, not just a blank order form."

Sales Representative

"When I'm out at a client's site, it would be really nice to be able to pull up their orders in our system and see what they ordered last month. Also, if some kind of billing problem occurs, I would like to be able to at least see what it is, and then I can sound knowledgeable when I call our billing clerks, rather than just calling up out of the blue without any information. I'd also love to be able to do some real-time ordering, rather than writing everything out longhand and then faxing it in the evening to the main office."

Billing Clerk

"A big drawback in the old system that we need fixed in the new system is that one of our bookkeepers has impaired vision and needs to look at things really closely. She has to find other, less valuable things to do because squinting at the screen gives her a headache. She's too valuable to lose, so we need to make it easier for her to work."

SECURITY

Like most firms, some variation exists in the security needs and requirements by employee position or role.

VP of Sales

The VP ought to be able to view any information that is desired. However, even the VP can't credit accounts or change invoices; that still needs to be done by a billing clerk.

Billing Clerk

Only billing clerks are allowed to change invoice information or to credit accounts for payments not received.

Sales Representative

Sales representatives should not be able to view or change contact information for another representative's client.

PERFORMANCE

Expectations around the performance of the new system vary. The following are some of the different views expressed by the VitaMobile employees.

VP of Sales

"I'm not really sure what kind of requirements we are going to have. We need to make sure that the computer isn't making it harder to sell and be interactive with the customer than if we did it by hand. If I start hearing complaints that our salespeople are sitting too long in customers' shops, then I'm going to know there is a problem."

continues

CASE STUDY: VitaMobile

continued

Programmer

"I think the connections from the remote laptops to our main PCs need to be made in about 15 seconds."

Data Entry Clerk

"I'm pretty fast at entering new orders into our current system. I can type ahead and the system keeps up with me. I hope the new system allows me to do at least as many orders per hour as I can do now. "

MAINTAINABILITY

A new system is only useful for as long as it continues to function properly. Maintainability is the measure of how easy it will be to keep things running smoothly.

VP of Sales

"Well, for the time being at least, our entire business is in this one building. Eventually, we're going to want to bring our customers closer to the business."

Development Manager

"Our current application is a mainframe-based terminal application running on an AS/400, and most of the people that worked on it have left. We're very careful with this stuff to make sure we don't break anything we can't fix. We're basically VB people here, but this application predates us all. The new system should be written in a language we know, Visual Basic, and it should be designed as components that can be upgraded

individually. No one here is a VB wizard, but if it's done properly, we can handle it."

AVAILABILITY

One of the things that can radically increase the amount of time it takes to develop and test a system is the requirements for availability. A system can simply require "business hours" availability, or perhaps it requires 24-hours-a-day, 365-days-a-year availability. In either case, knowing the level of expected availability is critical to delivering a satisfactory solution.

VP of Sales

"If we decide to put our eggs in this basket, we must have very high reliability. We won't have any other reliable processes in place to take manual orders, and with our planned expansions, most people won't even know we ever did it this way.

Although we've had a lot of complaints from our internal staff because they do not like using the terminals for their day-to-day work, it has been a very reliable system for us. Reliability for us equates to profitability. When our system is down, we lose money."

ANALYZING HUMAN FACTORS REQUIREMENTS

Analyze human factors requirements.

Any time we are going to try to understand how our users want to interface with a system, we have to discover who they are. After we know this, we can decide how they should be trained, what mobility requirements they have, or what kinds of special needs must get addressed.

Who Are Your Target Users?

The most important factor when considering the human-computer interface is to realize who your target users are. Simply put, this is because, just like shoes, one size does not fit all. With this in mind, the only way you can adequately design your interface is to start by understanding who your users are and then spending some time thinking about them and their motivations. You may be designing for a very task-oriented user group that is looking for very simple and specific systems. On the other hand, you may have very adept technical users who want much more flexibility in their use of the system, and who are willing to work harder to learn the system if it means they have more power.

Alan Cooper, an oft-quoted expert on human-computer interaction, has written a book titled *The Inmates Are Running the Asylum*. In it, he outlines a strategy for doing just this. He suggests that you build a "persona" that typifies a user of your system. You give this persona life by giving it a name, characteristics, hobbies, and even a photograph if possible. By being very specific, you are more likely to address those needs instead of your own. Developers often design a system to make things easy on themselves, when it is the users who ought to be the focus of the solution.

Nontechnical Target Users

Many times you will run across users who have either not been exposed to technology (for example, the work they do has not been automated at all to this point) or who have had experiences only with older, terminal-emulation-type machines. These people are often found in companies that are, as a corporate culture, slow to adopt technology or that are distrustful of its effects. They may even be in an industry where advances in technology have had a tendency to displace human workers. In this kind of an environment, the exposure to new technology is going to be very limited.

Generally speaking, when you are asked to provide a solution for this type of user group, it strongly suggests a path for design and implementation. This type of environment requires very specific solutions. Because the technology is not part of the corporate culture at this point, it will be very difficult to "sell" a solution that is very open ended and that has a lot of flexibility. A lot of flexibility inherently implies that there is less focus to the application because it can be used for many things.

On the up side, from a development perspective, this type of user group is much more likely to be impressed with the kinds of visual representations that well-designed Windows interfaces are capable of producing. This is a great benefit to a developer because creating graphical screens has become a fairly simple task (although creating *good* screens is a rare talent).

From a training perspective, a nontechnical user group is more likely to want specific, task-oriented help. Rather than a discussion of the "features" of an application, they are more likely to want a project manager to explain "how they take an order" with the new application.

One thing to especially be aware of among nontechnical user groups is the potential that the actual mechanics of using the system may be more trouble (in the minds of those not familiar with the metaphors, and so on) than the new features are worth. To combat this problem, make sure that the less technical your target audience is, the more you streamline the application to make it simpler to use. This is not to say that we ought to be removing functionality, but the priority should be on making the use of the software easily discoverable, rather than jamming in as many features as we can.

When you discover your target user group is largely nontechnical, you can expect the following:

◆ Simpler applications

◆ Step-by-step training

◆ More specific uses for software

Technical Target Users

Generally speaking, when you are presented with this type of target user group, it is important to look more at building a flexible tool. It is almost impossible to capture the diverse requirements of highly technical users in a single, very simple application. Instead, focus on providing a tool-based solution, which allows the end users more freedom to utilize the solution in the way they want.

Finally, from a training perspective, you will find this type of user group moving more directly to the functionality of the application. Rather than being impressed by user interface issues (most of which they have probably seen before), they will be curious about how, from a business perspective, they can use the application. The questions will likely be not as task-oriented, but will focus more on the capabilities of the tool set.

If you are targeting a moderately technical to highly technical user group for a solution—sometimes referred to as "power users"—expect to implement the following:

◆ More complicated applications

◆ Training focused on business uses of the application

◆ More flexible software, allowing more end user freedom in its use.

◆ Plentiful shortcuts (for example, "hot keys," command-line parsing)

Mixed Target Users

Of course, a third type of user audience exists—a combination of novice and expert. This type of user community seems to be the one that gives solution architects fits, and the one where, too often, *neither* group is satisfied with the outcome. Architects very often make the mistake of trying to "split the difference," creating an interface that is not too insulting to the expert but that is also not too big of a stretch for the novice. We give the novices more training, and we give the expert "hot keys" and move on. Usually, the better solution is to design separate interfaces for the two styles of interaction and allow the users to work with the one that makes them most comfortable. A one-size-fits-all interface actually slows down both the novice and the expert.

Which User Group Exists at VitaMobile?

Currently, the targeted users are not automating the process of ordering at all. This alone would not necessarily indicate a low-technology targeted user group. However, the automated systems they are currently using for other tasks are based on fairly old technology. The combination of these two factors make a strong argument for classifying this as a low-technology solution, at least from a Windows point of view.

R E V I E W   B R E A K

At this point, it is valuable to take a look at the differences among these three types of users to see the characteristics that help us create an optimal solution for that user group. The three aspects of our application that determine which class of user we are dealing with are the complexity of the interface, the amount and type of training required, and the flexibility of the application—versus being "task-driven" (see Table 4.1).

TABLE 4.1

TARGET USER TYPES

User Types	Application Interface Complexity	Training Type	Flexibility Requirements
Nontechnical users	Low complexity	Focused, task-oriented training	Low flexibility, highly specific application and help files

User Types	Application Interface Complexity	Training Type	Flexibility Requirements
Technical users	High complexity	Highly business oriented, tool usage	High flexibility, general, tool oriented, more general help files
Mixed users	Both	Both	Both

What Are Your Target User's Goals?

Just as architects who design homes should hold the owner's concerns as paramount above their own, so should human-computer interface designers hold the concerns of their users above their own.

Again in Alan Cooper's book, he points out that we should have a good understanding of the user's goals before we begin. A few examples of business goals that you might run across are as follows:

◆ Faster processing of orders

◆ More profit

◆ Higher customer satisfaction

In addition to business goals, users have personal goals. We often forget that users are human, with goals and desires that are different than the organization for which they work. These personal goals are as immutable as the business goals. If a solution falls short in either area, it has not met its objective. Some examples of personal goals might be the following:

◆ I don't want the software to make me feel stupid.

◆ I don't want the software to allow me to make unrecoverable mistakes.

◆ It should be better than or equal to what I have now.

This may seem like common sense. In fact, common sense is a good measuring stick to use when you design the interface.

Successful interface design centers around discovering the user's goals and then addressing them in the final solution. Unfortunately, even well-intentioned developers often get goals confused with features or tasks. Features are bullet points—things the software does. Features are a necessary part of a solution, but they are *not* goals.

Tasks are things the users do. Tasks are necessary things that the users of your system must do, but they are also not goals. They are how users get to their destination, but they are not the destination.

Some examples of things that are features or tasks rather than goals for a solution are the following:

◆ A database with referential integrity (feature)

◆ All command buttons are the same size (feature)

◆ Print an order (task)

◆ Change another user's password (task)

◆ Multithreaded processing (feature)

What Are the Goals at VitaMobile?

At VitaMobile, the main goal, as stated by the VP of Sales, is "...to take in orders from consumers more easily. We also need to speed up the processing of orders from both the consumers and our wholesale customers." That's pretty clear. The VP of Sales hinted at another goal later in the case study when she said, "Reliability for us equates to profitability. When our system is down, we lose money." Therefore, Vitamobile's goals for the new system seem to be the following:

◆ Customers can place orders easily.

◆ Order processing is fast and efficient.

◆ We do not incur outages that cause us to lose revenue.

Some of the features or tasks that will be utilized to accomplish these goals are things such as the use of laptops, accommodating the special needs of the billing department, building a reliable system, and building a better database.

Addressing the Needs of Mobile Users

In many cases, an application is used by someone who sits at a particular desk every day. It can be installed and set up in custom fashion just for them. In most workplace applications, this is the situation. A desktop computer is sitting at a particular user's desk. The application can be (but often is not) set up to know which user logs in from this machine.

However, this is not always the case. In some cases, such as electronic messaging, users will likely want to retrieve their messages from any desktop in the office. If they happen to be in a meeting, they would like to be able to use a nearby computer to check their electronic mail. This is the model used in many modern voice mail systems. From any phone, users can dial the extension and check their messages, even from across or outside the business.

As an even larger step toward mobility, users with portable computers may want the capability to work with the application anywhere they can take their computers.

Multiple Points of Access

This is the voice mail example previously discussed. In this model, an application prevents access to the overall system but allows any user to log in from any of the entrance points to the system.

Disconnected Access to an Application

Disconnected access to the application is access that is allowed to machines that change locations. In almost every case, this is a laptop machine. Two basic types of disconnected access are as follows:

- Internet-enabled applications
- Independently running applications

Internet-Enabled Applications

An Internet-enabled application allows the user to simulate a connection to the corporate network over the Internet, via a modem or across a LAN. It enables a laptop computer to continue working with an application from essentially any location, but it requires that the system be connected to the Internet or intranet, and thus to the corporate network, any time it is run. This is often achieved through technologies such as Virtual Private Networks (VPN).

Independent Applications

The most mobile of the user-system interfaces is the independent application. This enables a user to run completely without connection. A user with a laptop can simply open up the laptop and begin using the application. In this type of a model, a means of synchronization is usually provided, which allows changes made while the user was disconnected to eventually be recorded in a shared data store.

Mobility at VitaMobile

VitaMobile has several requirements for mobility. Most significant is the request from the salespeople to be able to "access orders for clients in real-time" and enable them to "look up billing issues." However, the salespeople make sales calls at various locations around the country, and they are certainly not always in a local calling area for the main offices. Consequently, if we are going to attempt to minimize the cost of using the system (that is, long-distance charges), we are probably looking at an Internet-enabled application with national dial-up accounts. This application would enable the sales staff to log in to the VitaMobile network and retrieve information while visiting a customer. This satisfies the requirements, but the downside is that it requires the salesperson to have access to a phone line to make the connection.

R E V I E W   B R E A K

If an application requires that users be allowed to "roam," it is important early on that the designer establish exactly what that phrase means in this context. As you have seen, it can have different meanings:

◆ Multiple points of access to an application within fixed positions

◆ Internet-enabled applications

◆ Independently running applications

Do Your Target Users Have Special Needs?

In any community of users, some will have special needs. Even one user can have special needs.

On one hand, this reminds us to be aware of these needs, to seek out those who might be out there today and to accommodate them as much as possible. On the other hand, it also points out that the goal of designing for special needs involves creating an application that can be extended to embrace new, unanticipated special needs, as well as to allow for current needs.

An example of special needs might be users who require "heads down" data entry, in which they need to focus their attention on a document rather than on the screen. This type of user cannot move between the keyboard and the mouse without substantially slowing down.

Accessibility Issues

Perhaps the most obvious and high-profile example of special needs in a system are users who are not able to productively use the standard Windows interface without modifications. Windows itself provides some of these features, but to make a system maximally accessible to users with special needs, you must analyze how the solution encourages users to work. Always be aware that in many subtle ways, particularly in UI design, well-intentioned, but poorly thought-out designs can make a system almost unusable to a portion of its target community.

A good example is drag-and-drop technology. If not implemented carefully, this is a classic case of a good idea gone bad for a portion of the user community. Drag-and-drop is a great *optional* tool, but it should never be the only way to do something. This is not simply because some users aren't able to use the mouse effectively, but also because many users would rather not constantly shift back and forth between the keyboard and the mouse. In either case, independent of any special user needs, the interface needs to support keyboard-based usage.

It might seem that we've concluded that the application developer is responsible for somehow anticipating and building in support for almost any conceivable problem in using Windows. However, this is not so. Not all accessibility issues rest on the shoulders of the application. For users who cannot effectively use the standard keyboard and mouse, many hardware products are available on the market, designed for users with different levels of mobility and control.

The key is to be aware of these issues while designing; begin investigating options early, so when the time comes that a problem needs to be addressed, you can provide information about the options and choices, both from a software and a hardware perspective.

Does VitaMobile Have Special Needs?

Yes, particularly from the perspective of one of the billing clerks. If you recall, one clerk made the comment that a bookkeeper had vision problems and had trouble looking at the current terminal-based screen for extended periods because the letters were too small. In this case, then, we may need to ensure that our application complies with the Windows specifications to use the Higher Contrast settings in the Control Panel.

Similarly, if VitaMobile is planning to increase consumer traffic on the Internet, as it says it is, it has opened itself up to a wide array of requirements. In the case of Internet-based customers, for example, an assumption is made that they have a way to use the Web browser, and so forth. These things are obviously outside the control of the Web application itself. However, you can ensure that things such as the font are either large enough to see or adjustable so that they can be made larger.

Not all accessibility issues are what would stereotypically be thought of as such. For example, a significant percentage of the population experiences partial or complete red/green color blindness. Although this may seem an insignificant inconvenience when it comes to computers, imagine a system that hard codes red as an indication that a value is inappropriate and green to indicate acceptable values. It might seem intuitive, but users who experience color blindness will be unable to distinguish between the two (or they will have great difficulty), and thus they will be unable to determine appropriate and inappropriate data.

NOTE

Special Needs Recognizing special needs among your user base, whether accessibility related or not, is an absolute essential when you design your system.

Localization Issues

Software localization is a very tricky issue to design for in an application. Localization is defined as enabling an application for use in different countries or for different languages. It is sometimes referred to as "internationalization." If it is a priority, it is important to be aware of it early. Essentially this introduces a level of indirection between your screen designs and the way those screens appear to the user. Rather than hard coding the labels for screens into the user interface itself, we can create lists, each of which populates the user interface with a set of labels in a language-specific format. These lists are stored in locale-specific DLLs. This allows us to compile a single EXE for the software itself and have multiple DLLs or resource files that can support the multinational locations.

This makes debugging an application much more challenging. If you are considering supporting a high degree of localization, make sure you consider all the issues associated with it. Linguistic experts should be engaged (native speakers, if possible, to capture idiom) to perform the translations.

The following are just some of the translation issues an application faces in an attempt to localize the code:

◆ Strings may be in a different language and thus, need to be replaced.

◆ Straight translation may not be possible in cases such as idioms (phrases that have a cultural meaning beyond the words that make them up). These need to have a context-based translation.

◆ Cultural symbols should be checked to ensure they retain their meaning between cultures.

◆ Particular attention should be paid to verify that no symbols have secondary meanings that might be offensive in a supported location.

◆ Text could run in the opposite direction, requiring repositioning of fields on the form, such as in Japanese Kanji.

◆ Care should be taken when sizing controls that hold text (for example, text boxes, labels, and combo boxes). The size of a message can vary with the language. This can present some very challenging screen layout issues.

◆ You might need an alternate set of characters, varying from just a few (French, Dutch, and so on) to a completely different alphabet (Arabic, Hebrew, Russian). This could require all the code in your application to be Unicode capable. Unicode uses two bytes for each character, significantly increasing the number of character codes.

Localization Issues with VitaMobile

VitaMobile says it is currently selling its product only in the United States. However, if it starts Internet sales or has increased consumer sales of any kind, the company may begin to attract business from other countries. In that case, it may be time to revisit the options for localization.

R E V I E W   B R E A K

Attempting to design a solution that will run seamlessly in multiple locales is a very difficult proposition. So many variables have to be accounted for in a complete language change that this kind of a design decision needs to be made early on, and it can dramatically affect your time specifications and/or cost estimates. It very often requires the development team to seek out specialized expertise in creating international-enabled applications.

Providing User Assistance

No matter how much we work at understanding our users or how sensitive we are to their needs, and no matter how well we train them, we aren't going to get everything completely perfect for everyone. And when end users have a problem with software, they do two things: they check the help menus, and then they call their help desk. Because every call to a help desk is basically more money being spent on the application, it is worthwhile to spend some time thinking about how user assistance can and should be provided.

Printed Documentation

One option—one that has been around for at least as long as any computer software—is to distribute a printed copy of documentation for the software. Normally this booklet contains information about installing software. It may also include a list of features and a few How To sections that outline basic operations with the software. The content of these manuals, however, is often strictly limited by the sheer weight of the booklets.

Electronic Documentation

It doesn't take long, after carrying around heavy manuals, to discover several problems with this approach. First, the book inherently carries a "knowledge versus weight" trade-off. Second, the proliferation of paper as more and more people use the application makes printing manuals for all who want them prohibitive. Lastly, an important issue exists related to updating this information. Errata sheets are a horrible way to do this, especially considering that no searches are available for errata sheets; they have to be manually referenced each time something is looked up to ensure that the manual is still correct.

It seems obvious, then, and it has become almost a standard practice, to include most of the help information in electronic form. Two methods of distribution for this information have been tried:

◆ Built-in help distributed with the application.

◆ Web-based help applications. These are Web sites with help information.

Built-in Help

A developer can build a set of compiled help screens into an executable file. One of the most common ways of doing this is using the Microsoft Help engine, which takes standard .rtf files and compiles them to allow them to be run inside the standard Microsoft Windows help interface. This file can then be distributed as part of the install process and can reside on each user's machine.

A newer version of this same utility can now compile HTML pages into a format that can be similarly used by Windows. The advantage of this is that it allows a much more straightforward construction of the help file, based on the Web metaphor. In the previous version, a fairly elaborate set of requirements exists for the layout of the RTF file that is going to be compiled. Microsoft uses this HTML format to distribute its MSDN and TechNet information to developers.

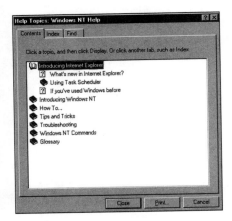

FIGURE 4.1
Windows help file interface.

Generally, two types of help are available. One consists of informational screens, offering the user information about what things mean or how they work. The other is a more task-oriented or tutorial help, breaking a particular topic down into step-by-step instructions. For example, for those needing to learn to draw tables, Word has a set of help screens that step through exactly how it is done.

This type of help is familiar to most users because it is the same interface included in products such as Microsoft Word, Excel, and even Windows itself (see Figure 4.1).

As Figure 4.1 illustrates, these help files generally have three views:

◆ A table of contents view, which allows a hierarchical navigation through topics in the help file, grouped by subject matter. This version essentially looks like an electronic version of a printed paper manual.

◆ An index tab, which behaves much like the index of a paper manual, providing completion for partially typed phrases.

◆ A Find or Search view, which scans the text and/or titles of pieces of the help file and reports any occurrences of the specified text.

Web-Based Help

An alternative gaining popularity lately, used in part to save space in distribution (whether on media or bandwidth), is to develop the user assistance application independently of the main solution. The help application, then, exists on the Internet, whereas the actual solution application is loaded onto local hard drives as always. Users then access help information via the Internet and a Web browser.

The advantages to this approach are numerous. First and foremost, maintenance and updates of the help file information are as simple as updating the Web server that hosts the help application. For the customer, the need to check help files for updates is no longer necessary because the newest help is always accessed when you visit the Web site.

However, like any big-advantage technical design, there are some pretty large disadvantages, as well. First, users who are not constantly connected to the Internet will likely become frustrated because of the requirement to dial up simply to use a help file. Second, your help application will now perform at the speed of the Internet, which means it may take an inordinate amount of time to connect, based on Internet traffic patterns and levels.

Other Help Strategies

In addition to the mainstream strategies previously mentioned for providing user help, several other tools are available in the developer's tool kit:

◆ **Frequently Asked Questions (FAQ) help**—Many business applications and commercial Web sites include a FAQ help area, where the answers to frequently asked questions are made available. These sections typically grow whenever the same question is repeatedly asked of customer service or support organizations. It is an inexpensive, albeit incomplete, version of "just-in-time" training.

◆ **ToolTips**—Familiar to every user of Windows and Windows applications, ToolTips are clearly a form of user help that is very effective.

◆ **"What's This?" help**—Enables the user to point to a specific control (text box, button, and so on) on the screen and request that the system explain the control's purpose.

◆ **F1**—As all programmers know, when in doubt, press <F1>. The user should have the same option.

User Assistance Design for VitaMobile

The user assistance needs for VitaMobile are probably best served with the Internet design for help. As we decided previously, the interface probably requires the users to be connected to the Internet when they are using the application remotely. So if the help files are also available primarily on the Internet, that isn't a big problem.

On the positive side, this allows us to have instantly updated help information that the remote sales team would never have to redownload and replace. We could potentially pay a performance penalty, but given the relatively small user base for the application (only the wholesale sales reps), it should be reasonably responsive.

To summarize, the user assistance types break down as shown in Table 4.2:

TABLE 4.2

USER ASSISTANCE TYPES

Help Types	Help File Location	Access Speed	Maintainability
Standard RTF/HTML help app.	Local hard drive, compiled form	Very fast	Difficult, manually redistributed to clients
Web-based help app.	Located on remote Web server, served to client Web browser	Could be much slower, Internet speed	Very high, no need to ever redistribute help files to clients
FAQ	Located on remote Web server, served to client Web browser	Could be much slower, Internet speed	Very high, no need to ever redistribute help files to clients
ToolTips, F1	Local hard drive, compiled form	Very fast	Difficult, manually redistributed to clients

Physical Environment Constraints

Sometimes planning, designing, and observing are not enough. If you have physical constraints on how you are allowed to provide the interface to your target users, you don't want to think of the constraints as ruining your design efforts. Instead, think along the lines that you are now being challenged to try to find the best solution *given the problems that you know exist*. For example, consider a system in which data must be transported across a telephone line. Clearly, this affects the architecture of the system. Consider the changes that would be necessary if the business validation logic used by an application were connected across a satellite WAN instead of a LAN that extends across the room.

Similarly, it is very possible that the type of environment will constrain some other aspects of the interface. For example, if the environment does not permit a group training session (for example, a distributed company where people do not work in physical proximity to one another), the ideal set of training exercises may not be possible. Instead, the training of users may be left up to the help files in an application. This puts most of the load of how the system gets used on only one aspect of the interface.

Other, more exotic, physical constraints often present themselves. Some applications support users on an industrial shop floor, where the environment makes the use of a mouse impractical.

The recent proliferation of Windows CE computers brings back a constraint that most developers thought was behind them—that of designing interfaces to fit within a 640 x 480 resolution screen.

CHAPTER SUMMARY

We've seen that after you recognize that most problems software is commissioned to solve begin with people and not with other software, the priority is clear. The only interface that really matters, in the end, is the interface with humans. If the users have their problems solved and their goals met, the ugliness behind the scenes isn't going to matter to them. If a user can be trained quickly and efficiently to use tools, then whether they are the most gracious tools will never enter that user's mind.

One of the most important ways that software designers can make sure they are solving the human problems that prompt software to be built is by making sure they know their target user group. Understanding this enables you to make intelligent decisions about what kinds of training the users will want for an application. It may help to create a fictitious user in excruciating detail, and then design the system to that user. An old saying goes, "When you try to please everyone, you end up pleasing no one."

In addition, by knowing your users, you can see to what extent they are currently (or are expecting to be) roaming. Roaming users are a special breed, and design decisions need to be made based on how many roamers are expected.

CHAPTER SUMMARY

KEY TERMS

- Accessibility
- Human-computer interface
- Localization
- Physical environment constraints
- Roaming users
- Target user group

Finally, getting to know the user group reminds you to address special needs. Many of the needs that currently exist may be something you are able to incorporate into the application. Equally important, however, is recognizing that the makeup of the target user group may change. This may result in new, unanticipated needs. The critical issue here is to design the system so that it is extensible to handle these issues down the line with minimal effort.

You should be aware of the goals for which you are designing—both business goals and personal goals. By meeting the user's goals in these two areas, you are more likely to "wow" them. It is a good feeling when users heap unsolicited praise on a system that you helped design.

Next, we looked at the effect that getting to know the users has on our distribution of the software. Specifically, when you know you may be distributing internationally or to primarily non-English speaking communities, you may have additional localization problems. In addition to obvious things such as translations of labels, you may also encounter problems of idiom that defy translation, metaphor differences between cultures, or even different screen layout requirements based on the user community.

We looked at various methods of user support. These methods enable an application to distribute extra information on system features or explain how to accomplish certain tasks within the system. This can be distributed as a book or a booklet, or in an electronic format. If it is distributed electronically, we can either do so to local machines, or if we are relatively confident of Internet access among users, we could put the help files online.

Finally, we looked at the reality of imperfect conditions. As computer software developers who are used to building everything ourselves, we often forget that a real, physical world exists outside of the software, and it may impact our ability to provide the kind of interface we would like for the software. Whether it is by constraining Internet access or because the physical locations of the users do not permit training sessions in the traditional sense, the physical environment in which a solution is deployed can constrain the human-computer interface.

APPLY YOUR KNOWLEDGE

Exercises

4.1 Styles of Help

Read each sample of a help statement below. For each of them, decide whether they are task oriented (TO), feature oriented (FO), or information oriented (IO).

TABLE 4.3

CLASSIFYING HELP STATEMENTS

Help File Statement	Help Type
"To enter new orders into the VitaMobile system, you begin by pressing the "n" key on the keyboard."	
"This button is the OK button, which will save your data and move on in the order process."	
"Pivot tables are a very powerful tool that can be used with our new data storage. The tables can be built into Microsoft Excel and can contain parent-child relationships."	
"Printing a report is simple; just start by going to the File menu."	
"This field will only accept dates in a proper format; all other data will be rejected."	

Answers: TO, FO, IO, TO, FO

Review Questions

1. If VitaMobile had been selling and supplying information on its products on the Internet for several years already, what effect would this have on your classification of the target user group?

2. What would be the effect on your project if a decision were made to move all users at VitaMobile to laptops? What specific area of appraisal would this impact most heavily?

3. How can you design your solution to make sure you've done your part in addressing special needs in the user base?

4. How does it change your solution if, in six months, VitaMobile decides to open two new marketplaces—Mexico and Brazil?

5. Under which circumstances would it clearly not be a good option to use Internet-based help files?

6. If you wanted to make sure the new system addressed the needs of the major users at VitaMobile, how many distinct profiles, or "personas," would you consider?

Exam Questions

1. Which of the following would be the logical starting point for identifying human factor requirements?

   A. Statement of problem.

   B. Identification of target users.

   C. Establish preferences among users.

   D. Classify users.

2. What would be the most effective way of providing for utilizing an application in several areas and potentially in multiple languages?

   A. Writing multiple executable modules for each locale.

APPLY YOUR KNOWLEDGE

B. Writing a single executable with options to select a language, which uses "lookup" DLLs for all text displayed to the user.

C. Separating the user interface from the business logic, and writing multiple user interfaces.

D. Constructing a single executable that uses a database to load locale information.

3. Which of the following is a characteristic of applications designed for a technical user base?

A. Training is geared toward process completion.

B. More specific uses for software.

C. The application tends to present a simpler UI.

D. User will often require greater flexibility from the application.

4. What kind of accessibility issues does the case study lead us to believe that VitaMobile has?

A. Keyboard independence

B. Blindness/eye strain

C. Mouse independence

D. Impossible to determine from facts given

5. Who are the target users of the solution for VitaMobile? (Choose all that apply.)

A. Sales reps

B. Billing and data entry clerks

C. Customers

D. VP of Sales

E. Programmers

6. Which of the following could be considered as goals for the new system? (Choose two.)

A. Setting up security so that the reps cannot change each others' orders

B. Allowing the sales reps to place orders while located at customers' sites

C. Internet-enabling the application

D. Allowing customers to place their own orders

7. You are the designer for the solution outlined above. It has been stated that support for mobile users is needed. In this situation, which type of remote use would be most practical?

A. Internet-enabling the application.

B. Building the application to run independently.

C. Either method is equally practical for this case.

D. There are no remote users.

8. Which of these would be a special need most likely to be found in the VitaMobile application? (Choose one.)

A. Large, onscreen fonts

B. Telephony capabilities for all users

C. Internet-based help

D. Verbal commands and audio interfaces

9. How does localization affect the VitaMobile solution?

A. It doesn't.

B. By offering the menu in other languages, more customers are reached.

C. Localization is a technical issue and never should affect a solution.

D. We don't need to know yet what the localization decisions are; they can come at a later time.

10. What does localization mean?

A. Customizing the delivery application based on local maps and information.

B. Only allowing delivery locally.

C. Building an application that can support multiple languages and/or cultures in its interfaces.

D. None of the above.

11. You are responsible for ongoing user assistance in the VitaMobile case study. Understanding that the system is designed to support a certain class of mobile users who will not be able to connect to a network, which of these would be the best means of providing for help documentation?

A. Printed documentation in a book format.

B. Documentation in a document format that can be printed loose-leaf style and carried.

C. Built-in help documents within the application.

D. Web-based help documents.

12. You are the designer for the VitaMobile application. A decision has been made to build a laptop-based solution for the sales reps. Which of these is least likely to become an issue because of the decision?

A. Supplying hardware to employees.

B. Deciding how this application will be connected (if at all) while the reps are at the customer site.

C. Whether to require the use of a mouse to use the application.

D. Support for sales reps with laptop problems (hardware or software).

13. Which of the following approaches would be useful to make sure that the target users of your application are pleased? (Choose all that apply.)

A. Use the "least common denominator" approach and design to your most novice user.

B. Build detailed profiles of typical users and build the system to support their goals.

C. Put yourself in the position of the user and design it the way you would want it.

D. Let the user's goals drive the features and the interface behavior.

Answers to Review Questions

1. Generally, clients who have been this exposed to the Internet and who trade over the Internet are probably fairly technically savvy, even if they are not technically proficient. This would likely move them from a low-tech to a mid-to high-tech user group. See "Who Are Your Target Users?"

2. This would radically increase the chances that we would have roaming users. The area that would require the most increased attention would be those services that supported mobile users. See "Addressing the Needs of Mobile Users."

APPLY YOUR KNOWLEDGE

3. As we've previously discussed, it is impossible to anticipate and address every single special need that may come up. However, one thing we can specifically do to make sure we're doing our part is to never build functionality into the application that *requires* the use of the mouse. See "Do Your Target Users Have Special Needs?"

4. Presumably, if they were going to sell in those markets, they would do so in the native languages. This would require our Web pages, perhaps, to support options to view the catalog in another language. In addition, because we had local salespeople in those areas, we would need to have our wholesale ordering software set up to use other languages to label and take orders. In both cases, we would need to add the support for language files, using compiled DLLs or resource files, to substitute text on a reusable "base" form. See "Localization Issues."

5. If the users were not normally expected to be logged on to the Internet (for example, salespeople at the client site normally would not be), then whenever they needed help, they would have to make a special point of getting logged on. Also, if Internet access is not part of the company's strategy, it would usually be inappropriate to establish a Web server just to support help. See "Web-Based Help."

6. At the least, we would define a customer, a salesperson, a billing clerk, and a data entry clerk. According to Alan Cooper, you would build a persona to represent each of these and then design specifically to meet their needs and goals. See "Who Are Your Target Users?"

Answers to Exam Questions

1. **B.** Human factor requirements are determined by the information passed back and forth between people and the computer. This can really begin only after we have reached a consensus on who the people are that need a solution. Statement of the problem may begin the process as a whole, but specifically for identifying human factor requirements, **B** is the correct choice. See "Who Are Your Target Users?"

2. **B.** A system that needs to run in multiple languages or among multiple cultures is said to have localization issues. These issues can most effectively be resolved by compiling a single executable, which 'looks up' string values for interfaces in one of several library files that can be distributed as DLLs (or resource files) with the application. See "Localization Issues."

3. **D.** Answers A, B, and C are all characteristics of a nontechnical user base. On the other hand, pressure to increase the flexibility of a tool or an application is often the sign of a technical user base, which is interested in and capable of applying a tool in ways that the designer has not anticipated. See "Technical Target Users."

4. **B.** From the facts we read in the case study, a reference is made to a user who has trouble seeing the screen. See "Accessibility Issues."

APPLY YOUR KNOWLEDGE

5. **A, B, C, D.** The system has specific uses for the sales reps, the VitaMobile clerks, and the customers. It seems reasonable to imply that the VP of Sales will be a user as well, probably to track the aggregate performance of all the sales reps. Failure to identify *implicit* users can often cause political issues later in the cycle. However, there is no indication that programmers will directly interact with the system after it is built. See the case study "Envisioned System."

6. **B, D.** Choice A is not a goal; it is a feature of the application. Likewise, C is a means to achieve choice D, not a goal in itself. See "What Are the Target User's Goals?"

7. **B.** The system will be roaming with sales reps who do not have a real-time connection. As such, the most practical method is to allow remote users by letting them carry the whole application with them. See "Addressing the Needs of Mobile Users."

8. **A.** The billing department has stated a special need for oversized fonts in the user interface. See "Addressing Special Needs."

9. **A.** It was stated explicitly that VitaMobile is only addressing business in the United States at this time. See "Localization Issues."

10. **C.** Localization is the process of building software so that it can be utilized by people using a different language or working in a different country. See "Localization Issues."

11. **C.** The system is designed to be used by different types of people, some of whom are not set up in an office setting. Consequently, the notion of printed manuals is probably not a practical one, whether they are printed as a bound manuscript or as loose sheets. Similarly, because users are not connected to the Web while they are on the move, stationing our help application on the Web will effectively prevent them from using it while they are conducting a large part of their day-to-day work. The most obvious answer, then, is to have a Windows help file built into the application. See "Providing User Assistance."

12. **C.** Although this might be an issue, no matter whether the users were remote, the information needs to be on the right screens; therefore, this decision would not have caused it to become an issue. On the other hand, each of the other issues would be raised by the decision. See "Physical Environment Constraints."

13. **B, D.** As stated in the text, try to please everyone and you will likely please no one. Therefore, A is an ineffective approach. C is also not correct because it presumes that the user has the same priorities as you do. See "Who Are Your Target Users?"

APPLY YOUR KNOWLEDGE

Suggested Readings and Resources

1. Cooper, Alan. *About Face: The Essentials of User Interface Design.* IDG Books, 1995.

2. Cooper, Alan. *The Inmates Are Running the Asylum.* Sams, 1999.

3. Heckel, Paul. *The Elements of Friendly Software Design.* SYBEX Publishing, 1991.

4. *Windows Interface Guidelines for Software Design.* Microsoft Press, 1995.

This chapter addresses the following exam objectives listed by Microsoft for this section of the Analyzing Requirements and Defining Solution Architectures exam:

Analyze the requirements for integrating a solution with existing applications. Considerations include

- **Legacy applications**

- **Format and location of existing data**

- **Connectivity to existing applications**

- **Data conversion**

- **Data enhancement requirements**

▶ An application that is deployed within an existing enterprise will often involve technical integration issues. The legacy of previously rolled-out applications influences how we look at data, connectivity, and application design itself. If backward compatibility must be maintained, it is important to find out in what ways they must be connected.

Analyze existing methodologies and limitations of a business. Considerations include

- **Legal issues**

- **Current business practices**

- **Organization structure**

- **Process engineering**

- **Budget**

- **Implementation and training methodologies**

- **Quality control requirements**

- **Customer's needs**

CHAPTER 5

Integration Issues

▶ Even if you are lucky enough to avoid a situation with a great deal of technical integration, you are probably ensuring an even greater amount of non-technical, business process integration.

▶ Part of the goal of system development should be to investigate the reason that work is done the way it is and to see whether, in the process of automation, we can also improve the way work is done.

▶ While a solution may offer efficiency and improvements in quality, a technical project will always be met with resistance if it tries to "take on" the standard means of doing business. It is almost never appropriate for a technical project to drive business change in an organization. Rather, it should be the other way around. Business should drive the technical direction of the project.

▶ Identify the primary ways in which a legacy application can affect development of a new solution.

▶ Identify some of the issues and approaches to dealing with connectivity to existing applications.

▶ Decide between various means of converting legacy data and determine which is appropriate in a given circumstance.

▶ Show how the current business practices in a situation can constrain or enhance your ability to provide an optimal solution for your client.

▶ Give examples of process engineering and show how it differs from simple reimplementation.

▶ List the major legal "land mines" to be aware of during solution design and implementation.

INTRODUCTION

Working with new solutions often involves replacing or augmenting older systems. This process is generally known as technical integration. As you might guess, a nontechnical form of integration also focuses on the business process and how the new solution should be built, used, taught, and executed.

CASE STUDY: THE COPY SHOP

BACKGROUND

The CopyShop is a chain of commercial, rapid-printing service shops. Each day, in more than 25 shops around the Denver, Colorado area, it runs 100,000 copy and special-print orders. Currently the stores are locally managed but centrally supplied, a situation that the main office would like to change. Complaints about quality control among offices has prompted a look at more centralized management of the offices.

PROBLEM STATEMENT

CopyShop is experiencing some problems of late with quality control. The various branch managers are running their shops independently of the directives of the central office. Because there is no good routing system for requests, approvals, and supplies, the movement of supplies is ineffective and mistakes are frequent.

Central Manager

"We have a communication problem. This company was built on strong communication among the employees, and lately, our growth has made that very difficult. We used to be in a single larger office, and people would just walk over and ask things. Now we're scattered all over the city."

Branch Manager

"No one at the main office knows what is going on. The process to get supplies seems to be getting more and more cumbersome each year. I can barely react to spikes in my business."

Supply Clerk

"About six months ago, when they realized what the problems were with the current system, the central management started to ask us to get approval for each supply order before we sent it. That's fine, but approval from who? Our software for managing inventory today doesn't even have places to type in where we send things—just the date they are sent out."

CURRENT SYSTEM

The current system at CopyShop is an older AS/400-based system located in the main office. Currently, no means exists of accessing this system from the branch offices. Consequently, all contact between the branches and the main office is done by phone, fax, and U.S. mail. The system tracks inventory only at the central office. For internal billing purposes, it keeps track of what each shop orders, but it stops short of tracking each shop's inventory.

Because the mainframe system utilizes a bar-code scanner for the warehouse, management would like keep the old system running and augment it with the new solution.

Branch Manager

"The system they use at the main office does nothing for us. I can't get at the system unless I want to drive over to their offices."

Shipping Clerk

"The system works pretty well for what it is. We've got some vendor-specific software we've used for years, which we can dump numbers out of into our inventory programs. This saves us

CASE STUDY: THE COPY SHOP

some time. We love the bar-code system. We can find anything in the warehouse in minutes. I hope they don't change that.

But on the other hand, the inventory program does a really lousy job of tracking inventory in the shops. We get a lot of emergency calls for supplies. We'd like to see that get fixed."

ENVISIONED SYSTEM

CopyShop has conceived a system that picks up where the current mainframe program leaves off. When inventory goes out the dock and to shops, the new system kicks in and provides a nearly seamless inventory-tracking system.

Central Manager

"Our new system needs to provide the shops with the capability to order their own supplies. It should automatically approve orders that fall within defined thresholds. If the branch managers abuse the system, we'll deal with that on the side. Maybe someday we can enhance the new system to completely replace the old system. It's getting harder and harder to find COBOL people to maintain the old stuff."

"We intend to use new technology so that we don't run into the same problem of being out-of-date. To make sure that we don't get in over our heads, we intend to roll out the solution to a pilot shop first. If all goes well, we can start the process of rolling out to the other shops."

Branch Manager

"All I really need are two things. First, I need an effective and fast way to get approval for new supplies and to get the order placed. Second, I need a way to keep track of inventory here in my shop. We often have to place urgent orders to the central office because we didn't have an accurate count of our supplies. We need to get that fixed."

Programmer

"We've got expertise in Visual Basic and SQL Server. Anything we build should use those technologies so that we can maintain it."

Supply Clerk

"I need to have a system that lets me keep better track of who orders what. Also, if we're going to have to continue to get approval for every order, I'd like to have the system handle making the request for me rather than always bothering people."

ANALYZING APPLICATION INTEGRATION REQUIREMENTS

Analyze the requirements for integrating a solution with existing applications.

Implementing a solution in an existing environment creates concerns that do not exist in a new environment. Most important is that when we replace one solution with another, it generally requires that functionality not be lost in the transfer.

This raises the issue of what applications are in use in the enterprise before the new solution is implemented. The common term for such applications are legacy applications, so named because they are the legacy of the existing system, and they must be carried on or accounted for in another way by any replacement system.

Therefore, our logical first step is to look at what legacy applications might exist that must be replaced or augmented by our new solution. The next step is to see how the different applications communicate and how that communication can be continued in a new system. Finally, we can look at the various options for data conversion from a legacy system to a newer one.

What Are the Legacy Applications?

A good place to start when you're designing a solution is to look at what solution already exists. As a designer deploying applications into existing enterprises (of whatever size), it is a necessity to think about the currently existing solutions. Am I replacing an old system? Am I expected to maintain connection points between other systems and the one I am specifically replacing? Am I going to need to interface with legacy data? Depending on the line of business for which you are designing a solution, an extensive archive of legacy data may needs to somehow be accessible in the new system.

Another important issue is the process that will be used to move the new solution into production. Does the crossover need to be totally seamless? Can there be downtime over the weekend to switch over to the new system? Sometimes, migration can be gradual, using pilot users or sites, and sometimes the migration needs to be accomplished in a few hours or less.

> **NOTE**
>
> **What Constitutes a Legacy Application?**   In this chapter, most of our examples place the legacy application on a mainframe. A legacy application could just as easily be another client/server application. All the same strategies apply. Legacy is a generic term that refers to any application that is built around older technology. These days, that could mean it was built last year.

In the next sections, we'll look at the major styles of integration with legacy solutions that can occur:

◆ Starting with a "clean slate"

◆ Retaining a legacy application

◆ Wrapping legacy code or screen scraping

Clean Slate

A clean slate could mean one of two things: Either no legacy solution exists, or the existing legacy solution is going to be completely replaced.

If no previous solution exists, this may seem to be the ideal situation from a design perspective. Indeed, it gives us a great deal of freedom to design the solution the way we would like. We have nothing to integrate with, we have nothing to emulate, no business rules must be reproduced, and our design is not constrained by preexisting conditions.

The downside of having no previous solution is almost the same list. If nothing exists to integrate with, we must do everything ourselves. If nothing is available to emulate, we must discover all the business patterns ourselves during analysis. If the business rules do not exist, we must build them from scratch rather than using "recover current design."

The bottom line is that if there is no existing solution, you must do all the analysis and design work from scratch. You must do the interviews, the flow charts, and the workflow analysis. With that extra work, however, comes the freedom to attack the problem in a fresh way, with fewer preconceived notions about how it ought to be done. The move into production is easier, as well, when there is no existing application, because you don't have to consider the issues related to switching over to the new application without interrupting business.

On the other hand, you may deal with a situation where there is an existing application, and you are asked to replace it with a better solution. The upside here is that analysis and design will go more quickly. You recover the business rules and work patterns from the legacy application. Your interview process is usually shorter because the users discuss improvements "piled on top of the current functionality." You don't have to start from scratch.

> **NOTE**
>
> **Recover Current Design** When existing code is to be replaced, we can often salvage useful information. This is known as recover current design. Most of the time, it is not an option. For example, if a business rule in a legacy application states that we cannot sell to any customer who is more than $1,000 past due, that rule needs to make its way into the new system. Some business rules are discovered the hard way, through mistakes and the passage of time. It would be inefficient and unwise to put the replacement application through the same learning curve.

The downside is that the design is often constrained by functionality that exists in the current system. Users are very reluctant to get a new system that is a "downgrade" from their current solution. You might hear things such as, "The screen is nicer to look at, but the old system was faster." Or "I had all the keystrokes to get from one screen to another memorized. Now I need to constantly switch between my keyboard and my mouse to get around."

Retaining a Legacy Application

Sometimes a solution is designed to extend or augment an existing application. In these instances, our new solution must coexist with the legacy application.

An example of this is a decision support system (see Figure 5.1). The legacy system houses the production data. Users perform their work against mainframe screens and mainframe databases. Work continues pretty much as it has since the legacy system was installed.

Our solution starts where the current system ends. Each night, a batch job grabs the day's activities from the database, aggregates the data at the appropriate level, and stores the results in specially built SQL Server tables. A new graphical application supports ad hoc and preconfigured queries against the new data stores.

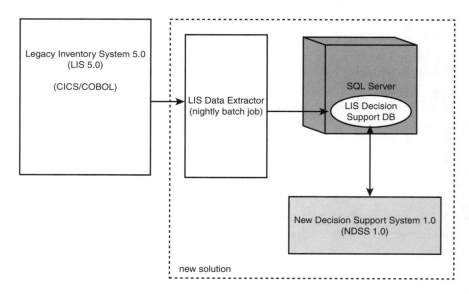

FIGURE 5.1

Augmenting an existing legacy solution.

In the preceding example, the two systems were related tangentially. Sometimes the integration is much more tightly coupled. An example that is common to most everyone (certainly everyone reading this book) is Microsoft Word for Windows (see Figure 5.2). Word is built upon the foundation established by Windows. It is written in a language that, at its core, makes calls to the operating system in such a way as to provide word processor capability out of the "ingredients" provided by various graphical, user, and computational API calls. Word depends on Windows. Word extends Windows; Windows existed first. Word was a clever way to augment the existing logic of Windows to provide new functionality.

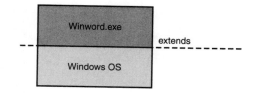

FIGURE 5.2
Tightly coupled integration.

Generally speaking, the important questions to ask when integrating with an existing solution are

◆ What is this new application using the existing application for?

◆ What kind of interaction is expected between the two applications?

◆ Does this interaction need to be real-time?

◆ Do the applications directly communicate, or is it enough to have them share a data store?

◆ What is the topology of the communication? Does it involve a LAN or a WAN? What languages or protocols are involved?

Wrapping Legacy Code or Screen Scraping

As we stated earlier, situations exist in which an enterprise is, by design, allowing two applications that perform the same business functions to coexist. The business reasons for this might range from budget constraints to technology challenges where the combined applications (old and new) can do something that neither of them can do alone. The reason might be to simplify user training, to retain mainframe performance, or to address time constraints that require the new solution to go live in a short time.

This may be the most difficult of the options for a developer or a development staff. Often, an appropriate way to approach this is to ask what is expected from the new application that is not present in the old one.

One common approach is to wrap legacy code in new components. An example is to make a connection between an old application and a new one. We can wrap the legacy code in a COM wrapper, allowing one or more new applications to communicate using current technology (COM) rather than older, proprietary protocols. In this way, we protect our entire investment in the old business rules, data stores, and such while allowing new components to interact more easily with the legacy code.

In Figure 5.3, the legacy system remains intact and is wrapped by the new code. We could use MSMQ or COMTI to connect the wrapper to the legacy code. How we choose to do so is abstracted from the new application. It knows only that it can call the wrapper as if it were a COM component and get information stored on the mainframe, utilizing any business rules built into the legacy application.

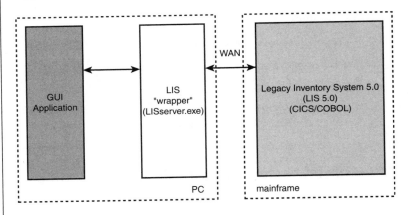

FIGURE 5.3
Wrapping legacy code.

NOTE

COMTI COMTI stands for COM Transaction Integrator. When we are discussing integrating PC applications with legacy applications that run on a mainframe, it is important to understand the benefits that COMTI can provide. COMTI allows MTS to run transactions on CICS or IMS on an IBM MVS mainframe. This allows the client/server architect to access and run legacy code directly, reusing all the analysis and design that went into it. This can speed up the development process significantly, in addition to using code that has already been tested and used in a production setting. When combined with MSMQ (see the note "MSMQ" in this chapter), this means that you can asynchronously trigger a CICS transaction to run on the mainframe and be notified when it completes. This opens up tremendous options for wrapping or reusing legacy code in an n-tier solution. For more information, see the MSDN article, "Using Microsoft Transaction Server 2.0 with COM Transaction Integrator 1.0."

The other strategy, which is used quite frequently in integrating a new solution with an existing one, is known as screen scraping. Screen scraping is the act of placing a new façade in front of an existing mainframe or character-based screen. ASCII characters are "scraped" off the screen, interpreted using static data that knows the location of "fields" on the screens, and rerepresented in a graphical format. The screen becomes the equivalent of production data, having already been subjected to the business rules that drive the mainframe screen. A single screen is analogous to a record in a table, and each piece of data on the screen (for example, Customer Name, Zip Code, Billing Date) is a field in that record. Several vendors offer 3270 and 5250 emulators that are COM-enabled and can serve as the integration point between the two worlds.

Screen scraping can add the Windows look and feel to a legacy mainframe application for far fewer dollars and in far less time than it would take to completely rewrite the system as a client/server solution. It can often extend the life of a legacy system by years. Often, it provides a better response than a client/server replacement because it is technically a two-tier, "fat client" architecture.

The other advantage of screen scraping is that the user services component can usually be built to extend functionality horizontally beyond what the legacy application provides (see Figure 5.4). Examples include enabling the sending of email through Microsoft Outlook from a legacy screen, using the Windows clipboard to store temporary data, or using the Windows registry to create an application that remembers information about the user and the user's preferences.

The downside of screen scraping is that you are restricted to the screen flow of the mainframe application. Although your application can allow the users to think that they are jumping directly from one screen to another, the code must send the appropriate keystrokes behind the scenes to navigate from one screen to another. This impacts the perceived response time to the user. Another downside is that you are really maintaining two applications. Both the mainframe application and the GUI application must be maintained, and changes to one must be carefully thought out because they may impact the other.

NOTE

MSMQ The majority of development has been and continues to be synchronous. In synchronous calls, the client calls the server to perform a task, and the client blocks until the server returns with some sort of results. Although ways exist to create asynchronous processing between components, MSMQ offers a new level of dependability and interaction between heterogeneous environments and long distances. MSMQ allows the developer to send asynchronous message to a queue, with guaranteed delivery to the destination. Although MSMQ does not use an email transport, it can be compared to email. MSMQ uses a "push" strategy where messages are packaged, sent to a queue, picked up later by the recipient, acted upon, and then a response is put back in the queue for later pickup by the original sender. This gives the architect freedom to do background tasks and still allow the user to do other work while the background task is processing elsewhere, probably on a different machine. For more information, perform an MSDN search on the keyword "MSMQ."

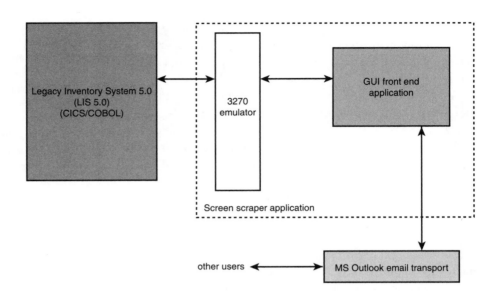

FIGURE 5.4
Mainframe "screen-scraping" integration.

Integration at the CopyShop

The obvious question here is to ask which of the integration styles we are dealing with in our case study. The legacy application seems to serve the needs of the central office just fine. In fact, the bar-code capability is exalted. Therefore, we are not dealing with a clean slate scenario.

The solution doesn't seem to call for a wrapper or a screen-scraper solution because the current system is incomplete. It isn't just a matter of adding a fresh interface to a competent system. The new solution needs to do things that the old system does not provide.

Therefore, it appears that we will be extending the existing system—that is, retaining a legacy application. We will need to connect to the CICS system, but our new solution begins where the existing system ends. The existing system will serve the needs of the central office and the new system will serve the outlying shops.

That will require us to spend time analyzing and designing the touchpoint—where the two systems meet.

Because the new solution addresses an area of inventory that doesn't even exist today, it appears that rollout (deployment) of the new solution will be less complicated. There is no need for a hard switchover date.

At this point, it is probably important to take a look at what we've seen about integration requirements. Legacy systems radically increase the amount of integration work that needs to be done. This is the case whether you are replacing a legacy system yourself, or whether other legacy applications are in the enterprise with which you must communicate.

Essentially, the three main categories for legacy applications are clean slate, fully retained legacy applications, and those with wrapped integration issues.

What Options Exist for Establishing Connectivity with Existing Applications?

One of the most challenging aspects of working with legacy systems—and in fact when working with integration in general—is analyzing the different methods of communication used by applications. In the past few years, several standards for interprocess communication were introduced that have been fairly widely adopted. However, if your legacy application is more than four years old, the odds are that it wasn't able to take advantage of these innovations.

Selecting the most appropriate communication method is critical in any attempt to integrate a solution into a set of enterprise applications. Essentially, you will find that the communication falls into one of the following four areas:

◆ Binary compatibility (COM)

◆ SNA server (or other Gateway-type products)

◆ Nonstandard connectivity

◆ Industry standard protocols

Binary Compatibility (COM)

In the middle and late 1990s, several binary standards in the PC/server area emerged. These standards proposed a new way of organizing communication between applications. They advocated a common standard for compiled binary code. In the Microsoft Windows world, this is accomplished by COM/DCOM/COM+, which is essentially an operating-system-level set of services. Every piece of software is entitled to behave as it likes internally, but it must maintain a standard interface when communicating with other components.

This allows applications to communicate with one another through a standardized mechanism, which should be very straightforward to reimplement in the new application.

We have already touched on this in our earlier example of wrapping legacy code. By doing this, we can make an application written in 1977 appear to be a component that was written last month.

SNA Server

Not all systems were written for PC computers—especially in larger legacy systems. Until very recently, they were almost 100 percent written for mainframes. At the last estimate, nearly 70 percent of the data stored in computers in the world was held on mainframes in a style that is not natively accessible to PCs.

In the past, the solution to this has been products that would enable the opening of a terminal window in the PC environment, allowing mainframe usage to continue as normal on the desktop. However, this completely fails to take advantage of the fact that the users normally do not have the green-screen mainframe terminals of the past, but fairly powerful desktop PCs.

To take advantage of this computing power, though, the location of the data becomes an issue. Microsoft's SNA Server is designed to allow connectivity to IBM mainframes and other, larger computer systems. This allows users to have a better experience than a simple terminal emulation mode when they use the application.

Before you can realistically think about implementing anything such as this, however, it is necessary to investigate what relation your project might have to the corporate mainframe data. In most cases, many applications will be using this data for different purposes. It is a very different skill-set that needs to be leveraged to properly design a fast, stable application in this space. Most mainframe data is stored and accessed using COBOL programs, so someone with those skill-sets will probably need to be leveraged if any significant effort in this area is undertaken.

SNA Servers connect the PC-based LAN to IBM host mainframes, supporting various standard protocols (for example, LU 6.2, APPC, 3270, and 5250 (AS/400) emulation).

SNA connectivity is very powerful. When you are connecting a PC-based LAN application to IBM mainframes, it can hardly be avoided.

The biggest benefit to the architect is that SNA Server consolidates mainframe connectivity in one place, creating a more stable solution that is less complicated than having each PC set up to connect to the mainframe directly. SNA Server offers LU "pooling" and reduces the load on client PC memory, allowing an underconfigured client PC to connect to the mainframe more reliably.

Nonstandard Connectivity

Sometimes we simply need to build our own connectivity. This usually happens when the solution calls for shared data stores or when the entire solution is "in house."

An example is an object model that gets its persistent data from the same place that the legacy application does. Connectivity is non-standard because it will work only at the company and for the application it was designed to integrate with.

Industry Standard Protocols

The computer industry has several very successful standards that assist developers in building applications at different times, by different people, that can interact with different development platforms or machines.

Common examples are HTML, TCP/IP, and EDI. Using industry standards has obvious advantages. Using industry standards in your solution allows you to more easily connect with other applications (or in the case of HTML, with browsers). Also, you do not need to design a comprehensive protocol. You can take advantage of a mature, tested protocol.

When communicating across machines or across applications within the PC area, using established standards is almost always a good move.

Connecting to the CopyShop

CopyShop does have connections, as we've seen, to an AS/400. However, the information clearly shows that it does not use the binary compatibility standards that we have described.

It appears that the best choice might be an SNA Server gateway that allows us access, either through COMTI or directly to the data stores, using one of the database-bridging technologies discussed in the next section.

To What Extent Must Data Be Converted Between Applications?

Probably the most common integration point of any large application is in relation to data. Normally at least some sort of pipeline allows data to be accessed by different applications.

The most common way of accomplishing this is with an enterprise database. This might be a database on the mainframe, as we've talked about before, or it might be a replicated database on a server somewhere. In either case, the idea is the same: to allow multiple applications to be able to utilize the same data.

From our perspective, as the designers of a new application, we need to have several database-specific questions answered:

◆ What is the format and location of existing data?

◆ What kind of data enhancements are required?

◆ Can we use any industry standard tools for data access, such as ODBC or OLE DB?

Format and Location of Existing Data

Obviously, the first question we have to ask when we're thinking about data is whether a legacy data source exists. Whether on the mainframe or a PC, a flat file or a relational database, it is important to establish that it exists and how it is formatted.

If sustaining the older database is a priority, whether the data is in a SQL-based database is going to have a great effect on what options are available. We will see how we might overcome this, though, later in this chapter.

Required Data Enhancements

One of the most common reasons for redesigning a system is that the data requirements have changed. Most often, redesigning is done so that the amount of information captured includes information that is relevant and helpful to business today, but that was either not available, not helpful, or not deemed a priority when the legacy system was built.

The data model must be designed or, in the case of an existing data model, redesigned to try to capture as many of these new elements as is feasible. However, a great deal of care needs to be taken with this because in many cases, the data model could be shared with other applications. In these cases, it is critical to remember that because our goal is to increase productivity, making changes that make it much harder (or even impossible) to get some data is obviously a bad thing. Remember, too, that you probably aren't familiar with all the ways that everyone uses the data. If changes are made without consulting all groups, negative fallout will almost surely occur. As carpenters often say, "Measure twice, cut once." Doing your homework in the analysis and design phases of a project will often pay off in big ways later in the project by avoiding embarrassing and visible outages.

Another dimension of data enhancements is that of data replication. Many more applications now utilize data replication than at any time in the past. It is a way of getting the data closer to the consumer while retaining a bidirectional flow of data.

Data Replication Know the basics of data replication for the exam. Know when it is appropriate to use data replication in a solution. Understand the concepts of the "publish and subscribe" data replication model. As is usually the case, MSDN is a good place to start reading more about Microsoft's data replication technologies. The MSDN CD ships with Visual Studio 6.0, or it can be accessed directly on the Microsoft Web site at `http://msdn. microsoft.com/library/default. htm`.

For example, Microsoft SQL Server uses a "publish and subscribe" model of data replication, which means that one database serves as the master, a publisher makes all decisions on what data needs to be published to replicated subscriber databases, and any number of subscribers can be present.

ODBC/OLE DB Bridging

Often, moving the data stores to a new location or server is impractical. The data, for various reasons, needs to stay where it is, but we need to access it as easily as we would a local, native database source.

Microsoft, over the last ten years, has delivered two major sets of APIs for solving this challenge. It is important that we review the strengths of each and describe how they can be used in an application. They are as follows:

◆ ODBC

◆ OLE DB

ODBC

ODBC and OLE DB ODBC and OLE DB are both major parts of Microsoft's UDA (Universal Data Access) strategy. Along with ADO and RDS, they are a very important element of the Solution Architectures exam. Knowing the best use of each of the UDA technologies mentioned (ADO, RDS, ODBC, and OLE DB) in addition to some of the older standards (for example, DAO, RDO) is a good idea. For more detailed coverage, check out the Microsoft Web site (`http://www.microsoft.com/data`), MSDN, and the books mentioned in the "Suggested Readings and Resources" section.

ODBC, or open database connectivity, was Microsoft's first success in the realm of database-neutral APIs. Its almost universal adoption by the industry demonstrates the value that it provides in the area of making connection to disparate data sources simpler. Its cloning into JDBC also demonstrates its popularity and value. A detailed examination of ODBC is well beyond the scope of this book (entire books are devoted to ODBC), so we will discuss it only at a high level. Essentially it is able to access many different data storage technologies (for example, SQL Server, ISAM, Jet, DB2) with a common set of APIs and commands. This enables, for example, any application written using ODBC with Access as the back end to be completely moved to Oracle, with almost no modification to code. All changes can be done in the database (to make matching tables), using a tool called the ODBC Administrator.

From a development perspective, essentially all ODBC-compliant databases can be treated similarly when considering the effects of development. For example, if you developed your application against Microsoft SQL Server and then discovered that the enterprise has an Oracle database located on the network, it would be a relatively simple switch to change between them.

OLE DB

ODBC is great, as far as it goes. But think about how much information out there is not stored in RDBMS. As we said earlier, much of the data in the world is still stored as flat files.

Microsoft took this information to heart and created a new API standard called OLE DB. Essentially, OLE DB allows many different kinds of data to be accessed using the same type of functionality as ODBC data sources. Now flat files, databases, and message queues can all be interchanged, one for the other, because OLE DB disguises the specifics of the implementation behind several software components. From a design perspective, this gives us another option. Data from virtually any source that we can gain access to through any means can be presented to our application in the same manner. This allows true anonymity of data sources, giving us more freedom in our application design rather than letting the data design determine how we can use it.

Examples of databases that have OLE DB providers written for them are DB2, SQL Server, Jet, Excel spreadsheets, and ASCII files.

Data Issues at the CopyShop

In the case of CopyShop, we have several data issues. First, data from the coexisting legacy application needs to be accessed. Also, we have a list of requests from the supply clerk to store more information. They would like to know to whom and where supplies are being sent, as well as knowing current inventory levels at the individual shops.

We have some design options. We can leave all the data on the mainframe and create ODBC or OLE DB links to the data from our new solution. Or we can move the data to a network database server when supplies leave the shipping dock of the central office.

Network latency is an issue that will help decide some of these details. At this time, because all shops are in the Denver area (no long-distance data transfers), we could limit the complexity of our solution by extending the mainframe data stores to include new tables or fields. Then we could create a link between our solution and the mainframe by using ADO combined with OLE DB or by using RDO combined with ODBC.

Data conversion is the most universal aspect of integration. In the best circumstances, when a user is willing to completely abandon an old application and has no legacy interfaces to support, the odds are they have a set of data that they want to persist. In this circumstance, some form of data conversion is necessary.

To perform the conversion, you first have to understand where the existing data is and what format it is in. Secondly, it is critical that we identify how we are expecting data in the new system to be different from the existing data. Will the format differ? Will the amount of data being collected change?

Finally, one of the best ways to enhance maintainability in your application is to hook up with one of the industry standards for database access. The two discussed here are ODBC and OLE DB.

Analyzing Existing Methodologies and Limitations of a Business

Analyze existing methodologies and limitations of a business.

Even if, by sheer chance, you were to stumble into an environment that has no legacy technical infrastructure, it is hard to even imagine how you could build a solution that had no existing methodologies in place or business practices that need to be adhered to.

What Are the Target User's Current Business Practices?

What are the common business practices of the company specific to the area your solution addresses? Are you asking people to begin using automation for processes they have always done by hand? Are you asking them to use a tool that may put many of them out of work? Are you taking authority away from people who are used to making business decisions? These are the kinds of questions that need to be thought through as you are looking at the business practices.

As these discussions occur, you must always keep in mind the goal of building any software solution: Things should be more efficient. Making things easier to do does qualify as making things more efficient. If you aren't doing this, however, this should be a red flag. Make sure you return to the basics and look at the following:

◆ Is the problem identified actually the real problem?

◆ Has the problem been addressed directly by the solution identified for it?

◆ Are there possible side effects from implementing the solution that I should consider?

To understand all the dimensions and ramifications of your solution, you should take several things into account:

◆ Implementation and training methodologies

◆ Process engineering

◆ Quality control requirements

◆ Organizational structure

Implementation and Training Methodologies

Within every organization, a group is responsible, either formally or informally, for the implementation of your solution. They are likely also to be responsible for the training of internal staff to make a successful transition to the new software (although in larger companies this may be by proxy). Designing a solution these people do not agree with or do not understand is going to make it all but impossible to have a successful implementation.

Just as nations often go to war over differing religious beliefs, architects can create "holy wars" over methodologies. Without getting into which one is the right one, at least take the time to find out if a development methodology is in place where the solution is to be built.

Examples of design methodologies include Andersen's Method/1, Rational's recently released RUP (Rational Unified Process), SDP (long an industry staple), and obviously, Microsoft's own MSF (Microsoft Solutions Framework).

Microsoft Solutions Framework (MSF) Because the 70-100 exam is about designing solutions and because Microsoft has a published framework for solutions design, it seems reasonable to suggest that you do some background research on this topic in MSDN or the MSDN Web site. Although we have tried to incorporate many of the basic precepts of the MSF (such as a three-tier design centered around User Services, Business Services, and Data Services), we have not explicitly addressed MSF as a separate topic anywhere in this book.

Similarly, if the organization will not buy in on a design, the training process will be less effective. Training for the end users should be focused at the experience level of the target group. For those who are very familiar with software, we need to illustrate features that can be used in the software and emphasize flexibility in the tool. Conversely, for less experienced users, we need to focus on task-oriented training, showing them exactly how to use the software for doing particular aspects of their business.

Although the solution architect rarely serves the role of training developer or user trainer, these things need to be considered during the analysis and design of the solution. Will a training database be needed? Will we need a "faux" trainer that works while disconnected from the production system? Does the system have the requested user-support features (see Chapter 4, "Human-Computer Interface Analysis")? Will the solution need to be discoverable by the user (for example, shrink-wrapped software)?

Process Engineering

It is important to understand, though, that you do not need to simply reimplement existing systems and processes. Part of the reason for application design is that users also want to address how the work is done—the process.

Process engineering is looking not only at how work gets done, but also at why it is done the way it is. This lets the software designer move into a role of helping the business reshape its practices to take advantage of new technology.

One place where this is especially important is in the instance of a first automation system. Most often, people will be used to a lot of strange, "short-circuit" processes put into place to relieve bottlenecks in the paper-and-pencil system. For example, in an order-entry system, an employee might just shout out orders to supply clerks while forwarding the actual written invoice to the billing clerks. Process engineering is all about looking at the steps that are taken and asking if these steps still make sense under a new solution.

One way to make sure that the solution enables rather than drives the business is to make decisions from fact-based information. Design decisions should be documented and defensible.

Quality Control Requirements

Many organizations have quality control processes that must be followed during a development cycle. These processes often require that milestones are placed where deliverables (usually documents) surface to those outside the team and are evaluated. Basically, two types of these deliverables exist. One type establishes and monitors the process of creating the application, whereas the other monitors the end product and its progression toward completion.

Finally, quality control dictates the quality of the final solution—the code. Often, companies are subject to rigorous quality control guidelines imposed from outside. Federal regulations issued by the FDA or the FTC require a certain level of quality to protect the public. Common sense also dictates quality requirements where the loss of life is at stake, such as at NASA, the airline industry, the health care industry, and so on.

Process Deliverables

Process deliverables offer insight into the procedure being used to develop the software. How are requirements gathered? How are people being solicited for input, and so on? The documents provide valuable reference materials if a need to determine the source of the requirement ever occurs.

These documents also serve the purpose of providing a reference for team members on their areas of responsibility. Process deliverables help us measure whether we are on track or off track early enough to make corrections before too much time or money is wasted.

Product Deliverables

This is primarily related to how the software itself is progressing, what features are supposed to be in the software, how complete the features are, and who is working on what. These things should all be documented in a way that someone outside the team can take them and understand. Only by doing so can those people paying the bills really track the software's progress toward completion.

Coding standards are an indication of process documentation. They signify that everyone on the team agrees to construct the solution in a standard way. This simplifies maintenance significantly and increases the overall quality of the code.

Frequent inspections at key project milestones are another example of process quality. When we subject our work to the review of others, improved quality is almost always the result.

A good way to distinguish the two is that process documentation is usually nontechnical and written to provide direction for the team, either in terms of their roles or what the software consists of. In contrast, product documentation includes discussions of schedule, feature completion level, people assigned to tasks, and so on. These are documents that either are technical or are about things technical.

Final Product Quality

As mentioned previously, this is the bottom-line quality of the solution—"where the rubber meets the road." Whereas the quality of the process and product documentation may be somewhat subjective, product quality can usually be measured quite precisely and objectively.

Metrics such as "bugs per 1000 lines of code," "mean time between failure," and "mean time to repair" are often used.

In situations where the public safety is safeguarded by government regulations, extensive validation tests are often required (and the documents are officially submitted).

Sometimes the quality requirements can be stated simply and with zero tolerance in mind. If we were designing an air traffic solution, we might build in safeguards, redundancies, and quality control to support the stated quality goal that "not a single life will be lost as a result of software failure in our air traffic system."

Formal QA testing is very often a part of an organization's quality requirements. Typically, these are people who were not involved in the building of the solution; therefore, they are more likely to "hammer away" on the software than would someone who doesn't want to look bad. Although this is often a frustrating phase for developers, good QA people are worth their weight in gold when it comes to rolling out the solution. The increase in user satisfaction and the decrease in support calls is worth it.

In summary, it is useful to know what quality standards the organization requires before completing the analysis phase of the project. In addition to affecting the scheduling, budgeting, and manpower estimates, it will often influence the overall design of the solution.

Organizational Structure

It might seem that the organizational chart of a company would be essentially irrelevant to application design. However, when it comes to enterprise applications (regardless of the size of the enterprise), this is a dangerous assumption.

In a highly structured organization, for example, there will be a much more structured approach to things such as workflow and approval processing. Furthermore, certain activities may be available only to people of a sufficient rank in the organization.

Political issues are very often relevant to the task of solution architecting. Policies pertaining to the approval of software purchases can often sidetrack a project. An organization's aggressiveness (or lack thereof) in regard to new technologies is significant to solution design. Knowing who has the final say-so on design decisions is important as well.

Without getting into all kinds of examples, suffice it to say that, to be effective, the solutions architect should be aware of the organizational structure and climate.

CopyShop Business Practices

The comments from the central manager indicate that this is a very successful business that has rapidly outgrown its infrastructure. Formerly a "one-shop" operation, it has grown into a collection of many "one-shop" operations, rather than growing into an expanded corporation.

CopyShop is using this software change as a change to reengineer what has become a very disconnected business process. The company intends to track inventory all the way to its final consumption at the various shops. This may excite some branch managers and dismay others. From comments made by the central manager, it seems that the shops will be given more authority over their own ordering (within thresholds).

A comment was made that newer technology will be used. This gives us some insight into the existing business practices.

We see the word "quality" mentioned in the case study, but not in a life-or-death context. We don't foresee any extraordinary requirements here. The concept of using pilot sites was mentioned. This is a form of quality management.

What Are the Budgetary Constraints on the Project?

In a perfect world, we would consider all the features and legacy applications, we would support all legacy requirements and enhance them with new technology, and everything would be worked on until it worked perfectly. However, we do not live in a perfect world. Remember our mantra—the project needs to increase efficiency. Increased efficiency saves money. A project that gets a chance to finish has to be one that convinces those around it that it can make money.

Most often, project budgets are set at the start. Make sure when you are designing an application that you are keeping in mind the funds available for it. If you build an application to the point of being 90% complete and are refused funding for the last 10%, the other 90% will not matter because no one will ever see it.

Estimated ROI

Often a time will come on a project when you must go to those paying the bills and ask for more time (and/or more money) to finish the project. One of your most powerful weapons in this kind of a conversation is to discuss the potential for savings after the project is implemented.

This is usually most effective when unanticipated areas of savings have been encountered in the course of the project. Some good examples are automation of formerly manual processes, faster responsiveness to customers, and so on. All these things are, for businesses, real savings that can justify giving a project the requested extension.

Scheduling

One way to avoid having this kind of conversation is by proactive scheduling and milestones.

Proactive scheduling means you don't just make up your schedule and then put it into a drawer for the next two months. You make the effort to find out the status of scheduled tasks, and then you manage the schedule. Milestones make this possible. Milestones create visibility in the mostly invisible act of designing and building a solution.

If you are consistently not able to meet the schedule, and if you've been tracking it all along, you can go to those who are paying the bills for the project and let them know exactly what the issues are. This will let you, early on, start making decisions about cutting back the project's scope or possibly expanding the budget to account for the difficulties.

As a protection, scope should be managed carefully. This does not always mean saying no to every request for a new feature. It does mean providing the user (or client) a cost estimate of what the new feature would mean to the project in terms of time, money, and resources. Contrary to many developers' experiences, scope can be managed successfully to pull a project in on time and within budget.

Budgetary Concerns for the CopyShop

Because this issue of communication and responsiveness to customer needs is so critical to management at the CopyShop, there shouldn't be an issue regarding initial funding. However a lot of focus is being placed on the estimated ROI for this solution, in terms of increased customer satisfaction and greater standardization of branches.

Consequently, it would probably be a good idea to go through all the perceived ROI for the project and review what kinds of expectations exist.

Scheduling of this project most likely would be pushed quickly. The management seems to perceive a serious problem in their current way of doing business, and they will likely be very aggressive in trying to correct it.

What Are the Legal Issues Surrounding the Project?

Software development has become an area, now more than ever, where legal considerations need to be factored in. When so many IT departments are outsourcing their technical development staff, several legal issues unique to software development arise:

◆ Noncompete clauses in employee and former employee contracts

◆ Software licensing

Noncompete Agreements

In the world of IT, a lot of external consultants are involved in mission-critical projects and rapid turnover in staff occurs, compared with most other aspects of the business. Because of this, many technical professionals are bound by noncompete clauses. This allows them to be exposed to the internal workings of business systems, with relatively low risk that the business secrets they might run across will be revealed to competitors.

Be sensitive to the fear among many project managers that business information may fall into the wrong hands. Especially if you are working on a project in a very competitive industry, investigate the possibility of asking employees to agree to a noncompete agreement.

Contractual obligations and professionalism are crucial for both parties. It is a time unlike any other in the history of business. Almost every company in the Fortune 500 has, to some extent, placed a significant amount of confidential information in the hands of "outsiders."

Just as significant is the concern that an external consultant may leave at an inopportune time, leaving the company high and dry, without sufficient knowledge to complete or maintain the solution.

These things do happen, but not as often as you might think. Just like the news, the bad stories get through, but the successes rarely make the front page.

Software Licensing

Software licensing is the other main issue unique to software designers. It is critical that you be aware of how many and what licenses are held by the company commissioning the project. If a product of a particular type is already in use in the enterprise, it will greatly increase both your ease of integration and the ROI (by decreasing costs) of your solution to use that product.

Also, designing a solution that incorporates a piece of software that the client doesn't have licenses for and doesn't have the budget to purchase wastes both your time and the client's. Make yourself aware of the environment the application will run in. If your solution requires that a piece of shrink-wrap software be deployed to 20,000 users, make sure you understand the pros and cons before including it as part of your solution. Being surprised late in the cycle by a hefty licensing expense can kill an otherwise successful project.

What Legal Concerns Should the CopyShop Have?

Generally speaking, CopyShop has few concerns of this type. The information is not sensitive enough that it is concerned about getting nondisclosure agreements, and it has already purchased licenses for software it needs.

Nevertheless, a quick confirmation that sufficient quantities of licenses exist would probably still be in order. In a switch of solutions, it is often easy to overlook the fact that you have only a five-client license on your database server.

What Needs Does the Customer Identify for Internal Integration?

The overriding concern for any software developer should be the customer's needs. What do they need this piece of software to do? To them, very little else matters. If a solution makes their work easier and more efficient, they are going to forgive a lot of technical compromises, and if it does not, then no amount of technical design is going to make them happy. The basic lesson here is the same one echoed throughout the chapter: software should make things more efficient for a business. Businesses are not in the software business; they don't appreciate the beauty of software for its own sake. They are in their own business and are using software only as a tool to increase their efficiency in serving their customers.

What Are the Needs of the CopyShop?

The CopyShop is placing a priority on effective communication between branch shops and the central office, particularly the management and supply divisions. Because of this, efforts need to be made to ensure that the solution demonstrates how this can be accomplished and to facilitate it actually happening.

CHAPTER SUMMARY

KEY TERMS

- COM
- COMTI
- Current business practices
- Data conversion
- Estimated ROI
- Legacy applications
- Noncompete agreements
- ODBC
- OLE DB
- Process engineering
- Screen scraping
- SNA Server
- Software licensing

All applications require some form of integration. The only question is what type of integration is needed. Essentially, as we've seen, it can be broken down into two major categories: integration with other applications and integration with existing business processes in the enterprise. For technically minded people, a tendency is to focus on the former and minimize the latter.

However, the integration with the existing business is where all solutions succeed or fail. If a good job is done combining this application into the processes the target users already perform, one of our primary goals of increasing user efficiency is being furthered.

Technical integration, too, can play a key part in fostering increased efficiency by removing redundant data entry or allowing interoperation of related, but different, "generation" applications.

APPLY YOUR KNOWLEDGE

Exercises

5.1   Analyzing Integration Requirements

In Exercise 5.1, review the list of solutions below; in the blank line after each, enter what you perceive as the most likely level of integration. Choose from either None, Coexisting, or Wrapped.

Estimated Time: 10 minutes.

1. XYZ Company has a mainframe program for tracking written customer correspondence. It does everything the company needs, but XYZ would like to make it accessible through a Web browser so that employees can work from home.

   _____

2. PQR Industries does department-level accounting through the use of a single Access database on a network drive. Each department enters its numbers into the database at the end of the month. Management has requested bar graphs in order to spot trends in revenue more easily. It has been decided that Excel will serve their needs without requiring extensive programming. Each month, a user will run a query that generates an Excel spreadsheet with the data. Then that same user will use macros to create the graph in the newly created spreadsheet.

   _____

3. GHI, Inc. has a COBOL program that tracks customer orders for gas burners. It likes the idea of offering the customer the capability to order directly through the Web. To make the entire process easier, GHI is planning to create a small

graphical interface and then migrate its data to SQL Server. After that is complete, they will pull the plug on the mainframe and use ASP to drive the Web page.

   _____

4. DEF Books is going object-oriented all the way. The only problem is that it cannot afford to rewrite all its legacy code. What the company would like to do is to shortcut the "recover current design" work and just access the business rules as if they were part of the application.

   _____

5. HIJKLMNOP Soup Company has a mainframe application that controls the large vats of soup. This application is so old that nobody wants to touch it. In addition, what it does, it does well. However, after the soup is poured into cans, the system does not provide good support for decision support. HIJKLMNOP executives would like to be able to roll up numbers and create production graphs. They have selected Visual Basic and Microsoft Graph to do this.

   _____

Answers:

1. Wrapped. Obviously, None is not the correct answer because a legacy application exists and is being retained. Coexisting, although close, does not define the relationship as outlined in the chapter text. We are not creating a new solution; we are placing a new façade on the existing legacy program.

APPLY YOUR KNOWLEDGE

2. Coexisting. This scenario reminds us that not all legacy applications are COBOL programs running on a mainframe and not all integration is automated. None does not work because an application already exists and is not being replaced. Wrapped is not accurate because the functionality of the two pieces is substantially different.

3. Clean slate. After the crossover period, no integration will occur. For that reason, this is classified as a clean slate integration.

4. Wrapped. Because the new solution will be accessing the legacy code as if it were just another object, Wrapped is more descriptive than Coexisting, which implies that each application will be integrated, yet more or less independent.

5. Coexisting. None is not appropriate because the old system will continue to work and will feed the new system. Wrapped is not correct because the functionality of the decision support solution is dissimilar to that of the mainframe application.

5.2   Analyzing Business Limitations

In Exercise 5.2, review Table 5.1, and in the column marked Applicable? enter Yes or No, depending on whether the fact should be considered as a business limitation on the solution architecture.

Estimated Time: 10 minutes.

TABLE 5.1

BUSINESS LIMITATIONS ANALYSIS

Business Statement	*Applicable?*
A. The solution will be a replacement to the company accounting system, which currently uses the principle of double-entry bookkeeping.	
B. he application is required to perform a long list of features, but the analysis shows that only about half of them will fall within the budgetary limitations placed on the project by management.	
C. Response time is more important than anything to the users of the new application.	
D. The new solution will be used to monitor the "vitals" of patients in an Intensive Care Unit. Information such as heart rate, respiratory rate, and blood oxygen level will be monitored against patient-specific thresholds. Any data that falls outside the threshold will set off an alarm at the nurses' station.	
E. The president of the company has stated, "Windows will be the only operating system installed in our company."	
F. Even the team leaders at We Code Until It's Done are technical.	
G. Big State College has a legacy enrollment system that stores data in DB2. The college wants to keep its data stored there and extend its legacy system by creating an ODBC connection to the data for the new solution.	
H. Generic Controls, Inc. has no time for training its users. The system must be intuitive and discoverable so that the users can "learn as they go."	

APPLY YOUR KNOWLEDGE

Answers:

A. No. Although this will certainly influence the design, it is not significant nor does it limit our architectural choices.

B. Yes. Because it can be reasoned that budget is tight, this will almost certainly influence the choice of architecture. An inexpensive architecture (that doesn't equate to hastily designed) seems most appropriate from the information given.

C. Yes. Performance is definitely an influencing factor on the type of architecture chosen. This falls under the classification of "customer's needs."

D. Yes. In this case, quality control overrides all other factors and clearly influences the architecture we require. Stability, response time, redundancy, and even security are all critical for a successful solution.

E. Yes. Assuming that the president of the company has the power that normally accompanies that title, all architectures that do not center around COM or other Microsoft technologies will not be the best choice. Architectures that support heterogeneous environments are unnecessary.

F. No. The technical expertise of the staff may influence design, but it does not limit our choice of architecture.

G. Yes. This is a bit tougher. We have to assume that the decision to keep the legacy system active is a business decision.

H. Yes. Training methodologies affect the selection of the architecture. We have a stated need for an intuitive application.

Review Questions

1. If CopyShop had no software-based system for tracking its materials (that is, it was tracking materials with note cards by hand), how would this affect an assessment of the technical integration requirements?

2. If connections need to be preserved to some mainframe applications, what would be the first option to investigate for making the connections?

3. If instead of being located on the mainframe, data is located in a PC database, what would be the most reasonable way of accessing the data?

4. How would our analysis of the solution change if CopyShop wanted to remain a largely decentralized operation?

5. What additional legal concerns might we be able to identify for CopyShop?

Exam Questions

1. From the following list of components, create a block diagram that represents a viable solution for CopyShop. Draw lines that indicate the flow of information through the system.

   - Mainframe data stores
   - Legacy application
   - Bar-code scanner
   - CopyShop store application
   - WAN
   - Legacy data ODBC connector
   - Central office decision support application

APPLY YOUR KNOWLEDGE

2. If a solution has a requirement to work simultaneously with a mainframe application, providing a graphical front end to a working IBM 3270 application, what is the integration situation?

   A. Clean slate

   B. Connected by data stores

   C. Screen scraping

   D. None of the above

3. If the enterprise wanted to begin rolling out a new voice-mail system, but it is not ready to roll it out to all users simultaneously, what kind of an integration situation is the solution required to handle?

   A. Clean slate

   B. Retain legacy application

   C. Wrap legacy code or screen scraping

   D. None of the above

4. Imagine a solution that requires you to manually handle the sockets of a TCP/IP connection and manually move data across that connection in a particular format. This would be an example of what type of connection?

   A. Custom connection

   B. Microsoft SNA Server

   C. Binary compatibility (COM)

   D. Industry standard protocols

5. Assume that your solution requires that you interoperate with a mainframe-based application. What would be the simplest solution to investigate first?

   A. Custom connection

   B. Microsoft SNA Server

   C. Binary standard

   D. None of the above

6. If your solution is being built new and is designed for a PC platform, which connection strategy makes the most sense?

   A. Custom connection

   B. Microsoft SNA Server

   C. Binary compatibility (COM)

   D. None of the above

7. Which of the following are the three main concerns for technical application integration? (Choose three.)

   A. Shared data requirements

   B. Current business practices

   C. Legacy connections

   D. Legacy software

8. If your solution only needs to pull data from two SQL-based data sources running on a PC, which method of data access is probably going to be most efficient to develop?

   A. Custom access through database-specific APIs

   B. ODBC

   C. OLE DB

   D. All methods are equal.

APPLY YOUR KNOWLEDGE

9. Assume your solution requires data from several SQL data sources, directory services, and flat file formats. In this situation, which method of data access is probably going to be the most efficient to develop?

   A. Custom access through database-specific APIs

   B. ODBC

   C. OLE DB

   D. All methods are equal.

10. You build a tool to solve a problem in a business, but the users complain that everything takes longer to do with this newer tool because of all the new features on it. This reaction illustrates what problem?

    A. Not understanding current business practices

    B. Poorly understanding legacy application

    C. Failing to adequately focus on the technical aspects of integration

    D. None of the above

11. Attempting to redesign the way a business works is better known as what?

    A. Process engineering

    B. Project management

    C. Quality assurance

    D. None of the above

12. If, in our case study, the manager started signing blank order forms to avoid being pestered for each new supply order, it would be an example of what?

    A. Short circuiting a process

    B. Process engineering

    C. Quality assurance

    D. None of the above

13. What is the difference between a process deliverable and a product deliverable? (Choose all that apply.)

    A. Process documents are technical.

    B. Product documents are technical.

    C. Process documents focus on interpersonal issues.

    D. Product documents include coding standards for developers.

14. An employee signs a document committing not to work for others in your industry, but takes a job with one of those companies anyway. What has the employee violated?

    A. Noncompete clause

    B. Licensing issue

    C. Employee retention clause

    D. None of the above

15. Which of the following best describes the business problem at CopyShop?

    A. Approval of orders for more supplies

    B. Need to keep the mainframe system operational

    C. Communication between home office and the shops as it relates to supplies

    D. Need to use newer technology

APPLY YOUR KNOWLEDGE

Answers to Review Questions

1. If there is no legacy system with which to work, we have much more limited concerns as far as integration is concerned. However, there would be a lot more work to do overall because we would have to create the inventory data stores from scratch. See "Analyzing Application Integration Requirements."

2. Microsoft SNA Server is designed to allow PC-based software to have a standardized way of connecting to some types of mainframe applications, particularly those that use CICS as a means of communicating between mainframe apps. See "SNA Server."

3. Microsoft is moving in the direction of OLE DB in many situations. In this case, it would still be the most maintainable solution to use OLE DB as a means of accessing the data. See "ODBC/OLE DB Bridging."

4. Our solution is designed to increase control at the central warehouse over how and when branch offices order supplies. If the goal instead were to facilitate a more flexible approach, there would be fewer places in our process where permission is requested from one group to another. See "What Are the Target User's Current Business Practices?"

5. If a high level of competition existed, based on having this kind of a solution, it might become an issue if people are leaving the project and going to competitors, creating a solution for them that CopyShop has paid the money to research and implement. See "What Are the Legal Issues Surrounding the Project?"

Answers to Exam Questions

1. The answer should look like Figure 5.5. See the entire chapter.

2. **C.** The solution does require integration; therefore, it can't be a clean slate situation. Because the mainframe application will still be active in the background and the new solution will be a front-end solution, screen scraping is the correct answer. See "Wrap Legacy Code or Screen Scraping."

3. **B.** In this case, the applications must exist simultaneously and must perform the same function. This is probably the most difficult scenario to resolve from an integration perspective because two applications will be attempting to manipulate almost the same data. See "Retain Legacy Application."

4. **A.** The handling of sockets manually and configuring a message to travel across those sockets is a classic example of manually creating a custom connection. See "Nonstandard Connectivity."

5. **B.** Microsoft's SNA Server is designed to enable communication between PC and mainframe systems. Although it does not always work, depending on your mainframe situation, it is certainly the simplest option to investigate first. If it works, it could save a great deal of development time. See "SNA Server."

6. **C.** If your solution is being built today, and if it has the capability to choose its own technology and is on the PC platform, the only way to build it for interoperability is to use COM. See "Binary Compatibility (COM)."

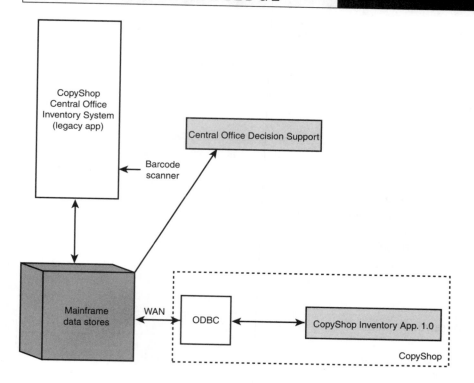

FIGURE 5.5
Solution architecture.

7. **A, C, D.** Current business practices are an integration point, but not a technical one. They are integration points related to the business into which the solution is being introduced. See "Analyzing Application Integration Requirements."

8. **B.** ODBC allows easy, efficient pulling of data from ODBC-compliant, SQL-based data stores. Although C is also a good answer, ODBC is more efficient when pulling from its subset of possible data stores, thus making it a better answer. See "ODBC/OLE DB Bridging."

9. **C.** In this case, we are pulling from a variety of data sources. Therefore, it is going to be most practical to use OLE DB to make all the different data sources look the same and thus increase development efficiency. See "ODBC/OLE DB Bridging."

10. **A.** The solution failed because we did not understand how the application was being used in the existing business model. We included features which, although probably valuable to the user, made the work less efficient. See "What Are the Target User's Current Business Practices?"

APPLY YOUR KNOWLEDGE

11. **A.** Redesigning how a business task is completed, in addition to automating it, is known as process engineering. See "Process Engineering."

12. **A.** When a user performs actions that are not part of the ideal process in order to speed up the rate at which the overall process occurs, this is known as a short circuiting. See "Process Engineering."

13. **B, C, D.** Process deliverables are not designed to be technical in nature but are written so that even nontechnical members of a project team can read and benefit from them. Product deliverables are technical and focus on issues related to functionality and schedule. See "Quality Control Requirements."

14. **A.** When the employee signs a document committing to not work for competitors, it is known as a noncompete clause. This is a common legal issue in software development practices. See "What Are the Legal Issues Surrounding the Project?"

15. **C.** Communication is the business problem. Choice A is not even an issue according to the case study. Choices B and D are technical issues, not business issues. See "Case Study: The CopyShop."

Suggested Readings and Resources

1. Kirtland, Mary. *Designing Component-Based Applications.* Microsoft Press, 1998.

This chapter addresses the following exam objectives:

Given a business scenario, identify which solution type is appropriate. Solution types are single-tier, two-tier, and *n*-tier.

▶ No such thing exists as a universally best solution type. Depending on the problem we are trying to solve and other factors about the project, different solution types will be appropriate. A *solution type* is an overall vision for the architecture of a system.

Identify which technologies are appropriate for implementation of a given business solution. Considerations include

- **Technology standards such as EDI, Internet, OSI, COMTI, and POSIX**

- **Proprietary technologies**

- **Technology environment of the company, both current and planned**

- **Selection of development tools**

- **Type of solution, such as enterprise, distributed, centralized, and collaborative**

▶ One of the decision areas that can make or break a project is the selection of the technologies that it will be based on. To further complicate the decision, technologies will often change in the middle of the development cycle.

CHAPTER 6

Defining the Technical Architecture for a Solution

Choose a data storage architecture. Considerations include

- **Volume**

- **Number of transactions per time increment**

- **Number of connections or sessions**

- **Scope of business requirements**

- **Extensibility requirements**

- **Reporting requirements**

- **Number of users**

- **Type of database**

▶ Part of the technical architecture of any solution is going to be how data is stored, or *persisted*, in the system. Normally, you will find that a database is the simplest and most efficient way to satisfy this requirement.

OUTLINE

STUDY STRATEGIES

▶ Identify the three main solution types and their strengths relative to one another.

▶ Make an intelligent choice of Microsoft's development tools for a given project and choose those which most easily will meet your goals.

▶ Identify what kind of a solution you are designing and explain what each kind of solution offers.

▶ Identify the reporting requirements of a business solution and its effect on your data architecture.

▶ Identify the scope of business requirements for persisting data.

▶ Explain the differences between various deployment strategies.

▶ Select the appropriate type of database for your solution.

INTRODUCTION

The most visible stage in designing a solution may be the one that we are about to discuss—that of designing the technical architecture. This is probably the 'glamour' part of the process. In this portion of the process, an application designer is allowed to think at a very high level about things and not become overly drawn into the details of the implementation. It is a time to push the envelope of the technology that is available, to explore options, and to make the decisions that will help the project as it moves forward.

Of course, conversely, it can become the time to chase your tail and make poor choices that will burden the project as it moves forward. What we will try to do here is make sure we can put the time we spend in this stage into the former category, rather than the latter.

CASE STUDY: GWA WINES

BACKGROUND

GWA Wines (GWA stands for "goes with anything") has more than 50 years of experience bottling the finest wines in the Portland area. Until now, the company has been largely a local phenomenon, but because it was recently honored as a top American vineyard by a national magazine, it expects much more national attention.

Because of its focus on local sales, at this point, GWA Wines does not have a standard way of supporting orders from customers not on the premises.

PROBLEM STATEMENT

GWA Wines, to take advantage of its national exposure, would like to enable customers to order its wine regardless of location. It already has an excellent setup for the delivery side (contracted through a shipping company). This was already in place for the local/regional orders the company was receiving.

What needs to be added is the capability to give national clients, who may never visit the winery personally, the ability to order their favorite wines by the bottle, cask, or case.

Currently, all orders are taken by hand, over the phone, without a catalog that customers can peruse. This results in several problems, not the least of which is decreased sales because customers do not know what is available.

Owner

"We just got a great review. Last year's winner of this award went from number 315 in the country to number 11. I talked to him after we got the award, and he said the best thing he ever did was prepare for a national presence for selling. That's what I want to do. It seems like everyone is buying everything online now, and if that

CASE STUDY: GWA WINES

works, great, because then I don't have to keep so many people answering the telephone."

Head of Marketing

"Using the Internet would be a perfect vehicle to do this, and to harness all this great publicity that we've got for ourselves here. I'd love to be able to put the Web page in the awards issue that is coming out in a month or so."

CURRENT SYSTEM

The current system at GWA Wines is mostly manual. The company has a fairly extensive order-processing program that helps get orders shipped correctly after orders are placed. What it doesn't have is a good way of letting people who aren't on the premises place these orders. Because most business has been local up until now, it hasn't been such a critical issue.

Owner

"Up to this point, we've had very few problems with our existing system, but it sure does tax our receptionist. She spends more time taking orders than she does anything else. And obviously, if the orders get a lot bigger, we're not going to be able to handle it. So we need to make it automated to fit into our existing delivery system."

Receptionist

"I have to say, I don't mind working, but it seems like every time I start to concentrate on something, that order phone rings. And that was before this award we just got. Now I won't be able to get anything done.

Some callers aren't familiar with our catalog, so I have to explain all the different types of wine before they place their order."

IS Manager

"We have an AS/400 in the back to do data processing. All the stuff we've got up until now is on there. The current application is a small COBOL application. It works fine, but it won't give us what we need to create a powerful Web presence."

ENVISIONED SYSTEM

GWA Wines doesn't want to reinvent its entire computer system. It just wants to build on what it has now.

Owner

"The whole point of the new system, in my mind, is to make it easier for us to take orders from people. Today, we seem to invest a lot of people time in getting an order placed. If we want to step up to the big leagues and play on a national level, we have to change that."

Programmer

"It would be nice to get some of the newer technology in here to make our lives easier. Maintaining the software we've got has been difficult. The programmer lives in Spokane and she can't always get here when we need her.

I spent some time at a previous company working with HTML and ASP. I think I can support the new system just fine after it's built."

continues

continued

ENVIRONMENT

GWA Wines intends to buy a new Web server with all the necessary memory and disk space needed. Because it can always use the telephone as a backup, the company is not planning on buying a backup server. All the internal sales people will use a new interface to make the entry of customer sales go faster.

IS Manager

"We're going to try to create a pass-through database on the server and keep our COBOL program running for now. If things go well, we might look at replacing the AS/400 program in a future release.

We want repeat users to be able to create a customized page that will make it even easier for them to order their favorite wines in bulk.

My staff and I have done some research on the latest technologies and we even performed a few proof-of-concept prototypes. We will probably use something like ADO to hook our Web page directly to the database. Customers can place orders directly into the system, look at inventory, and check their account status. We intend to support pictures of our wines as well."

MAINTAINABILITY

A new system is useful only for as long as it continues to function properly. Maintainability is the measure of how easy it will be to keep this happening.

IS Manager

"Our biggest problem with the existing system is getting the support when we need it. We have no expertise within the company, so all the work is done by outside people. This can get expensive when we have significant work to be done. We've tried giving our employees incentives to learn this, but it's 15-year-old technology. They just won't bite. So any new system must use technology we have some skill with in-house, and it must be new enough that employees will want to learn it.

The new system will be totally maintained by my three staff programmers. Two of them are in training right now to learn Visual Basic."

AVAILABILITY

GWA Wines does not seem to have severe requirements in the area of availability.

Owner

"I'd like, obviously, to have 100% availability. People can surf the Web 24 hours a day, 7 days a week, 365 days a year. But when I talk to my IS people, they tell me that that kind of availability means a really high price tag. So I guess what I want is the highest availability we can get without wasting a lot of money. There aren't going to be a lot of people who say, 'I can't order now, I guess I'll get a different kind of wine.' So, I'm a little flexible, but I wouldn't want that to happen very often."

CASE STUDY: GWA WINES

IT Manager
"We've decided not to purchase a backup server. We feel that we can survive a full day of downtime with very little impact overall on our business."

IDENTIFYING APPROPRIATE SOLUTION TYPES

Given a business scenario, identify which solution type is appropriate. Solution types are single-tier, two-tier, and *n*-tier.

One of the first decisions that must be made when designing a solution for any business problem is which type of solution is appropriate. Learning to design the right solution requires us to learn some general features of all the types, so that when the time comes to choose, we can make an informed decision.

The three options for solution types are

◆ Single tier

◆ Two tier

◆ *n*-tier

Single Tier

Single-tier, monolithic architecture is probably the oldest and the simplest to understand, and so we will begin here.

The model for this type of application can be seen in Figure 6.1. All the processing in a single-tier application is done on a single machine. In the cake business, this would be analogous to laying out a single sheet cake and frosting it. Also, we will see that, in essence, the advantages and disadvantages of a single-tier system will correspond fairly directly to those of a sheet cake.

NOTE

Approach to Single-Tier Architecture It should be noted that we are concentrating our analysis on PC client/server architectures. Although a mainframe system with a "dumb" terminal hanging off it satisfies the criteria for a single-tier application, it is not particularly relevant to the exam that is the focus of this book. We will discuss this again briefly at the end of this section.

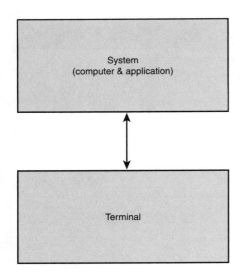

FIGURE 6.1
Single-tier architecture.

We should look at four main things when we are thinking about designing a single-tier PC solution:

◆ Simplicity of design

◆ Difficulty of maintenance

◆ Processing requirements

◆ Location of processing

Simplicity of Design

One of the primary reasons for baking a single sheet cake is the relative ease of designing it. There is no need to decide ahead of time where extra support is needed.

Similarly, one of the primary reasons for designing single-tier applications is ease of design. Design for this type of application is much simpler because there are very few choices to make. All the processing is done on the one-and-only machine in the architecture. Consequently, we have no need to build or design complicated cross-process communication mechanisms. Second, it makes the application itself location neutral. No machine is preferable to another when installing it; no options exist.

Another advantage of this type of solution relates to testing the solution. In modern IT shops, if you ask developers what single thing causes the most errors to slip past the testing process, you will often hear that the testing environment is not the same as the production environment. The problems are caused by many possible issues and simply can't be adequately re-created in a simulated production environment.

This problem is far less likely to happen in a single-tier architecture where, quite often, just a single program is involved. Dependency issues are far less common. Single-tier applications enable testers to build environments that much more accurately reflect production situations. This reduces the need for bug fixes (hopefully) and will correspondingly decrease the cost of maintenance for your software.

In short, much of the indeterminacy and the problems associated with custom-built applications can be removed by having just one machine involved in the processing. However, as we discuss next, this, like all technical trade-offs, carries a price.

Difficulty of Maintenance

When you distribute an application in this manner, some consequences exist for maintenance. As a single-tier system, the application must be present on whatever machine it runs on locally. As such, updates to the application (the result of maintenance) are much more difficult to roll out. Rather than having a central "pull" strategy for updating software, it will have to be "pushed" to each of the users every time an update is made, at least if it is expected that every user will have that update.

In essence, then, each maintenance cycle has with it a rollout cycle nearly as complex as the original rollout of the software. This radically increases the cost of maintenance for the application.

Add to this the concern about time-sensitive rollouts. Sometimes software has a particular point in time where it will stop working correctly. If your software has such problems in it, or something where time-based updates are critical, distribution suddenly goes from being a small, one-time issue to being a major, ongoing risk to your project.

Finally, the growing number of remote users and telecommuters makes this process just that much more complicated. This group is normally equipped with laptop computers and, depending on how the infrastructure of the company is set up, might access the program through the Internet or through a modem. This would not be the best way to download updates to a 50MB application.

We have identified three major downsides from a maintenance perspective for a single-tier application:

◆ Maintenance updates have a complicated update rollout cycle.

◆ Time-sensitive rollouts are much harder to coordinate with this kind of rollout, and risks to the project's success are increased.

◆ Supporting remote users is more difficult.

Nondistributed Processing

From a hardware perspective, single-tier applications may be the most costly option. Certainly, we will save money on the cost of servers (because we don't need one); however, we will spend much more money on end-user PCs than we would otherwise have to.

In single-tier applications, the machine that does the processing (the end-user machine) must have sufficient processing power to support all aspects of the application. Consequently, no capability exists to offload processor-intensive activities to another machine. This can have an impact on the solution's capability to scale.

The direct consequence is that each end-user machine needs to be of sufficient power to run the most demanding application on the system. As newer systems are developed, their increased demands will cause a need to upgrade all end-user hardware. This ongoing cycle creates, as applications get larger and more powerful, the need to be constantly upgrading end-user hardware.

This again becomes a critical issue when we consider the increasing role of laptops in an enterprise. The users with these systems may not be local, and if they are not local, they will be more likely to have a lot of files on the laptop that are not on the network.

Location of Processing

Up to this point, we have been focusing on the typical case of a single-tier application—the one in which an end-user PC contains software that runs on the local user's PC and allows increases of productivity.

However, this is not the only way to design a single-tier application. The only requirement we have discussed (in fact, the only requirement there is) is that only one machine exists on which processing takes place and that only one logical layer to the software is present on that machine.

Some software allows us to simulate a mainframe terminal connected to a mainframe (for example, 3270 emulators). This does not, however, make the application a two-tier approach. All processing, error checking and decision making is done on the server machine. No significant application intelligence is present on the client side.

Another technology is available, known as *thin client*. Thin client acts very much like a mainframe-terminal configuration, except that a PC server plays the part of the mainframe, and a Windows terminal plays the part of the terminal. Instead of sending ASCII characters, colored pixels are transmitted.

The single-tier application provides a great deal of simplicity in the design of the application. Rather than spending a lot of time coordinating communication between different chunks of the software, and potentially between different physical systems, single-tier design makes the assumption that the entire program will be loaded onto a single computer. When this can be arranged, it creates a much simpler design.

Conversely, it does make it more difficult to maintain and update software, by increasing hardware demands from software and requiring distribution to a much wider audience.

In some situations, employing the single-tier architecture is appropriate. Some examples are shrink-wrap software such as games or tax-preparation programs, small Excel or Access applications, demo CDs, and Windows applets (for example, Calculator).

Two Tier

One of the other limitations of the single-tier architecture, at least in the PC area, is that it is difficult to share data in a real-time capacity. Therefore, a natural evolution from single-tier architecture is the two-tier strategy, in which a shared database can be established. The definition of two-tier applications is fairly simple. A given application can be considered a two-tier architecture if pieces of the application have, by design, been created to execute as two separate layers. The layers can run on the same machine or, as is more typical, on different machines (see Figure 6.2). This is often referred to as client/server architecture.

As we have shown in the situation on the right in Figure 6.2, the portion of the application separated from the others is normally the database. This enables the data store to be shared between users and also enables much more powerful machines to be purchased for handling advanced data searches. Typically, it is a powerful, robust server on which the database is stored. All the business logic and services for the user interfaces are stored on the client machine, and data services are handled by the database machine.

FIGURE 6.2
Two-tier architecture (logical and physical).

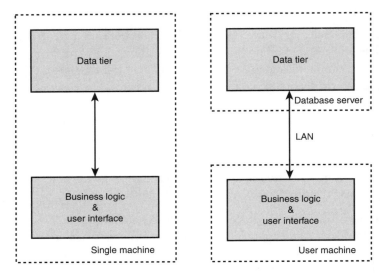

We can note four main features of a two-tier design that will help in deciding when it is a more appropriate solution than either single-tier or *n*-tier:

◆ Moderate level of design difficulty

◆ Improved maintenance over single tier

◆ Control over distribution of processing chores

Moderate Difficulty of Design

Design of two-tier applications is more difficult than single-tier applications. This isn't really a surprise when you consider that at least part of the application (usually the database) is now remote. This introduces two issues. First, the methods for communication between machines must be designed into the system. Second, communication between machines (and to a lesser extent between distinct processes) is expensive in terms of performance.

First, look at the issue of communication itself. It is obvious that the change from local to remote data sources is not going to be a trivial change. However, the changes are normally more than offset by the increased control of data and fewer synchronization issues that occur by having a single data store. This can be accomplished by various methods, depending on your data store. In many cases, if you are running a server-based RDBMS and are willing to communicate through ODBC (see Chapter 5, "Integration Issues," for more on ODBC), it is as simple as changing a driver and specifying the server on which the database resides.

However, it is not always this simple. Particularly if you either choose not to design for performance or are unable to find driver support for ODBC and your database. In that case, you may be back to making product-specific calls to your database software. Be aware that in many cases, this will require distributing some sort of software library with your final solution to support the calls. These calls will then handle the network-level information to access the database.

Now, take a look at our second issue, that of optimizing these calls. As we can see when we examine what has to take place to initiate a database call across the network, it is not an inexpensive item. Furthermore, most of the expense is data-request independent, which means that most of the time spent on an average query to a database is not spent running the actual query. It is spent acquiring from the system the resources that are necessary to run a query. Those resources are the scarcity point in the system. A scarcity point is a point in a design where something is consistently the limiting factor on throughput. In the case of databases, the acquisition of connection is a scarcity point, sometimes referred to as a bottleneck.

The moral to the story is this: the time taken to update or request an average-sized dataset may often be dwarfed by the time taken to connect to the data. Therefore, it is usually a good idea to look at batching updates. In essence, you collect a set of requests (whether for updating or adding or retrieving) and hold them for as long as is practical. Obviously, if the end user is waiting for information, that request must be made immediately. However, if other requests can wait for a certain length of time, this enables the system to make a single connection, spending time acquiring the resource only once, and then processing several requests one after another.

In a variation of this strategy, some applications perform a task known as *preconnecting*. Preconnecting is the practice of intentionally taking the performance hit for connecting to the database at a time when the user will be the least inconvenienced (usually at startup time or during idle time) in anticipation of the need to access the data later in the process.

NOTE

For Further Information To learn more about *preconnecting* and *connection pooling*, use the terms as search criteria in MSDN. Several good articles describe, in greater detail than we can here, the proper use of these two performance-improvement strategies.

A more sophisticated approach is a concept known as *database connection pooling*. In this strategy, utilized quite effectively by Microsoft Transaction Server (as well as by more recent versions of ODBC), database connections are preserved after the previous calling code is done with them. They can be reused for other queries unrelated to the previous one. It is a bit like keeping soup on a warmer, avoiding the lengthy time it takes to get the soup up to the proper temperature.

This kind of design obviously increases the technical requirements over the single-tier approach. However, it does solve a lot of the issues we raised when discussing a single-tier architecture.

Improved Maintenance

One of the greatest advantages that this approach introduced was the centralized control of the data store. Because all users of an application use the same data stores, it is possible to do more effective and more efficient reporting and analysis on the data. This allows those in decision-making roles to be much more confident in making decisions, because the data on which they are basing the decision is much more certain.

Second, this also enabled the creation and universal enforcement and change of data validation rules. If we need to make changes to those rules under a two-tier model, we can simply change them in the universal data store, and those changes should immediately go into effect throughout the system, without recompiling or downloading anything to client machines. The existence of this type of architecture gave rise to what are now known as data analysts. These people are those to whom the technical management and control of a centralized data source are given.

Do not, though, be deceived into thinking that the two-tier approach is the panacea of maintenance. Carefully note that the only logic we dealt with in our enhancement of maintenance was database activity. This is because traditionally, only database activity is removed from the end-user computer. All other business logic and user-interface functionality remains on the client systems and suffers from the same redistribution problems we have already identified. This is why many two-tier applications employ triggers, stored procedures, referential integrity, and validation rules right in the database. The more that can be accomplished in the database, the less that needs to be duplicated in the client code. This practice, although effective in a two-tier architecture, can get in the way if we move to *n*-tier architectures, as we will discuss later in this chapter.

Control Over Distribution of Processing Chores

Another important drawback we saw in single-tier applications was its effect on the hardware requirements for end users. In this, two-tier applications make some advances, but not without cost.

A user's machine, under this model, is relieved of the burdens of managing the database. Instead, it simply calls off to a machine on the network, and that machine handles all the processing, only reporting back that it has finished. This does indeed lessen the requirements for the end-user PC and will slow down the requirements for hardware upgrades.

The most obvious savings overall is that only one copy of the database exists, instead of one for each user. This is a substantial savings in disk storage over the network.

The centralization of database access, although perhaps slower in some ways (you have to go across the LAN to get there), provides more options for scalability. Database servers can be expanded and multiprocessed to provide far better performance than the equivalent dollars spent for every workstation to get a similar performance. Trains have one (sometimes two) locomotives to pull the whole train. You don't see an engine on each car. The cost would be prohibitive.

REVIEW   BREAK

The two-tier approach to application design enables us to loosen the coupling between certain aspects of the application. In essence, it allows us to remove the database from the local PC and centralize it. This increases our difficulty of design because we have to account for remote access to data, and we also have to be careful about performance when doing the data access.

However, a great deal of improvement in maintenance and reporting capabilities is gained from a single database versus a multitude of single-user databases. Also, it allows the near-simultaneous access of large volumes of corporate data to all users. We can do things with this strategy that were impossible or very difficult with a single-tier architecture.

In summary, two-tier architecture offers many advantages over single tier. It has served as the dominant architecture for many years. Even today, it has a place in many solutions. However, another evolutionary step addresses many of the deficiencies of the two-tier strategy. We'll discuss that next.

n-Tier Applications

We have looked at single tier and two-tier development already. It might seem logical to look at three-tiered development next. In fact, what we are going to look at was, and still is, known as three-tier architecture. However, excursions have been made into four and five-tier development, and designers began to realize that the changes aren't as significant as those between one and two tiers, or between two and three tiers. Consequently, it is common for architects to classify all designs containing more than two tiers under the common descriptor of *n*-tier. This, coincidentally, fits in with Microsoft's stated objectives for the Solutions Architecture exam.

As we discussed with the two-tier strategy, tiers are logical, not necessarily physical. A three-tier client/server solution does not need to reside on three separate machines (see the situation on the right in Figure 6.3).

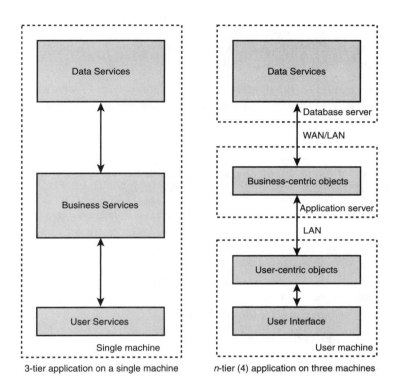

FIGURE 6.3
n-tier architecture (logical and physical).

Two-tier development essentially extracted the database layer of the application from the client computer, creating a second layer, or tier, in the application. Logically, then, *n*-tier designs are going to attempt to extract yet another layer of functionality from the client machine and place it in a centralized location. The target of *n*-tier development is business logic. It centers around the idea that business logic needs to be guaranteed to be identical across multiple users of the application. If, for example, a company validates or rejects an application for credit, it would be a very serious problem if somehow one operator could approve you, but another, given the same information, would not approve you. These kinds of errors are exactly the kind of problems people look to computers to solve.

Consequently, an *n*-tier design adds the concept of a business-services tier, or layer. This tier exists for the purpose of being a centralized place for the application to store business logic. The business logic, then, regulates all traffic between the user's screen and the database, ensuring that all the domain business rules are enforced and that the logic to validate and support user input gets executed consistently across all users.

The situation on the right in Figure 6.3 demonstrates an architecture that is becoming more popular these days because it solves some performance issues. The four-tier approach actually breaks the middle tier into two parts. The business-centric (or data-centric) services are in the application server, where they can be shared. This allows for resources and object pooling, security, and all the other things that middleware such as MTS can provide.

The user-centric objects (shown on the user's workstation) manage the attributes and methods necessary to provide a faster performing UI. The goal of this architecture is to cut back on the number of round trips made across the LAN every time the UI needs to validate some information. It does this while still keeping the UI ignorant of business rules. This keeps the UI thin and easily transportable to different technologies.

Before we proceed with the benefits and drawbacks to *n*-tier, we'll very briefly discuss the responsibilities of the three major tiers in Microsoft's model. We discuss each in much greater detail later in the book, so we'll move quickly through them here.

The *data services* tier is most well known to developers. It houses the data stores and is most often on a separate machine from the user's workstation. Under three-tier or *n*-tier design, we try to pull many of the business rules that were implemented using triggers, rules, and stored procedures out of the data tier and put them into the middle tier.

The *business services* tier, often referred to as the middle tier, houses the business and domain rules. If an object model is in the application, it usually exists here. The middle tier must package the data for the user tier and validate data before moving it to the data tier. It does things such as ensure that you don't submit a check request for a negative amount. The brains of the application reside in this tier.

If the business services tier is the brains of the outfit, the *user services* tier is the body. It is the part of the application that interacts with the outside world. Users enter and review data from this tier. Basic validation checks are sometimes performed (for example, valid date checking, simple math calculations) in the user services tier. User

> **NOTE**
>
> **What Constitutes a Tier?**
> Throughout this section, we may refer to *n*-tier as if each tier resides on a separate machine. This is done partly because this is a common practice when implementing *n*-tier and partly to make the text flow more smoothly, with fewer disclaimers. However, it is important to realize that tiers are logical constructs, not physical ones. The design should always allow for all tiers to remain on the same physical machine but should never make it a requirement that they do so. Just like a wedding cake, the tiers can be tightly coupled (touching) or they can be separated by distance (in the case of a wedding cake, typically small, white, plastic pillars).

support is often provided (for example, buttons enabled or disabled at the proper times, help systems) and the user is usually given feedback when processing is occurring (for example, hourglass cursor, "wait" pop-ups).

This three-tier model is evident in both the Microsoft Solutions Framework (MSF) as well as in the Microsoft Visual Modeler that ships with Visual Studio 6.

When compared to single-tier or two-tier architectures, *n*-tier applications are harder to test, harder to design, and more complicated in general because of all the dependencies and connection points. We'll explore the benefits and drawbacks in more detail as compared with the other two architectures:

◆ More difficult design and test

◆ Easier to maintain

◆ Highly decentralized processing requirements

◆ Distributed component approach

Difficulty of Creating a Good Design

As we can surmise, it is much more difficult to design a quality, effective, *n*-tier design than it is to design using either the single-tier or the two-tier architecture. That's not to say that it's rocket science. Most programmers could build a three-tier application. It's building one that is enterprise grade and that accomplishes all the PASS ME criteria that is difficult. By enterprise grade, we mean one that has sufficient quality to function successfully in an enterprisewide application. PASS ME was covered in Chapter 3, "PASS ME Analysis," so we won't go into that here.

Developing a good *n*-tier design is a lot like building a good three-layer wedding cake. Simply being good at baking each of the single cakes isn't enough. You need to have a good idea of where supports need to go, how the higher levels will be supported by the lower ones, and have a strong vision of how the whole thing goes from several smaller cakes and connects together to be one big cake.

Similarly, being an expert at designing each of the tiers in an *n*-tier solution is not the same as being an expert designer of an *n*-tier solution. A designer may have exactly the right software components (cakes), but without a good idea of how they all fit together and work to make things perform, they will remain just that—different pieces. This is why you often see specialists these days. With the rapid pace of technology, it is difficult to have a deep understanding of database technology, object technology (middle tier) and user-interaction design. We often see teams composed of these specialists, with a fourth specialist, the solutions architect, designing the big picture.

The glue which holds successful *n*-tier projects together is often called a *framework*. This enables each group of developers to focus on delivering appropriate functionality to the team while creating an atmosphere of confidence that, once complete, the pieces will be able to be assembled into a whole.

Part of the concept of an *n*-tier design is that information passing between the database and the user interface should rarely pass through in a "raw" state. This is in an effort to isolate these tiers from one another. Therefore, one of the most important aspects of designing an effective *n*-tier application is the ability to conceptualize each layer and how it relates to others within the application. In our wedding cake analogy, knowledge of how the cakes should be stacked up on one another (the framework) is at least as important as the knowledge of how each cake itself is made.

Designing a system so that it effectively addresses any bandwidth issues across LANs, WANs or telephone lines is more difficult in this style of architecture. Locating performance bottlenecks can be very difficult when the "moving parts" are spread across multiple machines. Designing the architecture so that locating the cause of a failure can be done efficiently is another challenge.

Testing the application also becomes more complex as it becomes more difficult to set up all the different permutations that could exist after deployment. A typical *n*-tier application could easily have 30 to 50 components that must all work in concert, along with the various operating systems that are involved.

Ease of Maintenance

One of the most critical aspects of *n*-tier design is the concept of abstraction of implementation. Each tier is a component of sorts, whose external behaviors are all that the other tiers know about. The internal implementation is hidden.

This approach is critical for maintenance of software because it allows a degree of interchangeability. For example, this makes it much simpler to change from one type of database to another. Without this modularity, it is a complicated, inherently risky process to try to replace one type of database with another.

Also, if we centralize our business logic on application servers, we have to update only one machine when business logic changes. Additionally, we have to update only the database server when data changes. Only in cases when we must update the actual physical user interface to an application must we experience all our previous issues with distribution.

Processing Distributed Across the Enterprise

The process that began with two-tier design is carried further in *n*-tier design. In two-tier design, the duty of database access is removed from the client computer and offloaded to a server. Similarly, in *n*-tier design, both the database and the business logic are removed from the end-user machine and are loaded onto separate logical machines.

Because of this offloading, we have a radical decrease in the processing requirements for the client machines. The client machine is now responsible only for displaying the user interface. However, as we have already seen in two-tier architecture, a certain trade-off has to be made. This trade-off is the existence of the application server. This machine will have to be powerful enough to funnel traffic between the database and user interfaces for all users.

However, one of the really helpful aspects of this design is that the logical application server can span one or more physical machines, enabling us to continue to use outgrown hardware, rather than having to remove it from the mix. This is one of the critical aspects that enhances the ROI of this type of project, and it compensates in many ways for the longer design cycle that needs to take place on this type of a solution.

Offloading all this computing to the servers may require more frequent updates to server hardware, but especially in larger enterprises, upgrading servers is almost always preferable to being forced to upgrade all the end-user workstations.

Overall, the use of application servers in an *n*-tier architecture increases scalability. Economies of scale can be applied. For example, we can utilize the concept of database connection pooling (discussed in Chapter 5, and earlier in this chapter) to decrease the overhead of establishing a connection to the database. Likewise, because of the reuse of connections, the database server benefits from having to service fewer connections overall.

Distributed Approach

How is all this tiering used in practice? The most common use of this technology is to distribute different aspects of the system across multiple machines. This is accomplished by building components that encapsulate business logic, database access, or user interface. Then, using one or more of several technologies designed for this purpose, the components are available for access across a network or even the Internet.

For us, the most notable technology of this type is Microsoft's DCOM protocol. This is essentially a means of taking your software components and being able to call these components from another machine. These machines might be end-user machines, application servers, or even database servers. Some of the components will be built as data access layers, which will enable the application to read and save data from a persistent storage mechanism. In this approach, the end-user computer (which houses the UI portion of the application) will make a call to a component residing on the application server. At some point, the application server components will probably need to retrieve some persisted data. To accomplish this, it will initiate requests to the database server.

This data is returned to the application server and its business logic components. At this point, business components use the data to make any necessary calculations and to verify against programmed business logic. This information, once translated, is provided to the user-interface computer (the end-user machine) in the format the client is expecting to receive it, independent of the format in which it was provided to the business components.

> **NOTE**
>
> **DCOM** We will discuss DCOM in more depth later in this book. For more information, consider the following two articles in MSDN: "DCOM Architecture" and "DCOM Solutions in Action."

As this book goes to press, Microsoft is consolidating DCOM and MTS into a single technology embedded in the operating system of Windows 2000. This platform is designed specifically to address the issues we have previously mentioned with inter-tier communication, as well as to simplify communication between machines (for example, a user workstation and an application server).

The history of *n*-tier applications is in large part still to be written. This approach has existed for years, but until recently, the hardware needed to run this type of application effectively has not existed. Much like a tiered wedding cake, it is a lot easier to build all the pieces of this type of application than it is to assemble it into a whole after the pieces are done.

Design for this type of application is always going to be more complex. Because of the complexities of making the various pieces fit together, a much greater need exists for trained architects who can craft a solution that will be stable, extensible, and powerful. With complexity comes power, but only if the solution is well architected.

R E V I E W   B R E A K

NOTE

For Further Information   To learn more about *n*-tier development, perform an MSDN search for the articles "Three-Tier Application Development" and "Integrate the Enterprise."

Solution Type at GWA Wines

To determine the best architecture, we'll use the process of elimination. If the idea is to enable remote customers to order wine, and the database is only going to be located at the winery, by definition we cannot have a single-tier solution.

However, we could have either a two-tier solution or an *n*-tier solution. One of the implicit technical desires in a program that (to some extent) must be made available to external users is to keep as much as possible internal to the company. Consequently, the way to keep as much of the system as possible on internal systems is to cut it into multiple tiers. The more tiers, the less that has to be sent to the client. Therefore, in our case study, GWA Wines would be better served by an *n*-tier solution type. Although we want to keep an open mind until later in the process, we can at least come up with a "strawman" architecture that has four tiers (see Figure 6.4). We'll go with that for now until we see a reason to reevaluate our decision.

R E V I E W   B R E A K

A few final thoughts before we move on to selecting the technology or technologies that will be utilized for our solution.

Microsoft supplies a tool, called Microsoft Visual Modeler, with Visual Studio that assists the developer in designing *n*-tier applications. Visual Modeler is based on the Microsoft Solutions Framework and the industry standard modeling language, UML.

Although well-defined rules surround the design of *n*-tier applications, it should be noted that there are times to break the rules. Just be sure to do it with your eyes open and be able to justify the reasons for those who must maintain or extend the application down the road.

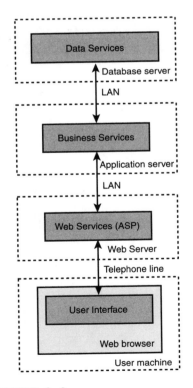

FIGURE 6.4
Proposed architecture for GWA Wines.

IDENTIFYING THE APPROPRIATE TECHNOLOGIES

Identify which technologies are appropriate for implementation of a given business solution.

After you have an overall vision regarding the application's solution type, the next step is to start making decisions about which technologies to use. There are three factors to take into consideration in making these decisions.

◆ Technology standards

◆ Selection of development tools

◆ Type of solution

Technology Standards

One of the greatest tools that exists today for decreasing development time on a custom application is the use of technology standards. The word "standard" is thrown around often in computer literature, and it is useful here to pause long enough to define it. In this case, we aren't talking about programming standards or development standards. Instead, we are talking about published standards for interoperation. A good example is file formats.

Through their publication to the software development community, they provide a good way to leverage someone else's work. For example, when someone writes software to display graphical images stored in a particular format, it eases all other software developer's burdens if they can store their images in that format and use existing technology to read and display the information. Some examples of successful file format standards are

◆ ASCII format (text files) and RTF format (Rich Text Format) for sharing of text

◆ PDF format (Adobe Acrobat) for combined text and graphics files

◆ BMP, JPG, and GIF formats for graphics files

◆ WAV, MID, and MP3 formats for sound files

There are really only two types of technology standards: open and proprietary. The primary difference between them has to do with whether the specification is shared openly with the public or has completely been designed and implemented by those who own the specification.

◆ Open standards

◆ Proprietary standards

Open Standards

Many open standards exist in the software development environment today. Some of the best known of these standards are the following:

◆ **HTML (HyperText Markup Language)**—This is the language through which basic Web pages are communicated. It is a standard because it enables files to be sent to the browser, which, of whatever type, knows how to read HTML files. An HTML file itself is just a string of text.

◆ **EDI (Electronic Document Interface)**—This is a defined structure for electronic commerce transfer.

◆ **ANSI 92-compliant SQL**—Standard commands for accessing relational databases.

- ◆ **ODBC (Open Database Connectivity)**—ODBC has been the de facto standard for connecting to different types of databases with a single API.
- ◆ **ActiveX/COM**—ActiveX and COM are now open standards, developed by Microsoft and maintained by the Open Group.
- ◆ **TCP/IP (Transmission Control Protocol/Internet Protocol)**—An industry standard network that serves as the foundation of the Internet.

You could choose to ignore a standard such as HTML and write your own technology that lets you stream documents over the Internet. However, what would be the point of doing so? In a business environment, the more of these standards that can be leveraged, the more stable your development cycle can be, and the less expensive it will be to build and maintain.

Open standards provide the following benefits:

- ◆ Extensive public information about features and limits of the standard let you know exactly what can be expected.
- ◆ Updates to the standard will be publicly documented and available.
- ◆ It is easier to purchase off-the-shelf add-ins and components that build on the standard technology.

Most often, open standards are drafted and submitted, as HTML was, to some political or official body. This process surrounding the creation of a standard creates a distinct set of advantages and disadvantages that we don't often see in proprietary standards. In fact, most of what makes the Internet possible is based around standards (for example, TCP/IP, HTML, ActiveX, Java).

Other examples of open-standard technologies include POSIX and OSI.

Proprietary Standards

Proprietary standards, as the name implies, are standards that belong to a particular company and are not published as public domain. Typically, though, the nature of these standards is such that the internal implementation is not important so long as the standard performs as advertised.

Good examples of these include Windows NT and RSA Encryption.

◆ **Windows NT**—This is Microsoft's proprietary operating system. Although Windows NT is owned by Microsoft, its functionality is exposed by publicly published APIs. This allows the industry to build products that rely on those APIs, but the code base remains proprietary.

◆ **RSA Encryption**—This is a model for the encryption of messages as they are sent from one location to another. The nature of the encryption is available, but the specifics of it are not public domain. The reason should be obvious, considering that the purpose of this standard is encryption; certain aspects of the encryption process cannot be made public, or it will not properly secure transactions.

Again, we might choose to ignore the options available commercially, either for an open standard or for a homegrown design. However, if you are not in the business of building and designing standards, choosing to do so opens up a whole new set of risks. If you can do it, it is almost always better to export this workload to a company that is already building such a standard. This is most easily done, obviously, by simply using a preexisting standard.

Using Standards at GWA Wines

Again for our case study, as in any other project, the use of these technical standards enables you to reduce the amount of time spent on things that cannot be directly assigned to an aspect of the project, such as writing standards for a language.

Instead, we might decide we want an *n*-tier Web-based application. As such, we are immediately adopting COM and HTML.

For database connectivity, because the data is stored in relational tables on a mainframe and because the owner has declared that he wants to focus on new technologies, we will go with OLE DB and ADO 2.0.

Technology Direction for the Company

Almost every company, as we have seen, has an existing application base. Usually, it also has some sort of an infrastructure base that predates the problem you are attempting to solve for them.

When you are designing an application for an enterprise, it is imperative to take into account any existing technological direction within the company or department.

Just as important is the direction in which the company plans to be heading in the future. If everything that is currently being deployed is Web enabled, and you attempt to display a non-Web based application, you may find that your solution is a square peg in a round hole. Probably, a strong push will be made to rewrite it sooner than if it had been consistent with the rest of the environment. Your application's capability to provide ROI is radically decreased when its life span is cut to a fraction of its original plan.

Current Direction

Be aware of your client's direction today. If it is a 100% mainframe shop and you've decided, without specific direction to do so, to implement a PC server-based solution, the client will most likely not be happy with it. It might be that what the client is discovering it needs isn't the newest and greatest of technology. It is normally your job to make people aware of the options and then to design a solution that meets their needs. If it ends up utilizing a legacy technology, at least you can be sure it meets the needs of the target users.

Conversely, departments that have made a commitment to focus on Microsoft technologies will influence the list of technologies from which to choose. COM is much more likely to be chosen than CORBA. VC++ is a more natural choice than Java.

A careful appraisal of the infrastructure of a company from a technology standpoint is important to make sure that the solution being envisioned is appropriate. Equally important, though, is to recognize that it's not only the physical infrastructure that must be taken into account. Perhaps even more important is an awareness of the technical environment and skill set of the staff. If the entire staff is already trained in a specific technology and will have to start over to learn a new one, this needs to be taken into account. In fact, it may even be the deciding factor.

Planned Future Direction

Many times, as you are rolling out a solution, you may find yourself involved in a corporate decision to change strategies from one technology or set of technologies to another. Many of us have lived through these types of projects as companies have moved data and applications off of mainframes that were being made obsolete by Y2K questions. Although these radical shifts are not always the case, it is important from a technology perspective to find out early on where the company is headed.

First, if the company is going to be radically changing its approach, you need to target that new position even more so than the existing one. If it means that it is a mainframe shop now and that it is committing to a change to PC-based development, you need to make sure you don't weigh the existing mainframe as heavily as if the company had made another 10-year commitment to the mainframe.

Second, investigate whether the company is planning to make these changes in the time span of your implementation. A classic example is a conversion to Windows NT. You might be building your application to roll out in six months, but if in four months, the company plans to be rolled into the NT server, you need to build the application for the NT box, not for the previous environment. If changes are being made to the production environment concurrent with the development and deployment cycle for your solution, you need to be doubly sure of what your target date is and what environment you are planning to deploy into. Changes in technology that will occur within the timeframe of your new solution usually must be considered dependencies when building a deployment schedule.

If you can anticipate changes to certain parts of your solution, you can *wrap*, or isolate, the main part of your code from these changes by providing abstraction classes. This technique is often used to create *vendor neutral* solutions. You simply unplug a wrapper to one vendor's interface and plug in another. This is usually used where your solution connects to the outside world.

Technology at GWA Wines

Although the company isn't quite ready to retire the AS/400, GWA Wines has made a commitment to moving into PC-based technology. This allows us to plan for the impending changeover. However, because of the statement that the COBOL application will not be retired in the first release of our solution, consideration should still be given on how to interoperate with the old environment.

Because of the statements that Visual Basic and HTML skills already exist, we can assume that Microsoft technologies are more likely to fit into the long-term plans of GWA Wines.

Selection of Development Tools

All development tools have an area of expertise that makes them the natural choice for a given solution. Some tools (Visual Basic, for example) are considered a better choice when rapid development is required. Even in the Microsoft world of COM, where a binary standard allows code to be developed and used without regard for tools, the selection of the right platform can make the difference between success and failure. Some of the issues involved in selecting development tools include:

- ◆ Rapid Application Development (RAD)
- ◆ Performance
- ◆ Cross-platform use
- ◆ Internet application design

Each of these issues is addressed to some degree by all the development tools, but as Microsoft itself will tell you, not all tools are equally good at doing all of them. To understand which tools should be used for which process is to come to a better understanding of how to make your application generate the maximum ROI by minimizing the amount of initial investment in development.

Visual Basic

Visual Basic is Microsoft's premiere Rapid Application Development (RAD) tool. It is designed around visual interfaces and is an excellent tool for any developer concentrating on user-interface aspects of an application. User-interface elements are in a toolbar on the side and are placed on a normal Windows screen by dragging and dropping them around the screen. They can be easily resized, and the properties of each element are menu driven and automatically type checked.

COM server creation is also exceptionally simple in Visual Basic, allowing developers to create components even when the details of COM and MTS are unknown to them. This is a huge advantage when you are starting a component-based solution with a team that has not done COM development before.

Many developers would probably identify their favorite feature of Visual Basic as its IDE. The debugger in VB is probably the most user friendly in the entire Visual Studio line. It enables line-by-line step-through of code, running multiple components via source code, and change and continue debugging. Essentially this means that a VB project can be run, and when an error is discovered it can be changed and the program can continue executing without being recompiled each time a change is made.

Finally, with the advent of version 6.0, Visual Basic has made enormous strides in the arena of Internet development. Two types of projects, WebClasses and Dynamic HTML applications, enable Visual Basic to create visually rich environments from HTML. These new features enable personalization of Web pages to reach a whole new level, and they also allow the code behind Web pages to remain in compiled format.

With its wide range of options, from wizard-generated code on the RAD side to the capability to call Windows APIs on the power side, VB is the most popular development tool in the world.

Visual C++

If we compared Visual Basic to a pickup truck, the workhorse of the Microsoft suite, then VC++ is a high-performance sports car. If speed and absolute control are essential, VC++ has what it takes.

The downside, of course, is that (to quote a famous saying) "with great power comes great responsibility." In our case this still holds true. Visual C++ developers take responsibility for implementing many of the details of Microsoft's COM architecture. No problem occurs with doing so; however, this now pushes component development into a much more elite group of developers who have an excellent understanding of how COM works. In essence, this power comes at the expense of ease of use, and thus decreases the number of developers capable of just "picking it up." The learning curve is significantly longer and the chance to make a coding error that can crash the PC is greater.

Also, because of the nature of C++ and its debugging, it is very difficult to engage in traditional, corporate-style RAD projects when using C++. Debugging a C++ project requires much more in the way of compiling, running, and recompiling than does VB. This results in a much slower development and design cycle, both because of the slower debugging and because of the increased need for design (for example, for COM functions that VB takes care of behind the scenes).

Internet development, for C++, is basically the same as any other development. It is complicated, but it is handled fairly straightforwardly. It is certainly not an easy way to do Internet development.

Performance in C++ applications varies (more so, in fact, than most other languages). However, in the hands of a qualified developer, this product, without question, builds the fastest applications in the Windows environment.

If you need exacting control over all aspects of the solution, such as when you're writing shrink-wrap applications such as word processors, games, and virus-scan software, VC++ is the tool to use. If complicated multithreading is a requirement, VC++ is probably the correct choice.

Visual J++

Continuing with our vehicle analogy, VJ++ would be the four-wheel-drive, go-anywhere utility vehicle. Although VJ++ and its genesis, Java, are still struggling to find their place in the industry, the possibilities are promising.

Java has a huge advantage over other applications when it comes to interoperability. It is the only language today that allows the production of applications that will run on multiple hardware platforms (for example, PC, UNIX, AS/400). This is obviously a huge plus for development.

However, performance on platform-independent applications basically has been abysmal compared with similar applications developed specifically for the platform. In an effort to level the playing field between this and other languages, Microsoft introduced an implementation of Java that enables calls to Windows-specific programs. This obviously undermines the cross-platform usage of Java, but in doing so, it dramatically improves performance when running in Windows.

In terms of its complexity, VJ++ lies somewhere between VB and VC++. It is certainly more difficult to use than VB, but because of its relatively limited set of functionality, especially when writing platform-independent code, it is simpler than Visual C++. Because it is an interpreted language, VJ++ is generally slower than both VB and VC++.

Java has long been touted as the next step in Internet development. It was the first time that anyone was able to put any form of compiled code on the Internet that would execute on client workstations rather than on the server. This opened up a whole new set of options for developers and catapulted Java to the forefront of Internet development.

Visual InterDev

Visual InterDev is a tool for Web application development. Using this tool, a development team can implement a client-server or n-tier solution that is distributed via Web pages to the user base.

However, comparisons between this tool and the others we have discussed are very difficult because Visual InterDev is not the same kind of tool as the others. HTML, the native tongue of Visual InterDev, is not a compiled language, but is instead an interpreted one. Obviously, then, this is going to be significantly slower than any compiled language.

This performance hit, however, is usually offset to some degree by the ease of distribution that Web pages bring to the game. This enables clients all over the world, who have had no contact with an application before and certainly have never installed anything on their PCs, to have access to your application. Nothing specific to your software needs to be running on the client. All the end-user's system needs is a Web browser, and the application information can be provided from various servers on the Internet or intranet. InterDev can create solutions targeted at specific browsers, or it can create solutions that are essentially browser independent.

Before the creation of Visual InterDev and other tools like it, the only option for Web developers was a sort of "change and try" method for debugging. With Visual InterDev and its high level of interaction with other tools, such as Microsoft's Internet Information Server (IIS), it is possible to do a line-by-line debugging of a Web page, with immediate notice of where it is failing.

Visual InterDev also brought to the forefront another technology for Web pages: scripting. Scripting, in essence, allows a Web designer to program a Web page as if it were a normal application, appealing to elements and forms. This allowed a whole class of developers who were already familiar with the Windows model for programming to gain quick entrance into the world of developing Web applications.

Other Development Tools

Although most serious client/server development will be done using one of the four tools mentioned previously, other options are open to a developer.

The entire family of Microsoft Office products now includes VBA (Visual Basic for Applications), which allows for powerful development bolted on to Word, Excel, PowerPoint, Outlook, and Access. Microsoft Access deserves a special mention because it could be considered a self-contained development platform in itself. All recent releases of Microsoft Office have included a product specifically for this purpose—Microsoft Office, Developer Edition.

Microsoft offers several other tools that can be selected to assist in the development effort—version control tools such as Microsoft SourceSafe and database design tools such as Microsoft Database Designer.

REVIEW BREAK

In Table 6.1, we have summarized the "Big Four" development platforms as well as the proper positioning of each in the selection of a language for the solution you are designing.

TABLE 6.1				
CONTRASTING STRENGTHS OF DEVELOPMENT TOOLS				
	Visual Basic	*Visual C++*	*Visual J++*	*Visual Interdev*
Internet Development	WebClasses DHTML Apps	Manual, very tough	Java is Internet-based	Tool for Internet development
Performance	Midrange	High speed	Slower than C++ or VB	Not compiled, N/A

	Visual Basic	*Visual C++*	*Visual J++*	*Visual Interdev*
RAD Tool	Premiere tool for RAD	Not a RAD tool	Not a RAD tool	Speeds up Web site building
Cross-platform use	Only WebClasses	Very limited, Web	Optional fully cross-platform	Most Web tools cross platform, some do not

As you can see, very specific circumstances exist under which we might want to use each of the tools. Microsoft has made it clear that it has no intentions of even attempting to make all tools equal. Instead, our role as application designers is going to grow, including a new task of deciding which tools should be used to build which pieces of the applications.

In addition to the differences that have been summarized previously, all these languages have some things in common. They all support access to disparate sources of data by supporting OLE DB. The UDA (Universal Data Access) framework provides a common architecture for them all.

Development Tools for GWA Wines

In our case study, several things are pushing us toward the use of Visual InterDev. First, the solution we are designing is probably most reasonably implemented as a Web site. If it is implemented as a Web site, InterDev offers the maximum flexibility of features.

This would enable us to build a 100% Web-based solution for accepting the orders. However, if we weren't sure a Web solution was where we wanted to go, we could implement it in Visual Basic, which includes functionality for building Web solutions, and additionally has a large set of non-Web features that could be leveraged. Because the IT manager stated that two of his people are already in Visual Basic training, this might be enough to tip the scales in that direction.

NOTE

For Further Information To learn more about tool selection, perform an MSDN search for the article "Building Successful Client/Server Applications" and scroll down to the section titled "Choosing the 'Right' Language." You may also want to read more about Microsoft's UDA strategy. Perform a search using UDA as the criteria.

What Type of Solution Are We Building?

Another important aspect to successful architecting is to have a solid vision for what type of solution you will be developing. This becomes a focal point, a single goal that team members can rally around and build toward as they work through the project. It also gives the designer a nice, high-level decision that can be used as an entree to engage users in the design process. Most often, the requirements from the user base will lead directly to one of these options. Also note that the types are not always mutually exclusive.

The types of solutions commonly proposed include the following:

◆ Enterprise

◆ Collaborative

◆ Communication

◆ Centralized

◆ Distributed

Enterprise

An enterprise application is usually defined as a large-scale, corporate application. The term *enterprise*, when used to describe a solution, usually denotes an application that has high visibility. Often, the company's success or failure can rest on the shoulders of an enterprisewide solution. These are known as *mission-critical* applications.

Enterprise applications are often "bet your business" types of applications, so they demand the highest levels of design, architecture, and quality. They are the skyscrapers of the IT world. Microsoft has created a model, called the Enterprise Application Model, that addresses the design of this type of application.

Because of the wide array of demands and various levels of technical expertise among their user community, these applications need to be especially robust and should be designed especially well in relation to user help.

When building this type of application, we need to be doubly sure that adequate work has been done to establish the goal of the application. Because it will affect so many users, it is critical that as many issues as can be resolved beforehand are resolved.

Don't be in a hurry to believe that a given application is at the enterprise level. Although it is true that such projects are generally high profile, with it they carry an increased set of risks. Many of the risks can only be minimally mitigated internally. Changing requirements, incompatible expectations, and/or limited patience for early test phases all serve to increase the risk of enterprise-level applications.

When you are working with a solution that has been identified as enterprise, expertise and skill in the architecture can make or break the project. It is not the time to just grab whomever is handy to design the solution.

Collaboration

These applications are designed to allow users to work together in new ways. This type of solution, when properly designed and implemented, can change the entire way a company does business. Examples of this type of application include things such as

◆ Video conferencing

◆ Shared whiteboard technology

◆ Document sharing

These types of applications enable users to collaborate on documents or other forms of data. It also prevents physical distance between employees from limiting the ability to communicate. It does this by allowing them to share a virtual whiteboard from locations across the planet the same way they might share a piece of paper and pencil in the same room.

An example of a collaborative application is Microsoft NetMeeting, designed to create a virtual conference room where audio, video, text, graphics, file transfer, and a free-form white board contribute to removing some of the issues of working remotely.

Communication

A solution type also exists that is devoted to enhancing collaboration. However, these applications are designed to work more within the traditional channels of communication. These applications, although not as revolutionary as collaboration software, often have an equally positive effect on productivity because they enhance existing work patterns.

Examples of this type of software include

◆ Fax software

◆ Email software

◆ Instant messaging software

These may seem like disparate types of applications, but they do have one thing in common. They replace existing work patterns with something that is technical, but of a similar style. Fax software replaces a traditional fax machine, email software can replace interoffice mail, and instant-messaging software can replace the widely distributed office memo.

Centralized

Centralized applications are ones in which the users typically are nearby and work from a single database. It often typifies home-office applications such as accounting software or order processing.

Centralized applications are usually easier to design because some amount of control over the user PCs is available. The network connections are usually of the LAN type, which simplifies design further by taking away the challenge of overcoming long latencies (although some LANs are so overworked that the same issues can come into play).

Data entry applications are usually centralized because they need to work against a single set of tables (for example, inventory data, customer records, order processing information).

Workflow that has tight timeframes or that is synchronous in nature would likely fall into this category. Often, the workflow task queue is just a centralized database table(s).

Most Internet applications fall into this category because the data stores and the code base are located on a central server and are requested on demand.

Distributed

Distributed applications are characterized by a more dispersed set of users. Often, this is accompanied by each user having an individual copy of the application and the data store, or a data store that is shared by an entire office but is separated from the central database.

These can be some of the hardest to design and to maintain. User machines are often configured differently. Even if they start out the same, it is very difficult to keep them under control as people download "stuff" from the Internet.

Another problem is data replication. Keeping multiple databases synchronized with a master copy is challenging.

Some workflow applications use this model, passing tasks through email or from database to database. It depends on whether the workflow is synchronous (which would be more likely to use the centralized model) or asynchronous (email).

Most shrink-wrap software falls into this category.

Solution Type at GWA Wines

The GWA Wines remote ordering software is primarily designed to replace a data entry application. Because all users will be funneled into a single data store and because the Web interface stores the application code at the server, this is considered a centralized solution model.

IDENTIFYING APPROPRIATE DATA STORAGE ARCHITECTURE

Choose a data storage architecture.

After we've chosen a development model, a development tool, and the overriding vision for the solution, the next step is to address how we will persist our information so that the application can actually store information and be useful to its target user group. Typically, the answer is some kind of database. However, user requirements may exist that will push you away from this type of solution.

We want to look at four main elements when deciding how to store data. They are

◆ The scope of business data storage needs

◆ Extensibility requirements

◆ Reporting requirements

◆ The type of database desired or required

Scope of Business Requirements

Choosing a persistence strategy is not simply a technical decision. It is usually driven just as much by business issues as by technology issues.

We'll look at some of the things that go into deciding what data needs to be stored and how much of it there will be. This process is sometimes referred to as volumetrics. Volumetrics can be analyzed in an number of different ways including:

◆ Volume of data

◆ Number of transactions per time increment

◆ Number of connections of sessions

◆ Number of users

Volume of Data

One of the most important factors to get a handle on at this point is the total amount of data that will be stored in the database. Volume is identified as the total number of rows estimated, multiplied by the width (in bytes) of a single record. An example of how this might look for a very small system is shown in Table 6.2.

TABLE 6.2

DATABASE VOLUMETRICS ANALYSIS

Table	Records	Bytes/Record	Total Bytes
Customer	5,000	1,200	6,000,000
InventoryDetail	200	500	100,000
Order (holds 1 yr.)	30,000	800	24,000,000
OrderDetail	60,000	100	6,000,000
Employee	60	1,500	90,000
StateTable (static)	51	50	2,550
Total			36,192,550

Thus, for our *very* simple example, we can expect more than 36MB of storage to be consumed by the end of the year. Some of this data, such as the StateTable and the Employee table, will not grow substantially throughout the year, but hopefully, the Order and OrderDetail tables will exceed our record volume estimates.

It should be noted that in our simplified math, we did not account for indexed fields. As many readers know, the storage requirements can come close to doubling depending on how many indexes are required. For various reasons, it is a good idea to set aside two to three times the anticipated storage determined in the preceding exercise.

Equally important to your decision will be the degree that old data needs to be kept online. For example, in the preceding fictitious solution, we have specified that information should be kept online for 12 months. Data that is more than 12 months old should be archived. We need to make sure to allow enough storage space for archived and/or decision support databases. Reducing the set of data can really improve performance, but it is necessary to get a handle on whether this solution is acceptable to your users.

Number of Transactions Per Time Increment

This is essentially an assessment of the minimum overall throughput required of a system. It is organized by transactions per time slice because typically, resources related to internal workings of the database are assigned and released on the basis of committing a transaction. Transactions per time slice basically means, "How many trips do I take to the database for a given period of time (for example, 40 reads/second)?"

The number of expected transactions will depend largely on the type of system you are building. If you are designing a data-entry system, obviously there will be a lot of transactions updating the system. If you are only reading data for a decision support application, there will be fewer transactions.

Equally important as the number is the context or content of the transactions. What is being transacted? Because of the changes in database speed depending on memory and what is cached, it is necessary to get a good idea of what kind of information may be updated. For example, it is important to know whether the information is all one table or if every table is equally likely to be updated. Are we are reading static data into cache? Are we doing live updates of records that could possibly be updated by another user at the same time? Are we doing lots of table joins? Is the data fully normalized or denormalized?

To measure this, using a simplified example, we might figure out how many simultaneous users will be accessing the database. This number is almost always lower than the number of real users because in a large percentage of the time, users are doing things that do not require active database transfers.

We take the count of users multiplied by the number of trips for data. Trips should be identified as read, write, delete, or insert. The trips should be counted and the expected number of bytes involved in the trip should be multiplied as well.

For example:

Static data (once at startup time, read only)

50 users × 10 trips × 30,000 bytes (averaged) = 15,000,000 bytes (between 8 a.m. and 9 a.m.)

Production data (queries against live data)

50 users × 200 trips × 3000 bytes (averaged) = 30,000,000 bytes/hour (using peak hour of 10 a.m. to 11 a.m.)

If decision support users were also accessing the same tables, they would have to be accounted for as well. Although we did not factor it into our simplified example, the trips should be characterized as to whether they are read or write. This information will help us better understand the amount of possible locking conflicts. Locking style (for example, pessimistic, optimistic, page, record) is also a factor in our analysis.

Number of Connections or Sessions

This number tells you what level of database use you will have in terms of licensing requirements and simultaneously managed connections. Connections and sessions are used by many databases as the means for deciding the number or the kind of license a site needs. This will also tell you something, when used in conjunction with the other measurements, about how powerful your database server machine needs to be.

We can use the typical number of simultaneous users from the previous section. We can expect about 50 users to be accessing the database at any one time. This means that we need to be able to support at least 75 connections (accounting for peaks). This is where MTS can show its stuff. By wisely using database connection pooling, we can make 500 users seem like 50 to the database server. The benefits are obvious.

Number of Users

This is the last of the main things that will be used to decide the scope of your data needs. In reality, however, it is most often used simply as a control variable. If the number of users on a system becomes twice what you had estimated, it is much easier to explain why the database may not be performing as expected. If these questions are asked, you will have answers, and you will be able to explain why more hardware or more licenses need to be purchased to make the system work as advertised.

This metric is not measuring simultaneous users, but total users. In our example, this is 5,060 (5,000 customers and 60 employees).

Extensibility Requirements

In essence, what we are looking for is an estimate of how long the solution is expected to be used. Also, after this is known, how much growth is expected in that time frame? It is important that this be estimated early in the process because if it is a fairly short-term solution or if growth expectations are minimal, the issues identified here may be fairly unimportant.

However, in a system that is going to be in place long term and that is constantly generating new data, gaining users, and expects to have growing sets of data to track, one of the primary duties of a system designer is to create a system that can be easily extended.

To do this, we will look at the four types of growth that can occur within a database architecture:

◆ Growth of data

◆ Growth of data set (items collected)

◆ Growth of usage

◆ Growth of functionality

Growth of Data

Data growth is simply a result of a system accepting input of new data from users, typically in the form of new table records. It is a natural process, and except in very rare circumstances, it is one that almost every application should count on having to account for.

The upside to this increased workload is that most relational databases handle this for us to a certain degree. As designers, we need to do only two things: First, make sure that we adequately set expectations for nontechnical users as far as the results on performance caused by increased data. Second, if the system is a high-data input system, considerations must be made as to when old data gets moved off the live system.

In some cases this may be never, but finding that out beforehand will allow planning to either cause it to happen or to set expectations accordingly.

Growth of Data Collected

This is also a growth of data, but whereas you might think of the first example as vertical growth in the data (adding more records), this is a 'horizontal' growth, adding more fields to existing tables or more tables. Essentially what it means is that users may discover they need to expand the set of data they are collecting for each record. If so, it can greatly affect your ability to meet performance goals.

Sometimes, these issues may be resolved simply. However, in the cases where they are not, it can be debilitating to the application's performance.

Growth of Usage

This is simply an increase in either the number of users accessing the system or in the amount of database activity by the same user set (for example, more complex queries).

Growth of usage is almost a given for a successful solution. Whether intentional or not, any solution will influence the way a company conducts its business. As its work patterns evolve, new and unanticipated uses for the data will become evident.

Growth of Functionality

In several areas of database design, new functionality might be incorporated into a system. Examples include things such as reporting requirements and data warehousing. If these functions are added to the database, additional time should be made for testing, development, and design. New functions may also affect performance, so additions of this sort should be planned out carefully.

Reporting Requirements

As we've stated previously, the best technical design won't mean anything to the end users (although a poor design will get their attention almost immediately). What they will most often be concerned about is their interaction with the program. One of the areas where users directly interact with the system is its ability to provide them with information served up in a way that is convenient to them and that addresses their business goals. Reporting requirements fall into this category.

When it comes to reporting, two types of requirements occur: frequency and complexity.

Frequency

Some applications may have requirements that, for example, support only daily summary reports. These reports could be generated in batches during the evening. This is a very low level of frequency for report generation, and the requirements for it are very easy to meet.

However, many applications contain requirements that will need on-demand styles of reporting. This is, in essence, the ability of an end user to make a request for a report at any time of the day and have it returned to them in real-time, either as a file or printed to a specified printer. This kind of frequency might cause a revisiting of the reporting architecture to verify that it is capable of performing at this level.

Complexity

Again, nearly as many levels of report complexity exist as there are applications. Some people will simply want, as we've already discussed, summary reports for daily activities. At other times, applications will require on-demand, dynamic, parent-child structure reports. These reports will be much more taxing on resources to run, both in terms of design resources and the data queries necessary to populate them.

These on-demand reports usually take one of two forms: *canned* and *ad hoc.*

Canned reports are the easier of the two. Users choose from a pre-built list of reports. The queries that form the basis of the reports have been tested and tuned to produce the proper results using safe and efficient SQL.

Ad hoc queries, on the other hand, are often designed by the user, on-the-fly, without any advance warning about how long the query will take or how big of a drain it will be on system resources. The nightmare scenario in this type of reporting scheme is to allow users to design a "Cartesian join" on two large tables, creating a massive number of records returned—if the system even finishes the query. When designing ad hoc query capability into a solution, it is best to place "guard rails" into the query designer screen to keep a novice user from taking down a production database. In case you are not aware of this, it is possible, with a poorly designed user query, to take down an entire IBM MVS mainframe running CICS. Enough said.

Knowing as soon as possible what kind of expectations users have for reports can enable you to prioritize the reporting components so that you can achieve your reporting goals. It is important that we all strive to resist the development tendency to think that reports can be worked out later; then they slip further and further down the priority list. Remember that reports are one of the few ways that an average user will evaluate your design. Let that be a guide in deciding on priorities for this part of the system.

Types of Databases

When the decision is made to store data, the next obvious question is how to store it. Several options are possible that aren't database related, but generally speaking, the appropriate method of persisting data is through the use of some type of database.

Indexed

This type of database allows a query to go to the nth record in a table but does not necessarily allow movement within a recordset (that is, go to the record before this one). Therefore, it does not carry the traditional recordset metaphor through all its construction, and it also does not enforce at the database level the concept of a primary or secondary key on a table.

An example of an indexed database is VSAM or IMS, both mainframe data storage techniques.

Hierarchical

The data structure returned from a hierarchical database will be a small relational database all its own. It will maintain records that are parent-child related. A good example is items on an order. Several ordered items are in a child relationship to one parent—the order.

Probably the most well-known example of a hierarchical database is the Windows registry. It is characterized by the tree-and-branches model.

Relational

Relational databases are those with which you are probably most familiar. They enforce primary keys and return structures called recordsets or resultsets, which enable relatively easy access to data. Microsoft SQL Server is an example of this type of database.

Relational databases support access through SQL (Structured Query Language).

This is the database you are most likely to use in an *n*-tier solution.

Object Oriented

This database type is a relatively new player on the market. Essentially, this technology allows a system to save objects in a database, rather than reading out the persisting properties and saving them in another style of database. The main drawback is that after you've decided on this system, you are almost forced to build all your software as object-oriented software.

This may all seem like a lot of work, and it is. Many of us have designed applications without taking some (or any) of these factors into consideration. We think storage is unlimited. However, at the server level, storage is *not* unlimited, and neither are CPU cycles.

EXAM TIP

Database Types Although the spectrum of database types is covered in this section to provide a comprehensive list, when the exam asks you to design a database, it will most certainly be a relational database. All of Microsoft's main-stream database products (SQL Server, Access, FoxPro) are considered relational databases.

Doing the math up front can save us from embarrassment and frustration down the road when the database server locks up one Friday afternoon, just as we are packing our bags to go home for the weekend.

Data Storage at GWA Wines

In our case study, very little discussion of data occurred, except to say that the legacy data is on an AS/400 machine. Because we are told that the legacy system is not going away just yet, it may be that the simplest thing to do is to work on interfacing with that machine. This is a classic example of where more work is needed to draw out requirements.

There was no mention of reports that the system must generate. In this type of solution, we are really just putting a new front on existing data, so it is uncharacteristic to see requirements for reports that don't already exist.

Because we basically are opening up our system directly to our customer base, we can anticipate large increases in the number of records we need to store. We must proceed with caution because when customers encounter slow response time, they may turn away, never to return.

In determining the database type, because we are staying with the existing tables, we can be pretty sure that data will be stored in a relational database. Any replicated data (server data) should follow the same pattern to retain efficiency.

These are the kinds of questions you need to ask, and this is the stage at which they need to be asked. You aren't being asked (generally) to reimplement a solution; you're being asked to solve problems. Make sure you know what the problems are before continuing.

CHAPTER SUMMARY

KEY TERMS

- Collaborative application
- Cross-platform compatibility
- Data Entry application
- Enterprise application
- Hierarchical database
- Indexed database
- Messaging application
- *n*-tier
- Object database
- Open standards
- Proprietary standards
- Rapid Application Development (RAD)
- Relational database
- Single tier
- Two tier
- Workflow application

The basis of any good solution is a sound and well-thought-out technical architecture. As we've seen, technical design must be thought out in several areas before any construction begins.

First, you need to decide what solution type is being sought. This is primarily a decision of how processing will be distributed across machines in the enterprise. Whether it is all isolated onto a single machine or distributed across multiple machines, decisions must be made in terms of design and maintenance.

In addition to the solution type, the technical environment for the solution should be taken into account. This includes the existing and planned environment, as well as things such as standards that can be implemented and types of tools that should be used for development.

The second main aspect of design to be undertaken at this point is an analysis of the data architecture. The important thing is to first assess the business requirements for data storage and then design something that will solve their problems.

APPLY YOUR KNOWLEDGE

Exercises

6.1 Selecting a Solution Type

For each of the solutions in Table 6.3, draw a line from the solution to the most likely architectural type.

Estimated Time: 5 minutes.

TABLE 6.3

ARCHITECTURAL TYPE AND CHARACTERISTIC SOLUTIONS

Single tier	Screen-scraper application
	Client/server
	Internet application
	Mainframe "green-screen" application
Two tier	DOS application
	Object-oriented application
	Component-based design
	MIDI player (sound files)
n-tier	Q-BASIC program
	Most scalable and extendable

Your solution should look like the following:

Single tier = "green-screen," DOS application, MIDI player, Q-BASIC

Two tier = Screen-scraper application, client/server

n-tier = Internet, object-oriented, component-based design, scalable, extendable

6.2 Choosing Technologies

For each of the requirements in Table 6.4, select the language(s) that match the requirement.

Estimated Time: 5 minutes.

TABLE 6.4

TECHNOLOGIES AND THEIR STRENGTHS

Visual Basic	Internet Development
	RAD
	HTML development
VC++	Cross-platform
	Short learning curve
	Best performance overall
VJ++	Most powerful when working with Windows APIs
	Largest contingent of available developers
	Simplified VC++
Visual InterDev	Interactive debugging capability

Your solution should look like the following:

Internet Development—all 4

RAD—Visual Basic

HTML development—InterDev

Cross-platform—VJ++, Visual InterDev

Short learning curve—Visual Basic, InterDev

Best performance overall—VC++

APPLY YOUR KNOWLEDGE

Most powerful when working with Windows APIs—VC++

Largest contingent of available developers—Visual Basic

Simplified VC++—VJ++

Interactive debugging capability—Visual Basic, Visual InterDev

6.3   Data Architecture

Given the following case study, determine the amount of storage space required for the database. Disregard overhead and space used by indexes.

Estimated Time: 15 minutes.

SmallTown Public Library wants to automate its card catalog system. The library estimates that it has about 2,000,000 books. Each book carries about 600 bytes of information (title, author, keywords, publisher, and so on).

About 5,000 cardholders can check out books. The system should track the cardholder's name (50 bytes), address (100 bytes), CardID (5 bytes), and expiration date (8 bytes).

At any one time, about 10,000 books are checked out. The system should carry the CardID (5 bytes), the BookID (8 bytes), and the date checked out (8 bytes). After books are returned, the table record is archived to a flatfile and the disk space is recovered.

With the previous three tables required, what is the minimum disk space that should be allotted? Record your answers in Table 6.5.

TABLE 6.5

SMALLTOWN LIBRARY DATABASE VOLUMETRICS ANALYSIS

Table	Records	Bytes/Record	Total Bytes
Book			
CardHolder			
Checkouts			
Total			

Answers can be found in Table 6.6.

TABLE 6.6

SMALLTOWN LIBRARY DATABASE VOLUMETRICS ANALYSIS

Table	Records	Bytes/Record	Total Bytes
Book	2,000,000	600	1,200,000,000
CardHolder	5,000	163	815,000
Checkouts	10,000	21	210,000
Total			1,201,025,000

We need at least 1.2GB of storage. Overhead, indexes, and room for growth would push us up to around 3.0GB.

Review Questions

1. If GWA Wines were trying to build an application for internal use, which of the solution types (single/two/*n*–tier) might become more desirable?

APPLY YOUR KNOWLEDGE

2. What would be a compelling reason to store files in HTML format rather than in a custom format?

3. If the future technology plan of GWA Wines were to change, how would this impact the solution?

4. What is an example of an enterprise solution type (distributed, centralized, and so on) that might be adopted by GWA Wines?

5. If the owner wanted to see, each week, how many bottles of each wine had been sold, which requirements would this change?

Exam Questions

1. What design strategies would be unavailable to us if we chose to make GWA Wines a two-tier architecture? (Choose all that apply.)

   A. Connecting a browser-based interface directly to the legacy data stores.

   B. Encapsulating business rules in the database.

   C. Creating a thin user interface that loads quickly to the user's browser.

   D. Establishing rules in business objects that do not load into the browser interface.

2. Which type of architecture might best describe the use of a 3270 emulator running a CICS COBOL program?

   A. Single tier

   B. Two tier

   C. Three Tier

   D. *n*-tier

3. Which type of architecture might best describe a screen scraping application?

   A. Single tier

   B. Two tier

   C. Three tier

   D. *n*-tier

4. Which of the following are characteristics of *n*-tier applications such as GWA Wines when compared with single- or two-tiered designs? (Choose two.)

   A. More difficult to design

   B. More difficult to maintain

   C. Easier to design

   D. Easier to maintain

5. How many physical machines are involved in an *n*-tier design?

   A. At least two

   B. Three or more

   C. One

   D. At least one

6. Which characteristics make the decision to use the *n*-tier model a more desirable architecture for GWA Wines? (Choose all that apply.)

   A. More extensible

   B. Quicker time to market

   C. Better fit for object-oriented and component-based design

   D. Better performance

APPLY YOUR KNOWLEDGE

7. Which of the following factors is not a reason to choose Visual Basic for GWA Wines?

    A. Expertise already exists in VB.

    B. Using Visual Basic, we can complete the solution more quickly.

    C. Visual Basic 6.0 offers tools to assist in Web development.

    D. Visual Basic can work directly with either ODBC or OLE DB.

8. Which of the following is an example of a proprietary standard?

    A. HTML, a public standard for document transfer

    B. EDI, a standard for document interchange

    C. PKZip, a file compression utility

    D. FTP, a file transfer protocol

9. What is the most important reason to know that GWA Wines may retire its mainframe application at some time in the future?

    A. So that we can choose its replacement now and code to that specification

    B. Because it will influence our choice of development platforms

    C. To make sure that we isolate the majority of our new solution from the location of the database through an abstraction layer

    D. To make sure that we account for Y2K issues in our new solution

10. Which development tool has been identified as most versatile for Internet development?

    A. Visual Basic

    B. Visual C++

    C. Visual InterDev

    D. Visual J++

11. Which of the following is not a criterion discussed for evaluating development tools?

    A. Language performance

    B. RAD tool

    C. Internet development

    D. Capability to access different types of data

12. The GWA Wines solution would be classified as which solution model?

    A. Distributed

    B. Collaboration

    C. Communication

    D. Centralized

13. Which is not a type of database used in applications?

    A. Indexed

    B. Hierarchical

    C. Publish and subscribe

    D. Relational

APPLY YOUR KNOWLEDGE

14. Which of the following strategies will help avoid an unplanned outage because of an overloaded database server? (Choose all that apply.)

    A. Proper sizing of the hard disk storage requirements

    B. Generating usage averages over a month's time to verify the appropriate size and power of the server

    C. Making sure that user ad hoc queries are limited to valid table joins

    D. Using MTS's capability to pool database connections

Answers to Review Questions

1. If the application is being built internally, the need to pull as much of the application as possible onto internal machines would be gone because all the machines are, by design, part of the enterprise already. Therefore, two-tier architecture would become more desirable. This does not mean, however, that *n*-tier is not the correct solution for GWA Wines. See "Identifying Appropriate Solution Types."

2. The compelling reason to choose HTML over a custom format is that HTML is a public standard. This makes it easier to develop initially and certainly makes it simpler to maintain than a custom format that might or might not continue to work as time goes on. See "Open Standards."

3. Future technology plans can definitely change our solution design. If, for example, GWA Wines planned on hiring several Visual InterDev developers, we would most certainly consider that as a stronger candidate for the development platform. See "Selection of Development Tools."

4. GWA Wines might institute a time-tracking program to see where the employees are spending their work day. This kind of a solution, because it is targeted for the entire corporation as a user group, is an enterprise application. In some respects, the identification as one of these models is arbitrary. Other characteristics should be taken into account. The main purpose in categorizing solutions in this way is to try to seek out patterns of reuse that can make design more efficient and more stable. See "What Type of Solution Are We Building?"

5. This kind of summary information viewed on a weekly basis would be an additional reporting requirement. This would change the reporting requirements and the overall data architecture requirements, which have to support the reporting. If the requirement was that more of this sort of data was needed during business hours, we might have to consider adding an offline, decision support database. See "Reporting Requirements."

Answers to Exam Questions

1. **A, C, D.** Choice A would be unavailable because we require a Web server between the legacy database and the browser interface. Choices C and D could not be accomplished because they require a middle, business tier. Choice B could be implemented in a two-tier system (although not as an Internet system). See "Identifying Appropriate Solution Types."

APPLY YOUR KNOWLEDGE

2. **A.** Although a piece of emulator software does exist on either the user's machine or as part of a browser-based interface, the emulator provides no substantial application-specific business logic. Therefore, in our architectural scheme, it is considered a single-tier architecture. See "Single Tier."

3. **B.** Unlike question 2, we have now added logic that is unique to our application in the user interface tier. This most typically will be a two-tier application, although the application could be designed to include additional, logical tiers if appropriate. See "Two Tier."

4. **A, D.** *n*-tier applications are more difficult to design but easier to maintain. It should be noted that for a specific application, *n*-tier may be easier to build because the use of component-based design can abstract the complexity and allow for testing at a lower level (unit-level testing versus systemwide testing). See "Identifying Appropriate Solution Types."

5. **D.** The different application design types we have discussed all reference *logical* tiers rather than actual physical machines. It is possible for an *n*-tier application to exist on one, two, or more machines. See "Identifying Appropriate Solution Types."

6. **A, C, D.** *n*-tier designs are easier to extend because they usually involve components and/or objects with well-formed interfaces that abstract the complexity. A well-designed solution can be extended by touching only one or two components, whereas in the older models, code is usually strewn throughout the application. It is almost unheard of to see a single-tier or a two-tier component-based application. (How *would*

you do that?) *n*-tier solutions cannot be characterized as faster to market than single or two-tier applications. Performance can also be considered a reason to chose *n*-tier, although this is not globally true across all solutions. This is discussed further in Chapter 11, "The Logic Tier." See "Identifying Appropriate Solution Types."

7. **D.** We can read that A and B are correct from the case study text. Early in the case study, the owner stated that he wanted to get the Web page up "in a month or so." Choice C is a correct and relevant statement. Although choice D is correct, the other technologies (VC++, VJ++, InterDev) also possess this benefit. See "Selection of Development Tools."

8. **C.** Although seemingly a standard in the industry (at least until WinZip arrived), PKZip is an example of proprietary software that is licensed. See "Proprietary Standards."

9. **C.** Choice A is incorrect because no need exists to select a replacement database product this soon. Choice B is incorrect because, thanks to OLE DB and ODBC, the actual database product is irrelevant. The location of the data, however, is important. It usually is wise to isolate your solution from the database activity by creating some sort of a *data access* or *data persistence* object. See "Planned Future Direction."

10. **C.** Visual InterDev was designed to be an IDE (Interactive Development Environment) for Web developers. Although many of the other Visual Studio tools may be capable of doing some level of Web development, only Visual InterDev was designed exclusively—and thus optimized—for Internet development. See "Visual InterDev."

APPLY YOUR KNOWLEDGE

11. **D.** All the tools mentioned in the text work with Microsoft's Universal Data Access (UDA) strategy. Through OLE DB and ADO, all the tools are on nearly equal footing in this respect. Performance may differ, but the capability to access heterogeneous data sources is common to all. See "Selection of Development Tools."

12. **D.** Choices B and C are incorrect because this solution does not facilitate communication between two human beings. It facilitates the customer's interaction with an order entry database. Choice A is also incorrect because the database is shared (not replicated to each user) and because the code base is managed centrally on the Web server. The UI code is downloaded to the Web browser on demand. As such, no concept of an installation process exists. All these factors characterize the GWA Wines solution as a centralized solution type. See "What Type of Solution Are We Building?"

13. **C.** Publish and subscribe is a data replication model (used by SQL Server) to keep subscriber databases synchronized with a master database. See "Identifying Appropriate Data Storage Architecture."

14. **A, C, D.** Choice A is obviously correct. If we run out of disk storage (physical or allocated), bad things will happen. Choice C is correct because a user who inadvertently creates a table join between two large tables on nonindexed fields (or even a Cartesian join) can cause a disruption to all other users. Choice D is correct because when pooling is utilized, the database server thinks it is serving fewer client applications than what actually exists. Reuse of connections increases performance on both sides of the middle tier. Choice B is incorrect because averages are of little value when sizing a database. Peak loads are much more important to manage. See "Identifying Appropriate Data Storage Architecture."

Suggested Readings and Resources

1. Williams, John. "Simplicity or Complexity?" *Component Strategies.* SIGS Publications, April 1999, p. 6.

2. Brown, Kent and Paul Tindall. "Impure Design," *Enterprise Development.* Fawcette Technical Publications, June 1999, p. 14.

3. *Developing for the Enterprise.* Manual Set for Visual Studio 6.0, Enterprise Edition. Microsoft Corporation, 1998.

This chapter addresses the following exam objectives listed by Microsoft for this section of the Analyzing Requirements and Defining Solution Architectures exam:

Test the feasibility of a proposed technical architecture.

- **Demonstrate that business requirements are met.**

- **Demonstrate that use-case scenarios are met.**

- **Demonstrate that existing technology constraints are met.**

- **Assess impact of shortfalls in meeting requirements.**

▶ After we have selected a "strawman" architecture, we need to validate it against the requirements for the solution. We need to ensure that we have selected the proper solution type, the proper technologies, and the proper data-storage techniques. Otherwise, we open ourselves up for failure later in the process.

Develop an appropriate deployment strategy.

▶ Finally, no solution can be complete while it remains installed only on the developer's machines. Although it may seem outside the typical duties of a system designer, it is important that the designer consider how the application will be deployed as part of the architecture. Anticipating how the deployment is to occur will make it more likely your application will succeed.

CHAPTER 7

Testing the Technical Architecture

► Identify the four tests of an architecture.

► Apply the four tests to the three areas of architectural focus—solution type, selected technologies, and data architecture.

► Develop an effective deployment strategy for a proposed solution.

INTRODUCTION

After we have designed an architecture for our solution, we need to make sure the architecture is a viable one. Probably as many different architectures exist as there are applications. What separates one from another is the degree to which it meets or exceeds goals for the project's infrastructure.

These goals can come from the general goals of all applications (performance, scalability, and so on), or they can be generated by application requirements, application use cases, or existing technologies.

TEST THE FEASIBILITY OF THE PROPOSED ARCHITECTURE

Test the feasibility of a proposed technical architecture.

After the architecture has been designed, we need to test it against reality. An eloquent architecture that doesn't address the needs of the business is a waste of time and money.

First, we'll discuss ways to test that the chosen architecture is compatible with the business requirements, the use cases, the technology constraints that exist in the company, as well as what the impact on the application would be if we failed to match these properly.

For each of the four dimensions, we'll analyze our architecture in terms of the three areas that we focused on in Chapter 6, "Defining the Technical Architecture for a Solution": solution type, technologies, and data architecture.

Finally, we'll validate the architecture that we designed in the last chapter for GWA Wines using the following criteria to see whether it is a good fit.

Does the Architecture Meet the Business Requirements?

We need to ensure that the architecture we have chosen (solution type, technologies, and data architecture) is compatible with the business requirements.

We went through the process of defining the business requirements in Chapter 1, "Analyzing Project Scope." Business requirements are basically the difference between the way things are now (present reality) and the way the business sponsors would like things to be (desired reality). Business requirements can be general or specific.

Examples of general business requirements are

◆ Increase bottom-line profits.

◆ Provide the capability for customers to place orders directly.

◆ Decrease accounts receivables.

◆ Measure pharmaceuticals' shelf life in compliance with FDA regulations.

Examples of specific business requirements are

◆ Must be able to send and receive faxes.

◆ Must connect to and use existing legacy data stores.

◆ Must be fully operational by August 21.

◆ User interface must be compatible with other applications in the department.

As we mentioned earlier in the book, business requirements must be written down. This documentation is important to the success of the project for several reasons. First, it enables us to ensure that we have designed an architecture that fits the business requirements.

Second, it enables us to better manage "scope creep." By clearly documenting from the outset what we are building, we can implement a change process that requires all changes to the original scope to be documented as such, along with the agreed upon change in time, schedule, and resources required to implement the new requirement(s).

It's actually easier than you might think to design any solution using any of the styles. A banking system could be *n*-tier; each layer is isolated from the other, with all users working against a single account database. Or it may be a monolithic mainframe program that uses CICS character-based screens to communicate with a program in a home office.

Therefore, the question is not, "Which one will work?" but rather, "Which one is best?"

We'll test our proposed architecture in each of the three dimensions covered in Chapter 6, "Defining the Technical Architecture for a Solution," and see how well it fits.

Solution Type

Is the selected solution type (single tier, two tier, n-tier) the best fit with the business requirements we have been given?

As we discussed earlier, you can build any solution using any of the solution types, but that doesn't mean you have designed the optimal architecture. We should assess the priorities in the requirements and pick the best fit. For example, if extensibility is a requirement, more tiers would be the logical selection.

If our requirement is, "Get it done fast. We lose $100,000 in opportunity every week that we are delayed," you may opt for a simpler design—single tier or two tier—and come back later to write a replacement. Before you raise your eyebrows in disbelief, consider the following. A $200,000 solution that is ready in 60 days and provides the users 90% of what they need is often better than a $2,000,000 solution that is ready in 18 months but that promises to meet 100% of the users' goals. As Voltaire said, "The best is the enemy of the good."

Are there any requirements that lead us toward one of the types?

For example, if you have a business requirement that states that the new solution "must deploy over the Internet, allowing our customers to place their own orders," we can already eliminate single tier, and probably two tier as well. We have a user interface that runs in the browser, we have our own order database, and we have a Web server.

Do we need to account for different back-end databases, now or in the future?

If we think that we might need to connect to heterogeneous databases or that the production database might change in the future, we would be more likely to isolate the user interface from the database by using a middle, or business, tier.

Do we have any PASS ME requirements that indicate the best solution type?

Is there anything in the business requirements that relates to Performance, Availability, Security, Scalability, Maintainability, or Extensibility that would suggest one of the solution types over the others?

Are any applications going to be single tier?

Single-tier and two-tier applications do have their place. As we discussed in the preceding chapter, at times they are the appropriate choice. Having said that, the majority of applications today utilize the *n*-tier concept. The main reason is that applications are getting more and more complicated. They also rely on interactions with components outside themselves (DLLs, OCXs, and so on). The best way to abstract the complexity as well as to isolate parts of the code from an ever-changing environment is through the use of *n*-tier, component architecture. Remember that tiers need not be on different physical machines. You could design an *n*-tier, shrink-wrap computer game that resides entirely on a customer's local hard drive.

Selected Technologies

Do the business requirements give us any clues as to technologies that we should utilize?

If the requirements state that the application should be completed in 60 days, that requirement pushes us in the direction of RAD development tools (for example, Visual Basic). If the requirements outline a plan to go to the Internet and work with any browser out there, we would likely avoid technologies that are not supported by all browsers, such as ActiveX controls, and lean toward HTML solutions and Visual InterDev.

Do we have any PASS ME requirements that would lead us toward a particular technology?

Does anything in the business requirements relating to Performance, Availability, Security, Scalability, Maintainability, or Extensibility suggest a particular technology? For example, if maintainability and extensibility are primary requirements and the current staff only knows Visual Basic, we would lean in that direction. If performance is the number-one issue, we would be more likely to choose VC++.

Do the business requirements eliminate any technologies?

Sometimes we get lucky. When requirements eliminate all but one or two technologies, our decision is easier to make and easier to defend, as well. The downside of this, of course, is that it often limits us and leads us into technologies that would not be our first choice under different circumstances.

One example is an application that would be a great fit for VC++, except that a requirement states that it should run on multiple, non-Windows platforms. This moves us toward selecting VJ++ as our development language.

Do any standards exist that we can (or should) implement based on the requirements?

If the requirements indicate that we must communicate daily with other vendors using EDI (Electronic Data Interchange), our decision is clear.

If, however, requirements state only that we must link all field offices to the home office, we must make a decision. Do we utilize ODBC or OLE DB and connect through the databases? Do we create a customized batch program that performs two-way transfers each night, using ASCII flatfiles as the medium?

Data-Storage Architecture

Is the choice of a back-end database made for us in the requirements?

If the requirements state that the new solution will use the same data stores as the existing legacy system, we have no decisions to make.

However, if there is no existing system, we may be free to choose the database vendor, the location of the database, whether replication will be utilized, and how data will be moved through the system.

Do the requirements hint at the right selection for a data-storage architecture?

If the requirements were for a small set of locally stored values, such as a shrink-wrap tax preparation program, for example, SQL Server would not be the best choice. Flatfile ASCII storage or a small Microsoft Access MDB would be simpler, faster, and more appropriate.

Conversely, if 200 users are entering order information from customers calling in over the telephone, an Access database would quickly wear out its welcome. A full-fledged SQL Server database with a designated database administrator would be more likely to fit the bill.

Do we get any information about reporting requirements for our solution?

Although this may not impact our choice of a database vendor, it might influence our design. If we are designing a pure data entry system with no reporting requirements, we can design a solution that optimizes the response time to the users' screens.

If our solution is, in all or part, a decision-support system, we will likely make very different choices. We might choose to denormalize the table structure. If we are also supporting live users, we might build a shadow database for the reports to run on, or we might limit reports to run only late at night.

We mustn't forget that complex decision-support queries, just because they display on a screen rather than go to a printer, should be still be considered reporting requirements. The load on the database is the same. The influence on the design is almost identical.

Do We Meet Business Requirements at GWA Wines?

We'll look back at Chapter 6 to see if we meet the business requirements established by GWA Wines.

The requirements were the following:

◆ Would like to enable customers to order wine

◆ Would like to use the Internet

◆ Want to continue to use the existing system (at least for now)

◆ New technology to be focused around Visual Basic talent already on staff

We selected a four-tier (*n*-tier) architecture type (see Figure 6.4). Considering the previous questions, this still looks like the best choice. Had the new solution been only for internal employees, we may have had to look more closely at other architectures.

Regarding technologies, we selected Visual Basic because that is what the staff was already familiar with. Although not in the requirements document per se, the owner stated that he wanted his own people to support the solution. This is an example of the business requirements overriding the technologically best choice. If we were free to pick the language platform for a Web solution based solely on technical merit, we would have more likely chosen Visual InterDev.

We also selected OLE DB and ADO because a stated requirement was to use newer technology.

The database architecture decision is made for us because the existing legacy data stores will continue to be used, at least for now. We chose to go with that, and the requirements back us up.

Does the Architecture Meet the Use Cases?

Over the past few years, use cases and use-case scenarios have become increasingly popular for solution architects. Use cases become the "Rosetta Stone" between the client's knowledge of the business and the designer's knowledge of the technology. They should be nontechnical and non-platform specific in their wording. They should define the behaviors of the system—not the "how" but the "what.""

Properly constructed use cases make team development easier and testing easier. They also make it more likely that the final solution will meet the needs of the users.

For all these reasons, it is important that any architecture we design must meet not only the requirements, which is more of a features list, but must meet the scenarios under which the solution is supposed to operate.

Solution Type

Is the selected solution type (single tier, two tier, n-tier) the best fit for the identified use cases?

If the use-case scenario states that the user "transmits the completed problem report to home office via electronic mail," then creating a monolithic mainframe solution, or even a two-tier solution, would not be a good fit.

We must look for clues in the use cases that would point us in a certain direction.

Having said all that, as we stated in the preceding section, most use cases these days will point to some style of *n*-tier technology. Because of its substantial benefits, it has become the default. A compelling reason must exist to choose one of the other solution types instead of going with *n*-tier.

This does not mean an end to the decisions. How many tiers? How should the components or objects inside the tiers be structured? What patterns should be considered when designing how the tiers will work internally and between each other? These questions are addressed in more detail later in this book.

IN DEPTH: THE ENCYCLOPEDIA GALACTICA OF ARCHITECTURE?

Of course, no book written to date has all the answers. First, issues such as patterns, anti-patterns, data persistence strategies, objects versus components, and so on are seemingly endless. Second, even if they did end, they would change tomorrow. Technology changes very rapidly these days. This is one of the causes of strong disagreement among experts about the best architectural approach. Finally, the book would have to be about 10,000 pages long!

Do we have any PASS ME requirements in the use cases that indicate the best solution type?

Any use cases where a customer is either face-to-face or on the telephone with users would seem to require a responsive architecture. Likewise, any use case scenarios such as "and then the system dispenses the proper amount of painkiller medication to the patient" would strongly indicate the need for high availability (stability).

Selected Technologies

Do the use cases give us any clues as to technologies and/or standards that we should utilize?

Because the use cases are theoretically done before any coding is started or any architectural decisions are made (if not, shame on you!), we can take our cue from the use cases. If a use case states that the output of a decision-support query should be imported into Microsoft Excel for graphing, we should consider Visual Studio or OLE DB.

Integration points with existing systems or technologies can very often cue us into technologies and standards that should be considered. If our use cases mention the digital storage of audio, we would likely choose from one of the available standards (WAV, MIDI, MP3) rather than creating our own technology from scratch.

Do the use cases help us answer the "buy versus build" question?

Every solution faces this question at some point in the design phase. Without trying to say which is best, we will suggest that the use cases are one place to look for an answer to this question. Sometimes, the answer is to go back and renegotiate the use cases to better match some piece of off-the-shelf software. With the advent of COM (and soon, COM+), it's easier than ever to take a piece of shrink-wrap software and extend it to meet the unique needs of your company.

Data-Storage Architecture

Hopefully, use cases don't have much to say in the area of data architecture. If so, then the use cases are written at a level of detail that is going to lock us into a particular path too early in the process.

However, from time to time you will be able to read between the lines and gain some insight into the persistence needs of the solution.

Do the use cases give us any clues as to a data architecture that we should utilize?

If we can get any clues at all from the use cases, they will likely be only hints. If the users' screens should reappear in the same place and be the same size as when they last used the application, this might suggest storing some values in the Windows registry.

Do We Meet Use Cases at GWA Wines?

The case study does not qualify as a use case. Therefore, we do not really have much to go on here. Entire books are devoted to the proper construction of use cases. We have added some of these references to the bibliography.

One example of a use case is the customer's interaction with the GWA Web site. The analogy of a shopping cart might be employed. The customer browses the various wines and chooses a few; he or she may even return some to the shelf. Finally, the customer is ready to make a purchase. Ah ha! We have just discovered, through a very short use case, the need for some sort of e-commerce technology. We need to enable the customer to purchase the wine over the Internet. This will influence our architecture as well as the standards we need to employ.

Does the Architecture Meet the Existing Technology Constraints?

Technology is changing faster than ever. Still, limitations exist to what technology can do—for example, limitations to the concept of data replication. Replication is not, and may never be, instantaneous.

Currently, bandwidth limitations exist for data, audio, and video transmission over long distances (WANs). Some companies may have technology limitations because of the hardware platform they select. For example, solutions that would benefit from touch-screen technology need touch-screen monitors, obviously.

Solution Type

Is our selection of solution type (single tier, two tier, n-tier) limited in any way by the technology currently in place or by the technology planned to exist when we deploy?

More and more companies are realizing that RAM and hard disk space, even for hundreds of users, is cheaper than extra development time. Applications are getting fatter and fatter. This may seem irresponsible, but at some level, it is just good business sense. If we saw a machine configured with 128MB of RAM and 8GB of disk space just four years ago, we would have concluded it was a server. However, these days it is just a typical user workstation, maybe even a laptop system.

The point of this is to determine the potential of the user workstation and the cost of adding more hardware to 200 PCs versus a single server. The answers to these questions are different than they were just a few years ago.

Does thin client computing offer some advantages based on the technology constraints that exist?

Thin client computing, to some degree, is a throwback to the days of mainframe computing. The user workstations are underpowered and fairly "dumb." The server does all the work, shipping colored pixels over the LAN instead of ASCII (or EBCDIC) characters over the wire.

Maintenance costs are one of the main targets for thin client, with the goal of eliminating configuration issues with DLLs and OCXs.

Selected Technologies

Is our selection of technologies for the new solution affected by existing technologies?

This is an important question. This is often where the Java (VJ++) issue crops up. If our solution must work on multiple, non-Windows platforms, we are more likely to choose a technology such as Java. If we create a browser-based application, HTML might be the best choice.

Conversely, if all our servers and all our workstations are running some flavor of the Windows operating system, we are very likely to include COM in our architecture.

If we are in a company that stores enterprise data in an indexed VSAM database and the company has no intention of migrating away from that, we would select OLE DB over ODBC.

A common challenge in this area occurs when we set out to build browser-based solutions. We must decide whether to support every browser out there or only certain browsers, as well as which legacy browsers to support (for example, Internet Explorer 3.0).

Data-Storage Architecture

Is our selection of data-storage architectures for the new solution affected by existing technologies?

We'll assume for a moment that our solution requires rapid screen-to-screen response and near-instantaneous updates. We'll also assume that all data will be stored in a single legacy database in Burlington, Iowa. If I am a user in Burlington, Massachusetts, my response time will not be acceptable unless some unusual technology exists to make that happen. Something has got to give. We may either have to rethink our response-time requirement, perform some intelligent prefetching of data, use some type of data-replication strategy, or spend a lot of money on a high-speed data link to the central database.

Do We Meet Technology Constraints at GWA Wines?

The technology constraints at GWA Wines are fairly common and straightforward. We are interfacing with a legacy system through the database tables. ODBC or OLE DB makes this a straightforward task. The new Internet solution is based on all new hardware, so no constraints are there.

Because the new interface is going to be browser based, the constraints here are well known. Our only decision is whether we want to use ActiveX. Because browser software can "sense" its browser environment, we can build an interface that uses standard HTML or VBScript but that is also able to take advantage of users with MS Internet Explorer.

How Would Requirements Shortfalls Impact the Solution?

The final "acid test" is to assess the impact on our solution's success should our proposed architecture fail to meet the requirements for the system.

Obviously, the spectrum extends from no effect at all to an expensive, time-consuming, career-ending total failure. Some projects recover; some never do.

Solution Type

What would be the impact on the success of our application if we selected the wrong solution type (single tier, two tier, n-tier)?

We stated in Chapter 6 that the major differences between the various solution types centered on complexity of design and complexity of maintenance. That would lead us to expect that the impact would be felt in one of the following areas:

◆ Cost of building the solution

◆ Cost of maintaining the solution

◆ One or more PASS ME requirements not met

We could find that the amount of time or money that it took to build the solution exceeded our estimates. Some companies handle this in stride; others go out of business. It often depends on the magnitude of the error.

The other possibility is that by choosing the wrong solution type, we cause maintenance and deployment issues. To keep a major application running on hundreds of user workstations, especially if a lot of dependencies exist on external components or DLLs, is no easy task. Locking down user workstations, an oft-used tactic, merely exchanges one problem for another.

Finally, any of the six PASS ME areas could be impacted if we choose the wrong architecture. How many and which ones depend on the solution itself. For example, if performance is crucial, fewer tiers might be more appropriate than more tiers.

Selected Technologies

What would be the impact on the success of our application if we selected the wrong technologies?

The impact of selecting the wrong technologies can often make or break a solution. Choosing a technology that is "not ready for prime time" can be dangerous for an enterprise solution. Departments often pride themselves on being at the "bleeding edge" of technology. It's called that for a reason.

Selecting new technologies that are incompatible with existing technologies can also be difficult, at best. This is where bridging technologies often appear. Bridges may be necessary, but they are rarely desired.

Utilizing a standard in your proposed architecture that is at odds with an existing standard can also cause problems. Imagine trying to deploy a solution based on EBCDIC characters to a Windows-based workstation.

Data-Storage Architecture

What would be the impact on the success of our application if we selected the wrong data-storage architecture?

Choosing the wrong data-storage architecture can have disastrous effects on our application. For example, if we choose an architecture that assumes only occasional incidents of record lock conflicts, and we experience severe and frequent record locks in production, the success of our solution is in jeopardy. Specifically, its performance, availability (stability) and scalability could all be threatened.

If we select data replication or data caching as a strategy, and it turns out that the data goes stale more than half the time and requires performance-draining arbitration to get things back in sync, we will find ourselves with an unpopular solution.

Shortfall Impact to GWA Wines

To test this, we'll ask the same three questions:

What would be the impact on GWA Wines if we selected the wrong solution type (single tier, two tier, n-tier)?

Because we selected n-tier, what would be the impact if we selected single tier or two tier?

Single tier would require that the Web browser become a pass-through to a monolithic mainframe application, a kind of emulator interface. This would eliminate the capability to use graphics or to provide any of the expected Internet user niceties. Sales would be affected. The users who remained would likely return to the telephone to make their purchases.

Using two tier, we would have to move all our business rules either into the database or into the user interface, probably both. This would increase the download time to the user's PC.

What would be the impact on GWA Wines if we selected the wrong technologies?

GWA Wines has onsite expertise in Visual Basic. If we selected VJ++ and sent the three GWA employees to classes, we might have problems down the road. VJ++ has a longer learning curve than Visual Basic (or Visual InterDev).

If working on various Web browsers is important, and we build lots of ActiveX controls, we should expect a large percentage of our customers to have trouble with our Web pages.

What would be the impact on GWA Wines if we selected the wrong data-storage architecture?

We have a requirement to work in tandem with the mainframe. If we were to choose a data replication strategy, holding customer order data in a SQL Server database that is replicated to the mainframe each night, we might acknowledge more orders than we can fulfill (especially for the very rare 1945 Cabernet).

Because we have customers from all over the country, we must be very careful not to design too much latency between the legacy data stores and the Web server.

DEVELOPING A DEPLOYMENT STRATEGY

Develop an appropriate deployment strategy.

When a solution is conceived, one area is almost always neglected by the designer. After the solution is completed, how will it be deployed? This is another of the areas where your application and end users interact. If installing your application either disrupts their work, or worse yet, negatively impacts other software on their machines, it won't be long before users begin to resent the software that caused all the problems. When this happens, they will likely be unwilling to give the software a chance to fulfill its mission, and the project will be chalked up as a failure.

The lesson here is simple. Although it is true that the actual performance of the installation is not a design issue, it is in the architect's best interest to consider deployment issues. Basically, two kinds of conversions exist, and we will take a short look at each. Then, we will wrap up with a brief look at some of the deployment vehicles available to us and some of the dependencies that we must consider.

"One Shot" Deployment

This strategy goes exactly the way it sounds. Changes are made all at once. The advantage of this is that no need exists to build complex migration strategies, as there would be in a more gradual move. It is also easier to support the system because only one design at a time must be supported.

The drawbacks to this position, however, are also fairly obvious. If you make the change and things do not work as they should, everything has to be backed out. Also, after this change has been implemented, it is highly likely that you will adversely affect other aspects of the business until your application is able to work correctly. This is a huge risk, especially if you aren't able to undo the change with a fairly short set of steps.

Gradual Deployment

Gradual deployment has the advantages of allowing conversion to occur one component at a time, or even one physical location at a time. Each allows for a greater flexibility in the rollout process.

However, problems clearly arise with gradual deployment that will cause more work. It almost always means that multiple versions of the application must be supported simultaneously. If that is the case, the question arises of whether you are spending more in this iterative install than you would going for the one shot we talked about earlier.

Gradual deployment often includes a concept known as piloting. Piloting is just another name for something we are all familiar with—Beta releases. It is based on the concept that subjecting 10 users to flawed software is better than subjecting 1,000 users to the same thing. We are hedging our bets. It keeps the department from having its entire business at risk because of a new piece of software.

The other major reason for implementing Beta, or pilot, releases is to study scalability issues with a smaller group before turning a large number of users loose on your database tables.

Deployment Vehicles

Several vehicles are available for deploying software. We are not going to cover an exhaustive list because it is unlikely that the exam will go into great detail in this area.

We can deploy using the traditional methods of floppy disk or CD installations. The use of deployment CDs is growing with the decrease in the cost of CD burners. Even very small companies can afford to purchase a CD writer for doing backups and software packaging.

A variation on media-based installations is network-based installations. The install image is located on a network drive instead of on a floppy or a CD.

Microsoft SMS is another tool available for deploying anything from single components to entire applications. Applications such as the Visual Basic Application Wizard or the commercially available InstallShield are used to build the packages, whereas SMS or CD-ROMs are used to deploy it.

Microsoft ships a tool called the Package and Deployment Wizard with Visual Basic that allows the developer to create CAB files for traditional or Internet deployment of your solution.

One last way that is growing in use in the corporate world is the concept of a user workstation image. Basically, a "gold" workstation image is created. Whenever new software is created, it is included in the image, tested as an entire environment, and if all goes well, deployed to hundreds of users at once.

This last concept relies on an assumption. Users must be very careful about what they save on their local drives. Ideally, it would be nothing. The upside of all this is that any users who inadvertently mess up their PCs can get a clean copy at any time.

PC manufacturers have been using this same concept for some time.

Deployment Dependencies

One of the things that can take the wind out of your sails is to do all the right things, only to have the application fizzle and die on the user's workstation. Almost every application has dependencies that, if not satisfied, can bring down the sturdiest architecture.

These dependencies may be hardware dependencies such as requiring a certain amount of RAM or hard disk space to work properly. It might be an assumption that LAN speeds in the field (or wherever the users are) are comparable to those of the developer's area.

Other environmental factors could be considered dependencies. Something as seemingly innocuous as the Windows color scheme can make a beautiful UI look like a preschool project. The version of Windows itself falls into this category.

Dependencies on other shrink-wrap products can cause trouble if everything is not verified in advance. Perhaps you are expecting a certain version of Microsoft's Jet database engine, a certain version of SQL Server that supports row locking, a certain release of Microsoft Office, or a particular release of Visio.

Finally, dependencies on certain components or DLLs can wreak havoc with your solution. We are probably all familiar with the pain of designing under one version of a DLL and then releasing to a machine with a different version, only to get a pop-up message about an "incompatible DLL version."

Deployment at GWA Wines

In our case, this is a relatively straightforward issue. We aren't converting from a former solution (other than a manual one), so no risk exists that it cannot be reinstated.

Most of the deployment is done on demand as users access the Web page. The business rules and application logic on the Web server are not really deployed because they exist only on a single machine.

However, the odds are the company will get only one try to make this strategy work. If the word goes out to order wine from the page, and it is not ready, we have problems. Therefore, the deployment is just as critical here.

CHAPTER SUMMARY

Designing an eloquent architecture serves no purpose if it doesn't address the needs of the business. Although this seems obvious, too often we don't take the time to validate our design before jumping into the construction phase.

Validation can best be accomplished by applying four tests to our proposed architecture:

◆ Does our architecture meet the needs of the stated business requirements?

◆ Does our architecture meet the needs of the stated use cases?

◆ Is our architecture compatible with existing technologies?

◆ What are the consequences of not meeting one of the other three preceding tests?

In Chapter 6, we divided our architecture into three areas: solution type, technologies, and data architecture.

We must apply the four tests to each of these three areas.

Finally, we discussed how important it is to be familiar with deployment strategies. Even if we are not the one who will be actually deploying the application, if we fail to account for all the issues, the value built into our solution will be overshadowed by a flawed implementation. The users don't know the difference; they just know it doesn't work.

Not only must we address initial deployment, we must plan for updates to our application, as well.

KEY TERMS

- Business requirements
- Buy versus build
- Scope creep
- Software pilot
- Thin client
- Use cases

Exercises

7.1 Validating Architectural Choices

Each of the statements in Table 7.1 may or may not fail one or more of the three tests described in this chapter. For each statement, identify which tests are violated, if any.

Estimated Time: 10 minutes.

TABLE 7.1

ARCHITECTURE FEASIBILITY

Statement	Fails Requirements	Fails Use Cases	Fails Technologies
A. We have selected a single-tier strategy. The application will utilize 3270 screen-scraping. All data should be validated before it goes to the mainframe. For example, when the user enters an invalid date, he should get a pop-up error message.			
B. We have selected a single-tier strategy. The solution is a highly specialized financial calculator that runs under Windows and provides bankers with a quick way to perform complex calculations needed to qualify people for loans.			
C. We are going to coordinate our new application with existing Microsoft Exchange information. Exchange stores workflow information and our application retrieves it. We have selected ODBC and VC++ as our technologies to accomplish this.			

APPLY YOUR KNOWLEDGE

Statement	Fails Requirements	Fails Use Cases	Fails Technologies
D. We are designing a Web application to enable customers to order books online. To provide the best service, we will use Active Server Pages.			
E. We have UNIX machines and Windows machines that must access the same data, stored in SQL Server. A different team is designing the UNIX solution. For our part, we have selected ODBC.			
F. The solution we are designing is a small standalone job aid that will be deployed to more than 300 users within the company. Therefore, we have selected a single-tier architecture. Although the users will not be sharing data, the application requires monthly changes to some static data tables that contain state statutes.			
G. The use cases call for the user to be able to send an email with the single click of a button. This will require manipulating Microsoft Outlook for some users and making calls to the Windows Messaging API (MAPI) for other users. We have selected Visual Basic.			

APPLY YOUR KNOWLEDGE

Answers:

A. Fails *requirements* and *use cases*. We cannot get the requested business rules into the user interface when selecting a single-tier architecture. We are also considering the request for a pop-up message as a use case.

B. Passes all rules. This solution requires no sharing of data among users and seems to fit the solution type selected.

C. Fails *technology*. ODBC will not access Outlook data directly; however, OLE DB could.

D. Passes all rules.

E. Passes all rules. We can use ODBC, and the UNIX development team can use something such as JDBC to access the SQL Server data. Connecting different technologies at the database is often the cleanest way to go.

F. Passes all rules. We might think that the solution fails requirements because of the need to frequently update more than 300 users. However, the application is described as a "simple applet." Designing an *n*-tier architecture might make maintenance easier, but it seems like overkill in this situation. We should consider when the creation of an infrastructure violates KISS (Keep It Simple, Stupid). We could add a small bit of code that causes the application to look in a server directory for updates, thus automating the monthly maintenance process. See Barlow in the "Suggested Readings and Resources" section at the end of this chapter.

G. Passes all rules. Visual Basic can communicate with Outlook through COM and can also make direct calls to the MAPI APIs needed.

7.2 Organizing Deployment Dependencies

We are about to deploy a new solution that will replace an existing application. To ensure that everything works as designed, we have identified several dependencies. Both hardware and software upgrades must be performed before our application will work properly. Order the tasks in Table 7.2 into the proper sequence to provide the most effective deployment of our solution.

Estimated Time: 10 minutes.

TABLE 7.2

DEPLOYMENT WITH DEPENDENCIES

Task	*Order*
A. Perform deployment test of "gold code" onto a test dummy (duplicate) of the user's machine.	
B. Upgrade database server software (SQL Server 6.0 to SQL Server 7.0).	
C. Upgrade workstation hardware.	
D. Deploy new solution to remainder of users.	
E. Deploy new solution to pilot group.	
F. Upgrade server hardware.	
G. Upgrade workstation OCXs needed for new solution.	
H. Deploy interim release of existing application to work with new or old database schemas (autoconfiguring based on Windows registry setting).	
I. Move production data to new table schema.	

APPLY YOUR KNOWLEDGE

The solution is shown in Table 7.3.

TABLE 7.3

ANSWER TO EXERCISE 7.2

Task	Order
A. Upgrade server hardware.	1
B. Upgrade workstation hardware.	2
C. Upgrade database server software (SQL Server 6.0 to SQL Server 7.0).	3
D. Deploy interim release of existing application to work with new or old database schemas (autoconfiguring based on Windows registry setting).	4
E. Move production data to new table schema.	5
F. Perform deployment test of "gold code" onto a test dummy (duplicate) of the user's machine.	6
G. Upgrade workstation OCXs needed for new solution.	7
H. Deploy new solution to pilot group.	8
I. Deploy new solution to remainder of users.	9

We have specified that all hardware upgrades should be performed first. Then, we perform upgrades that do not affect the current application (SQL Server). Next, we migrate the database, using a new release of the existing application to allow us to migrate the data prior to the new solution. This lessens the amount of work we must do later and also allows us to support a single database schema instead of two.

Next, we test our deployment package and move the new OCXs into all user workstations. The thorough testing has assured us that the newer OCXs will not break any existing software. One by one, we are

tackling our dependencies in advance of the solution deployment.

Finally, we deploy the solution, first to a small pilot group for a week, and then to the remainder of the users.

Review Questions

1. Why are most enterprise solutions suited for *n*-tier architecture?

2. What are five benefits that properly constructed use cases provide us as solution architects?

3. What are some of the challenges in successful deployment of a solution?

Exam Questions

1. What factor is most responsible for making GWA Wines a candidate for an *n*-tier architecture?

   A. Visual Basic is the chosen development language.

   B. Requirement to allow customers to enter orders from the Internet.

   C. A mainframe system already exists.

   D. The requirement that graphic images be included in the user interface.

2. Why was Visual Basic the best choice for a development language for GWA Wines? (Choose all that apply.)

   A. It supports Internet development.

   B. Expertise already exists for VB at GWA Wines.

APPLY YOUR KNOWLEDGE

C. It is the most natural fit for this type of solution, regardless of staff expertise.

D. It creates the "thinnest" user interface, speeding up download time over the Web.

3. Which of the following can be considered as benefits of properly constructed use cases? (Choose all that apply.)

A. Serves double-duty as business requirements

B. Helps in identifying flaws in the architecture

C. Enables better communication among all parties

D. Helps UI designers by supplying captions for the command buttons

4. Which of the following can be considered a dependency that must be considered for deployment?

A. Ergonomics of user workstation

B. Operating system on a Web-based user's workstation

C. Monitor size

D. Operating system on a client/server user's workstation.

5. GWA Wines is going to the Internet. Which of the following standards is not a good fit?

A. HTML

B. EDI

C. ASP

D. TCP/IP

6. If we were designing an internal application for a small company that still used Windows 3.11, which technologies would still pass the feasibility test? (Choose all that apply.)

A. ADO

B. DAO

C. ODBC

D. RDO

7. The disadvantage of using the "gold image" concept for PC deployment is what?

A. It cannot address the problem of a user picking up a virus on the workstation.

B. It requires a CD-ROM writer.

C. Any files stored on the local hard drive will be deleted.

D. It is unable to detect DLL version incompatibilities.

8. Which of these impacts is most likely if we select a technology that is incompatible with an existing technology? (Choose two.)

A. Our database could get corrupted.

B. Our application's performance may be slowed down by the need for bridging strategies.

C. We may not be able to deploy at all.

D. We may spend more money or time to get the solution working.

Answers to Review Questions

1. Because *n*-tier is a logical construct and not a physical one, it can be employed in any physical environment, even a single machine. Because applications are getting more complex and rely more heavily on interactions with external components, *n*-tier can isolate us from changes in those areas. The more we center our design around three or four tiers, the easier it is to replace or modify one of the tiers without making changes in the other tiers. Most applications these days, even computer games, benefit from these characteristics. See "Does the Architecture Meet the Business Requirements?"

2. Properly constructed use cases provide many benefits. Here are a few:

- Makes communication between client and developer more effective.

- Makes team development easier because tasks can be assigned based on use cases.

- Helps identify a flawed architecture.

- Serves as the contract between the client and the developers.

- Forms the basis for a good assembly test plan.

- Allows for creativity in design by not locking into the "right way" too early in the process.

- Provides a method of prioritizing features in a solution. Use cases can be identified as Core, Required, or Rare.

  See "Does the Architecture Meet the Use Cases?"

3. We can build an application that runs perfectly at our desk but that fails miserably when deployed. Some of the problems we might encounter are as follows:

- User workstation is missing a required DLL or has an older version of the required DLL.

- User workstation has a different version of Windows than the solution was developed under.

- User installs another application that overwrites required DLLs or OCXs with older ones.

- User workstation does not have enough RAM (memory) or disk space to run the application properly.

- User's LAN is overloaded, which causes frustration created by the lack of feedback. The user begins to "click and poke" impatiently, breaking the application in ways that were never tested for in the lab.

- User inadvertently deletes a file used by your application.

  We could go on and on. For all the preceding reasons, and for all the reasons not stated, the architect needs to address deployment. Otherwise, it's like a thoroughbred race horse that gets its stirrup stuck in the starting gate. You're behind before you even get going. See "Developing a Deployment Strategy."

APPLY YOUR KNOWLEDGE

Answers to Exam Questions

1. **B.** Requiring the solution to run on the Internet is the one requirement that has the most impact on the choice of *n*-tier. The other three factors could all be accomplished in single-tier or two-tier architectures. See " Does the Architecture Meet the Business Requirements?"

2. **A, B.** Visual Basic does offer expanded support for Internet development, especially since Visual Basic 6.0. Having staff that is already familiar with a language is a valid factor when choosing technology. VB is not the most natural choice for the Internet. Visual InterDev would probably be the correct choice if expertise existed (or if it was specified that new people were being brought in). Sometimes business requirements outweigh the natural selection from a purely technical perspective. See "Does the Architecture Meet the Business Requirements?"

3. **B, C.** Use cases do help locate flaws in our architecture, albeit indirectly. They also allow for better communication, both between the client and the developer and among developers, as well. This comes in handy when new developers enter the project team late in the process. Use cases are not requirements. They do not define features, environmental constraints, schedule requirements, and so forth. Use cases should not be detailed to the extent that they identify the "how." The use of command buttons and the caption of them should be left until later in the process. See "Does the Architecture Meet the Use Cases?"

4. **D.** The operating system is clearly a dependency for a client/server application. Monitor size and ergonomics, although relevant, do not affect deployment. The operating system versions for a Web-based user is basically isolated from being relevant. This is central to the success of the Internet. See "Deployment Dependencies."

5. **B.** EDI is not an Internet standard. See Chapter 5, "Integration Issues."

6. **B, C.** ADO and RDO are supported only in 32-bit operating systems. See MSDN.

7. **C.** The "gold image" strategy depends on being able to completely wipe the hard drive clean and start from scratch. See "Deployment Vehicles."

8. **B, D.** Choice A seems unlikely. Choice C, although it might occur, is less likely than B and D. These days, a way usually exists around any technological challenge. However, a price is usually paid in terms of performance and the time it takes to complete the solution for deployment. Most times, the solution is more complicated as well. See "How Would Requirements Shortfalls Impact the Solution?"

APPLY YOUR KNOWLEDGE

Suggested Readings and Resources

1. Barlow, Chris. "Create an Application Launcher," VBPJ, Fawcette Technical Publications, April 1999, p. 64.

2. Jacobson, Ivar. "The Last Word," *Component Strategies*, SIGS Publications, August 1999, p. 72.

3. Korson, Timothy D. "Constructing Useful Use Cases," *Component Strategies*, SIGS Publications, March 1999, p. 27.

4. Texel, Putnam P. *Use Cases Combined with BOOCH/OMT/UML*. Prentice-Hall, 1997.

This chapter addresses the following objectives listed by Microsoft for this section of the exam:

Construct a conceptual design that is based on a variety of scenarios and that includes context, workflow process, task sequence, and physical environment models. Types of applications include

- **SDI, MDI, console, and dialog desktop applications**

- **Two tier, client/server and Web applications**

- **_n_-tier applications**

- **Collaborative applications**

▶ The needs of the business should drive the solution, not technology. We must make sure that our design addresses the correct business problem. We ensure this by reviewing how the business will run under the new solution.

Assess the potential impact of the logical design on performance, maintainability, extensibility, scalability, availability, and security.

▶ After we have a "straw man" logical design for the solution, we need to determine its impact on the six PASS ME areas.

CHAPTER 8

Developing the Conceptual Design for a Solution

OUTLINE

▶ Construct a conceptual design for a solution using the context, workflow process, task sequence, and physical environment models.

▶ Construct a conceptual design for all the following application types: SDI, MDI, console, and dialog, desktop, two tier, client/server, Web, *n*-tier, and collaborative.

▶ Assess logical design decisions against the PASS ME parameters.

INTRODUCTION

As we get ready to leave the design section of our book, we need to explore a few tools and approaches that will serve as blueprints for the implementation phase.

If we compare the building of a solution to the building of a house, this is the phase where we create the final set of architectural floor plans that determine what the house will look like. In solution development, just like in construction, if we make a mistake at this point or take shortcuts, we will either find ourselves with an inferior final product or we will have to redo work already done.

Without this kind of forethought and planning, it is easy to let technology and whim lead the development effort. Too often when that happens, the end result is an application that either does not improve the efficiency of the enterprise or, worse yet, actually runs counter to such efficiency and ends up making things more difficult than they need to be.

We will explore two areas. First is the process that we must go through to construct a conceptual design and some of the tools that are available to us to help us built it. Second is reviewing our logical design or blueprint before we start the build process to see how it impacts the six PASS ME areas (see also Chapter 3, "PASS ME Analysis" and Chapter 13, "PASS ME and the Physical Design").

CASE STUDY: BOSTON FORMS, INC.

BACKGROUND

America's oldest and most prestigious producer of payroll check forms is Boston Forms, Inc. (BFI), founded in 1854. In addition to the printing of payroll checks (blank, of course), they produce other forms that are of a sensitive nature (for example, contracts, promissory notes, stock certificates). BFI has more than 12,000 corporate customers; 274 are in the Fortune 500.

BFI generally takes anywhere from four to six weeks to produce a run of a particular form for a client. In addition to the production, it also provides secure storage so that its larger clients do not need to store the final product.

PROBLEM STATEMENT

BFI's clients need a better way to access the inventory on hand at the various BFI warehouses. Also, when they place new orders or replenishment orders, they want to track them through the various stages: artwork, production, finishing, and packaging. No automated system is currently in place. Everything is done with manual processes and paper reports.

Owner

"Up until now, we've had no need to automate. Our manual processes are superb. We have some of the highest customer satisfaction numbers in the industry.

But, some of the original employees are leaving and the new hires don't have the same feel for the industry. Also, several of our clients would like a more efficient way to check their orders and their inventory."

CURRENT SYSTEM

Although BFI is not automated, it does have a mainframe system that it uses for inventory and billing purposes. The production floor is not hooked into it, and the system has no links to the outside world.

The present workflow proceeds as follows:

1. Client places an order for more copies of a specific form.

2. Production goes through the following process: artwork/design, printing, finishing (binding, perforating, embossing), and packaging.

3. Only at the end does the production floor update the mainframe to show that the new run is completed. The forms are then stored in a secure warehouse.

4. At any time, the client can call and request that forms be shipped to them, or they can request a count of how many forms are on hand.

5. Any client-initiated artwork changes are handled through fax or regular mail.

IT Manager

"Our current system is based on hard copy reports that get collected after the forms are ready. Any other information requires a call to a floor supervisor, who has to walk out onto the floor and check the order. If a client wants to know the status of a new run or check their inventory, they must go through their site rep.

continues

CASE STUDY: BOSTON FORMS, INC.

continued

The rep checks the inventory from a 3270 terminal. These reps spend a lot of time on the road, so they're not always that easy to reach."

ENVISIONED SYSTEM

BFI would like to create a new system that does six things:

- Allows clients to check on the status of new runs.

- Allows clients to check on inventory levels for form stock stored by BFI.

- Allows clients to set thresholds on those inventory levels that will flag the client if stock dips below a predetermined level.

- Allows clients to design their own forms using a built-in designer and then submit their design directly to the BFI art department.

- Allows clients to submit orders for additional runs on particular forms or to request shipment to their site of stock held by BFI.

- Allows clients to print hard copy output for all tasks or uses listed above.

In addition to these requirements, the system must be secure because of the sensitive nature of the forms being produced.

The new system should support the following flow:

1. Clients place orders through the system for more copies of a specific form.

2. Production goes through the following process: artwork/design, printing, finishing, and packaging. Each station has the capability to update the mainframe through a small industrial keyboard that updates the entire system within hours.

3. Clients can query the system as to the status of a new run at any time, finding out where it is in the process.

4. Clients can query the system at any time to find out their quantity on hand. Any user-established thresholds will trigger a visual flag if the inventory drops below that value.

5. Clients can use the system to request that the forms be shipped to their site.

6. Client can, at any time, print out reports of their status.

7. Clients can design and submit their own artwork changes through the system directly to the artwork department. These submittals are considered drafts and are rendered professionally and then returned for approval by the client, all without the use of paper mail.

VP of Sales

"My sales reps are spending so much time trying to close the next deal that they are often unavailable to answer a client's query about a current order in production. It would be helpful if that part of the business were taken off their plate."

CASE STUDY: BOSTON FORMS, INC.

Owner

"I got a referral to a consulting company from an associate. They came in and suggested that due to the complexity of our user interface, we use Visual Basic. We can then deploy the application by supplying a CD for the initial install and provide updates through the Internet, just like those virus-scanner companies do."

IT Manager

"Because of the complexity of the user interface—mostly the requirement for users to be able to draw their own forms in the system—we are unable to create a browser-based solution. However, we do think we can use the Web to transmit files and information back and forth. We just need to make sure we consider security in everything we do."

PERFORMANCE

Performance is not a major concern for BFI or its clients. Anything they provide will be faster than the telephone and the unfriendly mainframe interface that the sales reps use.

Developer

"We just want to make sure that the performance is not so slow that it is noticeable. This doesn't have to be a lightning fast system; it just can't be snail slow."

AVAILABILITY

The system should be available during normal business hours, 7 a.m. to 6 p.m. (in all U.S. time zones), Monday through Friday. With the telephone as backup, small outages will not be a serious problem, but anything that would annoy the clients should be avoided.

IT Manager

"Our uptime requirements are pretty straightforward. If I can't get the solution to meet this requirement, then we've got bigger problems."

SECURITY

Security is the largest concern of BFI. All data transfers will be encrypted and all access to the system from the client's side will be through multiple levels of password-based security.

Sales Rep

"If we make *one* mistake *one* time, we're in danger of losing that client. Also, if it can be proved that we caused a financial loss to our client, we are contractually obligated to compensate our client for those losses."

SCALABILITY

With more than 12,000 clients, scalability on the application server is something that should be an area of concern.

Owner

"I want to make sure that our clients can get into the server. I don't want a panic call late on a Friday afternoon that someone needs to know how many blank payroll checks they have in stock for next week's payroll."

continues

CASE STUDY: BOSTON FORMS, INC.

continued

MAINTAINABILITY

Although the system should be maintainable, no extraordinary requirements exist in this area.

EXTENSIBILITY

BFI has plans to move this out to its 300 European clients after it proves successful in the United States. As such, it should be possible to easily extend the application to other languages.

Owner

"In addition to our planned expansion in Europe next year, we are hoping to add new features to our system after the current requirements are met to our users' satisfaction.

We polled our clients for their ideas and have a list of 15 things we would like to add to the next major release. My IT manager has asked that we stay focused on the original requirements before we entertain system enhancements."

IT Manager

"I requested a "scope freeze" and a very high approval rating from our clients before we proceed with the next set of enhancements. We've left all that for v2.0."

CONSTRUCTING A CONCEPTUAL DESIGN

Construct a conceptual design that is based on a variety of scenarios and that includes context, workflow process, task sequence, and physical environment models.

There is significance to using the term "solution" in software development, rather than "programs" or "software." The reason is that the goal should not be simply to release software for its own sake, but to solve problems. Systems must not be only programs, but solutions to problems identified by the business.

With this in mind, a conceptual design should provide the instructions to the developers to guide the application so that it continues to address and resolve business problems. This is primarily accomplished through the use of four deliverables. The same as the building of a house requires several plans (for example, the floor plan, the electrical plan, the plumbing plan, the interior decoration plan), a solution requires different plans to create the total picture. The four deliverables that are likely to appear on the exam are the following:

◆ Context model

◆ Workflow process model

◆ Task sequence model

◆ Physical environment model

We'll look at the four models and how they might be used and then discuss some tools and approaches that aid the design effort.

The Context Model

A context model defines the boundaries of the project. At a high level, it describes what is part of the solution and what is not. This is typically called the scope of the project. If something is not a clearly defined business need, it is possible that it is out of context.

In solution design, a clearly defined goal is important. It helps us define the edges of our solution and prioritize our efforts.

Use Cases

One of the most common deliverables used to define the context of a solution are use cases. As discussed in the preceding chapter, use cases and use-case scenarios are a way to identify the boundaries of a solution as well as a vehicle for communicating with the users who are helping to design the system.

Because entire books are written about how to do use cases properly, we will just touch briefly on how a use case keeps a project on track.

A well-designed use case explains, in a technology-neutral fashion, what the system should do and how it should react. Use cases are a contract between the users and the developers. If the use case says, "Results should be displayed graphically in a multicolored bar chart," we know that we need to utilize something such as Microsoft Graph or Microsoft Excel.

Conversely, if a developer suggests that the system could easily be enhanced through the use of Microsoft Graph, but no requirement exists in the use cases, it is outside the context of the solution and should be considered a low priority.

If the blueprint for a house called for two doors, front and back, a carpenter wouldn't just add a third door, proclaiming, "It was easy. We had an extra door and I knew I could do it in just a few hours." That may seem silly, but developers do it all the time. Context tells us that the third door is out of scope.

Context Diagrams

Another vehicle that is often used is a context diagram. If we show the solution as a single large box (see Figure 8.1), we can show the services that support it—or that are outside of it—in the context diagram. This might look like a component diagram except that it includes dependent components that are not part of the solution.

In Figure 8.1, our dependency is on Microsoft Outlook. By definition, the building of an email engine is out of scope because the figure shows that we are using an existing component. The figure also shows that communicating with a legacy solution is in context. Before we design in a particular component or function, we need to be able to clearly answer the question, "Is this in scope?"

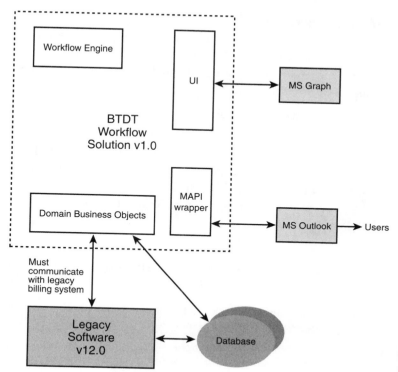

FIGURE 8.1
Context diagram.

The solutions architect should always be able to answer the question, "How do we want it to be?" This dovetails into the goal-driven design that we first discussed in Chapter 3.

The Context Model and Application Type

Because the context model deals with what is in and what is out of scope, the application type does make a difference. For example, in a browser application, the operating system is not in context, but the specific browser might be.

Likewise, different tier models create different situations. SDI and MDI applications imply a nonbrowser, Windows context. This means that services such as Windows API calls are available.

Collaborative applications, on the other hand, imply no such thing. Collaboration could be over the Internet, through email, or across a LAN.

BFI's Context Model

To determine what is in scope and what is out, we should revisit the requirements. Clients should be able to place orders, check order status, check inventory levels (using threshold alarms), design their own forms, and print reports.

We could draw a context model for this solution similar to what appears in Figure 8.2.

We can get a feel from the context diagram what is in scope and what is not. To complete the picture, we would spend the time to design use cases that would detail the interaction between the user and the system. A partial use-case scenario might be something like the following:

USE CASE SCENARIO: 12.0—CHECKING INVENTORY LEVEL

Preconditions: User must be logged on to the system, having passed through the security scheme.

1. User selects a form's correct part number from a list and requests a current inventory level. The system uses a secure Internet transmission to send the data to BFI.

2. The system queries all BFI warehouses and returns the results of the query to the user's workstation in less than 60 seconds, again using the Internet.

3. Data is compared to any user-established threshold settings. If any thresholds are violated, flags are displayed in addition to the date. Data is displayed in a grid.

We see from the use case that there is no mention of email, graphing capability, or ad hoc query capability (beyond choosing the particular form that the client is interested in). This helps us establish context.

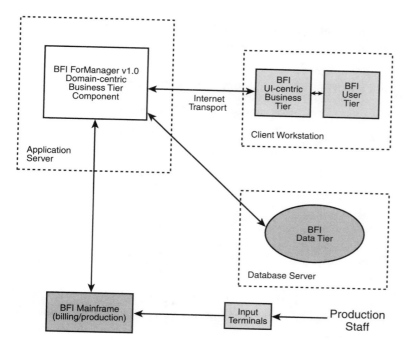

FIGURE 8.2
BFI context diagram.

The Workflow Model

A workflow process model is essentially a map of how work gets done in the context of the new solution—that is, who does what, who needs permissions to do what, and so on.

Workflow is an extension of the use cases we did in the last section. We can extend the use cases to include the work done by "actors" outside the system itself. A context diagram is more static, analogous to a UML class diagram. Workflow is more dynamic, typical of UML collaboration diagrams and sequence diagrams.

Workflows are perhaps one of the oldest and most used of all the design tools. As far back as the 1960s, when programmers were using Hollerith cards, flowcharting templates (squares, diamonds, and polygons) were used to model the logic flow through programs.

Because we are still discussing conceptual design, we are not yet ready for detailed sequence diagrams of object interaction. We are still focused on the movement of data and information through the system.

NOTE

UML Unified Modeling Language is a graphical language to aid in the construction of software solutions. It is most appropriate for object or component-based solutions. The UML specifications include many "views" of information. Tools such as class diagrams, sequence diagrams, and collaboration diagrams are available in an industry-standardized notation. For more information, you may want to read the books mentioned in the "Suggested Readings and Resources" section at the end of this chapter.

Workflow focuses around three types of entities: people, components, and the interactions between them.

For example, we'll create a scenario in which a fictitious company uses a system with the following, very simple workflow:

1. Customer places an order over the telephone to an operator.

2. Operator punches in the order on a terminal, which then transmits a request to the warehouse. This creates a hard copy "pick ticket."

3. The warehouse staff locates the item, sticks on the preaddressed label from the pick ticket, and sends it down a conveyer to the shipping dock.

From this, we could create the workflow diagram shown in Figure 8.3.

We can see by Figure 8.3 that four people are actually in the workflow. Two of the application components are displayed (the UI and the business logic), along with a printer and the order itself.

Creating workflow design helps us understand the interaction between different components of the solution as well as between humans and machine.

Figure 8.3 shows a successful workflow. We should also create workflow diagrams or use cases to represent unsuccessful scenarios (see Figure 8.4).

The Workflow Model and Application Type

Workflow through a system is influenced by the application model that is selected. SDI, console, and dialog applications are synchronous, sometimes called modal. MDI and collaborative applications are more asynchronous in nature. The user can go off in any direction. Workflow is more disconnected and unplanned. For example, you wouldn't really plan a detailed workflow model for a user working with five or six documents in Word or Excel. A data entry application such as the one shown in Figure 8.3 would be more representative of SDI.

Multiple-tier applications such as *n*-tier and client/server look very much like Web applications at this level. Until we get to the environmental details (coming up), the various diagrams will look very similar.

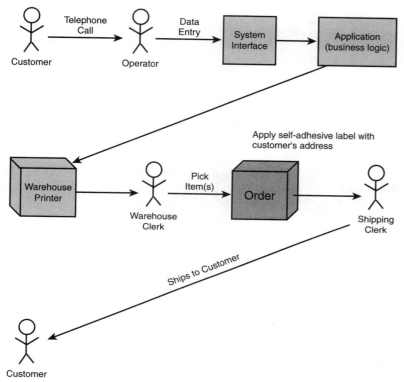

FIGURE 8.3
Sample workflow diagram.

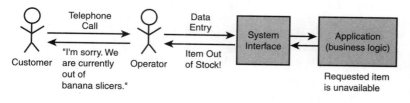

FIGURE 8.4
Sample workflow diagram—unsuccessful scenario.

BFI's Workflow Model

Next we'll review a partial workflow model for the part of the BFI solution where the users create a new draft for a particular form (see Figure 8.5).

As you can see in Figure 8.5, fewer humans are in it than in our earlier example. This is basically a secure, round-trip transaction between the client and a professional artist. Obviously, the latency involved in using regular mail can be cut substantially, perhaps accomplishing multiple iterations of redesign in a single day.

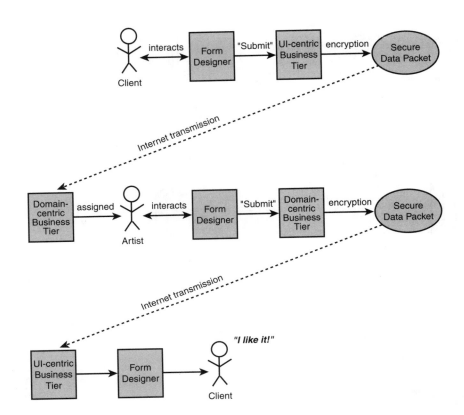

FIGURE 8.5
BFI workflow—form redesign.

The Task Sequence Model

As you may have noticed, each of these sections builds on work done in the previous section. First we establish the context of a solution. Then we create workflow diagrams of how data flows through the system. Now we need to fill in the details. What gets done at each step? This is where we begin to identify what functions a component must perform to add value to the entire process.

To illustrate this, we'll return to the scenario described in Figure 8.3. Although we have a workflow diagram, the details about what occurs at each step are vague. We'll add some more detail. To further the design process, we have italicized each action (verb) and underlined each object (noun).

1. <u>Customer</u> calls in to *place* an <u>order</u>. <u>Operator</u> receives the call and begins *entering* <u>customer information</u>.

2. <u>System</u> *verifies* that the customer has no overdue <u>credit balance</u>.

3. The <u>order</u> information is *taken* by the <u>operator</u> and *entered* into the <u>system</u>.

4. The <u>system</u> *verifies availability* of the <u>item</u> at the quantity specified.

5. When <u>order</u> is complete, <u>operator</u> clicks the *"Submit"* button on a <u>terminal</u>.

6. The <u>system</u> *calls* into a <u>clearinghouse</u> to *verify* the <u>credit card information</u> of the <u>caller</u> if the <u>order</u> was paid for by <u>credit card</u>.

7. The <u>system</u> *merges* <u>customer and order information</u> along with the <u>warehouse shelf location</u> of each <u>item</u> (from a separate database) to *create* a <u>pick ticket</u>.

8. The <u>system</u> *prints* the <u>pick ticket</u> at a <u>printer</u> located in the <u>warehouse</u>.

9. If not already paid for, the <u>system</u> *generates* an <u>invoice</u> that is then printed in the <u>Accounts Receivable department</u>.

10. The <u>warehouse staff</u> *locates* the <u>item(s)</u>, *sticks on* the <u>preaddressed label</u> from the <u>pick ticket</u>, and *sends* it down a <u>conveyer</u> to the <u>shipping dock</u>.

If you look closely at the preceding list, you will see the first glimmer of an object model; the nouns are the objects and the verbs are the methods. We could quickly assess that the system component must do the following:

◆ Verify past credit balance

◆ Verify item availability

◆ Verify credit card information

◆ Create and print a pick ticket

◆ Create and print an invoice (if needed)

In the task sequence model, we combine workflow with additional detail about who does what.

EXAM TIP

Exam Alert! The areas covered by this part of the chapter are likely to appear on the exam in some form. Questions requiring the creation of a workflow model using the new drop-and-connect question style or a task sequence model using the create-a-tree question style are very likely to appear. This is one of the areas where experienced architects may wonder "What's the big deal? It's common sense." It only seems intuitive after doing it 20 or 30 times. Newer developers or "pure programmers" may want to spend more time practicing the diagramming of solutions and drawing out nouns, verbs, and adjectives from case studies. Practice on case studies presented in programming trade publications or see Appendix E for more information.

The Task Sequence Model and Application Type

At this stage, we begin to see more influence over the model of the application type selected. We see in the following analysis of BFI's case study that the remote nature of the user forces encryption/decryption tasks. A desktop (in-house) application model is less likely to incur this sort of responsibility.

Multiple-tiered application types require that some thought go into where the tasks are placed. Putting the responsibility for ensuring Y2K-compliant dates in a business tier, for example, would be ill advised. For applications that exist entirely on a desktop (for example, MS Office, tax programs, games), it doesn't matter as much where the business logic resides.

BFI's Task Sequence Model

We'll take the previous workflow model from BFI and expand it into a task sequence model.

1. <u>Client</u> *loads* existing <u>form</u> into the <u>Form Designer tool</u> built into the BFI <u>interface</u>. The client could optionally start a new <u>form</u>.

2. <u>Client</u> *interacts* with the <u>Form Designer tool</u>, *using* built-in <u>aids</u> such as "add scanned image," rulers, and shape types. Although it is not Microsoft PowerPoint, the tool is similar in approach to PowerPoint's capability to assist users in their work.

3. <u>Client</u> *saves* the work and *returns* to the main <u>interface</u>. The client *submits* the new <u>artwork</u> to BFI.

4. The <u>UI-centric business logic</u> *locates* the new <u>artwork</u> based on a form number *supplied* by the <u>client</u>. The <u>system</u> *encrypts* the <u>file</u>, *initiates* an <u>Internet connection</u> to BFI's Web server, and *transmits* the <u>file</u>.

5. The BFI <u>domain-centric business logic</u> *sweeps* the <u>input queue</u> at regular intervals. When it *locates* a new <u>message</u>, it *decrypts* the <u>file</u> and *interrogates* the <u>header</u>.

6. The <u>business component</u> *determines* that this is an artwork submittal and *routes* the <u>file</u> to the appropriate <u>artist</u>. The <u>system</u>

is smart enough to *know* when artists are unavailable (vacation) and *reroutes* to a supervisor.

7. Artist *interacts* with the Form Designer tool, *putting* the finishing touches on the artwork submitted by the client.

8. Artist *submits* the final artwork back to the address that sent it.

9. The domain-centric business logic *encrypts* the file and uses Internet email to *send* the file back to the client.

10. The UI-centric business logic *decrypts* the incoming file, *flags* the client that a new design has been received, and makes it *available* to the client.

11. Client *accepts* design or *loops* back to step 1 and repeats the process.

We can learn a lot from the preceding design. We know, for example, that three human actors are present: client, artist, and supervisor.

We also see several names for the same object—the new form design. According to the preceding model, it is called form, artwork, or design. The encrypted packet is called a file or a message. We should be able to pick these out as two distinct objects.

We also get a better sense of the responsibilities of all the actors in the solution, both humans and application, through the italicized verbs.

The Physical Environment Model

The physical environment model takes into account, for the first time in the process, the actual physical constraints of implementing our solution. Until now, we have been working in an almost utopian environment, unconcerned about issues such as WAN latency, bandwidth, server capacity, and remote users.

After we design the components, sequence them, and determine what they need to do, we have to figure out where to put them. In some cases, few or no options exist. A browser interface must deploy to the user's Web browser, no matter where the user is located. When this is the case, we need to plan the most effective way to implement the component.

In other cases, we get to choose. How many servers? How smart should the user interface be? Should the data reside on the same machine as the application server?

As we mentioned earlier in the book, the concept of tiers is a logical concept, not a physical one. We could have all three tiers of a three-tier client/server system on the same machine or on three separate machines.

We should ask questions such as

- Where are the latency bottlenecks? Where is bandwidth going to impact the system most?

- What are the single points of failure in my design? Can I design redundancy?

- Where do remote users present a deployment or maintenance problem?

- Where should I employ asynchronous communication versus synchronous?

- Where is hardware capacity or capability likely to limit my solution?

These are just a few of the questions that need to be considered.

We'll use some examples to illustrate these points.

Latency issues usually come in one of three forms: LANs, WANs, or modems.

A Web browser-based application is a great example of latency concerns. The actual bandwidth is, for the most part, out of the hands of the company supplying the application. Some users, believe it or not, still have 14.4KB modems. If we are trying to create a good impression in the hope that the user might buy something, a Web page that takes five minutes to load may not be wise.

If a regular 4GL application needs to go out across a WAN to validate a text box entry, we have not created a smooth implementation. This was the main impetus behind the fourth tier in an *n*-tier architecture. By dividing the business or middle tier into two separate tiers, we can deploy some degree of business logic to the user interface. This keeps the UI from having to traverse a LAN or a telephone line every time it wants to verify the format of a social security number or that a past date is not allowed.

In Figure 8.3, all orders flow through a single printer in the warehouse. For all the sophistication and telephone skills of our operators, if the printer goes out—not even a software problem—our solution is out of business. This single point of failure should be considered. A backup printer, for example, might be a wise investment.

Environmental concerns should be addressed. The point is not to get bogged down in this model too early in the process or we may limit our possibilities. Otherwise, it is kind of like trying to make an unbiased decision when you prefer one of the choices. You bias all the information to lead you in that direction. Stay open to all possibilities as long as possible.

The Physical Environment Model and Application Type

This is where the application style chosen really matters. Questions such as operating system, scalability of a user's workstation, and bandwidth come into play.

A good example is the Web-based application style. With the benefits of easy deployment and maintenance comes the downside of a less-rich UI. The physical limitations of running within the browser "virtual machine" need to be evaluated carefully.

The network latencies between the user and the data stores is another issue, mostly for *n*-tier styles (this includes two-tier and client/server models). The reality of the environment may force us into using data replication, data caching, or intelligent prefetching of data.

BFI's Physical Environment Model

We'll revisit Figure 8.2, only adding notes regarding physical issues that should be accounted for.

As you can see in Figure 8.6, we've added notes to our earlier context model. In several places, data must traverse a LAN. Unless the LAN is notably overloaded (it can happen), we can concentrate our attention on the two areas with asterisks.

The single asterisk denotes our number-one concern. We have unknown and fluctuating bandwidth whenever we traverse the

EXAM TIP

Microsoft's Solution Philosophy
For obvious reasons, the Microsoft exam represents Microsoft's philosophy of solution architecture. Therefore, it is always helpful to locate insight into how Microsoft thinks about such things. One source of information that is very relevant is the Microsoft Solutions Framework (MSF). We have mentioned this in other chapters, but it bears repeating. MSF is typically a consulting service offered by Microsoft. Information is located at www.microsoft.com/msf. A search for "MSF" in the TechNet CD Online area (http://technet .microsoft.com/cdonline) is also recommended.

Internet. We also note an issue about security, which we believe we have addressed successfully. This has forced us into splitting the business logic into two parts, one of which is local on the client's workstation. Because of the robustness of the UI, this also cascaded into a decision to deploy the product on CD, using the Internet for updates only.

The other asterisked area is a notation that six production facilities are present across the country. The only way to tie all six into our corporate mainframe is with a WAN connection. This is less of an issue because we have already changed the granularity of the information from weeks to hours. The latency of a few minutes seems more than acceptable. In fact, this would be a candidate for asynchronous operation (for example, MSMQ), which would require us to place a workstation at each of the six facilities—a small concession.

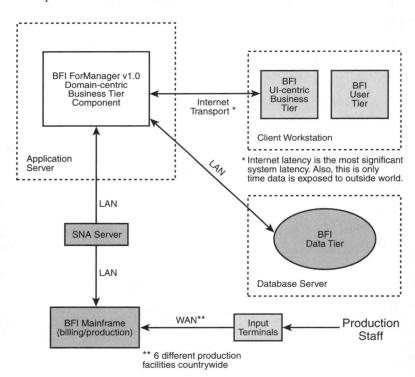

FIGURE 8.6
BFI physical environment.

Visual Modeler

Before we leave this section, we should briefly describe one of the tools provide by Microsoft to assist the developer in the work previously discussed.

Microsoft Visual Modeler is a fairly recent addition to the Visual Studio family (1998). Based on industry-standard UML, it is a way to design a solution, using diagrams, that can be shared between developers or between a developer and a client (see Figure 8.7).

An additional advantage to using Visual Modeler is that it can generate the code that creates the interface automatically from diagrams. As we discuss in other chapters, locking in the interface early is another key to good design.

> **EXAM TIP**
>
> **Tools, Tools, Tools**   In addition to Visual Modeler, a major design tool included in Visual Studio, you may want to familiarize yourself with the other available tools, such as installation wizards, Web-site designers (MS Site Designer), database designers, MTS administrators, and many more. See MSDN or TechNet for more, or better yet—take some time to browse through Visual Studio 6.0 Enterprise Edition.

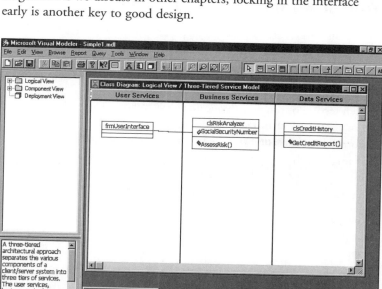

FIGURE 8.7
Microsoft Visual Modeler.

PASS ME REQUIREMENTS

Assess the potential impact of the logical design on performance, maintainability, extensibility, scalability, availability, and security.

Before we can declare our design complete and go on to the build phase, we must assess its capability to address any of the six PASS ME areas that are part of our solution requirements. We should also make sure we haven't neglected a PASS ME area that was not specified but that would cause our solution to fail.

One example is an *n*-tier application that did everything right from a pure object-oriented perspective, but that created an interface that was four times slower than the old character-based mainframe screens the user had before.

Because PASS ME is covered in several other places in the book, we will move quickly through the six areas, concentrating on how well the logical design addresses PASS ME criteria.

Performance

As we discussed earlier, performance can be the perceived performance on the part of the user or actual performance. Either way, very few solutions exist that don't have some sort of performance requirement.

When testing our logical design for performance issues, there is more guesswork than fact. It's very difficult to predict with any accuracy how moving 50 users to a single-application server or opening a Web server to the public will affect overall performance. Some of the very best have gotten it wrong in the past. So what are we to do?

After you have analyzed your design, looking for red flag areas where performance bottlenecks may occur, you can do at least two more things.

The first is to use Microsoft's Application Performance Explorer (see Figure 8.8). This program enables you to simulate certain application loads and network latencies and evaluate performance.

A more accurate but more costly method is often called a proof-of-concept prototype. A vertical slice of the application, typically all the way from the UI to the data stores, is built out and timed for the purposes of locating bottlenecks or technology risks. Obviously, this costs time and money, but the advantage of finding issues earlier rather than later usually makes it worthwhile.

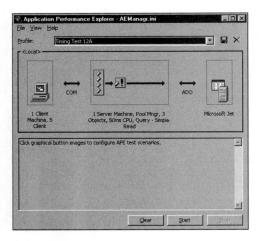

FIGURE 8.8
Microsoft Application Performance Explorer.

Performance at BFI

As mentioned in the case study, performance is not a major concern. The word "reasonable" would probably describe our performance requirement. Users expect queries to take some time, so we are probably OK with subminute response on inventory and production queries. Artwork submittal is an asynchronous process, so speed is irrelevant.

The only part of the system that should perform well is the form designer. Because it is an interactive process, we would expect performance equivalent to a desktop application. This is one of the reasons BFI chose to install it to the workstation.

Availability

Any system that is going to support an enterprise, or a portion of an enterprise, has certain requirements for its availability. Many of the tools we have used in the conceptual design will help us, not so much to increase availability as to mitigate the risks that present themselves when the system becomes unavailable in unplanned circumstances.

A synonym for availability, at least in solution development, is stability. All systems should strive to be stable. Little difference exists between a system that is down half the time and one that goes up and down regularly or that "sometimes works, sometimes doesn't."

Proper design can help mitigate stability issues, but some risks are unavoidable. Effective backup and contingency plans can turn bad situations into heroic rescue anecdotes that cement strong customer relationships.

Availability at BFI

The BFI solution should be available during normal business hours (in all time zones). Short outages for unforeseen situations such as power outages or heavy Internet traffic seem to be acceptable, as long as they are very infrequent in nature. This gives us plenty of time to work with the system on evenings and weekends to pilot new releases or fixes.

More important, the system should be stable. The BFI software is, at least in the client's eyes, managing sensitive and critical data. If it cannot be counted on to provide accurate counts of how many paycheck forms are in stock and thus a payroll is missed, severe issues could result.

BFI intends to use the telephone as its backup strategy for the time being.

Security

One of the concerns that managers almost always have, especially when connected to the outside world, is security of the system. With the onset of process automation, many managers feel as though they are losing the capability to properly secure their data, and they are looking to the technology to provide alternatives.

Fortunately, the industry has responded. Thanks in part to Windows NT's security-conscious operating system and standards such as Kerberos and eCommerce, security is manageable. It is not necessarily easy, but it is possible.

For people to feel comfortable sending their credit card number across the Internet, the industry has been motivated to create nearly airtight secure transmissions.

For strictly in-house solutions, security is easier. Through the use of the role-based security available in MTS and Windows NT security, solution developers can manage access in a fairly straightforward way.

Security at BFI

As mentioned in the case study, security is the number one concern for BFI. For data transmissions, BFI can choose between the CryptoAPI or Secure Sockets Layer (SSL). Both of these are discussed elsewhere in this book.

EXAM TIP

More on Security For more detailed information on security options, look up the Microsoft Internet Security Framework in MSDN, TechNet, or the Microsoft Web site.

Scalability

Scalability is key to enabling a successful deployment of an application. The greater the scalability, the more a business can expand without needing to rebuild its technology-based solutions.

Scalability is hard to figure in a design. All designs work on paper. What works great for 5 to 10 users could crash and burn at 15 users. This is where placement of the various logical tier components, choice of database locking schemes, and middleware usage come into play.

Scalability at BFI

Even though performance is not a serious concern, the clients should be able to get into the BFI server. One of the issues that needs to be analyzed carefully is whether peak periods of usage are likely. If so, the peaks are what matter, not the average.

By separating the application into four tiers, by putting some amount of business logic at the client workstation, by using MTS to pool database connections, and by separating the database server from the application server, scalability should be successfully addressed.

Maintainability

Maintainability is basically how easy it is to locate and address issues (bugs, bottlenecks, enhancements). This is one of the main reasons to move to component-based design strategies. For encapsulating much of the complexity inside a component, no single person needs to understand the entire application. Also, when something breaks or needs tweaking, good design points directly to the component that needs to be changed. In a major application with dozens of components, this is no small point.

Maintainability is also concerned with "How many copies do I need to keep current?" This includes all the supporting DLLs and OCXs as well.

Maintainability at BFI

BFI's only maintenance issue is deploying new releases of its user interface. To accomplish that, the company has built logic into its interface that goes to the BFI server looking for updated components. If it finds updates, it asks the user for permission and then redeploys itself. This allows BFI to release CD copies of its software only to new clients and for major new releases. Many virus checkers and Internet providers use this same strategy.

Extensibility

Extensibility in an application, much like scalability, is mostly a measure of how well the application will be able to grow in the enterprise it is released into. The main difference is that extensibility addresses growth in the functionality of the solution rather than growth in users.

One of the common mistakes developers make is to throw something together because it's only an interim solution, only to have it last for 10 years. After a solution exists, no matter how interim it is, the strong motivation to replace it dwindles. So does the funding. Plan to expand. Build to last.

Extensibility at BFI

Extensibility is an outright goal for BFI. This is not intended as an interim solution. We already know that we need to create a user interface that can be customized for multiple languages and that we have a "to do" list for the next release. Down the road, proper documentation, foresight, and well-designed component interfaces will aid BFI.

CHAPTER SUMMARY

After we have laid down a technical infrastructure, the next step is to start designing, from a conceptual level, what the system should be capable of doing. This is not done at a technical level. Instead, it is brought back to the origin of all projects—the business. What do we need the system for? What problems have we got? To what extent can we solve them? What are we not going to try to tackle this time through?

We should build the conceptual design around context, workflow, task, and environmental constraints.

The final design should be held up to the light and examined in relation to the six PASS ME areas that are integral to Microsoft's solution design methodology.

Finally, we need to remember that many tools are available in Microsoft Visual Studio to accomplish these tasks.

KEY TERMS

- Context model
- Physical environment model
- Task sequence model
- Workflow process model

APPLY YOUR KNOWLEDGE

Exercises

8.1   Modeling Conceptual Design

For each of the following statements in the left column, select whether it is best addressed in context modeling, workflow modeling, task sequence modeling, or physical environmental modeling.

Estimated Time: 10 minutes.

TABLE 8.1

ADDRESSING DESIGN ISSUES

Statement	*Model*
A. XYZ Corp has six plants around the world. It needs a component to pull together production data from six remote servers into a single resultset.	Context
B. Each component in an *n*-tier application needs to be able to restart itself in case of failure.	Workflow
C. A long-distance space probe must be programmed to be smart enough to make decisions on its own because of the communication latency between Jupiter and the Earth.	Task Sequence
D. An advertisement for a book publishing company—for example, one that specializes in high-quality exam prep books—must spin and play music in a Microsoft Internet Explorer browser but can just display in any other browser.	Environment
E. NR, Inc. has the capability to take orders over the Internet. Before an order is passed on to the shipping department, the customer's credit card number should be checked against a credit clearinghouse.	
F. Whenever a request stays in the queue for more than six hours, it is escalated to a supervisor.	

APPLY YOUR KNOWLEDGE

Answers to Exercise 8.1:

A. Environment. The problem is one of environment. If all the manufacturing were in the same building, the issue would not exist.

B. Task sequence. This references a capability of a component in some degree of detail, similar to a method or property.

C. Environment. If the satellite were back on Earth— in the next room, for example—the problem would not exist.

D. Context. This has to do with scope. The solution must work in Internet Explorer, but need not work in other browsers.

E. Task sequence. The scenario specifies how an action or a method should be performed. This is most characteristic of a task sequence model.

F. Workflow. This deals with the movement of data through the system.

8.2 Impact of PASS ME

For each of the six PASS ME areas, write two short scenarios that would cause a solution to fall short of success, and describe a possible fix for each.

Estimated Time: 20 minutes.

The following are some possible answers for Exercise 8.2. Obviously, there is no single right answer. The exercise is designed to promote a proactive design thought process.

Performance

1. Problem: Large amounts of graphical data required to be transmitted over the Internet.

Possible solution(s): Background transfers; prefetching, local caching; data compression; lowering the resolution of the images.

2. Problem: Business rules and UI separated by a busy, high traffic LAN. UI response is poor according to early feedback.

Possible solution(s): Basic rules validation done by UI-centric business logic at user workstation; stateless objects that lessen "chatty" interaction between physical tiers.

Availability

1. Problem: System must be up 24 x 365 (always).

Possible solution(s): Fully redundant hardware and software; extensive testing cycle; comprehensive design and code inspection process; partial failover (brownout).

2. Problem: After it is started, a transaction cannot fail in midstream without a full backout of all actions.

Possible solution(s): MTS or other transaction processing (TP) solution.

Security

1. Problem: Users who are not authorized should not be able to alter certain database tables.

Possible solution(s): Role-based security in MTS; stored procedures; Windows NT-based security.

2. Problem: Data transfers across both LANs and WANs must be secure from interception.

APPLY YOUR KNOWLEDGE

Possible solution(s): Kerberos security model, SSL (Secure Sockets Layer), or CryptoAPI.

Scalability

1. Problem: System works well with 20 users, but database server "locks up" with 40 users.

Possible solution(s): Better prototyping and load testing; MTS database connection pooling.

2. Problem: Application must occasionally spawn asynchronous tasks that slow down the user's PC, including the use of desktop office applications.

Possible solution(s): Migrate the load to remote DCOM components running on a server under MTS.

Maintainability

1. Problem: Application requires monthly updates to more than 5,000 users.

Possible solution(s): Use Web browser model to create an on-demand deployment, use a deployment server that is interrogated by the UI each time it launches (automated upgrade), or create a thin UI that runs against a centralized server that contains the business logic.

2. Problem: Spurious errors in a deployed application are hard to track down and fix.

Possible solution(s): Centralized error handler component that logs to NT Event log or text file; internal monitors that expose application internals for troubleshooting, debug trace stacks, and timing checkpoints.

Extensibility

1. Problem: Business rules are peppered throughout application. Changes are difficult.

Possible solution(s): Use component-based design to encapsulate business rules; use *n*-tier architecture rather than monolithic.

2. Problem: System needs to accommodate various languages and countries.

Possible solution(s): Create a thin UI that can be redesigned in various languages or configurations; use language-specific DLLs to translate text so that a single UI can be adapted on-the-fly.

Review Questions

1. How do use cases assist the conceptual design process?

2. Which of the PASS ME areas is most affected by a browser-based UI? Why?

3. How can the conceptual design be used to begin the process of managing scope?

Exam Questions

1. What is the purpose of a conceptual design?

    A. Design specification

    B. Establishing which business problems an application will solve, and how it will solve them

    C. Laying out how the technology will be used by the application

    D. Determining the number of tiers that are appropriate

APPLY YOUR KNOWLEDGE

2. What are potential benefits of Microsoft Visual Modeler? (Choose two.)

   A. Modeling database schemas

   B. Identifying problems in the enterprise

   C. Modeling a solution at the component level

   D. Generating code

3. The workflow model is best represented by which of the following?

   A. A list of methods and properties supported by an object

   B. A diagram or use case that describes the flow of data through a solution

   C. A description of components used to facilitate the solution (DLLs, OCXs)

   D. Manual processes that occur outside the automated solution

4. Security is clearly BFI's primary concern. What is its second highest concern?

   A. Performance

   B. Extensibility

   C. Scalability

   D. Availability

5. If BFI failed to accurately assess the user load on its Web server, what would be the likely impact?

   A. None—clients would try again later or use the telephone.

   B. If clients failed to get in or connections were slow, they would complain.

   C. Client confidence would drop. At some undetermined point, they would leave.

   D. Users would find a time of day when the load was lighter and alter their usage patterns.

6. Which of the PASS ME areas is most concerned with the addition of more users?

   A. Performance

   B. Extensibility

   C. Scalability

   D. Availability

7. How is a workflow process model useful in working with a set of users?

   A. Builds more robust applications

   B. Easier to explain concept of workflow

   C. Allows model to be communicated to users in a nontechnical way

   D. Shows how user interacts with the solution

8. What Microsoft tool is used to aid developers in creating Web-site layouts?

   A. Microsoft FrontPage

   B. Microsoft Site Designer

   C. Microsoft Visual Modeler

   D. Microsoft Visual InterDev

APPLY YOUR KNOWLEDGE

9. How does the remote nature of BFI users affect the conceptual design? (Choose all that apply.)

   A. Requires stricter security measures

   B. Requires more business logic in user workstation

   C. Requires the use of MTS

   D. Requires browser-based UI

10. How does the physical environment model potentially help improve performance? (Choose all that apply.)

    A. By identifying bottlenecks early

    B. By eliminating functionality that is not needed

    C. By allowing code to execute more quickly

    D. By locating design latencies

Answers to Review Questions

1. Use cases provide context, what is in scope, and what is out. They also demonstrate both workflow and task sequence. Well-constructed use cases have little to do with the physical environment. See "Use Cases."

2. Performance. The code that runs inside the browser is interpreted, not compiled, and most applications that use a browser interface (although not all) are anticipating some remote users, connected via unpredictable Internet bandwidths. See "Performance."

3. As soon as the conceptual design is complete, it will contain a context model. One of the key inclusions in the context model is to say which aspects of the identified problems are included in the solution. This can be used as the initial "line in the sand" for things such as scope creep. See "The Context Model."

Answers to Exam Questions

1. **B.** The purpose of a conceptual design is to lay out the business problems in an enterprise that an application is going to solve and state how the application will be able to solve them. See "Introduction."

2. **C, D.** UML-based Visual Modeler can model a solution at several levels as well as generate code. See "Visual Modeler."

3. **B.** Workflow is specific to the flow of data through a solution. See "The Workflow Model."

4. **B.** Extensibility. BFI already has a list of changes waiting in the wings, including expansion into Europe. A case could be made for Availability, which would probably be third. Establishing the image of a stable platform is crucial to the company's success. It doesn't take second place because it seems to be fairly straightforward to accomplish. See "Case Study: Boston Forms, Inc."

APPLY YOUR KNOWLEDGE

5. **C.** Unfortunately, users would disappear without warning. The majority of dissatisfied customers still "vote with their feet." No warning. Choice D would be optimal for BFI, but unlikely in the long run. See "Experience."

6. **C.** Scalability. Extensibility is more focused on the addition of functionality. Performance is more fundamental than the impact an increase in users would have. Availability is concerned with uptime. See "Scalability."

7. **C.** Workflow models arrange the process in terms of people and their individual pieces of work. It is much more straightforward for a business user to understand that than to try to explain the technical "under the covers" means of implementing workflow. See "The Workflow Model."

8. **B.** Site Designer is provided to help design the layout and flow of a Web site. FrontPage and InterDev are used to design the Web pages hemselves. Visual Modeler is used to design the tiers of a multitiered application. See "Visual Modeler."

9. **A, B.** MTS is not required just because the user is remote. Likewise, we are not required to use a browser-based interface just because the user is remote. See "Constructing a Conceptual Design."

10. **A, D.** After it is determined where the components will reside, we can assess the physical limitations and issues that this creates. See "The Physical Environment Model.

Suggested Readings and Resources

1. Booch, Grady. *Object Solutions: Managing the Object-Oriented Project.* Addison-Wesley, 1996.

2. Alvarez, Mike. "Make the Call Between VB and Web Clients," *Enterprise Development,* Fawcette Technical Publications, April, 1999, p. 49.

3. Rumbaugh, James, Jacobson, Ivar, and Booch, Grady. *The Unified Model Language Reference Manual.* Addison-Wesley, 1999.

4. Lhotka, Rockford. *Professional Visual Basic 5.0 Business Objects.* WROX Press, 1997.

5. Booch, Grady. *The Unified Modeling Language User Guide.* Addison-Wesley, 1999.

Suggested Web Sites

1. http://technet.microsoft.com/cdonline. TechNet/Database & Development Tools/MS Visual Basic/Technical Notes/Building Client/Server Applications

2. http://www.microsoft.com/msf

DEFINING SOLUTIONS

We have finished the conceptual design for our solution. It is time, therefore, to begin looking at our logical design alternatives. The material in this chapter corresponds to the following objective for the Microsoft exam:

Given a conceptual design, apply the principles of modular design to derive the components and services of the logical design.

▶ In previous chapters, you have seen the ways in which conceptual designs are brought into existence. Good design requires that, at a logical level, this conceptual design should be broken into several smaller pieces. These pieces are sometimes called *modules* or *components*.

▶ Every component is responsible for a specific, atomic area of the system's overall functionality. It produces this portion of the functionality by providing methods, functions, and properties that are collectively known as *services*.

CHAPTER 9

Building the Solution

OUTLINE

STUDY STRATEGIES

▶ Know the purpose of the data tier in an *n*-tier system design.

▶ Be able to name as many of the data-tier tools as possible.

▶ Understand the possible locations where data-tier components can be housed and the pros and cons of them all.

▶ Know the purpose of the logic tier in an *n*-tier system design.

▶ Be able to name as many of the logic-tier tools as possible.

▶ Understand the possible locations where logic-tier components can be "housed" and the pros and cons of them all.

▶ Know the purpose of the user interface tier in an *n*-tier system design.

▶ Be able to name as many of the user interface tier tools as possible.

▶ Understand the possible locations where user interface tier components can be housed and the pros and cons of them all.

INTRODUCTION

In this chapter, we turn our attention for the first time to issues surrounding the logical design of our system. The logical design represents a less abstract view of our solution's functionality than does the conceptual design. It is, however, still one level of abstraction higher than the physical design (which we will discuss later in this book).

The first step toward producing a good logical design from an existing conceptual design is *modularization*. In modularization, the various and sundry business objects identified during the conceptual design stage are related to specific components. Every component is then described in terms of the functionality and services that it should provide.

Three distinct kinds of components are sometimes said to exist on different tiers of a solution. These kinds, or tiers, are

◆ The data tier

◆ The logic tier

◆ The user interface tier

In this chapter, we will explain the significance of each of these tiers. We will then look at some of the tools that can be used in their construction and implementation. Finally, we will discuss the various locations that you may choose to use as "homes" for each of the tiers and whether they make good choices.

CASE STUDY: JUST TOGS

BACKGROUND

Just Togs specializes in the manufacture and sale of clothes designed to imitate recent creations by top fashion designers—only at much lower prices.

PROBLEM STATEMENT

The potential legal repercussions of "cloning" famous designers' fashions are growing even faster than Just Togs.

Owner

"The law says that there needs to be at least one material difference between the two in order for us to stay legal."

CURRENT SYSTEM

The system by which Just Togs garments are currently manufactured and sold is both simple and elegant.

Customer

Just Togs's direct customers are usually purchasing agents for large retail clothing stores. The process begins with the agents researching (at shows and in magazines) which fashions they think will become popular with the general public. They then contact Just Togs to determine whether copies of those garments can be manufactured. If so, a contract is signed, money is exchanged, and production of the cloned clothing begins. In a few weeks, Just Togs ships the final products directly to the customer's stores.

Seamstress

Seamstresses at Just Togs are paid much more than comparable workers at other organizations. Usually, their work begins with the receipt of a picture taken from a magazine or a "still" from a videotape of a fashion show. The reason for their higher rate of pay is that they are solely responsible at this point for determining what designs they must follow so that their products are legal. An initial prototype garment generally takes an entire day to produce. Thereafter, additional units can be produced at a rate of several hundred per factory per day.

Salesperson

The salespeople take the orders and ship them to the factories for fulfillment. A follow-up call is scheduled for one month after final delivery to ensure total customer satisfaction.

Developer

"We have several applications that are all designed to retrieve pictures and specifications for existing garments from differing data sources: fashion CDs, Web sites, and even emails! These all get translated and stored in a standardized format in an Access database.

Rather than using this database through file sharing, we wrote a single server application in Visual Basic. This one application is responsible both for retrieving and storing information, as well as for performing some of the more CPU-intensive graphical manipulations for its clients."

CASE STUDY: JUST TOGS

Software Project Manager

"Our current system uses a client/server architecture to help the seamstresses determine which modifications need to be made. The clients are standalone applications written with Visual J++ and the Windows Foundation Classes (WFC).

The problems with this are

- We have to redistribute the client applications every time we change them.

- The performance in the early clients was so poor that we had to offload most of the intense processing onto the server.

The only nifty part is that they can draw on the images to some extent using a graphics toolbox."

ENVISIONED SYSTEM

To answer the legal concerns of Just Togs, it is apparent that changes must be made. Some of those changes will be to the in-house information systems.

Software Project Manager

"As we add more seamstresses to our operation, we're starting to notice a lot more problems with our Access database. The request queue on the server never falls below three pending operations anymore. At peak usage (which falls around noon), it is not uncommon to wait upward of five minutes just to retrieve a single garment picture!

I've heard that SQL Server is the tool to move to after your Access database runs out of steam, but I'm not quite sure how to go about doing this. All our existing server code uses JET for database access. The client applications speak a home-brewed protocol directly over TCP/IP."

Salesperson

"I've been reading a lot of magazines and have decided that we should build an extranet. There should be a direct link between our customers' ordering systems and our own production systems. The only thing is that most of our customers have modems rather than dedicated network connectivity. Whatever software we build for them should store up any purchasing transactions during the day and transmit them all at night via a single telephone call. Similarly, our own systems should store any order updates for a customer and transmit them all during that same telephone call."

SECURITY

The use of computers at Just Togs has never extended to the financial side of the business, which is still conducted completely on paper. For this reason, security requirements at Just Togs are pretty low.

Owner

The owner should always, automatically, have the same rights and permissions as the salespeople. Whenever the salespeople's permissions change, so should the owner's.

continues

CASE STUDY: JUST TOGS

continued

Salesperson

Salespeople should be able to view all garment information in the system. They should not, however, be allowed to make any additions, modifications, or deletions. The data should be presented to them strictly as read-only.

Seamstress

The seamstresses should be able to add, modify, and delete any garment information in the database.

PERFORMANCE

Given the human-labor intensity of designing a garment clone, the performance of the automated systems at Just Togs has never been much of an issue. If the capabilities of this system are to be extended, however, new cause for concern will exist.

Developer

"I've been analyzing the performance of our server application and there seem to be two main bottlenecks. The first of these lies in the speed of the database engine that we are using.

The other challenge to improving performance, however, is the slowness of our graphics-manipulating code. It seems as if Visual Basic simply isn't executing fast enough to support the kinds of advanced mathematics that we need to do!"

Seamstress

"Marking up a given image is fine—that takes hardly any time at all. Switching between images, however, causes a very notable delay. I notice that the little E in the upper-right corner of my Web browser spins a little whenever I do this. What does that mean?"

MAINTAINABILITY

The level of technical competency available at Just Togs is considerable. For this reason, maintenance of its automated systems is thought of as an ongoing, proactive process.

Software Project Manager

"I'd really like to make use of DCOM and the other distributed component technologies now available when we redesign the system this time. That way, we can mix and match components as new situations arise.

We have a lot of analysis and design tools around here that are UML-enabled. Because we've already spent the money, we'd like to get as much use out of them as possible."

MODULARIZING A CONCEPTUAL DESIGN

Given a conceptual design, apply the principles of modular design to derive the components and services of logical design.

Modularizing a conceptual design requires that you break it into its constituent pieces or *modules*. These modules often take the form of components or objects.

Objects in the data tier are concerned primarily with the storage and retrieval of your solution's data. Those in the logic tier are charged with responsibility for accurately performing calculations and enforcing rules specific to the business in question. The user-interface components take the data and rules operating at lower levels and present them in a form that is pleasing and comprehensible to humans.

The Data Tier

The data tier exists, metaphorically, at the lowest level of an *n*-tier solution.

Purpose

The data tier in an *n*-tier application is intended to serve two main purposes. The first of these is to provide access to the solution's data. The second of these is to ensure data integrity.

Providing data access requires the implementation of a number of unique services. Some methods must be provided simply for retrieving data from storage. Typically, these take the form of object properties with names the same as (or similar to) the data that they are intended to provide. For example, a method named GetNumberOfCars might be used in an auto-dealer's system to retrieve from a database the number of cars sold on a given day.

In addition, methods should be provided for adding data to the database. To continue our earlier example, this might take the form of a method named addNumberOfCars and take an integer as a function parameter.

In this same vein, methods and functions should be provided for the updating of information already contained in the database. In our example, this would be closely related to the procedure for adding new data—perhaps a function called `changeNumberOfCars` that also takes an integer as a function parameter.

It may seem rather inefficient to you to have components in your system that do little or nothing other than talk to your database. You might ask, "Wouldn't it be better for me to simply talk directly to my database?" Ensuring data integrity is the best point in favor of using objects instead.

In our example, the component dealing with the car dealer's database could perform infinitely more complicated checks for data integrity than might otherwise be possible. For example, if we knew that the size of our lot could accommodate only 50 cars, we could add a rule to our data component that prevented an expansion greater than this number.

Figure 9.1 illustrates the series of events that might occur when a client application needs to know the total number of cars sold on a given date. In step 1, we see the application calling the `getNumberOfCars` method via COM or DCOM. The data-tier component creates the appropriate database query, and in step 2, this query is sent to the database engine using ODBC, OLE DB, or some proprietary networking protocol.

The response process begins with step 3, where the database engine returns a recordset containing the requested data. In this case, the data is a single row with a single field because this is all that was requested by the component. The data component extracts the contents of this record and uses it in step 4 as the return value for the original method call.

A fine line exists between the kinds of validation that are appropriate at this level and those that typically take place at the business-logic level. You learn more about this later in this chapter.

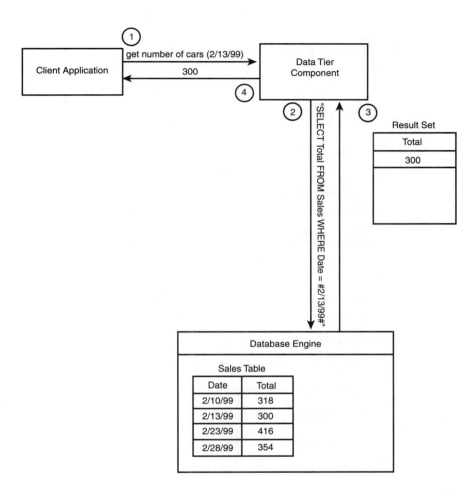

FIGURE 9.1
Typical data-tier component in action.

Tools

The most important tools used in the construction of your solution's data tiers are the databases themselves. Microsoft offers three important databases that you should be familiar with for the exam:

◆ Microsoft Access

◆ SQL Server

◆ Visual FoxPro

Microsoft Access is probably the most widely used and well-known of these products. It provides an easy way for small groups of users to store and retrieve relatively small amounts of data at acceptable levels of performance.

The engine that supports storage and retrieval of data in an Access format is known as the JET engine. The JET engine uses a file-level access methodology to interact with the data stored in an Access database. Three noteworthy disadvantages exist to this approach:

◆ An increased frequency of collisions while trying to access the same data as other users

◆ The requirement to install JET on any computer that will need to use an Access database

◆ The need to pull all the data across the network and run the query on the client machine

In contrast, SQL Server operates in a client/server architecture. Although data is still stored in one or more files by the server, access to them is provided via client connections over the network.

SQL Server is decidedly Microsoft's high-end database offering. Other advantages of SQL Server include

◆ 24-hour, 7-days-a-week support.

◆ Support for multiprocessors and 4GB of RAM.

◆ Online Transaction Processing (OLTP).

◆ Clustering support.

◆ Natural language interfaces.

◆ Queries are processed on the server, greatly reducing network traffic.

Finally, Visual FoxPro is something of a combination between a sophisticated, object-oriented programming language and a desktop-style database (such as Microsoft Access). Visual FoxPro utilizes a database format known as Xbase, which is also available on the Mac platform. One key reason for using FoxPro, then, is whenever data access on the Mac platform is essential.

Using queries stored on your database server to create data-tier modules is a very exciting way to leverage database technology. Typically, a database will know how to store and retrieve data within itself at much greater levels of efficiency than any outside system might suggest. For this reason, if your validation needs are simple, it often makes sense to try a stored-query approach to data-tier components first.

One example is a stored query named TotalCars that performs a query on all rows in the Lots table of our solution's database to determine the total number of cars in stock on all lots in the car dealership. Storing a simple query such as this on the server will be much more efficient in most cases. We show you in the next chapter why this is true.

Location

Data-tier components are typically located in the following two locations:

◆ Middleware

◆ The client computer

Middleware is a special term used to designate components that specialize in translating the protocols used by one level's components into those used by the components of another layer. For example, an Access database might use OLE DB (which you learn more about in the next chapter) as middleware when attempting to retrieve data from an unusual source such as email or a Web site.

When data-tier components are located on a client computer, it is typically an indication that a single-tier design is being used instead of an *n*-tier design. An application that stores and retrieves its information in a database is a good example. Rather than communicating queries and responses across a network, these kinds of databases are typically stored in proprietary file formats and accessed through simple file sharing.

The benefit to this approach is that very powerful client machines can sometimes achieve even better performance with small databases than with more sophisticated client/server designs. The reason is that they are able to leverage the full complement of their own resources (CPU, memory, and disk I/O) against the data-processing tasks rather than waiting to share the resources of a centralized server machine.

The disadvantage is that less-powerful clients will not be helped nearly as much by this approach. Also, very real limits exist to the size and number of users that this approach can support.

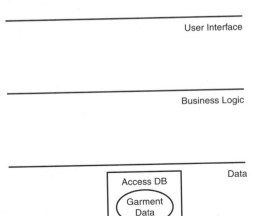

User Interface

Business Logic

Data

FIGURE 9.2
The data tier at Just Togs.

The Data Tier at Just Togs

The data tier at Just Togs currently consists of a single Access database. As we can see in the case study, Just Togs's server utilizes this database via the JET engine. Although this may provide slight performance benefits when working with an Access database, the performance of the system is probably suffering as a result.

The goal for Just Togs's data tier is a migration to the SQL Server database. One benefit to this migration is the availability of an OLE DB driver for this database server. OLE DB is a key component of Microsoft's Universal Data Access initiative.

Figure 9.2 illustrates the components of the data tier at Just Togs.

The Logic Tier

The logic tier of an *n*-tier application is, perhaps, the most interesting from a programming standpoint. It is at this level that the majority of your solution's "thinking" should take place. This thinking is usually related to performing CPU-intensive calculations and imposing sets of business rules on your users' actions. Therefore, the logic tier is often called the business-services layer.

Purpose

The primary purpose of the logic layer is to enforce the set of business rules that exist within an organization. Another benefit to shifting the bulk of your logic to a separate layer such as this is that it can help to ensure that all your target organization's solutions handle the same situations in approximately the same manner.

Business rules form the foundation of the way in which any organization does business. They provide the basic guidelines by which business is conducted. They prevent individuals from accidentally performing actions that could adversely affect the business's well-being. And they safeguard the company's assets against more intentional forms of abuse, such as embezzlement.

We'll look at an example of a business-logic component that would provide the benefits previously mentioned. Suppose our fantasy car dealership had a module called CarSales that evaluated offers made on the various models and brands in stock and decided whether they should be accepted. This would provide guidance for the sales staff by automating a large portion of their car-selling procedures. It would also prevent a salesperson from accidentally underselling or "gouging" through a simple error in arithmetic (for example, leaving out a decimal and selling a $13,000 car for $1300!) Finally, it would prevent intentional misconduct (such as selling a car below market value to a personal friend) by taking this authority away from the salespeople.

We also mentioned that abstracting all your business logic into a layer of components might have the benefit of ensuring consistency in the ways that all your applications respond to similar circumstances. Now suppose that our fantasy car dealership had a Web site. If we used the same component on the Web to accept or decline offers on our cars, we could be sure that people would not be able to find loopholes in the system. Whether customers visited us online or in person, our responses to their offers would always be the same!

Tools

Many, many tools can be used to assist in the creation and maintenance of your solution's logic tier. The reason for this profusion of tools is that the logic tier of your systems is composed entirely of code. The tools at your disposal, therefore, are all the Microsoft tools available for programming:

◆ Visual Basic

◆ Visual C++

◆ Visual J++

◆ Visual Modeler

◆ Microsoft Transaction Server (MTS)

◆ Microsoft Message Queue (MSMQ)

Visual Basic is the most popular programming language in the world and the flagship of Microsoft's line of programming languages. Reasons for using Visual Basic include

◆ The desire to create useful applications as quickly and as easily as possible

◆ The desire to leverage as many third-party components and tools as possible

◆ Existing code or technical expertise in Visual Basic

Visual C++ is, perhaps, the most powerful language in Microsoft's arsenal. The vast majority of commercial applications produced for Windows are, in fact, written in Visual C++. Reasons for using Visual C++ include

◆ An existing body of C or C++ code

◆ Existing C or C++ technical expertise

◆ A need for the absolute best performing code in your solution

Visual C++ is an object-oriented language. This enhances its capability to create reusable components, including COM-compliant ones.

Visual J++ is also an object-oriented language. It is thought to be somewhat easier to learn than Visual C++, and it captures much of that language's power and flexibility. The Windows Foundation Classes (WFC) for Visual J++ enable you to use most of the rich user-interface functionality available in Microsoft Windows right from Java! Reasons for using Visual J++ include

◆ The desire to run your application on multiple platforms without modification or recompilation

◆ Existing Java code or technical expertise

◆ The need to run your solution within the confines of Web browsers

Microsoft's three most popular programming languages can be most quickly compared and contrasted with each other as shown in Table 9.1.

TABLE 9.1

COMPARISON OF PROGRAMMING LANGUAGES

Language	Difficulty of Use	Third-Party Component Availability	Expertise Availability
Visual Basic	Least	Most	Most
Visual C++	Most	Middle	Middle
Visual J++	Middle	Least	Least

Although not a language, Visual Modeler should form an important part of any enterprise-level programming initiative. With Visual Modeler, you can diagram all the components and classes in your solution as you are formulating your designs. You can then assign these components to the data, business, or user interface tiers of your solution. Finally, Visual Modeler supports the generation of fundamental Visual Basic and Visual C++ code needed to implement the interfaces implied by your diagrams.

Other important features of Visual Modeler that you should know for the exam include

◆ UML support

◆ Reverse engineering

◆ Microsoft repository integration

Microsoft Transaction Server provides automatic support for transactions within your components. A transaction is a logical grouping of activities such that if any one cannot be properly completed, all are abandoned. For example, a common transaction in our car dealership model is selling an automobile.

The first activity in a car sale transaction is taking the customer's cash. The second activity is signing over possession of the car. If we can't sign over the car for some reason, we must return the customer's cash. The activities are united in a single transaction—you cannot stop midway. In real life, the police would stop you from running away with the customer's money. In the world of computers, Microsoft Transaction Server would stop you.

The precise details of how this works is beyond the scope of this book. Suffice it to say that your code must request that a transaction be started before initiating the first activity in that transaction. If something breaks along the way, it must request a rollback. If it gets to the end of the transaction without a failure, it can request that the transaction be committed.

The precise series of steps that your code must follow, then, are

1. Solution requests the start of a transaction.

2. Solution processes an activity on the list of things to do for this transaction.

3. If this activity is successfully completed, repeat step 2 until the last activity is finished.

4. If all activities have been completed successfully, the solution must request that the transaction be committed.

5. If any of the activities have failed, the solution must request that the transaction be rolled back.

In addition to providing support for transactions, Microsoft Transaction Server can also help to improve the performance of your components by maintaining a pool of them, ready to be used at all times. This way, you avoid the overhead of having to create a new instance from scratch every time one is needed.

The perfect example of this is keeping five CarLot components loaded into memory—assuming that your dealership has five car lots in real life. If memory were an issue, you might be able to get by with as few as you think are likely to be in use simultaneously.

In addition to transactions, Microsoft Transaction Server (MTS) allows you to secure the components in your solutions via role-based security. Using roles, users can be grouped and assigned to the varying levels of privileges and access on various MTS components. This makes securing your solutions much simpler and less time-consuming.

Other features of MTS that you should be familiar with for the Microsoft exam include

◆ Thread management to facilitate multiuser access to the same solution components

◆ DB access synchronization to prevent data contention locking

◆ Process isolation to prevent one faulty component from interfering with the operation of others

◆ Automated creation of distribution applications from the console to assist in configuring clients to remote access MTS components

◆ Pooling of solution resources, such as database connections

The final logic-tier tool that you should know about for the exam is Microsoft Message Queue (MSMQ). Using MSMQ, you can write networked applications that will continue functioning even in the absence of essential connections. The messages that would have passed over the connections in question will instead be stored by MSMQ until a time when the connections are restored.

An example of how you might use MSMQ in your solutions is in the case of salespeople with laptops. Salespeople might enter orders into client software on their laptops during the day while they are at customer sites. These messages would be stored in MSMQ queues on their laptops until they are able to connect via a modem in the evening. At this point, MSMQ would automatically transmit all the messages that had been stored during the day.

Location

The locations where business-logic components are kept are typically the same as those of database components. To review, this means that business logic may occur as part of

◆ The database

◆ Middleware

◆ The client

When business logic occurs within the confines of a database, it always takes the form of stored procedures. These may either be activated by code or triggered by actions taken on the data itself.

The most common location for business logic is on a middle server located between the client machines and a database server. Unlike data components, middleware logic components are not typically used to provide translation between competing protocols. Instead, they generally are used to provide common and/or intensive calculations required by clients in multiple applications. They can also be used for validation, formatting, logging, authorization checking, and many similar tasks.

Finally, logic components may be located on the same machines as the client applications that require them. In these cases, you are generally talking about a two-tier or single-tier client/server architecture. In this architecture, the responsibility both for processing and presenting information are given to the client computer. The only tasks that are offloaded are those dealing directly with the storage and retrieval of raw data from the database.

The Logic Tier at Just Togs

The logic tier of Just Togs is composed of the single Visual Basic server application. According to the case study, this server performs two main functions:

◆ Facilitating access to the database

◆ Performing CPU-intensive graphical computations

These two tasks differ quite a bit from each other. An architect might, for this reason, begin by considering dividing the functionality of this server into two or more separate applications.

In the particular case of Just Togs, we are told that the software project manager would like to begin using DCOM. DCOM is a distributed component technology that would make the partitioning of this application among several machines (as well as process spaces) much easier.

Figure 9.3 illustrates the components of the logic tier at Just Togs.

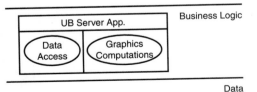

FIGURE 9.3
The logic tier at Just Togs.

The User Interface Tier

The user interface tier exists at the very top of any *n*-tier architecture. This is the part of a solution that users must actually work with to perform their jobs. Thus, a thorough understanding of how to properly design and implement this layer is essential.

Purpose

Your solution will, in all likelihood, deal with enormous quantities of data. Turning this data into information that a human can make ready use of is one of the most important purposes of the user interface level. The best reason for abstracting this functionality into a separate level of your solution is to create a common look and feel among the various applications at your target organization.

In the first chapter of this book, we discussed the various kinds of problems that a solution can be designed to solve. Two of the kinds that we said were particularly closely related—and easy to mistake for one another—are the Calculation and the Data Storage and Retrieval types. The difference, we pointed out, was that the former type dealt with data, whereas the latter kind worked with information.

Turning raw data into useful information is the most important purpose of the user interface layer. If your solution requires, for example, communicating the geographic distribution of your customer base around the country, a raw list of addresses is not likely to be very helpful output. Instead, you might want to design something such as a map of the country that covers itself in larger and smaller circles in areas of higher and lower customer concentrations.

Tools

Not long ago, it was very difficult to create user interfaces with pleasing looks and appropriate operations. The main reason was that the operating systems most people used provided only very low-level services for the creation of windows, controls, and the other parts of a modern user interface. Thankfully, modern operating systems such as Windows 98 provide many user-interface components straight out of the box.

The other thing that had been problematic in the area of user interface design had been the languages that were available to developers. Languages such as C were developed in the days when text-only monochrome monitors were considered state of the art. Languages such as COBOL had come into existence even before this, when the only way to "talk" to computers was with the aid of punch cards.

Fortunately, starting with Microsoft's introduction of Visual Basic, an increasing number of languages are being made available that fully support the simple creation of graphical user interfaces. The most common means of providing this support is through an IDE, or Integrated Development Environment. In languages with a graphical IDE, it is not uncommon to draw an entire user interface without writing a single line of code!

HTML is the final tool to be discussed for providing a user interface. Like Java, HTML's capability to create user interfaces that are both visually pleasing and functional has been limited by its insistence on 100% platform independence. HTML, however, has progressed much more rapidly than Java on this point because Java (as a multipurpose language) has had many more issues to contend with simultaneously than has HTML.

The future for HTML now seems to lie in offshoot technologies that will extend its functionality without sacrificing any of its current strengths. DHTML, which stands for Dynamic Hypertext Markup Language, allows client-side scripts to instantly change pages in a browser without talking to the server from which they came. The best support available for DHTML lies in Microsoft's Internet Explorer application. The Document Object Model (DOM) for Internet Explorer allows the manipulation of virtually every aspect of the page and browser via scripts running on the client.

Probably the most important use of DHTML in Internet Explorer is in support of Remote Data Services (RDS). Using RDS, a user can manipulate data retrieved from a server within the browser without requiring another round-trip to the Web server. For example, a list of customers can be sorted according to varying criteria multiple times without generating any additional network traffic—or wait time for the user.

XML, on the other hand, frees designers from the list of existing HTML tags used to construct pages, and it enables them to create their own on-the-fly. One advantage to this is that after a set of tags has been defined and implemented, additional pages can make use of the same tags to provide related information quickly and easily.

For example, a Web page that gives stock quotes can define a set of tags that analyze this information in various ways. Another site can then use its understanding of these tags to selectively repackage and reuse this information for its own purposes. The application continues to work for as long as the set of tags remains unchanged, regardless of changes to the format of the pages themselves.

Location

Ultimately, all user-interface components show up on the display of the client computer. The exact location where the binary codes composing these controls are stored, however, may be any computer on the network.

Imagine that your target organization needed another application that was supposed to show the geographic distribution of the company's stores around the country. Many reasons exist to want the output produced by this solution to be as close to that of the customer-distribution application as possible. One reason is for purposes of comparison and contrast between the two. Another reason is the decreased learning curve associated with teaching someone to use both applications from scratch.

One way to achieve common output would be to copy the user interface code manually into every new application that would use it. A much better way, however, is to create self-contained components that could be distributed and accessed across the network.

NOTE

VBA and Microsoft Office Microsoft Office applications, such as Excel and Word, are probably most often thought of strictly as end-user productivity tools. The most recent versions of these applications, however, have added powerful programming capability in the form of Visual Basic for Applications (VBA). Like VBScript, VBA is a subset of the popular Visual Basic programming language discussed earlier in this chapter. The presence of this technology means that all these programs should be considered as potential user-interface platforms on the Microsoft Exam.

EXAM TIP

Browser Interfaces Hosting your user-interface components in a browser will help to meet two of your solution's main requirements: maintainability and extensibility.

The reason that it is good for maintainability is that any problems that may arise with your solution can be fixed in a central location and will be distributed automatically the next time the page on which they are located is refreshed in a browser.

Similarly, they are more extensible because new functionality can be added and will be automatically distributed under the same circumstances.

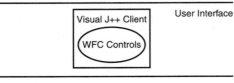

FIGURE 9.4
The user interface tier at Just Togs.

The User Interface Tier at Just Togs

The user interface at Just Togs is composed of the client application written in Visual J++. Because these clients utilize the Windows Foundation Classes (WFC), they are able to make much more extensive use of the rich user-interface functionality provided by Microsoft Windows.

Figure 9.4 illustrates the components of the User Interface tier at Just Togs.

CHAPTER SUMMARY

In this chapter, we introduced you to the purposes, tools, and locations of the three most common layers in *n*-tier architectures. To review, these layers are

- The data tier
- The logic tier
- The user interface tier

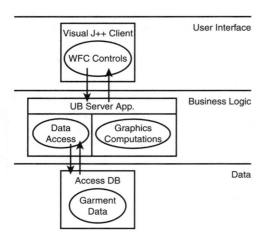

FIGURE 9.5
Three-tier layout at Just Togs.

Figure 9.5 illustrates the components of all three tiers at Just Togs and their relationship to each other.

The data tier exists to manage the storage and retrieval of the solution's data. Microsoft offers three database engines for this purpose: Microsoft Access, SQL Server, and Visual FoxPro. Access specializes in ease of use and the resulting decrease in development time. SQL Server is Microsoft's high-end database offering and has various features aimed at guaranteeing the safety and reliability of enterprise-level data access. Third, Visual FoxPro is a cross between a database and a programming environment that offers full inheritance and Mac compatibility.

The logic tier's purpose is to enforce the business rules that are used at a given organization. To ensure consistent application of these rules across multiple applications, these components may also be distributed to database servers or used as middleware. They may also be kept on the same machines as their client applications, but this will not serve the goal of multiapplication consistency nearly as well.

CHAPTER SUMMARY

The tools used to construct logic components include all programming languages: Visual Basic, Visual C++, and Visual J++. Visual Basic is the most popular language in the world and is well known for its capability to produce advanced applications quickly and with a minimum of effort. Visual C++ is the true powerhouse of the Microsoft family of languages and should be used whenever you need to create the smallest, best-performing code possible. Visual J++ is a Microsoft tool that enables you to access all the rich functionalities of Microsoft Windows from Java via the Windows Foundation Classes (WFC).

As its name implies, one of the key services Microsoft Transaction Server (MTS) offers is support for transactions. Transactions unite multiple-component activities into atomic units that must either succeed or fail as a group. Transaction Server can also improve the performance of your logic components by keeping a pool of them always on hand.

Microsoft Visual Modeler is an indispensable tool for the analysis and design of any component-based solution. Using Visual Modeler, you can illustrate, generate, and reverse engineer all kinds of COM components. In addition, Visual Modeler is UML-enabled to allow you to share your work with coworkers using other UML-enabled applications.

The user interface tier is the only level of architecture that your end users will typically deal with on a daily basis. It is this level's job to represent your solution's raw data in the form of information that can be readily understood and used by humans. The two major tools that can assist you in the creation of this tier are Integrated Development Environments that support the "drawing" of user interfaces, and HTML. User-interface components always execute on client computers, although their code may be stored at other locations.

You should remember for the exam that Microsoft Office applications also can be used as front ends to the business and data tiers of a distributed application. This is made possible via the support for Visual Basic for Applications (VBA) that is now a part of the Office software suite.

KEY TERMS

- Dynamic Hypertext Markup Language (DHTML)
- Extensible Markup Language (XML)
- Hypertext Markup Language (HTML)
- Integrated Development Environment (IDE)
- JET
- Microsoft Access
- Microsoft Transaction Server (MTS)
- Middleware
- Remote Data Services (RDS)
- SQL Server
- Stored queries
- Visual Basic
- Visual C++
- Visual J++
- Visual FoxPro
- Visual Modeler
- Windows Foundation Classes (WFC)

APPLY YOUR KNOWLEDGE

Exercises

9.1   Applying Modular Design to Get Components and Services

It is important to be able to recognize how the required features of a distributed application translate into specific components and services. In Exercise 9.1, you have the opportunity to practice making these decisions.

Estimated Time: 10 minutes.

QuickFix Software is the largest of the privately held Fortune 500 software companies. With regional offices located throughout the world, earnings for last year alone easily exceeded $12 billion. Unfortunately, many of its software products lately have been rushed to market too quickly to ensure adequate quality assurance. The development of an efficient and reliable

customer-support system is now QuickFix's most important project.

The features that such a system must provide are listed in the left column of Table 9.2.

Every feature listed in the right column should be provided as a service by one of the components in the left column. Draw lines to indicate the existence of these relationships. The number in parenthesis after the name of each component indicates how many services that component will provide in a correctly filled-out chart. The solution is provided in Figure 9.6.

TABLE 9.2

SYSTEM FEATURES AND COMPONENTS

User Interface Components
    TelephoneInterface (2)
    TroubleTicketEntry (1)
    EmailDisplay (1)
    PerformanceReports (1)
	Determine the number of calls abandoned each month.
	
	Forward incoming emails to the appropriate internal addresses.
	
	Place incoming calls into the proper queues.
	
	Automatically parse relevant information from incoming emails.
	
	Figure out how many emails come to technical support each week.
	
	Calculate the total percentage of calls responded to.

Business Logic Components
    EmailMonitor (3)
    TelephoneController (3)
	Allow the customer to make a few basic choices from the "phone tree."
	
	Communicate levels of technical support performance in all areas via bar graphs and pie charts.
	
	Store trouble ticket information.
	
	Retrieve trouble ticket information.
	
	Display caller information on technical support staff's computer screens.

Data Components TroubleTicketQueue (2)	Show header and body for incoming emails to support staff. Accept entry of trouble ticket information.

APPLY YOUR KNOWLEDGE

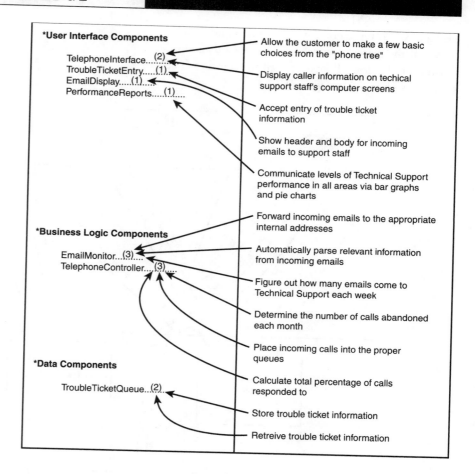

*User Interface Components

TelephoneInterface...(2)....
TroubleTicketEntry.....(1)....
EmailDisplay.....(1)....
PerformanceReports.....(1)....

Allow the customer to make a few basic choices from the "phone tree"

Display caller information on techical support staff's computer screens

Accept entry of trouble ticket information

Show header and body for incoming emails to support staff

Communicate levels of Technical Support performance in all areas via bar graphs and pie charts

Forward incoming emails to the appropriate internal addresses

*Business Logic Components

EmailMonitor...(3)....
TelephoneController....(3)....

Automatically parse relevant information from incoming emails

Figure out how many emails come to Technical Support each week

Determine the number of calls abandoned each month

Place incoming calls into the proper queues

*Data Components

TroubleTicketQueue...(2)....

Calculate total percentage of calls responded to

Store trouble ticket information

Retreive trouble ticket information

FIGURE 9.6
Solution to Exercise 9.1.

9.2 Components and Data Flows

Exercise 9.2 is intended to give you practice in analyzing the overall data flow between components in a distributed application.

Estimated Time: 5 minutes.

The seven components in Exercise 9.1 work with each other via nine distinct kinds of information. These are as follows:

- Number of abandoned calls
- Emails

- Telephone calls
- Number of inbound emails
- Total percent of calls responded to in less than 24 hours
- Phone tree choices
- Trouble tickets
- Caller information
- Email sender information

APPLY YOUR KNOWLEDGE

Using boxes to represent the components and lines to represent the pieces of information, draw a diagram illustrating the flow of data through the solution. The solution is provided in Figure 9.7.

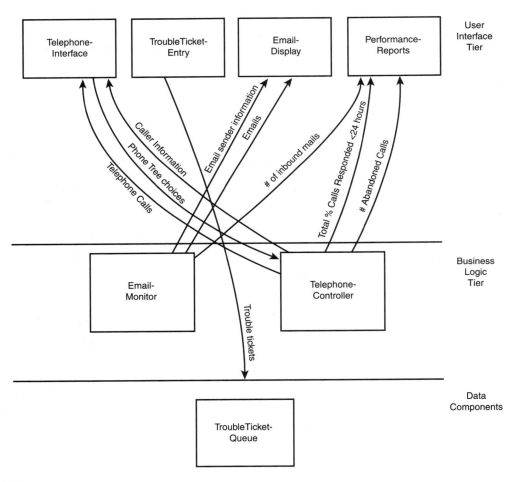

FIGURE 9.7
Solution to Exercise 9.2.

APPLY YOUR KNOWLEDGE

Review Questions

1. If you found that the entire data tier of Just Togs's solution was contained within the database server itself, what form would you think most likely for them to take?

2. Suppose the owner discovered that one seamstress's new application constantly recommended different modifications from that of another seamstress. How could Just Togs change the architecture of its new solution to ensure greater consistency?

3. The new solution seems to slow down whenever an application requires a new instance of the `WinterFashions` object. Which Microsoft technology might be used to lessen this performance hit?

4. Imagine that the `WinterFashions` component is needed by several applications in the Just Togs's new solution, but `SummerFashions` is only needed in one. How would you distribute these differently?

5. How could you choose to implement the user interface for Just Togs's new solution in a way that would address the company's needs for both maintainability and extensibility?

6. If Just Togs wanted its applications to run in a Web browser, what technology could they use to allow manipulation of the data without additional round-trips to the server?

7. Suppose the UML tools owned by Just Togs absolutely had to be used in any new solution that was built. What analysis and design tool from Microsoft could be used to diagram and generate classes with complete UML compliance?

8. The server at Just Togs simply isn't performing adequately when making large graphical computations. In which Microsoft language tool might you consider rewriting those portions to improve on this?

9. Suppose that Just Togs wants to build a Web site with information about its garments that can automatically be understood, analyzed, and included in its resellers' own Web sites. Assume that this must continue to work even if Just Togs's own site is completely redesigned without reseller notification. Which Internet standard could most facilitate such a project?

10. The owner of Just Togs would like to be able to take a copy of its garment database home at night to work on it. This is complicated by the fact that the owner has a Macintosh and the computer currently holding the Access database is a Windows machine. What language/database tool does Microsoft offer for Macintosh compatibility?

Exam Questions

1. Which of the following activities would be appropriate for data-tier components at Just Togs?

   A. Presenting garment information in a pleasing and easily understood fashion

   B. Guaranteeing that information recorded about each garment makes sense

   C. Storing and retrieving "raw facts" about garments

   D. All of the above

   E. None of the above

APPLY YOUR KNOWLEDGE

2. Ensuring that the one-to-one relationship between current garment projects and seam-stresses is never violated would be the job of which layer?

   A. The data tier

   B. The logic tier

   C. The user interface tier

   D. None of the above

3. What would a routine be called that is stored completely in SQL Server and is designed to delete all garment details after one month of storage?

   A. A trigger

   B. An object method

   C. A stored procedure

   D. Middleware

4. If a rule needed to be implemented in Just Togs's systems to prevent garment modifications from being too trendy, what tier would it most likely be created in?

   A. The data tier

   B. The logic tier

   C. The user interface tier

   D. None of the above

5. Which of the following activities would be appropriate for logic-tier components at Just Togs?

   A. Presenting garment information in a pleasing and easily understood fashion

   B. Guaranteeing that information recorded about each garment makes sense

   C. Storing and retrieving "raw facts" about garments

   D. All of the above

   E. None of the above

6. Which of the following would be the most natural choice for the construction of the logic tier?

   A. Visual Basic

   B. Internet Explorer

   C. SQL Server

   D. All of the above

7. It is important that when recording garment modifications, Just Togs's systems should record alteration instructions and cost estimates either together or not at all. If an attempt to store either piece of data fails, the other piece of data should not be stored either. What Microsoft product is intended to help ensure that this is the case?

   A. Transaction Server

   B. Exchange Server

   C. Internet Information Server

   D. Site Server

8. Which of the following activities would be appropriate for user-interface tier components at Just Togs?

   A. Presenting garment information in a pleasing and easily understood fashion

   B. Guaranteeing that information recorded about each garment makes sense

   C. Storing and retrieving "raw facts" about garments

D. All of the above

E. None of the above

9. User-interface components are executed at which of the following locations?

A. DB Server

B. Middleware

C. Client computers

D. All of the above

10. If Just Togs acquires a SQL Server and decides to use it in addition to (rather than in replacement of) its Access database, what kind of components will need to be developed?

A. Stored queries

B. Provider objects

C. Stored procedures

D. Middleware

Answers to Review Questions

1. Data-tier components that exist entirely within the confines of the database server itself are probably stored queries. See "Location" under "The Data Tier."

2. The best way to ensure consistency between the modifications recommended to the various seamstresses would be to distribute the components governing this to a commonly accessible server. That way, every seamstress's application will be using the same code to make these calculations. See "Location" under "The Logic Tier."

3. Microsoft Transaction Server (MTS) is the technology most likely to help with this performance problem. MTS maintains a pool of objects that are stored within it. This increases the chance of one already being on hand when a client application needs it. See "Tools" under "The Logic Tier."

4. If multiple applications need the same component, the most logical thing to do is to distribute it to a commonly accessible server. In this case, it would mean distributing the WinterFashions component and keeping the SummerFashions component local. See "Location" under "The Logic Tier."

5. Distributing your application via a browser is the best way to assure superior maintainability and extensibility. See "Location" under "The User Interface Tier."

6. Remote Data Services (RDS). Remote Data Services allow Internet Explorer to act as a sophisticated database client. An entire recordset of information is retrieved during a single connection to the Web server. After this, the data retrieved can be manipulated in various ways using RDS and DHTML without ever needing to establish another server connection. See "Tools" under "The User Interface Tier."

7. Visual Modeler. Visual Modeler is a tool designed to automate the process of analyzing and designing components for an *n*-tier solution. It supports Universal Markup Language (UML) for easy integration with the many other industry tools that support this. See "Tools" under "The Logic Tier."

8. Visual C++. For the absolute best performance available, Visual C++ is the programming language of choice. See "Tools" under "The Logic Tier."

9. Extensible Markup Language (XML). Using XML, developers can define their own tags, rather than being forced to use the limited set that already exists under HTML. Pages using these tags can then be freely redesigned with a substantially reduced risk of breaking other tools that might rely upon those pages' content. See "Tools" under "The User Interface Tier."

10. Visual FoxPro. Visual FoxPro uses Xbase technology, which is also available for Macintosh computers. The most notable other feature of this tool is its support for full object inheritance, unlike Visual Basic or Access. See "Tools" under "The Logic Tier."

Answers to Exam Questions

1. **C.** The purpose of the data tier is to store and retrieve a solution's data and to ensure low-level data consistency. Answer A is not correct because this is the job of the user interface tier. Similarly, answer B refers to a task that is the logic tier's responsibility. See "Purpose" under "The Data Tier."

2. **A.** This is an example of ensuring low-level data consistency, which is the responsibility of the data tier. Neither of the other two tiers mentioned as options should be concerned with this. See "Purpose" under "The Data Tier."

3. **C.** A logic-tier component that is stored entirely within the confines of the database server itself is known as a stored procedure. Provider objects and middleware components are not stored within the database server at all, but are instead completely standalone pieces of system functionality. Pruning trigger is not a piece of terminology covered in this chapter. See "Location" under "The Logic Tier."

4. **B.** The Logic Tier is the right choice for this job because it is an example of enforcing business logic. If it had been a more basic question of ensuring data integrity, the data tier might have been an option. Data validation at the user interface level would not extend to a level this involved. See "Purpose" under "The Logic Tier."

5. **B.** Making a decision of this sort is clearly a task for the logic tier. Presenting information is a user-interface tier task. Similarly, storing and retrieving data is for the data tier. See "Purpose" under "The Logic Tier."

6. **A.** Visual Basic is the only actual programming language on the list. Internet Explorer is more typically associated with the user interface tier of a distributed application. Similarly, SQL Server is more often thought of in the context of the data tier. See "Tools" under "The Logic Tier."

7. **A.** The need being described is for transaction support, which is one of the main purposes of Microsoft's Transaction Server software. Exchange Server is so-called groupware. Internet Information Server and Site Server are both Web servers. See "Tools" under "The Logic Tier."

APPLY YOUR KNOWLEDGE

8. **A.** The user interface tier's primary responsibility is to present data in the form of information that is readily usable by its human audience. Guaranteeing business sense is the job of the logic tier. And talking directly to the solution's data storage mechanisms is the duty of the data tier. See "Purpose" under "The User Interface Tier."

9. **C.** User-interface components always execute on the client computer(s). They may be stored anywhere, however. See "Location" under "The User Interface Tier."

10. **D.** Middleware is the term used to refer specifically to components that specialize in translating between different database protocols. Stored queries and procedures may play a part in this kind of software, as provider objects also might. See "Location" under "The Data Tier."

Suggested Readings and Resources

1. Caison, Charles and Johnny Papa. "Build a Simple OLE DB Provider." *Visual Basic Programmer's Journal.* Fawcette Technical Publications, December, 1998.

2. Hoag, Steve. "Together At Last: Microsoft Transaction Server and Visual Basic 6.0." *MSDN News*, September/October, 1998.

3. Hussey, Peter. "Designing Efficient Applications for Microsoft SQL Server." *MSDN Library*, January, 1999.

4. Lazar, David. "Microsoft Strategy for Universal Data Access." *MSDN Library*, January, 1999.

5. Sundblad, Sten and Per. "Scalable Design Patterns, Part I." *MSDN Library*, January, 1999

Having concluded our overview of all the tiers in a typical *n*-tier architecture, we will now begin to look at each tier in depth. Over the course of the next three chapters, we will focus on a different tier in each chapter. In this chapter, our discussion centers on the data tier and the relevant exam objectives from the areas of the exam Microsoft calls "Developing Data Models" and "Deriving the Physical Design."

Group data into entities by applying normalization rules.

▶ To satisfy this objective, you must learn how to properly design and lay out the tables that make up a typical relational database. You begin this process by determining the entities in your real-world model that the tables in your database must represent. You continue by applying sets of rules to your data that are known as the rules of data *normalization*. You should know three levels of data normalization for the exam: First-, Second-, and Third-Normal Form.

Specify the relationships between entities.

▶ After identifying and normalizing your data entities, you will connect them using relationships that imitate those found in your real-world situation(s). Some relationships are strictly one to one, as in the case of husbands and wives—a husband can have only one wife, and a wife can have only one husband. Other relationships are one to many, such as mothers and children—a mother may have many children, but every child can have only one mother. Finally, in many-to-many relationships, every entity on one side can be related to many entities on the other side and vice versa. Nieces and uncles are a good example of many-to-many relationships because a niece can have many uncles and any uncle can also have many nieces.

CHAPTER 10

The Data Tier

Choose the foreign key that will enforce a relationship between entities and that will ensure referential integrity.

▶ Relationships in relational databases are most often enforced through the use of *foreign keys*. Foreign key is the name given to one table's primary key when it occurs as part of another table. An example of this is a customer's social security number appearing in an Orders table. The social security number would be a likely primary key in the Customers table because it would uniquely identify every row in that table. In the Orders table, however, it serves as a foreign key, helping to link the two tables by identifying the customer associated with each order.

Identify the business rules that relate to data integrity.

▶ In addition to the referential integrity that foreign keys are intended to guarantee, the facts in your database should make sense. In relational databases, this is accomplished by identifying business rules and incorporating them into the database design. You will learn about three kinds of business rules in this chapter: translation, relational, and domain.

Incorporate business rules and constraints into the data model.

▶ You can take a number of approaches to establishing the rules used by your solution's data. In some cases, you may be able to enforce your rules simply through the design and normalization of your database. In other cases, standalone logic may be required to monitor and protect the correct form of your data.

Identify the appropriate level of denormalization.

▶ For various reasons, you will occasionally want to bend certain rules of database design. These are the occasions when you may want to denormalize your data. The most common reasons for doing this are related to improved performance.

Develop a database that uses general database development standards and guidelines.

▶ Many competing standards exist in the field of database technologies. In this book, we discuss the four that you are most likely to encounter on the Microsoft exam: SQL, QBE, ODBC, and OLE DB.

Evaluate whether access to a database should be encapsulated in an object.

▶ As you learned in the last chapter, objects in the bottom tier of an *n*-tier architecture typically focus on communicating directly with the database. In this chapter, you will learn how to go about identifying situations that require, tolerate, or absolutely proscribe the use of these kinds of objects.

Design the properties, methods, and events of components.

▶ In this chapter, we begin our coverage of the design of component properties, methods, and events. We show you the way the data-tier objects use properties to return data and meta-data from database engines. Methods, on the other hand, are more typically used for changing data and controlling the database engine itself. Finally, events are used for asynchronous notification of changes in data or server activities.

- ▶ Remember the requirements for data to be considered in first, second, and third normal form.

- ▶ Understand how to use foreign keys to specify whether entities are related in one-to-one, one-to-many, or many-to-many relationships.

- ▶ Identify situations in which second or third normal form may be abandoned to gain a potential improvement in your solution's performance.

- ▶ Define the attributes of an entity by name, fields, and ownership.

- ▶ Describe and distinguish between SQL, QBE, ODBC, OLE DB.

- ▶ Understand the validation, security, and relational concerns that typically underlie business rules relating to data integrity.

- ▶ Describe how stored procedure and provider objects may be used to incorporate business rules into your data model.

- ▶ Know the differences and similarities between data and meta-data as they relate to potential properties of data-tier components.

- ▶ Remember the three main functions typically provided by data-tier components: working with data, navigating through data, and manipulating the database engine.

- ▶ You should understand that data-tier components most often trigger events either in response to actions taken by other users of the same database or as callbacks to component requests made previously by the same user.

INTRODUCTION

This chapter is intended to give you a thorough understanding of the topics you are most likely to encounter on the Microsoft exam that deal with data-tier issues. We begin with a discussion of the best ways to go about developing your data models. Then, we examine the reasons why you may decide for or against encapsulating access to your solution's database in an object. For the situations in which you decide in favor of such encapsulation, we cover (in some depth) the proper design of data-tier objects.

The data tier of an *n*-tier application is the one that is responsible for interacting directly with whatever database(s) are used by a solution, if any. Therefore, it is extremely important that you are familiar with the proper design and implementation of this entire layer's many facets.

The design of the database itself proceeds from a simplified depiction of the solution's information stores, which is known as a data model. This model is produced by first identifying the various data entities involved in a solution, then describing them via the use of attributes. After this, the entities are related to one another and normalized.

After you have successfully completed the design of your database, you will want to evaluate whether it might be wise to encapsulate access to it in the form of an object. The need to ensure the validity, security, and/or relational integrity of your data will be factors to consider in determining the benefit of this approach. If you decide that this is the right way to go, you may elect to construct either stored procedures or components.

Components require appropriate properties, methods, and events. The properties of a data-tier component may represent either data or meta-data. The methods enable you to work both with the data and with the database engine itself. The events alert you to either the actions of other users or to the database's responses to your own queries.

EXAM TIP

The Most "Dangerous" Unit?
Of all the topics on the Microsoft exam, data-design issues seem to be the ones that give test takers the greatest fits. Therefore, you should proceed slowly and surely through this chapter. Make sure that you thoroughly understand all the material covered here before proceeding. It is particularly important that you familiarize yourself thoroughly with Microsoft's UDA strategy. In addition to the material presented here, you should review the suggested MSDN readings at the end of this chapter.

CASE STUDY: NEW RIDERS AIRLINES

BACKGROUND

In this era of increasing competition and shrinking profit margins, New Riders Airlines is increasingly turning to new technologies in an attempt to remain financially viable.

Line of Work

Most of New Riders' passengers are traveling as part of vacation packages that bundle food, lodging, and transportation into single, low-priced bundles.

Current Project

The vacation packages that have contributed so much to the growth of New Riders Airlines have always been beyond the company's direct control. Travel agents assemble them by working with airlines, car rental agencies, hotels, and so on. To win the business associated with these packages, New Riders Airlines has always had to offer substantial price reductions on its services.

New Riders Airlines would like to change this arrangement forever by beginning to arrange its own vacation packages. To do so, it needs a system that can keep track of available car rentals and hotel rooms in various cities, in addition to its own flight schedules.

At some point in the future, the company will want to allow its customers to make reservations via the World Wide Web. They will do this using IIS Web servers and an MS-SQL back-end database.

CIO

The chief information officer for New Riders Airlines has been involved in the design and implementation of information systems for more than 30 years.

Security

"Security isn't a terribly great concern with this system. The important thing is that every vacation plan that is purchased should be associated with a valid credit card number."

Maintainability

"We will be doing the maintenance on this system ourselves. To keep everything as simple as possible, I want the information from both of our current systems to be combined into just one database in SQL Server."

Extensibility

"We'll start off with the same information in our system about New Riders Airlines' flights as any of our competitors could access. This basically means just the standard fares that are booked in advance.

Eventually, though, we'd like to go beyond this and let our internal travel agents also see the reduced fares that sometimes arise from last-minute cancellations."

CASE STUDY: NEW RIDERS AIRLINES

USER SURVEY

To assess the strengths and weaknesses of the information systems currently in place at New Riders Airlines, a user survey was conducted.

Strengths

- **Reliability**—Generally, a consensus seemed to exist at New Riders Airlines that neither WILBUR nor ORVILLE, the two existing information systems, ever seem to go down.

- **Ease of use**—Most of the users surveyed agreed that WILBUR and ORVILLE both are exceptionally easy to use. Given the name of a city to depart from and another to arrive at, booking flights is as simple as pointing and clicking two points on a map! The software automatically translates the three-letter abbreviations used for identifying airports into their common names.

Weaknesses

- **Out-of-date information**—A consensus exists at New Riders Airlines that information about seating availability on flights is often obsolete by the time it is viewable.

- **Too forgiving**—A theme heard over and over again during the survey was that the current system allowed situations to arise that were not possible in the real world. For example, it is possible to enter a departure time into ORVILLE that isn't even on the clock—for example, 27:84 p.m.

WORKFLOWS

Over the years, New Riders Airlines has developed a number of procedures for carrying out the daily tasks involved in its operation. As the organization now prepares to evolve into a much wider scope of operations, many of these processes and procedures will need to change as well.

Reservations

Current:

1. Customer inquires about flight availability.

2. Employee queries WILBUR system.

3. Employee discusses availability with customer.

4. If customer is interested in a particular flight, the employee tries to book the customer on it using ORVILLE.

5. If the seating is still available, the reservation is accepted and the payment may be accepted. Otherwise, it is rejected and some portion of this process may be repeated.

6. Employee accepts payment into WILBUR and informs customer that tickets will be mailed.

7. If no problems are experienced with payment, customer receives tickets in two to three days.

continues

CASE STUDY: NEW RIDERS AIRLINES

continued

Desired:

1. Customer inquires about available vacations.

2. Employee queries VOYAGER system.

3. Employee discusses car, hotel, and flight availability with the customer.

4. If the customer is interested in a particular vacation, the employee tries to book the customer into it using VOYAGER.

5. Employee accepts payment.

6. Employee issues tickets on the spot.

Arrivals

Current:

1. Airplane pilot announces plane will land.

2. Flight attendants collect trays.

3. Airplane lands.

4. Passengers disembark.

5. Passengers collect baggage from automatic return machines.

6. Passengers leave New Riders terminal to find their own cars and hotels.

Desired:

1. Airplane pilot announces plane will land.

2. Flight attendants collect trays and distribute keys to hotel rooms and rental cars, along with maps featuring directions between airport and hotels.

3. Airplane lands.

4. Passengers disembark.

5. Passengers collect baggage and find rental cars—all within New Riders' terminal.

DATA DESCRIPTIONS

A unique social security number identifies each customer. We need to keep track of customer names, addresses, phone numbers, and total dollars spent with New Riders.

For hotels, we need to track names, cities, and the price per person for a one-night stay in a single, a double, or a suite within each hotel. For availability tracking, we will need to record the type of each room within each hotel, identified by the room numbers. Because hotels with the same name can exist within the same city, we will assign a unique ID number to every hotel.

CASE STUDY: NEW RIDERS AIRLINES

We need to track the city that every rental car is currently in as well as its price per day. Fortunately, cars are uniquely identified by their Vehicle Identification Numbers.

Every plane that we have must be tracked by its production number within the larger grouping of its manufacturer and model. For each one, we need to be able to look up its maximum seating and the price of a first-, second-, or third-class ticket.

We need to know where each flight is coming from and where it is going to, as well as the time when it will be leaving and arriving. We should also be able to assign and find out which customers are on which flights.

We should be able to assign and find out which customers are using which rental cars. We need to know when this use will be starting and when it will be ending.

Finally, we should be able to assign and find out which customers are in which rooms of which hotels. Each hotel reservation will have a specific starting and ending date.

DEVELOPING DATA MODELS

The first step in constructing the data tier for your solution is developing its data model. A data model is a simplified expression of the pieces of data that your solution will work with and the ways in which they must relate to each other. You should begin your development of a data model by using the rules of data normalization to group related pieces of data into entities.

Grouping Data into Entities

Group data into entities by applying normalization rules.

An entity is a single class of object represented by some of data in your model. This might represent the kind of thing that is found in the real world, such as cars or customers. Alternatively, it might represent an intangible concept used in the running of your business, such as weekly sales or organizational departments.

Each entity in your data model will typically become a single table in the construction of your solution's database(s). The pieces of data in your model that represent properties of these entities will become fields in your databases tables. For example, Balance could very easily become one field in the Customer table of your database if customers ever owe your business money.

The exact method by which entities and properties are implemented as tables and fields in your solution should be governed by the rules of data normalization. Data normalization is intended to encourage data consistency and reduce storage space requirements by carefully governing the permissible relationships between the pieces of data in your solution. To produce a perfectly normalized set of tables and fields, your data must pass through three distinct forms.

First Normal Form

The first form that is typically applied in data normalization is called, appropriately enough, First Normal Form. The most important requirements that your data must meet to be in this form are the following:

◆ All values are atomic.

◆ No repeating columns.

Having all your values be atomic means making sure that every property of every entity in your model contains exactly one value at every point in time. It is categorically forbidden to put lists in single properties.

As an example, suppose that you wanted to track all the dates on which your employees are calling in sick. Two basic objects, or entities, are being dealt with in this situation: employees and sick days. The correct way to model this, then, would involve two tables because every entity should have its own table in a normalized design.

You might, however, be tempted to create just one table, Employees, and a field within this table called SickDays. Every time an employee calls in sick, then, you could simply append the current date to whatever list was already stored in that field in that employee's record. It would look something like what is shown in Table 10.1.

TABLE 10.1

FIRST NORMAL FORM VIOLATION: NON-ATOMIC VALUES

Employee Name	Sick Days
Tom	1/1/97
Sarah	3/2/97, 4/8/98, 3/2/99
Dick	
Jane	4/20/97, 5/5/99

The reason that this is a bad idea is that it makes it much harder to get at specific values in the sick day lists later on. If you wanted to pull up a list of every employee that called in sick on 3/5/98, for example, your logic would have to search through the contents of the SickDays field in every row from start to finish. This is very inefficient.

To avoid this situation, you can try a slightly different approach. Unfortunately, this approach is equally in violation of First Normal form. In this approach, you limit the number of values you want to track to some small number, and then append a field to your table for each one of them. This approach is illustrated in Table 10.2.

TABLE 10.2

FIRST NORMAL FORM VIOLATION: REPEATING COLUMNS

Employee Name	Sick Day #1	Sick Day #2	Sick Day #3
Tom	1/1/97		
Sarah	3/2/97	4/8/98	3/2/99
Dick			
Jane	4/20/97	5/5/99	

It is only slightly easier to get at specific values using this approach than with the previous example of denormalized data. Your code won't have to search each field on a character-by-character basis, but it will have to look at three fields for every row.

The real problem with this approach, however, is that it has very static storage space availability that is not at all compatible with the dynamic requirements of the data being stored. Some employees, for example, will be sick much more than three days. Others won't ever be sick at all. In the case of the ones who are always sick, you will not be able to track all their sick days. In the case of the healthy ones, you will be wasting storage space because they will have three fields allocated, even if the fields are blank, just like all the other employees.

As we said earlier, the right way to approach this problem is to have two tables—one for each entity: Employees and SickDays. Such tables are shown in Figure 10.1.

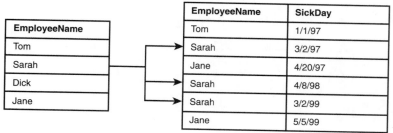

FIGURE 10.1

Employees and their sick days in First Normal form.

Now code designed to find all the employees that have been sick on a given day will not need to search fields on a character-by-character basis. This will help performance. Nor will it have to search through multiple fields. This will also help to improve performance.

An additional benefit to the preceding design is that sick days may be added and removed freely. No space needs to be reserved (and potentially wasted) for a predetermined number of days per employee, as in Table 10.2. Neither is it any longer a problem if a given employee has more sick days than we initially anticipate.

Second Normal Form

The requirements for your data to be considered to be in Second Normal form are even more stringent than for First. They are the following:

◆ Must be in First Normal form.

◆ All nonkey columns fully depend on the primary key and not on the constituent parts of a composite key.

◆ Each table should represent exactly one entity.

We described the meaning of First Normal form in some detail in the previous section, so we don't need to repeat it. Just note that all data in Second Normal form must also, by definition, be in First Normal form as well.

Second Normal form is intended to avoid situations where subgroups form within tables on a row-by-row basis. To see an example, examine Table 10.3.

NOTE

Relational Databases and Additional Rows   A skeptic might counter, "So what? Now you have more rows instead of more columns. What kind of an improvement is that?" As it happens, in relational databases, this is usually quite an improvement.

Most databases incorporate technologies that specialize in improving the performance of searches on whole-field values. For example, find all the rows that have the word John in the field CustomerName.

These technologies typically do not work nearly as well when the value being searched for only constitutes part of the value in a field. In the preceding example, this would be equivalent to John Jacob, Mr. John Jacob, or even Mr. John.

TABLE 10.3

SECOND NORMAL FORM VIOLATION

Employee Name	Sick Day	Total Excuses	Record Number	ExcuseCode
Tom	1/1/97	1	1	Alien abduction
Sarah	3/2/97	2	1	Lyme disease
Sarah	3/2/97	2	2	Death in the family
Jane	4/20/97	2	1	House burned down
Jane	4/20/97	2	2	Car won't start
Sarah	3/2/99	1	1	House burned down

> **NOTE**
>
> **Primary Keys**   For more information on primary keys, refer to the section "Specifying Relationships Between Entities" in this chapter. For now, it is enough to know that a primary key is a minimum set of columns that can be used to uniquely identify a given row in a table.

The problem with this is that we have some rows that are very clearly related to each other more than to other rows in the table. In particular, Sarah's rows for 3/2/97 and Jane's rows for 4/20/97 seem to form subgroups of rows. This is what it means to have columns that are not fully dependent on the primary key of the table.

You usually get this phenomenon when you are putting a container entity in the same table as the things that it is intended to contain. Take the issue of sick days, for example. It is possible that an employee could have more than one excuse for any given sick day. It would be a mistake to include multiple records for the same sick day in the same table, differentiated only by excuse. The reason is that you have now created logical subgroupings of related rows within a table.

To properly represent this kind of relationship, a minimum of two tables should be used, as shown in Figure 10.2.

FIGURE 10.2
Employees and their sick days in Second Normal form.

EmployeeName	SickDay	TotalExcuses
Tom	1/1/97	1
Sarah	3/2/97	2
Jane	4/20/97	2
Sarah	3/2/99	1

EmployeeName	SickDay	RecordNumber	ExcuseCode
Tom	1/1/97	1	1
Sarah	3/2/97	1	2
Sarah	3/2/97	2	3
Jane	4/20/97	1	4
Jane	4/20/97	2	5

Notice that this hasn't been terribly good to our storage requirements. We had been using one table with six rows in five columns (6 x 5 = 30 pieces of data). Now we've got two tables with a total of 10 rows in 7 columns between them (10 x 70 = 70 pieces of data)! It is clear from this example that the only benefit to Second Normal form is the clearer modeling of container relationships that it provides.

Third Normal Form

The requirements for your data to be considered to be in Third Normal form are even more stringent than for First and Second. They are the following:

◆ Must be in Second Normal form.

◆ A nonkey field must not depend on another nonkey field.

◆ No computed fields.

◆ No fields about entities that are just referenced.

We described the meaning of Second Normal form in some detail in the previous section, so it does not need to be defined here. The principle underlying the normal forms is the same: all data in Third Normal form must also, by definition, be in Second Normal form as well. And, as noted in the previous section, all data in Second Normal form must, by definition, also be in First Normal form.

Third Normal Form is intended to prevent storing data in your database that doesn't absolutely need to be stored there. The first kind of data that fits this description is needlessly repeated data. The other kind is data that can be easily determined by looking at other data in the database. A situation such as this is illustrated in Table 10.4.

Notice that the proposed solution to both outbreaks of Lyme disease was the same: contact an exterminator. Also note that the solution to both cases of houses burning down was the same: contact the fire inspector. We can deduce from this that a relationship exists between these two columns in which the proposed solution depends on the nature of the excuse.

TABLE 10.4

THIRD NORMAL FORM VIOLATION: INTERDEPENDENT
NONKEY COLUMNS

Employee Name	Sick Day	ExcuseCode	Solution
Tom	1/1/97	1	Call NASA.
Dick	3/2/97	2	Call an exterminator.
Sarah	5/8/97	3	Call the funeral home.
Harry	4/20/97	4	Call the fire inspector.
Jane	3/18/97	2	Phone an exterminator.
Emelda	3/2/99	4	Call the fire inspector.

Imagine if this list were a few hundred times longer, which is not an unlikely possibility in any good-sized company that has been around for a while. A table such as this might contain any number of duplicate excuses, and for every one of them, this table would be storing every character of the proposed solution.

One problem with this kind of design is the potential inconsistency that it can give rise to. For example, in Table 10.4, we made a point of starting the first member of either pair with "Call" and the second member with "Phone."

This is a trivial example in comparison to what will happen after your user community gets access to the data. Left to their own devices, people will find ways to phrase things that you wouldn't imagine in your worst nightmares. This will cause you endless torment when the time comes to finally generate reports from your data because your code will have to account for all possible phraseologies!

In Figure 10.3, we have shown you the proper way to implement Third Normal form for this data. The solution column that depends on the excuse given has been moved to a different table. Changes to proposed solutions now need to be made only in a single location to propagate throughout your solution.

FIGURE 10.3
Excuses and solutions in
Third Normal form.

Another thing that you should avoid when putting your data into
Third Normal form is calculated fields. Fields that can be calculated
on the basis of values stored in other fields should not be stored.
The reason is that the calculation should be performed by code
in the business (or even the user interface) tier of your solution.

Although the table in Figure 10.3 is perfectly within Second
Normal form, it is a good example of violating this rule of
Third Normal form. The value stored in its TotalExcuses column
could easily be calculated whenever needed by running a query
against the database that would count all the rows by salesperson.
If this seems vaguely inefficient to you, you may be right. We discuss
circumstances justifying reduced levels of data normalization shortly.

The final rule for putting your data into Third Normal form is
that none of the fields in any table should contain information
that properly belongs with a referenced entity. Table 10.5 shows
an example of a table that has clearly violated this rule.

TABLE 10.5

THIRD NORMAL FORM VIOLATION: COLUMNS FROM REFERENCED ENTITY

Employee Name	Phone Number	City	Sick Day	Excuse
Tom	Ext4305	Chicago	1/1/97	Alien abduction
Dick	Ext2525	Seattle	3/2/97	Lyme Disease
Sarah	Ext2112	Gibraltar	5/8/97	Death in the family
Harry	Ext2001	Calcutta	4/20/97	House burned down
Jane	Ext5050	Tokyo	3/18/97	Lyme Disease
Emelda	Ext4242	London	3/2/99	House burned down

This table seems to be suffering from something of a split-personality disorder! It starts out talking about the employee in the leftmost columns, and then it switches to the subject of their sick days. Again, because these are two separate entities, they should have two separate tables. This is illustrated in Figure 10.4.

FIGURE 10.4
Employees and sick days in Third Normal form.

Employee Name	Phone Number	City
Tom	Ext4305	Chicago
Dick	Ext2525	Seattle
Sarah	Ext2112	Gibraltar
Harry	Ext2001	Calcutta
Jane	Ext5050	Tokyo
Emelda	Ext4242	London

Employee Name	Sick Day	ExcuseCode
Tom	1/1/97	1
Dick	3/2/97	2
Sarah	5/8/97	3
Harry	4/20/97	4
Jane	3/18/97	2
Emelda	3/2/99	4

Grouping Data into Entities at New Riders Airlines

In this section, we step through all the criteria that we have established for the various forms and see how they might be applied in the development of a database for New Riders Airlines. Based on the information in the "Data Descriptions" section of the case study, we might create an initial set of proposed tables that resembles the following:

Customers: SS#, Name, Address, Phone

Hotels: ID#, Name, City, SinglePrice, DoublePrice, SuitePrice

HotelRooms: HotelID, Room#, RoomType

Cars: VIN#, City, PricePerDay

Planes: ManufacturerAndModel, ProductionNumber, MaximumSeating, 1stClassPrice, 2ndClassPrice, 3rdClassPrice, 4thClassPrice

Flights: ID#, ManufacturerAndModel, ProductionNumber, From, To, DepartureTime, ArrivalTime

FlightReservations: FlightID#, SS#

CarReservations: VIN#, SS#, StartDate, EndDate

HotelReservations: HotelID#, Room#, SS#, StartDate, EndDate

At this point, all the tables seem to satisfy the requirements for First Normal form except for two. The Planes and Hotels tables both violate the rule that forbids repeating columns. In the case of Planes, there shouldn't be the 1stClassPrice, 2ndClassPrice, 3rdClassPrice, and 4thClassPrice columns at the end. In the case of Hotels, the problem columns are SinglePrice, DoublePrice, and SuitePrice.

All these columns should be broken off and stored in additional tables, as follows:

Hotels: ID#, Name, City

HotelPricing: HotelID, RoomTypeID, Price

RoomTypes: RoomTypeID, RoomTypeName

Planes: ManufacturerAndModel, Production Number, MaximumSeating

PlanePricing: ManufacturerAndModel, Production Number, SeatClassID, Price

FlightClassList: SeatClassID, Seat

Please note that seat pricing is not normally done by plane, but rather by flight. We have taken a slight break from reality in this case to simplify our example.

After this correction for First Normal form is made, however, the tables seem to satisfy both this and the conditions for Second Normal form. The only remaining problem is the presence of the

DollarsSpent column in the Customers table. This could easily be computed at runtime from other information already present in the database. Thus, we must remove this column for our data to satisfy Third Normal form.

IN DEPTH: FOURTH AND FIFTH NORMAL FORMS

In addition to the three normalization forms that you have seen so far in this chapter, there are two more. They are known, logically enough, as Fourth (or Boyce-Codd, after its developers) and Fifth Normal forms. These are not nearly as common as the first three normal forms, however, and will not be on the Microsoft exam.

Specifying Relationships Between Entities

Specify the relationships between entities.

The entities in your data model do not exist apart from each other in a vacuum. An important part of the data normalization that we examined in the previous section was determining how to use the relationships between entities to reduce the storage of unneeded data in our model.

In this section, we look in greater detail at the use of foreign keys to establish relationships between the tables in your solution's databases. The relationships that are available for expression between entities in your models are the following:

◆ One to one

◆ One to many

◆ Many to many

Choosing Foreign Keys

Choose the foreign key that will enforce a relationship between entities and that will ensure referential integrity.

A primary key is the minimum set of columns (none of which can ever be null) needed to uniquely identify the rows in a table. In an

Employee table consisting solely of U.S. citizens, for instance, the primary key might be the social security number. This works because social security numbers are supposed to be unique across the domain of all U.S. citizens.

Sometimes, more than one column is needed to create a satisfactory primary key. If social security numbers are unavailable in the preceding example, you might choose to use both first and last names as a primary key. You must use both columns together because either column used individually could easily contain duplicate entries. A primary key with multiple columns is called a *combination key*.

When you want to relate two entities in your data model, you include the primary key from one in the fields of the other. When one entity or table's primary key occurs in the fields of another entity or table, it is called that table's *foreign key*.

Figure 10.5 graphically illustrates the concepts of primary and foreign keys using some of the tables shown earlier in this chapter.

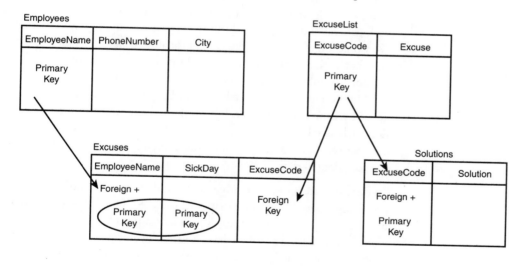

FIGURE 10.5
Primary keys and foreign keys.

Notice that we have replaced the text Excuses that we have been used to seeing with numbers called ExcuseCodes. The meaning behind these numbers is given by a new table, ExcuseList. A small, static table such as this, which uses foreign key relationships to translate codes into text, is often called a *lookup table*.

The important thing to remember in selecting foreign keys is that they will always be the primary keys of other tables. So, you are better off choosing your primary keys first. Then simply ask yourself what real-world process you would use, when given a specific instance of one entity, to find a related instance of another entity.

Kinds of Relationships

Three kinds of relationships exist: one to one, one to many, and many to many. These refer to the greatest possible number of entities that you may find when performing a lookup based on a foreign key.

As an example of a one-to-one relationship, suppose we had to store both general and confidential information about an employee. We would build an Employee table, probably using the Employee Number as the primary key. We would include information such as phone number, job title, and business address in this table. We would then create a second table called Employee_Personnel, also keyed by Employee Number. We would add confidential information such as salary, pay grade, and date of hire. By splitting the data between two tables, we can more easily restrict access to the confidential data.

To demonstrate a one-to-many relationship, we can extend the preceding example. Suppose that we have a requirement to maintain historical records of the employee's promotions and pay raises. We would create another table, related to Employee_Personnel, named Employee_Personnel_History. The table would be related on the Employee Number, but a Date field would also exist in the new table to create a unique primary key. Each employee can now have multiple pay increases, but each record in the History file will point back to only a single Employee.

Finally, we might decide to model something a little less typical, such as actors and movies. Now, how many movies can a given actor or actress be in during his or her career: just one or many?

Many, of course. What is the maximum number of actors and actresses that a single movie can have in it? Many. We have now discovered our first many-to-many relationship.

Unfortunately, this is a little more complicated than the previous situations. You can't use a single Actor or Movie column because both may require multiple entries. It is tempting, I know, to pluralize the column name into Actors or Movies and put a list in it, but recall that this is in violation of First Normal form (and it wouldn't allow proper lookups in a relational database, anyway).

The solution, which you will always need in a many-to-many situation, is the creation of a third table called a *junction table*. The purpose of the lookup table is to break a single many-to-many relationship into two separate one-to-many relationships.

The idea is this: first the two basic tables (in our example, Actors and Movies) stop referring directly to each other altogether. Then, a third table is created that contains only the primary keys from both tables. This is illustrated in Figure 10.6.

Notice in the tables that the two base tables no longer give any indication about external relationships. In contrast, the Starring lookup table gives information about nothing other than relationships between the two base tables.

Name	Address	Age
John Cleese	15 E. Jackson	21
Jeff Bridges	318 S. Wacker	73
Ewan McGregor	5252 N. Lasalle	41
Terry Jones	150 W. LaGrange	27

ActorName	MovieName
John Cleese	Holy Grail
Terry Jones	Holy Grail
Ewan McGregor	Shallow Grave
Ewan McGregor	Phantom Menace

Name	Country of Origin	Length
Shallow Grave	England	180
Phantom Menace	USA	90
The Big Lebowski	USA	90
Holy Grail	England	120

FIGURE 10.6
Actors, movies, and their "starring" relationships.

EXAM TIP

UML's Expanded Relationships
In Chapter 9, "Building the Solution," we briefly discussed the concept of UML compliance as a feature of Microsoft's Visual Modeler tool. Visual Modeler features an expanded set of relationships, derived from UML, that you are very likely to see on the exam.

One of these is zero or one to one. This is similar to a one-to-one relationship, except it specifically allows for the possibility of no related entities on one side of the relationship. Another UML-inspired type of relationship is zero or one to many. This is similar to a one-to-many relationship, except it specifically allows for the possibility of no related entities on one side of the relationship.

NOTE

One-to-One Relationships   In all honesty, these tend to be pretty rare in the real world. Most of the time, things that are related on a one-to-one basis wind up in the same table.

Specifying Entity Relationships at New Riders Airlines

In Figure 10.7, you see an entity relationship diagram for the entire data model at New Riders Airlines.

Notice first that no one-to-one relationships exist in the data model for New Riders Airlines.

Just a few one-to-many relationships are not part of larger, many-to-many relationships. The first of these is between Planes and Flights. A Plane can give many Flights during its lifetime, but any given Flight will involve only one Plane. Another one-to-many relationship exists between HotelRooms and Hotels. A Hotel will generally have many HotelRooms, but any one HotelRoom is a part of only one Hotel.

The final pairs of one-to-many relationships are connections between HotelPricing and RoomTypes and between PlanePricing and FlightClassList. In both of these cases, the pricing table is using rows in its related table to look up full text descriptions for the shorter codes that are stored within itself; for example, equating RoomTypeID 715 with Single Room, No Bath or SeatClassID 3 with First Class.

You might recall that we made some adjustments to the proposed layouts of these tables in the previous section on data normalization. In particular, we killed some repeating columns from Planes and Hotels and created two new tables: PlanePricing and HotelPricing. For more information, refer to the section "Grouping Data into Entities at New Riders Airlines."

Tables created for this reason also exist in a one-to-many relationship with the tables that they were "torn out of." One Plane can have many entries in PlanePricing, but a single entry there can correspond at most to only one entry in Plane. A Hotel can have many entries in HotelPricing, but a single entry there can correspond at most to only one entry in Hotels.

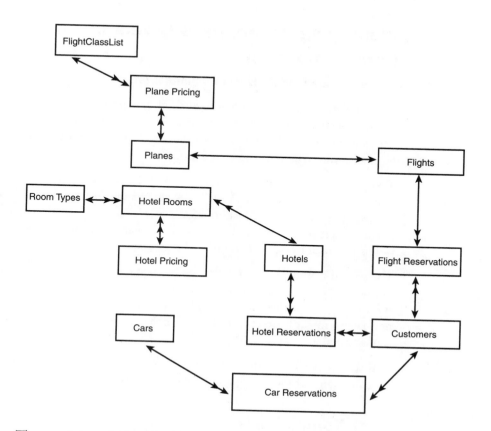

FIGURE 10.7
Entity relationships at New
Riders Airlines.

The remaining relationships in our data model for New Riders
Airlines are many-to-many, with the appropriate junction tables
sitting in the middle of each. These equate to the three kinds of
reservations that are possible under New Riders' new system: cars,
flights, and hotels. In all cases, more than one traveler may be
involved in making a single reservation (for example, multiple
people in one hotel room). Also, a single traveler may want to
reserve more than one of the possible items (for example, parents
getting an extra hotel room for their kids). These relationships are
made possible via the CarReservations, FlightReservations, and
HotelReservations tables.

Identifying Appropriate Levels of Denormalization

Identify appropriate level of denormalization.

Data models that adhere to the principals of data normalization t end to be better designed than those that completely ignore them. This having been said, it must be acknowledged that it is possible to normalize your data to the point of absurdity.

Two main circumstances exist under which data may be denormalized. The first of these is when data does not change, or when it changes only infrequently. Denormalization is acceptable under these circumstances because the full scope of functionality that normalization is intended to support will never be accessed.

The second reason for denormalization is when data is used for decision support and is particularly massive in size. The reason, in this case, is that queries and joins against information that is fully normalized might be have a detrimental effect on performance that is unacceptable.

In this section, we will discuss some of the reasons you might decide to ignore some of the principals of data normalization.

First Normal Form

Getting your data into First Normal form is almost always advisable. The only rule for this form that is commonly violated is the rule requiring atomic values within fields. In general, it is permissible to store a list inside a field if that list will almost always be referenced as a whole, rather than on an element-by-element basis.

Imagine a frame containing several check boxes on a form. All the check boxes refer to different reasons that a given customer should be accorded VIP status. Now, if your solution needs to allow people to search on a particular combination of these reasons, they should all be stored in separate fields. But if these values will only be made available as a group when a given customer's record is made current, they may be good candidates for First Normal form violation.

Second and Third Normal Forms

We saw, in the section on Second Normal form, that breaking a single entity into container and things contained tables (such as SickDays and Excuses) can work against the goal of reduced storage requirements. If you ever feel that this loss of storage space is not justified by the corresponding improvement in your data model's clarity, you may want to consider abandoning Second Normal form here. This is the reason why Second Normal form is much more often violated than is First Normal form.

Probably the singlemost commonly violated principal of data normalization is the requirement that computed fields not be stored as part of your database. In some cases, you may perform certain calculations on a fixed schedule that produce results that are historical in nature and, therefore, not subject to frequent changes. This occurs most often as part of decision support, or reporting databases.

An example is a field called LastYearsTotalPurchases in a sales-tracking database. Certainly, by combing your entire sales database for items from a given customer, you could write a procedure that would generate this figure from scratch every time it was needed. But this would probably eat up a lot more of your system's performance than simply doing it once a year and storing the results. Another example is recording employees' ages in a database, in addition to their dates of birth. The reason here, as in the previous example, is that the specifics of the date arithmetic required to calculate an age based upon a date of birth may be more complicated than we would like to bother with. In cases such as this, you will definitely want to consider violation of the Third Normal Form.

Denormalization at New Riders Airlines

Any violations of data normalization at New Riders seem unjustified based on the information in the case study.

Defining Data Entity Attributes

Now that we have discussed all the intricacies of data entity normalization and relationships, it is time for us to focus on the attributes of the entities themselves. Every entity in your model will have certain names and fields associated with it. There are also a few concepts of data entity ownership with which you should be familiar.

Entity Names

The name of a data entity is typically the name of whatever is being represented. This name is usually passed on to become the name of whichever table is used to represent the entity. For example, the employees at an organization are typically represented by an entity in our data model called Employees. This entity is then established in our actual, physical database as a table called Employees.

Fields

The fields in a table correspond to the properties of the entity that that table is intended to represent. Fields can usually be assigned specific data types that limit the kinds of data that they can contain. They can often also be given default values that will be used to fill their positions in new rows when no specific value is specified for them.

Every database engine supports different types of data for its fields and calls them something slightly different. The most basic abstraction of these data types that you should know for the Microsoft exam, however, are as follows:

◆ **Integer**—These are sometimes referred to as SHORT or LONG columns, depending on what range of numeric values is supported. These are numeric values where fractional components would be impossible in the real world. For example, the number of children—no one really has 1.5 kids, regardless of what the U.S. census department may claim! The number of incidents to which a given support person has responded, the number of countries forming an alliance, and the number of cars parked outside my house are all examples of integer values.

◆ **Double**—These are sometimes referred to as NUMBER columns. These are numeric values where fractional components are possible in the real world. Money fields are a good example of fields that should use this type. Billable hours, grade point averages, and the result of dividing 4 by 3 are also good examples of doubles and floats.

◆ **Text**—These are sometimes known as CHAR or VARCHAR columns. This is data that is strictly to be displayed "as is," without the possibility of arithmetic being performed on it. String data, such as Hello World and QWERTY, is the obvious example of data that should be stored in this kind of field. But identification numbers, although numeric, should also be stored as Text to make clear the fact that they will never be involved in arithmetic. For example, you will never add one employee's social security number to another's—they just aren't numbers that are used for that purpose. For this reason, social security numbers are a good example of numbers that should be stored as Text, rather than as numeric values. Telephone numbers are another example of a number that should be stored as Text data.

◆ **Time**—Different databases support this in different ways, but special support for Time/Date is widespread enough to be worth knowing about.

Ownership

The issues of ownership surrounding data entities are closely related to the concept of security that makes up the first S in our PASS ME themes. The creator of a data model can assign different ownerships to the following:

◆ Environments

◆ Databases

◆ Tables

◆ Fields

Environments are best defined as separate collections of databases that are typically supported by high-end database servers such as SQL Server and Oracle. Similarly, a database (for our purposes) is a collection of tables and stored queries and procedures. Finally, tables are collections of fields, although they can be more generally defined as any real-world implementations for data-model entities.

The fields in your databases are where information is actually going to be stored, so it is particularly important that you implement field-level decisions correctly. Possibly the most basic decision that you will have to make about your fields is what they should be named. Field names should neither be so short as to require interpretation nor so long as to be difficult to type and remember. The following list shows examples of good and bad ways to name the same field.

- **SocialSecurityNumbersUsedForCustomerIdentification**—
Too long. It gives us way more information than we need
to know.

- **ID**—Too short. In logic using this field later on, it might not
be readily apparent what kind of entity is being referenced by
this value.

- **CustomerID**—Perfect. Tells us the entity involved and
conveys the purpose of the field (identification).

The size of the fields you are using should also be wisely considered.
You don't want to reserve so little space that you wind up either
truncating large values or generating runtime errors. On the other
hand, you don't want to waste storage space by using huge fields to
hold tiny values. For example, the proper size for a Social Security
Number field is exactly nine characters because this is the exact size
of a social security number. If you chose three characters, you would
either truncate six digits every time you saved a row, or (more likely)
you would generate runtime errors. If you chose 255 characters in
this case, you would waste 246 bytes in every row.

Defining Data Entity Attributes at New Riders Airlines

We are told by New Riders' CIO, in the "Maintainability" section,
that she would like "the information from both of our current
systems to be combined into just one database in SQL Server."
Therefore, we know immediately that only a single database exists,
although we aren't given its name.

Figure 10.8 shows the finalized design of our tables and their
relationships to each other. If we make some educated guesses about
data type, as well, we can derive the following complete information
about data-entity attributes at New Riders Airlines:

- Customers: SS# (Text), Name (Text), Address (Text), Phone
(Text)

- Hotels: ID# (Text), Name (Text), City (Text)

- HotelPricing: HotelID (Text), RoomTypeID (Integer), Price
(Double)

- HotelRooms: HotelID (Text), Room# (Text), RoomType (Text)

- Cars: VIN# (Text), City (Text), PricePerDay (Text)

- Planes: ManufacturerAndModel (Text), Production Number (Text), MaximumSeating (Integer)

- PlanePricing: ManufacturerAndModel (Text), Production Number (Text), SeatClassID (Integer), Price (Double)

- Flights: ID# (Text), ManufacturerAndModel (Text), ProductionNumber (Text), From (Text), To (Text), DepartureTime (Time), ArrivalTime (Time)

- FlightReservations: FlightID (Text), SS# (Text)

- RoomTypes: RoomTypeID (Integer), RoomName (Text)

- HotelReservations: HotelID# (Integer), Room# (Text), SS# (Text), StartDate (Time), EndDate (Text)

- CarReservations: VIN# (Text), SS# (Text), StartDate (Time), EndDate (Time)

- FlightClassList: SeatClassID (Integer), SeatClassName (Text)

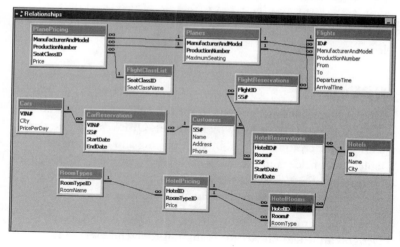

FIGURE 10.8
The finalized design of the tables and relationships.

Designing to General Standards and Guidelines

Develop a database that uses general database development standards and guidelines.

It could be said that everything done in the field of computer technologies ultimately boils down to the storage and retrieval of data. With this thought in mind, the profusion of established standards and guidelines for the processing of data should come as no surprise. Many of these standards vary from shop to shop. The standards we look at in this section are those that have gained industrywide standing.

SQL

SQL (Structured Query Language) is a language used to communicate requests for the storage, retrieval, and alteration of data. The industry standard for this language is set by ANSI (American National Standards Institute). It was last revised in 1992 (ANSI-92).

Variations on this industry-standard language are used by all the biggest database server products, including Oracle and Microsoft SQL Server. Although SQL can be a very powerful tool in the right hands, it suffers from a reputation of being somewhat difficult to learn.

QBE

One of Microsoft's first answers to the difficulty of learning and using SQL was QBE (Query By Example). QBE is a user interface allowing the creation of SQL by the dragging and dropping of tables, their fields, and the relationships between them. Although it lacks some of SQL's raw power and flexibility, QBE remains very popular with those new to database programming.

One example of a Microsoft tool that uses QBE is the Query Designer in Microsoft Access. Using this tool, end users can construct their own views of data by adding or removing tables and dragging their fields into the view-definition area at the bottom of the window. Joins between tables are as simple as dragging the linking fields between related tables.

ODBC

ODBC (Open Database Connectivity) was developed by Microsoft to allow databases made by different vendors to talk to each other. It has become one of the most important and universal industry standards, with almost every database vendor creating a driver for its engine that is ODBC-compliant. The one great limitation to ODBC going forward is its weak support for databases that are not relational in design.

OLE DB

OLE DB is Microsoft's successor technology to ODBC. Unlike ODBC, OLE DB is not limited to relational databases. This means that by using OLE DB, a developer should be able to provide access to data stored in email, graphics formats, and so on just as easily as in an Access or SQL Server database. This is Microsoft's newest technology and has been publicly stated to be the focus of almost all future development effort in the field of data access. For more information about these technologies, see Chapter 5, "Integration Issues."

Standards and Guidelines at New Riders Airlines

The case study avoids most topics of hardware and software, except for some comments about World Wide Web access in the section "Current Project." If we focus on just this subject, however, we can come to a few quick conclusions about the standards and guidelines that would currently be available in enabling such a project.

To begin with, New Riders plans to use an Oracle database. Oracle supports all the standards and guidelines mentioned in our text. However, the company also plans to use a UNIX Web server. This means we should largely rule out the Microsoft technologies, which are QBE, ODBC, and OLE DB/ADO. The focus of any such project then, from a data-access standpoint, should be on SQL and OLE DB or ODBC.

> **EXAM TIP**
>
> **ADO (Active Data Objects)** On the Microsoft exam, you are most likely to encounter several questions about OLE DB in the form of ADO. ADO refers to a layer of objects constructed to provide developers with easier access to the features and functionality of OLE DB. Although ADO is now Microsoft's preferred data access method for all development tools, this technology has strong historical ties to Active Server Pages. Virtually all Active Server Pages that do data access use Active Data Objects.

SHOULD DATABASE ACCESS BE ENCAPSULATED IN AN OBJECT?

Evaluate whether access to a database should be encapsulated in an object.

Sometimes it makes perfect sense for business logic and user-interface code to have direct access to a database. Other times, you will want to encapsulate this access into a layer of objects specifically designed for this purpose. In this section, we provide you with as much guidance as possible in how you might go about making this decision both in real life and on the Microsoft exam.

Identifying Business Rules for Data Integrity

Identify the business rules that relate to data integrity.

The first thing that you must do to evaluate whether access to your data should be encapsulated in an object is to identify your solution's business rules dealing with data integrity. You should know the three main kinds of data integrity rules for the Microsoft exam:

◆ Translation

◆ Relational

◆ Domain

Security rules can also be implemented in a data-tier object that will limit the access that various clients have to your data. In this way, you can give different users and applications only as much freedom to alter your data as you deem warranted.

Content Validations

A translation rule converts values stored in your database into values that your solution can use directly. Typically, this kind of rule is used when storing the solution-ready form of the value directly in the database would consume too much storage space. For example, you might elect to store two-letter abbreviations for state names in your database and then implement a translation rule in one of your data-tier objects to convert them into full names such as Illinois and Wyoming.

A relational rule ensures that the proper *n*-to-*n* relationships exist between specific entity instances within your solution's database. For example, it might ensure that every row in your ClassRoom table has exactly one related row in your Teacher table.

It might also take a more proactive approach and actively delete or update rows related to rows that are changed or deleted. This is called cascading updates and deletes and is most commonly seen in Microsoft's Access database product. When this kind of relational rule is applied, deleting a row in a Teacher table will delete all associated rows in the ClassRoom table. Another example: changing someone's name in the SchoolDistrictParents table would result in that name also being changed on the children's rows in the SchoolDistrictChildren table.

Finally, domain rules exist to ensure that values being stored in your database fall within the range of legitimate values for the fields in which they are being stored. A field named CleaningWeekday, for example, might use a domain rule to reject any number outside the range 1-7 (1 = Sunday, 7 = Saturday). Or a password field might refuse to accept any value that it could find in a standard English dictionary.

Security

A desire to safeguard the security of your data is the other likely reason for encapsulating access to it. On one hand, you might do this to protect your solution from maliciousness. On the other hand, you might be concerned about the effects of well-intentioned, but nevertheless incorrect, code running against your data.

The following are some examples of ways that data-tier objects can protect your data:

◆ **Restricted distribution**—The most basic way to protect your database. Forbid access to anything other than a given client-side component, then restrict distribution of this component to a handful of trusted computers and individuals.

◆ **Windows NT authentication**—Using logic in your data components to actually verify the identity of various users under the Windows NT security system. This requires a high degree of handshaking between your components and the underlying operating system.

◆ **Secret codes**—Embedding special identification and authorization codes within the client-side components that are used for data access. This can prevent access to components without the proper codes. It can also uniquely register which components have done what.

◆ **Encryption**—Components can provide encryption for data while it is in transit over the network. This is aimed primarily at preventing third-party snooping of important data.

Data Integrity at New Riders Airlines

In the "User Survey" section on strengths, we are told the following:

"The software automatically translates the three-letter abbreviations used for identifying airports into their common names."

This is an example of a translation rule that is already in place in the existing system.

In the "User Survey" section on weaknesses, we are told the following:

"it is possible to enter a departure time into ORVILLE that isn't even on the clock—for example, 27:84 p.m."

This is an example of the need for a domain rule in the solution that we are being asked to build.

All the many *n*-to-*n* relationships between New Riders' proposed tables are candidates for relational rules in our new solution. They could be designed to prevent situations from arising that would contradict the requirements of these relationships, or they could take the cascading approach and make whatever additional updates and deletions are needed to maintain referential integrity when a potentially damaging change is requested by the solution's user.

Incorporating Business Rules into Data Models

Incorporate business rules and constraints into the data model.

After you have identified all the business rules relating to data integrity, you may decide that you would like to incorporate some of them into your data model. Two primary ways of doing this are possible: stored procedures and components.

Stored Procedures

Stored procedures are bits of code that are kept and run entirely within the confines of your database server. From an architectural standpoint, this may allow you to dispense entirely with the need for an intermediate logic tier.

In addition to standard run-on-demand stored procedures, you should be familiar with a few other kinds for the Microsoft exam:

◆ **Alerts**—Defined sets of events and conditions that result i n notifications being sent to a defined set of people. For example, an administrator might create an alert to email him whenever the amount of storage space runs out. This is a feature of SQL Server.

◆ **Constraints**—Simple sets of requirements for data contents at the field level. This can be used to implement requirements that are too simple to justify data-object encapsulation. For example, fields that must be unique and/or non-null often express these requirements in the form of constraints.

◆ **Triggers**—These are used specifically for enforcing relational requirements after row-level events, such as INSERTS, DELETES, and UPDATES. A typical trigger might ensure that it is impossible to delete any row in one table that still has related rows in another table. This can be accomplished in Microsoft Access by choosing to Enforce Relational Integrity, but triggers are specifically found only in SQL Server. Triggers might also be used to create Access-style cascading updates and deletes in SQL Server.

The primary benefit to encapsulating business rules in the form of stored procedures is that you can protect your data from improper modification during database updates. Also, because stored procedures are kept within a database server, they can potentially make better use of whatever native query optimization is available on the server.

It should be noted that stored procedures are generally more effective with smaller transactions, typically under two-tier architectures. Procedures that are lengthy or complex are generally better implemented in the form of components.

Components

Components are standalone objects that exist within the middle, or logic, tier of your solution. You will have to use these for business logic relating to data integrity whenever the logic behind your code is particularly complicated.

One key advantage to implementing your rules in standalone components is superior access to multiple data sources. It is easier to write a component to simultaneously access a SQL Server database and an Oracle database, for example, than it would be to do so in stored procedures in either database server.

Finally, standalone components may be much better adapted to handling extremely large transactions, depending on the nature of the database being used. Typically, stored procedures would be a better choice for large transactions when the database server is something enterprise level, such as SQL Server or Oracle. On the other hand, if you are using a desktop database such as Access, you are probably better off creating a standalone database component for such purposes.

Business Rules at New Riders Airlines

Given New Riders' use of SQL Server, stored procedures are probably a better bet for encapsulating our business rules than standalone components. Nothing in the case study indicates a particularly complicated set of relationships. Neither are there multiple data sources to be simultaneously accessed. At this point, we have just become a two-tier client/server application.

DESIGNING OBJECTS

Design the properties, methods, and events of components.

At this point in our survey, if we are still committed to a three-tier architecture, we are ready to begin the work of actually creating our data-tier objects. (In the case of our airline, we have decided to use a simpler, two-tier client/server structure; therefore, they wouldn't need to do this.) Like all objects, the interfaces have three basic features: properties, methods, and events. We conclude this chapter with a look at some of the particulars of implementing these features on data-tier objects.

Properties

The primary purpose of properties in data-tier objects is to allow for the return of information from your solution's database(s). Most of the time, this information will be the data used by your solution. The rest of the time, it will be so-called meta-data.

Data

Your data objects may return your solution's data in several ways:

◆ Field values

◆ Recordsets

◆ Collections of recordsets

Field values are probably the most common return values for your data objects' properties. In this case, you would probably create an instance of an object for whichever row of data you planned on working with. Then you would have a property for each field in that row that you wanted to access—for example, a `Truck` object with a `NumberOfTires` property. Typically, the information for these objects will result from the performance of complex, multitable joins behind the scenes on the database server.

Sometimes, properties of data objects return entire recordsets. In this case, you would have one object for each table that you were interested in working with, methods for iterating row instances within that table, and properties for accessing the correct fields in whatever row was set to be current. To continue the example from the previous paragraph, you might now have one object called Trucks, still with the property NumberOfTires, but also with methods for NextTruck and PreviousTruck. Probably the most common implementation is to return entire recordsets from RDO or ADO.

Finally, carried to the extreme of abstraction, you might elect to create one database object for each database that your solution will be working with. In this case, you will need properties for each table within the database, each of which will return an entire recordset. Then, methods will be needed for iterating through these recordsets, other methods for iterating through rows within these recordsets, and properties for returning specific field values from these rows.

Meta-data

The other important kind of information that can be returned by your solution's data-tier objects is called *meta-data*. Meta-data is best described as data *about* data. In a table, for example, you would expect some meta-data to tell you about the data types of the fields. In a recordset, you would expect to find meta-data that would tell you how many rows were available for retrieval.

Because OLE DB is the foundation of Microsoft's UDA strategy, it is appropriate at this point to show you some examples of ADO properties that govern meta-data. Table 10.6 contains this information.

TABLE 10.6

META-DATA UNDER ADO

Property	Purpose
ActualSize	This is the length of the data that is currently stored in the field.
Attributes	Numerous meta-data facts about support for transactions, constraints, caching behavior, and read/write permissions.
DefinedSize	This is the number of bytes that the database has actually been designed to allow for this field.

Property	Purpose
Name	The name of the object being examined.
NumericScale	Tells you how many decimal places are supported by a field or a parameter.
Precision	Tells you how many total digits are supported by a field or a parameter.
Type	The data type of the field or parameter being referenced.

Data Object Properties at New Riders Airlines

Our options for data object properties at New Riders Airlines are much the same as they would be at any organization. However, in the previous section, we have decided to simplify our design to two tiers. We'll assume then, for example, that we had decided to use real data objects instead. What kinds of properties might they have?

Properties designed to return specific fields at New Riders might include any of the fields listed in the section "Proposed Tables" (including the modifications we suggested in the section on data normalization). You might, for example, elect to have an object called Plane with a single property for MaximumSeating.

Similarly, properties designed to return recordsets might use any of the tables from the "Proposed Tables" section as their basis. In that case, you might have a single object called Planes with properties for all that table's fields and methods, such as NextPlane and PreviousPlane.

Finally, you might elect to create just one big data object called BlueSky and create a property for each table that returned a omplete recordset. This would be considered a highly unusual design in common business practice, but we mention it for your consideration nevertheless.

Methods

The methods of data-tier objects typically exist to serve just a couple of purposes. One of these purposes is to allow a programmer to work with a solution's data. The other is to allow direct manipulation of the database engine itself.

Working with Data

Methods designed to work with the data in your database(s) are probably the most obviously needed. In a typical solution, you will need methods designed for updating and deleting existing data, as well as for inserting new data.

N O T E
Good Method Design   In both examples, the parameters passed were the minimum requirements for the identification of a specific row needing to be worked with—primary keys. Neither required additional parameters containing further information about what should be done with the row specified because each method was designed to serve exactly one purpose. This is the essence of good method design!

In our continuing example of employee sick days, the acts of updating existing data and inserting new data might be combined into a single IncrementSickDays method that takes an employee's social security number as a parameter. Similarly, a method for deleting existing data might be called MarkAsHavingComeInOn and take both an employee's social security number and a specific date as a parameter.

Methods designed to retrieve rows by passing SQL queries directly through to the database server are also very common. In Active Data Objects (ADO), this method is known as Execute and is found on the Connection object. In Data Access Objects (DAO), it is implemented as part of the database object's OpenRecordset method.

The final set of methods that your data objects should provide for working with your data is one made up of methods for moving through it. The most basic of these methods should provide the capability to move forward and backward through your retrieved rows on a step-by-step basis. Along with these, it would also be a good idea to provide methods for checking your current overall position in a recordset. In Microsoft's Data Access Objects (DAO), for example, a programmer can call PercentPosition and AbsolutePosition properties to find out approximately how far from the end of a recordset the current row is.

It is important to remember that Microsoft provides three essential object schemes for doing almost all this work: ADO, RDO, and DAO. It would be highly unusual for developers to create their own objects to navigate backward and forward through a dataset, for example.

Manipulating the Database Engine

Three main tasks are commonly enabled by data object properties designed to allow direct manipulation of the database server:

◆ Adjusting security

◆ Altering data definitions

◆ Triggering maintenance tasks

Methods designed to allow a programmer to design on-the-fly adjustments to a solution's security typically service administration applications only. Because of the potentially sensitive nature of these methods, it is important that you ensure their own security!

You can afford to be a little less paranoid when providing methods for altering your solution's data definitions. On the other hand, allowing your users to add and remove columns, tables, and stored queries themselves opens an entirely new can of worms. In general, these kinds of methods are best left to the default implementations provided by database DDL objects, such as SQL Server's DMO libraries.

Triggering maintenance tasks is the final purpose to which you might apply some of the methods on your data objects. Indexing is probably the most common of these because it is often required after large insertions of data to restore proper database performance. Replication is another maintenance task often performed by data object methods because remote users often require this to ensure that they are always working with the most recent sets of data possible. Because many enterprise-level database servers will simply cease functioning when their logs have filled up until some kind of truncation task is performed, this is also a very common task to automate in the methods of your data objects.

For example, a client application might call a method on a data-tier object called touch that went through and reindexed all the tables in the database. Or another method called ensureConsistency might cause your local database to replicate with one in another part of the world.

Data Object Methods at New Riders Airlines

It is usually a good idea to provide methods for working with your solution's data under all circumstances. New Riders Airlines is no exception to this fact.

Methods for directly manipulating the database server itself, however, should be implemented strictly on an as-needed basis. In this case, we know from the CIO's comments that security concerns are minimal, but was this really an informed analysis?

To begin with, people could easily book themselves into flights and hotels without paying for them if security is lax. Those people that weren't themselves hackers would also be very discouraged from using the system for fear that other people might look at when they were out of town. In this case, it would probably be a good idea to let the CIO know all the possibilities that are being left open and ask for another decision.

We are given no indication that data definitions will need to be modified on-the-fly.

Replication and log truncation are the only two database-engine methods that we might be able to make an argument for in this case. Replication might be needed because of the many remote locations (car rental agencies, hotels, and so on) that will need to access New Riders' database. Log truncation is an issue because we know that New Riders Airlines will be using a SQL Server database, which is an enterprise-level solution that may stop operating when its logs fill unless appropriate settings are made beforehand.

Events

The data objects that you create for your solutions may have events in addition to the properties and methods that we have already looked at. These events may be received by one user, but triggered by the actions of other users working with your solutions. More commonly, they will come in direct response to the actions of the same user. When this happens, they are known as callbacks.

Triggered by Other Users

When an application receives a data object event that was triggered by the actions of other users and applications on a shared database, the cause is generally some kind of lock being put on the data. Locking can occur at three main levels in most databases:

◆ **Record level**—The newest, best form of locking. Supported by SQL Server 6.5 and later.

◆ **Page level**—This level used to be the most common. Now this is found only in Microsoft Access. SQL Server used this prior to 6.5.

◆ **Table level**—Very rare, only in very old and primitive kinds of databases. No modern databases from Microsoft use this.

Of these options, record-level and table-level locking are probably the easiest to understand. In the case of record-level locking (for simplicity, we'll use the pessimistic locking strategy for our explanation), when one user or application starts accessing a given record, it locks it so that no other user or application can use it until the first application is finished. The same holds true for table-level locking, except the level at which the lock is placed is somewhat higher, so that no other application or user can work with an entire table while the first user or application is still using it.

Page-level locking is only a little more obscure. In this case, the amount of data that is exclusively locked depends on what the database server in question is configured to call a page. If the database has been set to use pages of 2KB, for example, then whichever 2KB block the data currently being accessed is on will be reserved exclusively for the use of whichever application gets there first. Any rows falling on the same page will be inaccessible to other applications and users until this first application is finished and releases the lock.

Often, when attempts are made by other applications to access locked data, events are fired by the data objects charged with making these attempts. The objects send these events as a warning to their client applications that whatever request was made of them will not be progressing according to plan. These might include the triggers and alerts described earlier in this chapter.

It is up to the client application, then, to decide what action to take in response. Sometimes it will cease its activities and alert the user.

At other times, it may simply elect to wait for the lock to be removed.

In Chapter 13, "PASS ME and the Physical Design," we discuss two approaches to locking—pessimistic and optimistic—that work in conjunction with the previously described varieties.

Callbacks to the Logic Tier

When the client application that receives an event is the same application that requested it, the event is referred to as a *callback*. Callback events are typically used so that you can ask an object—data tier or otherwise—to perform a task for you and then "call you back" whenever it is finished. This way, your client application may be able to go on to working on other tasks that don't require this response.

A general sequence of events is followed whenever a callback approach is being used:

1. The client application requests the return of some data or the performance of some action.

2. The object responsible for fulfilling the request returns control to its client application immediately.

3. The client application may continue working on any tasks that don't immediately require the data or action from step 1.

4. At some unpredictable point in the future, the object from step 2 raises an event to signal that it has either succeeded or failed in the performance of the task it was given.

5. The client application stops whatever it is currently doing to deal with the event.

Data Object Events at New Riders Airlines

In any system where multiple users and clients must access the same data simultaneously, the potential exists for locking conflicts. This potential is inversely proportionate to the smallest size of locks supported by a given database server. For example, a database server using row-level locking is much less likely to return locking conflicts than one that can lock only entire tables. The reason is that the odds of multiple users needing the same row simultaneously are not nearly as great as the odds of them needing the same tables simultaneously.

Fortunately, SQL Server supports record locking. This decreases the odds of a conflict, but it does not eliminate them. The need for callback logic depends on the exact nature of the code as it is being written. The best advice is that any opportunities to use this technology should be taken. Not using callbacks when you can essentially means opting to have your client applications sit idle when they could be completing important work. This would never be beneficial.

CHAPTER SUMMARY

In this chapter, we have given you a thorough overview of the purpose and functions of the data tier in any *n*-tier solution. We began by showing you how to apply normalization rules to properly group your data into entities. After you had your entities, we covered how you might decide whether to encapsulate access to them in the form of data-tier objects. For times when you decide that such encapsulation is appropriate, we gave you a good overview of the properties, methods, and events you might decide to implement.

The most basic rules of data normalization are known as the Normal forms: First, Second, and Third. In addition to covering these, we illustrated the proper way to specify relationships (one to one, one to many, and many to many) between your entities using foreign keys. We showed you how to recognize instances where normalization may be at odds with system performance. We concluded our study of entity creation with an overview of common entity attributes as well as database standards and guidelines.

In answering the question of whether to encapsulate access to your data in an object, we began by helping you to identify validation (translation, relational, and domain) and security rules relating to the integrity of your data. We then compared and contrasted the merits of stored procedures and components as vehicles for providing the required access encapsulation.

CHAPTER SUMMARY

KEY TERMS

- Callbacks
- Cascading updates and deletes
- Combination key
- Data model
- Data normalization
- Domain rule
- Entity
- First Normal form
- Indexing
- Locks
- Lookup table
- Meta-data
- Pages
- Primary key
- Relational rule
- Replication
- Second Normal form
- Third Normal form
- Translation rule

Finally, we showed you how to design data-tier objects whenever the need might arise. We began by showing you properties designed to return data in various forms, as well as those designed to return meta-data. Then, our attention turned to methods for working with your data and/or manipulating the database engine directly. Of course, no discussion would be complete without coverage of the numerous locking and callback events that you may want to design into your data-tier objects.

APPLY YOUR KNOWLEDGE

Exercises

10.1 Identifying Data Entity Attributes

In this exercise, we give you the opportunity to identify data entities and their attributes. When you are done with this exercise, you should be able to organize related pieces of data appropriately for use in a solution's data model.

Estimated Time: 5 minutes.

1. Review the bulleted list at the end of this exercise. Four of these items are actual entities, the rest are simply attributes of those entities.

2. Select the four entities and write their names in Table 10.7 in the column labeled Entities.

3. Use *all* remaining items as attributes of the four entities you have selected. Only one of these attributes is used more than once. Write these as a list in the column labeled Attributes.

4. Select one attribute from each entity that you think would make the best primary key. Write this attribute's name in the column labeled, Primary Key.

5. Don't worry about data normalization rules at this point; we will deal with this in future exercises.

TABLE 10.7

EXERCISE 10.1 WORKSPACE

Entities	Attributes	Primary Key

APPLY YOUR KNOWLEDGE

- ExpirationDate
- UsefulPurpose
- Company
- PatentNumber
- Name
- Inventor
- HomeAddress
- StateOfIncorporation
- InventorName
- InventionNumber

- SocialSecurityNumber
- AwardDate
- CompanyName
- Invention
- TaxRegistrationNumber
- TaxRateInStateOfIncorporation
- PatentNumber
- Patent
- AgeOfCEO

The solution is shown in Table 10.8.

TABLE 10.8

EXERCISE 10.1 SOLUTION

Entities	Attributes	Primary Key
Invention	PatentNumber, Name, UsefulPurpose, InventionNumber	InventionNumber
Inventor	InventorName, SocialSecurityNumber, HomeAddress	SocialSecurityNumber
Patent	AwardDate, ExpirationDate, PatentNumber	PatentNumber
Company	CompanyName, TaxRegistrationNumber, AgeOfCEO, StateOfIncorporation, TaxRateInStateOfIncorporation	TaxRegistrationNumber

APPLY YOUR KNOWLEDGE

10.2 Applying Normalization Rules and Identifying Appropriate Denormalization

In this exercise, we give you the opportunity to apply the three rules of data normalization. When you are done with this exercise, you should be able to identify design decisions that violate First, Second, and Third Normal forms. You should also be able to recognize circumstances justifying partial denormalization of your data.

Estimated Time: 5 minutes.

1. Ensure that your answer to Exercise 1 matches the solution.

2. A table in your database is called `TaxRatesByState`. In the first row of Table 10.9, name the entity and field that no longer needs to be included in your data model. In the column labeled Form Violated, write 1, 2, or 3, depending on which level of data normalization you think that retaining this field would violate. In the column labeled Reason, explain what principal you think would be violated.

3. A solution must print first, middle, and last names separately. On the second row of the table, name the entity and field that has made this difficult by violating data normalization. In the column labeled Form Violated, write 1, 2, or 3, depending on which level of data normalization you think has been violated by this field. In the column labeled Reason, explain what principal you think has been violated.

4. Imagine that it is a fact that all patents expire exactly 50 years after they are issued. In the third row of the table, name the entity and field that would no longer need to be included in your data model if this were true. In the column labeled Form Violated, write 1, 2, or 3, depending on which level of data normalization you think that retaining this field would violate. In the column labeled Reason, explain what principal you think would be violated.

5. The CEO's date of birth was originally going to replace one of the fields currently in the database. In the name of improved performance, however, slight denormalization has been chosen instead. In the fourth row of the table, name the entity and field that have been allowed to remain in the database against the standard rules of normalization. In the column labeled Form Violated, write 1,2, or 3 depending upon which level of data normalization you think is being violated by this field's retention. In the column labeled Reason, explain why you think that this denormalization is acceptable.

APPLY YOUR KNOWLEDGE

TABLE 10.9

EXERCISE 10.2 WORKSPACE

Entity	Field	Form Violated	Reason

The solution is shown in Table 10.10.

TABLE 10.10

EXERCISE 10.2 SOLUTION

Entity	Field	Form Violated	Reason
Company	TaxRateInState-OfIncorporation	2	Column is dependent on a non key column.
Inventor	InventorName	1	Column is not atomic.
Patent	ExpirationDate	3	Column values could be computed.
Company	AgeOfCEO	3	The CEO's age will change only once a year.

APPLY YOUR KNOWLEDGE

10.3 Specifying Relationships Between Entities

In this exercise, we give you the opportunity to specify the relationships between data entities. When you are done with this exercise, you should be able to distinguish between one-to-one, one-to-many, and many-to-many relationships.

Estimated Time: 5 minutes.

1. If you have not already done so, complete Exercises 1 and 2 in this chapter. Ensure that your answers match the solutions given.

2. Read the following short paragraph and note the relationships described between the entities that we have been working with in these exercises.

   "Companies retain the exclusive services of large numbers of inventors. These people work independently and on teams to create inventions. If an invention is particularly revolutionary, it may be responsible for the issuance of a patent."

3. In Table 10.11 at the end of this exercise, fill in the columns labeled Left and Right with One or Many, as appropriate.

TABLE 10.11

EXERCISE 10.3 WORKSPACE

Left Entity	Right Multiplicity	Left Multiplicity	Right Multiplicity
Company	Inventor		
Inventor	Invention		
Invention	Patent		

The solution is shown in Table 10.12.

TABLE 10.12

EXERCISE 10.3 SOLUTION

Left Entity	Right Multiplicity	Left Multiplicity	Right Multiplicity
Company	Inventor	One	Many
Inventor	Invention	Many	Many
Invention	Patent	One	One

10.4 Choosing Foreign Keys

In this exercise, we give you the opportunity to choose foreign keys. When you are done with this exercise, you should be able to enforce relationships between the entities in all your data models.

Estimated Time: 5 minutes.

1. If you have not already done so, complete Exercises 1 to 3 in this chapter. Ensure that your answers match the solutions given.

2. To properly establish the relationships described in Exercise 3, a number of columns must be added to your tables.

3. In Table 10.13, name the entity that must have a column or columns added to it to enforce the named relationship.

4. One of the relationships will require the creation of an entirely new entity—a junction table. For this relationship, simply use JUNCTION TABLE as the name of the new table.

APPLY YOUR KNOWLEDGE

TABLE 10.13

EXERCISE 10.4 WORKSPACE

Left Entity	Right Entity	Table Requiring New Columns	Column(s) to Add
Company	Inventor		
Inventor	Invention		
Invention	Patent		

The solution is shown in Table 10.14.

TABLE 10.14

EXERCISE 10.4 SOLUTION

Left Entity	Right Entity	Table Requiring New Columns	Column(s) to Add
Company	Inventor	Inventor	CompanyName
Inventor	Invention	JUNCTION TABLE	InventorName, InventionNumber
Invention	Patent	Invention	PatentNumber

10.5 Identifying and Incorporating Business Rules in Your Data Model and Evaluating Whether Access to a Database Should be Encapsulated in an Object

In this exercise, we give you the opportunity to identify and incorporate the business rules that operate within your data model. When you are done with this exercise, you should be able to distinguish between translation, relational, and domain rules. You should also be able to determine when these rules should be implemented in distinct data objects and when they may be implemented as server-side procedures.

Estimated Time: 5 minutes.

1. If you have not already done so, complete Exercises 1 to 4 in this chapter. Ensure that your answers match the solutions given.

2. In Table 10.15, six rules are listed that must be implemented by any solution using our data model from the previous exercises.

3. For each row, place an X in the appropriate column, depending on whether the rule described is Translational, Relational, or Domain.

4. For each row, place an X in the appropriate column, depending on whether the rule could be implemented as a stored procedure or would require a data object.

APPLY YOUR KNOWLEDGE

TABLE 10.15

EXERCISE 10.5 WORKSPACE

Rule	Translation	Relational	Domain	Stored Procedure	Data Object
A rule that states that every inventor must be associated with at least one company.					
A rule that uses sophisticated AI routines to convert patent numbers into International Technology Reservations (ITRs).					
A rule that applies complicated tax laws to determine whether submitted TaxRegistrationNumbers are valid.					
A rule that converts two-letter state codes into their full names, as stored in a lookup table.					
A rule to ensure that every inventor is associated with at least three inventions.					
A rule to require that every CEO is at least 18 years old.					

The solution is shown in Table 10.16.

TABLE 10.16

EXERCISE 10.5 SOLUTION

Rule	Translation	Relational	Domain	Stored Procedure	Data Object
A rule that states that every inventor must be associated with at least one company.		X		X	
A rule that uses sophisticated AI routines to convert patent numbers into International Technology Reservations (ITRs).	X				X

continues

APPLY YOUR KNOWLEDGE

TABLE 10.16 *continued*

EXERCISE 10.5 SOLUTION

Rule	Translation	Relational	Domain	Stored Procedure	Data Object
A rule that applies complicated tax laws to determine whether submitted TaxRegistrationNumbers are valid.			X		X
A rule that converts two-letter state codes into their full names, as stored in a lookup table.	X			X	
A rule to ensure that every inventor is associated with at least three inventions.		X			X
A rule to require that every CEO is at least 18 years old.			X	X	

10.6 Using Database Standards

In this exercise, we give you the opportunity to match various technologies to the database standards that they represent. When you are done with this exercise, you should be able to distinguish between SQL, QBE, ODBC, and OLE DB.

Estimated Time: 5 minutes.

1. If you have not already done so, complete Exercises 1 to 5 in this chapter. Ensure that your answers match the solutions given.

2. In Table 10.17, the column on the left lists a variety of technology uses during the construction and implementation of our data model.

3. In the table, the column on the right lists the four most important database standards to know for the Microsoft exam.

4. Draw a line connecting the use of technology on the left with the appropriate database standard on the right. All items should be used only once.

TABLE 10.17

EXERCISE 10.6 WORKSPACE

Uses of Technology	Database Standards
SELECT SocialSecurityNumber FROM inventor.	SQL
The database moves from Oracle to SQL Server, but none of the applications need to be rewritten because they all used this relational database access standard.	QBE
A patent clerk is able to graphically build a report on inventors and their inventions just by dragging and dropping tables and fields.	ODBC
An application is now able to pull data about patents directly from email storage without ever having to convert it to a form storable in a relational database	OLE DB

APPLY YOUR KNOWLEDGE

Solution:

SELECT SocialSecurityNumber FROM
inventor = SQL

The database moves from Oracle to SQL Server,
but none of the applications need to be rewritten
because they all used this relational database access
standard = ODBC

A patent clerk is able to graphically build a report
on inventors and their inventions just by dragging and
dropping tables and fields = QBE

An application is now able to pull data about patents
directly from email storage without ever having to
convert it to a form storable in a relational database =
OLE DB

10.7 Designing the Properties, Methods, and Events of Components

In this exercise, we give you the opportunity to
determine which features of our inventing data model
should be expressed as the properties, methods, and
events of components.

Estimated Time: 5 minutes.

1. If you have not already done so, complete
   Exercises 1 to 6 in this chapter. Ensure that
   your answers match the solutions given.

2. In Table 10.18, the column on the left lists many
   features that might be found on a data model for
   our invention-tracking system.

3. In the table, the column on the right lists the
   three kinds of services typically provided by
   data-tier objects.

4. Draw a line connecting the data-model feature
   on the left with the appropriate data-object
   service type on the right. All features should be
   used twice.

TABLE 10.18

EXERCISE 10.7 WORKSPACE

Uses of Technology	Database Standards
SocialSecurityNumber	Methods
changeInventionName	
PatentExpirationWarning	Properties
UsefulPurpose	
PatentInfringementAlert	Events
addYearToCEOAge	

Solution:

changeInventionName, addYearToCEOAge = Methods

SocialSecurityNumber, UsefulPurpose = Properties

PatentExpirationWarning, PatentInfringementAlert =
Events

Review Questions

1. What kind of *n*-to-*n* relationship exists between
   hotel floors and hotel rooms?

2. How would you be violating the rules of data
   normalization if you added a column to New
   Riders Airlines' Hotels table that showed an
   average room price for each row?

3. Imagine that the system you are about to build
   for New Riders Airlines will automatically reject
   any attempt to enter a hotel room price in excess
   of $300 per person, per night. What kind of data
   integrity rule is this?

4. The CIO of New Riders Airlines has decided to store a full complement of biographical information (name, birth date, and so on) about each principal pilot (ignoring copilots) in the Flights table, right next to whichever flights each pilot is responsible for making. Which standard Normal Form does this violate?

5. Suppose you talked the CIO of New Riders Airlines out of taking the approach described in the preceding question. How many tables will you now need to properly model the relationship between flights and pilots? Assume every flight has two pilots: principal and copilot.

6. Which two columns would be the best pick for a primary key (combo key) in the Hotels table if the ID# column were unavailable? Assume that two hotels might have the same name, but only if they are in different cities.

7. If New Riders Airlines needs to verify the existence of a real customer for every car that is reserved, what kind of data integrity rule is required?

8. The employees at New Riders Airlines want the new system to automatically enter the full name of each pilot whenever they type that pilot's initials. What kind of data integrity rule is this?

Exam Questions

1. Denormalization can be useful under certain circumstances. Choose the two situations from the following options that describe these situations.

    A. Frequently updated data

    B. Infrequently updated data

    C. Few or no joins

    D. Many joins

2. Data-tier objects can enhance the security of your systems in a number of ways. Which of the following options describes one such way?

    A. Normalized channels

    B. Silent channels

    C. NT authentication

    D. Windows authentication

3. Which of the following could you add to a data object to provide a means for changing a customer's name? (Select two.)

    A. A property

    B. A method

    C. An event

    D. All of the above

    E. None of the above

4. Which of the following are kinds of stored procedures provided by SQL Server? (Pick two.)

    A. Alerts

    B. Kernel panics

    C. Triggers

    D. Responses

5. Which kind of locking was the only kind provided by Microsoft Access prior to Jet 4.0?

    A. Table level

    B. Page level

    C. Row level

    D. Field level

APPLY YOUR KNOWLEDGE

6. Which of the following could you add to a data object to provide a means for finding out a customer's name?

    A. A property

    B. A method

    C. An event

    D. All of the above

    E. None of the above

7. Which of the following could you add to a data object to signal whenever another realtor was already looking at a particular house in the database?

    A. A property

    B. A method

    C. An event

    D. All of the above

    E. None of the above

8. Which kind of locking has been provided by SQL Server since version 6.5?

    A. Table level

    B. Page level

    C. Row level

    D. Field level

Answers to Review Questions

1. This is an example of a one-to-many relationship. A given hotel room will always be found on just one floor. On the other hand, a given hotel floor can have many rooms on it. See "Kinds of Relationships."

2. Adding an average room price column to the Hotels table violates Third Normal form. The reason is that Third Normal form prohibits the addition of computed fields. See "Third Normal Form."

3. This is a domain rule. Domain rules regulate the range of values that are allowed for fields within a database. In this case, the rule would be set to reject any value greater than 300 for the field containing the room's price. See "Content Validations."

4. Storing your pilots' information this way violates Second Normal form because Second Normal form requires that a single table in your database contains information for exactly one entity in your data model. If you do things as described, however, you will be dealing with two entities in one table: pilots and flights. See "Second Normal Form."

5. To correctly model the relationship between pilots and flights, you need three tables. The reason is that you are dealing with a many-to-many relationship, and these require one junction table in addition to a table for each entity. See "Kinds of Relationships."

6. If no ID# exists in the Hotels table, your next best choice for a primary key is to use the name in combination with the city. You won't have two hotels with the same name in the same city, so these two columns form a good combination key for this table. See "Defining Data Entity Attributes."

7. This is a relational rule. Relational rules ensure that the data's integrity will be maintained, avoiding orphaned records and similar data problems. See "Content Validations."

APPLY YOUR KNOWLEDGE

8. This is a translational rule. Translational rules convert short, easily entered and stored codes into longer, more easily understood values for presentation. See "Content Validations."

Answers to Exam Questions

1. **B, D.** Situations when there are a lot of joins and/or the data is infrequently updated make the best candidates for denormalization. This is usually, but not always, associated with decision-support systems. The other two options are the opposite of this. See "Identifying Appropriate Levels of Denormalization."

2. **C.** Windows NT authentication is a way for your data components to ensure that only certain accounts in your domain are allowed access to your data. Windows authentication is close, but not the proper name for this technology. The channels options are not even data access terminology. See "Security."

3. **A, B.** A property that could be written to as well as read from could provide a means for changing a customer's name. More typically, perhaps, a method could be used that would take as a parameter whatever the customer's new name should be. The benefit to this approach is that additional verification could be performed and complex status codes could be returned. See "Designing Objects."

4. **A, C.** Alerts are SQL Server tools that can send notifications under certain prespecified circumstances. Triggers are actions taken by SQL Server upon INSERTS, UPDATES, and DELETES. See "Stored Procedures."

5. **B.** Microsoft Access (prior to Jet 4.0) used page-level locking, which means that 2KB blocks were the finest degree of granularity possible. See "Triggered by Other Users."

6. **A.** A property is what is used to return information from a data object. Methods are used to perform actions upon that data and the server where it is contained. Events are used for asynchronous notification of occurrences outside the direct control of the user and/or client. See "Properties."

7. **C.** An event is used for asynchronous notification of occurrences (in this case another realtor's accessing of the database) that are outside the control of the user and/or client. A property is used to return information from a data object. Methods are used to perform actions on that data and the server where it is contained. See "Triggered by Other Users."

8. **C.** SQL Server uses row-level locking, which is the finest degree of granularity possible. See "Triggered by Other Users."

APPLY YOUR KNOWLEDGE

Suggested Readings and Resources

1. *SQL Server Books Online*—Database Design Considerations

   - Normalization
   - Data Security
   - Data Integrity

2. *DAO 3.5 SDK*

   - DAO Overview
   - Microsoft Jet Database SQL Reference

3. *Microsoft Data Access SDK*

   - ADO
   - ADO WFC vs. JDBC
   - OLE DB
   - ODBC4

4. Simsion, Graeme. *Data Modeling Essentials.* Van Nostrand Reinhold, 1994.

5. Hay, David C. *Data Model Patterns: Conventions of Thought.* Dorset House Publishing, 1996.

6. Codd, E.F. *The Relational Model for Database Management.* Addison-Wesley Publishing Company, 1990.

7. Web site

   - www.microsoft.com/data

8. MSDN resource

   - "MDAC Related White Papers (ODBC/OLE DB/ADO/RDS)"

Continuing what we started in the preceding chapter, we now turn our attention to the logic tier. This chapter addresses the following exam objectives as they relate to the logic tier:

Incorporate business rules into object design.

▶ One of the most powerful reasons for building object-oriented software is the capability to centralize and encapsulate various business-specific needs. If the user tier could be considered the visual body of an application and the data tier is the memory of the application, then the logic tier is the brains— the thought processes of the application.

Design the properties, methods, and events of components.

▶ Just like any particular development methodology, object development has its own set of requirements for design. Specifically, we'll see that it's necessary to start thinking of objects in terms of three types of things: What does the object know, what can the object do, and what can the object tell us that has happened?

CHAPTER 11

The Logic Tier

▶ Identify the ways in which including business rules in objects helps your application's maintainability. Show the difference between perceived and actual performance. Explain what MTS is and how it is used in object-oriented software. Explain the differences between properties, events, and methods.

INTRODUCTION

In the past three years, Microsoft has begun a new push in its development methodologies, adopting a strong push for "componentized" software. Essentially, this is software that has been broken into pieces and that communicates between those pieces to make the software function. Each piece exposes a public interface and hides the details. This enables developers to better manage the complexity present in most of today's solutions. It also makes it easier to divide the necessary work among several people or several teams, with each team needing to know only its part of the solution.

The next logical step then was for Microsoft to design technologies that support these kinds of designs. Both from a development and a maintenance perspective, Microsoft has been pushing object technology as a means of simplifying development and implementing component-based design. These technologies include COM, DCOM, and MTS.

As you go through this chapter, pay close attention to how to design objects and how to pull an object out of a case study and start assigning properties and methods to it. For a brief overview of how to focus on the nouns and verbs of a case study, see Appendix E.

CASE STUDY: GBS (GET BETTER SOON) HEALTHCARE

BACKGROUND

GBS HealthCare is a Chicago-based HMO with more than 1,000 listed doctors and nurses and almost 10,000 subscribers. Up to this point, it has been using a very simple client/server system. The clerical staff enters in patient-visit data and invoicing data through a well-designed but "fat" user interface. The system uses a series of reports to trigger activity in the accounts payable and accounts receivable departments, which then manually process the necessary paperwork.

PROBLEM STATEMENT

GBS is getting so large that it is having trouble tracking who qualifies for services and who does not. Accounts receivables are falling through the cracks and subscribers are getting services to which they are not entitled. GBS wants to add more business intelligence to its application.

HMO Manager

"We find out after the fact that we have authorized work for subscribers who are not covered for a particular procedure, who owe us significant amounts for past care, or who have dropped coverage with us altogether.

We want to do right by our paying clients, but we also need to do right by our stockholders. The system needs to be smarter. My people don't have the time to research each patient before they give approval for a doctor visit or a procedure."

HMO Clerk

"Our job is to approve or reject requests while we are on the phone with a clinic or a doctor's office. We don't have time to call Accounts Receivable, so if they show in our database at all, we just say yes and sort it out later. We pride ourselves on customer service."

CURRENT SYSTEM

The current system is a two-tier client/server application. It stores data in an older version of SQL Server. A conscientious but novice programmer wrote the UI in Microsoft Access. The tables are connected directly from Access to SQL Server through ODBC and although the UI is serviceable, what rules there are exist on each user's desktop in Access Basic.

IT Manager

"The current system has served us well. It was built in the early 1990s in a version of Microsoft Access that did not support classes and objects. We've upgraded to newer versions of Access, but no one wants to disturb the working code. I've recently hired two employees and a hot shot contractor to rewrite the program to be more component based and to include business rules that are currently enforced manually."

HMO Clerk

"The old program doesn't connect Accounts Receivable with the approval process. It also isn't smart enough to tell the difference between a procedure that requires a second opinion and one that should be approved right away.

continues

CASE STUDY: GBS (GET BETTER SOON) HEALTHCARE

continued

New clerks come in and apply the rules from their old employer or they wing it. We've had to implement manual approval processes to compensate. This slows the whole thing down."

Development Manager

"The problem with our existing system is that it doesn't have any smarts to it. You type in one screenful of data, and it connects to the database and puts it in, and then it gives you the next screen. I know this isn't ideal, but until recently, it was good enough that no one wanted to spend the money to change it."

ENVISIONED SYSTEM

GBS HealthCare would like to implement business rules into its system. It would also like to centralize those rules so that they can be changed quickly, in response to government regulations. The company intends to keep the existing data stores and to replace the UI with a Visual Basic component that talks to an application server.

The following are the main areas that it would like to address:

- Check Accounts Receivable for delinquent payments that would cause rejection of service.

- Check subscriber database to make sure the caller is still active.

- Check procedure code database to see if a second opinion is required.

- Maintain an audit trail of all approvals and rejections for service.

- Check pricing database to calculate customary pricing for specified procedure codes.

HMO Manager

"I've asked the IT department to interview all the people involved in the process and to try to emulate their practices in automated business rules.

An example is the check with Accounts Receivables. If subscribers owe more than a designated amount or are delinquent in their payments, we can refuse to cover them until it is rectified.

We also need to get a handle on people who are approved for medical procedures that are either overpriced or that require a second opinion."

Programmer

"In addition to the database server that houses SQL Server, we have a new application server that will house the business tier. We are going to try to use an *n*-tier architecture, keeping the UI as thin and as stupid as we can."

IT Manager

"We're using Visual Basic because it was easiest to find VB programmers. We've also discussed it and no overriding need exists for blazing speed or intricate API calls to Windows."

SECURITY

GBS's needs around security are minimal. No access is available to the system from outside the company.

CASE STUDY: GBS (GET BETTER SOON) HEALTHCARE

IT Manager

"We plan to use NT authentication as our security control. After users are on, we can use MTS security to control access to the right objects and data stores.

Because upper management is concerned that users follow the correct procedures, we will also be maintaining a log of all activity to a log table. The business tier will handle that as well."

PERFORMANCE

Performance is not a major concern for GBS, but at various times of the day the database server seems to slow down in the current system.

HMO Manager

"Well, I can't say that I'm unhappy with our current system, but we suspect that the database server is getting overloaded with connections from our 40 users. We are hoping to address that in the new solution by using MTS's capability to pool database connections."

MAINTAINABILITY

Right now, because the logic is spread out over 50 or so machines, GBS cannot easily make changes to the software.

HMO Manager

"The only thing that matters from my perspective is how much it costs to make changes. For example, three or four months ago we changed some of the rules. It took our development group two months to implement the changes, and the cost was way over what I thought was a reasonable budget. That has to change. I would like to be able to change certain rules up to twice a month."

IT Manager

"By centralizing our business logic, we can literally change the logic overnight. We do some tests in an offline lab machine, bring it to the production server on the weekend, and by Monday morning, everyone is using the new code."

Incorporating Business Rules into Objects

Incorporate business rules into object design.

NOTE

Components and Objects Because much of today's object-oriented design centers around components, especially within the Microsoft world, we use the word "component" generically to refer to larger-grained objects. It's a bit like saying that chairs are made of molecules; although we know that those molecules contain atoms, it gets awkward to always say "molecules/atoms." This will improve the flow of the text. If a statement applies only to objects, we will then use the word "object."

Business objects make designing, building, and maintaining an n-tier application simpler. They lend themselves to component-based design, which allows the architect to abstract or encapsulate much of the complexity. Programmers need to know only their part of the application, as well as the public interface of any components they interact with.

Replacing components or using off-the-shelf components is another advantage of centralizing business knowledge into its own tier in the architecture. In a large corporation, you may find that different departments or teams can share business components or objects, allowing one team to design them and other teams to consume them.

Maintenance is simplified when you physically separate the business components onto an application server. This enables you to have a single component that services all the users. Making changes then becomes a simple matter of replacing the component, rather than redeploying across all the users' workstations.

The practice is based on the concept of a well-defined interface. In this way, individual developers aren't aware of the specifics of the business rule's implementation. Instead, they need to be aware of what it does only at the functional level. Just as Windows exposes APIs, but not the code that implements those APIs, developers can create components with a particular set of behaviors, called an interface, and keep the implementation hidden.

Just as users of our application need to understand the user interface but should be shielded from the details inside, developers should need to know only the interface of another component, not its implementation. This is known as a black box component.

IN DEPTH: BLACK BOX VERSUS WHITE BOX

Whereas black box components completely hide the internal workings from the user, white box components require or allow some amount of knowledge about their internal implementation. A quick example would be the difference between a plug-and-play device installation and an installation under Windows 3.1. In Plug and Play, you plug in a device such as a scanner or a printer, and all the configuration details are automatically handled. In the past, under Windows 3.1 or DOS, the user needed to know things such as IRQ settings, memory addresses, and INI file setup.

Although most shrink-wrap components are considered black box, it seems that a high percentage of business components are designed under the white box strategy. A lot of factors go into this decision.

For example, if a business rule is that the mail order department cannot schedule a delivery for a Sunday, it makes sense to incorporate that into an object. Validation can be accomplished by checking the requested delivery date inside the object; if it is Sunday, an exception is returned, specifying the problem with the delivery date.

Developers who use this object do not need to know how it works. All they need to know is that when they submit a date, the object will either accept the date or reject it, based on rules that are abstracted from the caller.

With this in mind, then, it is necessary to think about why we want to go to the trouble of making these kinds of objects—and when we do, how we can use them.

Advantages of Using Objects

One of the most positive effects of programming with objects is one that end users don't directly see. It is essentially that although some projects have to build the objects, after they are built, they can be consumed by any other project in the enterprise. For example, our day-of-the-week validation software might also be useful for the service organization, which follows the same corporate calendar for its onsite service requests.

With this in mind, essentially four ways exist in which using object-oriented software will allow us to save effort from the development perspective:

◆ Greater reuse

◆ Central maintenance of applications

◆ Business logic consistently applied across applications

◆ Performance improvements

Less Need to Reinvent for Each Project

As we previously discussed, encapsulating things such as date validations, error handlers, and so on saves developers from having to write this code themselves over and over again on different projects.

When we're trying to build reusable business objects, we often run into opposition. Two of the common objections follow.

Objection 1: Code Reuse Is Almost as Good as Component Reuse

Many people claim they already have software reuse through the use of code repositories such as Microsoft Visual Source Safe. That is, they equate source code reuse with component reuse. Although they both have the goal of reusing previous work, a key difference exists between the technologies, which makes component reuse, where possible, clearly superior.

If Developer B attempts to use Developer A's code, Developer B will have to take time to understand how all the functions work and the reason for them so that all the relevant portions of code can be clipped. Developer B may forget to bring across other routines or constants that are needed for the code to work properly.

Those who have attempted to do this realize that the path is longer than it seems at the outset, and it is fraught with dangers unforeseen.

Source code reuse is better than no reuse, but it falls short of professionally designed components that have reuse engineered into them from the beginning.

Objection 2: These Business Rules Aren't Hard to Program, Anyway

This is better known as the NIH (not invented here) syndrome. When developers distrust the creator of a component, they forego using it in favor of rewriting all the business rules from scratch.

It is the component author's job to make sure the component does all the things it is supposed to do—and only those things.

In a corporate environment, proper design of interfaces in advance of implementation code, defensive programming, test harnesses, and test scripts can help to promote reuse. Most important, reuse must be a consideration from the beginning.

Central Maintenance for Applications

In non-object-oriented systems, business logic can be a very elusive subject, sometimes in one part of the application, sometimes in another. The one thing that is almost universally true is that it is mixed up in multiple functions and is in multiple places inside each application.

This causes huge maintenance headaches down the road. If, for example, a business rule changes and no objects encapsulate it, you have no choice but to go through each application and attempt to locate—and then change—each instance of the business logic.

It is not unheard of that a single business rule change could require hundreds of lines of code to be changed across many routines. In the fast-paced business world we now live in, this should be recognized as a bad thing. In contrast, objects enable us to encapsulate business rules. Consumers of the object will call it to gain access to the business functionality. Consequently, no other application (at least in theory) is duplicating this function within its own code. This means that changing a business rule should be as simple as changing the object that encapsulates the rule.

This alone is a justification for changing over to objects from nonobject procedural models.

Business Rules Consistently Enforced Across Applications

Changing a business rule is important, but in a day-to-day operation, what may be more important is how a business rule gets enforced across the enterprise. Some groups may understand the rule differently from others. Some groups may choose not to adopt the rule at all (because of an inability to understand requirements for the rule or because they were unaware of its existence).

Using an object-oriented approach to business rules allows us to give a very straightforward name to rules and encapsulate how they are determined. Nothing is more depressing than to discover that you have three or four interpretations of a business rule in your enterprise, and they are all mutually exclusive.

Object designs that encapsulate business rules enable us to enforce a consistent interpretation of business rules across a large application and between applications.

The Performance Advantage of Objects

Another reason to encapsulate business logic within components is to improve end-user performance by enabling components to run on other machines.

Intense Calculations on More Powerful Computers

Business rules are designed to be enforced in the middle tier of application design. This tier normally runs on what is called application servers. These machines act as central repositories for business logic components, and various end-user machines will call them.

Typically, the application servers are more powerful systems with many times the computing power of end-user machines. In many instances, they are multiprocessor, high-end servers.

These machines are much more capable of making high-demand calculations than are the end-user machines that run the application. The logic for this moving of the calculation is fairly simple. A given end-user's machine is likely to be engaged in a number of tasks. Word processing, email, spreadsheets—each task consumes large quantities of system resources.

Although the user's machine must be configured to run all these things, the application server can be tuned specifically to process the application in the most efficient manner. Consequently, it makes sense from a throughput perspective to move intense calculations to the more powerful application servers and simply report the relevant results back to the end-user computer.

Also, it is an important part of Microsoft's approach to this technology that multiple physical servers can be grouped together into a virtual application server. This can be handled several ways, the technical details of which aren't particularly relevant. The point of it is that we are no longer in a "replace everything" mode; rather, we can just add to the server group as our needs grow, making the lifetime of the application much greater and its corresponding cost lower.

Asynchronous Processing

One way to speed up processing is to send tasks to the server asynchronously. The client machine can then continue on until notified by the server that its request is completed. The reason such importance is placed on this issue is that the use of such technologies enables an improvement in perceived performance, even if actual performance is slowed down.

This is because users need not be aware of the total time to load an object. What they can see and what they will complain about, if it is too long, is the time it takes to display a screen. If a UI waits until all data has been loaded before it begins loading, valuable clock cycles are wasted on the client while the business objects load. The entire screen can be loaded without the data, and then repopulated. This will clearly be slower, in computer clock cycles, than waiting and populating all at once. However, in human time it appears more responsive. This, then, enables you to create increased performance for the users without really finding ways to make things run faster.

Microsoft Transaction Server (MTS)

In the past several years, Microsoft has recognized that a lot of time was being spent trying to make software objects run on remote systems. Three major issues had to be resolved.

First, a lot of security issues had to be addressed, as expected when one machine is allowed to create processes on another machine.

Second, fairly limited support existed for making sure that a proposed change to persistent data was completely updated. We had transactions inside a database, but what if we didn't want to commit them because another related component failed in its update?

For example, what if a component enters the items on an order, and then the component entering the order itself fails? Obviously, we would want to have the two databases kept in synch.

What was really needed was a set of transactional commands, much like those found in many databases, that would work at the business-object level. In essence, these transactional commands would allow commitment and rollback of data changes across multiple databases and multiple business components.

This would enable us to have an all-or-nothing approach to committing data to any number of databases.

Another performance strategy, multithreading, has always been complicated and daunting for all but the most accomplished of programmers. This puts the capability to take advantage of multiprocessor servers out of reach of the majority of developers.

Finally, we had performance issues to resolve. Each time we called a remote component, it had to start the whole component. It would be nice if a way existed to allow these objects to be reused.

Microsoft, then, conceived the Microsoft Transaction Server to handle all these concerns for developers. To do this, they addressed the following issues:

- ◆ Improving performance through pooling
- ◆ Protecting data through logical transactions
- ◆ Simplifying security through roles
- ◆ Providing multithreaded support without complex programming

Improving Performance Through Pooling

Objects that are instantiated on another machine are, in the normal course of things, destroyed when the calling machine has finished with them. Intuitively, this makes sense because the system should not be allowed to leave behind objects that don't belong to anything anymore. At that point, every server would eventually become overloaded and reach a failure point.

However, one of the things we have to come to terms with is that initially creating a component involves overhead. Consequently, repeatedly reinstantiating an object can consume a lot of time and negatively impact performance.

What would be nice, then, would be to have a pool of instantiated objects. These objects could be reused, and after a set time limit is reached (configurable all the way to "never delete"), the objects would be destroyed. This addresses our concern with having a system where objects just hang around indefinitely, and it also resolves the problem of the high percentage of time-instantiating objects.

Microsoft Transaction Server (MTS) is Microsoft's way of handling this issue. Microsoft has built a system that does exactly what we have outlined. Objects are created according to demand and then recycled through the calling machines. After you are done with a particular component, it returns to the pool and can be reassigned to another calling component.

This can radically increase performance, but it is generally most noticeable in a multiuser situation. It is more of an issue of scalability—or how an application will perform as the number of users increases.

An even bigger performance improvement than object pooling is database connection pooling. In short, MTS manages a small number of database connections, dispensing them to various operations as needed.

This has two benefits. First, as most developers know, it can take longer to establish a connection to a database than to run the SQL command. In a two-second operation, we could spend more than one second just getting the connection. Database connection pooling diminishes this by providing "warm" connections, with little or no overhead to the SQL command.

The second advantage is that the database server sees fewer connections. In a nonpooled environment, 50 users might result in at least 50 connections to the database server. Under MTS, through reuse, this could drop to fewer than 10. This decreases the load on the database server to manage all those connections.

Protecting Data Through Logical Transactions

MTS also enables a certain amount of transactional semantics. These semantics are designed to bring to business objects the same notion of a logical transaction as is already present in most relational databases.

Essentially, MTS creates a framework in which multiple database transactions can be open simultaneously, enabling them all to be simultaneously committed or aborted. This also applies to other, nondatabase-driven outputs of a component.

Therefore, although transactions do protect your data, it is a primary goal of the application designer to decide where in the application a transaction should be started and at what point it is considered complete. These decisions, more than anything else, will direct to what extent an application can actually take advantage of these features in MTS.

Simplifying Security Through Roles

One problem that can surface when one computer has the capability to start and stop processes on another machine is the issue of security.

Windows NT does have a security model built into the operating system for handling this type of interaction. However, because no shell exists around the entire process, all security measures have to be handled programmatically. This can be time consuming on the front end, and worse yet, when security issues are revisited, to implement any security changes actually requires coding changes.

MTS removes this issue by building a shell around all the security concerns. The advantage is that now all the security concern for remote activation can be handled with an administrative, rather than a programmatic, approach. In essence, security for components running under MTS can be set up externally to the component. This allows anyone with administration rights on a box to be able to set security on a component without having to recompile or redistribute anything.

The most obvious case where this would be useful is one in which you can write administrative functionality right into the normal component where it belongs, rather than in a separate admin component. Then only the administrator role in MTS can actually make calls to the function.

IN DEPTH: MTS AND STATEFUL OBJECTS

Although MTS brings many benefits to the solution architect, it is
not without cost. Typically, object-oriented programmers are used to
loading an object and then having it remain loaded, which is known
as a stateful object. MTS is considered by Microsoft to be a stateless object server. That means that client apps get on, do their
thing, and get off. This is MTS at its best. This does not always
sit well with OO purists. However, it is important information for
architects who may not already know it, and it may even be on the
exam. Articles are now appearing in magazines and in MSDN on
how to use MTS for stateful objects. The typical workaround to be
stateful is for objects not to participate in transactions. For more
information, check the MSDN article "Holding State in Objects with
Microsoft Transaction Server."

Providing Multithreading Support

One of the biggest areas for performance improvement can be the
use of multithreading. Basically, we break up a process into smaller
bits, or threads. Each thread processes on its own. As a thread completes, it returns to the client code that spawned it. When all threads
are returned, the process is complete.

Applications with processor-intensive tasks or applications that perform disparate tasks (that is, one takes a long time and one takes a
only a few milliseconds) can benefit from multitasking.

Before MTS, building a solution that supported multitasking was
difficult for all but a few expert programmers. Now, by creating an
in-process DLL as if it were going to be used by a single user, almost
any programmer can build a multithreaded component.

As with most transaction monitors, MTS abstracts developers from
the complexities and enables them to program just the business
logic. MTS 2.0 does this very well.

Using Objects at GBS HealthCare

Some of the issues at GBS are the following:

◆ Subscribers are getting services to which they are not entitled
because they are not covered for a particular procedure, they
owe significant amounts for past care, or they have dropped
coverage with GBS altogether.

◆ HMO clerks are not enforcing requirements for second opinions or procedures are consistently quoted too high.

◆ GBS needs to be able to make rule changes swiftly.

◆ GBS needs timely information when clinics are on the phone waiting for approvals.

By moving any existing business logic out of the user interface and into a separate tier, we can address all these issues.

We can connect each user to the Accounts Receivable business component so that any subscriber who has canceled coverage or who is delinquent beyond an established threshold is denied service until the problem is corrected. This not only benefits the subscribers who follow the rules, but it causes the more timely receipt of outstanding debt.

The other benefit is that we can create sophisticated rules that change almost daily when deciding what to approve or reject. A major surgery that is not accompanied by a recorded referral by the primary care physician into the database can be postponed until things are made right. Keep in mind that most of this was being done manually by the clerks.

By building a database of customary costs for specific procedures, coded by industry-standard procedure designations, we can quickly flag a cost that is out of range. This is something that would be almost impossible to implement manually.

Finally, by creating an application server, we address the HMO manager's request to be able to respond quickly to changes in governmental rules. Because we will have only a single copy of the business component, we can update it overnight if necessary.

Because 50 users are all accessing a single SQL Database Server, we would want to consider the benefits of using MTS. We could certainly take advantage of its capability to pool database connections. Although multithreading doesn't seem to be required here, the pooling of objects, the need for security, and the use of transactions could all benefit the final solution.

MTS is a big part of Microsoft's next generation of technology for developing this type of application. It primarily serves the following purposes:

▶ It introduces into business components the notion of a transaction and the all-or-nothing model.

▶ It increases scalability through the use of pooling.

▶ It supports multithreading with little or no coding.

▶ It uses an administrative model to take some of the busy work out of designing security for application servers.

As stated in the literature, future versions of Windows will have COM+, which includes MTS, wrapped right into the operating system. All solution architects should become familiar with what MTS can provide to their projects.

DESIGNING THE OBJECTS

Design the properties, methods, and events of components.

We've discussed how objects are good for development, how we can improve performance with them, and even some of the details of how they get utilized in an application. Next, we'll start looking at how to design objects well. In one sense, designing objects is very much akin to designing *n*-tier applications. For both, many tools are available that make it easy to build an application such as this. However, in both cases, the very ease with which they can be developed should cause designers to be more on guard. Designing an object is easy. Designing a good object, on the other hand, is definitely not easy. It is one part art, one part guesswork, and only a small part technical.

To understand how objects are designed, we will take a look at three main areas of their design:

◆ Designing properties

◆ Designing methods

◆ Designing events

Object Property Design

Properties are the pieces of information an object retains. This is the data of an object, which holds all the information we might want to input or retrieve after performing some action on the object. Whereas objects are most often nouns, such as a Person, an Order, or a Claim, properties are typically adjectives, such as Color or Height. This is why properties are sometimes called attributes.

Because objects are designed to encapsulate functionality, there is no way to know with certainty whether you are dealing with a raw variable or a property of an object.

For example, if we interrogate a `.Date` property, we don't know if it was just set a second ago by a "let" call to the same property or if it went out to a satellite circling the earth to get the date.

The final reason it is valuable to use properties on an object is for calculated values. Sales tax is one example. In all probability, no reason exists to store sales tax as an independent value in your database. It is simply some percentage of the total cost of all the items being purchased. You could develop a property, `SalesTax`, which simply adds up all the items in an order and multiplies by the correct percentage.

Properties let you build this kind of calculated functionality into requests for values in a way that isn't possible by simply exposing the value of a public variable. The calculated values can then be refreshed whenever the information is requested.

When you are designing an object, the proper means of deciding on a property is to ask, "What is it I need to know about this object or might need to have the object remember?" Each of those things, in all probability, is a property of the object.

One point to keep in mind while designing "stateless" components for use under MTS is that it is better not to have properties and instead pass or retrieve them as parameters to the method calls. For a remote component, every property access involves a network round-trip that can reduce scalability.

Object Method Design

Unlike properties, methods are not designed to convey information to the consumer about an object. Instead, they are designed to trigger a behavior. That is, they are to be used much the same way you might give a command to your dog. "Sit" or "Roll over" are perfectly valid methods on an object. We previously compared properties to adjectives; methods are most typically verbs (for example, GetRecord, DeleteCustomer) or a response to an inquiry (for example, IsValidState, RecordCount). This is why methods are also frequently called operations.

Object Event Design

The final aspect of object design that we need to look at is events. Events are essentially how a component tells its consumers that something has happened. Events fire without knowing for sure if anyone is listening. However, if an event handler exists, then that code runs before returning control to the code that fired the event. Although event handling is synchronous, the concept of events supports asynchronous processing.

Specifically, it enables business objects to call back to a UI component and indicate that it has finished being loaded. The UI component then knows how to "catch" the event and realizes it is time to read the data out of the business object.

CHAPTER SUMMARY

KEY TERMS

- Business logic
- Business rules
- Callbacks
- Code reuse
- Components
- Encapsulation
- Events
- Methods
- MTS
- Object pooling
- Properties
- Role-based security
- Transaction
- Transactional semantics

Business logic is one of the most critical—and most complicated—aspects of implementing a business application. One method that we have for mitigating these problems is by encapsulating the logic into objects.

This kind of encapsulation gives us three main advantages to saving programming effort. First, it allows us to reuse software in a new way, allowing reuse to occur without even looking at the code. Second, it creates a central spot for maintenance of business rules, enabling quick changes and allowing the application to keep up with rapidly changing business. Finally, it allows those business rules to be applied identically across the enterprise, rather than each team deciding its own interpretation of the business rules.

We can also experience performance gains from offloading processor-intensive activity to larger, more powerful application servers. In addition to this real performance gain, successful object design often creates an additional perceived performance gain because it allows activities to occur on another machine while the end-user's machine continues to work through the application.

Consideration of objects in the Windows environment would not be complete without MTS. Microsoft Transaction Server is Microsoft's solution for multithread support, pooling objects and database connections for performance, implementation of transactional semantics across multiple databases, and an administrative, standard, role-based approach to application security.

Each of these gives us an increased background as we approach actually designing business objects. Objects are pieces of software that have three types of features: properties (what an object knows), methods (what an object can do), and events (what an object can tell us).

APPLY YOUR KNOWLEDGE

Exercise

11.1 Using Objects in the Logic Tier

For each of the situations described next, determine whether the creation of a separate tier to hold business objects is beneficial. If so, choose the area that benefits the most: reuse, easier maintenance, consistent rules, performance. If no benefit exists, choose None.

Estimated Time: 15 minutes.

TABLE 11.1

BENEFITING FROM BUSINESS LOGIC OBJECTS

Situation	*Biggest Benefit*
A. With more than 200 users, the database server is spending more time keeping track of connections than running SQL.	Reuse
B. The UI needs to run either on a browser platform or as a standalone VB interface.	Ease of maintenance
C. Users complain that they must wait for a very long time before the screen appears that allows them to enter data.	Consistent use of rules
D. The Accounts Receivable department calculates its "Net Pay 30" late penalties based on business days, whereas the Cash and Carry department uses calendar days.	Performance
E. The spinning logo image on the user interface must be changed on every workstation each time the company goes through a buyout.	Not applicable
F. Interest rates for a mortgage company are changed daily, sometimes even hourly. Each user must have access to the latest rates when quoting refinances.	
G. One division in a pharmaceutical company has created a program for determining the shelf life of an over-the-counter drug. The algorithm would work for all pharmaceuticals, given the correct input parameters. This company also has a prescription drug and an animal medicine division.	

APPLY YOUR KNOWLEDGE

Answers to Exercise 11.1

A. Performance. A business tier allows us to utilize MTS database connection pooling, which reduces the number of active connections that the database server sees.

B. Reuse. We can create two separate UIs, each relatively thin, that use the same business tier.

C. Performance. By creating a business tier, we can trigger asynchronous operations that allow the UI to proceed even before all the data has been gathered for the form. This affects perceived performance.

D. Consistent use of rules. By accessing the same business object, the two departments could enforce the same method for calculating overdue payments.

E. Not applicable. The image is part of the UI and therefore is not affected by the addition of a business tier.

F. Ease of Maintenance. Rather than having to deploy a new rate table to 10 or 15 machines, the business rules are centralized and use a single table that is updated by an administrator.

G. Reuse. Each division can use the same component, assuming it was designed and built with reuse in mind.

11.2 Properties, Methods, and Events

For each of the following descriptions, assess whether it would best be implemented as a property, a method, or an event.

Estimated Time: 10 minutes.

APPLY YOUR KNOWLEDGE

TABLE 11.2

DETERMINING THE BEST IMPLEMENTATION OF OBJECT SERVICES

Statement	Property, Method, or Event?
A. The make and model of a car that was involved in an accident.	
B. The difference in age between two people.	
C. Display a stop sign icon when the disk space drops below 10MB.	
D. What is the age of the dog referred to by a specific "dog object," in dog years?	
E. Replace the word "pork" with the phrase "the other white meat" throughout the database.	
F. Link to a URL on the Web, get the latest Cubs score, and disconnect.	
G. A call to an object that returns another object.	
H. Run a series of SQL statements, blocking the caller's process thread at the same time, and then return a success or failure code.	
I. Run a series of SQL statements allowing the caller to do other things, and then return a success or a failure code.	

Answers to Exercise 11.2

A. Property. An adjective.

B. Method. Do something—in this case, perform a calculation.

C. Event. Asynchronous notification.

D. Property. Calculated from facts available within the object.

E. Method. Do something (a verb).

F. Method or property. If the server component is a generic component, this would be a method (do something). If this is a `.Game` object in a collection of `.TodaysGames`, then there could be a `.Score` property where the implementation of how to get the score is to use the Web.

G. The child object is a property of the parent object.

H. Method. This is an example of synchronous processing.

I. Event. We are utilizing asynchronous processing to do two things at once. This requires two separate threads to be effective (out of process server; see Chapter 13, "PASS ME and the Physical Design").

Review Questions

1. Give some examples of business objects in the case study.

2. How does MTS benefit an application?

3. What does an application need to do to take advantage of MTS?

4. Explain the difference between methods, properties, and events.

5. What is business logic, and how does it affect solution development?

APPLY YOUR KNOWLEDGE

Exam Questions

1. Which of the following statements is an example of a business rule that would apply to GBS HealthCare? (Choose one.)

   A. GBS is closed on Sundays.

   B. All kidney transplants require a second opinion before surgery can be approved.

   C. Bob Johnson owes GBS $5,000.

   D. All mail is sent with First Class postage.

2. Which of the following is not a benefit GBS would realize by going to a separate logic tier?

   A. Reuse of standard business objects in other solutions

   B. Centralized maintenance of rules

   C. Capability to use ADO

   D. Performance improvement by reducing overhead to the database server

3. What is the key difference between code reuse and component reuse?

   A. Component reuse uses objects; code reuse doesn't.

   B. Code reuse is at the source code level, whereas component reuse is reuse at a binary level.

   C. Code reuse is at the binary level; component reuse is at the source code level.

   D. Code reuse uses objects; component reuse does not.

4. What is the single biggest problem an enterprise faces in enforcing business rules?

   A. Business rules are difficult to decide on.

   B. Developers do not include business rules in applications.

   C. Different projects will take the same "English" business rule and implement it slightly differently in their software, creating inconsistent business rule enforcement.

   D. Some business rules are hard to code.

5. Where could a callback feature be used most effectively in the GBS case study?

   A. Between the UI and the logic tier.

   B. Between UI components.

   C. Between server components.

   D. There are no effective places to use callbacks in this application.

6. Which of the following would not be a justification for utilizing MTS on a project?

   A. Security is administrative rather than programmatic.

   B. Pooling improves performance.

   C. Simpler object design.

   D. Data is protected through transactions.

7. What are some reasons for role-based security in an application? (Choose all that apply.)

   A. Security is not part of the code; therefore, components don't need to be recompiled.

   B. Role-based security is administrative rather than programmatic.

    C. Role-based security is more effective than other forms.

    D. All of the above.

8. Which of the following roles would be logical choices for security in the GBS solution? (Choose all that apply.)

    A. HMO clerk

    B. Administrator

    C. HMO manager

    D. Customer (subscriber)

9. Select from the following all examples that could be transactions in the GBS system.

    A. Get an approval from Accounts Receivable, subscriber system, procedure database, and pricing database.

    B. An appointment that was scheduled is canceled and a monthly subscriber payment was received.

    C. An appointment that was scheduled is canceled and the subscriber copay should be subtracted from the subscriber database.

    D. Get an approval from Accounts Receivable, subscriber system, procedure database, and a supervisor.

10. What role do properties play in object design?

    A. They tell us what an object can do.

    B. They are what an object can report as having happened.

    C. They tell us about an object's state.

    D. All of the above.

11. Which of the following explains why encapsulation of variables protects data integrity?

    A. Data cannot be changed by users.

    B. External users can access data elements only in appropriate ways.

    C. Data is handled transactionally.

    D. None of the above.

12. What is a calculated value?

    A. A property that has variable values from the database.

    B. A variable that is calculated by the database.

    C. A property that is calculated in an object based on other values.

    D. A variable that is calculated.

13. What is the general purpose of an object event?

    A. Monitoring progress

    B. Connecting objects

    C. Allowing asynchronous processing between components

    D. Allowing synchronous processing between components

Answers to Review Questions

1. `AccountsReceivableCheck`, `SubscriberCheck`, `ProcedureSpecialInstructions`, `ProcedureCustomaryPricing`, `AuditServer`. See "Case Study: GBS HealthCare."

2. MTS can benefit an application in several ways. First, by allowing the pooling of objects and database connections, it can increase performance in a high-user environment. Second, it increases and protects data integrity by surrounding business logic with a single transaction, creating all-or-nothing processing. Finally, it allows for simpler security protocols by making security an administrative, role-based project rather than a programmatic one. See "Microsoft Transaction Server (MTS)."

3. Applications that are used by MTS must avoid holding state as much as possible. Also, they should be written to implement certain programming techniques that are needed to take advantage, for example, of the security model MTS enables. Finally, they need to be written as in-process components (DLLs). See "Microsoft Transaction Server (MTS)."

4. Properties are the information an object knows about itself. This is alternatively known as the object's state. Methods describe what it is an object can "do." Finally, events tell us what kinds of things an object will report to us. With these three characteristics, we can effectively model most behavior of actual things or ideas. See "Designing the Objects."

5. Business logic is a set of rules that are nontechnical in origin. These rules often relate in a nontechnical sense to the way a business runs. They are usually incorporated into business objects so that an enterprise can, for example, have an increased rate for service calls on Sundays. Essentially, the role of business logic in applications is to keep from having to teach every employee the business rules. Instead, the systems implement the business logic for the employees. See "Incorporating Business Rules into Objects."

Answers to Exam Questions

1. **B.** Choice B is stated in the case study. Although statements A and C may be true, they are not business rules. Choice D is a process rule that is not likely to be automated, at least not based on the case study we've been presented. See "Case Study: GBS HealthCare."

2. **C.** Use of ADO has nothing to do with using a logic tier. All the other choices are direct benefits of a separate logic tier. See "Incorporating Business Rules into Objects."

3. **B.** Code reuse focuses on a cut-and-paste approach to reusing work. Normally this is done at the code design level by trying to section off pieces of code that might be reusable later. Component reuse, in contrast, creates binary (compiled) code that has standard external interfaces. This can then be reused as a black box, without cutting and pasting code. See "Less Need to Reinvent for Each Project."

4. **C.** In a given enterprise, often more than one set of people will be developing applications. If this is the case, it is possible for each of these groups to interpret a business rule in a different way. Because such rules are written in English, not in formalized computer logic, it is possible that two teams may construct different formal interpretations of the rule. The effect of this is that two different business rules (in effect) are enforced throughout the enterprise. See "Business Rules Consistently Enforced Across Applications."

5. **A.** If it takes some amount of time to validate a request for service, the logic tier could be asked to go off and research the situation asynchronously and then report back to the UI. This would allow the user to continue to input information while waiting for approval, perhaps

APPLY YOUR KNOWLEDGE

not even knowing when the system requested information from the various services. See "Asynchronous Processing."

6. **C.** As we have observed, MTS adds a lot of functionality to a system. But, as we all also realize, in computers as in life, there is no such thing as a free lunch. Changes to the object's design must be made to take advantage of MTS. These changes, unfortunately, are not to make the object simpler. See "Microsoft Transaction Server (MTS)."

7. **A, B.** MTS is designed to enable role-based security. This really presents us with two main advantages. The first is that the security itself now becomes an administrative task (in the MTS explorer) rather than a programming task in components. Second, this method of security means that no need exists to recompile applications when security roles change, because they are implemented externally. See "Microsoft Transaction Server (MTS)."

8. **A, B.** An HMO clerk is someone who regularly interacts with the system and who must have a specific role as far as security goes. Similarly, it is only logical that some sort of an administrator of the system is needed to fix any potential technical problems or database errors. However, it is not clear that the HMO manager needs a specific security role apart from administrator. Finally, it is clear that because customers never interact with the system directly, they don't need a security level. See "Case Study: GBS HealthCare."

9. **A, C.** A and C demonstrate transactions that should process in an "all or none" fashion. Choice B shows unrelated system tasks, and choice D includes a nonautomated task that is outside the scope of the system. See "Microsoft Transaction Server (MTS)."

10. **C.** Properties are the portion of an object that tells us what an object knows or its information. This is otherwise known as the object's state. See "Object Property Design."

11. **B.** Encapsulation of data means that external clients are prevented from direct access to the data. Requests are accepted and processed when data needs to be altered, but no way exists for a client to directly manipulate an object's internal state in an inappropriate way. See "Designing the Objects."

12. **C.** Calculated values are a special kind of property. They are properties that, when they are requested, perform some series of calculations to determine the value to return. Normally they are not stored in the database, nor are their values determined in advance of the request. See "Object Property Design."

13. **C.** Events are used to allow one object to tell another object that something has happened. Its primary purpose is to allow a client to continue execution while waiting for another object to finish an operation. This is an asynchronous model for processing. See "Object Event Design."

APPLY YOUR KNOWLEDGE

Suggested Readings and Resources

1. MSDN: Windows DNA: Building Windows Applications for the Internet Age.

2. MSDN: Modeling a Distributed Inventory, Duwamish Books, Phase 2.

3. MSDN: A Guide to Reviewing and Evaluating Microsoft Transaction Server.

4. Kirtland, Mary. *Designing Component-Based Applications.* Microsoft Press, 1998.

5. Eddon, Guy. *Programming Components with Microsoft Visual Basic 6.0.* Microsoft Press, 1998.

6. Pattison, Ted. *Programming Distributed Applications with COM and Microsoft Visual Basic 6.0.* Microsoft Press, 1998.

This chapter addresses the following exam objectives listed by Microsoft for the "Designing a User Interface and User Services" section of the exam:

Given a solution, identify the navigation for the user interface.

▶ The user must be able to move from field to field and, if necessary, from screen to screen in your application. For this, a method of navigating the user interface must be available. We will investigate four major methods for enabling user navigation of the user interface.

Identify input validation procedures that should be integrated into the user interface.

▶ Every data item in an application has some kind of format to it. The user interface typically validates that the formatting is correct. However, it should not need to validate that the value is meaningful from a business perspective.

Evaluate methods of providing online user assistance, such as status bars, ToolTips, and help files.

▶ No matter how intuitive the application, it is never going to be 100% obvious to the users. Consequently, the role of user assistance in the application's user interface becomes critical. Each of these tools, ToolTips, status bars, What's This? help, and traditional help files offers a particular way of helping a user get the full advantage out of an application.

CHAPTER 12

The User Interface Tier

Construct a prototype user interface that is based on business requirements, user-interface guidelines, and the organization's standards.

- **Establish appropriate and consistent use of menu-based controls.**

- **Establish appropriate shortcut keys (accelerated keys).**

▶ After a user interface has been successfully designed, it is important for verification of the design by target users that a prototype of the interface be constructed as soon as possible. This prototype must follow the same guidelines the actual user interface will have to follow, just to verify that all the various standards being adopted are compatible.

Establish appropriate type of output.

▶ Applications have only one way to interact with the user, and that is through their output. Whether output is via the screen, hard-copy reports, or audio, each of these types of output must be designed so that it will meet the needs of the target user group.

Design the properties, methods, and events of components.

▶ Although this objective was covered in Chapter 10, "The Data Tier," and Chapter 11, "The Logic Tier," it is again addressed here, but now in terms of the user interface.

▶ Identify the main strategies for use with application navigation and identify the benefits of each.

▶ Explain Windows controls and how they are used to enable navigation in an application.

▶ Describe the different levels of input validation available in a user interface.

▶ Discuss the role ToolTips and status bars can play in providing user assistance.

▶ Identify and explain the purpose of various forms of system output.

▶ Define the various types of events on a control.

▶ Identify the types of properties on a control.

▶ Discuss the role of prototype development in user-interface design.

▶ Identify sources for user-interface design guidelines.

INTRODUCTION

The user of an application interacts with only one aspect of a solution, and that is the user interface. Therefore, great care needs to be taken when building the user interface. Great technology will not be given the chance to thrive if it is contained within a difficult or impossible-to-access user interface.

Wise solution architects don't treat the user interface as just the finishing touches to their application. They design around the needs of the interface and the needs of the user from the beginning.

Properly designed user interfaces should be consistent, helpful, and as intuitive as possible.

CASE STUDY: OFFICE EQUIPMENT SERVICES

BACKGROUND

Office Equipment Services (OES) was formed in 1983 through the merger and acquisition of several smaller office-equipment companies. One of these companies had implemented an application in the mid 1980s for tracking the core functions of the business. It was designed for a fairly small company, but it has continued to be utilized by OES as the company has grown.

PROBLEM STATEMENT

Although the business logic and data stores continue to function effectively, the principals of the company would like to bring the user interface "into the next millennium."

The original developers of the software have long since left the company. Further, the documentation for the system is currently either nonexistent or hopelessly out of date. Training in the use of the system, which is currently used by billing clerks, sales associates, and repair technicians, is two weeks for the clerks and the sales associates and almost a week for the repair technicians.

Sales Associate

"Our biggest problem with the software we are using is that the interface is difficult to use and difficult to learn. We can't get the information we need to get, and learning to use the system in the proper way is too daunting a task. We need to make things simpler."

Billing Clerk

"I'm spending way too much time just trying to figure out tasks. There is no real help for users of the system, so right now all the tricks are passed down like stories around a campfire. That's no way to get things done efficiently."

continues

CASE STUDY: OFFICE EQUIPMENT SERVICES

continued

Billing Clerk Manager

"The main problem I have with this system is that it is so much different from anything else out there today that I'm having to take people that have been in this industry for four years and send them to two weeks of training on the system. This can't continue. Even for myself, when I try to make something happen on the system, I'd better hope I haven't lost the cheat sheets that I made years ago."

Repair Technician Dispatcher

"I hire people to fix our office equipment. Generally these people are very good at what they do and are expecting to go right out into the field. Instead, I have to tell them that there is about a week of training that they have to go through. 'On the equipment?' they always ask. I end up having to tell them, 'No, it's not on the equipment; it's to report time into our system.' That's ridiculous and it costs us money."

CURRENT SYSTEM

OEI is currently running on a system developed in 1986 for a much smaller company. The system itself appears to have been well designed because it has scaled to many times its original targeted user base. However, the technological standards for user interfaces have passed the system by. This, coupled with a lack of documentation, is what is leading to the current problems.

The current system was developed in C++ as a 16-bit Windows program by developers who were used to building nonvisual components. Primarily for this reason, the business logic has scaled very well, but the user interface is weak. Fortunately, OES has been able to upgrade the database server over the years because of the three-tier architecture.

The sales associates and repair technicians access the system only once or twice a week, which classifies them as occasional users. The billing clerks, on the other hand, use the system almost constantly.

Billing Clerk

"I guess I am okay with the system. It's very difficult, though, to learn to do anything new in the system. I know how to do what I do on a daily basis mostly by trial and error and a long training program I had when I was hired."

"At month's end, when all the invoices are due, we go into a sort of mini data-entry mode. But the way the screens work, we basically have to use the mouse to move around the screen, and that's just a pain. It makes it impossible to get on a roll with entering things. Some screens have a Save button on the upper left of the screen and some screens have a Close on the lower right that does the same thing. We're always having to help out the new employees."

CASE STUDY: OFFICE EQUIPMENT SERVICES

Repair Technician

"I think I'm pretty good with computers. But this interface is so odd, and I just hate spending all this time figuring out how to do simple tasks.

Sometimes, when I click the OK button, I go to the Main menu. Other times, I go to a second page of data. It's also hard to tell when the system is actually doing something and when it's hung."

Sales Associate

"It's downright embarrassing to be with a client in the office and not be able to get the orders to process quite right. Just the other day, I accidentally typed in a bad date. The system tried to process my sales ticket and the last thing, just before it usually says Done, it comes back with 'Input data is invalid. Please reenter.' It took me a minute just to figure out what was wrong. And all this time, the customer is kinda chuckling. I felt like an idiot.

I'm constantly having to say OK to some pop-up message or other, and I don't even understand what some of the messages mean. The other day I got something like 'SQL failed on server port 5—Do you want to continue?' I don't know if I should say Yes or No."

ENVISIONED SYSTEM

OES understands that its current user interface is costing them time, money, and employee satisfaction.

OES would like to update the user interface of its main software application. It would like the screens to be consistent. It would like to create a more intuitive interface and add user support so that the training time can be cut back substantially.

OES would like the billing clerks to be able to do their work as fast as they can type, yet still allow the occasional users such as sales associates and technicians to be able to use the mouse.

Finally, OES would like some of the more basic data validation done in the user interface—before the data gets shipped across their overloaded LAN to the business tier.

Billing Clerk

"Well it would be nice if we could get a help file of some kind added to the system so we could figure out problems as they come up. Also, it would be nice if this system worked as much as possible like the rest of the applications on our PCs, like with cut and paste and things.

It would be nice if the new application had simpler screens so that we could figure things out for ourselves.

Also, Mark is color blind. It would be nice if the new system didn't try to use red text all the time to indicate required fields. Mark has to memorize all the fields because they look gray to him.

The last real issue we have is the way that we have to enter data. I don't like that currently we have to use the mouse to move between some sections of data entry. It breaks up the flow when I'm entering things."

continues

CASE STUDY: OFFICE EQUIPMENT SERVICES

continued

Sales Associate

"We need to add something to tell people what all the different buttons and things do. Right now its kind of a push-it-and-see mentality.

I'm hoping the new system will allow me to change to my favorite color scheme, eggplant, without looking like a patchwork quilt.

Also, I'd like better help when something goes wrong. I don't need all those techie messages. I need a message that tells me what I need to know on my level."

Repair Technician

"For me, I just want something easier. We aren't making anyone any money by sitting in the office watching these training tapes. I use a computer all the time at home. If it were just built the same way other things, like Microsoft Office, are built, I'd be much more comfortable with it."

PERFORMANCE

The new user interface should increase productivity. This is how OES plans to address what is otherwise acceptable performance out of its application.

Billing Clerk

"Well, like I said, there is a performance problem, but it isn't with the program itself. It makes us slow down while we're entering data. I mean, I can type a lot faster if I don't have to keep taking my hands off the keys to use the mouse."

Sales Associate

"It would save me a lot of wasted time if the system would just check simple things like dates and numbers before it tries to process an order that is clearly junk.

I've seen other systems that have push buttons and drop-down lists and little check boxes that help the user choose the proper type of data. Those sort of things would be really helpful. We have some fields that need a Yes/No answer, and I see people put in all sorts of things that don't make sense."

Repair Technician Dispatcher

"When I assign a call to a technician, I do it for a reason. It bothers me when the technicians swap the calls among themselves. The system should not allow the technicians to change the Assigned to field."

DESIGNING A USER INTERFACE

Given a solution, identify the navigation for the user interface.

Designing *n*-tier solutions to resolve technical issues is a lot of fun. At least it is for computer professionals. Realistically, though, the ultimate evaluators of software are the users. If they won't buy it or use it (whichever is the goal), it doesn't matter too much how wonderful and innovative the application design is.

The question then is one that Microsoft has made billions of dollars asking: "What is it about software that makes end users like or dislike it?" The answer starts from realizing what parts of the application a user has contact with.

Normally, this is composed primarily of a user interface. When end users interact with the application, it would be very rare indeed for them to notice the architecture. In fact, you might argue that if the users are even aware of the architecture, it isn't doing its job as well as it might.

What users are aware of, however, is the interface they are presented with. Good technology with an outdated or inefficient user interface will not be popular with the users. Because of this, much of the research done with end users on computer systems has been devoted to testing and gathering opinions related to what users like when it comes to user interfaces.

To make a solution that is both technically desirable and desirable to the user community it is designed to support, we have to spend some time focused on the user interface and how it is designed. To accomplish this, we need to look at the following set of areas:

◆ Navigational models for applications

◆ Controls used to facilitate navigation and usage

◆ Input validation procedures

◆ User assistance

◆ System output

What Are the Options for Navigational Models?

One of the most basic decisions that must be made when designing a user interface is what kind of navigation will be used within it. Sometimes, this is a simple choice because only one method will really work for the user interface. Unfortunately, those situations are the exception rather than the rule.

Normally, almost all these routes are open to a developer. The reason is fairly simple; very few of the options are mutually exclusive.

The most common models for navigation within an application are as follows:

◆ Single Document Interface (SDI)

◆ Multiple Document Interface (MDI)

◆ Browser model

As you may remember, we first discussed SDI, MDI, and browser models in Chapter 8, "Developing the Conceptual Design for a Solution." In this chapter, we focus specifically on how these models influence the user interface.

Single Document Interfaces (SDI)

The Single Document Interface, or SDI, is probably the most well-known and easiest-to-design Windows-based GUI. It is also the one with the longest history.

As we discussed in Chapter 8, the single document interface is essentially a model that presents a single screen of information at a time (discounting pop-ups). We referred to this as a *modal* solution.

One example of this is a wizard. Wizards are SDI implementations because, although you can go forward or backward, you will never have more than one "slide" in front of you at a time. Wizards are what are know as "constrained serial path" modal models because they control, to some degree, the path that the user can take through the slides.[7]

Some other examples of SDI design that everyone is familiar with are WinZip, most CD player applets, and the Windows calculator (see Figure 12.1).

FIGURE 12.1
The Windows calculator (SDI).

A more business style example of an SDI design is something like Figure 12.2.

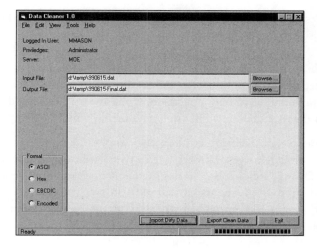

FIGURE 12.2
The Data Cleaner application window.

Figure 12.2 shows one of the screens for a fictitious DataCleaner application. Whereas the previous two examples are both small applications, SDI applications can have hundreds of screens, each taking up the entire Windows desktop.

The navigation strategy for SDI applications can be either constrained (as previously mentioned) or implied.[7] Constrained means that the user is locked into a navigation sequence that is optimal for the task at hand (see Figure 12.3). This usually appeals to a more novice or infrequent user of the system. Implied navigation allows the user more freedom. This would be typical of a tabbed interface (see Figure 12.4).

The main difference between the SDI model and the MDI model (which we will discuss next) is that each document or task gets its own window, complete with menus, toolbars, status bars, and so on. Each SDI screen is self-contained and autonomous from other copies of the same program.

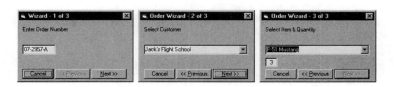

FIGURE 12.3
Constrained SDI navigation.

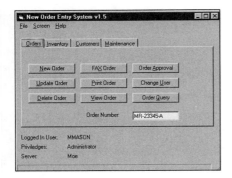

FIGURE 12.4
Implied SDI navigation.

The upside, however, is that each instance of the application will have its own button on the Windows taskbar. In the right circumstances, this is such an important benefit that Microsoft has chosen to redesign Word 2000 (in the upcoming release) to use the SDI model.

When should we consider using the SDI interface model?

The decision might have been made earlier as we designed the conceptual model of our application. If the application is modal, in which the user does only one thing at a time, then SDI is a good fit.

For example, an airline reservation clerk books one person into one seat on one flight before proceeding to the next booking. It would be confusing (although interesting) to allow for the simultaneous opening of multiple flights in multiple windows. As mentioned earlier, it is an excellent model when the notion of a document is not appropriate for your application. Specifically, it lends itself quite directly to data-entry applications. In this instance, most application users are entering data into the application and consequently, would be entering information one record at a time. The bottom line is that most custom business solutions end up using the SDI navigation model.

Multiple Document Interfaces (MDI)

As applications got larger and more functional and as the document-centric paradigm became more predominant, the need arose for an alternative to opening 10 copies of a program for 10 documents. Microsoft responded with a navigation model known as MDI.

MDI, simply stated, puts all the eggs into one basket. If you have 10 documents, they can all be opened under a single instance of the parent program.

IN DEPTH: WORD 2000 AND MDI

At the time this book was written, Microsoft Word was still using the MDI model. To keep the text from becoming awkward, we have used the MDI version of Word as an example. Even though Microsoft seems to be changing its approach, based on user feedback, it is still an example that should be familiar to you.

One example is that you wanted to play songs on five CDs in a random fashion. You could swap the CDs in and out of a single player; you could have five CD players, each with one CD loaded; or you could have a single CD player with five slots. The MDI model is analogous to a CD player with five slots.

To get back to the world of software, you could either launch and close Word between each document, launch multiple copies of Word, or manage multiple documents in a single container (see Figure 12.5).

The resolution of this issue for users was the MDI, or Multiple Document Interface. This presented many savings of effort to end users; it was done at the expense of increased complexity for software development. Two basic types of MDI models are as follows:

◆ Same document MDI

◆ Workspace MDI

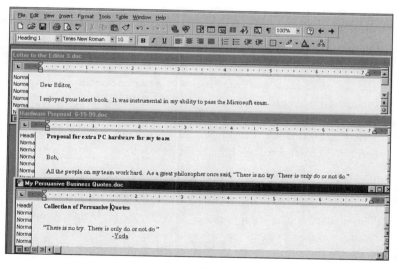

FIGURE 12.5
Word with Multiple Document Interface (MDI).

MDI Model in Which All Documents Are of the Same Type

The oldest and most well-known MDI model is one in which all documents are of the same type: spreadsheets, documents, and so on.

This model has several features that distinguish it from the SDI model:

◆ Allows more than one document to be opened

◆ Supports only one document type

◆ Generally more confusing to users

Allowing More than One Document to Be Opened

The MDI model addressed users' concerns about opening many instances of the same program by reinventing what the purpose of the application was to be. Rather than "being" the document, the applications began to change into containers for holding many documents. Whether a single document existed or many, the container (the new MDI) would simply wrap around all of them and hold them in an electronic basket (refer to Figure 12.5).

One obvious advantage is the savings in system resources. Application overhead increases very little as additional documents are opened. Menu bars, toolbars, macros, and so on are shared among all documents. Visually, all the documents must reside within the physical space of the MDI parent form.

MDI Generally Supports Only One Kind of Document

One of the barriers that remains even in most MDI applications is the type of files that are supported. Take, for example, Microsoft Word. It supports opening a variety of styles of documents. However, these documents all have one thing in common: They are all text documents. In the case of an Excel spreadsheet, for example, the Word system will not open this file.

This illustrates a fundamental limitation of the traditional MDI navigation model. It is normally limited to navigating within documents of a single format, or at the very least, a single family of formats (such as word processing documents). It does not allow a user to organize different files in the same container by idea.

NOTE

A Document by Any Other Name... We are using the word document in the generic sense. It should be noted, however, that documents can be spreadsheets, code modules, pictures, Web pages, and so on.

NOTE

Embedded Documents We should clarify that although you can technically open an Excel spreadsheet document in Word, it is treated as an embedded spreadsheet, not as a native Excel file. A definite difference exists between opening the spreadsheet in Word versus Excel.

Effect on the User Experience

For the user, there is one obvious effect. Instead of having 15 applications, each of which contains a single document, they now have only one application. However, this too comes with its price. The MDI model for navigation necessitates the appearance of another standard Microsoft Windows fixture, the Window menu (see Figure 12.6). This menu is responsible for the functionality related to having multiple windows open within a container. You will rarely see a Windows menu in an SDI navigation model.

Typically two kinds of functionality are in this menu. The first is a set of commands related to how to arrange the windows in the container. Choices are usually things such as Tile Vertically, Tile Horizontally, or Arrange All.

The second set of functionality is designed to make MDI applications easier to navigate. This menu item displays a listing of all the windows opened within a given container and allows the user to bring any one of those to the front for display and/or editing.

The other effect on the user has already been mentioned. If the application is MDI, only a single entry will be in the Windows taskbar, even if you have multiple documents open. In an SDI application, each application (or process) will have its own taskbar button. Some users are confused and unable to find their documents in the MDI model. Others complain that their taskbar gets cluttered with similar-looking buttons that, unfortunately, all start with the caption "Microsoft Word."

Uses for Traditional MDI Model

MDI applications are a common navigation mechanism in use today on desktops. Most productivity applications (such as word processors, spreadsheets, electronic mail) use this model to promote efficiency by allowing work on multiple documents at once. Microsoft Office applications use this interface as well.

MDI is a good choice for most document-centric applications. It allows the user the freedom to view, edit, and select from a multitude of documents without having to open and close files to do so.

Similarly, applications that are primarily decision-support tools are also good MDI applications. They use data in primarily a read-only model. Therefore, the synchronization concerns are gone. Also, remember that in a decision-support application, the user might

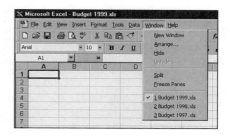

FIGURE 12.6
Windows menu (MDI).

have a very good reason for wanting to look at multiple sets of data at the same time.

The MDI offers increased flexibility over the single document interface. However, as we will see, still a lot of limitations are imposed by traditional MDI-based applications.

MDI Workspace Model

As the Multiple Document Interface is to the Single Document Interface, so is the workspace model to the MDI. It is essentially an extension of the concept of the MDI that allows for a variety of file formats. It provides a centralized container to hold documents of many types. This allows an end user to compose purpose-centric work areas, rather than it being arbitrarily divided by the technologies used to contain the ideas.

Understanding workspaces is critical to understanding the direction Microsoft itself is headed in terms of user navigation.

Before we continue, perhaps it would help to provide an example or two. Probably the most well-known example to the readers of this book is any of the Visual Studio suite (see Figure 12.7).

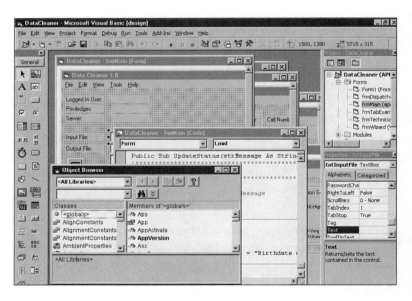

FIGURE 12.7
Visual Basic 6.0—workspace model.

In Figure 12.7, you can see code modules, forms, classes, object browsers, and so on. However, they all have one thing in common. They are all part of the studio window.

Another example is Microsoft Binder, which can store documents, spreadsheets, and PowerPoint presentations—all in the same container.

A final example that is probably more familiar to more people than any other is Microsoft Access. Access is a single workspace container that holds tables, queries, forms, reports, macros, and code modules.

Workspaces are based on the concept that users should be able to group what they are working on by the ideas the work contains, not by the file format in which it was saved.

The workspace model has several defining characteristics.

Allows Many Files to Be Opened

In the same manner as the MDI, workspaces allow the user to simultaneously open and work with different files. The goal is to increase productivity by allowing a user to use the workspace as a virtual desktop—to group the ideas that are being worked on. It's a highly focused version of the Windows desktop itself.

Supports Many Kinds of Files

The biggest conceptual advancement for the workspace is the proposal that a user ought to be able to pull various kinds of documents generated in different ways into a single place where they can be joined by content rather than separated by file format.

Instead of focusing on the file as a document, we have reached a point of "document as content." Users ask for the capability to put files from several sources all relating to the same content into a centralized interface for navigation. This is the workspace model.

An example of this is the supporting documentation for a solution design. The architect might want to bring together design documents done in Word with schedule and budget forecasts from Excel, flowcharts from Visio or Visual Modeler, PowerPoint system diagrams, and so on.

Although this is a legitimate navigation model, it should be pointed out that few enterprise solutions use this model.

Internet Browser

Over the last several years, a new contender has emerged in the world of application navigation models. This model takes advantage of the ubiquity of the Web browser on users' computers and builds an application that exists on a collection of Web pages.

The nature of this type of navigation is fairly simple. It takes the notion of a container that is used in MDI and workspaces, and it adds a twist. Rather than the developer writing the container in which to hold the various documents, a browser model uses the existing Internet browser on the user's desktop as a default container for the application. The browser is often referred to as a Submit type of data-entry tool. The user fills in all the necessary information and then clicks some button that acts on that information. This is very different from some of the "rich" user interfaces that characterize SDI and MDI applications.

Choosing Between the Models

We have presented three basic models of navigation. Choosing the correct model can have a significant impact on the success of your solution. Experience and common sense often steer us toward the correct solution, but we offer some guidelines for making the choice when it is not so clear.

First, we'll return to the four types of users[1] first discussed in Chapter 8, "Developing the Conceptual Design for a Solution":

◆ Data entry

◆ Super users

◆ Administrators

◆ Ad hoc users

Data-entry users care about speed. Ad hoc users require flexibility. Super users and administrators fall somewhere in between these two requirements. If you have a mix, you should lean toward the model that addresses the largest percentage of your users. The exception is if one of the three models (SDI, MDI, browser) precludes one of your users.

Data-entry users will almost always require the SDI model, using a 4GL such as VC++ or Visual Basic. They need speed, power, and robustness. Many data-entry users require a rich GUI that offers extensive feedback on a field-by-field basis, as well as the need to maintain state within the user interface. The choice between MDI and SDI usually depends on whether navigation is modal (one task at a time) or nonmodal (multiple, simultaneous tasks).

Ad hoc users, on the other hand, are more likely to be serviced best by a browser model using Active Server Pages.

Two last criteria that make a strong case for the browser model are the requirement to support remote users and the requirement for a simple deployment. Remote users from heterogeneous environments make the browser an obvious choice.

Choosing a Navigation Model for OES

The proposed solution for OES seems, at first glance, to be best suited for the SDI navigation model.

All users are in-house, using machines owned and controlled by the company. This eliminates the two strongest reasons for choosing a browser interface: remote users and the need to avoid an installation script.

The data-entry needs of the supply clerks seem to be best served by a modal SDI navigation model, taking one screen at a time.

We have two very distinct user personas (see Chapter 4, "Human-Computer Interface Analysis"): data entry (billing clerks) and ad hoc (sales administrators and technicians). We could consider designing a dual interface model. The billing clerks would get an ADI interface, and the field technicians and salespeople would get a browser interface that would be focused on their needs as well as allowing a minimal installation and remote access. Budget, time, and business considerations will probably help us make the decision between one or two interfaces.

How and What Controls Should Be Used to Navigate?

In a general sense, the role of controls in navigation is fairly straightforward. Controls are graphical representations of information and functionality related to navigating through the application. They can appear as many things but are often physical, visible items on the user interface designed to convey information or give a physical access point to some functionality.

These access points are some of the most common ways of gaining access to things such as secondary windows, which are windows that contain information not normally presented to a user. A good example of this is in Microsoft Word. The spacing option is not visible during normal operation. However, by using some controls on the screen, a user is able to gain access to the information in a secondary window.

We will take a look at four of the most common types of controls:

◆ Menus

◆ Command buttons

◆ Tabs

◆ Treeview control

Menus

Probably the most common navigation technique—one that has been around since DOS screens—is the concept of menus.

Menus don't need a lot explaining. We all know how they work, and most developers know how to build them. The one point that should be made is that a few standards relating to menus might appear on the exam.

Microsoft recommends a specific order to the menu bar (see Figure 12.8). Every menu bar should have a File menu to the far left. Other menus should appear in the same order as in the Microsoft interfaces (for example, Edit, View, Insert, Format, Windows) where appropriate. Finally, in the rightmost position (although not right-justified on the screen) is the Help menu.

Each menu should have a hotkey assignment. Figure 12.8 shows the minimum items the Help menu should contain.

Each of these will be covered in more detail later in the chapter.

Command Buttons

After menus, command buttons are probably the most familiar to end users of business applications. The traditional OK and Cancel are examples of command buttons. Command buttons are used to drive applications, being the primary means of opening secondary windows in an application. Clicking command buttons, whether in a bar or a single button, will enable users to open screens, save data to persistent storage, or perform virtually any other action the user might want to perform.

The role of command buttons in business applications is very significant. Normally, these are used as the means of moving between screens and indicating to the system that a particular "human time" task has been completed.

Windows Interface Guidelines for Software Design outlines several standards for command buttons.[3]

Just as important, the interface designer must work to maintain consistency in the placement and look of command buttons across all screens. It is also advisable that command buttons be enabled or disabled rather than turned invisible.

Another good practice is to have a standard and consistent behavior for all buttons labeled OK, Cancel, Apply, Done, Exit, and Close. Keep 'em guessing may work for a suspense movie, but it is not a good strategy for user-interface design. Refer back to Figure 12.2 for an example of command buttons on a form.

Tabs

As we saw in Figure 12.4, tabs can serve as a navigation control as well. In Figure 12.4, we could just as easily have designed four separate forms, with buttons on each to move in between forms. However, users are familiar with the tab metaphor, and it usually provides a cleaner, simpler navigation model.

FIGURE 12.8
Microsoft's menu standards.

EXAM TIP

Interface Guidelines *Windows Interface Guidelines for Software Design* outlines several standards for command buttons. It would be good to browse this book prior to the exam. As one example, Microsoft recommends that command buttons used for navigation be right-justified in the lower-right corner of a form, aligned from most-frequently accessed on the left to least-frequently accessed on the right. An online version of the book is available within the MSDN Library CD or on the Web at: `http://msdn.microsoft.com/library/default.htm`.

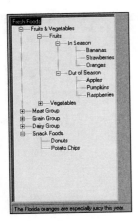

FIGURE 12.9
Treeview control.

One caution: Make sure that your users can access the tabs by using the keyboard, either through a hotkey or from within the tab sequence of the form.

Treeview

With the release of Windows 95 and Windows NT 4, Microsoft revealed a new control for working with data that is organized in a hierarchical fashion: the treeview control.

The treeview is essentially a means of displaying hierarchical data. Each tree has roots, with nodes that are arranged as children of the roots. This is the control that Windows itself uses in the Windows Explorer (see Figure 12.9).

Business applications have increasingly taken advantage of the treeview control in recent years. Data stores for business solutions are often organized in a hierarchical style, natural for relational databases. We can see in Figure 12.9 that the user can navigate directly from one food or group to another the same as a Windows user jumps between file folders in Windows Explorer.

It should be mentioned that the treeview control is not appropriate for all users. The metaphor is nonintuitive for some users. As with all user-interface design, "know thy users."

Controls for Navigating at OES

In reality, we will probably use all the controls previously mentioned, with the exception of the treeview. Commands buttons and menus exist in virtually all applications. Because the solution seems to support different users and different functions, we may find the tab control useful.

We will return to an analysis of control usage later in the chapter when we discuss input validation and shortcut keys.

What Procedures Are Needed for Input Validation?

Identify input validation procedures that should be integrated into the user interface.

When users enter things into a text box, they can enter two types of data. They might enter appropriate data, which the business components can correctly interpret into data. However, the user might also enter data that is completely nonsensical for that information. For example, a user who is typing in a data input application might accidentally enter the name John Brown into the telephone number text box. Obviously, the name John Brown is not going to be parsed correctly as a telephone number. The user interface needs to have a strategy for dealing with incorrect data formats.

To provide comprehensive input validation, we should explore two areas. First, we should analyze how to best constrain the data. Second, we should analyze when to validate the data.

Constraining the Possible Entries

Many ways exist in which we might decide to constrain entries for data fields. The most common of these is to add logic behind the form to check the data in a text box at some point in the entry process. For example, we might ask the user for a required social security number. With code behind the form, we can make sure that the user has not left the field blank and also that it is in the format nnn-nn-nnnn. We might ask that a date entry require a four-digit year. Another practice is to add code to various events behind the form (for example, Form_Load) that enables or disables various controls. This keeps unauthorized data entry from occurring and also avoids the need to pop up all kinds of extraneous message boxes such as, "You are not authorized for this function."

The other standard practice for ensuring valid data is to use different controls that limit the user's options only to valid choices. Examples of these types of controls are

- ◆ Check boxes
- ◆ Option buttons
- ◆ Drop-down lists and combo boxes
- ◆ Slider bars

FIGURE 12.10
Proper use of option buttons.

Check boxes are used when a question has only a yes or no answer. For example, if the user is supposed to ask customers on the telephone whether they are "generally satisfied," if the answer is "Yes, the user can simply check the box.

Option buttons are used when the number of correct choices is very small, but involves more than a simple yes or no. For example, if we wanted to enter the sex of an employee, we wouldn't have a check box that was labeled "Male?." It would be both confusing and improper to do so. We would have a small group of mutually exclusive option buttons labeled Male, Female, Unknown (see Figure 12.10).

Although adding an Unknown option to the preceding example was done whimsically, it should be stated that properly constructed option buttons should provide the user an out. If we do not know the sex of the employee, perhaps because they have not been contacted yet, we must have an option to indicate so. Otherwise, if a user accidentally clicks male or female, no way exists of undoing the selection. Often, option buttons should present a quad-state choice: Yes, No, Unknown, and Incomplete.

Drop-down lists and combo boxes are used to constrain input to a larger list of choices than those that would be appropriate for option buttons. Anything with more than six or so choices should lean toward the use of a drop-down list or combo box rather than a series of option buttons.

By convention, drop-down lists restrict users to what is already on the list, whereas combo boxes provide users with choices, but also allows them to type in a response not found on the list. Slider bars work to constrain the user to entering a number within a range. A good example is the slider bar that allows the user to choose screen resolution (see Figure 12.11). Only a few choices are acceptable.

The biggest advantage to input validation is the standardization of information in your data stores. If the user can type Yes, yes, Y, True, OK, or sure into a field, it is very hard to construct a query that ensures that all affirmative responses are counted.

Methods for Checking Entries

After all the constraint models have been selected for fields, it is time to get down to the nuts and bolts of how to verify that the

FIGURE 12.11
Slider bar example.

constraints are followed. Don't worry—we won't be getting into code. What we will be getting into, and what we, as user-interface designers, need to be most concerned about, are the various times where it might make sense to put in validation information. We will focus on these four spans of time:

◆ On Character Input

◆ On Change of Focus

◆ On View Complete

◆ On Submit

On Character Input

It is possible that we might choose to validate each character of input. This is particularly effective if, for example, only numeric or alphabetic characters are valid. It enables a system to throw away all characters that do not meet a particular standard.

The most common usage for something of this type is for numeric and date fields. It prevents nonnumeric characters, which would always be invalid for these fields, from being entered.

Under this model, because no invalid character inputs are acknowledged, no need exists for a subsequent check of the information when the field is complete or when the total information is input. This presents some performance advantages. However, this can be used only in certain cases.

For example, when dates are required, simply restricting the entry to numeric values is not going to be enough to make sure that a particular string of numbers is a valid date.

This is the most immediate form of input validation. It is also the most intensive form. Every time a key is pressed, some of your application code is running and validating that it is a key that can be echoed into the appropriate control on the form.

How to signal to users that a keystroke has been discarded is often a tough decision. As mentioned earlier, it helps to know your user base. A beep that indicates an invalid keystroke may not be heard. A color change on the screen may not show up under different color schemes.

IN DEPTH: USING COLOR TO INDICATE ERRORS

The use of specific colors to indicate error or validation problems is generally not recommended. Remember that most users are free to adjust their Windows color schemes. In that scenario, red text against a mauve background may not have the desired effect. Furthermore, studies show that 8% of men are color blind in the red-green spectrum.[12]

Several ways exist around this. One is to always use the system colors rather than coding specific colors into your application.

The other suggestion is to use small icons or symbols to indicate errors. An example is the small, yellow triangle with an exclamation mark inside—the same one that the Windows MsgBox uses. This can be displayed or hidden, depending on validation rules.

The best practice is usually the simplest. Simply discarding the keystroke and optionally placing a message in the status bar usually works best.

On Change of Focus

A second option serves things such as date fields particularly well. It allows any characters to be entered into a field. However, when the user attempts to exit a given field, the user interface checks what has been typed into the box against the validation rules that have been created for that item.

Consequently, in a date field, a user might type in an alphabetic value. This obviously won't transfer into a date. When the user clicks Enter or a tab or clicks the mouse on another control before the cursor is placed at another location, this method attempts to validate the information that is in the box. If, as in this case, the information is invalid, a message is delivered to the user to check the field's validity; the user will not be allowed to move on in the data entry until this is corrected.

The obvious advantage of this technique is that it allows less checking to go on when users are typing larger input fields. However, it does make it more disruptive to the users because they will likely be prompted to fix the problem immediately.

This is sometimes known as a *rich user interface*. It provides quicker feedback than the other techniques do, but it can be irritating under certain circumstances. One that most developers are probably familiar with is when a user leaves a field with invalid data to try to click a Cancel button or close the form. The system forces the user to clean up the bad data before allowing them to discard the entire screen.

All these issues can be worked around, but for various reasons, this model is less popular than in years past.

On View Complete

A view can best be explained as a subset of all the data currently being used by the application. Views, in this case, are sets of data that are grouped by subject matter and location in the user interface. When the user finishes entering a section of data, validation occurs for all members of the group.

In an application that enables a large amount of data access, particularly "power" data entry, it is probably advantageous to disrupt the rhythm of the user's typing as little as possible. In those cases, it may be worthwhile to simply validate at the end of a given view of information.

This is most useful in situations where there are a lot of tabs, or frames of data. It allows the user to efficiently enter data into the entire section and to leave bad data until all data in that section is entered. It does potentially leave more to go back and fix if an entire section was entered incorrectly, but that is offset by the fact that it allows for more efficient data entry when only a single mistake is made.

This strategy works well when a user is dealing with a customer on the telephone. The caller often takes the call in different directions. Rather than saying, "Can we please finish discussing your medical history before we go into your education?" the user can move through the tabs, checking a Completed box when each tab has all the required information.

On Submission Action

At the opposite extreme from character-by-character validation is the On Submission validation. That is, validation is only attempted when the user interface begins to pass its contents to a middle tier or persistent storage mechanism.

This is by far the least disruptive and the most often used of the validation models. However, it is also the method that potentially makes it hardest to correct errors. Instead of validating and revealing errors every character or field, or even every section, this method waits until the data has been completely finished and the user believes it is ready to be saved.

This method has several drawbacks. Most notably, if your users are prone to typos or miskeys, it seems like a long time to wait to point out that a user accidentally hit "3" instead of "e" on the third field that was entered. It also requires the user interface to be able to display more than one validation exception at a time.

In general, then, the fewer typographic mistakes your users are likely to make, the fewer the number of times per screen that you ought to be checking to validate data.

Browser interfaces use the on submit model almost exclusively. In a primarily stateless environment where the performance cost of round-trips between the user interface and the business logic are unpredictable, this is the least disruptive mode of validation.

Integrated Validation

In most applications, a single method of validation is not going to be sufficient. Some fields will be validated best on a character-by-character basis. Others will be validated best at a field level. The combination of the two will often result in a powerful validation plan. Checking to make sure that all the digits entered into a phone number are numeric is great, but the data also needs to be checked to ensure that the number entered is a valid phone number (in length).

Input Validation at OES

The important thing to realize in the case of OES is that the users who are most likely to be impacted are the billing clerks. When the bills begin rolling in for the month, this group sets up as a small data-entry shop to get all the payments processed for equipment. Because of this, they are the most affected by the current system's validation procedures.

The new user interface should try to take advantage of some of the controls previously mentioned. Also, data that is required to be in a certain format, such as dates, may be validated best by using the *lost focus* method.

It seems, from some of the comments in the case study, that validation is not done before the system starts its processing. Doing a thorough validation right after the user clicks OK and displaying user-focused messages when rules are not met would be improvements over the existing system.

Evaluate Methods of Providing Online User Assistance

Evaluate methods of providing online user assistance, such as status bars, ToolTips, and help files.

Another important aspect of the user interface is how an application provides user assistance.

We can approach user assistance in several ways. One ways that is used less and less is a printed manual. At this point, almost no software has its sole means of user assistance in a printed book distributed to the user. Instead, a "bootstrap" help book may be supplied, which is a help book designed to get the application installed and to deal with installation troubles.

Functional user assistance, however, is almost always distributed electronically. User assistance can be supplied in many ways, and in this section we focus on some of the most important ways:

◆ ToolTips

◆ What's This? help

◆ Help files

◆ Internet hyperlinks

◆ Status bars

FIGURE 12.12
ToolTip text.

ToolTips

ToolTips are probably the single aspect of user assistance that users themselves see most often. A ToolTip is a type of caption for a control that was first envisioned and implemented by Microsoft. Essentially, as a user pauses the mouse pointer over a control of any kind (whether a button, text box, check box, or anything else), the control can display a message explaining what it is that using this control can do. This is demonstrated in Figure 12.12.

In Figure 12.12, new users may not be familiar with the Order Approval button. Rather than forcing the users to click the button to see what will happen, we use ToolTips to teach them "just in time."

ToolTips can be used in almost every aspect of user-interface development. They are part of Microsoft's standard recommendations for style in the user interface, especially for toolbar buttons.

What's This? Help

A variation on ToolTip help is the What's This? help. The user can either go to the Help menu or press the Shift+F1 key combination. The cursor changes to a pointer with a question mark next to it. The user can then point to any control on the screen and click the mouse. Instead of executing the control, a small pop-up window appears that gives more detail about the control than what will fit into a ToolTip. Although What's This? is the predecessor to ToolTips, it still has a use for controls whose purpose needs some explaining.

Help Files

Any application that is developed needs to have an associated help file. Even if that file simply says who developed the application and where to go for technical support on the application, it still needs to be there. Users expect to be able to access help files and be able to investigate their problems with the software from there.

Currently, two means are available of providing help files:

◆ Windows help files (.hlp)

◆ New compiled HTML help files (.chm)

Windows Help Files (.hlp)

For several years, Microsoft had a technology that allowed them to convert specifically formatted files (RTF files) into Windows help files, with extension HLP. This was the standard means of providing help, and it was loaded into the standard Windows help file engine. Whenever the user chose Help from the menu bar, a form like Figure 12.13 would appear.

From a development perspective, a huge benefit is gained in using this engine. It enables applications developed by widely diverging groups of developers to present a single face for application assistance. Every application that creates Windows help files generated an essentially similar file. This enables users who are familiar with Windows in general to gather information on almost any other application simply by using what they already knew about Windows help files.

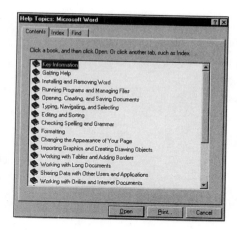

FIGURE 12.13
Windows help.

New Compiled HTML Help Files (.chm)

As Microsoft rushed to embrace the World Wide Web, someone began to notice how closely Web pages resembled what they were doing with Windows help files. In fact, they were almost exactly like them, except that they offered some additional benefits. They were written in (relatively) standard language, they were about as extensible as anything on the market, and most developers were already conversant in producing Web pages at the quality level needed for help files.

However, a few problems occurred. First, HTML was an interpreted language in the browser. This meant that distributing normal HTML files as help files amounted to sending out text files that anyone could change and redistribute—spreading incorrect, or even malicious information. What was needed was a way to make HTML files into a format that could not be changed with a text editor. The other issue is that each Web page is a separate HTML file. Therefore, it would take hundreds of separate files to do what a single Windows help file could do.

Microsoft set out to build a tool for turning HTML pages into a compiled file. This was accomplished, and Microsoft introduced the CHM extension, an abbreviation for Compiled HTML, to the developer community. This protected the help files from casual alteration by users, and at the same time, provided all the ease of normal HTML from a file-creation standpoint.

Today, Microsoft distributes MSDN (Microsoft Developer Network) and the help for Visual Studio in this CHM format. Microsoft and other software vendors have committed to moving help to this format for more products as they move ahead in versions. See Figure 12.14 for an example.

Internet Hyperlinks

We have looked at HTML-based help, but we only compiled HTML pieces that are located on the user's machine. Obviously, a potential exists for using HTML pages on the Web to create user help information. The relative ease of creation, as well as the capability to dynamically change content, make this option very attractive.

However, this approach is not without problems. Imagine www.microsoft.com, which receives millions and millions of hits a day. Now, imagine if the help file for Microsoft Office were on that site, and any user who asked for help would attempt to create an Internet connection to that site. You can only imagine how many new Internet servers and increases of bandwidth Microsoft would have to undertake to make the site even capable of responding, let alone in a timely manner, to the questions of the users.

FIGURE 12.14
HTML help example (MSDN).

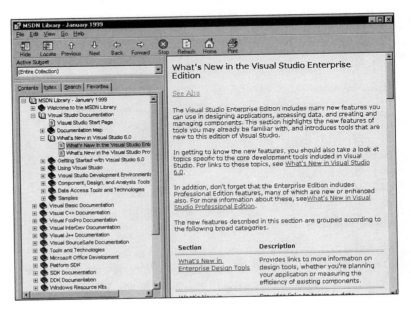

Another issue is simply the availability of an Internet connection and the bandwidth to support help downloads at a speed acceptable to users.

Status Bars

Status bars are not exactly user assistance in the sense of the other methods we have discussed. All the other instances we have discussed are initiated by some action on the part of the user. ToolTips have to do with where the user places the mouse pointer. Help files or Internet hyperlinks are resources that a user chooses to take advantage of.

The status bar is different from all these in that it is programmed by the developer with what information to display and when. Essentially, it acts as an indicator to the user of different pieces of information (see Figure 12.15).

In many cases, the status bar is used to indicate to the user that a time-consuming process is still progressing according to plan and that the user should not react as though the software has ceased functioning according to plan. Progress bars can be contained within status bars for this purpose as well.

In other cases, it informs the user of relevant details concerning the current state of the application. If it is a data-centered application, it may inform the user how many records currently exist, at what position the currently presented record lies, and so on.

The status bar is also often used to indicate things such as flags for the user interface. Some good examples of this are Caps Lock, Num Lock, and Overtype. Each of these affects the way that the user interface behaves in a particular way, and it is often useful for users to be able to see this while they are using the system. Similarly, many systems will include time/date areas in their status bar.

One final note about status bars—do not assume that the users will see what you place there. Studies have shown that the status bar is very often ignored. The status bar is better suited for secondary information.

FIGURE 12.15
Status bar example.

User Support at OES

Based on the case study comments, user support is probably the area where the OES can benefit most from a rework of the system. It seems that on almost every measurable level, there has been a failure to provide user assistance.

One of the sales associates stated that buttons do not clearly indicate their purpose, to the point that users have a "hope for the best" attitude. This is a classic scenario in which it would be appropriate to use ToolTips on the system. No button that begins processing should be without a ToolTip describing its purpose.

Second, the system they are currently using appears to have no help file at all that can be used. Given that no legacy help file exists that would have to be imported or converted to the newer format, nothing is preventing the new development effort from completely targeting the newer CHM format for help files. With this, the help files could also be much more easily converted into a Web-based application if that becomes necessary (or desirable).

Third, status bars will allow the system to offer useful information regarding order status to the sales staff or to the billing clerks. Each screen that is used could potentially be tracking different information in the status bar. Again, because currently no use is being made of such technology, it is much easier to include such things. Specifically, throughout the application, there seems to be a feeling that the users are unsure exactly what is happening. Because the original system was designed for a much smaller user base, some processes are much slower than users normally expect. This is a perfect opportunity to use a status bar to reassure the user that all is in order, and it is simply taking longer than the user expects.

Establish Appropriate Type of Output

Establish appropriate type of output.

Users interact with the system by inputting data into it and manipulating it through the system. However, many times users may need to take that information and go to a site where they do not have access to the system that the information came from. Whether it is to do work at home or to take information to a meeting with a business partner, the same requirement exists. As the users input data, so too do they expect the system to be able to output data to them.

One of the most important aspects of any new application, from an end-user perspective, is what kind of output the system can generate and how users can gain access to it.

A system creates several categories of output, ranging from hard copy to the screens themselves and to audio and visual support inside an application. Because of this, we will look at several areas related to what types of output the application produces:

◆ Hard copies of information

◆ Audio and video support

Need for Hard Copies of Information

Probably the single most important aspect of output from a system is the hard copies of the information. Whether it is reports, graphs, or lists, it is critical that these needs be addressed. Because we've already gone into some detail in earlier chapters about how to determine reporting requirements, we won't go over that again here.

However, it is important that we realize that it isn't just data analysts that need reports about the data. A user needs to have clear access to information and reports containing information. Assessing this need is one of the most important things that must be done from a user perspective. Users will not interact on a daily basis with the data architecture; however, they will interact with reports on the data on nearly a daily basis.

Audio and Video Support for Applications

As systems become more advanced, a new option is that applications might offer some form of audio and video output. When we approach their usage in the application, we should be asking two main questions:

◆ Are there places where A/V support would be valuable to a typical user?

◆ Are there special needs among the users that would lead us to incorporate audio and video?

Audio/Video Usage for Typical Users

The first issue is a fairly straightforward one. In many cases, it might be useful to record additional information about a help topic as an audio file that the user could listen to while performing the task being described. This avoids a lot of the flip-flops that users sometimes complain about when they try to follow an example in help files.

However, it is also important not to put anything only in audio or video, unless you are willing to state that the application requires a sound card to perform correctly.

Special Needs Driving Audio Incorporation

In some cases, an existing special need drives incorporation of A/V into the application. Sometimes it may be accessibility issues, where a particular employee or group of employees would be better able to function with the software if some of the features were available with audio support.

However, although it is not often thought of in these terms, audio incorporation for an application usually has nothing to do with accessibility. Many software packages that are used by mobile users, particularly drivers, have audio components for parts of the software for when they specifically do not want the user looking at a screen. Similarly, many products that make it possible to view presentations, for example, can function only if an audio component is designed into them.

Audio and video are, in a lot of applications, a luxury. In some, such as the driver program previously described, it is a necessity. It is critical that a designer decides which is the case for a given application.

Output Requirements for OES

In our case study, the only form of output that is required is to the screen. It does not appear that we have any hard copy or A/V requirements.

Essentially, the screen is not appearing to users in a way that seems equivalent to the applications they use on a daily basis and understand, at an intuitive level, how to use. This will be addressed by the other changes we discussed earlier.

DESIGNING USER-INTERFACE OBJECTS

Design the properties, methods, and events of components.

User interfaces consist of controls and code components. These both have objects, which consist, as we saw in the previous chapter, of properties, methods, and events. However, the user interface presents an entirely new set of challenges for the developer of components. Now, visual requirements must be met instead of calculation and computational ones.

Again, as we discuss objects, the rational way to break them down is into the three constituent pieces that make them up:

◆ Properties

◆ Methods

◆ Events

Properties

User-interface objects can be divided into two types. First, we can consider the code objects. These objects, in terms of structure of the code, look much like middle-tier business objects. However, they are not designed to govern middle-tier object interaction, but instead to work with the other user-interface tier objects.

The second type of user-interface objects is controls. Most, but not all, components have a visual aspect to them.

In either case, these controls typically have many properties, and we will examine two of the main categories:

◆ Appearance

◆ Input acceptance

Control Appearance

A large number of properties of user-interface objects are designed to control the appearance of the controls. Many of these properties translate directly into visual effects for the users. For example, text box controls have a Background Color property. This sets the color of the background on the text box.

Also, controls exist whose very shape and attributes are largely determined by properties. Microsoft's FlexGrid control allows properties to be set that determine how many rows and columns are in the grid.

Some control properties can be set only at design time, some can be set only at runtime, some can be set at design time or runtime, and others are read-only.

Capability to Accept Input

Some properties of the controls do not affect the actual physical appearance of controls. Instead, they affect the inner workings of the control. For example, text boxes have a Locked property. If this property is set to True, then no user can change the value that is displayed in the text box. This property does not affect the appearance of the text box at all, but it does affect the text box's capability to accept input from the user.

Properties also exist that affect the formatting of the input. Many controls have properties that allow a developer to set the *mask* for input into the control. A mask is simply a means of specifying formats for the data. It automatically formats the data input by the user into the mask's format. Note, however, that this technique does not replace validation; typically, it will not be able to react to different types of keystrokes.

Methods

Controls on the user interface have a wide array of methods available to them. Generally, these methods can be divided into two categories. First, they are related to changing the appearance of the control. Second, they relate to how the control responds to or initiate contact with the rest of the application and environment.

An example of a method that changes the appearance of a control is a Move method. Move performs an action rather than describing the control.

The second category of methods on controls are those that allow or cause responses between the control and the rest of the application and OS environment. These methods are normally used to perform actions more complex than a simple property setting. If a property could be considered as an adjective or noun (for example, Visible, Name), then methods are verbs (for example, Drag, Move).

An example of methods that respond to the environment are `Refresh or SetFocus.`

Events

Perhaps the single most important aspect of controls in the user-interface layer is their events. Using events, it is possible to monitor what a user has done on the user interface and to react accordingly.

Events, as we've previously discussed, are the way that components— or in this case, controls—let others know what they are doing. These events fire in particular sequences based on what the user is doing in the interface, and other controls have code in them, which "listens" for these events and reacts to them.

A classic example is to have a text box disable itself (deny any input) after a particular check box has been unchecked. In this case, in the Click event of the check box, code would disable the text box.

Basically, a control can produce two kinds of events. Each of these should be examined so that a larger picture of how controls can be used in the user interface is given. They are as follows:

◆ Input events

◆ Focus events

Input Events

Input events are essentially designed to indicate that the control is receiving some kind of input from the system. This may be in the form of characters typed into the keyboard, but it doesn't have to be. A common input event is the mouse click. This simply indicates that the user has clicked the mouse on the control. For some controls, this may not mean anything. However, in the case of a check box, this means the value of the control must change. If it is checked, it must now be unchecked, and vice versa.

Input events often include, where appropriate, information about what was input. For keystroke-related events, it has an argument that indicates what key was pressed and whether Shift or Control, for example, was depressed when it happened. In the case of the mouse, it will often report which button was clicked and where the cursor was pointed when it occurred. Using this information, a developer can lay out what should happen in the user interface because the user took that action.

One of the biggest mistakes that is made in a lot of user-interface code is to start thinking, "Well, this value should always be one of these three values because that's how the business works." Although this may be true now, it does not always have to be true. If those rules change, only one place in the application should be where they are changed.

By beginning to interpret those business rules at the user-interface level, you are violating the hope that we can have a single source for all business-level logic. The benefit is clear when it comes to maintenance. If business rules change, no need exists to be concerned about the user-interface layer—only the business-object layer.

Conversely, if business logic is being validated in the user-interface tier, if a different user interface is proposed, it is also going to have to reimplement the business-logic validation.

Focus Events

Focus events are designed to let controls know when a particular control has been activated or deactivated. This allows the developer to have some control over how a control is presented to the user (in both its activated and deactivated state). For example, a control may display data entered in a currency format when the field doesn't have the focus. However, after the field is given the focus, the dollar sign ($) is cleared to make it easier to edit the data.

Focus events are also useful for dynamic data. If your choices in a list box, for example, are determined by other data options on the screen, it is useful to be able to recalculate them every time the user attempts to view the choices in the list box. This can be handled by recalculating the values each time the list box gets the focus.

Often, focus events are used to trigger validation if it is handled at the field level.

The last purpose for this type of event is to allow special features of the control to be activated when the user attempts to set the focus to the control.

BUILDING A PROTOTYPE OF THE USER INTERFACE

Construct a prototype user interface that is based on business requirements, user-interface guidelines, and the organization's standards.

After you have designed a user interface, the next step to implementing it in a real application is to attempt to build a prototype for the interface. The best prototypes avoid constricting the design alternatives too early in the process. Two other things should be remembered when constructing the prototype.

First, the design was done for a reason, so try to stick as close as possible to the design when building a prototype. In theory, the design phase includes creating what are known as *lo-fi screen sketches.*[9] These are simple screen sketches that precede actual implementation. If you find that you are making a lot of changes to the low-fidelity design, take a closer look at your design techniques.

In general, three types of prototypes exist: throwaway, reusable, and progressive.[2]

Throwaway prototypes are done either to create very quick faux screens for user feedback or to perform proof-of-concept experiments. Faux, or stubbed, screens can sometimes help the user visualize the finished application's behavior. Proof-of-concept prototypes usually test out a theory and mitigate the riskier parts of the solution in advance. In both cases, no attempt is made to create industrial-strength code because the prototype is slated for destruction.

Reusable prototypes are designed with the intention that small pieces, or subcomponents, may find their way into the final solution, but overall, the code will be discarded.

Progressive prototypes are like sketches. The outline is built with the intention that the details will be filled in over time—basically iterative design. Much of the prototype code will find its way into the final product.

The second thing to remember is that usually standards exist for user interfaces, both at the business level and at the operating-system level. For the former, the requirement is obvious. If a business has a requirement for how its applications look, it probably ought to be followed. Similarly, however, if the operating system has a standard way of accomplishing certain tasks, refusing to do them that way will simply serve to confuse the users.

To avoid this, we look at two of the system standards for how user interfaces should be built:

◆ Menu-based controls

◆ Shortcut keys and access keys

Menu-Based Controls

Menu-based controls are simply what they say. Windows has developed a standard interface for menus and menu-based controls. Users, as a group, have developed a high level of understanding of how the menu structures of traditional Windows applications are used. Windows has essentially broken menus into three categories, which we can examine more closely:

◆ Traditional menu bar

◆ Toolbar

◆ Context menus

The Menu Bar

The menu bar is one of the most common forms for a menu interface. It is a special area displayed across the top of a window (refer to Figure 12.8). It shows directly below the title bar for a window, and it holds the various text menus that the application may support. These menus contain standard elements that were covered in the section on navigation.

The new generation of menu bars also has a handle that users can grab to move the menu bar from its standard position—on top, just beneath the toolbar—to other locations along the bottom or side of the application window. This allows users to customize the user interface to better meet their needs.

Toolbars

Toolbars are very similar to menu bars. However, they are typically icon based rather than text based. Generally speaking, they are made up of a row or a column of icons. In some cases (usually indicated by a small down arrow next to the icon), depressing the arrow will drop down a list of text items. A good example is the Back arrow in Internet Explorer. Depressing the icon itself results in the screen moving back to the previous Web address. However, clicking the small arrow next to the Back icon results in a drop-down list of the previous few pages loaded.

Many applications have more than one toolbar. In this case, it is important to allow the user to customize the toolbar(s). Additionally, much like the menu bar, toolbars have the capability of being moved from place to place to be positioned for the user's convenience.

Context Menus

The final set of menu controls we need to look at doesn't appear on the user interface in the same way as the others we have discussed. A context menu is a menu that is not displayed in the normal menu-bar hierarchy. Instead, it is made visible in the user interface when a user presses the second button (typically the right button) of the mouse or trackball (see Figure 12.16).

When that button is clicked, a context menu will appear if a control has one. This menu behaves just like traditional menu-bar menus in that it can have access keys and submenus. However, its key element is that in a given form, different context menus may be available for different controls.

Most often these context-sensitive menus have elements on them designed to exploit specific functionality of a control. For example, if a control supports special functionality related to data access, it may be used through a context menu. Similarly, common control-based

FIGURE 12.16
Context menu.

functionality (such as cut and paste) might be implemented on this menu in addition to the normal location. As a general rule, the context menu should not be the only way to get to a function.

Using Shortcut Keys and Access Keys

Shortcut keys are keyboard commands that give access to functions in the user interface that are normally accessed by the mouse and pointer. These are usually combinations of keys, often including the Control or Shift keys. Similarly, access keys are designed to allow users to gain access to particular menus or controls related to the caption property. Normally, these are indicated in the user interface by underscoring a letter that is the access letter for a particular control. Pressing and holding the Alt key while pressing the access key "accesses" the menu option or control.

Shortcut keys can be assigned to any function in the application. They enable a user to stay focused on the keyboard, using the mouse only for graphical-based functions such as drawing or dragging.

An access key can be used to indicate a menu on the application's menu bar. It drop downs the menu and selects the first item on it. The user can then use other access keys (if they are defined) to select items in the menu, or the arrow keys can be used to scroll to the correct menu item that is being sought.

An access key can be used to reference one of the other controls on a screen. By setting the access key of the caption for the control, a user can then use that access key (with the Alt key) as a way to gain quick access to a control and set the focus to it appropriately.

The main difference between the two is that shortcut keys execute system features regardless of whether the menu or command button is visible. For access keys to work, the control must be visible. For example, Ctrl+V performs a paste command regardless of whether the Edit menu is showing.

Access and shortcut keys are beneficial to the user-interface design in two ways. First, they enable people who may not be able to use a pointer effectively a way to gain access to the full functionality of the user interface.

Secondly, they enable users who are keyboard-centric to avoid, as much as they like, the use of a mouse. Some users, particularly those who do high-volume data entry, do not want to remove their hands from the keyboard to point to a menu. By putting access and short-cut keys into the interface, these users can continue to the use the keyboard as their sole means of interacting with the system.

It may seem as though shortcut keys are a panacea for solving our access issues. Although they are a very useful tool, utilizing them presents a new set of problems and concerns that developers need to be aware of. One of these is that the idea of shortcut keys actually came from Windows, and Windows gets to "see" keys pressed before any application does. Therefore, if both your application and Windows are using the same shortcut key, your application will not be able to respond to it because Windows will take control of the system when the shortcut key is pressed. A classic example is Control+Alt+Delete. This is a valid shortcut key, but it belongs to Windows. No application written to take advantage of this key set would ever be able to do so.

As if it weren't problematic enough to implement the application's shortcuts and access keys when Windows is grabbing them, you must also be aware that other applications may be using certain shortcuts and access keys during a Windows session.

One situation exists in which this is particularly evident and particularly dangerous—that of programming access keys for a system that is designed to run inside of an Internet browser. The browser stands in the same relation to applications running inside it as the operating system does to programs running inside of it. The browser receives keystrokes, and after it has decided that there isn't any reason for it to use the keystroke, it passes it on to the application running inside the browser.

So far, so good. That is exactly what we want the Web browser to do with our application. We want it to ferry data into and out of the browser for us. However, what if the browser runs into a situation in which it believes it should intercept the communication?

This is exactly the analogous case to applications having their access keys hidden because Windows is already using them. If the browser is using access keys, then any application that runs inside the browser runs a risk. The risk is that the access keys in the application will overlap the access keys present in the browser, thus making the access key permanently inaccessible.

There are ways to mitigate this problem. A developer can look at the current versions of popular browsers and try to make sure that the access keys are not duplicated. This does leave, however, two large, outstanding risks.

First, because only the popular browsers are being considered (which at one point, for example, would not have included Microsoft's Internet Explorer), if a change in market share occurs and a previously untested browser moves into competition, access key conflicts may be present.

Similarly, although a developer can verify against current versions of Internet browsers, no protection or verification can be insured against any future versions of browsers, which may contain different access and shortcut keys.

Although shortcut keys are a valuable resource for developers, enabling faster keyboard-based movement within applications, they must be designed in and not simply thrown in at the last minute.

It should also be mentioned that developers can cause problems within their own applications if they inadvertently assign an access key to two controls. The behavior of the access key will vary, depending on where the focus happens to be at the time. The bottom line, then, is to use access and shortcut keys wisely.

A Prototype at OES

OES is currently suffering from two things that we can pick out as being all or partly resolved by our discussions in this section.

First is the issue of requiring the mouse for data input. Apparently, the current application is not able to allow tabbing or shortcut keys to move between data elements. This, in an application that is used at least part of the time as a data-entry application, is not an acceptable situation. Effective data entry requires that users do not remove their hands from the keyboard between all the fields.

To rectify this problem, we can use combinations of shortcut keys and access keys. This can enable a user to access any control on the user interface from the keyboard. This will resolve the problem the billing clerks identified related to use of the data-entry system.

The second issue that can be addressed, at least in part, is the complaint from several people that the system does not work like other systems they use. In part, this is a result of having a system that would have been implemented for Windows 3.1 rather than for the Windows 95/NT shell. Another part of it, however, is to allow things such as toolbars and pop-up menus with which to interface. These kinds of tools, combined with traditional menu structures in the menu bar itself, will allow users familiar with common Windows applications, such as Word, to use the application more effectively.

CHAPTER SUMMARY

Often developers, in their fascination with new technology, forget that the ultimate consumers of their work are not their peers or the technical magazines they subscribe to. The only consumer that will ultimately matter is the targeted user group.

As we mentioned in Chapter 4, users have both business goals and personal goals. The user interface should respect both of these. The business goals should be met with a powerful user interface that allows data entry to be smooth, efficient, and as unerring as possible. Wherever possible, input should be constrained to the proper subset of values by choosing the most appropriate control. Data validation should be done at the point where it is most effective for the solution being designed. The proper navigation model should be selected (SDI, MDI, browser) for the work at hand.

Users' personal goals are important, as well. The proper amount of help should be designed into the solution so that users can figure it out for themselves. Buttons and controls should behave in a way that is standard and easy to anticipate.

A properly designed user interface will make the user more productive while simultaneously keeping them from feeling stupid.

KEY TERMS

- Access keys
- Input validation
- Menu bars
- Multiple Document Interface
- Shortcut keys
- Single Document Interface
- Status bars
- ToolTips
- Treeview

APPLY YOUR KNOWLEDGE	

Exercises

12.1 Selecting the Most Appropriate Navigation Model

Selecting the most appropriate navigation model for your solution is important to the overall success of the application. We have used the term "most appropriate" because many solutions could work under different models, but usually one is a better fit (see chapter text). For each of the scenarios in the following table, select the most appropriate navigation model from the list at the right.

Estimated Time: 10 minutes.

TABLE 12.1

CHOOSING THE MOST APPROPRIATE NAVIGATION MODEL

Scenario	Navigation Model
A. A wizard that helps the user through the steps to build an ad hoc decision-support query.	SDI
B. Corporate telecommuter employees logging in from home on their own PCs to run the application.	MDI
C. Computer game.	Browser/ASP-based
D. Email program.	
E. "Heads down" data entry of customer complaints received in the mail.	
F. An inventory system for a warehouse that uses a bar-code scanner.	
G. A system that allows library cardholders to reserve books, renew books, and query the card catalog, all from their home.	
H. A small helper applet that assists corporations in setting up a connection to a network printer.	
I. A system for organizing disparate information for police reports, such as officer reports, audio clips of witness and suspect interviews, scene diagrams, expert reports, and crime-scene photographs.	
J. An ATM screen.	

APPLY YOUR KNOWLEDGE

Answers to Exercise 12.1:

A. SDI. Most wizards are SDI because they employ a constrained-path structure.

B. Browser. Employee's home machines are an unknown quantity. A browser user interface is the one most isolated from the OS and the environment of the PC. Also, it simplifies deployment and maintenance significantly.

C. SDI. Most computer games require power and speed. They also rarely have multiple screens up simultaneously.

D. MDI. This could be traditional MDI or workspace MDI, depending on whether you are going to allow the simultaneous opening of both mail and appointments, or only mail.

E. SDI. Navigation must be structured and able to use the power of a 4GL language for validation and for maintaining a keyboard-centric user interface.

F. SDI. Most inventory systems use SDI models.

G. Browser. With remote users, especially thousands, using an established vehicle (the Internet) and no installation procedure is the best fit.

H. Browser. This could have gone SDI, but for small applets, using the browser avoids maintenance and deployment headaches. The applet is described as

simple and seems to be run very infrequently. Therefore, we can simply make it accessible from the employee's desktop browser.

I. MDI. This would be a workspace MDI. We are bringing together different file types into a single workspace.

J. SDI. A prototypical modal activity—moving through a series of screens, finishing one screen before going to the next.

See "What Are the Options for Navigational Models?"

12.2 Data Validation

Ensuring valid data is crucial to being able to draw business conclusions from stored data. Current technology allows for more ways to maintain valid data than just firing a message box in the user's face. Selecting the proper control can create a more silent application.

From the list of situations in the following table, choose the most appropriate strategy to ensure valid data.

Estimated Time: 15 minutes.

TABLE 12.2

ENSURING VALID DATA

Situation	Validation Strategy
A. User must enter patient's sex: Male or Female.	Check box
B. User can choose from one of 50 company names or enter the name if it is not in the database.	Drop-down list
C. The Delete button is available only to database administrators.	Text box rules

continues

APPLY YOUR KNOWLEDGE

TABLE 12.2 *continued*

ENSURING VALID DATA

Situation	Validation Strategy
D. User must choose one of 16 basic colors.	Option buttons
E. User is talking with telephone customer and needs to record the answer to the question, "Does your family have a dog?"	Form-level rules
F. User must choose between Good, Bad, or Indifferent.	Slider bar
G. Free-form text is allowed—no special characters (%, ?, #, &, /, \, *).	Combo box
H. Nonmanagers cannot alter the "Percent Discount" given to customers.	
I. Users can choose any number between 0 and 24.	
J. User must select a valid state code.	
K. User should be able to indicate which records are Y2K compliant so that a simple query can locate all the noncompliant records.	
L. The user can type in any date, but the date must include a four-digit year.	

Answers to Exercise 12.2:

A. Option buttons. The choice is not Yes or No (check box), nor does it have a large range of choices (drop-down list).

B. Combo box. Combo boxes allow the user to pick from a list or type in a free-form entry.

C. Form-level rules. When the form first loads, it checks the user's security or group and disables or enables the button.

D. Drop-down list. The number 16 is too large for an option-button array. Microsoft suggests using drop-down lists or combo boxes. Because the situation did not say the user could choose outside the 16 colors, we can use a constraining drop-down list.

E. Check box. Questions that have a Yes/No or True/False answer are usually best served by check boxes.

F. Option buttons. When the choices are restricted and small in number, a set of option buttons is usually the best fit (space permitting).

G. Text box rules. Each keystroke can be interrogated and special characters discarded.

H. Form-level rules. When the form first loads, it checks the user's security or group and disables or enables the control.

I. Slider bar. A slider bar restricts choices to numbers only and confines the choices to a predetermined range.

J. Drop-down list. The user can choose from only one of 51 (or so) entries.

K. Check box. The answer to the question is Yes or No.

L. Text box rules. At "lost focus," the text can be examined to see whether it contains a valid four-digit year. In certain circumstances, this could also be a form-level rule, enforced on the Done button.

APPLY YOUR KNOWLEDGE

See "What Procedures Are Needed for Input Validation?"

12.3 Choosing a Help Strategy

Providing good help avoids support calls, decreases training costs, and keeps the user from feeling stupid. Therefore, using the proper tools can make your solution more popular.

From the list of scenarios in the following table, choose the most appropriate help strategy.

Estimated Time: 10 minutes.

TABLE 12.3

CHOOSING A HELP STRATEGY

Scenario	Help Strategy
A. Keep user informed as to the progress of a lengthy query run.	Online (Web) help
B. Developer wants the user to have a small amount of detailed information about the purpose of the Reason for Detention field on the form.	FAQ
C. We need to provide the user with a quick way to learn how to set up an ad hoc query.	Windows help file
D. The Help Desk for XYZ Corp. gets asked the same business question about five times a week. They would like to cut back on this phone support.	Status bar
E. The developer wants the function of each button in the "query builder" toolbar to be clear. For example, the stop sign causes a running query to cease.	ToolTips
F. System use information changes frequently. Users need accurate and current advise on system functionality.	What's This?

APPLY YOUR KNOWLEDGE

Answers to Exercise 12.3:

A. Status bar. The status bar is the only one of the selections that is always showing.

B. What's This? Concise, but able to display more than a ToolTip.

C. Windows help. No need to go out on the Web. A local help file will do.

D. FAQ. Frequently Asked Questions is a way to provide answers to oft-asked business or application usage questions. It is usually more informal and more frequently updated than standard help.

E. ToolTips. ToolTips are strongly recommended by Microsoft for all toolbar buttons.

F. Online help. Online help is easier to keep current because only a single copy exists on the server, which is accessed by all users. Can be updated daily if necessary.

See "Evaluate Methods of Providing Online User Assistance."

12.4 Establishing Output

In addition to the forms themselves, which we have covered extensively in the other exercises, two main forms of output exist: hard copy and audio-video.

Take a few minutes and create a list of three solution scenarios in which hard-copy output, audio output, and video output would add value to the solution presented to the user.

Estimated Time: 10 minutes

Answer to Exercise 12.4

Obviously, many correct answers to this exercise are possible. The point of the exercise is to provoke thought about using these alternatives in a solution. We have provided just a few of the options next.

Hard copy: Decision-support reports and graphs, production reports, hard-copy security log files, electronic mail, material for distribution to others (for example, presentations), user-support information, and so on.

Audio: Event sounds (for example, Windows sound schemes) that notify the user of some sort of exception condition, musical accompaniment to a computer game or Internet site, audio recording of spoken text (for example, police witness interviews, legally recorded telephone conversations, adaptive tools for users with challenged eyesight, and so on.

Video: Expanded help, self-paced instruction, DVD entertainment, teleconferencing (for example, MS NetMeeting), and so on.

See "Establish Appropriate Type of Output."

12.5 Building a Prototype

Building a prototype allows the architect to combine all the user-interface strategies covered previously. It is like a scale model to a building architect. Better to find a flaw in a $5,000 model than in a $500,000,000 building.

Using the information from the OES case study, design two prototype screens, one for the repair dispatcher and one for the repair technician. Use the following supplemental information.

The two screens should be similarly designed. The following fields should appear: Service Call Received Date & Time (automatically entered by the system), Service Call Scheduled Date & Time, Service Call Number (assigned by the system), Customer Name (should match the list of customers registered in the database), Customer Address/City/State/Zip (inserted

APPLY YOUR KNOWLEDGE

by the system based on selected customer), Technician Assigned (also restricted to list of technicians), Problem Description (free form), Problem Resolution (free form) Time Arrived Onsite, Total Hours Spent. Away should also be provided to identify that the call is Closed. The technician is allowed to enter only into the Problem Resolution, Arrived Onsite, and Total Hours Spent fields. They can also close a call.

The dispatcher should be able to identify the problem as either a Hardware, Software, Network, or Unknown problem.

OES requests instant feedback from the customer on all service calls, using a scale from 0 to 10, with 10 being perfect and 0 meaning that the customer could not be contacted. Only the dispatcher is allowed to change the rating.

Both types of users need to be able to navigate to Reports and Maintenance screens.

Several user-support (help) aids should be designed into the screen as well.

Estimated Time: 45 minutes.

Hint: Do the Dispatcher screen first.

Answers:

We have used many of the controls we discussed earlier for validation. Combo boxes, check boxes, slider bars and option buttons all ensure clean data.

A standardized menu bar and help has also been incorporated into the prototype, although they don't show well in a static prototype screen shot. ToolTips do not exist only because we have not implemented a toolbar in our prototype.

Controls where no user is allowed to enter (read-only data) utilize flush label controls.

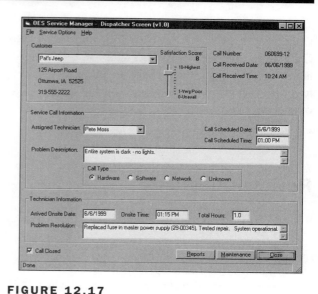

FIGURE 12.17
Exercise 12.5—Dispatcher screen (prototype).

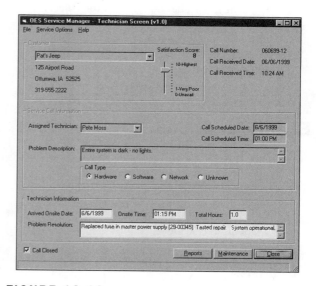

FIGURE 12.18
Exercise 12.5—Technician screen (prototype).

APPLY YOUR KNOWLEDGE

The only real difference between this screen and the Dispatcher screen is that the Customer and the Service Call frames have been disabled. The use of frames makes this easy to do when the form first loads. We have also changed the background color of disabled controls as a visual cue.

See "Building a Prototype of the User Interface."

Review Questions

1. If OES needed an application strictly for decision-support style issues, why might we switch to another navigation model?

2. Which version of user-assistance help files is the most conservative choice and is most likely to be usable by the user base?

3. When designing validation rules, why is it so important not to be too strict in the rules?

4. How can the treeview control, when used in combination with a listview control, be used for effective navigation?

Exam Questions

1. What is the main difference between a traditional Multiple Document Interface (MDI) navigation model and a workspace MDI navigation model?

   A. Both MDI models support multiple documents at once.

   B. Workspaces support multiple format types.

   C. Traditional MDIs are more flexible.

   D. Workspace MDIs are more popular.

2. How does the decision to use an SDI navigation model affect their use as OLE Automation objects?

   A. Each OLE use creates a new instance of the application.

   B. All OLE use uses the same instance of the application.

   C. SDI applications cannot be OLE Automation objects.

   D. SDI applications cannot be built to be multithreaded.

3. If OES wants to be able to group similar kinds of files together by customer or subject, which would be the best navigation model?

   A. SDI

   B. Traditional MDI

   C. Workspace MDI

   D. Internet Browser

4. What is the primary use of controls as it relates to navigation through an application?

   A. Accessing secondary windows

   B. Starting the application

   C. Input of data

   D. None of the above

5. When the dispatchers at OES are finished changing information on a screen, which of the following controls is most likely to be used to indicate completion?

   A. Text box

   B. Command button

APPLY YOUR KNOWLEDGE

C. Treeview

D. Menu bar

6. What common component of the Windows 95/NT operating systems uses the treeview control?

   A. Network Neighborhood

   B. Windows Explorer

   C. Control Panel

   D. ODBC Manager

7. What are the two steps that need to be addressed in designing input validation for forms in an application? (Choose two.)

   A. Designing input constraints

   B. Coding validation

   C. Choosing an input validation implementation style

   D. All of the above

8. When designing value constraints, developers should

   A. Never do it in the user interface.

   B. Err on the side of not controlling data tightly enough.

   C. Always do it in the user interface.

   D. Err on the side of too strictly controlling data.

9. Which of these is not a valid technique for validating user input?

   A. Monitoring keystrokes

   B. Monitoring words

C. Monitoring fields as they are left

D. Monitoring entire forms as they are complete.

10. What is the primary function for the user of a ToolTip?

   A. Offer instructions to user

   B. Offer explanation about what control is

   C. Trigger system help file.

   D. Give tips about when it is appropriate to use a tool

11. Which of the following are valid file formats for help files? (Choose all that apply.)

   A. CHM

   B. DLL

   C. HLP

   D. RTF

12. A property of a control that assures all data entered for social security numbers contains dashes is what kind of property?

   A. Appearance control

   B. Input acceptance

   C. Input mask

   D. None of the above

13. An event is raised from a control as the user moves the cursor to another control. What kind of event is it?

   A. Input events

   B. Validation events

C. Focus events

D. None of the above

14. Which are two of the best reasons to use access and shortcut keys in an application?

   A. Users may have difficulty using pointers and this is an alternative.

   B. Data entry will be faster with shortcut keys available.

   C. All users would rather not use the mouse.

   D. Unless other reasons are present, no reasons exist to do so.

Answers to Review Questions

1. One of our primary motivations for adopting the Single Document Interface navigation model was concerns about data entry and also questions about what value would be gained in allowing the user to have multiple calls open at once. If that were the case, an MDI environment might be more effective. See "What Are the Options for Navigational Models?"

2. Old-fashioned Windows help files (HLP) are probably the most conservative choice. These files have been in use for several years, and as long as the system has a version of the Windows 95/NT shell installed, the help files will be able to work. The CHM format, because it is newer, may not be available on all desktops yet. See "Evaluate Methods of Providing Online User Assistance."

3. Validation rules that are too strict may accidentally exclude valid data. For example, an application that, in good faith, invalidated the "/"

on address information would be unable to capture the address of individuals who lived at, for example, 151 1/2 37th Street. Unanticipated data is the single biggest risk in data validation and must be carefully sought out. See "What Procedures Are Needed for Input Validation?"

4. Microsoft itself demonstrates how this can work. A treeview on the left side of a screen makes a natural hierarchical arrangement. On the right side of the screen then, we can display those things that are contained in each element of the hierarchy via a list box. This powerful combination is the model for Microsoft's Windows Explorer, the Microsoft Management Console for MTS, and other server-side applications. See "How and What Controls Should Be Used to Navigate?"

Answers to Exam Questions

1. **B.** Workspaces are designed to allow files of different formats to be associated based on their content. MDI models allow multiple files but are not capable of supporting multiple format types as the workspace is. MDI models divide up work by format rather than by content. See "MDI Workspace."

2. **A.** Because the application has no capability to generate multiple instances within a single container, each instance must have its own container. This means that each OLE object must have its own instance of the application to use. Statements C and D are incorrect. See "Single Document Interfaces (SDI)."

APPLY YOUR KNOWLEDGE

3. **B.** The use of multiple files of any kind rules out the SDI interface. Because the files are of a similar format, it is most likely that a traditional MDI interface would be best. See "Choosing Between the Models."

4. **A.** The primary purpose of the controls, as it relates to navigation, is to allow the user to access windows that are not actually visible in the default display. These are called secondary windows. See "How and What Controls Should Be Used to Navigate?"

5. **B.** Command buttons are most often used to indicate that human tasks are done. When a person has completed some extra-system task, they click the button to indicate it is acceptable to proceed. See "How and What Controls Should Be Used to Navigate?"

6. **B.** The Windows Explorer is built with a tree-view control on the left side of the application. A and C are both built with the listview but not with the treeview. See "How and What Controls Should Be Used to Navigate?"

7. **A, C.** Two main things must be done in the design. First, decide what are the input constraints we want to put on controls. Second, decide when we want the validation to take place. Coding is never part of design, so B is not true. See "What Procedures Are Needed for Input Validation?"

8. **B.** The danger in applying validation rules is not that a lot of inappropriate data will be entered. Normally, this data is easily spotted and corrected if need be. The bigger danger is that we accidentally define as invalid an actually valid value, causing the end users to not be able to complete their work. Regarding choices A and C, "never" and "always" are poor and inflexible guidelines for design. See "What Procedures Are Needed for Input Validation?"

9. **B.** The system lacks the capability to monitor words—in contrast to keystrokes or entire fields. See "What Procedures Are Needed for Input Validation?"

10. **B.** The primary purpose of a ToolTip is not to start the help system or to give detailed instructions. Instead, it is a short name—more often than not simply a label—which gives an indication about what the control is and perhaps an indication of how it should be used. But instructions are certainly not the primary purpose of the ToolTip. See "ToolTips."

11. **A, C.** Neither DLLs nor RTF files are valid file formats for help files. RTF files can be compiled into HLP files, but are not themselves valid formats. See "Help Files."

APPLY YOUR KNOWLEDGE

12. **C.** This property is controlling the format of the text that is typed into a control. This is handled by an input mask property of the control. See "What Procedures Are Needed for Input Validation?"

13. **C.** The event we are discussing is a lost focus event. Essentially its purpose is to indicate that a user has decided to leave a control. This is part of the functionality discussed under the headings of Focus events. See "What Procedures Are Needed for Input Validation?"

14. **A, B.** Some users may have special needs that make keyboard interfaces more palatable than pointer-based interfaces. Specifically, those with movement difficulties or those who have visual difficulties will likely find it easier to control an application that has these keys. Second, it will speed up any attempts at power data entry because those entering won't have to remove their hands from the keyboard to use the mouse. See "Using Shortcut Keys and Access Keys."

Suggested Readings and Resources

1. Alvarez, Mike. "Make the Call Between VB and Web clients." Enterprise Development, April, 1999, p. 49. Fawcette Technical Publications.

2. Rofail, Ash. "Adopt a UI-Driven Architecture." Enterprise Development, June 1999, p. 46. Fawcette Technical Publications.

3. Windows Interface Guidelines for Software Design. Microsoft Press, 1995.

4. Cooper, Alan. *The Inmates Are Running the Asylum.* Indianapolis: Sams, 1999.

5. Cooper, Alan. *About Face: The Essentials of User Interface Design.* IDG Books, 1995.

6. Carter, Matthew. "A Method to End the Madness." WEBBuilder, August 1998, p. 20.

7. Fowler, Susan. "Modes for Better GUI Navigation." Software Development, November 1998, p. 43. Miller-Freeman.

8. Zetie, Carl. *Practical User Interface Design.* McGraw-Hill, 1995.

9. Constantine, Larry. "Prototyping from the User's Viewpoint." Software Development, November 1998, p. 51. Miller-Freeman.

10. Ritter, David. "Déjà vu All Over Again." Intelligent Enterprise, November 1998, p. 76. Miller-Freeman.

11. Brown, Kent. "A New Model for Data Validation." Enterprise Development, January 1999, p. 52. Fawcette Technical Publications.

12. Fowler, Susan. "Spit and Polish." Software Development, January 1997, p. 49. Miller-Freeman.

At this point, we have examined those things you should consider when designing each layer in your *n*-tier architecture. We will conclude this book, then, with a look at how various physical design implementations may affect the "PASS ME" aspects of your finished solution. Microsoft lists the following relevant exam objective:

Assess the potential impact of the physical design on performance, maintainability, extensibility, scalability, availability, and security.

▶ Throughout the text of this book, we have referred to the solution aspects identified in this objective as the "PASS ME" themes. Reordered according to our mnemonic acronym, the themes are

- Performance
- Availability
- Security
- Scalability
- Maintainability
- Extensibility

▶ We have explained the meaning and significance of these terms many times previously in the text of this book. In this chapter, we focus on how the decisions you make when implementing your solution's physical design have an impact on these aspects.

CHAPTER 13

"PASS ME" and the Physical Design

OUTLINE

OUTLINE

- ▶ Remember that indexes generally improve data retrieval performance but impede the progress of data updates.

- ▶ Understand how proper use of queues and proper structuring of queries can improve your solution's performance.

- ▶ Explain why your choice of data types, early-binding versus late-binding, and use of string concatenation can also exert a considerable influence over your solution's performance.

- ▶ Know the problems likely to be exhibited by a solution using too many controls on its forms and/or too many forms or dialog boxes.

- ▶ Understand how your solution's availability can be detrimentally affected by downtime required for maintenance, inability to recover from disasters, and scalability lockouts.

- ▶ Understand the potential impact that end-of-period routines and poor reliability can have on your solution's availability.

- ▶ Know the ways that views, encryption, and auditing can contribute to the security of a solution.

- ▶ Remember how your solution's security can be enhanced through the use of passwords, automated logoffs, and challenge/response authentication.

- ▶ State the differences and similarities between the various levels and types of database locks, as well as the many querying technologies that can exert a considerable influence over the scalability of your solutions.

- ▶ Know the scalability ramifications of choosing to instantiate objects of varying life spans locally, out of process, or remotely.

- ▶ Explain how needing to clear logs and compact your data can adversely affect your solution's maintainability.

- ▶ Understand the concept of source control and how it relates to the maintainability of your solutions.

- ▶ Explain why a solution that stores its caption strings in a resource file is likely to be more maintainable than one where they are hard coded.

- ▶ Know the drawbacks to using a physical database design that relies on a certain ordering of fields and/or rows to achieve extensibility.

- ▶ Remember how COM's strengths in language independence and versioning support contribute to its usefulness in making your solutions more extensible.

INTRODUCTION

The physical design decisions that you make in putting together your solutions will exert a profound influence on the PASS ME themes that we have been discussing throughout this book. In this chapter, we illustrate the specific influences that each of the three tiers in an *n*-tier solution may exert.

CASE STUDY: BOOKWARE, INC.

BACKGROUND

In the field of electronic books, one name stands out above all others: BookWare. Founded last year as a breakaway venture by an ex-employee of Trey Research, the hype surrounding this company has made it a Wall Street sensation.

Line of Work

BookWare, Inc. specializes in the production of hardware and content for electronic books.

CURRENT SYSTEM

The company has been in a position to actually conduct business for only a few months now. Already, however, a few chinks in the armor have appeared.

Author

"To begin with, adding my submissions to the central repository seems to take forever.

Also, why is it that I can't work on a certain part of my submissions at the same time as my editor? I've gotten some weird errors about "database contention" before, and whenever I've called technical support at BookWare, they've said that it was because my editor was already working on my submission."

Editor

"We are assembling a massive central repository of author texts that we intend to make available for customer purchase. I can search the entire repository for any set of words or phrases amazingly quickly."

ENVISIONED SYSTEM

BookWare would like to revise the system it currently uses for receiving author submissions.

Author

"I would like to be able to do everything in Microsoft Word and just email it to my editor. Any translations that need to be done after this to get it into electronic format should be BookWare's problem."

Editor

"In speaking with some of my colleagues working in non-English-speaking countries, I have heard stories of poor system performance when working in other languages. For example, many of our editors working in Japan seem to think that the UI controls in our editing applications are laid out in a very illogical manner!"

continues

Case Study: BookWare, Inc.

continued

Programmer

"To make their submissions and revisions, our authors and editors all have to use software that we have built from scratch . We'd like to work toward a thinner client layer and greater code reuse by redesigning our system for a three-tier architecture.

Most of the logic needed by the authors' and editors' software should be stored in objects derived from our ElectroBooks themselves and stored on our central servers here at BookWare. They should gain access to these using DCOM.

We really need some kind of source-control software."

Network Manager

"Right now, the only time that editors and authors have to connect to our network is when they are actually submitting their final works. All this talk of DCOM has me worrying that we are going to have to increase our network's band-width capacity.

What concerns me most about the increased traffic, though, is that I have no idea how I can keep track of all the additional accesses. What if someone unauthorized gets in and starts mess-ing with our data? If we have three times as many people using the system as we do now, I can guarantee that I will see a problem in time!"

DBA

"Maintaining the BookWare ElectroBooks Library is fairly simple and straightforward. We keep everything in a single SQL Server database.

Things are largely automated, except for the big database reindexing that I have to do at the end of each month.

My most important task is creating all the queries that development requests. They are pretty much basic SQL, except for some parts of them that are supposed to hold variables.

I would really like to save disk space by dropping any unneeded indexes."

USER SURVEYS

Before starting work on the system redesign, engineers at BookWare, Inc. wanted to satisfy themselves that they were addressing all issues currently being experienced. To this end, they conducted a survey of all authors and editors currently using the system.

Strengths

- **Ease of searching**—Editors seemed to agree that it was very easy to find things based on target words and phrases in the current system. But they'd be just as happy being able to search by section titles.

- **Specificity of functionality**—Editors and authors liked the fact that their custom software allowed them to access features (such as animations) that would not be available in standard print media.

CASE STUDY: BOOKWARE, INC.

Weaknesses

- **Performance**—Some level of acknowledgement seemed to be present among all parties surveyed that the system seems to slow down around the end of each month.

WORKFLOWS

The workflows at BookWare, Inc. have been hastily assembled to keep pace with the company's dynamic growth.

Author Submissions

Current:

1. Authors type their manuscripts directly into ElectroBook's Authoring Software (EAS).

2. Authors connect to BookWare's internal network to transmit their submissions.

3. Authors disconnect from BookWare's internal network.

Proposed:

1. Authors connect their computers into BookWare's internal network.

2. Authors create their manuscripts using Microsoft Word.

3. VBA Macros in Word access shared components over the network (via DCOM) to provide ElectroBook-specific functionality from within Microsoft Word.

4. When authors are finished, they use a VBA Macro to upload their submissions.

5. Authors disconnect from BookWare's internal network.

Editorial Reviews

Current:

1. Editors connect to BookWare's internal network.

2. Editors find the submitted manuscripts they are looking for by searching on the names of authors from whom they are expecting submissions.

3. Editors download these submissions into their ElectroBook's Editing Software (EES).

4. Editors disconnect from BookWare.

5. Editors make their revisions using either manual (keyboard) controls or the voice interface.

6. Editors reconnect to BookWare's internal network.

7. Editors upload their corrected submissions.

8. Editors disconnect from BookWare.

Proposed:

1. Editors connect to BookWare's internal network.

2. All submissions on the network that belong to an editor are automatically downloaded if they have not been downloaded before.

3. Editors make their revisions in Microsoft Word, using VBA Macros to access special ElectroBook components via DCOM across the network.

4. Editors upload their corrected submissions.

5. Editors disconnect from BookWare.

PERFORMANCE

Performance is a gauge of how much work your system can accomplish in a given amount of time.

The Data Tier

Many aspects of your data tier's physical design can exert a tremendous influence on the performance of your solutions. In this section, we focus on three of the most important ones:

◆ Indexing

◆ Queuing

◆ Query structure

Indexing

A database's index is much like the index of a book. On one side, you have a list of things that might need to be looked up. Next to each of these, you have a list of places in the work (be it a book or a database) where they occur. Trying to find any of these things without an index may require a row-by-row search from start to finish in order to find them.

You can see from this description of indexes that the primary benefit to having one is that it speeds up searches and, to use database terminology, data retrievals. On the other hand, you should also know that indexes may slow down the addition of new data. This occurs because any new piece of data that is to be added must also have a new entry made for it in the index. If this new entry occurs in the middle of an index, a performance-costly reordering may also be required.

Just like the additional pages consumed by an index in a book, indexes in databases consume additional storage space. If data storage is a bigger concern than performance, you may seriously want to reconsider the wisdom of including an index.

Here, briefly, are a few general guidelines for indexing properly:

◆ Index fields used in table joins.

◆ Index fields used in WHERE clauses.

◆ Index fields that are mostly unique, but not entirely.

IN DEPTH: INDEXES

For more information on the topic of indexing, please refer to "Converting the Application to ODBC and SQL" and "Microsoft SQL Server Performance Tuning and Optimization for Developers" in the MSDN Library.

Queuing

Queuing is a technology that allows a solution that is designed to use some form of network connectivity to continue functioning even when such connectivity is unavailable. For example, if an application makes heavy use of a database server, a queuing system might temporarily hold requests during periods of high database usage so that the application can continue with its work while waiting for the database to respond to its queries.

> **EXAM TIP**
>
> **Microsoft Message Queue** The queuing technology that you are most likely to encounter on the Microsoft exam is the Microsoft Message Queue. Most often, this tool is simply referred to as MSMQ, and it occurs in combination with SQL Server.

Query Structure

It should come as little or no surprise that probably the single biggest physical design decision in your data tier affecting performance lies in the structure of your queries. Poorly designed queries can have an extremely adverse impact on the performance of your solutions.

What exactly constitutes a good design in contrast to a bad design varies from database to database. A few general principals have been demonstrated to hold true under virtually all circumstances, however. They are as follows:

◆ Avoid joining tables on fields of different types.

◆ Avoid restricting results on nonindexed fields.

◆ Put calculations only in the highest levels of your queries.

The Data Tier's Impact on Performance at BookWare

At one point, the author interviewed states that making her submissions "seems to take forever." This strongly suggests that every word in her submissions is being added to some kind of running index. Although the editors cited being able to search the text as a strength of the current system, they also said that they would be just as happy searching only on section names. The DBA also was quoted as saying that he'd like to save disk space by dropping any unneeded indexes. The suggested course of action would seem to be that of redesigning the index to work only on section names. This would achieve the following:

◆ Improve submission performance by requiring fewer index entries.

◆ Retain the minimal searching functionality required by the editors.

◆ Save disk space by requiring fewer index entries.

The Logic Tier

Many aspects of your logic tier's physical designs can exert a tremendous influence on the performance of your solutions. In this section, we focus on three of the most important ones:

◆ Choice of data types

◆ Early-binding

◆ String concatenation

Choosing Data Types

The data types that you choose for storing and passing information and performing calculations in your solutions can have a serious impact upon their performance. It is important for the Microsoft exam that you be aware of several of the more common mistakes that you can make in your physical designs.

If possible, it is generally best to choose long integers for arithmetic. This has to do with the structure of the underlying Windows APIs, which typically use longs for parameters. Using anything else will, therefore, usually require a type conversion before a Windows API can use it.

Another thing that can adversely affect the performance of your solutions is the use of Collections rather than arrays for storing simple data. In languages where Collections are not easily available (such as C++), this is not much of an issue. But in Visual Basic, where Collections provide an attractive alternative for the dynamic storage of complicated object hierarchies, it is important to remember the considerable overhead that comes with their use. This overhead is primarily because Collections in Visual Basic utilize variants for most of their data storage.

Use Collections only when absolutely necessitated by the complex nature of the data you must store. Designing and implementing your own data structures will create more work for you as a developer but improve performance considerably.

Early Binding

Early binding occurs whenever you declare—at compilation time—that a piece of memory will be used for the storage of a particular kind of COM object. Simply declaring that a piece of memory will be used for the storage of some kind of COM object is not sufficient for early binding. What will happen instead is that at runtime, the client application will have to rediscover all the methods and properties available on your object *every time it is used.* This will cause an obvious performance hit.

For example, in Visual Basic an early-binding code snippet might take the form

```
Dim x as BillingStuff.Invoice
```

Whereas a late-binding bit of code would look like the following:

```
Dim x as Object
```

So, clearly one key difference between early binding and late binding is that early binding requires that a programmer know as he or she is creating a solution what kind(s) of data will need to be stored at various points in the code. The payoff for this knowledge and planning,

> **NOTE**
>
> **Data Type Conversions**   Where performance is concerned, remember a simple rule: Converting between data types is always expensive. Avoid it by using the appropriate data type from the start wherever possible.

however, is that the time required to instantiate these objects at runtime is greatly reduced. Also, the memory required to store these objects is much less.

For more information on this topic, see "How Binding Affects ActiveX Component Performance" in the MSDN Library.

Avoiding String Concatenation

The final common blunder related to performance in creating a solution's physical design is to rely on string concatenation. An example is combining the string "ABC" with the string "XYZ" to create the string "ABCXYZ." Because of the multiple pointer manipulations and memory-to-memory copying operations that must be performed by the OS to support this, it is better to avoid these operations whenever possible.

The Logic Tier's Impact on Performance at BookWare

The potential logic tier performance blunder at BookWare might lay in the difference between early and late binding. Until recently, Microsoft Word was not generally able to early bind with components.

Fortunately, more recent versions of Microsoft Word have included Visual Basic for Applications (VBA). This is a subset of the Visual Basic language that allows for the setting of object references at design time, thus enabling the use of early binding.

All this is relevant at BookWare because of its plans to redesign its author submissions and editorial revisions process using Microsoft Word to control objects over the network via DCOM. If early binding could not be used in this process for some reason, the performance hits involved in instantiating these objects could become quite significant.

The User Interface Tier

Of all the layers in your *n*-tier solutions, the user-interface tier will probably be the least essential to achieving satisfactory real performance in your solutions. It will behoove you on the exam, however, to have a good understanding of the general kinds of user-interface issues affecting your solution's performance.

Number of Controls

A direct relationship exists between the number of ActiveX controls on a form and the amount of time that it takes for a computer to load and display that form. The reason is that the code for each control must first be located, then loaded into the memory of whichever computer is displaying the form in question.

The situation is made even worse if the form in question happens to be running in a browser across a slow network. It is not uncommon for a single ActiveX control to be larger (in bytes) than the entire rest of the page on which it is located. This can add considerably to the load time of a page.

Number of Active Forms or Dialog Boxes

A direct relationship exists between the number of active forms or dialog boxes in an application and the amount of time that it takes for a computer to load and execute that application. The reason is that the code for each form or dialog box must first be located, and then loaded into the memory of whichever computer is running the application in question.

The User Interface's Impact on Performance at BookWare

As is true in most cases, the user interface at BookWare has made little, if any, impact on performance.

> **NOTE**
>
> **Perceived Performance** Although the user-interface layer's impact on real performance may be minimal, recall from Chapter 3, "PASS ME Analysis," that issues of perceived and expected performance must be addressed. The user-interface layer's role in affecting these kinds of performance can be considerable.

AVAILABILITY

Availability determines when and how people can use your system to perform their work. In planning the physical designs for your solutions, you will make many decisions that may exert an influence over their ultimate availability. These design influences can occur on each of the three tiers in an *n*-tier solution.

The Data Tier

The data tier can influence your solution's availability in three primary ways:

◆ The amount of downtime required for maintenance

◆ Disaster recovery

◆ Scalability lockouts

Downtime Required for Maintenance

Every time that you have to take your system down for maintenance, it becomes unavailable to the people who need to use it. This, obviously, will have an effect on the perceived availability of your solution. Two kinds of maintenance downtime are possible—scheduled and unscheduled.

Scheduled maintenance downtime is usually considered the lesser of two evils in business. On one hand, it is downtime, and downtime is never a good thing. On the other hand, the fact that it can be announced ahead of time usually gives people a chance to work around whenever the outage will occur.

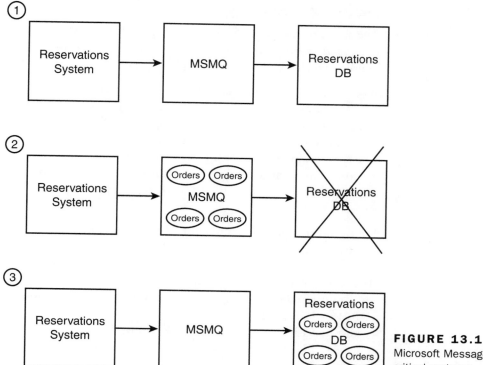

FIGURE 13.1
Microsoft Message Queue and mission-critical systems.

Unscheduled maintenance downtime is always bad. This occurs whenever something in a system breaks to the point where a repair is needed immediately before it can continue functioning. For example, a hard-disk crash that makes all data on the device instantly unreadable constitutes such unscheduled maintenance.

Sometimes even unscheduled maintenance downtimes are preceded by warning signs that allow for some degree of advanced notice to the user community. In the previous example of a hard-disk crash, this might be the faint whirring sound that often signals an approaching drive disaster. Also, recall the concept of alerts that we discussed in Chapter 10, "The Data Tier." Using these, it might be possible to arrange for a warning to be sent to a SQL Server administrator whenever disk space is almost full.

Disaster Recovery

The ability to restore a system when things go horribly wrong is called *disaster recovery*. Disaster recovery comes in two main flavors: built-in and technical support.

If you can afford the time and resources to build disaster-recovery routines into your solutions, the availability of your system will be greatly enhanced. One benefit to this approach is that recovery can begin the instant that a disaster occurs, rather than having to first be discovered by a human being. Another advantage is that this approach can ultimately be cheaper to the solution's owner than having to retain the services of personnel specially trained to deal with such emergencies.

On the other hand, occasions occur when a technical-support approach to disaster recovery is probably just as good as (if not better than) a built-in one. One example is on a large, enterprise-level database system (such as SQL Server) where the maintenance tasks are complex and ongoing enough to justify a full-time staff position (DBA) anyhow. In cases such as this, it might be just as well to entrust the task of disaster recovery to a human being. After all, someone will have to be charged with performing ongoing maintenance whether a disaster happens or not.

Scalability Lockouts

The single most common way that a busy system will find its availability affected by its physical design is in the form of scalability lockouts. A scalability lockout occurs whenever the number of users and clients contending for system resources exceeds that system's total capacity. In cases such as this, a few outcomes are possible.

The first way in which a scalability lockout can be brought about is by exceeding the capacity of a network link. In these instances, the amount of traffic that is attempting to travel to and from a server in a system becomes too great. This problem typically manifests itself in the form of network timeouts.

Even when the network is capable of handling the amount of traffic being sent and received, the server itself sometimes cannot. Sometimes the amount of work that is being requested of a server exceeds the amount of memory available on that server. Other times, the sheer complexity of the calculations being requested exceeds the speed of its processor. A third possibility could be that the number of connections permitted by the server's license is exceeded. In all these instances, the server will be forced to ask its clients to wait a little bit longer, and this will reduce your solution's overall availability.

The Data Tier's Impact on Availability at BookWare

One potential stumbling block to availability exists in the physical design of BookWare's data tier. The DBA claims that he must do a rather lengthy database reindexing at the end of every month. The case study doesn't say whether system access is affected during such times, but we can be reasonably sure that system performance cannot possibly be as good as at other noncompacting times.

The Logic Tier

The logic tiers in your solutions can have a direct impact on their availability. In short, your system's availability will be reduced by logic tier requirements for so-called end of period procedures. The reliability of the code in this tier to do what it is supposed to do is another key factor in determining the ultimate availability of your solutions.

Downtime Required for End-of-Period Routines

In the previous section on the data tier and availability, we discussed the negative effect that maintenance can have on availability. End-of-period routines are similar to this concept, but they occur in the logic tier rather than in the data tier.

An end–of-period routine is any series of procedures that must be run on a periodic basis to transform the information in your solution appropriately. For example, an accounting package might need to close the books on a fiscal year every July 1.

Some end-of-period routines purposely block continued access to a solution to make for a logical cut-off in some kind of chronological grouping. In the case of our accounting application, this grouping would be a single fiscal year's financial transactions.

More commonly, solutions will continue to be available during end-of-period routines, but at the cost of noticeably degraded performance.

Reliability

The great wildcard in system availability is the reliability of the code in your logic tier. Code is reliable if it consistently does what it is intended to do. It is unreliable if it does not. You can increase the reliability of the code in the logic tiers of your solutions in four good ways:

◆ Testing

◆ Bullet-proofing

◆ Logging

◆ Simplicity of design

Testing your code is probably the most obvious of these three. Good testing is difficult to do properly, however. In general, proper code testing begins with a sufficient sample size. This means putting your code through plenty of potential situations, both correct and incorrect, to observe how it behaves.

A logic-tier component governing withdrawals from a bank account, for example, should be tested with deposits of negative amounts as well as positive. This is to ensure that the code responds correctly even in the absence of correct input.

Another important aspect to proper testing is guaranteeing a testing group that is large enough and diverse enough. This is to guarantee that a wide cross-section of possible situations will be thought of and tested for ahead of time.

Bullet-proofing your code is the art of making sure that your solution will avoid completely melting down, even when the inputs it receives are absolutely insane. Probably the classic case of this is the "I clicked it twice" syndrome. In short, any application that you build will have at least one user who insists on performing the most critical step twice every time he or she uses it.

Now, consider the case of a credit card charging program. What if this problem user hits the Start button twice. Will everyone's credit cards get charged twice? A bullet-proofed application will keep track of how many times such an event should occur and politely refuse to exceed that number.

The very least that you can do to ensure the reliability of the logic in your solutions is to provide some capacity for logging. When your code is put into a mode where it is logging, it should keep track of every step that it performs. That way, if something proves to have been done in error, at least the exact nature of the error will be known so that efforts at reversing the damage can be more intelligently directed.

In the example of our credit card charging program, a log for the application would show credit card numbers showing up twice within the same batch. This would be an obvious sign that something went wrong and would greatly assist in generating a charge reversal batch for the credit card processor.

The final way that your logic tier can enhance the reliability of your application is through the simplicity of its design. The key rule to remember here is K.I.S.S.—Keep It Simple, Stupid. For example, having one application preprocess a file and drop it into a directory where it will be downloaded and used by another application is inherently unreliable. There are too many moving pieces, links in the chain, or (put simply) "things to go wrong." A better idea in this case is to write a single application that is capable of processing the data where it lives.

The Logic Tier's Impact on Availability at BookWare

It is important to reinforce the difference between scheduled maintenance and an end-of-period routine at this point. The database compacting mentioned in the case study is scheduled maintenance because it may require making the system unavailable so that the technologies involved (that is, the database server) can do the job (compacting) properly.

If this had been an end-of-period routine, any loss of availability would have been required by the nature of the business logic involved. In our case study, this would most likely be an end-of-year routine required to properly assess tax liabilities or similar financial circumstances.

SECURITY

Security is the art of preventing people from doing anything that they aren't supposed to do. The effectiveness of your solution in performing this prevention will ultimately depend on the strength of your physical design.

At the most basic level, your data tier should focus on preventing unauthorized access to the information used and produced by your solution. The logic tier, on the other hand, should focus on restricting use and visibility of the business rules governing your solution's operations. And at the highest level, your user-interface components should provide the means to control access to the controls and feedback mechanisms used in the operation of your solution.

The Data Tier

The data tier of any solution has the ultimate responsibility for ensuring the security of any data stored by that solution. The best mechanisms for securing your solution's data are the following:

◆ Using views

◆ Encrypting transmissions

◆ Auditing

Using Views

Views are database objects that look like tables but that actually contain no data themselves. Instead, views present certain perspectives on the data contained in other tables within the same database. In this sense, the queries in Microsoft Access can be thought of as views.

The main use for views in securing your solution's data is to limit the columns that can be seen within a given table. For example, Table 13.1 shows some sample sales records for an imaginary company.

TABLE 13.1

SAMPLE SALES TABLE

Salesperson	Product	Customer	Revenue	Commissions
Michael Nesmith	Liquid Paper	Rhinegold Industries	$32.00	$3.20
Micky Dolenz	Stationery	Valkyrie Production	$84.75	$9.00
Peter Tork	Ballpoints	Sigfried Corporation	$18.82	$1.88
Davy Jones	Ballpoints	Twilight Limited	$47.50	$4.75
Michael Nesmith	Glue	Sigfried Corporation	$22.19	$2.21
Micky Dolenz	Stationery	Valkyrie Corporation	$32.00	$4.00

Notice that everyone is getting paid 10 percent commissions in this table except for Micky Dolenz, who is getting slightly more (10 percent rounded up to the nearest dollar). Because letting the other sales people find out about this might lead to internal dissension, your first reaction might be to prevent all access to the information in this table.

But what if some of it is needed by the salespeople so that they can do their jobs? Suppose, for example, that every salesperson is expected to turn over customers calling to whichever salesperson first serviced that customer. In this case, the wise course of action would be to create a read-only view based on the preceding table that shows only the name of the salesperson and the company (See Table 13.2). We could safely give our salespeople access to this view.

TABLE 13.2

SAMPLE SALES VIEW

Salesperson	Customer
Michael Nesmith	Rhinegold Industries
Micky Dolenz	Valkyrie Productions

continues

TABLE 13.2	*continued*

SAMPLE SALES VIEW

Salesperson	*Customer*
Peter Tork	Sigfried Corporation
Davy Jones	Twilight Limited
Michael Nesmith	Sigfried Corporation
Micky Dolenz	Valkyrie Corporation

In actual practice, it might also be wise to sort this view on company name and remove duplicate entries.

The capability to do this using a simple view or query varies from database to database, however.

Encrypting Transmissions

Encrypting the transmission of the data in your solution is another approach to increasing your system's security. This will assist you because, without encryption, it may be possible for other people on the same network as your solution to snoop (that is, intercept and examine) data packets as they flow between users and your solution. If the network used to connect your solutions and their users is the Internet, you can imagine how many potential eavesdroppers exist on a network as big as this! The technologies that you should be most familiar with for the Microsoft exam are called SSL and the Cryptography API (CryptoAPI).

SSL stands for Secure Sockets Layer. This is supported by both the Netscape and the Internet Explorer browsers, as well as most popular Web servers. SSL is used primarily for encrypting transmissions on the World Wide Web. You are using SSL whenever you visit a Web site with a URL that begins with "https" rather than "http." The idea is that every piece of information sent while in this mode is encrypted using public-key encryption, guaranteeing that only the server at the other end of the transmission is able to decode and understand your information.

The Cryptography API (CryptoAPI) is Microsoft's way of providing a standardized framework for applications that need to encrypt and decrypt information using public-key encryption. The actual functionality for performing this work requires the presence of one or more cryptography providers that implement the prescribed Microsoft interfaces. Like all public key encryption, the possession of a public-key certificate and key is also required.

Auditing

Auditing is intended not to prevent unauthorized access to your system, but instead to detect when such access has occurred. This enables you to respond quickly and take whatever measures (for example, unplugging the affected computer from the network or phone line) are needed to stop the break-in as soon as possible.

Three important requirements for successful auditing are the following:

◆ Monitor who is doing what.

◆ Monitor failed access attempts.

◆ Log all changes to data.

To begin with, by using your system's auditing features, you should be able to figure out all the people currently using your system at any point in time. Also, you should be able to get a pretty good general idea of what these people are doing.

Failed access attempts should be brought immediately to your attention without your having to go looking for them. This might take the form of an email. Or in particularly serious cases (for example, a failed attempt to log on as Administrator or root), you might want to have the entire system become unavailable until it is reset in some special way.

Finally, your systems should all provide a way to go back and see all the changes that have been made to their data. This need not go back to the very dawn of time. It should, however, go back as far as you think it would take for malicious damage to show up. In other words, if you think it would take a week for damaged data to show up, be able to see changes going back a week. If it would take just a day, you need to go back only a day.

NOTE

Administrators, Clients, Guests, and Groups   Recall from Chapter 3 that four primary roles are associated with security implementation. Administrators are the only security roles empowered to alter the security setting of others. Clients are internal users of your solutions. Guests are external users, such Web browsers. Groups are collections of one or more of the previous three roles.

The Data Tier's Impact on Security at BookWare

The greatest security risk at BookWare would be that an author's submissions might be stolen while in transit. Whether this is an entirely valid concern depends on the nature of BookWare's network connectivity.

If any part of the BookWare network uses the Internet to transport data from the authors to their internal servers, a certain danger exists of submissions being stolen. This is because a message may pass through many servers on the Internet before reaching its final destination. On the other hand, if the network at BookWare is strictly a private one, probably no need exists to worry about packets being snooped.

The Logic Tier

The logic-tier components in your solutions also have an effect on the ultimate security or insecurity of your solutions. To increase the security of your solutions, you should begin by designing your components in a way that makes it difficult to use them for intentionally malicious purposes. Beyond this, you should endeavor to strictly control who can access your distributed components at all.

Distributed Component Security

A properly designed business-logic tier component will make it difficult for a user to intentionally perform malicious acts through its use. One thing you should look at in ensuring that this is the case with your components is the methods you provide with your objects. The other thing you should examine closely is the parameters for those methods.

In deciding on the methods you will provide on your business objects, think twice before adding one that has an obviously malicious purpose. For example, a business object designed to facilitate the administration of a disk farm might reasonably include a method called Format that would format a given disk. In a secure environment, however, you would probably opt to avoid automating such a potentially disastrous activity in favor of requiring a manual approach.

This approach is roughly analogous to removing all the really sharp knives from your kitchen under the pretense that somebody might get stabbed. This is logical only under circumstances where a danger is truly present. Remember this before depriving yourself of potentially useful methods in your business objects.

IN DEPTH: INTERFACES AND MTS

One benefit to using MTS for distributed systems is its capability to specify different permissions for each interface on a single COM component. It does this through close integration with the underlying NT security system and its role-based permission structure.

It should also be noted that seemingly innocuous methods can occasionally be used in ways that can prove disastrous, whether through intentional malice or simple ignorance. For example, a method designed to check someone's social security number might take a single string as a parameter. If someone passes a string consisting of several gigabytes worth of whitespace, the danger of memory exhaustion exists.

Therefore, a well-designed business object always implements strict controls on the range of values that it permits as parameters for its methods and properties.

The final concept that must looked at when examining the security of your logic-tier components is the degree of control available over who can use your objects in the first place. Under DCOM, all component access is controlled by so-called ACLs, or Access Control Lists. Access Control Lists simply are lists maintained by DCOM for each distributed component indicating which usernames (as provided by the operating system in use—invariably Windows NT) are allowed to use them.

The Logic Tier's Impact on Security at BookWare

The existing system at BookWare presents little or no great dangers to security in its middle tier because all business logic at BookWare is currently included in the clients and servers themselves, without any use of distributed components. All this may change in the proposed solution, however.

In the proposed solution, Microsoft Word will serve as a client for both authors and editors accessing ElectroBook-specific functionality over the network via DCOM. It will be very important under this new system to ensure that these objects are not accessible by nonemployees.

The User Interface Tier

All good security begins at the user interface tier. Concepts affecting security at the user interface level that you should be familiar with for the Microsoft exam include the following:

◆ Password protection

◆ Automatic logoffs

◆ Cookies

Password Protection

Using a password to prevent unauthorized access to your solutions is probably the simplest and most familiar approach to security. Using this approach, users are considered valid if they can provide a certain secret phrase that is known only to the system and (hopefully) legitimate users.

The first problem with this approach is that the text of passwords can usually be found fairly easily in code. This means that you should try to avoid coding something along the following lines:

```
If attempted_password = "sesame" then
        LetThemIn()
Else
        TurnThemAway()
End If
```

If you do put something like this in your code, someone is bound to come along sooner or later and find the sesame password in your code. This can be done even after compilation!

A better approach is to store the actual password in a database, where access can be strictly controlled. The only problem here is that the user will still have to type the password. If this password is sent across the network for any reason, it can still potentially be seen and stolen.

Even if you avoid both of the pitfalls, a final factor must be considered. Except in the case of very large and/or obscure passwords, it is usually possible to run programs that will produce successful "cracks" in a relatively short period of time. These kinds of programs try every word in the dictionary, common keyboard patterns, and so on and so forth. To safeguard against these, you must implement strict guidelines in your code and organization that prohibit easily guessed passwords.

The following are some examples of common rules for business passwords:

◆ Nothing that can be found in a standard dictionary

◆ No names of friends, relatives, or pets

◆ Must contain at least one letter

◆ Must contain at least one number

◆ Must be at least five characters in length

Automatic Logoff After Time Lapse

Even after you have successfully navigated the pitfalls of proper password security, your solution may still not be entirely safe. If a legitimate user logs in to your solution and then leaves the computer unattended, it is possible for unauthorized personnel to access your system using that terminal.

The best way to eliminate this possibility is to design your solution to automatically log off users after a certain period of inactivity. You will want to take the nature of your solution carefully into account when determining how much inactivity is too much. For example, if your application has to perform many advanced calculations requiring hours to produce a final answer for your users, you should not set the timeout length to anything less than this. Otherwise, it will be quite impossible for your users to ever get their answers!

A good compromise is probably to design your application to lock rather than to log out. This way, all the work that is in progress at the point of inactivity will be retained. All that is required to return to business as usual is the repeated entry of the user's password.

Cookies

Although not entirely a user-interface issue, an issue of security remains that you should be aware of for the Microsoft exam: cookies. A cookie is a piece of information that is sent to a browser by a Web server and that is stored on the client computer.

This is how an electronic commerce site can seem to remember you from one visit to the next without always having to ask who you are. Each time you visit the site, it asks for the cookie it stored on your computer. If your browser is able to supply it, the site is able to identify you. If not, you must log in again.

It is important to note that a cookie cannot contain any information about you or your computer that you have not already given the site that put it there. The information in the cookie must be given by the server creating it, and it would have no way of knowing anything about you unless you (or your browser) told it.

The other important thing to remember is that a site can ask for your browser to send it only the cookies that it has placed there itself. It would not be possible, for example, for Microsoft's Web site to ask for all the cookies that Sun may have put there. Whether it would want to and what it might do with them if it could is left as an exercise for the readers' imagination.

The User Interface's Impact on Security at BookWare

Authors or editors could be required to enter a password every time that they log in to BookWare's network. For further security, users could be automatically logged off of BookWare's network after a certain period of inactivity. Writing and editing really shouldn't involve any considerable sitting and waiting for responses and computations, so we can set the threshold fairly low—three minutes, for example.

SCALABILITY

Scalability is the degree to which any system you build can continue to function efficiently as its input levels rise and fall. The ideal is that a solution should be able to run on the most basic and inexpensive machinery when the demands upon it are very light. Then, as demand continues to grow, more sophisticated and expensive machinery should be able to be added. All three tiers in an *n*-tier solution must play a part in ensuring that this is the nature of a solution's scalability.

The Data Tier

The data tier of a solution is probably the tier most often looked at as the source of scalability victories and defeats. This is the reason why scalability is one of the most frequently heard buzzwords in any advertisement for Oracle or SQL Server. To a large extent, this attitude is justified.

The most important factors influencing solution scalability at the data-tier level are

◆ Lock levels

◆ Locking philosophies

◆ Querying technologies

◆ Data-housing philosophies

Lock Levels Used

A lock is a hold placed on a database resource that prevents other users and processes from trying to update it while another user or process is already doing so. The granularity of locking provided by a database engine is one of the key factors influencing database *concurrency*. Concurrency is the measure of how many users and processes can interact with the same database at the same time without stepping on each other's toes. This is one of the key measures of scalability at the data tier.

Both SQL Server and Oracle now provide row-level locking. This means that a given user or process is now denied write access if—and only if—they are trying to access the same row at the same time as another user or process. This is considered much better (and more conducive to concurrency) than page-level locking, which is what was offered by SQL Server prior to release 7.

For more information on lock levels, see the section "Events Trigger by Other Users" in Chapter 11, "The Logic Tier."

Lock Types Used

The other key influence on concurrency at the data-tier level is the type of locking used by a solution. There are two kinds of locking: pessimistic and optimistic. As their names imply, the appropriate kind for you to use has much to do with your estimation of the likelihood of a collision between competing data access requests.

The pessimistic approach puts a lock on as soon as a cursor reaches the needed data. This is done regardless of whether any intention exists to write to or otherwise change it. In other words, the lock is placed whether it is needed or not. It is not removed until the cursor has completely moved off the affected record.

Figure 13.2 graphically contrasts the amount of time required to establish both kinds of locking. Notice that pessimistic locking requires substantially more time than optimistic locking.

In contrast, the optimistic approach won't lock until it actually begins a read/write operation. This is done strictly to ensure that the data isn't switched by another process midway through the current process's input/output procedure.

The benefit to optimistic locking is that the row or page (depending on the locking level) remains available for general use longer than with pessimistic locking. The benefit to pessimistic locking is a reduced risk of multiple processes being able to alter each other's data.

Optimistic locking is better for concurrency; therefore, it is better for scalability. Use it whenever you are reasonably sure that the chances of coinciding requests for the same areas of the database are slight. On the other hand, when you know that the chances of data contention are high, you may want to consider pessimistic locking. Pessimistic locking is better for ensuring data *consistency* rather than concurrency.

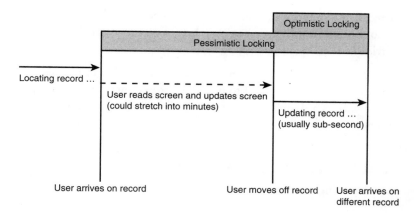

FIGURE 13.2
Optimistic versus pessimistic locking.

Querying Technology

One additional way exists in which your solution's data tier can affect your solution's scalability. This is through the querying technology that it uses to produce its results.

The most primitive of all querying technologies is sometimes called a *forward searching*, or table scan approach. This is a fancy way of saying that any piece of data you request will be looked for by the database engine starting at the very beginning of all records and proceeding one-by-one until it has found the right answer.

Forward-searching technologies can produce reasonably good results with small data sets and whenever the requested data happens to fall close to the start of the data set. Their performance worsens quickly as the amount of data in the database increases.

Hashing technologies are an improvement on this approach. Using hashing, a formula is applied to all data that is intended for storage in a database. This formula produces a result (generally a number) indicating where in the database the data should be stored. When the time comes to retrieve the data, the database applies the same formula in reverse.

Variations on binary searching form the basis for most of the high-end database engines available. To perform a binary search, data must first be sorted. A record exactly in the middle of the data is then read. If this is the record being sought, the search is finished. Otherwise, the database now at least knows that half of the data is either too high or too low and can be removed from further consideration in this search. The process repeats until the correct record is found with the remaining half of data always being itself divided in half.

The benefit to binary searching is that, as the number of records increases, the time required to perform a search increases only very slightly. In fact doubling the amount of data from 2 million to 4 million rows requires only one additional database lookup!

Data Housing Philosophies

Data housing refers to the approach that your organization takes to the location and storage of its data. At one end of the spectrum, you may decide to store everything that ever passes through your system in the same place for all eternity. At the opposite end, you might elect to retain only the last few days' transactions and completely drop everything else.

Probably the most common compromise between these two extremes is an archiving system that retains some nucleus of data in easily accessible storage and moves the rest offline. For example, an Internet Service Provider is probably interested in the call records of its users only over the past couple of months. Everything older than this can probably be moved to tape or optical recordings kept in a vault.

A variation on the preceding approach is when, rather than using tape or optical storage, the older data is simply transferred to another nonproduction system, called a data warehouse. This system is designed and implemented specifically for such tasks as decision support and market analysis. This typically entails a greater degree of denormalization, which we discussed at some length in Chapter 10.

The Data Tier's Impact on Scalability at BookWare

Next, we will illustrate all three querying technologies described in the preceding section as they might be applied at BookWare. The task at hand will be that of locating the author associated with a given social security number.

The forward-searching process is the simplest. The very first author record is read and its social security number examined. If this is the one being sought, the search is finished. Otherwise, the next author's record is examined. This process repeats until the end of the database is reached or the social security number is found.

A hashing algorithm, on the other hand, applies some (largely arbitrary) formula to the social security number being sought. For the sake of the example, we'll say that it adds all the digits and uses this as the number of bytes from the beginning of the database to begin looking. Given the social security number 434-72-9029 then, the database first looks for the credit card number 40 bytes into the database. If it doesn't find it, the database proceeds in a forward-searching manner from this location until either the end of the database is reached or the social security number is found.

Finally, a binary search requires that all the authors are sorted first according to social security number. Then, the record exactly in the middle of the database is examined. This record has a social security number that is either correct, too high, or too low. If it is too high, the top half of the current data is dropped from further consideration. If it is too low, the bottom half is dropped. In both of these cases, the procedure repeats until the correct number is found.

The Logic Tier

The influence exerted by your solution's logic tier over its scalability is determined largely by the qualities of the technologies used to distribute its components. For example, a certain instantiation overhead is associated with every new object created by your solutions. Similarly, the life span of these objects will affect your solution's scalability by consuming resources that could otherwise be used in the operation of your systems.

Instantiation Overhead

The performance hit that occurs every time one of your solutions needs to create a new object for itself is called that object's *instantiation overhead*. Some of this overhead takes the form of additional memory requirements. Some of it is the processor cycles needed to properly initialize your new objects.

Logic-tier servers tend to come in a few, distinct varieties:

◆ In-process

◆ Out-of-process

◆ Remote

An in-process server runs in the same process space as the process that requests its creation. These are, by far, the most efficient components to create and maintain. The first time one of your solutions needs a component of this type, the code for it will be loaded into memory. After this, the overhead for creating additional instances of the same type is negligible. In a Windows environment, in-process servers are typically stored in DLL and OCX file types.

One possible performance drawback exists to using in-process servers, however. If the component is single-threaded, it will "borrow" the thread of its client to get its work accomplished. In this instance, the work of its client will be blocked until the component finishes. From a performance standpoint, this is no better than having the component's code as a built-in part of the client application itself.

Out-of-process servers run in the address space of a process external to the one that requests their creation. This requires additional overhead for as long as the component is in use because some kind of communications medium must be maintained between the two process spaces. The work of maintaining this communications medium is called *cross-process marshalling*.

In general, cross-process marshalling places a performance burden on your solutions that might not otherwise be there. To begin with, a certain level of security checking must take place to ensure that the calling process(es) have the permissions required to access the target process(es). Most important, however, the parameters used by your components must be specially packaged and unpackaged for use in remote procedure calls. Depending on the complexity of the data types used in your procedures, the overhead required for this may prove very nontrivial.

The performance hit that occurs at the time of component creation differs depending on the exact variety of out-of-process server being called. Out-of-process servers come in two varieties: multiuse and single-use.

A multiuse out-of-process server requires the creation of an external process only upon instantiation of the first object of its type. Every additional object of its type created thereafter will exist within the address space of that same process. With this kind of out-of-process server, the first object of a type created requires the worst performance hit.

The neediest kind of out-of-process server of them all is the single-use variety. These components spawn a separate process for every object created. The only benefit to this approach is that the objects involved are supremely isolated from each other. Using this scheme, it is very difficult for one component to interfere with the operations of another.

Remote servers are the most intense of all in their performance requirements. The reason is that communications between separate processes must not only be maintained, but they must be transmitted across some kind of networking environment as well. Because the fastest network is still not nearly as fast as the internal wiring of an average computer, remote components can be a real drain on your solution's performance and, therefore, on scalability as well.

Figure 13.3 illustrates the process and machine boundaries involved in the creation and use of all these kinds of components. In panel 1, Process A is making use of a single in-process server that is located (by definition) entirely within the confines of its own process space. In panel 2, two processes (A and C) are making joint use of a single out-of-process server located within its own process space (Process B). Panel 3 is also an illustration of out-of-process component use, but in this case the server has been set to single use, forcing the creation of a separate process for every instance of the same server (Processes B and D). Finally, panel 4 shows a process (A) calling a remote server via DCOM on a different machine.

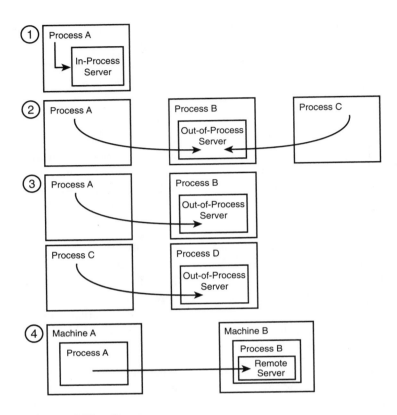

FIGURE 13.3
In-process, out-of-process, and remote
servers.

Object Life Span

The life span of an object can affect the scalability of your solution
by tying up valuable resources that could be otherwise utilized. In
most cases, the resources associated with an object should be
returned to general availability as soon as the object is no longer
needed. The quicker this turnaround can be achieved, the better.

You may wonder how a system can know when an object is no
longer in use. Under COM, a count of the number of references to a
given object is maintained at all times. When this count reaches 0,
the object is removed from memory and all resources are released
back to the operating system.

Software that maintains a constant pool of available objects, such as
Microsoft Transaction Server, can have a positive impact on solution
scalability. Because objects are usually already on hand when needed,
the constant overhead of instantiation is greatly reduced. On the
other hand, improperly designed MTS objects that are kept constantly on hand may consume valuable resources!

Therefore, any components that you intend to utilize with MTS should be designed to be stateless. In other words, they should be designed in a way that allows them to be created, to do useful work, and to be destroyed. No persistence of data should be required between steps.

IN DEPTH: CONTEXT SWITCHING

The time that an operating system spends coordinating the CPU's shift from process to process is called context switching. On computers with many simultaneous processes and limited processing power, this may wind up consuming the bulk of the processors' time. For this reason, it is usually wise to limit the number of processes running for a given solution based on the number of processors available on a given computer.

The Logic Tier's Impact on Scalability at BookWare

The components proposed for BookWare's new solution are all of the remote variety. They are not in-process because they won't be running in the same process space as Microsoft Word, which will be serving as their client. In fact, they won't even be running on the same machines. Instead, they will be running across the BookWare network on some server machines located at the company's facilities.

Making this matter worse is the fact that the proposed connectivity between the clients and the servers are analog phone connections. Analog modems provide the absolute slowest forms of network connectivity, and this will become painfully obvious in doing DCOM across them. Bookware will have to pay particular attention to issues of cross-marshalling performance as it designs its new solution. Among other things, this means using the simplest parameter types (integer, string, and so on) possible for its remote procedure calls. It may also justify some loosening of security restrictions on the components that must be accessed over the analog lines.

The User Interface

The scalability of a solution is probably least affected by the physical design of its user interface.

Valid Value Ranges for Controls

It is possible to make the upscaling of an otherwise good design more difficult by making the controls and indicators on a user interface with ranges that are just too small. For example, a progress bar might be used to indicate how close to its threshold the pressure on a submarine's hull has become. If the maximum level is known to be 3 tons per inch, then 3 tons might be hard coded at the extreme end of the bar with marks for 1 and 2 along the way.

Now, what happens when the technology behind submarine hulls improves and we can now pilot subs to much greater depths without worrying about implosions? Suppose we can go up to 15 tons per inch. Of course, we can redesign our progress bar, but a more scalable solution wouldn't even require that we take this step.

A better idea, in this case, would probably be to design the progress bar using percentages right from the start. After all, what we're really interested in knowing about under these circumstances is how close we are to imploding. With percentages, 100 percent of capacity is 100 precent of capacity—whether capacity is 3 tons or 15.

The User Interface's Impact on Scalability at BookWare

With regard to solution scalability, no readily apparent flaws are present in the user interface tier at BookWare.

MAINTAINABILITY

Maintainability is a measure of how easy it is to keep your solution as useful to its users as it is when you first put it into production. The data tier contributes to this mainly in terms of the ease of its operation and the severity of whatever ill effects might arise from its neglect. The manner in which the logic tier is built is more relevant to its maintainability than to its final content. The user interface's main contribution to maintainability involves the location where its caption strings are stored.

The Data Tier

Two important procedures determine the data tier's contribution to solution maintainability. The first of these is whether it is a database that uses logs and, if so, whether it is capable of clearing them itself. The second is whether it is able to compact itself at appropriate times.

Clearing Logs

Most enterprise-level databases, such as SQL Server and Oracle, generate logs of all activity as they operate. One of the ideas behind this is that if anything goes wrong, the logs can be used to reverse some or all of the damage.

A danger in using this kind of system is that the space (typically disk space) available for storing the logs will run out. Without space to store additional logs, Oracle and SQL Server will cease accepting requests for additional activities. Fortunately, both servers offer options for automatic handling of logs when all available space is consumed. Sometimes they can be automatically archived to a different location, Or in the absence of an additional location, they can always be truncated.

If the database server your solution uses is the type that will stop functioning when log space is exhausted, the maintainability of your solution will be reduced. If it is the sort that should be able to deal with logs on its own (such as Oracle and SQL Server), much of this loss in maintainability is recovered.

Reindexing

Most enterprise-level databases, such as SQL Server and Oracle, allow their indexes to fall gradually into a state of disrepair during everyday use. The reason is that the procedure for restoring indexes to complete accuracy is rather resource intensive.

The problem with never reindexing your databases, however, is that without this procedure your indexes will probably continue to grow obsolete until finding data takes forever.

If your database can be set to automatically reindex itself periodically or at times when it senses minimal use, the maintainability of your solution is improved. In SQL Server, this functionality is provided via the Maintenance Plan Wizard. If not, the maintainability of your system must be estimated in somewhat less-optimistic terms.

The Data Tier's Impact on Maintainability at BookWare

The DBA tells us that he has to do a manual database reindexing at the end of each month. Given BookWare's use of SQL Server, this would suggest that the DBA is not familiar with the use of the Maintenance Plan Wizard.

The Logic Tier

The way in which you create the logic-tier components for your solutions will be the ultimate determiner of whether they are maintainable. Exactly which practices make for the most and least maintainable code is debatable. For the Microsoft exam, you should be familiar with the following concepts:

◆ Advantages to general-purpose components

◆ Source control

◆ Modified Hungarian-naming standards

General-Purpose Nature of Components

In developing the physical designs for your solutions, you may often be tempted to create components that are obscure or special interest in nature. For example, you might want to have an object for Cans in one application and another one for Bottles in another. If, however, both applications are being developed for the same beverage-packaging corporation, it would be better to have a single object named Container and find ways to make it work in both applications.

The first benefit to doing this is that you will have to write that much less code because you will need to develop only one component rather than two. Another advantage to this is that general-purpose components are going to be easier for outsiders (for example, newly hired staff and/or consultants) to understand and begin using immediately.

In addition, it gives you more of an incentive to name your methods and properties reasonably. The names of methods and properties are probably a component's single greatest source of documentation, so this factor should not be taken lightly.

For example, we'll return to our bottle versus can versus container example. If you used bottles and cans, you would most likely have an unscrew method for bottles and a pop method for cans. Now, quick, what do those two methods do? You can't be nearly as certain as if we had just used a single object called container and named the method open.

Source Control

Source control is a system whereby changes made to a set of files (source code, documentation, executables) are carefully controlled and coordinated. Typically, files are all checked in to a central repository shortly after the time of their creation. The various members on a development team must all then check out a file before they may work on it and make changes.

When the files are then checked back in, the changes made by different people are merged into a finished product. Conflicts are noted and resolutions are required before the files can be checked back in. Because all changes are tracked, bad ideas can be undone using rollbacks.

Naming Standards

In addition to the names that you give to your components and their properties and methods, the names that you choose for the variables in your code are also extremely important to your solution's ultimate maintainability. The naming standard that Microsoft has demonstrated a decided preference for over time has been the so-called modified Hungarian approach.

> **EXAM TIP**
>
> **Microsoft Visual SourceSafe** The source-control technology that you are most likely to encounter on the Microsoft exam is the Microsoft Visual SourceSafe.

In this naming style, the first few letters of every private (or public, but not exposed via a public interface) variable name indicate its data type and scope. For example, a global string designed to hold a customer's social security number might be called `gstrSocNumber`. As you can tell, it is also traditional to keep the first few letters all lowercase, then capitalize at the start of each word thereafter. A few more examples follow:

◆ `lintNumberOfSales` = local, integer, number of sales

◆ `sobjPhoto` = static, object, a photo

◆ `gdblTotalDue` = global, double, total due

Note that it is a serious mistake to use this naming for variables and functions that are exposed through a public interface. This will violate encapsulation by forcing the renaming of existing methods and functions if the data types involved in their use ever change.

The Logic Tier's Impact on Maintainability at BookWare

At one point in the case study, the programmer remarks that "We really need some kind of source-control software." Of course, this is Microsoft Visual SourceSafe. If the development staff at BookWare finds and uses this to bring their development under source control, the maintainability of their solutions will be greatly increased.

The User Interface Tier

The user interface tier of your solution contributes to its maintainability through the location of its caption strings and other visual components.

Resource Files

Taken in its narrowest sense, a resource file is a Windows concept. This concept is embodied in a file used to hold various visual (and sometimes nonvisual) components, or resources. The benefit to putting these resources into a standalone file rather than hard coding them is that they become easier to swap out with other resources whenever the need may arise.

When might the need arise? The most notable example (and one with which you should be familiar for the Microsoft exam) is in the case of internationalization. If you put all your application's messages directly in your code, your task will be much harder when the time comes to ship your application to a place where they don't speak the same language. You will have to alter and recompile all your code specifically for each locality.

A better approach is to put all your caption strings into resource files appropriately labeled and maintained for each locality. This way, you can ship the same application code to all your different locations with only their resource files exchanged.

When designing interfaces for possible internationalization, it is important to provide more space than you might currently need for labels, text boxes, and so on. It is quite possible that the same text in a different language from the one currently used in your application may consume significantly more space. A good rule to follow when no other indications are available is to provide double the amount of space that would appear needed.

The User Interface's Impact on Maintainability at BookWare

The key thing to note in the case study (and to remember for the Microsoft exam) is that some international users have complained about components seeming to be arranged oddly. In the section on the Envisioned System, the editor cites Japanese colleagues on this point. The most likely cause for this is components being arranged in the standard, western top-to-bottom, left-to-right orientation.

In Japan, writing flows from right to left (and flows down a column). Therefore, a properly designed solution will be able to adapt and take on a conforming user interface when needed. Currently, the BookWare user interface does not.

EXTENSIBILITY

Extensibility is a measure of how easy it is to add to the functionality of your solution after it is in place. All three tiers in an *n*-tier solution contribute to that solution's level of extensibility.

EXAM TIP

Localization via Multiple DLLs
The approach most often recommended on Microsoft exams is to use a different DLL for each locality.

EXAM TIP

Layout Order of Components It is important to know that the proper layout for components in any application designed for internationalization is that in which the target country's language is read. For example, the components in an American application should tend to flow top to bottom and left to right. An application destined for Israel, however, should still flow top to bottom, but right to left. The reason is that Hebrew, one of the official languages of Israel, is written this way.

The Data Tier

The data stored by your solution should be completely free from assumptions about the exact position in which it is stored. Failure to refrain from making such assumptions is guaranteed to reduce your capability to extend your solutions.

On the other hand, accessing your data via parameter queries is a very good thing.

Assumptions About Row Order

Referring to rows in a database in a way that expects the data to exist in some specific order is a serious design mistake. One example is code that utilizes the binary searching techniques, which we showed you earlier in this chapter, without first verifying that the data in question has been sorted appropriately.

The danger here is that someone may have to index the tables in question differently to extend the solution's functionality. If this happens, you run the risk of having your solution break or begin returning erroneous information just as in the previous section. The code in the physical tier of any solution should always check to ensure that data is sorted as expected so that it remains extensible. This may be accomplished as simply as adding an explicit ORDER BY clause to your SQL code.

Using Parameter Queries

The best approach that can be taken to ensure extensibility at the data-tier level of your physical designs is to make extensive use of so-called parameter queries. Parameter queries are strongly related to the normal kinds of queries offered by most database engines. Unlike these simpler kinds of queries, however, parameter queries allow variables to be used in their coding that are not filled in until they are executed. The mechanism calling on the parameter query to execute provides the value for the variable.

Consider a query designed to return all the sales orders associated with a given customer. If this were built without the use of parameters, the best that could be done would be to create a query returning all the sales orders in the database. There wouldn't be any way to tell the query in advance exactly which customer's sales orders we were interested in. The solution calling the query would then have to sift through all the sales orders returned by the query looking for ones associated with the correct customer.

If a parameter query had been used, however, things would be much simpler and more efficient. The parameter query could contain logic that caused it to return only those sales orders associated with the customer represented by a certain variable. It would then be the job of the application calling the query to fill in that parameter with the customer currently being examined.

The Data Tier's Impact on Extensibility at BookWare

The DBA tells us that he creates a lot of queries that are "pretty much basic SQL, except for some parts of them that are supposed to hold variables." This is, more or less, the definition of parameter queries. It is important to note, however, that parameter queries can be created using technologies other than SQL (although this is pretty rare).

The use of parameter queries at BookWare will improve its solution's extensibility greatly. Without them, the addition of new authors and products might have necessitated the creation of entirely new queries to work with them—or worse yet, additional code in the business-logic tier components to sift the right information out of more general queries' responses.

The Logic Tier

The technology that you use to create the objects in your applications can have an enormous impact on their extensibility. Because COM (and DCOM) are the most important technologies for you to know for the exam, this section focuses on some of the unique benefits associated with these Microsoft inventions.

Language Independence

COM is a binary-level, rather than a source-level, standard for the creation of objects. One of the most important significances of this is that it is a language-independent standard. This means that a

COM object can be created in VC++ and used in a system otherwise comprised entirely of code written in Visual Basic. Conversely, a COM object can be created in Visual Basic and used in a system otherwise comprised entirely of code written in VJ++.

This is really neat and something to get quite excited about because it means that you can mix and match languages based upon what they're good for. Perhaps you like to write most of your stuff in Visual Basic because it is an excellent general-purpose language with a fairly easy-to-understand syntax. However, suppose you have some small piece in one of your applications that requires a three-dimensional object to be drawn and rotated in every conceivable direction per the user's request (CAD/CAM, for example). Visual Basic may prove too slow for this requirement, so you might write the code for this in VC++ and use COM to tie it all together.

COM technologies also exist for a variety of other languages. So long as you use Microsoft's JDK software, you can do the same thing with VJ++ objects. One reason for doing this might be if you had one small portion of an application that you thought you might like to use on other platforms at some point in time.

Versioning Support

The problem of versioning in systems comprising multiple components has always been very tricky. Suppose, for example, that you have a pharmaceutical application designed to automatically prescribe drugs and watch for possibly harmful interactions. Furthermore, suppose that this application uses version 2.0 of a popular third-party component called Chemist for doing its in-depth chemical analysis.

What should happen if someone tries to install another application on the same machine that includes version 1.0 of Chemist? If the installation software overwrites version 2.0, a good chance exists that your pharmaceutical application will stop working. Fortunately, COM provides versioning information in the Windows registry that prevents most installation software from making this mistake.

Now, what about the case where your pharmaceutical application uses version 1.0, and the other software contains version 2.0? In the days before COM, allowing this replacement would often break a client application as well because the order and types of parameters might vary greatly between component versions.

COM solves all this by requiring components complying with its standards to provide certain basic interfaces that automate access to all the other methods and properties within a component. The most commonly referred to of these interfaces are IUnknown and IDispatch. A COM client will always know how to find the methods provided by one of these two interfaces, and it will use these to find whatever additional functions it needs.

Imagine, for example, a component designed to verify that submitted passwords meet the minimum security requirements described earlier in this chapter. The initial version of this component, v1.0, might have a function called isThisAcceptable that takes a submitted password as its only parameter (a string) and returns a Boolean signaling acceptance or rejection. Version 2 of this component, however, might be enhanced to also take a second parameter—an integer specifying the degree of strictness with which the security rules should be applied in determining whether a given password is acceptable.

Without COM, a client application expecting version 1 would break when the version 2 component was installed because it would be passing only a single parameter where two were expected. Under COM, the original method would be retained as part of the original interface and the second, modified method would be found on a new, versioned interface with a different Interface GUID (IID). IUnknown and IDispatch would work to redirect clients to the interface appropriate for their expectations.

For example, imagine a geometry component that implemented an interface called IShapes. On the IShapes interface are methods such as Square, Circle, and Triangle. In the initial version of the component, Circle takes only a single parameter—the point at which the circle should be centered. After considerable user feedback, it is decided to include a second parameter—the diameter of the circle—on the second version of the component.

Under COM, this change in the signature of the Circle method would require the definition of an entirely new interface—call it IShapes2. Because all methods calls in COM must ultimately route through either IUnknown or IDispatch, these interfaces will redirect clients appropriately based on the version of the interface that they are expecting. A version 1 client would call Circle and get the IShapes version. A version 2 client would call Circle and get the IShapes2 version.

Figure 13.4 illustrates the way that COM provides versioning support for version 2 of the geometry component.

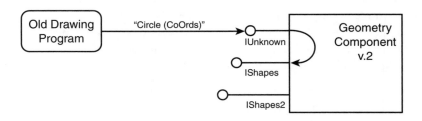

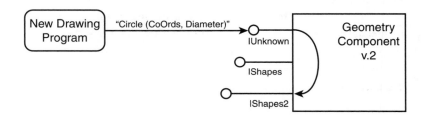

FIGURE 13.4
Why new COM components don't
break old COM clients.

The Logic Tier's Impact on Extensibility at BookWare

BookWare's programmer has indicated the company's intention to use DCOM in the construction of its envisioned systems. DCOM is a variation on the COM standard that allows for the distribution of COM components over a networked infrastructure. It provides all the same benefits in language independence and versioning support. Therefore, the logic tier's impact on extensibility at BookWare must be judged to be positive.

CHAPTER SUMMARY

In this chapter, we have endeavored to give you clear insight into the ultimate ramifications that your physical design decisions can have for the PASS ME qualities of your solutions. As defined many times previously in this text, PASS ME refers to the recurring Microsoft exam themes of performance, availability, security, scalability, maintainability, and extensibility. In this chapter, we covered each tier of a typical three-tier application's contributions to the PASS ME successes and failures of a solution.

We began this chapter by examining the impact of indexes, queues, and queries on performance. Indexes are beneficial to lookups, but not to the addition of new data. Queues allow applications disconnected from network connectivity to continue operating as if they were still connected. And queries can lead either to victory or ruin, depending on the observance of some key rules of design.

We then continued on to look at how performance can be improved through the use of early binding instead of late binding.

Forms using too many controls are likely to take longer to become visible because every control must be loaded into memory. Similarly, applications with too many forms or dialog boxes are likely to be slower in general because they consume more memory.

At this point in the chapter, we turned our attention to improving your solution's availability through superior physical design decisions. All downtime requirements are bad, but unscheduled downtime without warning is considered the absolute worst. On the other hand, a system that offers built-in disaster recovery is likely to be quite ahead of the curve in availability. In any event, however, a system that uses too much memory or network traffic can always reach a point where lockouts begin to occur.

Whenever possible, systems should be designed in a way that avoids the need to make your solution unavailable for end-of-period processing. This, combined with a process of testing, bullet-proofing, and logging for the reliability of your code can help to achieve a greater degree of availability for your solutions.

Probably the most important facet of solution development is security. At the data-tier level, we have seen how using views can help control user access to sensitive information. Encrypting

CHAPTER SUMMARY

transmissions with SSL can reduce the chance of this information being intercepted en route over a network. Providing a comprehensive capability to audit security logs in your applications will help to reduce the damage whenever security breeches may happen.

The components in the logic tier of your solutions may be secured in a number of ways. When using DCOM, the method of choice is to use access control lists (ACLs) specifying the rights and privileges of every possible user against every possible component. MTS enhances these security features by allowing access to be restricted on an interface-by-interface level to specific and predetermined roles.

At the user interface level, asking for passwords is probably the simplest and most effective approach to increasing security. Beyond this, however, it is often a good idea to provide some kind of automated logoff capability for whenever users inadvertently leave a session with your applications open.

Although technically not a part of the user interface tier, we also told you a little about cookies. These pieces of information stored on your computer by Web servers are considered mostly harmless, but they allow most of your favorite Web sites to remember things that you tell them about you on subsequent visits.

The kinds of locks provided by your solution's database engines can have a profound effect upon the scalability of your data-tier components. Optimistic locking provides greater concurrency than pessimistic locking for your solution's users, but it may come at the cost of data consistency. Similarly, row-level locking provides greater concurrency, but usually without any associated loss of consistency.

Forward searching is the most primitive of data-access technologies, essentially starting at the beginning of a set of data and looking through it until the requested data is found or the end of the data is encountered. Hashing is a major improvement that calculates the best locations for storing data by applying arbitrary formulas that convert your data into byte offsets. Binary searching is probably the most efficient of all, using a recursive approach to split a data set into smaller and smaller search areas until the correct data is found or acknowledged as missing.

CHAPTER SUMMARY

Local, in-process components can enhance solution scalability by not requiring cross-process marshalling. If they share the same threads as their clients, however, they can cause blocking in the client code that is detrimental to performance.

Out-of-process components require cross-process marshalling. Additional performance barriers exist in the case of single-use, out-of-process components because every new object instantiated will require the creation of an additional process. On other hand, these kinds of components use their own threads in the execution of their code.

Remote, out-of-process components require cross-process marshalling as well as cross-machine marshalling over network connections. The performance barriers in this case can be most pronounced over slow data connections. This can be addressed most effectively by confining development to the use of simpler data types in remote procedure parameters. The great advantage to remote components is that, in addition to their own threads, they harness the resources of additional machines for your solution's work.

COM maintains a count of all clients currently referencing every component that you instantiate under Windows. When this count falls to zero, the object is unloaded from memory and all resources associated with it are reclaimed.

The greatest challenge to scalability at the user interface level of your application is the range of your controls. If you use absolute ranges, such as real numbers on a progress bar, your applications won't be as scalable as if you use percentages.

The need to clear logs and reindex your database manually must be seen as detrimental to the maintainability of your solutions. It is better if your database engine has the capability to clear or archive its own logs when space for them is exhausted. Similarly, a database that can reindex itself on schedule or during periods of low usage is superior from a maintenance standpoint.

Creating fewer, more general-purpose components rather than more numerous special-interest components is a good way to physically design your logic tier for maintainability. Using a source-control system, such as Microsoft Visual SourceSafe, will also help you at

CHAPTER SUMMARY

KEY TERMS

- Binary searching
- Cookies
- Early binding
- Hashing
- Index
- In-process components
- Instantiation overhead
- Late binding
- Modified Hungarian naming
- Optimistic locking
- Page-level locking
- Pessimistic locking
- Queuing
- Remote components
- Resource files
- Row-level locking
- SSL
- Views
- Out-of-process components
- Visual SourceSafe
- Versioning support

this level. Finally, Modified Hungarian naming is the Microsoft-preferred method for naming variables. This approach uses the first few letters of a private (or hidden) variable's name to instantly communicate type and scope information to someone reading the code.

Another issue should be considered in physically designing your solution for greater maintainability. All the captions and other locality-dependent items in your user interface should be stored in resource files. This will greatly assist you if your ever need to internationalize your solution.

The extensibility of your solutions can be endangered by a physical design at the data-tier level that expects fields and rows to remain in a consistent order. The addition or removal of fields, or the reindexing of a table can easily upset this scheme. On the other hand, parameter queries enhance the extensibility of your solution by reserving a portion of their code for variable content that can be easily modified as your data needs change.

COM is a Microsoft technology that you should know as much as possible about for the exam. It benefits the extensibility of your solutions in two key ways: It allows you to mix and match components written in different languages. The other benefit to COM is its support for versioning your components via standard interfaces rather than byte offsets.

APPLY YOUR KNOWLEDGE

Exercises

13.1 Assessing the Impact of the Physical Design

In this exercise, we examine the impact that various physical design decisions can have on your solution's performance, availability, security, scalability, maintainability, and extensibility.

Estimated Time: 10 minutes

1. Examine Table 13.3. The left column lists a variety of physical design decisions that might be made during the construction of a solution. The right column lists ways in which these decisions might impact the usability of that solution.

2. Draw a line connecting each decision on the left to only one PASS ME entry on the right. A one-to-one relationship should exist between both sides of the table.

TABLE 13.3

EXERCISE 13.1 WORKSPACE

Physical Design Decision	*PASS ME*
Using pessimistic locking	Improved Performance
Implementing versioned component releases via COM interfaces	Degraded Performance
Avoiding the need for end-of-period routines	Improved Availability
Using SSL for all Internet transmissions	Degraded Availability
Using optimistic locking	Improved Security
Choosing a database server that stops running when its transaction logs fill	Degraded Security
Buying fewer database server licenses than you have clients	Improved Scalability
Choosing a database server that automatically reindexes itself	Degraded Scalability
Assuming a particular order for the rows in a database table	Improved Maintainability
Using collections rather than arrays	Degraded Maintainability
Turning off all auditing logs for your solution	Improved Extensibility
Indexing a mostly unique, read-only field	Degraded Extensibility

APPLY YOUR KNOWLEDGE

Answers:

Using pessimistic locking = Degraded Scalability

Implementing versioned component releases via COM interfaces = Improved Extensibility

Avoiding the need for end-of-period routines = Improved Availability

Using SSL for all Internet transmissions = Improved Security

Using optimistic locking = Improved Scalability

Choosing a database server that stops running when its transaction logs fill = Degraded Maintainability

Buying fewer database server licenses than you have clients = Degraded Availability

Choosing a database server that automatically reindexes itself = Improved Maintainability

Assuming a particular order for the rows in a database table = Degraded Extensibility

Using collections rather than arrays = Degraded Performance

Turning off all auditing logs for your solution = Degraded Security

Indexing a mostly unique, read-only field = Improved Performance

Review Questions

1. Suppose that the DBA at BookWare decides to remove all indexes from the ElectroBooks database. How would you expect this to affect your solution's performance?

2. In the user interface tier, what could be causing the editor's software at BookWare to load slowly?

3. What availability problem could be expected if the memory and network connectivity of the servers at BookWare housing components for DCOM access were suddenly and sharply reduced?

4. You are trying to devise some means for detecting when credit card numbers are being improperly used for the purchase of ElectroBook texts. What is the term for this kind of after-the-fact investigation of security breaches?

5. Suppose that BookWare wants to start offering the texts for its ElectroBooks for sale via its own site on the World Wide Web. If it wants to avoid asking repeat customers to give their names and credit cards every time they visit the site, what technology should they use for storing this information in an easily retrieved form on their customers' own computers?

6. If BookWare's DBA suddenly decides to switch from a row-level to a page-level locking scheme, what is most likely to suffer in your solution's availability?

7. BookWare informs you that it has decided to use an optimistic-locking scheme with its databases rather than pessimistic-locking. How should this improve the availability of your solutions?

8. Someone at BookWare has decided to package all the components needed to use its editor's and author's software with the software itself. This will remove the need for network access to these components via DCOM. What would now be the most efficient physical design for accessing these components instead?

APPLY YOUR KNOWLEDGE

9. All the page-count indicators in BookWare's software max out at 1,000 pages. To which of the PASS ME themes is this likely to prove detrimental?

10. The programmers at BookWare want to replace a current component called SpellChecker. If they do so using two components, called Author-Speller and EditorSpeller, why would this be a good or bad thing?

11. If BookWare wants to continue packaging its software in a single executable, what will it have to do to internationalize its solutions?

12. How would you expect a variable named gstrAuthorName to be scoped and typed?

13. Imagine that modifications are made to BookWare's author's software. Suddenly, the editor's software already in production starts breaking. If COM isn't being used, what limitation in the component technology is probably causing this?

14. The DBA at BookWare reindexes all the tables in the ElectroBooks database without warning, and all the software using it breaks. What is the most likely mistake in the physical design of the data tier?

Exam Questions

1. How could designing the electronic books' screens without scrollbars prove to be a poor design decision?

    A. Better maintainability in the user interface

    B. Poorer maintainability in the user interface

    C. Better scalability in the user interface

    D. Poorer scalability in the user interface

2. What technology could cause a drop in performance during write-intensive database operations?

    A. Versioning

    B. Instantiation overhead

    C. SSL

    D. Indexes

3. Which of the following tools can allow for the reversal of source code changes after they have already been saved?

    A. Notepad

    B. Microsoft Project

    C. Visual SourceSafe

    D. Late binding

4. Consider the problems inherent in versioning standalone components. Which of the following technologies solves most of these problems by providing versioned interfaces?

    A. COM

    B. CORBA

    C. OLE

    D. SSL

5. At what point would the decision to identify employees by the contents of a single-byte field in a database begin to hamper the extensibility of a human resources system?

    A. When the 257th employee is hired

    B. When the 1,027th employee is hired

APPLY YOUR KNOWLEDGE

C. The first time any employee is fired

D. When the 1,027th employee is fired

6. The owner of an aerospace company that builds fighter planes wants (as much as possible) to avoid altering existing code for recording his planes' flight data. Which of the following technologies could best be used to facilitate the temporary local storage of telemetry data whenever network connectivity becomes unavailable?

A. Indexing

B. Queuing

C. Early binding

D. Late binding

7. The Microsoft technology that is intended to standardize the way in which encoding services are provided is called

A. The Context Switching API

B. The Cryptography API

C. The Cross-Process Marshalling API

D. The Decision-Support API

8. When parameters are passed between processes running on different machines, what is the process called of packaging them for transmission from the client and then unpackaging them at the server?

A. Context switching

B. Cryptography

C. Cross-machine marshalling

D. Decision support

Answers to Review Questions

1. The performance of additions to BookWare's databases would be greatly improved because additional entries in an index would not need to be made for each new row. On the other hand, the performance of lookups would be greatly reduced because all data would have to be located in a forward-searching method. See "Indexing."

2. Too many forms or dialog boxes will cause software to load slower because every form or dialog box must be loaded into memory before an application can be started. See "Number of Forms or Dialog Boxes."

3. Reducing the memory and network connectivity on any machine intended as a server may cause scalability lockouts. A scalability lockout occurs when available memory on a server is not sufficient to allow the loading of an additional process for an additional user or when network connectivity is not enough to support communications with another user. See "Scalability LockOuts."

4. Auditing. Auditing is the review of logs made by the security implementation of a solution. This is done in an attempt to locate improper access after it has already occurred. See "Auditing."

5. Cookies. Cookies are pieces of information stored by a Web server on the client computers that connect to them. In this case, the cookies would contain the names and credit card numbers of customers. See "Cookies."

6. Changing from row-level to page-level locking would reduce the potential concurrency of a solution's data tier because the likelihood of a collision between the data-access requests of different users and processes would be much greater. See "Lock Levels Used."

APPLY YOUR KNOWLEDGE

7. Changing from pessimistic to optimistic locking would improve the potential concurrency of a solution's data tier because the likelihood of a collision between the data-access requests of different users and processes would be much less. See "Lock Types Used."

8. Under these circumstances, the most efficient way to access components would be as local, in-process objects. The reason is that local processes do not require cross-process marshalling. In fact, in-process components don't even require the maintenance of communications channels between processes. See "Early-binding."

9. This physical design would impose a limitation on the extensibility of this solution. The solution could not be extended for page counts in excess of 1,000 pages. See "Valid Value Ranges for Controls."

10. This would be a very bad decision from a solution-maintainability standpoint. The problem is that the programmers are substituting two special-interest components for a single general-purpose component. See "General-Purpose Nature of Components."

11. To internationalize a solution designed in this way, locality specific pieces will have to be stored in multiple resource files or DLL files. Then the same executable could be packaged for each targeted locality with a different resource file or DLL. See "Resource Files."

12. You would expect this variable to be a global string. The g at the start of a variable, under Modified Hungarian naming, is taken as the scope indicator—global. The str is intended as a type indicator—string. See "Naming Standards."

13. This would most likely be traceable to a lack of support for proper versioning. COM solves this problem by requiring certain standard interfaces through which all other methods and properties are accessed, regardless of the version of a component. See "Versioning Support."

14. The software composing the solutions at BookWare probably made assumptions about the ordering of rows in the databases' tables. Reindexing is one of many actions that can be taken on a database that will upset this ordering. See "Assumptions About Row Order."

Answers to Exam Questions

1. **D.** A screen that cannot adapt to displaying more text than called for in an initial design will have a greatly impaired scalability in its user interface. In this chapter, the only issues of user-interface maintainability that we discussed were those of Internationalization via resource files and DLL's. See "Valid Value Ranges for Controls."

2. **D.** Inserting data into a database is adversely affected by the presence of an index. Versioning is an issue of maintainability. Instantiation overhead is an issue of scalability. SSL could slow the performance of transmissions as they are encrypted, but no indication that SSL is being used exists whatsoever in the question. See "Indexing."

3. **C.** A source-control tool is what is being sought. In a Windows environment, the best tool to know for the exam is Microsoft Visual SourceSafe. Notepad allows the performance of Undo operations but generally cannot revert to a

APPLY YOUR KNOWLEDGE

stage prior to that in which a file was opened. Late binding is completely irrelevant, as is Microsoft Project. See "Source Control."

4. **A.** COM is Microsoft's proposal for object standards. CORBA is a competing technology that stands for Common Object Request Brokering Architecture. OLE is sometimes used interchangeably with the name COM but is generally thought to refer to a smaller, older subset of this technology. SSL is used for encrypting transmissions over unsecured TCP/IP networks. See "Versioning Support."

5. **A.** A single byte will run out of bits to hold a distinct identification number before reaching the 257th entry. This will, obviously, occur long before the hiring of a 1,027th employee. Firing employees, however, should not present any problem at all. See "Valid Value Ranges for Controls."

6. **B.** A queuing application can allow solutions intended to work over a network to continue functioning normally, even in the absence of a network connection. In the case of our fighter's telemetry, the messages being sent would automatically be stored or "queued up" in the fighter's hard disk until the plane returned to the ground, when network connectivity could be restored and all data offloaded to the ground systems. Indexing is an issue of data-tier performance. Early binding and late binding are issues affecting instantiation overhead, which is of concern to the logic tier's scalability. See "Queuing."

7. **B.** This is provided by the Cryptography API (CryptoAPI). Context switching occurs when a CPU changes the process that it is currently working on. Decision support refers to a kind of database that contains archived information and is usually somewhat denormalized. See "Encrypting Transmissions."

8. **C.** Cross-machine marshalling is the way in which DCOM establishes and maintains procedure calls across process boundaries. Context switching occurs when a CPU changes the process that it is currently working on. Decision support refers to a kind of database that contains archived information and is usually somewhat denormalized. See "Early Binding."

APPLY YOUR KNOWLEDGE

Suggested Readings and Resources

1. Chappell, David. "Microsoft Message Queue Is a Fast, Efficient Choice for Your Distributed Application." *Microsoft System Journal,* July 1998.

2. MSDN Library suggestions:

   • "Visual Studio Documentation— Optimizing Database Retrieval"

   • "The Cryptography API, or How to Keep a Secret"

   • "Converting the Application to ODBC and SQL"

   • "Microsoft SQL Server Performance Tuning and Optimization for Developers, Part 1: Overview of Performance Issues"

   • "How Binding Affects ActiveX Component Performance"

3. Brockschmidt, Kraig. *Inside OLE.* Microsoft Press, 1995.

4. Lhotka, Rockford. *Professional Visual Basic 5.0 Business Objects.* Wrox Press, 1997.

   • Chapter One: Introducing Business Objects

   • Chapter Two: Application Architecture with Business Objects

   • Chapter Three: Business Object Analysis

5. Saganich, Al. "The Basics of ActiveX." *Visual J++ Developers Journal.* February 1998.

PART

III

FINAL REVIEW

Fast Facts

Study and Exam Prep Tips

Practice Exams

The thirteen chapters of this book have covered the objectives and components of the Analyzing Requirements and Defining Solution Architectures exam. After reading all those chapters, what is it that you really need to know? What should you read as you sit and wait in the parking lot of the testing center right up until the hour before you go in to pass the test and finish one more step toward your first (or next) Microsoft certification?

The following material covers the significant points of the previous 13 chapters, and it provides some insight into the information that makes particularly good material for exam questions. Although there is no substitute for real-world, hands-on experience, knowing what to expect on the exam can go a long way toward a passing score. The information that follows is equivalent to *Cliffs Notes*, providing the information you must know in each of the seven sections to pass the exam. Don't just memorize the concepts given; attempt to understand the reason why they are so, and you will have no difficulties passing the exam.

For more exam-taking help and suggestions specifically oriented to the case-study aspects of the exam, please refer to Appendix E, "Using the Exam Gear, Training Guide Edition Software."

ANALYZING BUSINESS REQUIREMENTS

Businesses use a wide variety of strategies and approaches in their never-ending quest for market share. It is important, therefore, to first achieve a clear understanding of whatever processes are currently in use at any given organization. It is through this understanding that a solution developer may eventually understand a company's unique blend of challenges and opportunities.

Fast Facts

SOLUTION ARCHITECTURES

Analyzing Project Scope

The kind of technology that an organization already has in place can have a profound influence on the scope of projects at that organization. Organizations with very little technology can require that more be built. On the other hand, such situations save you the difficulty of ensuring interoperation with existing technologies. Table 1 provides a comparison of this situation with cases in which existing technology is either easily integrated into your new solution ("Beneficial") or provides a further challenge("Difficult").

TABLE 1
COMPARISON OF EXISTING APPLICATION SITUATIONS

Situation	Amount to Build	Difficulty of Integration	Return on Investment
Starting from scratch	Most	N/A	Most (perceived)
Beneficial	Least	Least	Middle (perceived)
Difficult	Middle	Most	Least (real)

The scope of a project can also be affected by planned changes in a solution's environment. For example, an organization may intend to change the operating system under which new solutions must run. A few features exist in any new operating system that may help to decrease the scope of your project:

◆ A better user interface

◆ Superior Internet integration

◆ Support for a wider range of hardware

In addition to the technological environment of your solution, changes may also be planned for its business environment. A rapid increase in the number of new hires may require that your solution be more capable of scaling than would otherwise be the case. However, plans to downsize may

◆ Create additional problems

◆ Remove essential players in your solution

◆ Require that your solution be easy to learn and use

Generally speaking, a direct correlation exists between the expected life span of your solution and the scope of your project. Short-term solutions offer the following benefits:

◆ Shorter time for things to break

◆ More user "buy in" to project success

◆ Better user understanding of solution

◆ Fewer business changes for system to cope with

Rapid Application Development (RAD) can allow your users to gain many of the benefits of using your solution more quickly, and an iterative release strategy can provide payback and feedback before your solution is completely finished.

In contrast, longer-term solutions have the benefit of more time over which your solution may be able to justify the expense of building it.

On any solution-building project, you will find yourself working with four primary resources: time, labor, money, and benefits. Time represents the total number of hours, days, weeks, and so on that remain until your solution must be delivered. Labor refers specifically to the availability of skilled personnel for working on your project. Money can be used to reward hard work on your project as well as to buy various labor-saving items such as prebuilt components. Benefits represent the sum total of all business advantages encapsulated by your new solution.

Analyzing the Extent of Business Requirements

It is important to remember for the exam that the best statement of any problem in business is the difference between an ideal and reality. For example, imagine a situation in which wait staff are supposed to be delivering food orders to a chef in a speedy and accurate fashion. If orders are being lost, the problem is specifically that orders are not always being delivered. This reliability issue should be clearly distinguished from issues of accuracy or speed.

When taking the Microsoft exam, you may find it useful to remember four general types of problems. Communications problems involve ensuring the swift and accurate transportation of information. Calculation problems require the transformation of disparate pieces of information into useful information. Similarly, automation problems involve transformation, but in this case, it is the transformation of people, materials, and information into useful products. Finally, storage and retrieval problems take data and cause it to persist on some kind of media for later use.

Upfront costs can be reduced by a conscious decision to use more of the people and systems already in place at an organization. If the level of workforce expertise and availability at an organization is not great enough, this may require a slower rollout than would normally be the case.

Two important ways exist to reduce the ongoing or "maintenance" costs associated with keeping a solution in operation. The first of these is to build a solution to a higher degree of quality and reliability right from the start. This way, fewer resources are expended in an attempt to keep the system functioning at an acceptable level. Another approach is to work on reducing the amount of external administration (such as database compaction and log truncation) that must be performed for a solution to continue operating.

You can calculate your solution's ROI by figuring out the savings it produces (usually labor costs) and subtracting the costs associated with building it (hardware, software, development time, and so on) For example, if three billing clerks have to spend 10 hours per week sending out late notices, and the clerks each make $10/hr, over the course of a 52-week year this will cost a company

$$3 \text{ clerks} \times 10 \text{ hours} \times \$10/hr \times 52 \text{ weeks} = \$15,600$$

If a solution to solve this problem requires purchasing Visual Basic ($500) and having a developer work on the project for a single 40-hour week at $50/hr, the cost of producing the automated solution is

$$\$500 \text{ VB software} + (\$50/hr \times 40 \text{ hours}) = \$2500$$

The ROI for our solution, then, is

$$\$15,600 - \$2500 = \$13,100$$

In addition to the two approaches previously described, encapsulating your solutions' logic in the form of components can also help to increase their return on investment. You will be able to more easily reuse the code involved in creating your solutions in new and different solutions if they are components. This will reduce the cost of creating these additional solutions.

You will also want to consider the organizational constraints that may impact requirements for your solution.

In addition to financial constraints at an organization, the politics, the technical acceptance levels, and the training needs should also be considered. Politics may feature either static decision-making flows, which tend to offer reliability at the expense of quick resolutions, or dynamic ones that are the exact opposite. In general, lower technical acceptance levels will bring increased training needs, which will figure prominently in the business requirements for your solutions.

Arguments in favor of faster and slower implementations should be the final thing that you consider as you collect business requirements for your solution. The obvious benefit to a quicker rollout is that your organization could begin getting the benefits of your solution that much sooner. On the other hand, when training needs are sizable and the costs of failure are high, a slower solution may be demanded and justified by circumstances.

PASS ME Analysis

It is important to understand all six of the PASS ME factors as they relate to the business requirements for any solution that you plan on building. These are

- Performance
- Availability
- Security
- Scalability
- Maintainability
- Extensibility

Three kinds of response times relate to the performance requirements for your solution. Real performance is the kind that can be objectively measured. Perceived performance, on the other hand, is a subjective sense that an end user might get as to how your solution is performing.

The third kind of response time is an expected response time. This is a performance estimate of how much work a customer thinks your solution should be able to accomplish in a given amount of time on the basis of

- Other systems
- Previous uses of the same system
- Published technical specifications

The performance requirements for any solution can be stated in terms of peak and average requirements, as well as capacity. Peak requirements refer to the amount of work that a system should be able to perform at the height of its use. Average requirements, on the other hand, refer to what your system should be able to handle during typical usage. Capacity is the measure of exactly how many transactions or users your system can tolerate before breaking.

Four principal factors influence the requirements for your solution's performance. The first of these is workload growth, by which we mean any expected increase in the total amount of work that your solution will be called upon to perform. The second is hardware—that is, the processing power of the machines that will run your systems. Architectural design is the third factor influencing the performance of your system. The fourth factor is the means by which your solution's data is accessed, which will exert a profound influence over its performance.

It is important to know as early as possible in the development of your solutions what kind of availability is expected. In some cases, a need will exist for your solution's availability to be limited. This means specifically ensuring that no one can access your solution during certain times. Other instances will be the exact opposite and require guaranteed 100 percent uptime, as in the case of a hospital or a 24-hour convenience store. Between these two extremes are the cases of flexible availability where 100 percent uptime would be nice, but nothing is going to go horribly wrong in the case of an occasional, short outage. Stability is another way to look at availability. If your solution is up 98 percent of the time but crashes four times a day, taking users' work with it, you have an availability problem.

The geographic scope of your solutions can also exert an influence over their availability. The cost of maintaining constant network links to other countries, for example, may be prohibitive.

As previously mentioned, the effects of downtime on your solution's users can vary widely between different availability requirements.

For the Microsoft exam, you should know the four important people, or roles, involved in the security of any solution. They are

◆ **Administrators**—The only users of your solution with the privileges needed to set other users' security.

◆ **Groups**—Convenient groupings of administrators, guests, and clients.

◆ **Guests**—Users external to the organization in which your solution is primarily deployed; for example, suppliers linked to your solution via an extranet.

◆ **Clients**—Users internal to the organization in which your solution is primarily deployed.

The time and effort that you put into designing airtight security for your solutions should largely be governed by the likelihood and consequences of a potential break-in. In situations where an attempted break-in is highly unlikely—where a solution is not even connected to a modem or a network, for example—it may be acceptable to spend less time worrying about security. In a similar vein, if the potential impact of a break-in is minor (finding a few trivial Word files, perhaps), you may be well advised to spend your time on other parts of your solution.

You should remember two key things in trying to design security for your systems:

◆ Backing up your security database

◆ Auditing your system's security logs

Any remote access privileges that might be needed to provide technical support and maintenance after a solution has gone into production should be accounted for during the design phase.

It is important to realize that more security may mean more time required by end users to perform the same basic tasks. The reason is that they will have to negotiate the same security barriers as an intruder.

It is important to come to an agreement with your target organization as early in the design process as possible regarding who will be responsible for maintaining which parts of your solution. Note that in the PASS ME scheme, this is primarily considered to be an availability issue.

For the exam, you should know the three primary ways for providing for third-party extension of your solutions. These are as follows:

◆ **Source code**—Most flexible, but also the most dangerous. Harder to support and more likely to be ripped off.

◆ **APIs**—A little less flexible, but easier to support. Exposes system functionality only in preapproved, C-style function calls.

◆ **Components**—The easiest approach to support and potentially the most powerful. Components are Microsoft's favorite tool for the exam and should be understood at a semi-instinctive level!

Human Factors

If you do not consider your users, their problems, and their goals, a solution—no matter how beautifully conceived and designed—is likely to fail. Therefore, as a designer, being aware of the unique characteristics of the users, understanding the business problems thoroughly, and meeting their needs (as opposed to the developer's needs) is critical.

You should be able to identify who the target user base is for your solution. Remember, if it does not solve the problems from the user's point of view, it solves nothing.

Users can be technical, nontechnical or mixed. When you discover your target user group is largely nontechnical, you can expect the following:

◆ Simpler applications

◆ Step-by-step training

◆ More specific uses for software

If you are targeting a moderate to highly technical user group for a solution, sometimes referred to as "power users," expect to implement

◆ More complicated applications

◆ Training focused on business uses of the application

◆ More flexible software, allowing more end-user freedom in its use

◆ Plentiful shortcuts (for example, hot keys, command-line parsing)

Users have both business goals and personal goals that must be met. Unfortunately, even well-intentioned developers often get goals confused with features or tasks. Features are bullet points—things the software does. Features are a necessary part of a solution, but they are not goals. Tasks are things the user does. Tasks are necessary things that the users of your system must do, but they are also not goals. They are how users get to their destinations, but they are not the destination.

When you're designing the human-machine interface, don't forget about remote or disconnected users. Two basic types of applications are run by remote users:

◆ Internet-enabled applications

◆ Independently running applications

Make sure you understand any special needs that your users have. Do you need to build accessibility into your interface? Do you have any localization issues (different languages, different countries)?

User assistance can be provided in hard copy or electronic form. If electronic, it can be built-in help, Web-based help, FAQ (frequently asked questions) or ToolTips.

Finally, when you're designing the human-machine interface, notice whether any physical constraints exist, such as noisy or dirty shop floors, mouseless operation (for example, kiosks), or the need to support the smaller screens on Windows CE machines.

System Integration Issues

As a designer deploying applications into existing enterprises, you must think about the currently existing solutions. Am I replacing an old system? Am I expected to maintain connection points between other systems and the one I am specifically replacing? Am I going to need to interface with legacy data?

Integration can take one of three basic forms. First, we may have a "clean slate" scenario. This means that either there is no existing system to integrate with or the existing system is being totally replaced by the new solution. Second, we may have a solution that is designed to extend or augment an existing application. In these instances, our new solution will need to coexist with the legacy application.

Third is the concept of basing the new solution on the logic of the old, but providing the legacy system a "face lift" by wrapping it as an object or using a technique known as screen scraping.

Integration can be accomplished by using technologies such as CICS emulator software or Microsoft COM TI. Microsoft MSMQ also has a place in integrating with existing solutions when an asynchronous style of communication is best.

When you're establishing communications between a new solution and a legacy solution, four major options exist:

◆ Binary Compatibility (Microsoft COM)

◆ Microsoft SNA Server (or other Gateway-type products)

◆ Nonstandard protocols

◆ Industry standard protocols

COM provides intercomponent communication within the Microsoft world, regardless of the language used to create the component. SNA connects the PC world with the mainframe world. Industry standard protocols are used to communicate between platforms and languages outside of the Microsoft COM world. Nonstandard protocols are a last resort when no existing industry standard serves the needs of the solution.

Often, connection between the old and the new is through the data stores. ODBC has long been an industry standard for connecting with disparate SQL-based data stores (for example, Oracle, DB2, SQL Server, Jet). OLE DB and ADO are more recent additions to the available options. OLE DB goes beyond ODBC to allow access to non-SQL-based data stores. Data replication is another technique used to integrate between the new solution and the legacy solution.

Finally, consider the philosophies presented in the Microsoft Solutions Framework (MSF).

Analyzing Existing Business Practices

In addition to the technical integration issues, most application developers know that current business practices and methodologies are important. A successful solution is one that molds itself to the personality of the company that is using it. If a company is a risk taker, newer technologies are appropriate. If a company is more conservative, established, stable languages and technologies are more likely to be the right choice.

A company's quality processes and standards should be taken into account when you're building a solution. What is the expected mean time between failures or bugs per 1000 lines of code metric?

What are the financial constraints of the project? Is the schedule firm or soft? What is the budget? Is it flexible?

Should any legal issues be considered when designing a solution? Noncompete agreements? Nondisclosures?

ROI and Controlling Development Costs

One of the most risky aspects of developing software in a corporate environment is the question of cost. How does a business recoup the cost of (and thus justify building) a significant software project?

This question has two answers. The first involves a conscious effort to realistically appraise costs. Costs, in the context of ROI consideration, are not simply the cost of the proposed solution. It is also an analysis of how much money is spent accomplishing the task without the solution in place.

For example, if the users currently send reports via U.S. Mail to the main office, we can be relatively sure they are spending at least 33 cents per message on stamps. Additionally, they are spending money for paper and envelopes. If we can replace such a thing with an email-based reporting system, then at least 33 cents per message can be saved. Although this is certainly not, in itself, a reason to build the system, it does illustrate a very concrete way in which a system can save money.

The second part of the analysis considers the possibility of revenues that can be increased and/or created by constructing the solution.

Given that we will always have constrained resources on a project, not all functionality can always implemented. The important thing, then, is to choose the pieces of the solution that have maximum ROI for the business.

Two Sets of Tasks

The Analyzing Business Requirements unit, at first glance, seems daunting. When you examine the contents of this unit, it seems to be combining an awfully large set of directives. It feels, on the surface, as if it is simply saying "understand everything." However, application of a more critical eye to this unit will show that just two types of tasks are listed in the objectives.

The first is simply to gain an understanding of what the business situation is and what the users are expecting of the solution you are designing. If someone has been sold a bill of goods, it is best to find out right now that you're not going to be able to create such a solution for them—and let them know it.

The second set of tasks is to take this understanding of the businesses expectations and translate them into technical requirements. Whether it is in terms of scalability, performance, maintainability, or any of the other "usual suspects," the results are almost 100 percent driven by what the users need from the solution.

Don't confuse the two and start asking end users about technical requirements. They will do one of two things: answer without the knowledge base to answer with authority, or not answer at all. In either case, it is better to wait.

DEFINING THE TECHNICAL ARCHITECTURE FOR A SOLUTION

The technical architecture for a solution can be thought of as analogous to a design for a house. It lays out where the walls are and shows which walls will be load-bearing, but it doesn't go into the details of what color things are or what particular type of woodwork will be added to the home. Instead, it is focused on creating the infrastructure, the plumbing and wiring, which will support the rest of these details. This infrastructure, then, needs to be capable (within reason) of supporting whichever details of construction the builder decides to opt for.

How Many Tiers?

The architect's first decision is how many tiers. Should the solution be a monolithic-style, single-tier application? Although they are the simplest to design, they are the hardest to maintain. A lot of hype is published in journals, books, and Web sites about *n*-tier applications. "They're more scalable, they're more robust, they're just plain better." Although this is true, there is still a place for single-tier and two-tier architectures.

Should it be a traditional two-tier client/server solution with the logic and data separated? The biggest downside with two tier is the necessity to include business rules within the user interface. This causes deployment challenges. Also, each user has a separate connection to the database server. This may have a negative influence on scalability.

Or should the application be an *n*-tier architecture? For business solutions, *n*-tier will certainly constitute the majority of the solutions, but architects need to remain open to all the options. Be warned that the more tiers there are, the longer the design process will be. However, maintenance does become easier.

It should be noted that tiers are a logical construct. It is possible to have a three-tier solution on a single workstation. Microsoft favors a three-tier concept. The three tiers are named User Services, Business Services and Data Services. Within each of these, it is possible to add additional tiers, creating *n*-tiers.

Choosing the Proper Technology

The developer needs to determine whether to use industry standard formats such as ASCII, BMP, or WAV, open standards such as HTML, ODBC, or COM, or proprietary standards such as Windows NT.

The other decision is whether to use Visual Basic, VC++, VJ++ or Visual InterDev. Requirements such as speed of development (RAD), speed of operation, or cross-platform support will help decide which platform is the best fit. Table 2 provides a comparison of development tools by such requirements.

TABLE 2
CONTRASTING STRENGTHS OF DEVELOPMENT TOOLS

	Visual Basic	*Visual C++*	*Visual J++*	*Visual Interdev*
Internet development	WebClasses DHTML Apps	Manual, very tough	Java is Internet based	Tool for Internet development
Performance	Midrange	High speed	Slower than C++ or VB	Not compiled, N/A

continues

TABLE 2 *continued*
CONTRASTING STRENGTHS OF DEVELOPMENT TOOLS

	Visual Basic	*Visual C++*	*Visual J++*	*Visual Interdev*
RAD Tool	Premiere tool for RAD	Not a RAD tool	Not a RAD tool	Speeds up Web-site building
Cross-platform use	Only WebClasses (client-side only)	Very limited, Web (client-side only)	Optional fully cross-platform	Most Web tools cross platform, some are not (client-side only)

In closing this discussion of the technical architecture, remember the six areas of Microsoft's Enterprise Application Model (see Chapter 1 of the book *Developing for the Enterprise* that comes with Visual Studio 6.0, Enterprise Edition): Business Model, User Model, Logical Model, Technology Model, Development Model, and Architecture (physical) Model.

Data Storage Decisions

Choosing a persistence strategy requires us to analyze what data needs to be stored and how much of it there will be. This is sometimes called *volumetrics*. Volumetrics can be based on some or all of the following:

◆ Volume of data

◆ Number of transactions per time increment

◆ Number of connections or sessions

◆ Number of users

Volume is basically the number of rows multiplied by the bytes of each row. *Transactions per time* is an analysis of how many transfers will take place in a predetermined time slot (for example, an hour). Connections will help assess whether the database server is going to be overwhelmed by user connections. This may help determine whether MTS ought to be considered. The number of users is helpful in determining licensing requirements as well as the upper limit of peak activity.

Testing the Architecture

After we have designed an architecture for our solution, we need to make sure the architecture is a viable one. Specifically, we should assess our choice by applying four tests:

◆ Demonstrate that business requirements are met.

◆ Demonstrate that use-case scenarios are met.

◆ Demonstrate that existing technology constraints are met.

◆ Assess the impact of shortfalls in meeting requirements.

Each of these tests should be applied to the selected solution type (single tier, two tier, *n*-tier), the selected technologies (VB, VC++, VJ++, Visual InterDev), and the selected data-storage architecture. Iterative development and a prototype are effective ways to ensure that the architecture will be successful.

We also need to make sure that we have developed an effective deployment strategy.

DEVELOPING THE CONCEPTUAL AND LOGICAL DESIGN FOR AN APPLICATION

Without forethought and planning, it is easy to let technology and whim lead the development effort. The business requirements and goals should be the driving factor in any solution.

The conceptual design serves as the blueprint to the solution developers. It comprises four views or models that describe the solution before it is firmed up. This gives the architect and the users a chance to validate the design prior to construction. These are

◆ Context model

◆ Workflow process model

◆ Task sequence model

◆ Physical environment model

A context model defines the boundaries of the project. At a high level, it describes what is part of the solution and what is not. It can involve the creation of use cases or context diagrams. Use cases serve as a scenario-based contract between the developers and the users as to how the system will behave in specified situations. It can easily double as the basis for a system acceptance test.

A workflow process model is essentially a map of how work gets done in the context of the new solution. Who does what? The workflow model is similar to the well-worn practice of flowcharting a system.

Task sequence modeling is answering the question, "What gets done at each step?" This is where we begin to identify what functions a component will need to perform to add value to the entire process. We do this by identifying the nouns, verbs, and adjectives in a case study and by building a conceptual set of properties and methods. This practice works well for case studies found in exams as well.

The physical environment model takes into account, for the first time in the process, the actual physical constraints of implementing our solution: issues such as WAN latency, bandwidth, server capacity, and remote users. It requires us to ask such questions as

◆ Where are latency bottlenecks? Where is bandwidth going to impact the system most? (LANs, WANs, modems)

◆ Where do remote users present a deployment or maintenance problem?

◆ Where is hardware capacity or capability likely to limit my solution?

The models previously described should take into account the architecture type selected (SDI, MDI, browser, collaborative).

The solutions architect should take advantage of the plethora of tools provided by Microsoft: Visual Modeler (based on UML), Site Designer, Database Designer, Application Performance Explorer, and so on.

Finally, the selected logical system design should be inspected in relation to each of the six PASS ME areas to make sure that all explicit and implicit system requirements are met.

Another excellent source of information on conceptual and logical design is the Microsoft Solutions Framework (MSF).

BUILDING THE SOLUTION

Three tiers exist in the typical distributed application. Their purposes, possible locations, and the tools that might be used to create them are summarized next in Table 3.

TABLE 3
THE THREE TIERS OF A DISTRIBUTED APPLICATION

Tier	Purpose	Tools	Locations
Data	Storing and retrieving raw data from the solution's database	SQL Server, ADO, OLE DB, stored procedures, and provider objects	DB Server, middleware, or client computer
Business	Encapsulating the business rules by which an organization conducts business	MTS, all programming languages, MSMQ	Middleware or client computer
Presentation	Receiving user input and displaying raw data in a form that constitutes information for the user	Integrated Development Environments, HTML, ActiveX controls, and so on	Client computer

Components and Objects

One of the additional tasks that has been created as we have moved more toward the component-based architecture that Microsoft presents us with today is the necessity of laying out the logical designs of (and interrelations between) the components that compose our application.

The components package objects into a redistributable format. The objects have properties and methods, which serve to give us lists of the state and behavior of a particular object, respectively.

By laying out these objects in advance, we can begin to see how one object can provide services to several others. For example, a given object might be designed to talk to the database. Rather than all objects talking to the database, all objects instead talk to this one object, which in turn retrieves and returns the data necessary.

Components and the objects they contain are also used to encapsulate business rules. These rules come in many flavors but have one thing in common. They are all designed to convey information that is not obvious from the data itself. For example, merely requiring a date to be entered into a field does not guarantee that someone will not enter July 1, 1066. However, the odds are that this value is not going to be a valid one for most businesses.

As such, business rules can act to regulate these technically valid but contextually meaningless values. The appropriate place to house these rules is within business objects, which allows for centralized maintenance of these rules rather than having them scattered throughout all the code.

Impact of Choices on the PASS ME Requirements

Logical design choices can have obvious impacts on the primary areas of application design. These are performance, maintainability, extensibility, scalability, availability, and security.

Unfortunately, it is sometimes very difficult to deduce where a problem may be found. In general, be aware of the consequences of choices. In making a choice to distribute the application, we are negatively impacting performance and security. The issue, then, becomes one of degree. How much are we negatively impacting them?

All designers make similar decisions, which negatively impact each of the PASS ME concepts. This allows us, many times, to at least identify trouble spots. What a look at our logical design cannot tell us, however, is the degree of problem a given problem spot presents. This will have to either be gleaned from experience or tested in a physical model.

DEVELOPING DATA MODELS

Data is the lifeblood of any system, and an effective model for the data is one of the surest ways of gaining efficient access to the data.

Following Standards

Probably the singlemost important thing to do when developing a data model is to define and adhere to standards. Some standards are industry standards; others simply need to be consistent across a given enterprise. However, nothing is more frustrating and difficult to maintain than data models with three or four different sets of naming conventions being used in different parts of the database.

Similarly, field names need to have a naming convention, which enables administrators to follow the flow of the database more easily. Without these standards, it rapidly becomes nearly impossible to follow a data model. This slows down development and database administration.

The most important database standards for you to know for the Microsoft exam are as follows:

◆ **SQL**—Standard Query Language, an industry standard language for querying databases.

◆ **ODBC**—Open Database Connectivity, an industry standard (started by Microsoft) for allowing interoperation between different relational database engines.

◆ **OLE DB**—OLE Database, a Microsoft standard for Universal Data Access. Often used in Active Server Pages via ADO (Active Data Objects).

Normalization

Normalization attempts to build a database that is more maintainable by removing repetitive or redundant columns in tables. This is accomplished through the use of several *normal forms*. The ultimate extension of this idea creates many tables, which contain possible values and which generate tables with foreign keys to those values.

Highly normalized databases make it very easy to change the description attached to a foreign key, without needing to change multiple records or potentially breaking the rest of the application.

Denormalization to Increase Performance

However, highly normalized databases radically increase the number of joins (connections between tables) that have to be made to execute a request. As a result, performance on highly normalized systems will sometimes begin to degrade.

With this in mind, one of the main attractions of denormalization is that it allows some of that processing time to be reclaimed. Essentially, it involves re-folding some of the tables holding values back into the main table.

For example, instead of having a foreign key on the order table to a State table, it could simply allow a freely keyed entry for the state. Yes, it is possible that someone might enter an invalid state name. However, if that is judged to be relatively unlikely, it might be worthwhile to not have to make that database join each time a record is requested.

Specifying and Enforcing Relationships Between Entities

As objects are to components, so entities are to databases. In essence, they are collections of data that describe a particular instance of data. For example, an order might contain the customer who ordered a product, a shipping address, and order items data. All these entities (the customer, the order, and the order items) stand in particular relation to one another. The customer stands in a one-to-many relationship to an order (meaning that one customer can have many orders). These relationships are critical to the function of the application and the database itself and need to be maintained, not just by the goodwill of the developers, but by enforcement within the database through the use of foreign keys.

In our previous example, each order has a foreign key to the customer table. That is, it picks out of the customer table a unique customer to whom the order belongs. This relationship should be designed into the database to ensure that no one enters an order for a nonexistent customer.

The Data Tier

To be in First Normal form, a data entity must meet the following requirements:

- ◆ All values are atomic.
- ◆ No repeating columns.

To be in Second Normal form, a data entity must meet the following requirements:

- ◆ Must be in First Normal form.
- ◆ All non-key columns fully depend on primary key.
- ◆ Each table should represent exactly one entity.

To be in Third Normal form, a data entity must meet the following requirements:

- ◆ Must be in Second Normal form.
- ◆ All non-key columns are mutually independent.
- ◆ No computed fields.
- ◆ No fields about entities that are just referenced.

Data entities are typically related to one another by including the primary key of one table as the foreign key of another table. In this case, one entry may be on the primary-key side for every one on the foreign-key side, in which case the relationship is said to be a one-to-one relationship. Alternatively, the relationship may be many-to-one or many-to-many.

The data tier of your solutions should implement three kinds of rules for ensuring the integrity of your database. They are

- **Translation**—For converting lookup codes stored in the database (such as RTM) into data for application use (such as Read the Manual).

- **Relational**—For ensuring that every object intended to be in a master-detail relationship is satisfied on both sides of the relationship. For example, this would make sure that every invoice has at least one sales item and every sales item is on exactly one invoice.

- **Domain**—These rules make sure that every value stored in the database falls within the logical range of possibilities for that piece of data. For example, a distance in miles should always be a number, not a text or a picture.

It is important to know that meta-data is the data stored by your database *about* the data that it is storing. It is meta-data, for example, that can tell your solution how many rows are in a table and what kinds of data are stored within each of its columns.

The objects in the data tier of your solutions should allow for three main kinds of methods:

- Adjusting security

- Altering data definitions

- Triggering maintenance tasks

Data-tier events arise as the result of two occurrences. The first of these is a locking conflict with another user or process. The other possibility is that the event is occurring as a callback requested by your own solution.

DESIGNING A USER INTERFACE AND USER SERVICES

Wise solution architects don't treat the user interface as just the finishing touches to their application. They design around the needs of the interface and the needs of the user from the beginning. The user interface should be designed and constructed to make it as simple as possible for users to accomplish their goals within the application.

Properly designed user interfaces should be consistent, helpful, and as intuitive as possible. This begins as the design initially addresses how users will navigate through the application. It becomes even more important as we address the users' need to provide input and receive responses in an efficient manner.

Prototyping is often the only really effective way of pinning down how the users would like a screen or set of screens to appear.

Choosing a Navigation Model for the Application

The most common models for navigation within an application are

- Single Document Interface (SDI)

- Multiple Document Interface (MDI)

- Browser model

The SDI is essentially a model that presents a single screen of information at a time (discounting pop-ups). This is otherwise called a *modal* solution. Also, each SDI screen is self-contained and autonomous from other copies of the same program.

The MDI model is more nonmodal. Users are allowed to open many things and interact with all of them in a basically random fashion. Another way of saying this is that the user is unconstrained by the interface. Traditional MDI applications focus on a single document or file type. Word processor or spreadsheet programs typify this model. Workspace MDI applications also exist that allow the opening of different file types. This is more similar to the Visual Studio interface style.

The third major navigation style is the Web browser interface model. Navigation is focused on the Submit button or hypertext *jump*.

When choosing the best model for our solution, we need to be familiar with the prevalent style of our users. Data entry users care about speed and power. The SDI model will usually be the best fit here. Ad hoc users require flexibility; therefore, the browser model is often the best fit. Remote users or users that require a simple deployment strategy will also respond better to the browser model.

Controls and Components

A few controls do the majority of the navigational tasks in any solution. They are menus, command buttons, tabs and the treeview control.

Menus should always be placed in a specific order, which is best typified by Microsoft Word. The order is File, Edit, View, followed by any custom menus, followed by a Window menu (if appropriate), followed by Help.

Command buttons are part of almost every business solution. The interface designer should strive for consistency of wording, placement, size, and behavior as much as possible.

Tab controls are sometimes used to clean up what would otherwise be a confusing or busy screen. They work best when the metaphor fits a situation that the user would likely be able to intuit.

Finally, the treeview control is used more and more when the data is organized in a hierarchical manner and the user needs to be able to jump around or drill down to even deeper levels of the hierarchy.

Validation of User Input

The best way to protect the integrity of your solution's data is to reject or constrain the user input. This is done by enforcing rules at the form level, at the text box level, or by using controls that allow only valid data to be entered. Any opportunity to constrain the input by using special controls, avoiding a message such as "Invalid entry. Choose again.," is going to make the user more effective. Check boxes, option buttons, drop-down lists, combo lists, and slider bars are typical controls used to constrain input.

Another choice is to enable or disable controls based on user authority when the form first displays. The developer can also define data validation rules that are enforced either on a per keystroke basis, when a control loses focus, or when the user attempts to submit the data to the system (for example, a Done button). Color should not be used to indicate an error condition because users may have altered their Windows color scheme settings or the user may be colorblind.

User Assistance

Help for users is a critical factor in the success or failure of any business enterprise. An application can provide help to the users in many ways. ToolTips, for example, provide an onscreen, real-time indication of what a button or control is designed to do. These indications can help a user, particularly in the case of icon-based toolbars, where there are no other written indications of what functionality is being requested.

Help files are perhaps the most common form of user assistance. The access to these help files, according to Microsoft standards, should be a menu item at the extreme right of your menu bar entries. The help files themselves are compiled with a tool from Microsoft and built from Rich Text Format files (RTF) or HTML help files (CHM files). The option also exists to include What's This? help or support for the F1 key (always a trigger to launch the help system in all Microsoft standard solutions).

User Interface Prototyping

The user interface is, by design, the only piece of your application architecture that your targeted user base has direct contact with. As such, it is most directly affected by the desires of the users. Most of the design for the middle and data tiers can be driven by users, but they don't really care how they look. If they are badly designed, as long as it doesn't affect their own performance, they aren't too worried about it. This is not the case with the user interface.

Therefore, the user interface, more than any other part of the application, should be put through several series of prototypes. These are used to work out kinks in the presentation and to verify with users that we have achieved the layout that will make it more efficient, rather than less so, to perform their work.

Generally speaking, however, these prototypes need to have little, and initially probably none, of the functionality that will eventually be in the application. All it really is designed to test is whether the proposed physical design of the user interface will fulfill the business's needs. In fact, the first set of prototypes should probably be on paper, not using any technology at all. Remember, the sooner you lock into an approach, the sooner you lock out alternatives that might be better.

DESIGNING A BUSINESS SERVICES TIER

Sandwiched between the data tier and the user interface tier is the business services tier, at least in three tier or higher solutions.

The logic tier enables the solution architect to take advantage of component-based design, one of the most powerful approaches available for the design of reusable, stable, scalable applications. The interfaces of each component are designed first, leaving the implementation details encapsulated within. This helps address issues caused by the growing complexity of applications today.

The middle, or business, tier also allows the designer to move business rules out of the user interface and back to a central server or component. This improves maintainability, reuse, scalability, and deployment. It also allows for a more consistent use of business rules across an enterprise.

Finally, it allows the architect to take advantage of MTS and what it can provide—database connection and object pooling, transaction processing, a role-based security model, and support for multithreading without requiring complex coding changes. Remember that MTS prefers stateless objects, although by forgoing the transactional nature of MTS, stateful objects can also be supported.

Components and objects are generally composed of three types of interface access points: properties, methods, and events.

Properties tell you something about the object. They are analogous to adjectives in a case study (for example, Name, Height, EmployeeNumber, AmountOwed).

Methods are actions, or verbs, that an object or component can perform (for example, CalculatePayment, ReleaseSession, DeleteRecord).

Events are a way for a component to communicate that something has happened in an asynchronous fashion (for example, DiskFull, TransactionCanceled, FormLoaded).

DERIVING THE PHYSICAL DESIGN

After you have determined the services that your solution's components will provide, you can begin the process of building them. The physical implementation that you give to your solution will be the ultimate determiner of whether it satisfies the PASS ME portions of your business requirements.

PASS ME and the Physical Design

Indexing some of the columns in your database(s) will help retrieval but adversely affect INSERT operations. Queues can improve your solution's performance by allowing it to operate in a largely asynchronous fashion.

The way that you build your queries can either help or harm your solution's performance. In particular

◆ Avoid joining tables on fields of different types.

◆ Avoid restricting results on nonindexed fields.

◆ Put calculations only in the highest levels of your queries.

A physical implementation that uses a lot of casting between types and doing string concatenation will perform poorly. So will one with too many control or dialog boxes.

Most important, your solutions should make use of early binding whenever possible. Early binding allows a compiler to know in advance what kind of object will be referenced by a given variable. The opposite of this, late binding, requires the discovery of type information at runtime. In addition to producing more error-prone code, the runtime type information discovery produces a noticeable degradation in real performance.

The availability of your solutions can be reduced by end-of-period routines (such as nightly database compactions).

Views provide a way to increase the physical security of your solution by limiting access to your data at a column-by-column level within your database. Encryption can increase security of information while in transit over unsecured networks.

Most important, good auditing should be provided for instances when all else with security fails. Good auditing should

◆ Monitor who is doing what.

◆ Monitor failed access attempts.

◆ Log all changes to data.

The data tier of your application influences the scalability of your solutions most notably through the style of locking that you choose. Optimistic locking is better for concurrency, but pessimistic is better for data integrity. Row-level locking is better for concurrency; page-level locking is worse.

The kinds of components that you use in your solution also affect its scalability. Local, in-process components (ActiveX DLLs) can be instantiated the quickest and with the least cost in system resources, but they cannot be easily accessed by other users and processes. Out-of-process components (ActiveX EXEs) on the same computer require more system resources and are only a benefit insofar as they offer some isolation of potentially dangerous operations from the rest of your solution's processes. Remote objects are the most resource intensive of all, involving long periods of network latency, but they are required to properly distribute an application among multiple machines.

The maintainability of your solutions can be degraded by physical implementations that require recurrent clearing of logs or database compaction. Source control, on the other hand, can improve your solution's maintainability by allowing changes to be tracked and (if need be) reversed. Storing location-dependent resources in resource files and/or .dll files is also an excellent way to make your physical implementation more maintainable.

Extensibility is the final aspect of your physical implementation that you should consider when taking the Microsoft exam. COM is arguably Microsoft's most important technology and assists extensibility in two important ways. First, it is a language–independent, binary-level standard that can assist extensibility by allowing you to create new components in whatever language you deem most appropriate for the task at hand. Also, COM has built-in support for component versioning through multiple interfaces that will prevent client applications expecting a previous version of your component from breaking when a newer version is installed.

At the user interface or presentation level, it is important that your components do not hard code any assumptions about the containers in which they will be used. A Web browser is one example of a container—a Visual Basic form is another. On the other hand, components that are capable of automatically resizing themselves to retain an appropriate appearance at whatever size is required will be much more platform independent and extensible.

Object Implementation (Components)

In Microsoft Windows development, COM components are used as the physical deployment mechanism for objects. Methods, properties, and events are exposed in classes within these components. Components themselves are packaged either as DLLs or EXE files and can run either remotely (on another system) or locally. The highest performance set of options is a component packaged as a DLL, running locally. Conversely, the slowest combination is a component packaged as an EXE and running remotely.

Remote components run through a mechanism called Distributed COM (or DCOM). DCOM is simply a means of distributing components across multiple machines and allowing the components themselves to remain location neutral.

Encapsulating Database Access Through Objects

Database access can be one of the more complicated aspects of a system design. Because it is, almost by definition, interaction with resources that are external to our solution (such as connections to a database server), it is critical that database access be a highly optimized set of functionality.

One solution to this problem is to wrap our database access functionality in an object. This object is then packaged as a component (either a DLL or an EXE) and can be utilized by the entire development team.

This allows the team to spend a lot of time optimizing database access, and as long as the object doesn't change the way it looks from the outside, optimizing internal performance shouldn't affect anyone else.

The tradeoff here, though, is that building the access into a component creates some performance overhead that we may not be able to accept in the solution.

Impact of Physical Design on the PASS ME Concepts

Physical design is probably the thing which can most surreptitiously undermine our objective of addressing the PASS ME considerations (performance, availability, scalability, security, maintainability, and extensibility). Each of these, no matter how well envisioned and designed, has to be implemented in a physical format in a particular way.

The variety of options available causes a whole new set of problems. Internal physical implementations and physical designs can take an application from meeting performance goals to being orders of magnitude too slow.

Similarly, scalability, extensibility, and maintainability are all dependent on physical designs. The best-designed systems for these traits are all going to fall apart without a well-thought-out physical design.

The danger in all this is that these kind of problems probably won't show up on the whiteboard when you're diagramming systems. In some cases, it will not be apparent that problems exist in the physical design until some form of a protosystem is up and running.

This chapter provides you with some general guidelines for preparing for a certification exam. It is organized into three sections. The first section addresses your pre-exam preparation activities and covers general study tips. This is followed by an extended look at the Microsoft Certification exams including a number of specific tips that apply to the various Microsoft exam formats. Finally, changes in Microsoft's testing policies and how they might affect you are discussed.

To better understand the nature of preparation for the test, it is important to understand learning as a process. You probably are aware of how you best learn new material. You may find that outlining works best for you, or you may need to "see" things as a visual learner. Whatever your learning style, test preparation takes place over time. Obviously, you can't start studying for these exams the night before you take them; it is very important to understand that learning is a developmental process. Understanding it as a process helps you focus on what you know and what you have yet to learn.

Thinking about how you learn should help you recognize that learning takes place when we are able to match new information to old. You have some previous experience with computers and networking, and now you are preparing for this certification exam. Using this book, software, and supplementary materials will not just add incrementally to what you know; as you study, you actually change the organization of your knowledge in order to integrate new information into your existing knowledge base. This will lead you to a more comprehensive understanding of the tasks and concepts outlined in the objectives and of computing in general. Again, this happens as a repetitive process rather than a singular event. Keep this model of learning in mind as you prepare for the exam, and you will make better decisions concerning what to study and how much more studying you need to do.

Study and Exam Prep Tips

STUDY TIPS

There are many ways to approach studying just as there are many different types of material to study. However, the tips that follow should work well for the type of material covered on the certification exams.

Study Strategies

Although individuals vary in the ways they learn information, some basic principles of learning apply to everyone. You should adopt some study strategies that take advantage of these principles. One of these principles is that learning can be broken into various depths. Recognition (of terms, for example) exemplifies a more surface level of learning in which you rely on a prompt of some sort to elicit recall. Comprehension or understanding (of the concepts behind the terms, for example) represents a deeper level of learning. The ability to analyze a concept and apply your understanding of it in a new way represents a further depth of learning.

Your learning strategy should enable you to know the material at a level or two deeper than mere recognition. This will help you do well on the exams. You will know the material so thoroughly that you can easily handle the recognition-level types of questions used in multiple-choice testing. You will also be able to apply your knowledge to solve new problems.

Macro and Micro Study Strategies

One strategy that can lead to this deeper learning includes preparing an outline that covers all the objectives and subobjectives for the particular exam you are working on. You should delve a bit further into the material and include a level or two of detail beyond the stated objectives and subobjectives for the exam. Then expand the outline by coming up with a statement of definition or a summary for each point in the outline.

An outline provides two approaches to studying. First, you can study the outline by focusing on the organization of the material. Work your way through the points and sub-points of your outline with the goal of learning how they relate to one another. For example, be sure you understand how each of the main objective areas is similar to and different from another. Then do the same thing with the subobjectives; be sure you know which subobjectives pertain to each objective area and how they relate to one another.

Next, you can work through the outline, focusing on learning the details. Memorize and understand terms and their definitions, facts, rules and strategies, advantages and disadvantages, and so on. In this pass through the outline, attempt to learn detail rather than the big picture (the organizational information that you worked on in the first pass through the outline).

Research has shown that attempting to assimilate both types of information at the same time seems to interfere with the overall learning process. Separate your studying into these two approaches, and you will perform better on the exam.

Active Study Strategies

The process of writing down and defining objectives, subobjectives, terms, facts, and definitions promotes a more active learning strategy than merely reading the material does. In human information-processing terms, writing forces you to engage in more active encoding of the information. Simply reading over it exemplifies more passive processing.

Next, determine whether you can apply the information you have learned by attempting to create examples and scenarios on your own. Think about how or where you could apply the concepts you are learning. Again, write down this information to process the facts and concepts in a more active fashion.

The hands-on nature of the Exercises at the ends of the chapters provide further active learning opportunities that will reinforce concepts as well.

Common-Sense Strategies

Finally, you should also follow common-sense practices when studying. Study when you are alert, reduce or eliminate distractions, take breaks when you become fatigued, and so on.

Pre-Testing Yourself

Pre-testing allows you to assess how well you are learning. One of the most important aspects of learning is what has been called "meta-learning." Meta-learning has to do with realizing when you know something well or when you need to study some more. In other words, you recognize how well or how poorly you have learned the material you are studying.

For most people, this can be difficult to assess objectively on their own. Practice tests are useful in that they reveal more objectively what you have learned and what you have not learned. You should use this information to guide review and further studying. Developmental learning takes place as you cycle through studying, assessing how well you have learned, reviewing, and assessing again until you feel you are ready to take the exam.

You may have noticed the practice exam included in this book. Use it as part of the learning process. The *ExamGear* test simulation software included on the CD also provides you with another excellent opportunity to assess your knowledge.

You should set a goal for your pre-testing. A reasonable goal would be to score consistently in the 90-percent range.

See Appendix D, "Using the ExamGear, Training Guide Edition Software," for more explanation of the test simulation software.

EXAM PREP TIPS

Having mastered the subject matter, the final preparatory step is to understand how the exam will be presented. Make no mistake, a Microsoft Certified Professional (MCP) exam will challenge both your knowledge and your test-taking skills. This section starts with the basics of exam design, reviews a new type of exam format, and concludes with hints targeted to each of the exam formats.

The MCP Exam

Every MCP exam is released in one of two basic formats. What's being called exam format here is really little more than a combination of the overall exam structure and the presentation method for exam questions.

Each exam format uses the same types of questions. These types or styles of questions include multiple-rating (or scenario-based) questions, traditional multiple-choice questions, and simulation-based questions. Some exams include other types of questions that ask you to drag and drop objects on the screen or reorder a list. It's important that you understand the types of questions you will be asked and the actions required to properly answer them.

Understanding the exam formats is key to good preparation because the format determines the number of questions presented, the difficulty of those questions, and the amount of time allowed to complete the exam.

Exam Format

There are two basic formats for the MCP exams: the traditional fixed-form exam and the adaptive form. As its name implies, the fixed-form exam presents a fixed set of questions during the exam session. The adaptive form, however, uses only a subset of questions drawn from a larger pool during any given exam session. The Solution Architectures exam is a fixed-form exam, but it includes Case Studies that serve as the basis for answering the various types of questions.

Fixed-Form

A fixed-form computerized exam is based on a fixed set of exam questions. The individual questions are presented in random order during a test session. If you take the same exam more than once, you won't necessarily see the exact same questions. This is because two or three final forms are typically assembled for every fixed-form exam Microsoft releases. These are usually labeled Forms A, B, and C.

The final forms of a fixed-form exam are identical in terms of content coverage, number of questions, and allotted time, but the questions are different. You may notice, however, that some of the same questions appear on, or rather are shared among, different final forms. When questions are shared among multiple final forms of an exam, the percentage of sharing is generally small. Many final forms share no questions, but some older exams may have a 10–15 percent duplication of exam questions on the final exam forms.

Fixed-form exams also have a fixed time limit in which you must complete the exam. The *ExamGear* software on the CD-ROM that accompanies this book provides fixed-form exams.

Finally the score you achieve on a fixed-form exam, which is always reported for MCP exams on a scale of 0 to 1,000, is based on the number of questions you answer correctly. The exam's passing score is the same for all final forms of a given fixed-form exam.

The typical format for the fixed-form exam is as follows:

- ◆ 50–60 questions
- ◆ 75–90 minute testing time
- ◆ Question review is allowed including the opportunity to change your answers

Adaptive Form

An adaptive-form exam has the same appearance as a fixed-form exam, but its questions differ in quantity and process of selection. Although the statistics of adaptive testing are fairly complex, the process is concerned with determining your level of skill or ability with the exam subject matter. This ability assessment begins by presenting questions of varying levels of difficulty and ascertaining at what difficulty level you can reliably answer them. Finally, the ability assessment determines if that ability level is above or below the level required to pass that exam.

Examinees at different levels of ability will see quite different sets of questions. Examinees who demonstrate little expertise with the subject matter will continue to be presented with relatively easy questions. Examinees who demonstrate a high level of expertise will be presented progressively more difficult questions. Individuals of both levels of expertise may answer the same number of questions correctly, but because the higher-expertise examinee can correctly answer more difficult questions, he or she will receive a higher score and is more likely to pass the exam.

The typical design for the adaptive form exam is as follows:

◆ 20–25 questions

◆ 90 minute testing time (although this is likely to be reduced to 45–60 minutes in the near future)

◆ Question review is not allowed, providing no opportunity for you to change your answers

The Adaptive-Exam Process

Your first adaptive exam will be unlike any other testing experience you have had. In fact, many examinees have difficulty accepting the adaptive testing process because they feel that they were not provided the opportunity to adequately demonstrate their full expertise.

You can take consolation in the facts that adaptive exams are painstakingly put together after months of data gathering and analysis and that adaptive exams are just as valid as fixed-form exams. The rigor introduced through the adaptive testing methodology means that there is nothing arbitrary about what you'll see. It is also a more efficient means of testing, requiring less time to conduct and complete.

As you can see in Figure 1, a number of statistical measures drive the adaptive examination process. The most immediately relevant to you is the ability estimate. Accompanying this test statistic are the standard error of measurement, the item characteristic curve, and the test information curve.

The standard error, which is the key factor in determining when an adaptive exam will terminate, reflects the degree of error in the exam ability estimate. The item characteristic curve reflects the probability of a correct response relative to examinee ability. Finally, the test information statistic provides a measure of the information contained in the set of questions the examinee has answered, again relative to the ability level of the individual examinee.

When you begin an adaptive exam, the standard error has already been assigned a target value that it must drop below for the exam to conclude. This target value reflects a particular level of statistical confidence in the process. The examinee ability is initially set to the mean possible exam score (500 for MCP exams).

As the adaptive exam progresses, questions of varying difficulty are presented. Based on your pattern of responses to these questions, the ability estimate is recalculated. At the same time, the standard error estimate is refined from its first estimated value of one toward the target value. When the standard error reaches its target value, the exam is terminated. Thus, the more consistently you answer questions of the same degree of difficulty, the more quickly the standard error estimate drops, and the fewer questions you will end up seeing during the exam session. This situation is depicted in Figure 2.

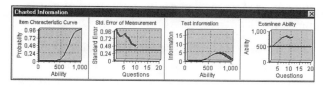

FIGURE 2
The changing statistics in an adaptive exam.

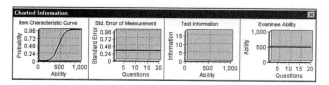

FIGURE 1
Microsoft's adaptive testing demonstration program.

As you might suspect, one good piece of advice for taking an adaptive exam is to treat every exam question as if it is the most important. The adaptive scoring algorithm attempts to discover a pattern of responses that reflects some level of proficiency with the subject matter. Incorrect responses almost guarantee that additional questions must be answered (unless, of course, you get every question wrong). This is because the scoring algorithm must adjust to information that is not consistent with the emerging pattern.

New Question Types

A variety of question types can appear on MCP exams. Examples of multiple-choice questions, drag and drop, and ordered list questions appear throughout this book and the ExamGear, Training Guide Edition software. Simulation-based questions are relatively new to the MCP exam series.

Simulation Questions

Simulation-based questions reproduce the look and feel of key Microsoft product features for the purpose of testing. The simulation software used in MCP exams has been designed to look and act, as much as possible, just like the actual product. Consequently, answering simulation questions in an MCP exam entails completing one or more tasks just as if you were using the product itself.

The format of a typical Microsoft simulation question consists of a brief scenario or problem statement, along with one or more tasks that you must complete to solve the problem. An example of a simulation question for MCP exams is shown in the following section.

A Typical Simulation Question

It sounds obvious, but your first step when you encounter a simulation question is to carefully read the question (see Figure 3). Do not go straight to the simulation application! You must assess the problem

that's presented and identify the conditions that make up the problem scenario. Note the tasks that must be performed or outcomes that must be achieved to answer the question, and then review any instructions you're given on how to proceed.

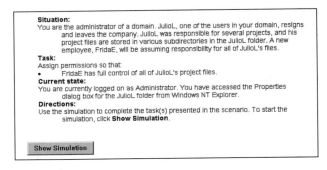

Situation:
You are the administrator of a domain. JulioL, one of the users in your domain, resigns and leaves the company. JulioL was responsible for several projects, and his project files are stored in various subdirectories in the JulioL folder. A new employee, FridaE, will be assuming responsibility for all of JulioL's files.
Task:
Assign permissions so that:
• FridaE has full control of all of JulioL's project files.
Current state:
You are currently logged on as Administrator. You have accessed the Properties dialog box for the JulioL folder from Windows NT Explorer.
Directions:
Use the simulation to complete the task(s) presented in the scenario. To start the simulation, click **Show Simulation**.

Show Simulation

FIGURE 3
Typical MCP exam simulation question with directions.

The next step is to launch the simulator by using the button provided. After clicking the Show Simulation button, you will see a feature of the product, as shown in the dialog box in Figure 4. The simulation application will partially cover the question text on many test center machines. Feel free to reposition the simulator and to move between the question text screen and the simulator by using hotkeys or point-and-click navigation, or even by clicking the simulator's launch button again.

It is important for you to understand that your answer to the simulation question will not be recorded until you move on to the next exam question. This gives you the added capability of closing and reopening the simulation application (using the launch button) on the same question without losing any partial answer you may have made.

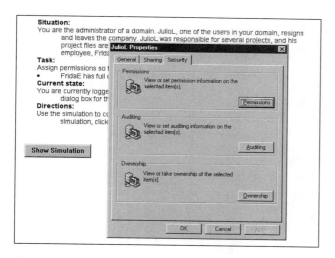

FIGURE 4
Launching the simulation application.

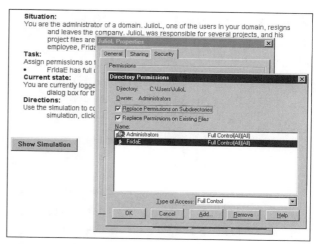

FIGURE 5
The solution to the simulation example.

The third step is to use the simulator as you would the actual product to solve the problem or perform the defined tasks. Again, the simulation software is designed to function—within reason—just as the product does. But don't expect the simulator to reproduce product behavior perfectly. Most importantly, do not allow yourself to become flustered if the simulator does not look or act exactly like the product.

Figure 5 shows the solution to the example simulation problem.

Two final points will help you tackle simulation questions. First, respond only to what is being asked in the question; do not solve problems that you are not asked to solve. Second, accept what is being asked of you. You may not entirely agree with conditions in the problem statement, the quality of the desired solution, or the sufficiency of defined tasks to adequately solve the problem. Always remember that you are being tested on your ability to solve the problem as it is presented.

The solution to the simulation problem shown in Figure 5 perfectly illustrates both of those points. As you'll recall from the question scenario (refer to Figure 3), you were asked to assign appropriate permissions to a new user, Frida E. You were not instructed to make any other changes in permissions. Thus, if you were to modify or remove the administrator's permissions, this item would be scored wrong on an MCP exam.

Putting It All Together

Given all these different pieces of information, the task now is to assemble a set of tips that will help you successfully tackle the different types of MCP exams.

More Pre-Exam Preparation Tips

Generic exam-preparation advice is always useful. Tips include the following:

◆ Become familiar with the product. Hands-on experience is one of the keys to success on any MCP exam. Review the exercises in the book.

◆ Review the current exam-preparation guide on the Microsoft MCP Web site. The documentation Microsoft makes available over the Web identifies the skills every exam is intended to test.

◆ Memorize foundational technical detail, but remember that MCP exams are generally heavier on problem solving and application of knowledge than on questions that require only rote memorization.

◆ Take any of the available practice tests. We recommend the one included in this book and the ones you can create using the *ExamGear* software on the CD-ROM. As a supplement to the material bound with this book, try the free practice tests available on the Microsoft MCP Web site.

◆ Look on the Microsoft MCP Web site for samples and demonstration items. These tend to be particularly valuable for one significant reason: They help you become familiar with new testing technologies before you encounter them on MCP exams.

During the Exam Session

The following generic exam-taking advice that you've heard for years also applies when you're taking an MCP exam:

◆ Take a deep breath and try to relax when you first sit down for your exam session. It is very important that you control the pressure you may (naturally) feel when taking exams.

◆ You will be provided scratch paper. Take a moment to write down any factual information and technical detail that you committed to short-term memory.

◆ Carefully read all information and instruction screens. These displays have been put together to give you information relevant to the exam you are taking.

◆ Accept the Non-Disclosure Agreement and preliminary survey as part of the examination process. Complete them accurately and quickly move on.

◆ Read the exam questions carefully. Reread each question to identify all relevant detail.

◆ Tackle the questions in the order they are presented. Skipping around won't build your confidence; the clock is always counting down.

◆ Don't rush, but also don't linger on difficult questions. The questions vary in degree of difficulty. Don't let yourself be flustered by a particularly difficult or verbose question.

Fixed-Form Exams

Building from this basic preparation and test-taking advice, you also need to consider the challenges presented by the different exam designs. Because a fixed-form exam is composed of a fixed, finite set of questions, add these tips to your strategy for taking a fixed-form exam:

◆ Note the time allotted and the number of uestions on the exam you are taking. Make a rough calculation of how many minutes you can spend on each question, and use this figure to pace yourself through the exam.

◆ Take advantage of the fact that you can return to and review skipped or previously answered questions. Record the questions you can't answer confidently on the scratch paper provided, noting the relative difficulty of each question. When you reach the end of the exam, return to the more difficult questions.

◆ If you have session time remaining after you complete all the questions (and if you aren't too fatigued!), review your answers. Pay particular attention to questions that seem to have a lot of detail or that require graphics.

◆ As for changing your answers, the general rule of thumb here is *don't*! If you read the question carefully and completely and you felt like you knew the right answer, you probably did. Don't second-guess yourself. If, as you check your answers, one clearly stands out as incorrect, however, of course you should change it. But if you are at all unsure, go with your first impression.

Adaptive Exams

If you are planning to take an adaptive exam, keep these additional tips in mind:

◆ Read and answer every question with great care. When you're reading a question, identify every relevant detail, requirement, or task you must perform and double-check your answer to be sure you have addressed every one of them.

◆ If you cannot answer a question, use the process of elimination to reduce the set of potential answers, and then take your best guess. Stupid mistakes invariably mean that additional questions will be presented.

◆ Forget about reviewing questions and changing your answers. When you leave a question, whether you've answered it or not, you cannot return to it. Do not skip any question either; if you do, it's counted as incorrect.

Simulation Questions

You may encounter simulation questions on either the fixed-form or adaptive-form exam. If you do, keep these tips in mind:

◆ Avoid changing any simulation settings that don't pertain directly to the problem solution. Solve the problem you are being asked to solve and nothing more.

◆ Assume default settings when related information has not been provided. If something has not been mentioned or defined, it is a non-critical detail that does not factor into the correct solution.

◆ Be sure your entries are syntactically correct, paying particular attention to your spelling. Enter relevant information just as the product would require it.

◆ Close all simulation application windows when you complete the simulation tasks. The testing system software is designed to trap errors that could result when using the simulation application, but trust yourself over the testing software.

◆ If simulations are part of a fixed-form exam, you can return to skipped or previously answered questions and change your answers. However, if you choose to change your answer on a simulation question or even attempt to review the settings you've made in the simulation application, your previous response to that simulation question will be deleted. If simulations are part of an adaptive exam, you cannot return to previous questions.

Case Studies and Case Study-Based Questions

This new question format calls for unique study and exam-taking strategies. Therefore, this book includes Appendix E, "Quick Tips for Analyzing an Exam Case Study," which is designed to help you acquire those strategies. Read it carefully and follow the recommended approach to taking the exam.

FINAL CONSIDERATIONS

Finally, a number of changes in the MCP program will impact how frequently you can repeat an exam and what you will see when you do.

◆ Microsoft has instituted a new exam retake policy. The new rule is "two and two, then one and two." That is, you can attempt any exam twice with no restrictions on the time between attempts. But after the second attempt, you must wait two weeks before you can attempt that exam again. After that, you will be required to wait two weeks between subsequent attempts. Plan to pass the exam in two attempts or plan to increase your time horizon for receiving the MCP credential.

◆ New questions are being seeded into the MCP exams. After performance data is gathered on new questions, the examiners will replace older questions on all exam forms. This means that the questions appearing on exams will regularly change.

◆ Many of the current MCP exams will be republished in adaptive form in the coming months. Prepare yourself for this significant change in testing as it is entirely likely that this will become the preferred MCP exam format.

These changes mean that the brute-force strategies for passing MCP exams may soon completely lose their viability. So if you don't pass an exam on the first or second attempt, it is likely that the exam's form will change significantly by the next time you take it. It could be updated from fixed-form to adaptive, or it could have a different set of questions or question types.

Microsoft's intention is not to make the exams more difficult by introducing unwanted change, but to create and maintain valid measures of the technical skills and knowledge associated with the different MCP credentials. Preparing for an MCP exam has always involved not only studying the subject matter, but also planning for the testing experience itself. With the recent changes, this is now truer than ever.

This exam consists of case studies and exam questions representative of the types that you should expect on the actual exam. There are four case-study sections or "testlets," which include a case study and a set of questions relevant to the case. A fifth section consists of multiple-choice questions.

The answers to all questions appear in their own section following the exam. We strongly suggest that when you take this exam, you treat it just as you would the actual exam at the test center. Time yourself, read carefully, and answer all the questions to the best of your ability.

Practice Exam

CASE STUDY 1: PEARSON ROOFING

Line of Work

Pearson Roofing specializes in the installation and maintenance of roofs in and around the Sante Fe, New Mexico area.

Problem Statement

The entire installation crew of Pearson has been outsourced in an attempt to cut costs. This has, however, made scheduling new jobs very difficult. Although many talented installers are in Sante Fe, they are not always available when needed.

Pearson has very limited warehousing facilities, so they dare not order new supplies too far in advance. On the other hand, the turnaround times of Pearson's suppliers vary widely.

Installers

Installers are the contract workers responsible for actually constructing or repairing roofs.

Current System

Pearson places advertisements in local trade papers and union halls looking for just enough installers to cover an imminent job. Installers who are interested and available to work respond with resumes. Pearson reviews all resumes received and picks all qualified installers until they have enough. If enough installers are not found, the impending job has to be postponed.

Suppliers

Suppliers manufacture the shingles, tar, and other tools used in the construction and repair of roofs.

Current System

Pearson has worked out semiformal relationships with a number of suppliers in the Sante Fe area. In return for their exclusive patronage, these suppliers are willing to sell goods to Pearson at some level of discount. These discounts vary from 5 percent to 15 percent.

A sample transaction between a supplier and Pearson would begin with Pearson discovering that it is running low on a certain item. Pearson then mails or faxes an order for that item to one of its official suppliers. The supplier, in turn, checks with the manufacturer to determine availability.

The supplier then either orders the item from its manufacturer and ships it to Pearson, or back orders it. Payment from Pearson to the supplier is expected within 30 days of accepting delivery.

Proposed System

Many of the suppliers have multiple applications that they would like to link into Pearson's systems via an extranet. They should all have some common way of uniquely authenticating themselves into the system. The code behind this will probably change infrequently.

CASE STUDY 1: PEARSON ROOFING

Consultant

Pearson has retained the services of an experienced IS consultant to analyze the rules that should govern its new database solution.

Rules

The solution that we are going to build for Pearson needs to implement a variety of rules at the data-tier level. Some of these are

- A rule that converts installers' ID codes into their full names

- A rule that states that all customer balances must be positive

- A rule for converting suppliers' ID codes into their full names

- A rule stating that every supplier in the database must have at least one manufacturer

- A rule stating that every manufacturer must have at least one supplier in the database

- A rule stating that the average turnaround time for a manufacturer cannot exceed one month

- A rule that converts manufacturers' ID codes into their full names

- A rule stating that every customer must have at least one address in the system

- A rule that converts customers' Social Security numbers into their full names

- A rule stating that every telephone number in the database must be of the form (XXX) XXX-XXXX

Manufacturer

The manufacturers are responsible for producing the materials and equipment sold by the suppliers. They are located all across the United States.

Current System

Manufacturers under the current system are only indirectly involved with Pearson Roofing. The process begins when one of Pearson's suppliers realizes that it is out of a given piece of equipment or supplies that they usually sell. This invariably doesn't happen until Pearson actually places an order for the equipment or the supplies.

At this point, the supplier places an order for the goods with a manufacturer. Many manufacturers are capable of producing any given piece of equipment or supplies. The decision is usually made semirandomly on the basis of previous dealings.

The manufacturer may already have sufficient quantities of the goods on hand, in which case the sale takes place immediately. Otherwise, the manufacturer may have a factory that is not currently busy, and the goods can be produced and sold within 24 hours. In the worst case scenario, the manufacturer will neither have the goods nor an available factory, in which case the goods will have to go on back order until they can be produced.

A mainframe computer in Pearson's possession is capable of performing at least 50,000 I/O operations per second.

continues

CASE STUDY 1: PEARSON ROOFING

continued

Proposed System

Pearson would like to establish greater control over the manufacturers used by each of its suppliers. That way, if one manufacturer is unable to produce goods that are desperately needed, suppliers may be directed to use alternate sources.

Most of the manufacturers have multiple applications that they use to estimate the amount of time required to produce new pieces of equipment. Their estimates could be much more accurate if they could directly communicate with similar applications used by suppliers for generating shipping time estimates. The code involved in the manufacturer/ supplier collaboration components will probably change frequently, as manufacturing and shipping technologies evolve.

Features

"In the new system, I would like to be able to enter a telephone number and get back a name. I've seen other automated phone book systems where this kind of stuff can be done in the blink of an eye, and I want our stuff to be every bit as fast!

I also want a single application to compare and contrast the discount rates offered by all our suppliers. Their pricing structures tend to be pretty complicated and change often.

Finally, I want a single application to help me keep track of our installers' availability. This will probably be a very static, unchanging kind of application."

Owner

The owner of Pearson has been involved in measuring the productivity of his own employees for a very long time. He sees no difference between this and setting goals for his new information system.

Exam Questions for Case Study 1

1. Based on the owner's requirements for features in a new solution, on which columns would you place an index? (Choose all that apply.)

   A. Name

   B. TelephoneNumber

   C. SocialSecurityNumber

   D. CurrentBalance

2. In Table 1, select the appropriate data entities and attributes from the list on the right. Categorize each of these in a tree to the left with tables at the top level of the tree, and Primary Keys, Foreign Keys, and Other Attributes all arranged on sub-nodes underneath them. Be aware that not all the items listed will be used in building a correct answer, and some items will be used multiple times.

TABLE 1

CREATE THE TREE

Create the Tree in the Column Below:	Data Entities and Attributes
	Address
	AmountBilled
	AmountDue
	AverageTurnaround
	CurrentBalance
	Customers
	Discount
	ID
	Installers
	ManufacturerID
	Manufacturers
	Name
	OrderNumber
	Orders
	SocialSecurityNumber
	SupplierID
	Suppliers
	SuppliersManufacturers
	TelephoneNumber

3. Which of the following components described in the case study make the best candidate for remaining on a central server and being accessed strictly through DCOM?

   A. The supplier/manufacturer collaboration component for estimating the time required to produce new equipment

   B. The component for helping Pearson's owner track installer availability

   C. The components for uniquely authenticating each supplier into Pearson's extranet

   D. The component for helping Pearson's owner compare and contrast various suppliers' discount rates

4. A number of steps must be processed whenever someone at Pearson wishes to change the information stored about a given supplier. Pick the steps from the following list that would be performed by data-tier components and order them appropriately.

   ◆ If any manufacturer has been left without associate suppliers, remove them.

   ◆ Locate the record keyed on the given username and retrieve its password field.

   ◆ Encrypt the password given according to MD5 encryption standards and compare it to the one returned from the database.

   ◆ Verify that the discount given for the supplier is less than their annual revenue.

   ◆ Display a brief welcome screen.

   ◆ Report an error if the given code isn't associated with any supplier.

   ◆ Verify that any new manufacturer actually exists in the database.

continues

continued

◆ Return all records matching a given supplier code.

◆ Warn user if the solution is being executed on the third day of March.

◆ Report a successful login or a failed password.

◆ Save the updated information.

◆ Request and accept the entry of a supplier ID code.

5. The consultant at Pearson Roofing has identified a number of rules that any new solution must implement correctly. Using Table 2, categorize each of these rules according to whether they are Domain, Translation, or Relational rules. Draw a line from each rule on the right to the appropriate rule type on the left.

TABLE 2

DRAW A LINE FROM THE RULE TO THE APPROPRIATE RULE TYPE

Rule Type	Rules
Domain	• A rule that converts installers' ID codes into their full names
	• A rule stating that all customer balances must be positive
	• A rule stating that every supplier in the database must have at least one manufacturer
	• A rule stating that everymanufacturer in the database must haveat least one supplier
Translation	• A rule stating that the average turnaround time for a manufacturer cannot exceed one month
Relational	• A rule that converts manufacturers' ID codes into their full names
	• A rule stating that every customer must have at least one address in the system
	• A rule that converts customers' Social Security numbers into their full names
	• A rule stating that every telephone number in the database must be of the form (XXX) XXX-XXXX

6. A great deal of information changes hands in systems currently surrounding Pearson Roofing. Connect the seven entities listed in Table 3 with arrows representing the pieces of information that are also listed. Clearly label each arrow with the piece of information it is intended to represent, and make sure that the direction of flow is obvious. Note: some pieces of information are used more than once, so beware!

TABLE 3

CONNECT THE ENTITIES WITH THE APPROPRIATE PIECES OF INFORMATION

Entities	Pieces of Information
Contractors	Back orders
Customers	Discounts
Installers	Estimates
Manufacturers	Hiring decisions
Newspapers	Orders
Pearson Roofing	Printed ads
Suppliers	Quotes
	Resumes
	Submitted ads

7. Which of the following is a comment on "real" performance made in the case study?

    A. Installers will perceive slowness as malfunctions.

    B. The mainframe can do 50,000 I/O operations in a second.

    C. The owner is expecting his automated phone book to work as fast as all the others he has seen.

    D. The mainframe can do 25,000 I/O operations in a second.

8. Given the description of Pearson's installers and their needs, what model for software distribution and use seems most advised?

    A. Standalone applications delivered via mass mailings to prospective, current, and former employees

    B. ActiveX documents that automatically load into Internet Explorer and operate similarly to standalone Windows applications

    C. Password-protected HTML applications designed to work in any browser on any operating system

    D. Standalone applications delivered via shared network directory

9. Given the relationship between suppliers and manufacturers, how could you best model this using components and collections?

    A. Many supplier objects and many manufacturer objects.

    B. Many supplier objects, each with its own manufacturers collection.

    C. Many manufacturer objects, each with its own suppliers collection.

    D. Many supplier objects, each with its own collection of manufacturer objects. Every manufacturer object also contains its own suppliers collection.

10. Of all the different ways to implement software for the installers, which method would probably create the fastest-running applications?

    A. Single-use, out-of-process components

    B. In-process components

    C. Multiuse, out-of-process components

    D. Components accessed remotely via DCOM

CASE STUDY 2: NR CAFE

Background

NR Cafe is the largest of all multinational fast-food chains.

Current Project

The management of NR Cafe would like to ensure the consistency of recipes followed by its chefs all over the world. For example, a plate of NR Cafe spaghetti should be made the same in Rome, Italy, as in Tokyo, Japan.

Also, every NR Cafe restaurant must currently have at least three chefs on duty whenever it is open. This is because of the excessive amount of time required to produce a single entree.

The excessive time is thought to result largely from the tendency among NR's chefs to want to make each new entree a little different from the last. This level of personalization costs the company time and money through the cost of extra ingredients and customers lost due to slow responses.

In response to these problems, NR Cafe is trying to develop an automated system that will

- ◆ Reduce time spent gathering ingredients
- ◆ Increase the consistency of entree recipes
- ◆ Eliminate much of the wait staff

Chef

Every entree prepared at a NR Cafe restaurant is the unique creation of a single chef. Every chef works at just one NR Cafe restaurant and, therefore, naturally develops a certain feeling of loyalty to that particular branch of the organization.

Workflows

The current workflow is as follows:

1. A waitress pins a piece of paper with an order written on it to a metal wheel outside the kitchen.

2. A chef grabs whichever piece of paper on the wheel is next.

3. The chef rotates the wheel to move the next piece of paper into position.

4. The chef reviews the order and, if needed, consults the recipe books in the kitchen.

5. The chef gathers all needed ingredients from the pantry.

6. The chef makes the requested entrees.

7. The chef places the food next to the metal wheel with the original piece of paper on top of it.

8. A waitress picks up the finished order and delivers it to the customer.

CASE STUDY 2: NR CAFE

The proposed workflow is as follows:

1. A customer places the order directly at the table, using some kind of electronic device.

2. The proposed solution finds the company-mandated recipes for all entrees in the order.

3. Robotic devices in the pantry, under the control of the proposed solution, gather all required ingredients and drop them onto a conveyor belt.

4. The conveyor belt delivers the ingredients to a chef as soon as that chef finishes preparing his previous entree.

5. A computer display in front of the chef displays the required recipe.

6. The chef prepares the entree in accordance with the recipe and places it on the conveyor belt.

7. The conveyor belt delivers the entree to the customer as another batch of ingredients and recipe are given to the chef.

Customer

Research has shown that the typical NR Cafe customer is looking for food that meets just a few, basic requirements.

Basic Requirements

◆ **Variety**—The flavor of dishes varies enough from one NR Cafe to the next to keep things interesting.

◆ **Nutrition**—Most of the customers surveyed seemed to think that when they were eating at NR Cafe, they were eating healthy food.

The customers seem to have only one need that is not being met by NR Cafe.

Unmet Requirement

◆ Speed of Service—The amount of time needed to be served at NR Cafe is generally seen as excessive.

Software Engineer

NR Cafe employs a total of 30 full-time software engineers, all of whom hold a minimum of bachelor's degrees in computer science.

Envisioned System

"We just finished doing a study here that indicated that we've been completely rewriting our entire information infrastructure from scratch every two years! This has got to come to a stop. We're talking millions and millions of lines of C code here.

continues

CASE STUDY 2: NR CAFE

continued

Any new system we build must take two important things into account. First, the amount of business taken in by each of our restaurants tends to double every year. Second, based on past experience, we are going to want to add a lot of new features to anything we build—constantly!

The most important thing to me is that we should be able to change even the smallest detail in the implementation of our solutions at all times."

DBA

There is one MS MCDBA at NR Cafe.

Envisioned System

"Many of our applications seem to take a long time to start. In actuality, they all just tend to start with a lot of database requests. It would be nice if all our applications continue working on something else while they wait for our database to respond to them."

Security

"Some of the tables in our database contain columns that need to be seen by everyone; they're mixed in with columns that should be seen only by a few people. For example, our Entrees table lists the retail price for each dish, which everyone should be able to see. But, then it also lists the production cost, which should be available only to accounting employees.

Our network managers are the only people at NR Cafe that should be allowed to change security settings."

Network Manager

Three network managers are employed at NR Cafe. They work in shifts designed so that one network manager is always at work at all times. It is the network manager's job to ensure that all restaurants remain connected to the company's central office at all times.

Envisioned System

"We've been maintaining our own WAN with microwave technology for the last few years. It has done a good job for us, but it is very expensive. In whatever new solution we construct, it would be much cheaper to use the Internet."

Availability

"We have restaurants open 24-hours a day, so our network must be available constantly."

Exam Questions for Case Study 2

1. A number of steps must be processed whenever a customer orders food at a NR Cafe restaurant. Pick the steps from the following list that would be performed by the user interface tier components and order them appropriately.

   ◆ Customer is informed that his or her credit card, if invalid, is being rejected.

   ◆ Name, birth date, and a credit card number are requested.

   ◆ Ingredients are gathered.

   ◆ All recipes involved are retrieved.

   ◆ Any beverages containing alcohol are made unavailable if no one over 21 is in the party.

   ◆ Tip amount is requested.

   ◆ Any tip amount less than 15 percent is rounded up to this level.

   ◆ Appropriate recipes are displayed for the chef.

   ◆ The final charge for the meal is displayed and the customer is thanked.

   ◆ The customer's credit card is charged.

2. Given the software engineer's description of his envisioned system, how would you try to design the objects for NR Cafe's new solution?

   A. Fewer, simpler objects

   B. Fewer, more complicated objects

   C. More numerous, simpler objects

   D. More numerous, more complicated objects

3. Suppose that NR Cafe wants to allow its chefs to access the main recipe database from home via the World Wide Web. What technology could prevent unauthorized interception of secret recipes as they travel across the Internet?

   A. Active Server Pages

   B. Internet Information Server

   C. Cookies

   D. Secure Sockets Layer

4. NR Cafe operates restaurants all over the world. What is the best design for an application that must be used in every location where they operate?

   A. A single executable and many .dll files

   B. Multiple executables and one .dll file

   C. No executables—just resource files

   D. None of the above

5. NR Cafe operates restaurants all over the world. What is the best layout for user interface controls in any given location where they operate?

   A. Top to bottom, left to right

   B. Top to bottom, text component left to right, and graphical components in whichever order seems most logical

   C. Whichever order text is read in the location's native language

   D. None of the above

6. Classify the methods and properties in Table 4 according to the components that they would most likely be a part of.

TABLE 4

CLASSIFY THE METHODS AND PROPERTIES BY COMPONENT

Component	Method/Property
Recipe	TotalOrderPrice
	makeWithoutFat
	calculateAge
Customer	verifyFormat
	gatherIngredients
	deliverOrder
Credit card	charge
	restrainCustomer
	lookupMenu
Robot	IsAlcoholic
	lookupRecipes
	Ingredients
Librarian	addTax
	addTip

7. The DBA at NR Cafe expressed a desire that the applications could continue to work on "other things" while waiting for database responses. Which of the following technologies could best be used to achieve this result?

   A. Indexes

   B. Callback functions

   C. Polling

   D. All of the above

8. Which of the following constitutes the best statement of NR Cafe's problem?

   A. Making food that tastes good and that is nutritious is the only thing that NR Cafe is doing properly.

   B. Chefs need to be forced to follow the recommended recipes.

   C. Customers need to be warned ahead of time about the time required for their entrees.

   D. Entrees are not being prepared in an acceptable amount of time.

9. Based solely on the software engineer's desire to be able to constantly tweak even the smallest details of NR Cafe's solutions, what method of extension seems the most advisable?

   A. Source code

   B. APIs

   C. Components

   D. Requirements analysis

10. NR Cafe offers a selection of more than 3,000 exotic (and alcoholic) beverages. Suppose a company policy is put into effect that prohibits serving more than a single alcoholic beverage to a customer during a single visit. What, then, would be the best way of presenting this choice of beverages to customers?

    A. Radio buttons

    B. A drop-down list

    C. Check boxes

    D. A slider bar

11. Classify the factors in Table 5 according to the aspect of performance that they would influence.

TABLE 5

PERFORMANCE ASPECTS AND INFLUENTIAL FACTORS

Aspects of Performance	Factors
workload	Late binding
	Single tier
hardware	Digital Alpha
	New stores
architectural design	Optimistic, row-level locking
	Obsolescence
data access	Binary tree searching
	Single-use components
	128 Megabytes of SDRAM

12. Every entity in the left column of Table 6 represents a single participant in NR Cafe's business. Each one corresponds to exactly one security role in the right column of the table. Specify which relate to which.

TABLE 6

PARTICIPANTS AND SECURITY ROLES

Participants	Roles
Technical staff	Client
Customer	Group
Network manager	Administrator
Chef	Guest

13. You would like to provide a way for customers to order multiple dishes. What button should you put on the order form to send their orders without closing the window?

A. Test

B. Submit

C. Apply

D. Refresh

MULTIPLE-CHOICE EXAM QUESTIONS

1. A Microsoft Windows help file is a compiled version of a specially constructed file of what type?

A. hlp

B. doc

C. txt

D. rtf

2. MTS can register which of the following types of objects?

A. ActiveX EXE Server

B. ActiveX DLL Server

C. Non-COM Exe

D. All of the above

3. What is the benefit of Unicode in relation to localization?

A. Language translation

B. Ease of implementation

C. Expanded character set

D. None of the above

4. What is the logic behind the partitioning of a system into multiple tiers?

   A. Separation and encapsulation of functionality.

   B. It increases single-user performance.

   C. It simplifies development.

   D. All of the above.

5. How will deploying ADO and OLE DB in an application increase the solution's flexibility over ODBC?

   A. ADO performs faster than ODBC.

   B. ADO permits binding to non-SQL data sources.

   C. ODBC is an API; OLE DB is not.

   D. COM makes ODBC slower.

6. What is the purpose of a business object?

   A. To increase the speed of an application

   B. To allow for transactions

   C. To connect the user interface as the data tier

   D. To allocate a logical location to apply business rules.

7. You are writing an application in which the primary need is a strong user interface and a short development cycle. Which tool makes the most sense to consider for development?

   A. Visual C++

   B. Visual J++

   C. Visual Basic

   D. Visual InterDev

8. What is the best way to provide help on demand for specific controls on a form?

   A. ToolTips

   B. Status bar captioning

   C. Online help

   D. What's This? help

9. You are designing an application with a toolbar. You want little captions to appear next to the pointer whenever a user hovers the mouse pointer over one of your toolbar's buttons. What kind of help is this?

   A. ToolTips

   B. Status bar captioning

   C. Online help

   D. What's This? help

10. What is the appropriate position for "Help" on an application's menu?

    A. Left edge of the application's menu bar

    B. Right edge of the application's menu bar

    C. First menu option running left to right, regardless of absolute position within application's window

    D. Last menu option running left to right, regardless of absolute position within application's window

CASE STUDY 3: DAVIDSON AUTOMOBILES

Background

Davidson has been building cars in this country for more than 50 years. During that time, the company has built an effective and efficient means of manually managing materials inventory and dealer supply.

The key to its continued profitability is to perpetuate the effective management of materials supply. Davidson simply doesn't have the warehousing space to store raw materials indefinitely, and it cannot afford to have huge overheads of these materials just sitting and waiting. The target for the company's process is that never more than one day of excess materials should be at a factory at any time.

Davidson has two main plants. One is in Marietta, Georgia. The other is in Phoenix, Arizona. Each employs approximately 5,000 workers at various levels. Management at the plants comprise approximately another 150 employees.

Problem Statement

The overall problem for Davidson is a fairly simple one. Because it has had some excellent manual processes for accumulating warehouse efficiency metrics, it has delayed automation of this system as the company continued to grow. Now, however, it is beginning to reach a point where this manual process is costing the company more than building an automated process for it would cost.

The key result of the manual process overload is the amount of time it takes to spot a problem. As the process is now completed, the AS/400 system generates certain reports that are an indication of usage and production. However, they are not generated for a typical executive decision-maker. Instead they are statistical analysis documents. These documents are distributed to a team of statisticians.

At this point, end-user reports in Microsoft Excel are created by the statisticians and distributed to the two district managers. These individuals are then responsible for making sure that the report is reviewed and that ordering is modified accordingly.

This process has been getting more complex over the past 10 years as more and more steps are added to the process. If the profitability of the company is going to be maintained for the long-term, a substantial decrease must occur in the time it takes for this information to get to the district managers.

Current System

The current system for managing inventory and production at Davidson is less an automated system and more a human process. Virtually no automation of the process has occurred, which is where many of the problems originate.

New raw materials coming in are tracked very carefully and are entered into a SQL-based data source. This is used also for verification of receipt before invoice payment.

The machinery that is used to assemble the automobiles has the capability to track how many cars have been assembled at any given point.

continues

CASE STUDY 2: DAVIDSON AUTOMOBILES

continued

This information is fed into an AS/400, where a mainframe program generates statistical output about the usage of materials. The program currently runs once a day and calculates the usage over the entire day.

This information is then output to a line printer and is delivered to an engineer who plays the role of statistician. This person performs the necessary translation to make this report meaningful to decision makers and inputs the new data into a Microsoft Excel spreadsheet. This file is then available to be electronically distributed to the appropriate people. This usually takes most of the morning, and the information is normally not available for a given day until after the plant in Georgia has gone home for the day.

Inventory Manager

"It is amazing to me, and a credit to our people, that things have run as smoothly as they have for as long as they have. However, some definite problems exist with our process, especially in terms of turnaround time on the information. We have to hold far more materials in warehouse than is necessary, simply because we don't have a fine-grained enough approach to managing the inventory.

The ideal scenario would be to receive and consume our entire inventory each day. I know that isn't literally doable, but I'd like to see us get closer to that than we are now. To do that, we need information hourly, not daily."

IS Director

"I've got one of my most talented developers (who happens to also be a statistics graduate) working at least half-time on simply translating all the information that comes out of our monitoring equipment into meaningful data for executives. I realize it's necessary, but it could be automated so that it would free him up to work on other things."

Plant Manager

"My bottom line is directly impacted by how long I have to store raw materials. It currently takes us days to see how changes to procedure have affected this. That's just not going to be acceptable as higher and higher levels of profitability are targeted.

What I really need is a system that can give me this information in a format that can be easily used. Sometimes I want to be able to analyze how productivity and consumption varies across a 24-hour period, not just in one big block, midnight to midnight."

Envisioned System

The new system, as it is currently envisioned, needs to have a faster turnaround time for results than what currently exists in the process.

To accomplish this goal, the system is going to be collecting the data from bar-code scanners placed at each raw material disposition site. As all material is dispensed to the assembly line, the material usage is recorded into the database instantaneously.

CASE STUDY 3: DAVIDSON AUTOMOBILES

The scanner data feeds into a mainframe database, and it is then replicated into a new SQL Server data warehouse created for our solution and made available to the inventory managers to be queried, sliced, or analyzed in any way that they choose. The managers still want to be able to use the charting capability of Excel, so it is a requirement that the solution export data directly into Excel spreadsheets.

For the end user, this will all be accessible through a user interface that is hooked into the database via access to the stored procedures.

This interface will allow the end user to request information of various types and have it preprocessed by the stored procedure into a format that makes sense to a decision-making end user.

This will also be exportable to Microsoft Excel so that users who perform specific functions with the data will be able to continue to do so.

Availability

The plants each run two shifts per day. The first shift runs from 7:00 a.m. to 4:00 p.m., the second from 4:30 p.m. to 1:30 a.m. Additionally, they operate six days each week, usually with five holidays during a year.

Plant Manager

"My foremost concern is that this system should not impact our ability to keep working. Even if this new system completely goes down, I don't want it to impact our ability to perform our primary business, which is making the best cars in the world.

The truth is, we can recover from losing some information about how fast we use up car doors. What we can't recover from, though, is having one of our plants stop working—while we're paying our workers—because of a problem with recording information."

Scalability

Today, the reports are directly distributed only to the two plant managers. With the new system, however, it would be valuable to be able to distribute it to the entire management team at Davidson. This consists of approximately 75 individuals.

Plant Manager

"When there was just one report, it was possible, although not efficient, to have the two of us be the conduit for the report. However, if everyone is going to be able to request his or her own reports, we need to provide the automatic ability to give it back to the proper person automatically. After all, we don't run a clearinghouse here in my office for reports."

IS Director

"If we're going to allow managers to design and run their own queries, the system should expect performance spikes. We will try to design enough intelligence into the interface and into stored procedures so that the managers can't run a query that will take down the mainframe."

Exam Questions for Case Study 3

1. What solution type is being represented here?

   A. Single tier

   B. Two tier

   C. *n*-tier

2. As an application designer building this application, why would it be valuable to use stored procedures for data access? (Choose all that apply.)

   A. Easier to develop

   B. Abstraction of data, enabling some database change

   C. Easier to deploy business logic

   D. Better performance

3. Using the preceding information, sketch a workflow process diagram for the current business process at Davidson when it comes to inventory management.

4. Using the following pieces, sketch the conceptual architecture of the solution: database, warehouse, bar-code interface software, Excel worksheet, user interface/analysis software, bar-code scanner, stored procedures. Add a dotted box around the pieces that exist on the mainframe and the pieces that exist on the user's PC.

5. As a system architect, what would be reasonable for you to create as an availability requirement based on the preceding information?

   A. Monday – Saturday, 7:00 a.m. EST to 4:30 a.m. EST

   B. Monday – Saturday 7:00 a.m. EST to 1:30 a.m. EST

   C. Monday – Friday 8:00 a.m. EST to 5:00 a.m. EST

   D. Monday – Friday 7:00 a.m. EST to 1:30 a.m. EST

6. Why is process engineering such a major part of this project for an application designer?

   A. No processes are in place.

   B. No automated processes are in place.

   C. No business rules exist to analyze the data.

   D. Processes need to be reworked because they are broken.

7. What have we done from a process standpoint to make the solution more scalable?

   A. Removed the necessity of human contact from it.

   B. Decreased the code base used.

   C. Partitioned the application over more machines.

   D. We have not increased scalability from a process standpoint.

8. How is the required uptime for our solution related to the required uptime for the production line?

   A. Dependent; when our application goes down, both do.

   B. Dependent, but can be separated.

   C. Independent; our application can go down without affecting the system.

   D. Independent, but it has to be manually separated.

9. Which of the following technologies would be appropriate for this solution? (Choose two.)

   A. ADO

   B. Visual InterDev

   C. ODBC

   D. MTS

10. Which aspect of our solution illustrates our integration with existing processes?

   A. Maintaining existing Excel reports

   B. Changing distribution methods

   C. Altering the flow of the reports

   D. Changing the time intervals for reports

11. As the solution designer, how can you illustrate that the solution really does solve the business problem?

   A. By showing the reports that the system generates

   B. By ensuring that the database design enforces referential integrity

   C. By asking a user if the solution has achieved the result

   D. By checking the deployed solution against use cases

CASE STUDY 4: Z PRODUCE, INC.

Background

Z Produce is the second largest commercial producer of produce in the United States. Its corporate office is based in Los Angeles, CA. However, the bulk of the company is not at this location; it is scattered throughout dozens of farms and thousands of acres around the country and, to a smaller extent, internationally.

The company has been profitable over the last few years. However, over the last two quarters profitability has decreased sharply, and although they are not yet losing money, investors are starting to notice the lower-than-expected profits.

After some analysis of sales and production, one of the main things that changed during the past few years is the predictability of supply. Because of some extraordinary extremes in weather over the past few months, the company was unable to accurately predict what the internal supply of given commodities would be.

Because they were not able to identify in a timely manner an upcoming shortfall, Z Produce was forced to pay a premium to suppliers for certain fruits and vegetables.

Problem

Currently, the first time that Z Produce analysts have any knowledge of how the product is coming is when it is harvested.

If any circumstances exist that will change the amount of produce harvested (either positively or negatively), an employee must take the initiative to inform someone of the problem.

continues

continued

As a company that bases many of it profit-making decisions on the supply of given commodities it can provide, not having this type of information is a critical mark against long-term profitability.

Current System

Currently, Z Produce has a good system for inventory after the commodities are harvested. This system uses a series of Windows NT Servers located at the main office, which runs a SQL Server to track the levels of harvested produce.

This system is populated by a PC running Windows NT Workstation on each of the farms. The farm managers input the data that is discovered from the harvest, and these values are used to decide whether and/or how much of a given commodity should be bought.

What is not currently in place is a process for formalized tracking of the conditions of the crops and estimates as to the normal yield of the field. Instead, if an obvious problem occurs, informal processes are in place to email someone in the main office. Too often, however, those emails are either not sent or they are incomplete, insufficient, or simply are overlooked or ignored.

Farmer

"I have farmed in the county here for twenty years. I could have told them three months ago that the bean yield was down about a quarter. We did tell the manager here on the farm. He says he sent an

email to someone about it, but you know how those email things are. Sometimes it doesn't work like it is supposed to. And even if it did, it isn't necessarily going to get their attention when it counts."

Envisioned System

The envisioned system is basically a supplement to the existing system.

The solution involves putting into the hands of the farmers a tool to report on the conditions in individual fields. A number of additional PCs will be placed in the main office of each of the farms (the number proportional to the number of farmers working). Each farmer will keep track of the situation on paper (if necessary) and input their forecasts into the system.

This software will be using the current Windows NT Workstation computer as a server to maintain a local data store. At the end of each day, replication procedures will synchronize the local data store's new entries with the centralized SQL Server at the main corporate offices. In this way, information about the various crops can be analyzed and delivered to appropriate decision makers in a timely and systematic manner.

Farmer

"I guess I don't care which one we try to do, but I don't want to spend hours doing it. It needs to be easy. I've got a system at home. If I could dial in to the server, that would be best."

CASE STUDY 3: Z PRODUCE, INC.

Security

This information is being requested for a very specific, profit-related reason. If it were to leak out to other companies or to individuals within those companies, a great deal of damage could result.

This is one reason that an Internet-based solution was viewed as impractical. Given that trunk lines already exist to support the other aspects of the system that run directly between the farms and the main office, it was considered a needless security risk to open up the system to the Internet.

Extensibility

Crop predictions are just one way in which people who are on the ground on a day-to-day basis could improve profitability. Information about the soil, weather patterns, and even the pervasiveness of certain crop-based pests can all be tracked through this type of system.

Consequently, we need to make sure that there is a means of allowing the application to be applied to other circumstances. Specifically, we might construct it to allow different data to be collected.

Maintainability

The big priority with maintainability in this situation is that the application should be relatively self-contained. Centralization is not going to be part of this installation. However, creating a system that has a relatively straightforward installation/deinstallation procedure will take a large step toward allowing simpler maintenance.

Exam Questions for Case Study 4

1. From the perspective of an application designer, which type of interface would most directly achieve the goals of Z Produce, Inc.?

   A. Single document interface

   B. Multiple document interface

   C. Workspace interface

   D. Internet browser interface

2. Why would it be so critical to include online help in this solution?

   A. Users are less attentive.

   B. Less opportunity exists for training.

   C. The application is more complex.

   D. Both A and C.

3. When considering the design of a system, how will the proposed solution decrease the total cost of ownership (TCO)?

   A. Machines are less expensive than people.

   B. Z Produce stands to increase its profits through better information.

   C. Much of the existing infrastructure is used.

   D. The application is reusing code from a legacy application.

4. How would you classify the type of solution that we are designing for Z Produce, Inc.? (Choose all that apply.)

   A. Communication

   B. Data entry

   C. Workflow

   D. Messaging

5. When designing the application, how would you sketch the newly planned flow of work? Label which connectors represent a LAN and which represent a WAN (potential latency issue). Also label where the solution is synchronous and where it is asynchronous.

6. What unique technical issues are imposed by our proposed solution?

   A. Maintenance of a data store.

   B. Data synchronization across the WAN.

   C. User-interface design issues.

   D. Asynchronous database update from the user interface.

7. Which technologies would be appropriate for this solution? (choose all that apply.)

   A. MSMQ

   B. ADO

   C. Visual Basic

   D. MTS

8. How can the system be designed to meet the level of security required?

   A. Individual logins to the NT Client machines

   B. Database user logging to monitor changes

   C. Not exposing application to external network

   D. Locking down system based on time of day

9. Performance is a consideration in any system. How has our system design been able to increase performance?

   A. More clients to a server

   B. Local data stores that synchronize with the main one

   C. Servers on each site

   D. Using MTS to build an n-tier solution

10. How are you meeting your goals for extensibility in the solution?

    A. Building the infrastructure that other systems can take advantage of

    B. Making the application programmable, to collect other kinds of data

    C. Making the source code for the application public

    D. None of the above

11. What are the difficulties we have created in regard to maintaining the solution based on our design? (Choose all that apply.)

   A. No centralization of application code

   B. No automatic installation of the application

   C. Client-based solution, rather than server based

   D. Widely distributed location of machines

ANSWERS TO EXAM QUESTIONS

Answers to the case study exam questions and the multiple-choice exam question are listed next.

Answers to Exam Questions for Case Study 1

1. **B.** You should always place an index on the column that a lookup will be based on. In this case, you want to find a name based on a given telephone number. Putting an index on the name, therefore, would be like arranging the index in a book to tell you what contents were on which pages, rather than which pages different topics were on.

2. See how closely your drawing represents the contents of Figure 1.

   Only a few things here may surprise you. The first of these is the absence of a CurrentBalance column in the Customers

table and an AverageTurnaround column in the Manufacturers table. They have been removed because they are computed fields and are therefore a violation of Third normal form.

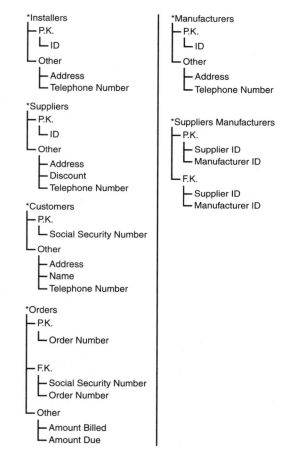

FIGURE 1
Answer to Case Study 1, question 2.

3. **A.** The best candidate component for distributed access will be one that is subject to frequent changes and one that is reused in multiple applications. The component we chose was described in the case study as being both of these things. Although the case study did not say so, functionality that is packaged in distributed components should also have loose performance requirements and should not be frequently accessed.

4. All the records except those listed next belong either to the user interface or the logic tiers of the solution. The rule about ensuring that every installer record has a matching entry in the suppliers table is, indeed, a data-tier procedure. Unfortunately, it is not even remotely required by the solution that we are trying to build.

    1. Locate the record keyed on the given username and retrieve its password field.

    2. Return all records matching a given supplier code.

    3. Verify that any new manufacturer actually exists in the database.

    4. If any manufacturer has been left without associated suppliers, remove it.

    5. Save the updated information.

5. A domain rule regulates the range of values that are allowed for fields within a database. The following rules met these criteria:

    ◆ A rule that states that all customer balances must be positive

    ◆ A rule that states that the average turn-around time for a manufacturer cannot exceed one month

A translation rule is a rule that converts values stored in your database into values that your solution can use directly. The following rules met these criteria:

◆ A rule that converts installers' ID codes into their full names

◆ A rule that converts suppliers' ID codes into their full names

◆ A rule that converts manufacturers' ID codes into their full names

◆ A rule that converts customers' ID codes into their full names

◆ A rule that states that every telephone number in the database must be of the form (XXX) XXX-XXXX

A relational rule is a rule that ensures that the proper n-to-n relationships exist between specific entity instances within your solution's database. The following rules met these criteria:

◆ A rule stating that every supplier in the database must have at least one manufacturer

◆ A rule stating that every manufacturer in the database must have at least one supplier

6. See how closely your drawing represents the contents of Figure 2.

The bit about whether back orders flow from the manufacturers to the suppliers or vice versa is completely arbitrary, so don't beat yourself up if you have that arrow going in the opposite direction. The rest of the drawing should look pretty similar, however.

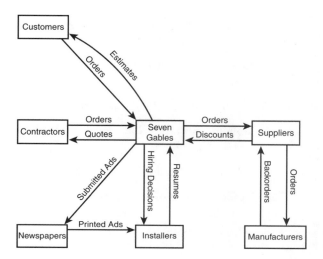

FIGURE 2
Answer to Case Study 1, question 6.

7. **B.** Real performance statements should include some kind of accurate measurement of the performance being observed. Although the installers' reaction to system slowness is definitely relevant to performance, it lacks the kind of quantification needed for our purposes. The owner's experience with other phone book applications is an example of expected response times. A real performance measurement would be 25,000 I/O operations, but it disagrees with the 50,000 cited in the text.

8. **C.** Microsoft considers HTML in a browser to be the ultimate in maintainability and extensibility. This is what the case study tells us any solution used by the installers must be. Mailing software is not nearly as instant as delivering it via a network. ActiveX documents and shared network directories would require more of the installers' hardware and operating systems than the case study would lead us to believe we should expect of them.

9. **D.** The only proper modeling for the relationship between suppliers and manufacturers has two collections. This is because the two exist in a many-to-many relationship. All other proposed solutions would reduce at least one side of the relationship to a singular status.

10. **B.** In-process components will always outperform the other kinds of components. The benefit to out-of-process components running on the same machine is that they can run more independently, allowing the use of so-called call-backs to improve *perceived* performance (sometimes). Out-of-process components have their own execution thread, so they can perform work independently of whatever calls them. They are also much less likely to crash your application if they are improperly coded.

Remote components are the basis of distributed computing and allow for incredible levels of code reuse. They tend to hamper solution performance, however, because of the slowness of network links in comparison to that of the data buses inside modern computers.

Answers to Exam Questions for Case Study 2

1. All the records except those listed next belong either to the data or the logic tiers of the solution.

    1. Name, birth date, and a credit card number are requested.

    2. Customer is informed that his or her credit card, if invalid, is being rejected.

    3. Appropriate recipes are displayed for the chef.

4. Tip amount is requested.

5. The final charge for the meal is displayed and the customer is thanked.

2. **C.** The software engineer wants us to bear in mind the addition of stores and the need to keep adding functionality. This corresponds to the PASS ME goals of scalability and extensibility. Using only a few complicated objects tends not to scale as well as multiple, simple objects because their attempts to do too much often keep vital resources in use.

3. **D.** The solution could use Secure Sockets Layer to encrypt information for transmission across the Internet. Cookies store information on the NR Cafe client computers via Web browser interactions. Active Server Pages and/or Internet Information Server could also be used in building this kind of solution, but they are not needed.

4. **A.** The idea is to put the locale-specific portions of your application into different .dlls. Then you can distribute the same .exe with whatever .dll is appropriate for the target installation. Resource files are also good for internationalization, and they hold the additional advantage of being able to store noncode objects such as graphics. They must, however, be used in conjunction with some kind of executable code.

5. **C.** Microsoft suggests laying out the elements in your applications as closely as possible to the order in which text is read in your target environments. Top to bottom and left to right is just how we happen to read text in Western cultures.

6. The correct answers are given next. Robot is perhaps the most highly abstract of the components listed—consider correct answers for this component as bonus points.

- ◆ Recipe = IsAlcoholic, Ingredients, makeWithoutFat

- ◆ Customer = calculateAge, addTip, addTax, TotalOrderPrice

- ◆ CreditCard = verifyFormat, charge

- ◆ Robot = gatherIngredients, deliverOrder, restrainCustomer

- ◆ Librarian = lookupMenu, lookupRecipes

7. **B.** A callback function is used whenever your application has other work that it can attend to while awaiting a response from another process or machine. Polling is an active process of waiting, which is not covered in this text and is not important for the Microsoft exam. Indexes are used to improve the performance of some kinds of database queries and are not related to this question.

8. **D.** This is the only statement that tells us specifically what is going wrong. The first statement, answer A, essentially tells us exactly the opposite—that is, what is still working all right at NR Cafe. The remaining two options are actually suggestions for fixing the problem—not statements of the problem itself.

9. **A.** Source code allows for the greatest degree of control over the behavior of a solution. APIs would be nice from the standpoint that C is a heavily used language at NR Cafe, but it is not as flexible. Components are the least flexible of all and are geared more toward reusability and ease of learning. Requirements analysis is a step in the creation of a solution; it is not a method of extension.

10. **B.**   A drop-down list is the most appropriate choice for a single-choice decision when the alternatives are very numerous. Most monitors wouldn't have room for enough radio buttons. Check boxes generally are a bad idea in this case because they are supposed to be used for multiple-choice situations. A slider bar is usually an appropriate choice only when selecting a difficult-to-quantify value from between two extremes.

11. Workload = new stores (increasing) and obsolescence (decreasing)

    Hardware = Digital Alpha (a kind of CPU) and 128 Megabytes of SDRAM (memory)

    Architectural Design = Late binding (slower kind of resource allocation), single tier (as opposed to two tier or *n*-tier), and single-use components (which require a new process for each object instantiated)

    Data access = Optimistic, row-level locking (the best kind for concurrency) and binary tree searching (the quickest method for data that is already sorted)

12. Clients are internal users and applications that use your solution—in this case, the chefs. Groups are logical groupings of administrators, clients, and guests—in this case, the technical staff. Administrators are security audience members empowered to change security policies, permissions, and accounts, and the only person at NR Cafe fitting that description is the network manager. Finally, guests are people and programs that use your solution, but they are typically external to the organization for which your solution was developed—for example, the customers.

13. **C.**   An Apply button is the Microsoft-prescribed method for making changes in a solution without closing the dialog box where the changes are being made. In standard Windows Interface Design, no such thing exists as a Test button. Submit and Refresh typically are found on Web pages. Submit, however, usually closes a form after sending the requested information. Refresh, on the other hand, completely clears the form being filled out.

Answers to Multiple-Choice Exam Questions

1. **D.**   Microsoft Windows help files have the extension .hlp, but they are created with a special compiler from properly formatted Rich Text Files. These files use the extension .rtf.

2. **B.**   MTS cannot accept any non-COM-based object, therefore answer C cannot be the case. Additionally, EXE Servers cannot be loaded under MTS. ActiveX DLLs, however, as both COM objects and DLL Servers, can be loaded under MTS.

3. **C.**   Unicode is a specification that lays out two bytes for each character. Rather than the ANSI standard sets of possible characters, there are literally thousands of possible characters. This allows the display of an expanded set of characters, enabling applications to be written for multiple languages, thus benefiting localization.

4. **A.**   Partitioning a system allows it to encapsulate certain aspects away from the rest of the system. It decreases single-user performance and makes development more difficult.

5. **B.** ADO and OLE DB bring the capability to bind to non-SQL based data sources, such as email stores or flatfiles, to the table. ADO is not faster than ODBC, and OLE DB is an API, as is ODBC.

6. **D.** Business objects do not increase the speed of an application. Nor do they, of themselves, allow for transactions. In a two-tier application, the data tier and the user interface are directly connected, so that is not the purpose, either. The purpose of a business object is to create a place in the code for business rules to be applied.

7. **C.** Visual C++ and Visual J++ both have longer development cycles than does Visual Basic. Furthermore, Visual Basic is targeted at RAD development and is focused on providing a rich user-interface experience. InterDev probably has a longer debugging cycle and certainly lacks the rich control of the user interface that VB provides.

8. **D.** What's This? help is considered the appropriate method for providing user assistance on demand for questions pertaining to nontoolbar portions of the user interface. ToolTips are for use with toolbars only. Status bar captioning will occur without a specific request from the user. Online help is not recommended for questions pertaining strictly to questions of the user interface.

9. **A.** ToolTips are provided and recommended precisely for providing these kinds of floating captions for toolbars. Status bar captioning would also work, but not as well because the captioning text is located on a different part of the screen from the pointer (and the user's attention). Online help is not recommended for any questions pertaining strictly to the user interface. Finally, What's This? help is a good choice for user-interface questions, but ToolTips are superior where toolbars are concerned.

10. **D.** The proper place for help in the Microsoft Windows world is immediately to the right of all other menu options. Putting it all the way to the right is the kind of thing that you might see in an Apple interface. Nothing is wrong with putting help to the left of all your menu options, but it is not standard and will not earn you any points on the exam!

Answers to Exam Questions for Case Study 3

1. **B.** Because the system, as described, is directly connected to the database without a middle tier of components separating it, it is not an *n*-tier solution. Similarly, because the database is on a different physical machine (and a different logical layer), it is not a single-tier application. Because it has a user interface tier and a data tier only, it is a two-tier application.

2. **A, B, C, D.** These are all good reasons for using stored procedures. Data access development is simplified by using stored procedures. Because much of the specifics of the data retrieval is hidden, there is at least a certain level of abstraction. Deployment of database-level business rules is simplified because only a single copy exists. Finally, stored procedures perform better than ad hoc queries against a database because they can be optimized in advance.

3. The answer to this question is shown in Figure 3.

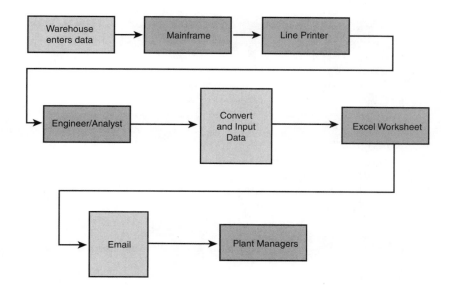

FIGURE 3
Answer to Case
Study 3, question 3.

The current system starts when the warehouse enters the receipt and the consumption of raw materials into the mainframe. The mainframe program prints out a hard copy that is interpreted and *reentered* by an analyst into an Excel spreadsheet. The spreadsheet is then mailed to the appropriate distribution list.

4. The answer to this question is shown in Figure 4.

The warehouse will use a bar-code scanner to track receipt and consumption of raw materials. This scanner will feed scanner software that updates the AS/400 database. The user's PC will access the database through stored procedures from a user interface that also includes any analysis logic that cannot be represented by stored procedures. Finally, the user interface has the capability to export to Excel.

5. **A.** Because the system collects the material usage data as well as being the decision-support tool, the system must run Monday through Saturday because that's when the production line runs. It also has to run until 1:30 a.m. Pacific time to make sure the final shift in California has time to wrap up. This is 4:30 a.m. Eastern time.

6. **B.** The process to this point has been largely a manual one. Therefore, process engineering will be needed to convert the process into an electronic one. Business rules do exist, but they exist in the informal, manual interventions of people.

7. **A.** In terms of time to execute, time spent with humans is far less efficient than time spent internally calculating. Therefore, the more that a process does not require human intervention, the more scalable it can become.

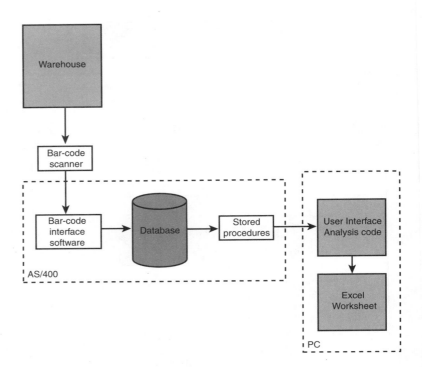

FIGURE 4
Answer to Case
Study 3, question 4.

8. **C.** Although the company hopes that the solution will be available at all times during production line activity, its independence was a critical system requirement. The production line cannot go down because a piece of software that reports off of it malfunctions. It is more important to not impact the actual line of business. We would likely see a manual system used as a backup so that no data would be lost.

9. **A, C.** Both ADO and ODBC would be appropriate for this solution (although we would choose one or the other). MTS would not apply because no business-object tier really exists, and Visual InterDev is not a good choice—primarily because the case study does not mention a browser-based interface.

10. **A.** Integration with existing processes is simply making our new solution continue to support certain aspects of existing business processes. The use of Excel spreadsheets is an existing process that we will need to continue to support.

11. **D.** The verification of the deployed solution with the use cases that were created during the design phase is the best measure of how well we met our requirements. Answers B and C do not provide a good measuring stick for whether we built the solution that was intended.

Answers to Exam Questions for Case Study 4

1. **A.** The MDI and the workspace interface both address a need to have multiple documents of a given type open at the same time. The case study

contains no clear need to have such a thing. Although it might be possible to enter data about multiple fields, each in a separate window, it is unclear exactly how this would benefit the user's experience of the application. The Internet browser interface, too, makes an assumption that the application will be running in the browser. We saw earlier that a decision was made to not make this application Internet enabled, and although this will not preclude the Internet browser interface, the reasons for not including Internet access (simplicity of development and security) would tend to also argue against the use of the browser. Consequently, although all possible choices *could* be used as a solution, the SDI model seems like the best fit.

2. **B.**   The users are around the country and the planet, and they will use this system only for a small fraction of their day. As such, the company will likely have a very limited expectation for the cost of training. As such, users will have to be able to pick up its usage on their own.

3. **C.**   The existing enterprise data store is being used, and the existing network is being reused. The machines that act as clients in the other system's design are acting as servers in our design. This means much less expense than in other scenarios. Choice B is incorrect because that is an impact on ROI but not TCO.

4. **A, B, D.**   The purpose of this application is to enable the decision makers at the main office to gain the information that those who work in the field already have. In this sense, then, it is a communication application. It is designed to replace the standard communications (phone, email) and replace them with something more concrete. On the other hand, it is also a data-entry application because it is enabling the farm employees to enter the information so that it can be stored and analyzed at the corporate office.

The asynchronous nature of the data updates also has the characteristics of a messaging system such as MSMQ. However, although it might change the workflow of the employees and the managers, it is not a solution that, in itself, is designed to monitor or manage workflow.

5. The answer to this question is shown in Figure 5.

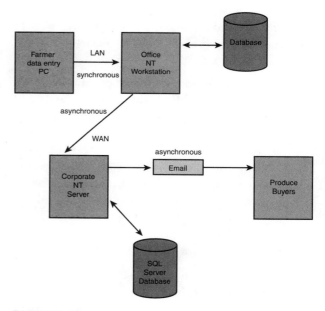

FIGURE 5
Answer to Case Study 4, question 5.

The new solution requires the addition of some PCs for the farmer's data entry. The code running here is part of the new solution. From there, information is stored in a local database at the farm office's site. Each night (or at whatever intervals are designated), data is shipped asynchronously to the corporate office. This could be done using a data replication technique or something such as MSMQ. The data is merged with all the other farms and mailed to the decision makers.

6. **B.** In any case, we will have the need to design a user interface, or else no one could actually use the application we've designed. Similarly, no matter what kind of application is designed, a need exists to maintain a data store somewhere in the application. Finally, our design for the application takes the asynchronous processing away from the user interface because it updates a local data store in real-time. Our primary, new technical issue, then, is how the databases can be synchronized across the WAN to ensure that data entered at each of the farms is available to the decision makers at the main office.

7. **B, C.** ADO and Visual Basic could be used in this solution. MSMQ is redundant to the data replication strategy we have selected, although it could be used as an alternative to send updates between the farms and the corporate office. ADO can be used for data access, both in the field and at headquarters. Visual Basic would be one language that could be used to build the SDI interface that was discussed earlier. It's not clear where MTS would fit in our solution because it is not a true *n*-tier solution.

8. **A, B, C.** Security, because of the nature of the application, is an important consideration. Unauthorized access could directly result in a loss of profits for the company. As such, a flexible, highly maintainable, high-level of security is important. This can be accomplished first and foremost by using the security inherent in the NT operating system. Second, the conscious decision not to support application access externally makes it much easier to maintain security because far less risk exists of hostile interception of information. Finally, in all our considerations, we didn't discuss dangers specific to one time of day. As such, it isn't clear how locking down the system would help us.

9. **B, C.** Two primary things were done to increase the system's performance. First, the system is designed, instead of communicating over the network to the main server, to communicate with an onsite server and utilize that system's data store to input data into, letting the data store then synchronize with the main store at the corporate office. Second, the servers were utilized on each site, allowing only a small number of clients to be expected to connect at each one. We did not design an *n*-tier solution, so using MTS was not undertaken.

10. **B.** Answer A does, in fact, create better reuse, but it has little to do with actually making your application extensible. It could also be used to build a completely separate application just as easily. Making source available does not count as extensibility either. Extensibility, at the application level, means that we are able to add additional functionality to an existing application. Making the application a programmable framework that could collect other data as well would allow for extensibility.

11. **A, C, D.** Automatic installation, assuming that all these computers are on the network (an assumption that this solution makes all the way along), is possible. Without such things as Internet CAB distribution, it does become more complicated. However, it is possible. Maintenance is made difficult, though, because application code is not centralized onto servers, making it a client-based rather than a server-based solution. This is further complicated by the wide range of locations where machines must be physically located

APPENDIXES

Glossary

80/20 Rule   The principle in software engineering stating that approximately 80 percent of a customer's problem can usually be solved at a justifiable level of expense. On the other hand, the remaining 20 percent often will be too cost prohibitive to solve.

A

Acceptance testing   Testing performed by the customer to answer the question, "Did our solution provider's plans really take into account what we need?"

Access keys   A key or combination of keys, usually involving the Alt key, that allows access to a particular menu item or control. The access key is always indicated by an underscore beneath a letter of the menu's caption (for example, File), command button (for example, Exit) or control.

Accessibility   A term used to group the collections of features available, both in the operating system and in specific applications, to help individuals who have trouble productively using the traditional Windows interfaces. Examples include increased visual contrast, hotkeys, alternate input devices, and so on.

Administrators   Members of a solution's audience who are empowered to change its security policies, permissions, and accounts.

API   Application Programmers' Interface. This allows programmers to control much of the functionality of your solutions simply by making function calls.

Auditing   Reviewing security logs kept by your system for indications that security breeches have been attempted.

Average requirements   Average requirements represent the amount of work that a solution must be able to do during more "normal" periods of use.

B

Binary searching   Using a recursive approach to split a data set into smaller and smaller search areas until the correct data is found or acknowledged as missing.

Business logic   Pieces of code that ensure that the rules and processes necessary to execute the day-to-day work of an enterprise are followed. Most often these business rules implement restrictions against data that does meet the correct technical type but is not a meaningful value.

Business requirement   The documented features and functions that a solution must provide, as well as the technologies that it must use and the deadlines for its completion. Business requirements are often measured in terms of the performance, availability, security, scalability, maintainability, and extensibility that must be obtained for a solution to be considered successful or useful to an organization. See PASS ME.

Business rules   Business rules are designed to codify the way in which a business works. These rules are used to generate the business-logic portion of an application. They are usually related to validating data for appropriateness or to the complex calculation of rules or algorithms.

Buy versus build   The decision that almost every project must go through to decide whether to buy shrink-wrap software that may be only a partial fit or to build custom code from scratch.

C

Callback   A means of letting one component communicate with another component. Distinct from events or objects in that it is not a broadcast, but it is sent to a specific component.

Capacity   The measure of the most work that a solution can possibly do.

Cascading deletes   Actively deleting the related rows in child tables when a given row is deleted.

Cascading updates   Actively updating the related rows in child tables when a given row is updated.

Clients   Internal users and applications that use your solution.

Code Reuse   The effort to create applications in which pieces of code (or binary components) are written in a way that they can be utilized by more than just the piece of software for which they were originally written.

Collaborative application   Applications that are designed to allow new ways for knowledge workers to communicate with each other. The most common instance of this is the shared whiteboard type of application, which allows multiple users to view a shared screen and add to it.

Combination key   A primary key in a database table consisting of more than one field.

Commodity skill set   A set of programming skills that are available widely enough on the market that it is no longer considered a specialty. This results in much more competitive pricing, both in employee salaries and external consulting prices.

Component   A piece of physical software that encapsulates some functionality within its internal implementation and exposes one or more interfaces to allow access to these functions while hiding the implementation.

COMTI   COM Transaction Integrator. Microsoft's solution to moving data between the COM world and the IBM CICS environment.

Context model   A conceptual design document that outlines what the perceived business problems are and which aspects of the problem are within the scope of the proposed solution.

Cookies   Pieces of information stored by a Web server on client computers accessing it so that it can retrieve them at a later time. Cookies are typically used for the maintenance of state information between multiple Web pages on the same site.

Costliest Bits First (CBF)   Solving the bits of a problem first that are costing the target organization the most money. The benefit to this approach is that you may get a better return on your investment.

Cross-platform compatibility   A term used to indicate that a particular piece of code can be run on various operating systems. This term is most often used in conjunction with Java.

Cycle of use   The life cycle of a typical information solution. It begins in a new, underused phase. It then reaches a peak of use during the established phase. Finally, it sinks into disuse again near the end of its useful life.

D

Data entry application   An application whose primary purpose is to allow for the insertion of information into a persistent store for later management. Most order entry systems fall into this category.

Data model   A model showing the various relationships and entities that compose the database involved in a useful set of business processes.

Data normalization   The process of bringing a data model into compliance with First, Second, and Third Normal forms.

Design document   A formal document outlining the exact means by which a solution provider intends to meet the business requirements of the target organization.

Domain rule   A rule that regulates the range of values that are allowed for fields within a database.

Downsizing   Cutbacks in spending (typically in the form of job cuts) for the purpose of increasing revenues.

Downtime   This is time, whether scheduled or not, during which the system is not operating. Within this larger category are two distinctions: planned and unplanned downtime. The former simply is time when the system does not need to operate; the latter is usually caused by a failure somewhere in the system.

Dynamic Hypertext Markup Language (DHTML) An extension to standard HTML that allows runtime modifications of Web pages using client-side scripts.

E

Early binding   A way of implementing automation that uses a virtual table to perform compile-time syntax checking and to provide faster runtime applications.

Easiest Bits First (EBF)   Solving the easiest bits of a problem first to allow you to solve the most problems with the fewest resources.

Encapsulation   A principle of object-oriented programming that asserts that a properly designed object should not expose internal implementation to its consumers. Instead, only the necessary methods or properties of an object should be available to a consumer (through an interface), and the implementation is kept private.

Enterprise application   A piece of software whose target audience spans an entire business, including most (if not all) of its various aspects. Most often these systems include things such as productivity applications, time tracking applications, and so on.

Entity   A single object in a data model comprising a name, fields, and possibly a certain number of methods.

Events   Attributes of an object that allow a client to receive notice that a particular situation has occurred.

Expected response times   A comparison of how long the users of your system think that it takes your solution to respond to their requests against how long they think that it *should* take.

Extensible Markup Language (XML)   An extension to HTML that allows the definition of custom tags. This can allow information to be described in terms that are tailored to the nature of the subject matter.

F

Fault tolerance   The attempt to build a system or subsystem in such a way that the failure of one piece of hardware or software will not necessarily bring down the entire system. This is often accomplished through redundant systems and backups.

First normal form   A state in which a single entity or table contains all atomic values and no repeating columns.

G

Groups   Logical groupings of administrators, clients, and guests, which are used to facilitate security administration.

Guests   People and programs that use your solution but are external to the organization for which your solution was developed. This puts them outside the scope of entities normally found within your solutions' security databases.

H

Hashing   Applying an arbitrary formula to a piece of data to generate a number that is then used as a byte offset into a database to determine where that data should be stored and/or looked for.

Hierarchical database   A persistent storage mechanism based on the parent-child relationships between information.

Human-computer interface   The various means (including screens, reports, and user assistance) by which the electronic portion of a system enables interaction between itself and the users of the system.

Hypertext Markup Language (HTML)   The language in which pages are most often currently written on the World Wide Web.

I

Index   A piece of a database that speeds data retrieval and slows data storage. It contains entries for every piece of data that indicate where that data may be found in the database.

Indexed database   A persistent storage mechanism based on numbered rows in tables.

Indexing   The process of producing the entries in an index. This typically takes place during data storage and slows that process because of the reordering of the index that is typically required.

In-process components   Components that exist entirely within the address space of their client process.

Input validation   Code or processing that exists in a user interface to ensure that the data a user provides to the system is of the proper type and format. Most often used to verify that a date is entered in a correct field or that a number is entered when a number is expected.

Instantiation overhead   The amount of system resources (typically CPU time) consumed to create a new object of a given type or class.

Integrated development environment   A system for the production of source code in a given language that makes compilation and execution readily available. Currently, it is also becoming more common to provide a means for constructing (using a toolbox of visual components) a graphical user interface for whatever application is being created.

Integration testing   Testing performed by the solution provider to ensure that all of a system's individual pieces are capable of working together as an effective solution.

Interim releases   Application versions that are knowingly built and distributed without certain functionality to enable the enterprise to gain value from what is complete. Eventually, these are followed by complete releases, which implement all the functionality. This is the deliverable of an iterative development strategy (see next definition) that is part of the Microsoft Solution Framework philosophy.

Iterative development   A process by which pieces of a solution are rolled out as quickly as possible, and then modified and extended in response to user comments while in production. This approach allows delivery of some of a solution's benefits to a customer as quickly as possible.

J

JET   The database engine under which Microsoft Access runs.

Junction table   A table created to break down a many-to-many relationship between two tables into two one-to-many relationships. The junction table contains the primary keys of the two tables with the many-to-many relationship.

L

Late binding   Requiring an operating system or virtual machine to determine at runtime what kind of object is referred to by a given variable. This prevents the direct use of the IUnknown interface, typically requiring the less efficient IDispatch mechanism.

List view   A Microsoft ActiveX control that is designed to allow for the implementation of a complex list structure for data. Normally, list views have several

settings, exposing different levels of detail. For an example of a list view control, see the right side of the Windows Explorer.

Local Area Network (LAN)   A Local Area Network that provides connectivity typically no greater in scope than the building-wide level.

Localization   The process of constructing software in such a way that it can support being run internationally and still retain cultural significance and utilize the correct language. Much of this technology is based around the Unicode specification.

Locks   A hold placed on a database resource that prevents other users and processes from trying to access it while another user or process is already doing so.

Logical tier   One part of an *n*-tier architecture. Logical implies that it need not exist on a separate machine. It denotes a virtual layer.

Lookup table   A small table used to translate short codes into their more verbose descriptions. For example, a lookup table for an airport might contain an entry for "ORD" that provides the name "O'Hare International."

M

Menu bars   A group of words that serves as a navigation aid to other screens or adds functionality within the application.

Messaging application   An application that is designed to facilitate and replace existing communication mechanisms. Examples include things such as email software, which replaces memos and inter-office mail.

Meta-data   Data *about* data. A client finds out about the schema of a database used by its solution via meta-data.

Methods   Operations of an object that tell a client what the supported behaviors of an object are. Also used by the clients to request a behavior from an object. Specifies actions that an object or a component can take.

Microsoft access   Microsoft's entry-level database solution specializing in ease-of-use and RAD issues.

Microsoft Transaction Server (MTS)   A piece of software that provides services for security, object pooling, database pooling, multithreaded processing, and transactional semantics at the business object level.

Middleware   A translation layer between the user tier and the database tier.

Mission critical   Any system where an outage can have a show-stopping effect on the organization as a whole.

Modified Hungarian naming   A naming standard in which the first few letters of every variable name indicate its data type and (sometimes) its scope.

Multiple Document Interface (MDI)   A user interface model that potentially contains more than one form and that might have multiple files of the same type open at the same time. Each of these can be worked on in nonmodal windows.

Multithreading   A way for a program to do many things simultaneously, without requiring the overhead of multiple processes.

N

n-**tier**   An application in which the user interface, business logic, and data persistence code is broken out onto separate logical machines.

O

Object pooling   Destruction of component objects does not lead to their literal unloading from memory. Instead, they are returned to a pool of objects from which another client may request an object. The purpose is to avoid the creation and teardown time of objects that are used repeatedly.

Open standards   Open standards in software are those that are typically owned by a public standards body, such as the World Wide Web Consortium or ANSI.

Optimistic locking   A style of locking that won't place a lock until the database actually begins a read/write operation.

Out-of-process components   Components that exist outside the address space of their client processes but on the same computer.

P

Page-level locking   Denying a user or a process access to the database if they are trying to access a page at the same time as another user or process.

Pages   An arbitrary number of rows that constitutes the standard amount of data that is read from or written to a database during a single access.

PASS ME   Performance, Availability, Security, Scalability, Maintainability, and Extensibility. These are the six solution attributes most stressed by the Microsoft exam.

Peak requirements   The absolute hardest that your solution will ever have to work to meet your target organization's requirements.

Peak longevity   How long it will take a solution to break when forced to continue running at maximum capacity.

Perceived response times   A measure of how long the users of your system *think* that it takes your solution to respond to their requests.

Pessimistic locking   A style of locking that places a lock as soon as the database reaches the record on which a read/write operation will be performed.

Physical environment constraints   A factor that limits the design of a solution and is related to the location in which it is to be deployed, either in terms of location in a geographic sense or the layout of the location.

Physical environment model   A design document that lists the various physical locales and tasks to be completed and outlines which tasks must be performed at which locations. This is often a useful tool in enterprise applications, to discover where effort is being wasted in traveling between locations.

Primary key   The minimal set of fields needed to uniquely identify any row within a given table.

Properties   Attributes of an object that tell a client the state of an object.

Proprietary standards   These are software development or deployment norms that are typically owned by a particular company or a small group of companies.

Q

Quality assurance   Testing conducted immediately before or simultaneously with acceptance testing to ensure that a solution performs at a level meeting or exceeding organizational standards. The PASS ME themes of performance, availability, security, scalability, maintainability, and extensibility are usually measured during this process.

Queuing   A technology that temporarily holds requests during periods of high system usage or network latency (or total unavailability) so that an application may continue with its work while waiting for the database to respond to its queries. For example, messages sent from one business partner to another via an extranet might be queued in Microsoft Message Queue until a weekly dial-up connection is made between the two.

R

Rapid Application Development (RAD)   An approach to application design and deployment that emphasizes speed of development over the more traditional approaches. Support for RAD is one of Visual Basic's key selling features.

Real response times   A measure of how long it takes for your solution to actually do the work that it is being asked to do.

Real-time system   A piece of software that controls external physical systems that need to run at particular intervals. These systems are particularly challenging to develop because deviance from the proscribed performance absolutely cannot be tolerated.

Relational database   A persistent storage mechanism using key values to link multiple tables of information.

Relational rule   A rule that ensures that the proper *n*-to-*n* relationships exist between specific entity instances within your solution's database.

Remote component   A component that exists both outside the address space of the client component and on a different machine.

Remote Data Services (RDS)   A Microsoft technology enabling data to be manipulated within Internet Explorer without requiring additional calls to the server.

684   Appendix A   GLOSSARY

Replication   A process whereby the data in one database is intelligently merged with and/or transferred to the data in another database.

Resource files   A file (usually under Windows) designed specifically to hold text strings, graphics, and sound that might be used in common with multiple applications.

Response time   This is the measurement of the length of time it takes for a computer to respond to a particular request. It is often used as an overall criterion for performance in a system. For example, the total response time for loading an order should be less than five seconds.

Return on Investment (ROI)   All the benefits produced by the use of your solution, minus the total cost of its ownership.

Review meeting   A meeting held for the explanation and inspection of code created by people working on the construction of a solution.

Roaming users   Persons who use a solution but who are not always in the same physical location. Most often this is accomplished by the use of a laptop or palmtop portable computer.

Role-based security   A system for controlling access to an application or set of applications based not on the user name, but on a set of independently defined groups, which can be maintained separately from the physical security of systems and networks.

Row-level locking   Denying a user or process access to the database if they are trying to access a row at the same time as another user or process.

S

Scope   Factors influencing the difficulty and number of requirements for a solution to be useful to an organization.

Scope creep   Additions to the solution's scope or requirements after the design and build process has begun. Scope creep, if mismanaged, has the potential to kill a project.

Screen scraping   The PC-based process of reading characters off a mainframe emulator screen, essentially using the screens as IO ports into the IBM mainframe transactions. Screen scraping is a way to inexpensively place a graphical user interface on top of a character-based screen.

Second normal form   A state in which a single table is in First Normal form, represents exactly one entity, and has all nonkey columns fully dependent on the primary key.

Secure Sockets Layer (SSL)   This is the de facto standard for encryption on the World Wide Web.

Shortcut keys   A key or combination of keys that allows access to a particular screen or function directly, rather than via the pointer/menu interfaces.

Sign-off   A semibinding statement of official approval. Almost always in writing.

Single Document Interface (SDI)   A user-interface model that displays a single form at a time as the main point of interaction. All other interaction is pop-up modal dialogs on the form.

Single tier   An application that contains user interface code, business logic code, and a means of persistent storage all located on one logical machine.

Software pilot   An early release of a product that is subjected to a smaller audience than the final targeted user group. This is done to test the waters, in terms of stability and scalability. It keeps a company from taking down its entire business should an unexpected problem occur early in the release cycle.

Source control Software that requires developers to check code (or documents) in and out of a central repository before working on it. This allows greater coordination and lessens the chance of conflicting modifications.

SQL Server Microsoft's high-end database solution, specializing in enterprise-level data storage needs.

Stateful objects Objects that retain information between calls from a client object. For example, a person object that remembers height, weight, age, and name is said to retain state.

Stateless objects Objects that are short-lived, where the client application invokes the object, uses it to perform a function, and then destroys the object almost immediately. This is the object style favored by MTS.

Status bars A control, usually placed on the bottom of forms. It is used to convey information to the users either about the user interface or progress on a task.

Stored procedures Pieces of code (usually SQL) kept on the database server that return specific sets of data when requested.

T

Target user group The set of people for whom the solution being designed solves a problem and who will utilize the proposed solution.

Task sequence model A design document that breaks down a particular piece of work into the tasks that compose it. This is often useful when attempting to duplicate a given piece of work in automation because it explicitly lays out each task in its proper order, ensuring that the automated process maintains this order of operations.

Technology churning The tendency of technological process to render lengthy projects obsolete even before they are completed.

Thin client A relatively recent technological approach that focuses all the processing and file management onto the server, leaving the user's workstation to manage only display functions. It is basically a revival of the mainframe/dumb terminal structure of the past, except with a GUI display.

Third normal form A state in which a single table is in Second Normal form, has all columns mutually independent, contains no computed fields, and contains no fields about any entities that are merely referenced.

Threshold tolerance The length of time that you can continue using a system at its peak capacity before certain system failure. For example, the length of time that a database can process 1,000,000 transactions per second without needing to be restarted represents such a time period.

ToolTips Floating pop-up windows that offer insight into the purpose of a particular piece of a user interface. This window is normally activated when a user hovers the pointer over a particular area of the user interface. For example, floating above the floppy disk icon in Microsoft Word creates a window with the word Save. This is the functionality of clicking the icon.

Total cost of ownership The sum of all resources spent in the initial creation and deployment of a solution, plus all resources expended in its maintenance and extension throughout its useful life.

Transaction A logical unit of work, which must be atomic, consistent, isolated, and durable (ACID). A system will either commit a transaction or cancel it in entirety.

Transaction frequency A measure of how often transactions are sent through a system for processing.

Transaction intensity A measure of the total resources (memory, CPU cycles, and so on) required to process a given transaction.

Transaction server See Microsoft Transaction Server.

Transactional semantics The formal grammar of working with transactions. In this context, it is working with MTS transaction support.

Translation rule A rule that converts values stored in your database into values that your solution can use directly.

Tree view A Microsoft ActiveX control designed to allow for the implementation of hierarchical structures of data. For an example of a tree view control, see the left side of Windows Explorer.

Two tier An application that partitions user-interface code, business logic code, and data storage into two logical machines. Most often it is by partitioning the data storage onto one logical machine and the business and user-interface code onto a second.

U

Unicode A specification that expands the ANSI single-byte reference to characters to two bytes. This is a means of displaying thousands of characters and enabling the display of other languages. Implementation of Unicode is a standard method of handling localization of software.

Unit testing Testing conducted against each component of a system in isolation from all other components. This is intended to verify that each piece or component performs as expected on an individual level.

Upsizing Increases in spending (typically in the form of hiring) aimed at increasing revenues.

Use-case document A scenario-based document describing a number of situations and the desired behavior for a solution built to operate under those circumstances. Use cases can become acceptance criteria or a contract between the users and the developers of a solution.

Use cases See Use-case document.

V-Z

Versioning support The capability of an object technology (such as COM) to facilitate the use of components of versions different than those that their clients are originally designed to work with.

Views Reduced sets of columns and/or rows taken from tables already existing in a database, usually created to allow access to some information in tables while keeping the rest of it out of reach.

Virtual Private Network (VPN) Used for encrypting transmissions over the Internet to allow the sending and receiving of sensitive information over an otherwise insecure (but cheap) medium.

Visual Basic Microsoft's most popular tool for RAD development.

Visual C++ The Microsoft programming language capable of producing the most powerful and efficient code.

Visual FoxPro A combination between a desktop database and an advanced, object-oriented programming environment. Notable for its support of the Xbase data storage format, which is also available on the Macintosh.

Visual J++ Microsoft's implementation and extension of the Java programming environment.

Visual Modeler   A UML-enabled tool for facilitating the analysis and design stages of component-based solutions. Diagramming, reverse engineering, and automatic code generation are a few of the salient features.

Visual SourceSafe   A Microsoft tool for source control. See Source Control.

Wide Area Network (WAN)   Used for providing network connectivity between locations more spread out than a single building but (usually) less than international in scope.

Windows Foundation Classes (WFC)   A set of classes that allows Visual J++ code to leverage much of the rich UI functionality available in Microsoft Windows.

Workflow application   An application designed to control or direct the flow of information and required actions through an enterprise. A piece of software that routes orders from entry through approval and delivery falls into this category.

Workflow process model   A design document that illustrates the flow of information between people and objects in an enterprise. It is often used to map out how and where processes need to be automated or preserved.

Workspace   A user-interface model that potentially contains more than one form and which might have multiple files of different types open at the same time. Each of these can be worked on in nonmodal windows.

Overview of the Certification Process

You must pass rigorous certification exams to become a Microsoft Certified Professional. These closed-book exams provide a valid and reliable measure of your technical proficiency and expertise. Developed in consultation with computer industry professionals who have experience with Microsoft products in the workplace, the exams are conducted by two independent organizations. Sylvan Prometric offers the exams at more than 1,400 Authorized Prometric Testing Centers around the world. Virtual University Enterprises (VUE) testing centers offer exams at more than 500 locations.

To schedule an exam, call Sylvan Prometric Testing Centers at 800-755-EXAM (3926) or VUE at 888-837-8616 (or register online with VUE at http://www.vue.com/student-services/). Currently Microsoft offers seven types of certification, each based on specific areas of expertise.

TYPES OF CERTIFICATION

- **Microsoft Certified Professional (MCP).** Persons with this credential are qualified to provide installation, configuration, and support for users of at least one Microsoft desktop operating system, such as Windows NT Workstation. Candidates can take elective exams to develop areas of specialization. MCP is the base level of expertise.

- **Microsoft Certified Professional+Internet (MCP+Internet).** Persons with this credential are qualified to plan security, install and configure server products, manage server resources, extend service to run CGI scripts or ISAPI scripts, monitor and analyze performance, and troubleshoot problems. Expertise is similar to that of an MCP but with a focus on the Internet.

- **Microsoft Certified Professional+Site Building (MCP+Site Building).** Persons with this credential are qualified to plan, build, maintain, and manage Web sites using Microsoft technologies and products. The credential is appropriate for people who manage sophisticated, interactive Web sites that include database connectivity, multimedia, and searchable content.

- **Microsoft Certified Database Administrator (MCDBA).** Qualified individuals can derive physical database designs, develop logical data models, create physical databases, create data services by using Transact-SQL, manage and maintain databases, configure and manage security, monitor and optimize databases, and install and configure Microsoft SQL Server.

- **Microsoft Certified Systems Engineer (MCSE).** These individuals are qualified to effectively plan, implement, maintain, and support information systems with Microsoft Windows NT and other

Microsoft advanced systems and workgroup products, such as Microsoft Office and Microsoft BackOffice.

◆ **Microsoft Certified Systems Engineer+Internet (MCSE+Internet).** Persons with this credential are qualified in the core MCSE areas and also are qualified to enhance, deploy, and manage sophisticated intranet and Internet solutions that include a browser, proxy server, host servers, database, and messaging and commerce components. An MCSE+Internet-certified professional is able to manage and analyze Web sites.

◆ **Microsoft Certified Solution Developer (MCSD).** These individuals are qualified to design and develop custom business solutions by using Microsoft development tools, technologies, and platforms. The new track includes certification exams that test users' abilities to build Web-based, distributed, and commerce applications by using Microsoft products such as Microsoft SQL Server, Microsoft Visual Studio, and Microsoft Component Services.

◆ **Microsoft Certified Trainer (MCT).** Persons with this credential are instructionally and technically qualified by Microsoft to deliver Microsoft Education Courses at Microsoft-authorized sites. An MCT must be employed by a Microsoft Solution Provider Authorized Technical Education Center or a Microsoft Authorized Academic Training site.

NOTE

For up-to-date information about each type of certification, visit the Microsoft Training and Certification World Wide Web site at http://www.microsoft.com/train_cert. You also may contact Microsoft through the following sources:

◆ Microsoft Certified Professional Program: 800-636-7544

◆ mcp@msource.com

◆ Microsoft Online Institute (MOLI): 800-449-9333

CERTIFICATION REQUIREMENTS

An asterisk following an exam in any of the lists below means that it is slated for retirement.

How to Become a Microsoft Certified Professional

To become certified as an MCP, you need only pass any Microsoft exam (with the exception of Networking Essentials).

How to Become a Microsoft Certified Professional+Internet

To become an MCP specializing in Internet technology, you must pass the following exams:

◆ Internetworking Microsoft TCP/IP on Microsoft Windows NT 4.0, #70-059

- ◆ Implementing and Supporting Microsoft Windows NT Server 4.0, #70-067

- ◆ Implementing and Supporting Microsoft Internet Information Server 3.0 and Microsoft Index Server 1.1, #70-077

  OR Implementing and Supporting Microsoft Internet Information Server 4.0, #70-087

How to Become a Microsoft Certified Professional+Site Building

To be certified as an MCP+Site Building, you need to pass two of the following exams:

- ◆ Designing and Implementing Web Sites with Microsoft FrontPage 98, #70-055

- ◆ Designing and Implementing Commerce Solutions with Microsoft Site Server 3.0, Commerce Edition, #70-057

- ◆ Designing and Implementing Web Solutions with Microsoft Visual InterDev 6.0, #70-152

How to Become a Microsoft Certified Database Administrator

To become an MCDBA, you must pass four core exams.

Core Exams

- ◆ Administering Microsoft SQL Server 7.0, #70-028

- ◆ Designing and Implementing Databases with Microsoft SQL Server 7.0, #70-029

- ◆ Implementing and Supporting Microsoft Windows NT Server 4.0, #70-067

- ◆ Implementing and Supporting Microsoft Windows NT Server 4.0 in the Enterprise, #70-068

Elective Exams

You must also pass one elective exam from the following list:

- ◆ Designing and Implementing Distributed Applications with Microsoft Visual C++ 6.0, #70-015

- ◆ Designing and Implementing Data Warehouses with Microsoft SQL Server 7.0 and Microsoft Decision Support Services 1.0, #70-019

- ◆ Internetworking with Microsoft TCP/IP on Microsoft Windows NT 4.0, #70-059

- ◆ Implementing and Supporting Microsoft Internet Information Server 4.0, #70-087

- ◆ Designing and Implementing Distributed Applications with Microsoft Visual Basic 6.0, #70-175

How to Become a Microsoft Certified Systems Engineer

You must pass four operating system exams and two elective exams to become an MCSE. The MCSE certification path is divided into two tracks: Windows NT 3.51 and Windows NT 4.0.

The following lists show the core requirements (the four operating system exams) for both the Windows NT 3.51 and 4.0 tracks and the electives you can take for either track (of which you must pass two).

Windows NT 3.51 Track

The Windows NT 3.51 track will probably be retired with the release of Windows 2000. The Windows NT 3.51 core exams are scheduled for retirement at that time.

Core Exams

The four Windows NT 3.51 track core requirements for MCSE certification include the following:

- ◆ Implementing and Supporting Microsoft Windows NT Server 3.51, #70-043*

- ◆ Implementing and Supporting Microsoft Windows NT Workstation 3.51, #70-042*

- ◆ Microsoft Windows 3.1, #70-030*

  OR Microsoft Windows for Workgroups 3.11, #70-048*

  OR Implementing and Supporting Microsoft Windows 95, #70-064

  OR Implementing and Supporting Microsoft Windows 98, #70-098

- ◆ Networking Essentials, #70-058

Windows NT 4.0 Track

The Windows NT 4.0 track is also organized around core and elective exams.

Core Exams

The four Windows NT 4.0 track core requirements for MCSE certification include the following:

- ◆ Implementing and Supporting Microsoft Windows NT Server 4.0, #70-067

- ◆ Implementing and Supporting Microsoft Windows NT Server 4.0 in the Enterprise, #70-068

- ◆ Microsoft Windows 3.1, #70-030*

  OR Microsoft Windows for Workgroups 3.11, #70-048*

  OR Implementing and Supporting Microsoft Windows 95, #70-064

  OR Implementing and Supporting Microsoft Windows NT Workstation 4.0, #70-073

  OR Implementing and Supporting Microsoft Windows 98, #70-098

- ◆ Networking Essentials, #70-058

Elective Exams

For both the Windows NT 3.51 and 4.0 tracks, you must pass two of the following elective exams for MCSE certification:

- ◆ Implementing and Supporting Microsoft SNA Server 3.0, #70-013

  OR Implementing and Supporting Microsoft SNA Server 4.0, #70-085

◆ Implementing and Supporting Microsoft Systems Management Server 1.0, #70-014*

  OR Implementing and Supporting Microsoft Systems Management Server 1.2, #70-018

  OR Implementing and Supporting Microsoft Systems Management Server 2.0, #70-086

◆ Microsoft SQL Server 4.2 Database Implementation, #70-021

  OR Implementing a Database Design on Microsoft SQL Server 6.5, #70-027

  OR Implementing a Database Design on Microsoft SQL Server 7.0, #70-029

◆ Microsoft SQL Server 4.2 Database Administration for Microsoft Windows NT, #70-022

  OR System Administration for Microsoft SQL Server 6.5 (or 6.0), #70-026

  OR System Administration for Microsoft SQL Server 7.0, #70-028

◆ Microsoft Mail for PC Networks 3.2-Enterprise, #70-037

◆ Internetworking with Microsoft TCP/IP on Microsoft Windows NT (3.5–3.51), #70-053

  OR Internetworking with Microsoft TCP/IP on Microsoft Windows NT 4.0, #70-059

◆ Implementing and Supporting Microsoft Exchange Server 4.0, #70-075*

  OR Implementing and Supporting Microsoft Exchange Server 5.0, #70-076

  OR Implementing and Supporting Microsoft Exchange Server 5.5, #70-081

◆ Implementing and Supporting Microsoft Internet Information Server 3.0 and Microsoft Index Server 1.1, #70-077

  OR Implementing and Supporting Microsoft Internet Information Server 4.0, #70-087

◆ Implementing and Supporting Microsoft Proxy Server 1.0, #70-078

  OR Implementing and Supporting Microsoft Proxy Server 2.0, #70-088

◆ Implementing and Supporting Microsoft Internet Explorer 4.0 by Using the Internet Explorer Resource Kit, #70-079

How to Become a Microsoft Certified Systems Engineer+Internet

You must pass seven operating system exams and two elective exams to become an MCSE specializing in Internet technology.

Core Exams

The following seven core exams are required for MCSE+Internet certification:

◆ Networking Essentials, #70-058

◆ Internetworking with Microsoft TCP/IP on Microsoft Windows NT 4.0, #70-059

◆ Implementing and Supporting Microsoft Windows 95, #70-064

  OR Implementing and Supporting Microsoft Windows NT Workstation 4.0, #70-073

  OR Implementing and Supporting Microsoft Windows 98, #70-098

◆ Implementing and Supporting Microsoft Windows NT Server 4.0, #70-067

◆ Implementing and Supporting Microsoft Windows NT Server 4.0 in the Enterprise, #70-068

◆ Implementing and Supporting Microsoft Internet Information Server 3.0 and Microsoft Index Server 1.1, #70-077

  OR Implementing and Supporting Microsoft Internet Information Server 4.0, #70-087

◆ Implementing and Supporting Microsoft Internet Explorer 4.0 by Using the Internet Explorer Resource Kit, #70-079

Elective Exams

You must also pass two of the following elective exams for MCSE+Internet certification:

◆ System Administration for Microsoft SQL Server 6.5, #70-026

◆ Implementing a Database Design on Microsoft SQL Server 6.5, #70-027

◆ Implementing and Supporting Web Sites Using Microsoft Site Server 3.0, # 70-056

◆ Implementing and Supporting Microsoft Exchange Server 5.0, #70-076

  OR Implementing and Supporting Microsoft Exchange Server 5.5, #70-081

◆ Implementing and Supporting Microsoft Proxy Server 1.0, #70-078

  OR Implementing and Supporting Microsoft Proxy Server 2.0, #70-088

◆ Implementing and Supporting Microsoft SNA Server 4.0, #70-085

How to Become a Microsoft Certified Solution Developer

The MCSD certification is undergoing substantial revision. Listed below are the requirements for the new track (available fourth quarter 1998) as well as the old.

New Track

For the new track, you must pass three core exams and one elective exam. The three core exam areas are listed below, as are the elective exams from which you can choose.

Core Exams

The core exams include the following:

Desktop Applications Development (one required)

◆ Designing and Implementing Desktop Applications with Microsoft Visual C++ 6.0, #70-016

  OR Designing and Implementing Desktop Applications with Microsoft Visual Basic 6.0, #70-176

Distributed Applications Development (one required)

◆ Designing and Implementing Distributed Applications with Microsoft Visual C++ 6.0, #70-015

  OR Designing and Implementing Distributed Applications with Microsoft Visual Basic 6.0, #70-175

Solution Architecture (required)

◆ Analyzing Requirements and Defining Solution Architectures, #70-100

Elective Exam

You must pass one of the following elective exams:

◆ Designing and Implementing Distributed Applications with Microsoft Visual C++ 6.0, #70-015

  OR Designing and Implementing Desktop Applications with Microsoft Visual C++ 6.0, #70-016

  OR Microsoft SQL Server 4.2 Database Implementation, #70-021*

◆ Implementing a Database Design on Microsoft SQL Server 6.5, #70-027

  OR Implementing a Database Design on Microsoft SQL Server 7.0, #70-029

◆ Developing Applications with C++ Using the Microsoft Foundation Class Library, #70-024

◆ Implementing OLE in Microsoft Foundation Class Applications, #70-025

◆ Designing and Implementing Web Sites with Microsoft FrontPage 98, #70-055

◆ Designing and Implementing Commerce Solutions with Microsoft Site Server 3.0, Commerce Edition, #70-057

◆ Programming with Microsoft Visual Basic 4.0, #70-065

  OR Developing Applications with Microsoft Visual Basic 5.0, #70-165

  OR Designing and Implementing Distributed Applications with Microsoft Visual Basic 6.0, #70-175

  OR Designing and Implementing Desktop Applications with Microsoft Visual Basic 6.0, #70-176

◆ Microsoft Access for Windows 95 and the Microsoft Access Development Toolkit, #70-069

◆ Designing and Implementing Solutions with Microsoft Office (code-named Office 9) and Microsoft Visual Basic for Applications, #70-091

◆ Designing and Implementing Web Solutions with Microsoft Visual InterDev 6.0, #70-152

Old Track

For the old track, you must pass two core technology exams and two elective exams for MCSD certification. The following lists show the required technology exams and elective exams needed for MCSD certification.

Core Exams

You must pass the following two core technology exams to qualify for MCSD certification:

◆ Microsoft Windows Architecture I, #70-160*

◆ Microsoft Windows Architecture II, #70-161*

Elective Exams

You must also pass two of the following elective exams to become an MSCD:

◆ Designing and Implementing Distributed Applications with Microsoft Visual C++ 6.0, #70-015

◆ Designing and Implementing Desktop Applications with Microsoft Visual C++ 6.0, #70-016

◆ Microsoft SQL Server 4.2 Database Implementation, #70-021*

  OR Implementing a Database Design on Microsoft SQL Server 6.5, #70-027

  OR Implementing a Database Design on Microsoft SQL Server 7.0, #70-029

◆ Developing Applications with C++ Using the Microsoft Foundation Class Library, #70-024

◆ Implementing OLE in Microsoft Foundation Class Applications, #70-025

◆ Programming with Microsoft Visual Basic 4.0, #70-065

   OR Developing Applications with Microsoft Visual Basic 5.0, #70-165

   OR Designing and Implementing Distributed Applications with Microsoft Visual Basic 6.0, #70-175

   OR Designing and Implementing Desktop Applications with Microsoft Visual Basic 6.0, #70-176

◆ Microsoft Access 2.0 for Windows-Application Development, #70-051

   OR Microsoft Access for Windows 95 and the Microsoft Access Development Toolkit, #70-069

◆ Developing Applications with Microsoft Excel 5.0 Using Visual Basic for Applications, #70-052

◆ Programming in Microsoft Visual FoxPro 3.0 for Windows, #70-054

◆ Designing and Implementing Web Sites with Microsoft FrontPage 98, #70-055

◆ Designing and Implementing Commerce Solutions with Microsoft Site Server 3.0, Commerce Edition, #70-057

◆ Designing and Implementing Solutions with Microsoft Office (code-named Office 9) and Microsoft Visual Basic for Applications, #70-091

◆ Designing and Implementing Web Solutions with Microsoft Visual InterDev 6.0, #70-152

Becoming a Microsoft Certified Trainer

To understand the requirements and process for becoming an MCT, you need to obtain the Microsoft Certified Trainer Guide document from the following WWW site:

    http://www.microsoft.com/train_cert/mct/

At this site, you can read the document as a Web page or display and download it as a Word file. The MCT Guide explains the four-step process for becoming an MCT. The general steps for the MCT certification are as follows:

1. Complete and mail a Microsoft Certified Trainer application to Microsoft. You must include proof of your skills for presenting instructional material. The options for doing so are described in the MCT Guide.

2. Obtain and study the Microsoft Trainer Kit for the Microsoft Official Curricula (MOC) courses for which you want to be certified. Microsoft Trainer Kits can be ordered by calling 800-688-0496 in North America. Those of you in other regions should review the MCT Guide for information on how to order a Trainer Kit.

3. Take the Microsoft certification exam for the product about which you want to be certified to teach.

4. Attend the MOC course for the course for which you want to be certified. This is required so you understand how the course is structured, how labs are completed, and how the course flows.

> **WARNING**
>
> You should consider the preceding steps a general overview of the MCT certification process. The precise steps that you need to take are described in detail on the WWW site mentioned earlier. Do not misinterpret the preceding steps as the exact process you must undergo.

If you are interested in becoming an MCT, you can obtain more information by visiting the Microsoft Certified Training WWW site at `http://www.microsoft.com/train_cert/mct/` or by calling 800-688-0496.

What's on the CD-ROM

This appendix is a brief rundown of what you'll find on the CD-ROM that comes with this book. For a more detailed description of the newly developed ExamGear, Training Guide Edition exam simulation software, see Appendix D, "Using the ExamGear, Training Guide Edition Software."

EXAMGEAR, TRAINING GUIDE EDITION

ExamGear, Training Guide Edition is an exam simulation environment developed exclusively for New Riders Publishing. It is, we believe, the best exam software available because it closely emulates the format and question types of the Microsoft exams. In addition to providing a means of evaluating your knowledge of the exam material, ExamGear, Training Guide Edition features several innovations that help you to improve your mastery of the subject matter.

For example, the practice tests allow you to check your score by exam area or category to determine which topics you need to study more. In another mode, ExamGear, Training Guide Edition allows you to obtain immediate feedback on your responses in the form of explanations for the correct and incorrect answers.

Although ExamGear, Training Guide Edition provides the full functionality of the retail version of ExamGear (including the exam format and all question types), this special version includes fewer cases and questions. It is designed to aid you in assessing how well you understand the Training Guide material and allow you to experience the question formats you will see on the actual #70-100 exam. However, it is not as complete a simulation of the exam as you would expect to see in the full ExamGear retail product.

Again, for a more complete description of ExamGear, Training Guide Edition features, see Appendix D, "Using the ExamGear, Training Guide Edition Software."

EXCLUSIVE ELECTRONIC VERSION OF TEXT

The CD-ROM also contains the electronic version of this book in Portable Document Format (PDF). The electronic version comes complete with all figures as they appear in the book.

COPYRIGHT INFORMATION AND DISCLAIMER

New Riders Publishing's ExamGear test simulator: Copyright 1999 New Riders Publishing. All rights reserved. Made in U.S.A.

Using the ExamGear, Training Guide Edition Software

This training guide includes a special version of ExamGear—a revolutionary new test engine that is designed to give you the best in certification exam preparation. ExamGear, Training Guide Edition offers sample and practice exams for many of today's most in-demand technical certifications. This special Training Guide edition is included with this book because it has the features that allow it to emulate the new approach Microsoft has taken to the Solution Architectures exam. In the rest of this appendix we describe in detail what ExamGear, Training Guide Edition is, how it works, and what it can do to help you prepare for the 70-100 exam. Note that although ExamGear, Training Guide Edition includes all the test simulation functions of the complete retail version, it does not contain as many questions or offer the degree of online support that the full product does.

EXAM SIMULATION

One of the main functions of ExamGear, Training Guide Edition is exam simulation. To prepare you to take the actual vendor certification exam, ExamGear, Training Guide Edition is designed to offer the most effective exam simulation available.

Question Quality

The questions provided in the ExamGear, Training Guide Edition simulations are written to very demanding standards of quality. Each question pertains to a specific exam objective as defined by the vendor offering the certification. No "fluff" questions are in ExamGear, Training Guide Edition. Each skill that you must have to pass the exam is tested by ExamGear, Training Guide Edition. If the question is included in ExamGear, Training Guide Edition, you can rest assured that it pertains directly to the vendor's learning objectives for certification, and you will need to know it to pass the actual exam.

Interface Design

The ExamGear, Training Guide Edition exam simulation interface offers you the same sort of look and feel as the actual certification exam. This enables you to effectively prepare for taking the exam by making the test experience a familiar one. Using the ExamGear, Training Guide Edition test simulation can help eliminate the sense of surprise or anxiety that you might experience in the testing center, because you will already be acquainted with the test process and the test interface.

Case Study-Based Testing

With the Solutions Architecture exam, Microsoft has sought to test MCSD candidates in a novel way—one that they believe is most appropriate to the kinds of problems solution developers face. ExamGear, Training Guide Edition enables you to practice testing in this new exam mode to familiarize yourself with this testing method and to ensure that you are completely prepared to take the actual exam.

STUDY TOOLS

ExamGear provides you with learning tools to help prepare you for the actual certification exam.

Effective Learning Environment

The ExamGear, Training Guide Edition interface provides a learning environment that not only simulates the actual certification exam, but also teaches the material you need to know to pass the exam. Each question comes with a detailed explanation of the correct answer and provides reasons why the other options were incorrect. This information helps to reinforce the knowledge you have already and also provides practical information you can use on the job.

Automatic Progress Tracking

ExamGear automatically tracks your progress as you work through the test questions. From ExamGear, Training Guide Edition's Item Review tab (discussed in detail later in this appendix), you can see at a glance how well you are scoring by objective, by unit, or on a question-by-question basis (see Figure D.1). You can also configure ExamGear, Training Guide Edition to drill you on the skills you need to work on most.

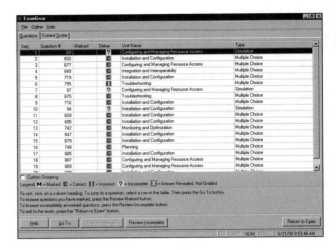

FIGURE D.1
Item review.

HOW EXAMGEAR, TRAINING GUIDE EDITION WORKS

ExamGear comprises two main elements: the interface and the database. The *interface* is the part of the program that you use to study and to run practice tests. The *database* stores all the question-and-answer data.

Interface

The ExamGear, Training Guide Edition interface is designed to be easy to use and provides the most effective study method available. The interface enables you to select among the following modes:

◆ **Study Mode**—In this mode, you can select the number of questions you want to see and the time you want to allow for the test. You can select questions from all the objective groups or from specific groups. This enables you to reinforce your knowledge in a specific area or strengthen your knowledge in areas pertaining to a specific objective. During the exam, you can display the correct answer to each question along with an explanation of why it is correct.

◆ **Practice Exam**—In this mode, you take an exam that is designed to simulate the actual certification exam. Questions are selected from all test-objective groups. The number of questions selected and the time allowed are set to match those parameters of the actual certification exam.

◆ **Adaptive Exam**—In this mode, you take an exam simulation using the adaptive testing technique. Questions are taken from all test-objective groups. The questions are presented in a way that ensures your mastery of all the test objectives. After you have a passing score, or if you reach a point where it is statistically impossible for you to pass, the exam is ended. This method provides a rapid assessment of your readiness for the actual exam. Although this exam format is not likely to ever appear in the 70-100 exam because of the case study approach, we include it as an option here to give you the opportunity to experience testing in this format.

Database

The ExamGear, Training Guide Edition database stores a group of test questions along with answers and explanations. At least two databases are included for each ExamGear, Training Guide Edition product. When you purchase ExamGear, Training Guide Edition, you get an *activation key* that gives you access to the databases for a specific exam. Each ExamGear, Training Guide Edition product comes with at least one activated database. Depending on which version you've purchased, additional demonstration exams may be on the CD as well. Additional exam databases may also be available

for purchase online and are simple to download. Look ahead to the section "Obtaining Updates" in this appendix to find out how to download and activate additional databases.

INSTALLING AND REGISTERING EXAMGEAR, TRAINING GUIDE EDITION

This section provides instructions for ExamGear, Training Guide Edition installation and describes the process and benefits of registering your ExamGear, Training Guide Edition product.

Requirements

ExamGear requires a computer with the following:

◆ A computer running Microsoft Windows 95, Windows 98, or Windows NT 4.0.

Pentium or later processor recommended.

◆ Microsoft's Internet Explorer 4.01.

Internet Explorer 4.01 must be installed. (Even if you use a different browser, you still need to have Internet Explorer 4.01 or later installed.)

◆ A minimum of 16MB of RAM.

As with any Windows application, the more memory, the better your performance.

◆ A connection to the Internet.

An Internet connection is not required for the software to work, but it is required for online registration, product updates, downloading bonus question sets, and for unlocking other exams. These processes are described in more detail later.

Installing ExamGear, Training Guide Edition

Install ExamGear, Training Guide Edition by running the setup program that you found on the ExamGear, Training Guide Edition CD. Follow these instructions to install ExamGear, Training Guide Edition on your computer:

1. If you purchased ExamGear, Training Guide Edition on CD, insert that CD in your CD-ROM drive.

2. Click Start, Run. In the Open line, type the path to the SETUP.EXE program. If you purchased ExamGear, Training Guide Edition, this is the path to the root directory of your CD-ROM drive (for example: D:\SETUP.EXE).

3. The Installation Wizard appears onscreen and prompts you with instructions to complete the installation. Select a directory on which to install ExamGear, Training Guide Edition (the Installation Wizard defaults to C:\Program Files\ExamGear).

4. The Installation Wizard copies the ExamGear, Training Guide Edition files to your hard drive, adds ExamGear, Training Guide Edition to your Program menu, adds values to your Registry, and installs ExamGear, Training Guide Edition's DLLs to the appropriate system folders. To ensure that the process was successful, the Setup program finishes by running ExamGear, Training Guide Edition.

5. The Installation Wizard logs the installation process and stores this information in a file named INSTALL.LOG. This log file is used by the uninstall process in the event that you choose to remove ExamGear, Training Guide Edition from your computer. Because the ExamGear, Training Guide Edition installation adds Registry keys and DLL files to your computer, it is important to uninstall the program appropriately (see the section "Removing ExamGear, Training Guide Edition from your Computer").

Registering ExamGear, Training Guide Edition

The Product Registration Wizard appears when ExamGear, Training Guide Edition is started for the first time, and ExamGear, Training Guide Edition checks at startup to see if you are registered. If you are not registered, the main menu is hidden, and a Product Registration Wizard appears. Remember that your computer must have an Internet connection to complete the Product Registration Wizard.

The first page of the Product Registration Wizard details the benefits of registration; however, you can always elect not to register. The Show This Message at Startup Until I Register option enables you to decide whether the registration screen should appear every time ExamGear, Training Guide Edition is started. If you click the Cancel button, you return to the main menu. You can register at any time by selecting Online, Registration from the main menu.

The registration process is composed of a simple form for entering your personal information, including your name and address. You are asked for your level of experience with the product you are testing on and whether you purchased ExamGear, Training Guide Edition from a retail store or over the Internet. The information will be used by our software designers and marketing department to provide us with feedback about the usability and usefulness of this product. It takes only a few seconds to fill out and transmit the registration data. A confirmation dialog box appears when registration is complete.

After you have registered and transmitted this information to New Riders, the registration option is removed from the pull-down menus.

Registration Benefits

Remember that registration allows you access to download updates (see "Obtaining Updates and Additional Exams") from our FTP site using ExamGear, Training Guide Edition.

Removing ExamGear, Training Guide Edition from Your Computer

In the event that you elect to remove the ExamGear, Training Guide Edition product from your computer, an uninstall process has been included to ensure that ExamGear, Training Guide Edition is removed from your system safely and completely. Follow these instructions to remove ExamGear, Training Guide Edition from your computer:

1. Click Start, Settings, Control Panel.

2. Double-click the Add/Remove Programs icon.

3. You are presented with a list of software that is installed on your computer. Select ExamGear, Training Guide Edition from the list and click the Add/Remove button. The ExamGear, Training Guide Edition software is then removed from your computer.

It is important that the INSTALL.LOG file be present in the directory where you have installed ExamGear, Training Guide Edition should you ever choose to uninstall the ExamGear, Training Guide Edition product. Do not delete this file. The INSTALL.LOG file is used by the uninstall process to safely remove the files and Registry settings that were added to your computer by the installation process.

USING EXAMGEAR, TRAINING GUIDE EDITION

ExamGear is designed to be user-friendly and very intuitive, eliminating the need for you to learn some confusing piece of software just to practice answering questions. Because the software has a smooth learning curve, your time is maximized because you start practicing almost immediately.

General Description of How the Software Works

ExamGear has three modes of operation: Study Mode, Practice Exam, and Adaptive Exam (see Figure D.2). All three sections have the same easy-to-use interface. Using Study Mode, you can hone your knowledge as well as your test-taking abilities through the use of the Show Answers option. While you are taking the test, you can expose the answers along with a brief description of why the given answers are right or wrong. This gives you the ability to better understand the material presented.

The Practice Exam section has many of the same options as Study Mode, but you cannot expose the answers. This way, you have a more traditional testing environment with which to practice.

The Adaptive Exam questions continuously monitor your expertise in each tested topic area. If you reach a point at which you either pass or fail, the software ends the examination. As in the Practice Exam, you cannot reveal the answers.

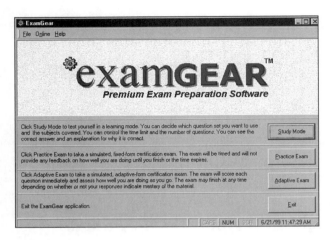

FIGURE D.2
The opening screen offers three testing modes.

Menu Options

The ExamGear, Training Guide Edition interface has an easy-to-use menu that provides the following options:

File	Exit	Exits the program.
Options	Study Mode	Takes you to the Study Mode configuration screen.
	Practice Exam	Takes you to the Practice Exam configuration screen.
	Adaptive Exam	Takes you to the Adaptive Exam configuration screen.
Online	Registration	Starts the Registration Wizard and allows you to register online. This menu option is removed after you have successfully registeredthe product.
	Check for Product Updates	Downloads product catalog for Web-based updates.
	Web Browser	Opens the Web browser. Non-hierarchical on the main menu, but the Web Browser menu becomes hierarchical after the browser is opened.
Help	Help	Opens ExamGear, Training Guide Edition's help file.

Options

The Options menu allows you to configure the testing options for a particular type of exam. Three options are available from the Options menu: Study Mode, Practice Exam, and Adaptive Exam. The Options screen that appears when you select either the Study Mode or the Practice Exam is essentially the same.

Online

In the Online menu, you can register ExamGear, Training Guide Edition, check for product updates (update the ExamGear, Training Guide Edition executable as well as check for free, updated question sets), surf Web pages, and participate in threaded discussion groups. The Online menu is always available, except when you are taking a test.

Registration

Registration is free and allows you access to the newsgroups and mentoring. Registration is the first task that ExamGear, Training Guide Edition asks you to perform. You will not have access to the free product updates if you do not register.

Check for Product Updates

This option takes you to ExamGear, Training Guide Edition's Web site where you can update the software. Registration is required for this option to be available. You must also be connected to the Internet to use this option. The ExamGear Web site lists the options that have been made available since your version of ExamGear, Training Guide Edition was installed on your computer.

Web Browser

This option provides a convenient way to start your Web browser and connect to the New Rider's Web site while you are working in ExamGear, Training Guide Edition. Click the Exit button to leave the Web browser and return to the ExamGear, Training Guide Edition interface.

Starting a Study Mode Session

Study Mode enables you to control the test in ways that actual certification exams do not allow:

◆ You can set your own time limits.

◆ You can concentrate on selected skill areas (units).

◆ You can reveal answers or have each response graded immediately with feedback.

◆ You can restrict the questions you see again to those missed or those answered correctly a given number of times.

◆ You can control the order in which questions are presented (random order or in order by skill area [unit]).

To begin testing in Study Mode, click the Study Mode button from the main Interface screen. You are presented with the Study Mode configuration page (see Figure D.3). This is the same page that is accessed by selecting Study Mode from the Options menu.

At the top of the Study Mode configuration screen, you see the Exam drop-down list. This list shows the activated exam that you have purchased with your ExamGear, Training Guide Edition product, as well as any other exams you may have downloaded or any demo exams that were shipped with your version of ExamGear, Training Guide Edition. Select the exam with which you want to practice from the drop-down list.

Under the Exam drop-down list, you see the question sets that are available for the selected exam. Each exam has at least two question sets, and if you have registered your ExamGear, Training Guide Edition product, you will also have access to the Bonus question set. You can select from any individual question set or any combination of the question sets available for the selected exam.

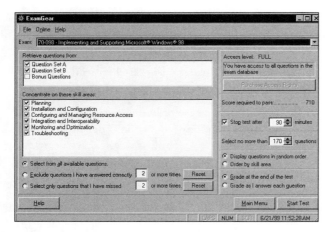

FIGURE D.3
The Study Mode configuration page.

Below the Question Set list is a list of skill areas or units on which you can concentrate. These skill areas are derived directly from the categories of exam objectives defined by Microsoft for the 70-100 exam. Within each skill area you will find several exam objectives. You can select a single skill area to focus on, or you can select any combination of the available skill areas to customize the exam to your individual needs.

In addition to specifying which question sets and skill areas you want to test yourself on, you can also define which questions are included in the test based on your previous progress working with the test. ExamGear, Training Guide Edition automatically tracks your progress with the available questions. When configuring the Study Mode options, you can opt to view all the questions available within the question sets and skill areas you have selected, or you can limit the questions presented. Choose from the following options:

◆ **Select from All Available Questions**—This option causes ExamGear, Training Guide Edition to present all available questions from the selected question sets and skill areas.

◆ **Exclude Questions I Have Answered Correctly X or More Times**—ExamGear offers you the option to exclude questions that you have previously answered correctly. You can specify how many times you want to answer a question correctly before ExamGear, Training Guide Edition considers you to have mastered it (the default is two times).

◆ **Select Only Questions That I Have Missed X or More Times**—This option configures ExamGear, Training Guide Edition to drill you only on questions that you have missed repeatedly. You may specify how many times you must miss a question before ExamGear, Training Guide Edition determines that you have not mastered it (the default is two times).

At any time, you can reset ExamGear, Training Guide Edition's tracking information by clicking the Reset button for the feature you want to clear.

At the top-right side of the Study Mode configuration sheet, you can see your access level to the question sets for the selected exam. Access levels are either Full or Demo. For a detailed explanation of each of these access levels, see the section "Obtaining Updates" in this appendix.

Under your access level, you see the score required to pass the selected exam. Below the required score, you can select whether the test will be timed and how much time will be allowed to complete the exam. Select the Stop Test After 90 Minutes check box to set a time limit for the exam. Enter the number of minutes you want to allow for the test (the default is 90 minutes). Deselecting this check box allows you to take an exam without any time limit.

You can also configure the number of questions included in the exam. The default number of questions changes with the specific exam you have selected. Enter the number of questions you want to include in the exam in the Select No More than *XX* Questions option.

You can configure the order in which ExamGear, Training Guide Edition presents the exam questions. Select from the following options:

◆ **Display the Questions in Random Order—** This option is the default option. When selected, it causes ExamGear, Training Guide Edition to present the questions in random order throughout the exam.

◆ **Order by Skill Area—**This option causes ExamGear, Training Guide Edition to group the questions presented in the exam by skill area. All questions for each selected skill area are presented in succession. The test progresses from one selected skill area to the next, until all the questions from each selected skill area have been presented.

ExamGear offers two options for scoring your exams. Select one of the following options:

◆ **Grade at the End of the Test—**This option configures ExamGear, Training Guide Edition to score your test after you have been presented with all the selected exam questions. You can reveal correct answers to a question, but if you do, that question is not scored.

◆ **Grade as I Answer Each Question—**This option configures ExamGear, Training Guide Edition to grade each question as you answer it, providing you with instant feedback as you take the test. All questions are scored unless you click the Show Answer button before completing the question.

Before ExamGear, Training Guide Edition begins each test, you are presented with Startup screens that display copyright information and general instructions for completing the exam. If you want to go directly into the exam without viewing these screens, select the Skip Startup Screens check box.

You can return to the ExamGear, Training Guide Edition main startup screen from the Study Mode configuration screen by clicking the Menu button. If you need assistance configuring the Study Mode exam options, click the Help button for configuration instructions.

When you have finished configuring all the exam options, click the Start Test button to begin the exam.

Starting Practice Exams

This section describes practice exams and adaptive exams, defines the differences between these exam options and the Study Mode option, and provides instructions for starting them.

Differences Between the Practice and Adaptive Exams and Study Modes

Question screens in the practice and adaptive exams are identical to those found in Study Mode, except that the Show Answer, Grade Answer, and Item Review buttons are not available while you are in the process of taking a practice or adaptive exam. The Practice Exam provides you with a report screen at the end of the exam. The Adaptive Exam gives you a brief message indicating whether you've passed or failed the exam.

When taking a practice exam, the Item Review screen is not available until you have answered all the questions. This is consistent with the behavior of most of Microsoft's current certification exams. In Study Mode, Item Review is available at any time.

When the exam timer expires, or if you click the End Exam button, the Examination Score Report screen comes up.

Starting an Exam

From the ExamGear, Training Guide Edition main menu screen, select the type of exam you want to run. Click the Practice Exam or Adaptive Exam button to begin the corresponding exam type.

What Is an Adaptive Exam?

To make the certification testing process more demanding, and therefore make the certification itself more valuable, many vendors in the industry are using a testing technique called *adaptive testing*. In an adaptive exam, the exam "adapts" to your abilities by varying the difficulty level of the questions presented to you.

The first question in an adaptive exam is typically an easy one. If you answer it correctly, you are presented with a slightly more difficult question. If you answer that question correctly, the next question you see is even more difficult. If you answer the question incorrectly, however, the exam "adapts" to your skill level by presenting you with another question of equal or lesser difficulty on the same subject. If you answer that question correctly, the test begins to increase the difficulty level again. You must correctly answer several questions at a predetermined difficulty level to pass the exam. After you have done this successfully, the exam is ended and scored. If you do not reach the required level of difficulty within a predetermined time (typically 30 minutes) the exam is ended and scored.

Why Do Vendors Use Adaptive Exams?

Many vendors who offer technical certifications have adopted the adaptive testing technique. They have found that it is an effective way to measure a candidate's mastery of the test material in as little time as necessary. This reduces the scheduling demands on the test taker and allows the testing center to offer more tests per test station than they could with longer, more traditional exams.

Studying for Adaptive Exams

Studying for adaptive exams is not different from studying for traditional exams. You should make sure that you have thoroughly covered all the material for each of the test objectives specified by the certification exam vendor. As with any other exam, when you take an adaptive exam, you either know the material or you don't. If you are well prepared, you will be able to pass the exam. ExamGear, Training Guide Edition can allow you to familiarize yourself with the adaptive exam testing technique. This will help eliminate any anxiety you might experience from this testing technique and allow you to focus on learning the actual exam material.

ExamGear's Adaptive Exam

The method used to score the adaptive exam requires a large pool of questions. For this reason, you cannot use this exam in Demo mode. The adaptive exam is presented in much the same way as the practice exam. When you click the Start Test button, you begin answering questions. The adaptive exam does not allow item review, and it does not allow you to mark questions to skip and answer later. You must answer each question when it is presented.

Assumptions

This section describes the assumptions made when designing the behavior of the ExamGear, Training Guide Edition adaptive exam.

◆ You fail the test if you fail any objective, earn a failing overall score, or reach a threshold at which it is statistically impossible for you to pass the exam.

◆ You can fail or pass a test without cycling through all the questions.

◆ The overall score for the adaptive exam is Pass or Fail. However, to evaluate user responses dynamically, percentage scores are recorded for units and the overall score.

Algorithm Assumptions

This section describes the assumptions used in designing the ExamGear, Training Guide Edition Adaptive Exam scoring algorithm.

Unit Scores

You fail a unit (and the exam) if any unit score falls below 66 percent.

Overall Scores

To pass the exam, you must pass all units and achieve an overall score of 86 percent or higher.

You fail if the overall score percentage is less than or equal to 85 percent, or if any unit score is less than 66 percent.

Inconclusive Scores

If your overall score is between 67 and 85 percent, it is considered to be *inconclusive*. Additional questions will be asked until you pass or fail or until it becomes statistically impossible to pass without asking more than the maximum number of questions allowed.

Question Types and How to Answer Them

Because certification exams from different vendors vary, you will face many types of questions on any given exam. ExamGear, Training Guide Edition presents you with different question types to allow you to become familiar with the various ways an actual exam may test your knowledge. The Solution Architectures exam, in particular, offers a unique exam format and utilizes question types other than multiple choice. This version of ExamGear, Training Guide Edition includes cases— extensive problem descriptions running several pages in length, followed by a number of questions specific to that case. Microsoft refers to these case/question collections as testlets. This version of ExamGear, Training Guide Edition also includes regular questions that are not attached to a case study. We include these question types to make taking the actual exam easier because you will already be familiar with the steps required to answer each question type. This section describes each of the question types presented by ExamGear, Training Guide Edition and provides instructions for answering each type.

Multiple Choice

Most of the questions you see on a certification exam are multiple choice (see Figure D.4). This question type asks you to select an answer from the list provided. Sometimes you must select only one answer, often indicated by answers preceded by option buttons (round selection buttons). At other times, multiple correct answers are possible, indicated by check boxes preceding the possible answer combinations.

You can use any one of three methods to select an answer:

◆ Click the option button or check box next to the answer. If more than one correct answer to a question is possible, the answers will have check boxes next to them. If only one correct answer to a question is possible, each answer will have an option button next to it. ExamGear, Training Guide Edition prompts you with the number of answers you must select.

◆ Click the text of the answer.

◆ Press the alphabetic key that corresponds to the answer.

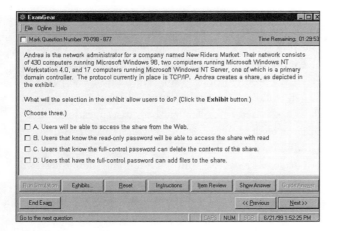

FIGURE D.4
A typical multiple-choice question.

You can use any one of three methods to clear an option button:

◆ Click another option button.

◆ Click the text of another answer.

◆ Press the alphabetic key that corresponds to another answer.

You can use any one of three methods to clear a check box:

◆ Click the check box next to the selected answer.

◆ Click the text of the selected answer.

◆ Press the alphabetic key that corresponds to the selected answer.

To clear all answers, click the Reset button.

Remember that some of the questions have multiple answers that are correct. Do not let this throw you off. The *multiple correct* questions do not have one answer that is more correct than another. In the *single correct* format, only one answer is correct. ExamGear, Training Guide Edition prompts you with the number of answers you must select.

Drag and Drop

Drag-and-drop questions present you with a number of objects and connectors. The question prompts you to create relationships between the objects by using the connectors. In the preceding image, the gray squares on the left side of the question window are the objects you can select. The connectors are listed on the right side of the question window in the Connectors box. An example is shown in Figure D.5.

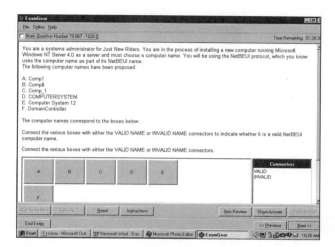

FIGURE D.5
A typical drag-and-drop question.

To select an object, click it with the mouse. When an object is selected, it changes color from a gray box to a white box. To drag an object, select it by clicking it with the left mouse button and holding the left mouse button down. You can move (or drag) the object to another area on the screen by moving the mouse while holding the left mouse button down.

To create a relationship between two objects, take the following actions:

1. Select an object and drag it to an available area on the screen.

2. Select another object and drag it to a location near where you dragged the first object.

3. Select the connector that you want to place between the two objects. The relationship should now appear complete. Note that to create a relationship, you must have two objects selected. If you try to select a connector without first selecting two objects, you are presented with an error message like that illustrated in Figure D.6.

FIGURE D.6
The error message.

Initially, the direction of the relationship established by the connector is from the first object selected to the second object selected. To change the direction of the connector, right-click the connector and choose Reverse Connection.

You can use either of two methods to remove the connector:

◆ Right-click the text of the connector that you want to remove, and then choose Delete.

◆ Select the text of the connector that you want to remove, and then press the Delete key.

To remove from the screen all the relationships you have created, click the Reset button.

Keep in mind that connectors can be used multiple times. If you move connected objects, it will not change the relationship between the objects; to remove the relationship between objects, you must remove the connector that joins them. When ExamGear, Training Guide Edition scores a drag-and-drop question, only objects with connectors to other objects are scored.

Ordered List

In the *ordered-list* question type (see Figure D.7), you are presented with a number of items and are asked to perform two tasks:

1. Build an answer list from items on the list of choices.

2. Put the items in a particular order.

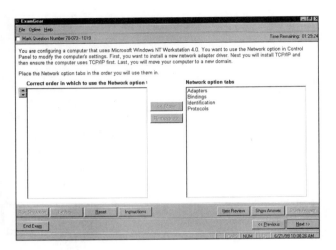

FIGURE D.7
A typical ordered-list question.

You can use any one of the following three methods to add an item to the answer list:

◆ Drag the item from the list of choices on the right side of the screen to the answer list on the left side of the screen.

◆ From the available items on the right side of the screen, double-click the item you want to add.

◆ From the available items on the right side of the screen, select the item you want to add; then click the Move button.

To remove an item from the answer list, you can use any one of the following four methods:

◆ Drag the item you want to remove from the answer list on the left side of the screen back to the list of choices on the right side of the screen.

◆ On the left side of the screen, double-click the item you want to remove from the answer list.

◆ On the left side of the screen, select the item you want to remove from the answer list, and then click the Remove button.

◆ On the left side of the screen, select the item you want to remove from the answer list, and then press the Delete key.

To remove all items from the answer list, click the Reset button.

If you need to change the order of the items in the answer list, you can do so using either of the following two methods:

◆ Drag each item to the appropriate location in the answer list.

◆ In the answer list, select the item that you want to move, and then click the up or down arrow button to move the item.

Keep in mind that items in the list can be selected twice. You may find that an ordered-list question will ask you to list in the correct order the steps required to perform a certain task. Certain steps may need to be performed more than once during the process. Don't think that after you have selected a list item, it is no longer available. If you need to select a list item more than once, you can simply select that item at each appropriate place as you construct your list.

Ordered Tree

The *ordered-tree* question type (see Figure D.8) presents you with a number of items and prompts you to create a tree structure from those items. The tree structure includes three levels of nodes, each marked with distinct colors and shapes:

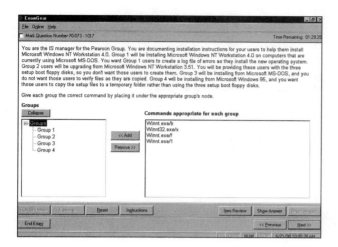

FIGURE D.8
A typical ordered-tree question.

◆ Red triangles indicate nodes to which you cannot add items.

◆ Blue squares indicate nodes to which you can add items.

◆ Green circles appear next to items that you have added to nodes.

An item in the list of choices can be added only to the nodes that are marked with blue squares. Do not think that after you have selected an item on the list of choices, it is no longer available for selection. If you need to add an item from the list of choices more than once, simply select that item again and add it to the appropriate node. A node can have more than one item added to it from the list of choices. You cannot add or remove blue or red nodes.

You can use either of the following two methods to add an item to the tree:

◆ Drag the item from the list of choices on the right side of the screen to the appropriate node of the tree on the left side of the screen.

◆ Select the appropriate node of the tree on the left side of the screen. Select the appropriate item from the list of choices on the right side of the screen. Click the Move button.

You can use either of the following two methods to remove an item from the tree:

◆ Drag an item from the tree to the list of choices.

◆ Select the item and click the Remove button.

To remove from the tree structure all the items you have added, click the Reset button.

Simulations

Simulation questions (see Figure D.9) require you to actually perform a task. Because the Solution Architectures exam is not task-based but conceptual in nature, no simulation questions are on the exam. However, they appear in increasing numbers on the other Microsoft exams and so we include them here.

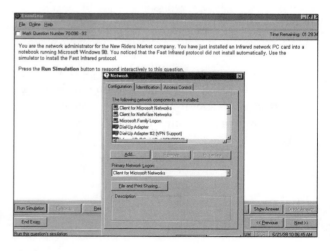

FIGURE D.9
A typical simulation question.

The main screen describes a situation and prompts you to provide a solution. When you are ready to proceed, you click the Run Simulation button in the lower-left corner. A screen or window appears on which you perform the solution. This window simulates the actual software that you would use to perform the required task in the real world. When a task requires several steps to complete, the simulator displays all the necessary screens to allow you to complete the task. When you have provided your answer by completing all the steps necessary to perform the required task, you can click the OK button to proceed to the next question.

You can return to any simulation to modify your answer. Your actions in the simulation are recorded, and the simulation appears exactly as you left it.

Simulation questions can be reset to their original state by pressing the Reset button.

Hot Spot Questions

Hot spot questions (see Figure D.10) ask you to correctly identify an item by clicking an area of the graphic displayed. To respond to the question, position the mouse cursor over a graphic. Then press the right mouse button to indicate your selection. To select another area on the graphic, you do not need to deselect the first one. Just click another region in the image. Again, these don't appear in the Solution Architectures exam, but you will encounter them on other Microsoft exams.

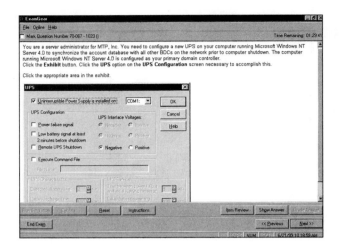

FIGURE D.10
A typical hot spot question.

Standard ExamGear, Training Guide Edition Options

Regardless of question type, a consistent set of clickable buttons enables you to navigate and interact with questions. The following list describes the function of each of the buttons you may see. Depending on the question type, some of the buttons will be grayed out and will be inaccessible. Buttons that are appropriate to the question type are active.

- ◆ **Run Simulation**—This button is enabled if the question supports a simulation. Clicking this button begins the simulation process.

- ◆ **Exhibits**—This button is enabled if exhibits are provided to support the question. An *exhibit* is a bitmap image or text file that provides supplemental information needed to answer the question. If a question has more than one exhibit, a dialog box appears, listing exhibits by name. If only one exhibit exists, the file is opened immediately when you click the Exhibits button.

◆ **Reset**—This button clears any selections you have made and returns the question window to the state in which it appeared when it was first displayed.

◆ **Instructions**—This button displays instructions for interacting with the current question type.

◆ **Item Review**—This button leaves the question window and opens the Item Review screen. For a detailed explanation of the Item Review screen, see the "Item Review" section later in this appendix.

◆ **Show Answer**—This option displays the correct answer with an explanation of why it is correct. If you choose this option, the current question will not be scored.

◆ **Grade Answer**—If Grade at the End of the Test is selected as a configuration option, this button is disabled. It is enabled when Grade As I Answer Each Question is selected as a configuration option. Clicking this button grades the current question immediately. An explanation of the correct answer is provided, just as if the Show Answer button were pressed. The question is graded, however.

◆ **End Exam**—This button ends the exam and displays the Examination Score Report screen.

◆ **<< Previous**—This button displays the previous question.

◆ **Next>>**—This button displays the next question on the exam.

◆ **<<Previous Marked**—This button is displayed if you have opted to review questions that you have marked using the Item Review screen. This button displays the previous marked question. Marking questions is discussed in more detail later in this appendix.

◆ **<<Previous Incomplete**—This button is displayed if you have opted, using the Item Review screen, to review questions that you have not answered. This button displays the previous unanswered question.

◆ **Next Marked>>**—This button is displayed if you have opted to review questions that you have marked using the Item Review screen. This button displays the next marked question. Marking questions is discussed in more detail later in this appendix.

◆ **Next Incomplete>>**—This button is displayed if you have opted to review questions, using the Item Review screen, that you have not answered. This button displays the next unanswered question.

Mark Question and Time Remaining

ExamGear provides you with two methods to aid in dealing with the time limit of the testing process. If you find that you need to skip a question, or if you want to check the time remaining to complete the test, use one of the options discussed in the following sections.

Mark Question

Check this box to mark a question so that you can return to it later using the Item Review feature. The adaptive exam does not allow questions to be marked because it does not support item review.

Time Remaining

If the test is timed, the Time Remaining indicator is enabled. It counts down minutes remaining to complete the test. The adaptive exam does not offer this feature because it is not timed.

Item Review

The Item Review screen allows you to jump to any marked or incomplete question. ExamGear, Training Guide Edition considers an *incomplete* question to be any unanswered question or any multiple-choice question for which the total number of required responses has not been selected. For example, if the question prompts for three answers and you selected only A and C, ExamGear, Training Guide Edition considers the question to be incomplete.

The Item Review screen enables you to review the exam questions in different ways. You can enter one of two *browse sequences* (series of similar records): Browse Marked Questions and Browse Incomplete Questions. You can also create a custom grouping of the exam questions for review based on a number of criteria.

When using Item Review, if Show Answer was selected for a question while you were taking the exam, the question is grayed out in item review. These questions can be returned to, but they cannot be reanswered or included in a browse sequence.

The Item Review screen contains two tabs. The Questions tab lists questions and question information in columns. The Current Score tab provides your exam score information, presented as a percentage for each unit and as a bar graph for your overall score.

The Item Review Questions Tab

The Questions tab on the Item Review screen (see Figure D.11) presents the exam questions and question information in a table. You can select any row you want by clicking in the grid. The Go To button is enabled whenever a row is selected. Clicking the Go To button displays the question on the selected row. You can also display a question by double-clicking that row.

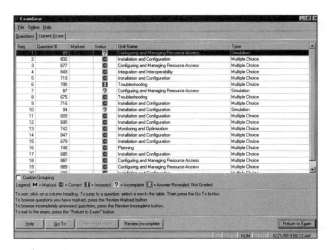

FIGURE D.11
The Questions tab on the Item Review screen.

Columns

The Questions tab contains the following six columns of information:

◆ **Seq**—Indicates the sequence number of the question as it was displayed in the exam.

◆ **Marked**—Indicates a question that you have marked using the Mark Question check box.

◆ **Incomplete**—Indicates an incomplete question.

◆ **Unit Name**—The unit associated with each question.

◆ **Type**—The question type, which can be Multiple Choice, Drag and Drop, Simulation, Hot Spot, Ordered List, or Ordered Tree.

◆ **Question Number**—Displays the question's identification number for easy reference.

To resize a column, place the mouse pointer over the vertical line between column headings. The mouse pointer changes to a set of right and left arrows. When the mouse pointer changes, you can drag the column border to the left or right to make the column more or less wide. Simply click with the left mouse button and hold that button down while you move the column border in the desired direction.

The Item Review screen enables you to sort the questions on any of the column headings. Initially, the list of questions is sorted in descending order on the sequence number column. To sort on a different column heading, click that heading. You will see an arrow appear on the column heading indicating the direction of the sort (ascending or descending). To change the direction of the sort, click the column heading again.

The Item Review screen also allows you to create a *custom grouping*. This feature enables you to sort the questions based on any combination of criteria you prefer (see Figure D.12). For instance, you might want to review the question items sorted first by whether they were marked, then by the unit name, then by sequence number. The Custom Grouping feature allows you to do this. Start by checking the Custom Grouping check box. When you do so, the entire questions table shifts down a bit onscreen, and a message appear at the top of the table that reads `Drag a column heading here to group by that column.`

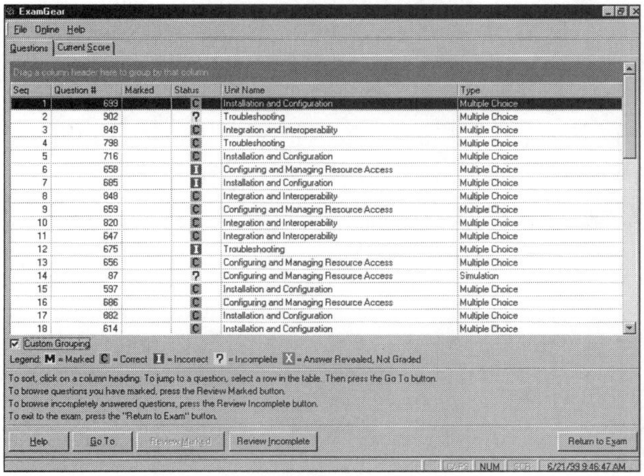

FIGURE D.12
Custom grouping.

Simply click the column heading you want with the left mouse button, hold that button down, and move the mouse into the area directly above the questions table (the custom grouping area). Release the left mouse button to drop the column heading into the custom grouping area. To accomplish the custom grouping previously described, first check the Custom Grouping check box. Then drag the Marked column heading into the custom grouping area above the question table. Next, drag the Unit Name column heading into the custom grouping area. You will see the two column headings joined together by a line that indicates the order of the custom grouping. Finally, drag the Seq column heading into the custom grouping area. This heading will be joined to the Unit Name heading by another line indicating the direction of the custom grouping.

Notice that each column heading in the custom grouping area has an arrow indicating the direction in which items are sorted under that column heading. You can reverse the direction of the sort on an individual column heading basis using these arrows. Click the column heading in the custom grouping area to change the direction of the sort for that column heading only. For example, using the custom grouping created previously, you can display the question list sorted first in descending order by whether the question was marked, in descending order by unit name, and then in ascending order by sequence number.

The custom grouping feature of the Item Review screen gives you enormous flexibility in how you choose to review the exam questions. To remove a custom grouping and return the Item Review display to its default setting (sorted in descending order by sequence number), simply uncheck the Custom Grouping check box.

The Current Score Tab

The Current Score tab of the Item Review screen (see Figure D.13) provides a real-time snapshot of your score. The top half of the screen is an expandable grid.

When the grid is collapsed, scores are displayed for each unit. Units can be expanded to show percentage scores for objectives and subobjectives. Information about your exam progress is presented in the following columns:

◆ **Unit Name**—This column shows the unit name for each objective group.

◆ **Percentage**—This column shows the percentage of questions for each objective group that you answered correctly.

◆ **Attempted**—This column lists the number of questions you answered either completely or partially for each objective group.

◆ **Correct**—This column lists the actual number of questions you answered correctly for each objective group.

◆ **Answer Shown**—This column lists the number of questions for each objective group that you chose to display the answer to using the Show Answer button.

The columns in the scoring table are resized and sorted in the same way as those in the questions table on the Item Review Questions tab. See the earlier section "The Item Review Questions Tab" for more details.

A graphical overview of the score is presented below the grid. The graph depicts two red bars: the top bar represents your current exam score and the bottom bar represents the required passing score. To the right of the bar graph is a legend that lists the required score and your score. Below the bar graph is a statement that describes the required passing score and your current score.

Clicking the End Exam button terminates the exam and passes control to the Examination Score Report screen.

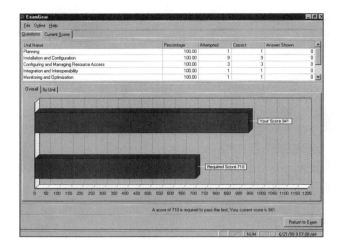

FIGURE D.13
The Current Score tab.

The Return to Exam button returns to the exam at the question from which the Item Review button was clicked.

Note that the Options pull-down menu does not appear when the Current Score tab is selected.

Review Marked Items

The Item Review screen allows you to enter a browse sequence for marked questions. When you click the Review Marked button, questions that you have previously marked using the Mark Question check box are presented for your review. While browsing the marked questions, you will see the following changes to the buttons:

◆ The caption of the Next button becomes Next Marked.

◆ The caption of the Previous button becomes Previous Marked.

Review Incomplete

The Item Review screen allows you to enter a browse sequence for incomplete questions. When you click the Review Incomplete button, the questions you did not answer or did not answer completely are displayed for your review. While browsing the incomplete questions, you will see the following changes to the buttons:

◆ The caption of the Next button becomes Next Incomplete.

◆ The caption of the Previous button becomes Previous Incomplete.

Examination Score Report Screen

The Examination Score Report screen (see Figure D.14) appears when the Study Mode or Practice Exam ends—as the result of timer expiration, completion of all questions, or your decision to terminate early. The adaptive exam does not offer an Examination Score Report because of its pass/fail format.

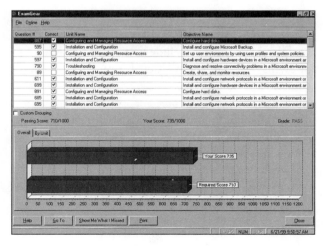

FIGURE D.14
The Examination Score Report screen.

This screen provides you with a graphical display of your test score, along with a tabular breakdown of scores by unit. The graphical display at the top of the screen compares your overall score with the score required to pass the exam. Buttons below the graphical display allow you to open the Show Me What I Missed browse sequence, print the screen, open online help, or return to the main menu.

Show Me What I Missed Browse Sequence

The Show Me What I Missed browse sequence is invoked by clicking the Show Me What I Missed button from the Examination Score Report or from the configuration screen of an adaptive exam.

Note that the window caption is modified to indicate that you are in the Show Me What I Missed browse sequence mode. Question IDs and position within the browse sequence appear at the top of the screen, in place of the Mark Question and Time Remaining indicators. Main window contents vary, depending on the question type. The following list describes the buttons available within the Show Me What I Missed browse sequence and the functions they perform:

◆ **Score Report**—Returns control to the Examination Score Report screen. In the case of an adaptive exam, this button's caption is Exit, and control returns to the adaptive exam configuration screen.

◆ **Run Simulation**—Opens a simulation in Grade mode, causing the simulation to open displaying your response and the correct answer. If the current question does not offer a simulation, this button is disabled.

◆ **Exhibits**—Opens the Exhibits window. This button is enabled if one or more exhibits are available for the question.

◆ **Instructions**—Opens the online help file to display instructions for using the Show Missed screen.

◆ **Print**—Prints the current screen.

◆ **Previous/Next Buttons**—Displays missed questions.

Checking the Web Site

To check the New Riders Home Page or the ExamGear, Training Guide Edition Home Page for updates or other product information, choose the desired Web site from the Web Sites option of the Online menu. You must be connected to the Internet to reach these Web sites. When you select a Web site, the Internet Explorer browser opens inside the ExamGear, Training Guide Edition window and displays the Web site.

OBTAINING UPDATES

The procedures for obtaining updates are outlined in the following sections.

The Catalog Web Site for Updates

Selecting the Check for Product Updates option from the Options menu shows you the full range of products you can either download for free or purchase. You can download additional items only if you have registered the software.

Product Updates Dialog Box

This dialog box appears when you select Check for Product Updates from the Online menu. ExamGear, Training Guide Edition checks for product updates from the New Riders Internet site and displays a list of products available for download. Some items, such as ExamGear, Training Guide Edition program updates or bonus question sets for exam databases you have activated, are available for download free of charge.

Types of Updates

Several types of updates may be available for download, including various free updates and additional items available for purchase.

Free Program Updates

Free program updates include changes to the ExamGear, Training Guide Edition executables and runtime libraries (DLLs). When any of these items are downloaded, ExamGear, Training Guide Edition automatically institutes the upgrades. ExamGear, Training Guide Edition will be reopened after the installation is complete.

Free Database Updates

Free database updates include updates to the exam or exams that you have registered. Exam updates are contained in compressed, encrypted files and include exam databases, simulations, and exhibits. ExamGear, Training Guide Edition automatically decompresses these files to their proper location and updates the ExamGear, Training Guide Edition software to record version changes and import new question sets.

CONTACTING NEW RIDERS PUBLISHING

At New Riders, we strive to meet and exceed the needs of our customers. We have developed ExamGear, Training Guide Edition to surpass the demands and expectations of network professionals seeking technical certifications, and we think it shows. What do you think?

If you need to contact New Riders regarding any aspect of the ExamGear, Training Guide Edition product line, feel free to do so. We look forward to hearing from you. Contact us at the following address or phone number:

New Riders Publishing
201 West 103 Street
Indianapolis, IN 46290
800-545-5914

You can also reach us on the World Wide Web:

`http://www.newriders.com`

Technical Support

Technical support is available at the following phone number during the hours specified:

317-581-3833

Monday through Thursday, 10:00 a.m.–3:00 p.m. Central Standard Time.

Friday, 10:00 a.m.–12:00 p.m. Central Standard Time.

Customer Service

If you have a damaged product and need a replacement or refund, please call the following phone number:

1-800-858-7674

Product Updates

Product updates can be obtained by choosing ExamGear, Training Guide Edition's Online pull-down menu and selecting Products Updates. You'll be taken to a private Web site with full details.

Product Suggestions and Comments

We value your input! Please email your suggestions and comments to the following address:

`certification@mcp.com`

LICENSE AGREEMENT

YOU SHOULD CAREFULLY READ THE FOLLOWING TERMS AND CONDITIONS BEFORE BREAKING THE SEAL ON THE PACKAGE. AMONG OTHER THINGS, THIS AGREEMENT LICENSES THE ENCLOSED SOFTWARE TO YOU AND CONTAINS WARRANTY AND LIABILITY DISCLAIMERS. BY BREAKING THE SEAL ON THE PACKAGE, YOU ARE ACCEPTING AND AGREEING TO THE TERMS AND CONDITIONS OF THIS AGREEMENT. IF YOU DO NOT AGREE TO THE TERMS OF THIS AGREEMENT, DO NOT BREAK THE SEAL. YOU SHOULD PROMPTLY RETURN THE PACKAGE UNOPENED.

LICENSE

Subject to the provisions contained herein, New Riders Publishing (NRP) hereby grants to you a nonexclusive, nontransferable license to use the object-code version of the computer software product (Software) contained in the package on a single computer of the type identified on the package.

SOFTWARE AND DOCUMENTATION

NRP shall furnish the Software to you on media in machine-readable object-code form and may also provide the standard documentation (Documentation) containing instructions for operation and use of the Software.

LICENSE TERM AND CHARGES

The term of this license commences upon delivery of the Software to you and is perpetual unless earlier terminated upon default or as otherwise set forth herein.

TITLE

Title, ownership right, and intellectual property rights in and to the Software and Documentation shall remain in NRP and/or in suppliers to NRP of programs contained in the Software. The Software is provided for your own internal use under this license. This license does not include the right to sublicense and is personal to you and therefore may not be assigned (by operation of law or otherwise) or transferred without the prior written consent of NRP. You acknowledge that the Software in source code form remains a confidential trade secret of NRP and/or its suppliers and therefore you agree not to attempt to decipher or decompile, modify, disassemble, reverse engineer, or prepare derivative works of the Software or develop source code for the Software or knowingly allow others to do so. Further, you may not copy the Documentation or other written materials accompanying the Software.

UPDATES

This license does not grant you any right, license, or interest in and to any improvements, modifications, enhancements, or updates to the Software and Documentation. Updates, if available, may be obtained by you at NRP's then-current standard pricing, terms, and conditions.

LIMITED WARRANTY AND DISCLAIMER

NRP warrants that the media containing the Software, if provided by NRP, is free from defects in material and workmanship under normal use for a period of sixty (60) days from the date you purchased a license to it.

THIS IS A LIMITED WARRANTY AND IT IS THE ONLY WARRANTY MADE BY NRP. THE SOFTWARE IS PROVIDED "AS IS" AND NRP SPECIFICALLY DISCLAIMS ALL WARRANTIES OF ANY KIND, EITHER EXPRESS OR IMPLIED, INCLUDING, BUT NOT LIMITED TO, THE IMPLIED WARRANTY OF MERCHANTABILITY AND FITNESS FOR A PARTICULAR PURPOSE. FURTHER, COMPANY DOES NOT WARRANT,

GUARANTEE, OR MAKE ANY REPRESENTA-
TIONS REGARDING THE USE, OR THE
RESULTS OF THE USE, OF THE SOFTWARE
IN TERMS OR CORRECTNESS, ACCURACY,
RELIABILITY, CURRENTNESS, OR OTHERWISE
AND DOES NOT WARRANT THAT THE
OPERATION OF ANY SOFTWARE WILL BE
UNINTERRUPTED OR ERROR FREE. NRP
EXPRESSLY DISCLAIMS ANY WARRANTIES
NOT STATED HEREIN. NO ORAL OR
WRITTEN INFORMATION OR ADVICE
GIVEN BY NRP, OR ANY NRP DEALER, AGENT,
EMPLOYEE, OR OTHERS SHALL CREATE,
MODIFY, OR EXTEND A WARRANTY OR IN
ANY WAY INCREASE THE SCOPE OF THE
FOREGOING WARRANTY, AND NEITHER
SUBLICENSEE OR PURCHASER MAY RELY ON
ANY SUCH INFORMATION OR ADVICE. If the
media is subjected to accident, abuse, or improper use;
or if you violate the terms of this Agreement, then this
warranty shall immediately be terminated. This warran-
ty shall not apply if the Software is used on or in
conjunction with hardware or programs other than
the unmodified version of hardware and programs
with which the Software was designed to be used as
described in the Documentation.

LIMITATION OF LIABILITY

Your sole and exclusive remedies for any damage or loss
in any way connected with the Software are set forth
below.

UNDER NO CIRCUMSTANCES AND UNDER
NO LEGAL THEORY, TORT, CONTRACT, OR
OTHERWISE, SHALL NRP BE LIABLE TO YOU
OR ANY OTHER PERSON FOR ANY INDIRECT,
SPECIAL, INCIDENTAL, OR CONSEQUENTIAL
DAMAGES OF ANY CHARACTER INCLUDING,
WITHOUT LIMITATION, DAMAGES FOR LOSS

OF GOODWILL, LOSS OF PROFIT, WORK
STOPPAGE, COMPUTER FAILURE OR MAL-
FUNCTION, OR ANY AND ALL OTHER
COMMERCIAL DAMAGES OR LOSSES, OR FOR
ANY OTHER DAMAGES EVEN IF NRP SHALL
HAVE BEEN INFORMED OF THE POSSIBILITY
OF SUCH DAMAGES, OR FOR ANY CLAIM
BY ANOTHER PARTY. NRP'S THIRD-PARTY
PROGRAM SUPPLIERS MAKE NO WARRANTY,
AND HAVE NO LIABILITY WHATSOEVER, TO
YOU. NRP's sole and exclusive obligation and liability
and your exclusive remedy shall be: upon NRP's
election, (i) the replacement of our defective media;
or (ii) the repair or correction of your defective media
if NRP is able, so that it will conform to the above
warranty; or (iii) if NRP is unable to replace or repair,
you may terminate this license by returning the
Software. Only if you inform NRP of your problem
during the applicable warranty period will NRP be
obligated to honor this warranty. SOME STATES
OR JURISDICTIONS DO NOT ALLOW THE
EXCLUSION OF IMPLIED WARRANTIES
OR LIMITATION OR EXCLUSION OF CONSE-
QUENTIAL DAMAGES, SO THE ABOVE
LIMITATIONS OR EXCLUSIONS MAY NOT
APPLY TO YOU. THIS WARRANTY GIVES YOU
SPECIFIC LEGAL RIGHTS AND YOU MAY ALSO
HAVE OTHER RIGHTS WHICH VARY BY STATE
OR JURISDICTION.

MISCELLANEOUS

If any provision of the Agreement is held to be in
effective, unenforceable, or illegal under certain circumstances for any reason, such decision shall not affect
the validity or enforceability (i) of such provision under
other circumstances or (ii) of the remaining provisions
hereof under all circumstances and such provision shall
be reformed to and only to the extent necessary to
make it effective, enforceable, and legal under such

circumstances. All headings are solely for convenience and shall not be considered in interpreting this Agreement. This Agreement shall be governed by and construed under New York law as such law applies to agreements between New York residents entered into and to be performed entirely within New York, except as required by U.S. Government rules and regulations to be governed by Federal law.

YOU ACKNOWLEDGE THAT YOU HAVE READ THIS AGREEMENT, UNDERSTAND IT, AND AGREE TO BE BOUND BY ITS TERMS AND CONDITIONS. YOU FURTHER AGREE THAT IT IS THE COMPLETE AND EXCLUSIVE STATEMENT OF THE AGREEMENT BETWEEN US THAT SUPERSEDES ANY PROPOSAL OR PRIOR AGREEMENT, ORAL OR WRITTEN, AND ANY OTHER COMMUNICATIONS BETWEEN US RELATING TO THE SUBJECT MATTER OF THIS AGREEMENT.

U.S. GOVERNMENT RESTRICTED RIGHTS

Use, duplication, or disclosure by the Government is subject to restrictions set forth in subparagraphs (a) through (d) of the Commercial Computer-Restricted Rights clause at FAR 52.227-19 when applicable, or in subparagraph (c) (1) (ii) of the Rights in Technical Data and Computer Software clause at DFARS 252.227-7013, and in similar clauses in the NASA FAR Supplement.

Quick Tips for Analyzing an Exam Case Study

Part of the challenge in any "real life" case study is breaking down the important points accurately, filtering out unimportant details, and organizing what is important in an efficient and usable fashion. The purpose of this appendix is to help you draw out the key words and design objectives from a case study. This should assist you in architecting quality software solutions.

This appendix has been organized around Microsoft's Solution Architectures exam (#70-100). The principles, however, apply equally well to real client/server development. Specifically, this appendix uses the Microsoft case study-based test demo for the 70-100 exam (http://www.microsoft.com/mcp/exam/stat/sp70-100.htm) as a working model.

THE SIX OBJECTIVE AREAS

Microsoft has divided the process of architecting into six areas:

◆ Business Requirements

◆ Technical Architecture

◆ Logical Design

◆ Data Model

◆ User Interface

◆ Physical Design

> **NOTE**
>
> **Remembering the Six Areas**
> Although you won't be tested on the six categories per se on the exam, you might want to remember the main functional areas of focus. Here's a useful mnemonic device: **B**uild **T**o **L**ast; **D**on't **U**nderestimate **P**rocess. You will certainly benefit from knowing and understanding these topic areas because this is how the Microsoft exam writers see the organization of the concepts underlying the exam.

In addition to the six major objectives for the exam, six attributes of a well-crafted solution run like a thread through the Microsoft objectives. To help remember them we have invented an acronym: PASS ME. PASS ME stands for Performance, Availability, Security, Scalability, Maintainability, and Extensibility. Microsoft features these six attributes several times in their exam objectives, so it will be important for you to understand how they interact to create a better solution architecture. These are covered in more detail in other parts of the book. You'll also find more information on them later in this appendix.

Let's see how we might analyze case study information for each of the six objective areas.

In order to facilitate our discussion, we'll work with a fictitious college called Big State College. BSC wants to make their enrollment processes more efficient, taking advantage of a new site agreement with Microsoft.

The Big State solution centers around an upgrade to their enrollment system. They currently have an IBM AS/400 that maintains class schedules and enrollments with an old PL/1 program. The gradual loss of college employees who know PL/1 has motivated the college to move to a SQL Server database, gradually phasing out the AS/400. BSC wants a new graphical user interface to replace the character-based screens in their current application. They intend to work with the old system and the new together for six months and then migrate totally to the new system.

Because the college teaches both SQL Server and Visual Basic, they have graduate assistants who are fluent in those areas who will be responsible for maintaining the system after it is built. The instructors have requested that the system be simple to maintain because new graduate assistants rotate through each year.

The college intends to upgrade both the hardware and the software in all their PCs and has also planned a major upgrade for the application server targeted to support the new system.

There are basically three levels of users: the course administrator, registrars, and the students themselves. There is only one course administrator, but there are 12 registrars and around 10,000 students.

The students will use the system by reviewing course schedules online from any of the 40 computer kiosks placed strategically around the campus. The students submit their requests via e-mail functionality built into the program. Responses will also be through e-mail, typically arriving within a few hours after the request is submitted. A simple ID/password system provides a link to the system. The course administrator and registrars will be directly connected to the system.

Big State is expecting about 6,000 students to take advantage of their new e-mail registration. Registrars can average 10 student enrollments per hour. The registrars are paid $20 per hour, so the college is hoping the system will pay for itself in three years (six semesters). Due to the low enrollments for the summer semester, BSC has decided to base all their calculations on two semesters per year. As it is at many colleges, cost is an issue.

A short development cycle is also part of the college's requirement. The new system should be up in time for fall enrollments, just eight months away.

In between enrollment periods, the system will see minimal usage. However, during the enrollment period (which usually lasts three weeks), the system needs to be up close to 24 hours a day every day.

Business Requirements

Business requirements, as defined by Microsoft, include such things as scope, integration with existing applications, business issues, security, performance, maintainability, extensibility, scalability, and availability. This is a lot to draw out of a case study and keep track of in an exam situation.

One of the most useful strategies for extracting information from case studies is to take notes, draw diagrams, or make lists as you read the case study.

While reading a case study, you should jot down a few notes that will help you answer the questions. Figure E.1 shows what these notes might look like for the BSC case study. All the essential information is there. All duplicated or extraneous information is filtered out.

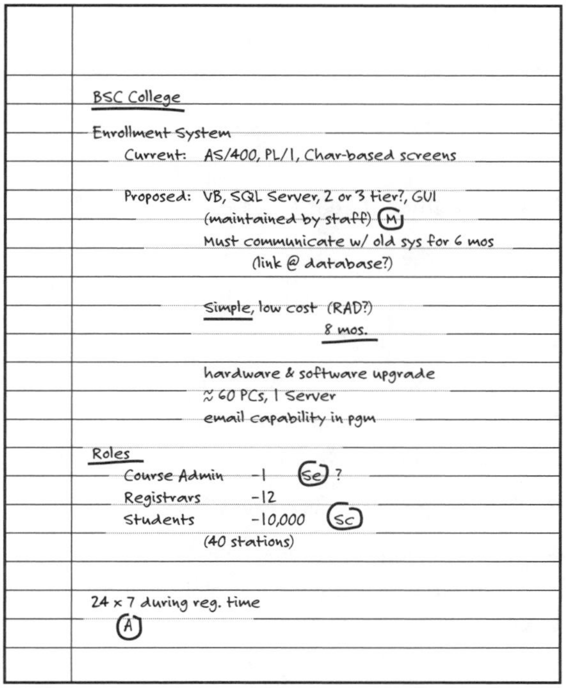

FIGURE E.1
Notes taken on the business requirements of the case.

Notice that these notes focus heavily on the *nouns*, *verbs*, and *adjectives*. When building requirements, nouns help you understand the *existing system* (such as "AS/400"), the *scope* of the new system ("enrollment system," "e-mail"), and the *roles* involved ("course administrator," "student"). Adjectives like "simple" and "low cost" are also helpful in defining *business issues*, both when reading a case study and when designing a system in the real world. The verbs help you identify things like *availability* requirements (for example, "up 24 hours a day"). You should also watch for verbs like "submit" and "reviewing" to give you clues.

The "requirements" phase is one of the times when the six PASS ME areas are important. PASS ME requirements are noted in Figure E.1 by circled letters. It appears from Figure E.1 that only four of the six PASS ME areas are significant to the system requirements.

As one last issue, whenever you see hourly wages in a case study, it is possible that you will be expected to calculate ROI (Return On Investment) for a solution. You can quickly step through the calculations to see what the college is expecting to pay for this solution.

They expect 6,000 students to do their own enrollment, saving the cost of the registrar's wages for those students. Given that registrars can register six students each hour and earn $20 per hour, you can determine the cost savings for a single semester as follows:

$$(6{,}000 \ / \ 6) \times \$20 = \$20{,}000$$

If you apply the savings over six semesters (they mentioned a goal of getting payback within three years and also discounted any summer semester registrations as financially insignificant), you can calculate that they expect to pay around $120,000 for this solution.

$$\$20{,}000 \times 6 = \$120{,}000$$

Before you move out of the analysis phase, here are just a few more tips regarding "Business Requirements":

◆ *Business requirements should be documented.* This creates a paper trail that will be useful late in a project cycle when tension is high and deadlines approach.

◆ *Interview, interview, interview.* The case studies on the Microsoft exam should serve as a reminder that most of the useful information needed to build a quality solution comes as a result of interviewing users and accurately identifying a way to address their needs and goals.

◆ *Create use cases.* There are several good books on use cases; simply stated, they are small "scenarios" that describe how an application should respond in various situations. They can be the basis of communication between the client and the developers, as well as among the developers. They also serve as a basis for the acceptance tests that will come later in the development cycle.

The business requirements make up what is known as the "analysis" phase. The remaining five objective areas constitute the "design" phase.

Technical Architecture

Before we start into our design, let's briefly return to Big State and learn more about their needs as they apply to choosing the appropriate technical architecture.

Big State College enrolls more than 9,000 students in an average of four classes each semester. It is expected that a third of these registrations will come in through registrars and two-thirds through the new e-mail process (which guarantees a "first come, first served" strategy).

Enrollment records are small (less than 1,000 bytes each), but enrollments are stored for 10 years.

The system is expected to generate course schedules for bulletin board display, invoices for billing purposes, and class rosters for the instructors.

Technical Architecture includes issues like choice of tiers, choice of technology(s), data storage architecture, and so on.

As you read the case study and take notes, try to pull out answers to the following questions:

◆ How many users? Will each have his own machine?

◆ How many different locations?

◆ What is the physical distance from the farthest user to the central mainframe or server database?

◆ What technology is current (mainframe, older PCs, state-of-the-art, Internet)?

◆ Volume of data transfer (record size times number of records)?

◆ Reporting requirements (batch or real time)?

◆ What are your developers experienced in? Technology decisions often boil down to what the available people know best.

From the case study and your notes, you can determine the following:

◆ There are 12 registrars, each with his or her own machine. The 9,000 students (6,000 of whom are expected to enroll via e-mail) will use 40 PC stations.

◆ All parts of the system are within the confines of the campus. It is unclear where the server will reside, but it seems like a three-tier logical architecture would be appropriate. The client PCs (student kiosks and registrar PCs) will make up the "User Services" tier. The "Business Services" tier will reside on a central server. And the SQL Server database, although residing on the same server, will be logically separated to simplify maintenance as well as to make it easier to scale up if future expansion is required.

◆ You have some information regarding data transfer volumes: 9000 students × 1000 bytes × 4 classes = 36MB of data for each semester. Additional data traffic will support "reviewing" course schedules and replying to e-mails ("You are enrolled in CIS100-10" or "You are NOT enrolled in CIS100-10"). You also know that you will need to archive 36MB × 2 semesters × 10 years worth of data, or 720MB.

◆ Reporting requirements are pretty specific: course schedules, invoices, and class rosters.

◆ It was also very clear what skill sets the onsite support personnel have: Visual Basic and SQL Server. In fact, this practically makes the technology decision for you. If the college were teaching VC++, you might have considered that, but the requirements for RAD (Rapid Application Design) and "keep it simple" drive you toward using Visual Basic.

Just as in the previous section, focusing on key words and phrases seems to give you all the information you need.

Logical Design

Logical Design requires you to choose an application "model" from a list that includes the following: SDI, MDI, *n*-tier, Web, and so on.

Let's look at some of the activities and questions that would help you solidify your choice for a logical design:

◆ Draw a simple system block diagram, component level. Show major data flow and any substantial latencies (for example, a slow WAN).

◆ Does the case study provide any clues to the best logical design? For example, is there any mention of needing access to multiple documents at the same time?

◆ What impact would decisions made have on the "PASS ME" areas (see the second bullet in the following list)?

◆ Does the technical architecture dictate any logical design constraints?

From the BSC case study, you can draw the following conclusions:

◆ By requiring students to submit requests via e-mail, you can expect to deal with a single transaction at a time. You can also see from the case study and your analysis of nouns, verbs, and adjectives that there is no requirement for Web or Internet functionality. The request for a "graphical user interface," combined with the information above, leads toward an SDI application model.

◆ Reviewing the "PASS ME" areas, you can see that *availability* is an issue four times a year. *Performance* and *security* do not seem to be an issue. *Scalability* might have been an issue, but the fact that the 6,000 forecasted students must all funnel their requests through 40 PCs places the bottleneck outside the system (as students stand in line for their turn).

This section is a bit more difficult if you have not participated in designing actual applications in the different models. Each has its pros and cons. It is a good idea to review the most appropriate situations for each before going to the exam.

You can also create a quick component diagram that may help you visualize the solution. Figure E.2 is a sample of such a drawing for the Big State College solution. It shows all the major parts of the system, as well as the connection to the existing enrollment system.

In Figure E.2, you see the beginnings of a system block diagram. When you're taking the exam, this can help keep your thoughts straight and expose the "big picture." In real life, such a document is very useful for communication with clients, team members, and anyone else with an interest in the solution. If you are required to connect to other applications or components, this diagram shows those connection points, perhaps exposing design flaws early in the process when they are easier and cheaper to fix.

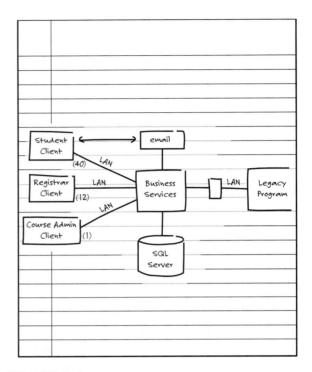

FIGURE E.2
A sketch of the components of the solution.

Data Model

You have analyzed the business requirements, designed a technical architecture, and selected an appropriate logical model (or pattern) for the proposed solution. At this point, then, it is appropriate to spend time designing a data model to support the solution.

Before you can do that, you need some additional information from the business experts at BSC who are helping design the system.

The concept, piloted by the BSC PL/1 program, is to archive the data at the end of each enrollment period and clear the master tables (delete all records) in preparation for the next semester. This eliminates the need to stamp each record with a year and semester.

Each student is assigned a unique ID number. The student's name, major, grades, and financial status are also required for enrollment processing. Obviously, each student is in one or more classes. Students who are not in any class are considered "dormant" and are removed from the enrollment database for the semester being processed.

Each class is assigned a name and section (such as "CIS0100-10") that uniquely identifies it. Classes are filled with students up to the assigned class limit.

Instructors, also assigned unique IDs, can be assigned to more than one class, but at BSC, no class has more than one instructor.

BSC provides dorms for students who live elsewhere. Although each dorm can house upward of 500 students, not all students live on campus. Therefore, some students do not have a dorm assignment.

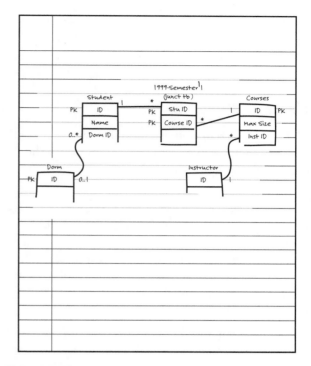

FIGURE E.3
A sketch of the database diagram.

In the "Data Model" area, you are most concerned with issues such as normalization, table relationships, keys (primary and foreign), integrity rules, and attributes.

The best way to work on this area is by drawing a table design on paper. Figure E.3 provides an example of what that might look like for the BSC case study. The sketched data model will basically look like a paper version of work you would do in Microsoft Access or Microsoft Database Designer. If done properly, it will make answering the exam questions much easier, especially the database diagram.

As you work on the model, make sure you do the following:

◆ Draw the tables as you read the case study. Fill out attributes as they present themselves.

◆ Note primary and foreign keys on the diagram.

◆ Look for relationships between tables. Note the proper cardinality of each relationship (using MS Visual Modeler syntax):

  • One to zero or more (1 to 0..*)

  • One to one (1 to 1)

  • Zero or more to one (0..* to 1)

  • Many-to-many (two tables joined with a junction table in the middle)

  • Zero to three (or any exact number) (0..3)

If done properly, this drawing can serve to solidify your thoughts and make it easier to answer the exam questions without doing a lot of re-reading.

User Interface

Much of the design work is now done. But the part of your design that will have the biggest impact on the success of your application is yet to come—the user interface.

In a real application, designing the interaction between your program and the user is a combination of logic, common sense, and art. For purposes of the exam, it is much simpler. You need to know what pieces of information to make available to the user and whether the user should be allowed to make changes to that information.

Additionally, you may need to know some of the Windows user interface design guidelines, such as those listed here:

◆ Where does the "help" menu belong?

◆ Under what circumstances should a form be modal? Non-modal?

◆ What are the proper guidelines for each of the standard Windows controls (list boxes, radio buttons, and so on)?

In order to get the information you need to design a high-quality user interface for the BSC enrollment system, you must continue your "interview."

When a Big State student accesses the system, she can view course information such as Name, ID, class date/time, cost, and maximum size. She is allowed to enter her ID and up to four requested course IDs (for example, CIS0100-10). When the information is ready, she clicks a "Submit" button. A reply to her request will be returned via e-mail within two hours.

Because new students are always entering the college, a simple help system is required. The user interface should also be as intuitive and "discoverable" as possible.

Registrars have basically the same screen; the main difference is that they receive instant notification of whether the enrollment is accepted or refused. Registrars are also able to perform searches to locate alternatives when a requested class is full.

The course administrator controls the cost of each course, the assigned instructor (via a drop-down list), the date and time of the course, and the maximum class size. He or she can also update the name of the course, although the ID is assigned automatically by the system.

While focusing on the user interface, you need to concern yourself with such things as user navigation, input validation, user assistance, prototype, and output.

While reading the case study, try to pull out answers to the following questions:

◆ How sophisticated are the users? Are there different levels of users?

> **NOTE Dealing with a Wide Range of User Experience**   One of the most challenging situations for user interface designers is to successfully address the needs of novice users and expert users without designing multiple interfaces. Similarly, the user interface should "grow" with the user. Aids that seem necessary or cute at first can become wearisome over time. Users need well-designed preference settings (as one approach) to allow them to control the efficiency of the interface.

◆ Do the users use the system infrequently? Daily? Constantly?

◆ Are there any requirements for online documentation or user support (help)?

◆ What unique input requirements exist? "Heads-down" data entry?

> **NOTE "Heads-Down" Data Entry**   "Heads-down" data entry requires a user interface to provide exclusive keyboard control with little or no mouse usage necessary. It is called "heads down" because the user typically does NOT look at the screen. He reads a document of some type and expects the system to respond predictably to memorized keystroke sequences. These types of users are often very demanding of an interface. Even small changes (like adding an extra Tab or carriage return into an existing process) can upset the timing of a serious heads-down data entry person. (It's almost like adding another key to a piano.) Every effort should be made to offer a way to perform tasks with either the keyboard or the mouse, but without requiring the user to switch back and forth.

◆ What output does the system need to produce? Look for the keywords "report," "analyze," and "generate." Are any of the items on your list of nouns output (for example, the bill)?

In addition to the questions above, you may want to take notes regarding the fields that should be displayed on the user interface, broken out by role. Again, focusing on the nouns will do almost all the work for you. If you were taking notes for the Big State user interface, you might create something like that shown in Figure E.4.

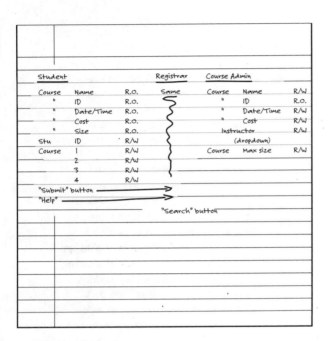

FIGURE E.4
Proposed user interface elements.

Essentially, this is a list, based on hints in the case study, of all the data elements needed for each of the three roles the solution must support. Additionally, an "R.O." designates elements that are read-only, and an "R/W" designates those that are read/write (editable by the user).

Using this approach, you can see that the solution almost designs itself. If you were asked to design a tree on the exam, a diagram like the one in the figure would make the task much easier.

If this were a real application, you would take the information in Figure E.4 and create what is known as a "lo-fi" (low fidelity) UI design. The "lo-fi" design is basically a sketch of the proposed user interface. This would then lead to a prototyped user interface ("hi-fi") with stubbed out behaviors.

Physical Design

You are almost done. All that remains is to bring your theoretical design into the light of day to implement it in the physical domain.

In the exam, as in the real world, this is usually an opportunity to draw another diagram—one that shows the connections of application components as well as the flow of data through the system. Additionally, you need to diagram bottlenecks or latencies in your implementation. When reading the case study, keep an eye out for any of the following words or phrases: LAN, WAN, network, satellite, delay, bridge, phone line. Also watch for statements that hint at the number of users (such as "from any of the 40 computer kiosks placed strategically throughout the campus").

You need to spend just a few more minutes with your client at Big State to see if you can gather the information needed to design the physical layout of the solution.

The new enrollment system takes requests from two areas: student kiosks and registrar workstations.

In both cases, they go through a basic validation processor. If all the required information is present, the request is sent to a holding database.

A business rules component does a more thorough completeness check. It then checks the student's financial status. If he does not exceed established thresholds, the financial component approves the request. The enrollment is then matched against course availability. If there is an available seat, the student is enrolled, and a positive response is returned to him (via e-mail). His enrollment is then sent, through a database "persistence" layer to the main SQL Server tables.

Anything that will cause denial of the enrollment triggers a negative e-mail response to the student.

The registrars go through basically the same process. However, their replies are immediate; no e-mail is involved.

Finally, in physical design, you concern yourself with performance, maintainability, extensibility, scalability, availability, security, and properties/methods/events. Therefore, follow these guidelines:

◆ Look for operations (methods) that the target system may need to perform. Create a list of these from the list of the verbs.

◆ Look for properties (nouns and adjectives) such as "class size," "name," and "cost."

◆ Identify geographical constraints, and identify unusually large distances between tiers.

◆ Look for workflow through the system. This is particularly important for the Microsoft exam.

A strategy that can prove very useful for the exam is to draw a "workflow diagram" that shows the flow of data through the system. Using numbers to indicate sequence may also be helpful for certain question styles. The drawing in Figure E.5 is a sample of what this might look like.

You've covered strategies for reading and drawing out information for the six major areas of the Microsoft exam. Now, let's quickly review the "PASS ME" areas. This will be brief because they have already been covered in the main text of the book.

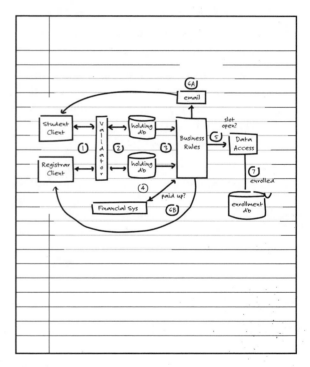

FIGURE E.5
Sketch of a workflow diagram.

"PASS ME"

Microsoft has defined six areas of constant focus for application architects/developers. These six factors should be considered during each phase of development:

◆ **Performance.** How fast? Is the anticipated response time acceptable to the users?

◆ **Availability.** What are the requirements? 24/7? 8am–5pm? 90% uptime? 100% uptime?

◆ **Security.** Who has the right to get at what?

◆ **Scalability.** If you double the number of users, how will the application behave?

◆ **Maintainability.** Are the application and the source code easy to maintain? Does it require an "expert" developer, or can a medium-skilled developer find and correct defects? Is the application solid or is it fragile?

◆ **Extensibility.** How flexible is the solution in scope or requirements if changes are needed?

How can you draw information relative to these factors from a case study? Ask yourself the following sorts of questions.

Performance

Have existing systems already set user's expectations around response time?

Can it be determined at what tier the application will need to maintain state (data, business, user)? State simply questions whether the object remembers information between calls. If you load a "customer" object with information like address, account balance, and such, and then come back later and update the account balance, it is said to be *stateful.* If you "get on, do your thing, and get off," an object is said to be *stateless.*

> **NOTE**
>
> **Interface Style** One of the first things you should try to decide is whether the user interface style is "rich" (data validation feedback on each field or on each keystroke), "batch" (typified by the "Submit" button paradigm, where validation and data tier updates do not take place until a final button click), or somewhere in-between. Does the case study provide any guidance (user requirements), or is this left to the architect to decide?

Availability

Are any availability requirements stated outright in the case study? If not, based on your personal knowledge of the business described in the case study, what would be your expectation for application availability?

Security

What "roles" exist? What level of access should each role have? Analyze access in terms of **CRUD** (**C**reate new records, **R**ead records, **U**pdate record data, **D**elete records). Analyze access in terms of "need to know." Analyze access in terms of explicit statements in the case study. One way to do this is to attach a *role* from the previously created list to another *noun* (an object) with a *verb* in-between. For an example, see Table E.1.

TABLE E.1

SECURITY ANALYSIS

Role (Noun)	Action (Verb)	Object (Noun)	CRUD
Student	Reviews	Course schedule	R
Course administrator	Updates	Class cost	C, R, U, D

Scalability

What is the expectation for concurrent users? What is the potential for that number to increase? If the number of concurrent users hits the largest possible value, how will the application respond? Is that acceptable? Is the design "client heavy," requiring the installation of complete application packages on your client machines? Or is it "client thin," perhaps running as VBScript in a Web browser?

Maintainability

Are good coding practices in place that will make the application easy to maintain (variable naming standards, comments and white space, and so on)? Has component technology been used effectively to abstract the complexity of the entire application? Is the deployment strategy the easiest to maintain in regards to versioning issues?

Extensibility

With fast-paced changes in business objectives, can the application design respond easily to changes in scope, both during the development cycle and after?

SUMMARY

Using the strategies outlined in this appendix, you should be able to improve your comprehension of the case studies and improve your score by organizing your thoughts. In short, read the case study from front to back with a pencil in your hand before starting in on the questions.

These same principles should also serve you well in the real world of designing solutions. The key is to ask a lot of questions and do your homework before jumping to an answer. Just like in the shoe business, "one size does NOT fit all."

Index

J-K

L

M

N

O

P

TRAINING GUIDES
NEXT GENERATION TRAINING

MCSE Training Guide:
Networking Essentials,
Second Edition

1-56205-919-X,
$49.99, 9/98

MCSE Training Guide:
TCP/IP, Second
Edition

1-56205-920-3,
$49.99, 10/98

A+ Certification
Training Guide,
Second Edition

0-7357-0907-6,
$49.99, 10/99

MCSE Training Guide:
Windows NT Server 4,
Second Edition

1-56205-916-5,
$49.99, 9/98

MCSE Training Guide:
SQL Server 7
Administration

0-7357-0003-6,
$49.99, 5/99

TRAINING GUIDES
FIRST EDITIONS

MCSE Training Guide: Systems Management
Server 1.2, 1-56205-748-0

MCSE Training Guide: SQL Server 6.5
Administration, 1-56205-726-x

MCSE Training Guide: SQL Server 6.5
Design and Implementation, 1-56205-830-4

MCSE Training Guide:
Windows NT Server 4
Enterprise, Second
Edition

1-56205-917-3,
$49.99, 9/98

MCSE Training Guide:
SQL Server 7 Database
Design

0-7357-0004-4,
$49.99, 5/99

MCSE Training Guide: Windows 95, 70-064
Exam, 1-56205-880-0

MCSE Training Guide: Exchange Server 5,
1-56205-824-x

MCSE Training Guide: Internet Explorer 4,
1-56205-889-4

MCSE Training Guide: Microsoft Exchange
Server 5.5, 1-56205-899-1

MCSE Training Guide: IIS 4, 1-56205-823-1

MCSE Training Guide:
Windows NT
Workstation 4,
Second Edition

1-56205-918-1,
$49.99, 9/98

MCSD Training Guide:
Solution Architectures

0-7357-0026-5,
$49.99, 10/99

MCSD Training Guide: Visual Basic 5,
1-56205-850-9

MCSD Training Guide: Microsoft Access,
1-56205-771-5

MCSE Training Guide:
Windows 98

1-56205-890-8,
$49.99, 2/99

MCSD Training Guide:
Visual Basic 6 Exams

0-7357-0002-8,
$69.99, 3/99

FAST TRACKS

The Accelerated Path to Certification Success

Fast Tracks provide an easy way to review the key elements of each certification technology without being bogged down with elementary-level information.

These guides are perfect for when you already have real-world, hands-on experience. They're the ideal enhancement to training courses, test simulators, and comprehensive training guides.

No fluff—simply what you really need to pass the exam!

MCSE Fast Track: Networking Essentials
1-56205-939-4, $19.99, 9/98

MCSE Fast Track: Windows 98
0-7357-0016-8, $19.99, 12/98

MCSE Fast Track: TCP/IP
1-56205-937-8, $19.99, 9/98

MCSE Fast Track: Windows NT Server 4
1-56205-935-1, $19.99, 9/98

MCSE Fast Track: Windows NT Server 4 Enterprise
1-56205-940-8, $19.99, 9/98

MCSE Fast Track: Windows NT Workstation 4
1-56205-938-6, $19.99, 9/98

A+ Fast Track: Core/ Hardware Exam & DOS/Windows Exam
0-7357-0028-1, $29.99, 3/99

MCSE Fast Track: Internet Information Server 4
1-56205-936-X, $19.99, 9/98

MCSE Fast Track: SQL Server 7 Administration
0-7357-0041-9, $29.99, 4/99

MCSE/MCSD Fast Track: SQL Server 7 Database Design
0-7357-0040-0, $29.99, 4/99

MCSD Fast Track: Visual Basic 6 Exam 70-175
0-7357-0018-4, $19.99, 12/98

MCSD Fast Track: Visual Basic 6 Exam 70-176
0-7357-0019-2, $19.99, 12/98

MCSD Fast Track: Solution Architectures
0-7357-0029-x, $29.99, 10/99

HOW TO CONTACT US

IF YOU NEED THE LATEST UPDATES ON A TITLE THAT YOU'VE PURCHASED:

1) Visit our Web site at www.newriders.com.

2) Click on the Product Support link and enter your book's ISBN number, which is located on the back cover in the bottom right-hand corner.

3) There you'll find available updates for your title.

IF YOU ARE HAVING TECHNICAL PROBLEMS WITH THE BOOK OR THE CD THAT IS INCLUDED:

1) Check the book's information page on our Web site according to the instructions listed above, or

2) Email us at support@mcp.com, or

3) Fax us at 317-817-7488 ATTN: Tech Support.

IF YOU HAVE COMMENTS ABOUT ANY OF OUR CERTIFICATION PRODUCTS THAT ARE NON-SUPPORT RELATED:

1) Email us at certification@mcp.com, or

2) Write to us at New Riders, 201 W. 103rd St., Indianapolis, IN 46290-1097, or

3) Fax us at 317-581-4663.

IF YOU ARE OUTSIDE THE UNITED STATES AND NEED TO FIND A DISTRIBUTOR IN YOUR AREA:

Please contact our international department at international@mcp.com.

IF YOU WISH TO PREVIEW ANY OF OUR CERTIFICATION BOOKS FOR CLASSROOM USE:

Email us at pr@mcp.com. Your message should include your name, title, training company or school, department, address, phone number, office days/hours, text in use, and enrollment. Send these details along with your request for desk/examination copies and/or additional information.

Fold here and tape to mail

- -

New Riders
201 W. 103rd St.
Indianapolis, IN 46290